Experiencing Stanislavsky Today

This pioneering introduction to Stanislavsky's methods and modes of actor training covers all of the essential elements of his System. Recreating truthful behaviour in the artificial environment, awareness and observation, psychophysical work, given circumstances, visualization and imagination, and Active Analysis are all introduced and explored.

- Each section of the book is accompanied by individual and group exercises, forming a full course of study in the foundations of modern acting.
- A glossary explains the key terms and concepts that are central to Stanislavsky's thinking at a glance.
- The book's companion website is full of downloadable worksheets and resources for teachers and students.

Experiencing Stanislavsky Today is enhanced by contemporary findings in psychology, neuroscience, anatomy and physiology that illuminate the human processes important to actors, such as voice and speech, creativity, mind-body connection, the process and the production of emotions on cue. It is the definitive first step for anyone encountering Stanislavsky's work, from acting students exploring his methods for the first time, to directors looking for effective rehearsal tools and teachers mapping out degree classes.

Stephanie Daventry French has directed over 40 productions using Stanislavsky's Active Analysis. She teaches the Stanislavsky System integrated with many other techniques as head of the Acting for Theatre, Television and Film track at East Stroudsburg University.

Philip G. Bennett has been an actor, teacher and director of the Stanislavsky System since 1969 – Artistic Director of the San Francisco Theatre Academy 1976–1984, the Bennett TheatreLab & Conservatory 1984–present, and Assistant Artistic Director to Russian emigré teacher, Sonia Moore, American Stanislavski Theatre, 1969–1975.

Experiencing Stanislavsky Today

Training and Rehearsal for the Psychophysical Actor

Co-authored by Stephanie Daventry French

and Philip G. Bennett

LONDON AND NEW YORK

First published 2016
by Routledge
2 Park Square, Milton Park, Abingdon, Oxon OX14 4RN

and by Routledge
711 Third Avenue, New York, NY 10017

Routledge is an imprint of the Taylor & Francis Group, an informa business

© 2016 Stephanie Daventry French and Philip G. Bennett

The right of Stephanie Daventry French and Philip G. Bennett to be identified as authors of this work has been asserted by them in accordance with sections 77 and 78 of the Copyright, Designs and Patents Act 1988.

All rights reserved. No part of this book may be reprinted or reproduced or utilized in any form or by any electronic, mechanical, or other means, now known or hereafter invented, including photocopying and recording, or in any information storage or retrieval system, without permission in writing from the publishers.

Trademark notice: Product or corporate names may be trademarks or registered trademarks, and are used only for identification and explanation without intent to infringe.

British Library Cataloguing-in-Publication Data
A catalogue record for this book is available from the British Library

Library of Congress Cataloging-in-Publication Data
French, Stephanie Daventry
Experiencing Stanislavsky today : training and rehearsal for the psychophysical actor / Stephanie French and Philip G. Bennett.
pages cm
Includes index.
1. Stanislavsky, Konstantin, 1863-1938. 2. Acting--Psychological aspects. I. French, Stephanie. II. Title.
PN2062.B48 2015
792.02'8--dc23
2015010688

ISBN: 978-0-415-69394-3 (hbk)
ISBN: 978-0-415-69395-0 (pbk)
ISBN: 978-0-203-15247-8 (ebk)

Typeset in 9/12 Sabon LT Pro
by Fakenham Prepress Solutions, Fakenham, Norfolk NR21 8NN

Printed and bound in the United States of America by Sheridan Books, Inc. (a Sheridan Group Company).

This book is dedicated to our hundreds of students, as well as our teachers and artistic collaborators. Thank you for sharing your light.

"The teacher and the taught together create the teaching."
—Anonymous Chinese Proverb

Contents

List of Illustrations ix
Preface xii
Illustration Acknowledgments xvi
Acknowledgments xxiv

1. An Invitation to the Quest for Inspiration 1

Part 1: Psychophysical Conditioning 13
2. The Actor's Palette: Interconnected Elements of Action 15
3. The Creative State: Preparing for Inspiration 37
4. Yoga and Acting: Dedication to the Creative Space 62
5. The Psychophysical Instrument: Exploring the Mind-Body Connection 77

Part 2: Psychophysical Action: Engaging Others 115
6. Communion: Deepening Communication and Mutual Influence 117
7. Discovering and Endowing Circumstances 137
8. Nonverbal Action: Communicating through Behavior 155
9. Embodying Voice 193
10. Activating Speech 215
11. Verbal Action: Communicating with Words and Subtext 243
12. Orchestrating Emotions 267

Part 3: Active Analysis 299
13. Active Analysis: Reconnaissance of the Play 303
14. Active Analysis: Reconnaissance of the Character 322
15. Active Analysis through Events and Actions 346
16. Active Analysis in Rehearsal 386
17. Entering the Collaborative Process 406
18. The Actor of Living Experience 450
19. The Creative Life: Communion with Audience and Society 465

Part 4: Honoring Our Acting Legacy 489
20. The Evolving Stanislavsky System 491

Appendix I—A Selected Glossary: Terminology of the Stanislavsky System with Supplemental Terms 541
Appendix II—10 Yoga Poses 556
Appendix IIIa—Basic and Intermediate Improvisation Worksheets 558
Appendix IIIb—Intermediate and Advanced Improvisation Worksheet 561

Appendix IV—Additional Actions for Selection and Practice 563
Appendix V—Sample Text Analysis: *Three Sisters* by Anton Chekhov, Act 2,
    Scene 2 (Andrei and Ferapont) 565
Appendix VIa—The Properties of Vowels (with IPA Vowel Articulation Chart) 567
Appendix VIb—The Properties of Consonants (with IPA Consonant
    Articulation Chart) 570
Appendix VII– Full List of Exercises and Improvisations by Category 574
Bibliography 579
Index 585

Illustrations

0.1	Stanislavsky writing his book	xii
1.1	Bamboo forest, Kyoto, Japan	2
1.2	Sarcophagus of the Muses	7
1.3	Paul, Germany's Octopus Oracle	8
1.4	Ancient meditation garden in Kyoto, Japan	12
2.1	The Actor's Palette of colors from the Stanislavsky System	16
2.2	Jamil Joseph and Jannel Armstrong in *Spike Heels* by Theresa Rebeck	18
2.3	Gabryal Rabinowitz and Kirsten Walsh in *Blithe Spirit* by Noel Coward	22
3.1	Benicio del Toro as Dr. Gonzo in *Fear and Loathing in Las Vegas* (1998)	39
3.2	Ziyi Zhang as Moon in *Hero* (2002)	40
3.3	Positions for meditation—watching the breath	46
3.4	Primary brain regions	49
3.5	Selected and shared brain hemisphere functions	51
4.1	Stanislavsky's Plan of Experiencing, 1935	64
4.2	Communication pathways of the central nervous system (brain and spinal cord) and the peripheral nervous system	65
4.3	Diagram of the chakras (energy centers of the body)	65
4.4	Taneshia Davis, Esther Joseph, and Mary Dennis prepare for a performance of *Sold!*	70
4.5	Stage management team, director, writers, cast, and crew of *Sold!* East Stroudsburg University, 2011	71
4.6	Tyler Adams checks his messages before a performance of *Sold!*	73
5.1	Prone position with a thin book under the head	85
5.2	Alternate position for relaxation (often preferred by females)	85
5.3	Alternate position for relaxation (often preferred by males)	85
5.4	Rising without tension	88
5.5	Rolling up the spine	89
5.6	Parts of the spine	89
5.7	Preferable and problematic alignment	95
5.8	Rolling down from plow	96
5.9	Swinging twist	97
5.10	Seated twist	98
5.11	Lying-down twist	98
5.12	Positions for disobeying hands	100
5.13	The synaptic gap	101
6.1	Dave Ausem and Christi Berlane in *The Hobbit*	119
6.2	The opera *Sino alla Morte* at the University of California, San Diego	124
6.3	Janel Martinez in *Polaroid Stories* by Naomi Iizuka	133
7.1	Suppose you were at a baseball stadium …	138
7.2	Assuming and conveying status	143
7.3	Getting what you want	147
8.1	Aftermath of the Loma Prieta earthquake	169
8.2	Burned-out vehicle after the Oakland fire	170
9.1	The anatomy of voice and speech	196
9.2	Healthy and problematic alignment	199
9.3	Additional components of breath	201

9.4	Voice class with Dr. Margaret Joyce Ball	203
9.5	Physical movement for Tai Chi Breaths	206
10.1	Swollen tonsils and the uvula	219
10.2	Front, central, and back consonants	226
10.3	Combining consonants and vowels	227
10.4	Projection	233
11.1	Kirsten Walsh as Ruth, Shannon Leigh Christmann as Elvira, and Gabryal Rabinowitz as Charles in *Blithe Spirit* by Noel Coward	254
11.2	Douglas James Brehony as Tartuffe and Raj Shankar as Orgon in Molière's *Tartuffe*	255
11.3	Brandon Cabrera as Andrew, and Jamil Joseph as Edward, in *Spike Heels* by Theresa Rebeck	256
11.4	Selena and Shwanda Farber in *Sold!* by Stephanie Daventry French and Ahleea Zama	259
12.1	Psychological burden: Merrill McGuinness in *Polaroid Stories* by Naomi Iizuka	277
12.2	Analogous emotions: Brandon L. Cabrera as Jeffrey, and Aaqilah Lewis as Dorcus, in *Sold!* by Stephanie Daventry French and Ahleea Zama	282
12.3	Targeting an emotion: Mary K. Dennis as Lydia, and Jannel Armstrong as Georgie, in *Spike Heels* by Theresa Rebeck	285
12.4	The path of the vagus nerve	294
12.5	Key aspects of the limbic system for emotional response	295
13.1	*A Streetcar Named Desire* by Tennessee Williams	311
13.2	Molière's *Tartuffe*	314
13.3	Christi Berlane as Stella, Dave Auseum as Stanley, and Angel Berlane as Blanche in *A Streetcar Named Desire* by Tennessee Williams	319
14.1	Sample character/relationship map for Blanche in *Streetcar*	325
14.2	Sample character dichotomy for Blanche in *Streetcar*	325
14.3	Sample character adjectives chart from *Streetcar*	326
14.4	Elyse Burnett as Gret, Eldee as Lady Nijo in *Top Girls* by Caryl Churchill	330
15.1	"Exit, pursued by a bear." Philip G. Bennett in Shakespeare's *The Winter's Tale* at the Rogue Theatre	355
15.2	The Exploding Trunk episode in *A Streetcar Named Desire* by Tennessee Williams	363
15.3	Yunzhou "Elldee" Gao recalls her lost child; from *Top Girls* by Caryl Churchill	368
15.4	Symbols for Script Notation	376
15.5	Example: A graphic analysis of text	378
15.6	*Three Sisters* by Anton Chekhov	380
15.7	A notated script	381
16.1	Forgiveness. *The Crucible*, by Arthur Miller	387
16.2	Dancing in the woods. *The Crucible*, by Arthur Miller	388
16.3	Hysteria. *The Crucible*, by Arthur Miller	389
16.4	"God is dead!" *The Crucible*, by Arthur Miller	389
16.5	Act 3: Mary confesses. *The Crucible*, by Arthur Miller	390
16.6	Avoiding Salem. *The Crucible*, by Arthur Miller	393
16.7	Act 4: final moments. *The Crucible*, by Arthur Miller	401
16.8	A breakdown of main and secondary events. *The Crucible*, by Arthur Miller	404
17.1	A curtain call for *Twelfth Night* at East Stroudsburg University	406
17.2	Primary theatre stage formats	409
17.3	Shakespeare's *Twelfth Night* at East Stroudsburg University	412
17.4	The SITI Company's *Who Do You Think You Are?*	417
17.5	Stages of design for *The Devil's Music* at the George Street Playhouse in New Brunswick, New Jersey	418
17.6	Consultation between charge artist and scenic designer, Yoshi Tanokura	419
17.7	Sample headshot and résumé: Carla Harting	420
17.8	Stage area map—a proscenium with apron	428
17.9	Blocking created through Viewpoints in the SITI company's *bobrauschenbergamerica*	429
17.10	Actors' body positions in relation to the audience	430
17.11	Actor coaching	432
17.12	Maria Picon (Persephone) in *Polaroid Stories* at East Stroudsburg University	435
17.13	*The Threepenny Opera* at the San Diego Repertory Theatre	436
17.14	*Bruja*, by Luis Alfaro, at Borderlands Theatre Company, Tucson, Arizona	437

ILLUSTRATIONS

17.15	*The Tragical History of Dr. Faustus,* by Christopher Marlowe	438
17.16	The good and bad angels, *The Tragical History of Dr. Faustus,* by Christopher Marlowe	439
17.17	Mixing sound	439
17.18	Giving notes after a run of *A Christmas Carol*	440
17.19	Noel Coward's *Blithe Spirit* at East Stroudsburg University	441
17.20	Circuiting strip lights	442
17.21	Costume design concept	444
17.22	Actor notes during tech	444
18.1	Stanislavsky's Plan of Experiencing, 1935	452
18.2	The Anatomy of Experiencing (Philip G. Bennett's translation)	453
18.3	Jamil Joseph and Jannel Armstrong in *Spike Heels* by Teresa Rebeck	462
19.1	Samantha Crawn and Christopher Centrella in *Polaroid Stories* by Naomi Iizuka	466
19.2	Joseph Bednarchik and Samantha Crawn in *Polaroid Stories* by Naomi Iizuka	472
19.3	David Ausem and Angel Berlane in *A Streetcar Named Desire* by Tennessee Williams	472
19.4	*The Threepenny Opera* by Bertolt Brecht	479
19.5	*Edipo,* by Luis Alfaro at Borderlands Theatre Company	483
19.6	Mask making	485
19.7	Ariel Princeton Mota and Ian Owstrovski in *The Phantom Tollbooth,* by Susan Nanus	486
20.1	Stanislavsky in the late 1800s, Moscow Art Theatre company	494
20.2	Stanislavsky and Nemirovich-Danchenko, circa 1935	498
20.3	First reading of *The Seagull,* Moscow Art Theatre company	502
20.4	Leopold Sulerzhitsky	507
20.5	Vsevolod Meyerhold	513
20.6	Evgeny Vakhtangov	515
20.7	Cubist set design for Vakhtangov's production of *Princess Turandot,* by Carlo Gozzi	516
20.8	Mikhail Aleksandrovich Chekhov (Michael Chekhov)	517
20.9	Sonia Moore	526
20.10	Bertolt Brecht	528
20.11	Jerzy Grotowski	529

Preface

"Before attaining the beguiling heights of inspiration, we have to deal with the conscious technique for achieving it"[1]

—Konstantin Stanislavsky

0.1 Stanislavsky writing his book.
Photo: Fine Art Images/Heritage Images/Getty Images.

Why This Book?

As a creative artist, an actor, you will invariably develop your own approaches to the art. Whether you are acting for the very first time or supplementing your knowledge with additional training, basic acting technique gives you a strong foundation upon which to build. From our deep artistic and personal experience in the theatre, we offer you some of the riches we have found.

This book represents our abiding respect for the legacy of Konstantin Stanislavsky.[2] One of the purposes in writing it is that many of Stanislavsky's

---

[1] Stanislavsky, *An Actor's Work*, p. xxvi (original draft Preface).
[2] Stanislavsky is sometimes spelled with a *y* and sometimes with an *i*. Both are used widely in publication. This is because in Russian there is a different alphabet known as Cyrillic. We will generally use *y* except when quoting or referencing other sources that use the *i*.

PREFACE

techniques are misunderstood and thus summarily dismissed, or only partly understood and thus not taught or practiced in the ways that can best serve the actor. This is no fault of the fantastic teachers who teach aspects of his System but rather a collection of issues that have led to misunderstandings such as 1) mistranslations in publication, 2) vital parts cut from publications, 3) Soviet censorship in publication, and 4) an oral tradition that in some cases was transmitted according to earlier periods of Stanislavsky's development of the System, which he later revised. Also, it is now rare, at least in North America (except in a very few conservatory programs), for a student to be steeped in one technique for a period of the 3–4 years required for mastery (in Russia and China the System is taught as a 4-year technique). As most of us in the West do not have this luxury in training time, we have written the book to be flexible so it can be used in a variety of training structures such as 2–4 year programs, B.A., and conservatory formats (M.F.A, B.F.A., private non-accredited) and even at performing arts high schools (US) or for A-levels (U.K.).

What's in a Name? The System, Method of Physical Actions, and Active Analysis

Stanislavsky called his overall technique that encompasses both actor training and work on a play the "system," humbly putting it in the lower case. Out of respect, we capitalize it as a proper noun and call it the Stanislavsky System or the System. His new techniques for work on a play he called the Method of Physical Actions; however, some of his students, particularly Maria Knebel, who participated in the final *Tartuffe* experiment, preferred the name The Method of Active Analysis through Physical Actions. We have selected Active Analysis so as to clear up any ambiguity that may confuse the approach to the System in this book with Lee Strasberg's Method Acting. (Strasberg considers his Method his own approach. It is not inclusive of Stanislavsky's final experiments or final understanding of the System as driven by psychophysical action.) We also choose to further distance our understanding from the Soviet-imposed philosophical revisions of the System sometimes associated with the name the Method of Physical Actions.

This book offers actors:
- a solid foundation in acting technique based on the logic and sequence of human action that can serve as a stimulus for truthful content and great theatricality;
- clear instructions on *how* to use the System's conditioning exercises so that the creative principles are experienced and assimilated, thus creating new neurological pathways between mind, body, breath, and emotions;
- a palette of techniques that can be mixed differently according to the needs of each actor's unique artistic nature, the demands of the dramatic source material, and the cultivated aesthetic tastes of the actor and director;
- a comprehensive, systemic approach to empower actors as creative artists capable of making significant contributions to the collaborative process of theatre production;
- clarification of some commonly misunderstood ideas about Stanislavsky's technique;
- illumination of the principles and important sources behind the evolving Stanislavsky System; and
- a glimpse at how these theories align with findings in contemporary science.

The companion teacher's guide also includes:
- a master chart of the book that outlines terms, active techniques, and exercises in each chapter;
- comprehensive guidance for teaching the System sequentially through psychophysically based training methods (including some sample lesson plans);
- learning outcomes and assessment for each phase of the training;
- additional background and detail on many of the exercises;
- a variety of approaches and techniques to address common acting challenges;
- uses of Active Analysis on non-realistic style plays;
- suggestions on how to use the System in a variety of training formats, including quarterly and semester structures and B.A. or B.F.A./conservatory programs; and
- tips for teaching the System in large classes with time limitations.

How to Use This Book

Experiencing Stanislavsky Today is organized in four distinctive parts to train you in acting tasks with increasing challenges at each step. The first step is conditioning the inseparable mind and body, the psychophysical instrument, while actively learning the foundational Elements of Action. Exercises are accompanied by points of discussion and reflection and supported by relevant scientific findings. Next, you learn to affect others through action, first nonverbal and then verbal actions, with increasing layers and complexity. The third phase involves an engaged rehearsal process for work on a play through Active Analysis. All of this leads to the final phase of experiencing the role in communion with your artistic collaborators, the audience, and your community in performance. The techniques in this book not only give you insights but also help you to develop direct applications of those insights so that they are embodied opportunities rather than purely intellectual ideas.

Honoring Our Artistic Lineage

There are many branches of actor training that have grown from Stanislavsky's teachings (some of the primary ones include Chekhov, Ouspenskaya, Vahktangov, Tovstonogov, Knebel, Strasberg, Stella Adler, Grotowski, and Sonia Moore). Although a book can never take the place of a master teacher, we strive with this work to provide the teachings as passed to us from Stanislavsky through Vahktangov and Sonia Moore (and thereby from Bennett to French).

The tradition of a teacher trained in the evolving Stanislavsky System is to honor the master's legacy through continuous research, development, and contributions to the Art. Our understanding of acting in the System is supplemented by reading and research into the rich scholarship around the legacy of Stanislavsky and the Moscow Art Theatre. We integrate this through training actors in a culture that supports the aesthetic, technical, and ethical principles that it took Stanislavsky a lifetime to discover and perfect.

As direct inheritors of Stanislavsky's legacy through the oral tradition we have attempted through this book to both honor the tradition and move the System forward for today's actors. Our work has been honed by our own artistic endeavors in acting and directing, decades of teaching, and training in a wide variety of other acting, voice, and movement approaches. We also wanted to share with you some of the emerging science relevant to acting. The more precise scientific measures now available can observe many human systems while in action. Their findings, if at all relevant to human systems used in acting, support Stanislavsky's insights and findings from his acting experiments of a century ago. Our hope is that you, as part of a new generation, will master and expand the teachings and pass on the legacy through your art and perhaps through your teaching.

Sources for the Exercises

This book is filled with exercises for training at each step of the System that come directly from our oral Stanislavsky legacy. These are supplemented with ones we have created to teach specific aspects of the System. We have included additional exercises from traditions outside of the Stanislavsky legacy that develop important acting, movement, voice or speech skills, or rehearsal goals. Wherever possible, we have attributed the exercises to the sources, using the initials of the source teacher next to the exercise (such as KSS for Konstantin S. Stanislavsky), with a footnote for the first time that teacher is referenced. In very many cases, exercises have been adjusted and developed for specific training goals or to address specific acting challenges in our different student populations. In this case, we have noted in parentheses that it is an adapted exercise; for example, SM/PGB Sonia Moore adapted by Philip G. Bennett. Exercises passed on to us through a variety of oral acting traditions were not always attributed in classes and workshops. For some exercises, we were able to track down the original sources and for some we were not. If you have further information about any exercises, we welcome your feedback for future editions of the book.

Illustration Acknowledgments

Preface

Figure 0.1 Stanislavsky writing his book. Photo: Fine Art Images/Heritage Images/Getty Images.

Chapter 1

Figure 1.1 Bamboo forest, Kyoto, Japan. Photo: Stephanie Daventry French.
Figure 1.2 Sarcophagus of the Muses. Photo: © Araldo de Luca/Corbis.
Figure 1.3 Paul, Germany's Octopus Oracle. Photo: © Wolfgang Rattay/Reuters/Corbis.
Figure 1.4 Ancient meditation garden in Kyoto, Japan. Photo: Stephanie Daventry French.

Chapter 2

Figure 2.1 The Actor's Palette of colors from the Stanislavsky System. Original illustration by Darlene Farris Labar.
Figure 2.2 Jamil Joseph and Jannel Armstrong in *Spike Heels* by Theresa Rebeck. Direction: Stephanie Daventry French; Design—Scenic and Costume: Yoshi Tanokura; Lighting: Annie Weigand; Sound: Asia Burnett. Photo: Bob Weidner, courtesy of East Stroudsburg University.
Figure 2.3 Gabryal Rabinowitz and Kirsten Walsh in *Blithe Spirit* by Noel Coward. Direction: Stephanie Daventry French; Design—Scenic and Costume: Yoshi Tanokura; Lighting: Wil Bonnell; Hair and Makeup: Stephanie Carifi. Photo: Bob Weidner, courtesy of East Stroudsburg University.

Chapter 3

Figure 3.1 Benicio del Toro as Dr. Gonzo in *Fear and Loathing in Las Vegas* (1998). ©1998 Universal City Studios, Inc. Courtesy of Universal Studios Licensing LLC.
Figure 3.2 Ziyi Zhang as Moon in *Hero* (2002). Photo: © Russel Wong/Corbis.
Figure 3.3 Positions for meditation—watching the breath. Original illustration by Darlene Farris Labar.
Figure 3.4 Primary brain regions. Original illustration by Darlene Farris Labar.
Figure 3.5 Selected and shared brain hemisphere functions. Original illustration by Darlene Farris Labar.

ILLUSTRATION ACKNOWLEDGMENTS

Chapter 4

Figure 4.1 Stanislavsky's Plan of Experiencing, 1935. Original diagram courtesy of the Moscow Arts Theatre Museum.
Figure 4.2 Communication pathways of the central nervous system (brain and spinal cord) and the peripheral nervous system. Original illustration by Darlene Farris Labar.
Figure 4.3 Diagram of the chakras (energy centers of the body). Original illustration by Darlene Farris Labar.
Figure 4.4 Taneshia Davis, Esther Joseph and Mary Dennis prepare for a performance of *Sold!* by Stephanie Daventry French and Alheea Zama (adapted from the novel by Julius Lester), 2011; Direction: Stephanie Daventry French; Design—Scenic and Costume: Yoshi Tanokura; Lighting: Wil Bonnell; Hair and Makeup: Stephanie Carifi. Photo: Bob Weidner, courtesy of East Stroudsburg University.
Figure 4.5 Stage management team, director, writers, cast, and crew of *Sold!*, 2011. Photo: Bob Weidner, courtesy of East Stroudsburg University.
Figure 4.6 Tyler Adams checks his messages before a performance of *Sold!*. Photo: Stephanie Daventry French.

Chapter 5

Figure 5.1 Prone position with a thin book under the head. Original illustration by Darlene Farris Labar.
Figure 5.2 Alternate position for relaxation (often preferred by females). Original illustration by Darlene Farris Labar.
Figure 5.3 Alternate position for relaxation (often preferred by males). Original illustration by Darlene Farris Labar.
Figure 5.4 Rising without tension. Original illustration by Darlene Farris Labar.
Figure 5.5 Rolling up the spine. Original illustration by Darlene Farris Labar.
Figure 5.6 Parts of the spine. Original illustration by Darlene Farris Labar.
Figure 5.7 Preferable and problematic alignment. Original illustration by Darlene Farris Labar.
Figure 5.8 Rolling down from plow. Original illustration by Darlene Farris Labar.
Figure 5.9 Swinging twist. Original illustration by Darlene Farris Labar.
Figure 5.10 Seated twist. Original illustration by Darlene Farris Labar.
Figure 5.11 Lying-down twist. Original illustration by Darlene Farris Labar.
Figure 5.12 Positions for disobeying hands. Original illustration by Darlene Farris Labar.
Figure 5.13 The synaptic gap. Original illustration by Darlene Farris Labar.

Chapter 6

Figure 6.1 Dave Ausem and Christi Berlane in *The Hobbit*, an adaptation by Markland Taylor based on the novel by J. R. R. Tolkien. Direction: Stephanie Daventry French; Design—Scenic and Costume: Yoshi Tanokura; Lighting: David Dougherty; Sound: John (AJ) Scognamiglio; Hair and Make-up Artist: Michelle DiBella. Photo: Yoshinuri Tanokura.
Figure 6.2 The opera *Sino alla Morte* at the University of California, San Diego. Photo: Jim Carmody.

Figure 6.3 Janel Martinez in *Polaroid Stories* by Naomi Iizuka. Direction: Stephanie Daventry French; Design—Scenic and Costume: Yoshi Tanokura; Lighting: Pierre A. Clavel; Sound: Wonderful Bere. Photo: Charles Perry Hebard, Courtesy of East Stroudsburg University.

Chapter 7

Figure 7.1 Suppose you were at a baseball stadium … Photo: Karoline Culler.
Figure 7.2 Assuming and conveying status. Photo © François Guillot /AFP/Getty Images
Figure 7.3 Getting what you want. Photo © Photographee.eu/Shutterstock

Chapter 8

Figure 8.1 Aftermath of the Loma Prieta earthquake. Photo: © Chris Wilkins/AFP/Getty Images.
Figure 8.2 Burned-out vehicle after the Oakland fire. Photo © Morton Beebe/Corbis.

Chapter 9

Figure 9.1 The anatomy of voice and speech. Original illustration by Darlene Farris Labar.
Figure 9.2 Healthy and problematic alignment. Original illustration by Darlene Farris Labar.
Figure 9.3 Additional components of breath. Original illustration by Darlene Farris Labar.
Figure 9.4 Voice teacher: Dr. Margaret Joyce Ball; voice students: Shannon Faegan Long and Alex Misurella. Photo: Philip Stein, courtesy of East Stroudsburg University.
Figure 9.5 Physical movement for Tai Chi Breaths. Original illustration by Darlene Farris Labar.

Chapter 10

Figure 10.1 Swollen tonsils and the uvula. Photo: © Suzanne Tucker/Shutterstock.
Figure 10.4 Projection. Photo: iStock © Alija.
See also p. 242 for text acknowledgements for this chapter.

Chapter 11

Figure 11.1 Kirsten Walsh as Ruth, Shannon Leigh Christmann as Elvira, and Gabryal Rabinowitz as Charles in *Blithe Spirit* by Noel Coward. Photo: Bob Weidner, courtesy of East Stroudsburg University.
Figure 11.2 Douglas James Brehony as Tartuffe and Raj Shankar as Orgon in Molière's *Tartuffe*. Direction: Stephanie Daventry French; Scenic: Sarah Lambert; Costumes: Jennifer Tiranti; Lighting: Sooyuen Hong; Actors: Douglas James Brehony

ILLUSTRATION ACKNOWLEDGMENTS

as Tartuffe and Raj Shankar as Orgon; Sound: Dave "Doc" Dougherty. Photo: David Dougherty.

Figure 11.3 Brandon Cabrera as Andrew, and Jamil Joseph as Edward, in *Spike Heels* by Theresa Rebeck. Photo: Bob Weidner, courtesy of East Stroudsburg University.

Figure 11.4 Selena and Shwanda Farber in *Sold!* by Stephanie Daventry French and Ahleea Zama. Photo: Bob Weidner, courtesy of East Stroudsburg University.

Chapter 12

Figure 12.1 Merrill McGuinness in *Polaroid Stories* by Naomi Iizuka. Photo: Charles Perry Hebard, courtesy of East Stroudsburg University.

Figure 12.2 Brandon L. Cabrera as Jeffrey, and Aaqilah Lewis as Dorcus, in *Sold!* by Stephanie Daventry French and Ahleea Zama. Photo: Bob Weidner, courtesy of East Stroudsburg University.

Figure 12.3 Mary K. Dennis as Lydia, as and Jannel Armstrong as Georgie, in *Spike Heels* by Theresa Rebeck. Photo: Luis Vidal.

Figure 12.4 The path of the vagus nerve. Original illustration by Darlene Farris Labar.

Figure 12.5 Key aspects of the limbic system for emotional response. Original illustration by Darlene Farris Labar.

Chapter 13

Figure 13.1 *A Streetcar Named Desire*, at the Young Vic and broadcast through the National Theatre Live progam. Director: Ben Andrews (with Nick Wickham for live broadcast); Gillian Anderson as Blanche, Ben Foster as Stanley, Vanessa Kirby as Stella. Photo: Nigel Norrington/ArenaPAL.

Figure 13.2 Molière's *Tartuffe*. Photo: Dave Dougherty.

Figure 13.3 Christi Berlane as Stella, Dave Auseum at Stanley, and Angel Berlane as Blanche in *A Streetcar Named Desire* by Tennessee Williams. Direction: Stephanie Daventry French; Scenic, Costume Designer: Jesse Berlane; Lighting Designer: Q. Brian Sickels; Sound: David Dougherty. Photo: Stephanie Daventry French.

Chapter 14

Figure 14.1 Sample character/relationship map for Blanche in *Streetcar*. Original illustration by Darlene Farris Labar.

Figure 14.2 Sample character dichotomy for Blanche in *Streetcar*. Original illustration by Darlene Farris Labar.

Figure 14.3 Sample character adjectives chart from *Streetcar*. Original illustration by Darlene Farris Labar.

Figure 14.4 Elyse Burnett as Gret, Eldee as Lady Nijo (and in background, Naomi Snyder as Pope Joan, and Michelle Jones as Griselda) in *Top Girls* by Caryl Churchill. Direction: Stephanie Daventry French; Design—Scenic and Costume: Yoshi Tanokura; Lighting: Wil Bonnell; Still Projections and Video Clips: Brandon Cabrera; Sound: Rhi Milliard. Photo: Bob Weidner, courtesy of East Stroudsburg University.

Chapter 15

Figure 15.1 "Exit, pursued by a bear." Actor: Philip G. Bennett (Antigonus) in *The Winter's Tale* at the Rogue Theatre. Director and Costumer: Cynthia Meier; Lighting Designer: Clint Bryson. The Bear was designed and created by Matt Cotten. The operators of the Bear were Lee Rayment, Christopher Johnson, Dylan Page and Marissa Garcia. Photo: Tim Fuller.
Figure 15.2 The Exploding Trunk episode in *A Streetcar Named Desire* by Tennessee Williams with Christi Berlane, Angel Berlane, and David Ausem, East Stroudsburg University, 2007. Photo by Charles Perry Hebard.
Figure 15.3 Yunzhou "Elldee" Gao recalls her lost child; from *Top Girls* by Caryl Churchill. Photo: Bob Weidner, courtesy of East Stroudsburg University.
Figure 15.6 *Three Sisters* by Anton Chekhov. Director: Philip G. Bennett, The San Francisco Theatre Academy: Stanislavsky Ensemble, 1981. Director: Philip G. Bennett; Design—Lighting: Rosanne Groger; Set: John Dennis; Costumes: Franco Barone; Makeup: Jon Henn; Technical Director/Stage Manager: (and Nina the maid) Robin Miller. Photo: Robbie Tucker.

Chapter 16

All pictures in this chapter are from *The Crucible,* by Arthur Miller, San Francisco Theatre Academy Company, 1979; Direction and Stage Design: Philip G. Bennett. Costumes: Franco Barone; Lighting: Kent Fillmore.
Figure 16.1 Actors: Kent Fillmore (John Proctor), Dolores Neese (Elizabeth Proctor). Photo: © Robbie Tucker.
Figure 16.2 Actors: Joanne Lucich (Abigail Williams), Patricia Walker (Tituba). Photo: Philip G. Bennett.
Figure 16.3 Hysteria. *The Crucible*, by Arthur Miller, performed at the San Francisco Theatre Academy Ensemble Company, 1979. Photo: Philip G. Bennett.
Figure 16.4 "God is dead!" Kent Fillmore (John Proctor). Photo: Philip G. Bennett.
Figure 16.5 Act 3: Mary confesses. Actors (L to R): Jim Peters (Judge Danforth), Cynthia Cristelli (Mary Warren), Kent Fillmore (John Proctor). Photo: Philip G. Bennett.
Figure 16.6 Avoiding Salem. Kent Fillmore (John Proctor). Photo: Philip G. Bennett.
Figure 16.7 Act 4: final moments. Actors: Dolores Neese (Elizabeth Proctor), Kent Fillmore (John Proctor). Photo: Philip G. Bennett.

Chapter 17

Figure 17.1 A curtain call for *Twelfth Night* at East Stroudsburg University. Direction: Stephanie Daventry French; costume design: Jennifer Tiranti Anderson; scenic and lighting design: Q. Brian Sickels. Photo: Stephanie Daventry French.
Figure 17.2 Primary theatre stage formats. Original illustration by Darlene Farris Labar.
Figure 17.3 Shakespeare's *Twelfth Night* at East Stroudsburg University. Photo: Brian Sickels.
Figure 17.4 The SITI Company's *Who Do You Think You Are?* Premiered March 2008; conceived and directed by Anne Bogart; created and performed by SITI

ILLUSTRATION ACKNOWLEDGMENTS

Company; Lighting Design: Brian H. Scott; Set and Costume Design: James Schuette; Sound Design: Darron L. West. Scenic designer and photographer: Yoshinori Tanokura. Photo: Michael Brosilow.

Figure 17.5a–d Stages of design for *The Devil's Music* by Angelo Parra at the George Street Playhouse in New Brunswick, New Jersey. Conception and Direction: Joe Brancato; Design—Scenic Designer: Yoshinori Tanokura; Lighting: Jeff Nellis; Costume: Toni Leslie-James; Sound: Christopher J. Bailey and Ryan Gravett; Actor/Singer: Miche Braden (as Bessie Smith). Band: Bass: James Hankins; Tenor Sax and Clarinet: Anthony Nelson; Pianist: Scott Trent.

Figure 17.6 Designer Yoshinori Tanokura consulting with work-study students Chris Walters and Tyler Adams on scenic painting. Photo: Stephanie Daventry French.

Figure 17.7 Sample headshot and résumé: Carla Harting (as of 2014). Photo: Laura Rose.

Figure 17.8 Stage area map—a proscenium with apron. Original illustration by Darlene Farris Labar.

Figure 17.9 Blocking created through Viewpoints in the SITI company's *bobrauschenbergamerica*, by Charles L. Mee; world premiere at the 2001 Humana Festival of New American Plays at Actors Theatre of Louisville, Louisville, KY; Direction: Anne Bogart. Created and Performed by: SITI Company. Designs—Set and Costumes: James Schuette, Lighting: Brian H. Scott; Soundscape: Darron L West; Choreography: Barney O'Hanlon; Properties Design: Jason Szalla, Dramaturg: Tanya Palmer, Actors (L to R): Will Bond and Barney O'Hanlon. Photo: Michael Brosilow.

Figure 17.10 Actors' body positions in relation to the audience. Original illustration by Darlene Farris Labar.

Figure 17.11 Actor coaching. Director Stephanie Daventry French coaching Merril McGuinness in Naomi Iizuka's *Polaroid Stories* at East Stroudsburg University. Photo: Charles Perry Hebard (courtesy of East Stroudsburg University of Pennsylvania).

Figure 17.12 Maria Picon (Persephone) in *Polaroid Stories* at East Stroudsburg University. Photo: Yoshinori Tanokura.

Figure 17.13 *The Threepenny Opera* by Bertolt Brecht and Kurt Weill at the San Diego Repertory Theatre. Direction: Sam Woodhouse, Musical Direction: Mark Danisovszky, Choreography: Javier Velasco, Design—Scenic: Mark Danisovszky, Costume and Makeup: Jennifer Brawn Gittings, Lighting: Trevor Norton, Assistant Director and co-dramaturg: Stephanie Daventry French, co-dramaturg Dawn Moore. Actors (top): Gale McNeeley (as Jackie "Tiger" Brown, on box), Jeffrey Meek (MacHeath), Amanda Kramer (Polly Peachum); on floor: Lyle Kanouse (Jonathan Peachum), Leigh Scarritt (Mrs. Peachum), Lisa Payton (Jenny Diver), Amy Biedel (Lucy), Ruff Yeager (Matt), Paul Kruse (Smith), and Bryan Barbarian, Karson St. John, Shawn Goodman Jones, Jim Mooney, and Danny King. Photo: Ken Jacques.

Figure 17.14 *Bruja,* by Luis Alfaro, at Borderlands Theatre Company, Tucson, Arizona. Direction: Eva Tessler, Design—Sound: Jim Klingensus, Lighting: Frank Calsbeek, Set: Andres Volovsek Urisic, Costumes: Kathy Hurst, Actors: Ester Almazan (Vieja), Angelica Rodenbeck (Bruja), Robert Encilla (Jason), Philip Bennett (Creon). Photo: Andres Volovsek.

Figure 17.15 *The Tragical History of Dr. Faustus*, by Christopher Marlowe, at the San Jose Repertory Theatre, 2013. Direction: Kirsten Brandt, Lighting and Multimedia Design: David Cuthbert, Actors: Mark Anderson Phillips (Faustus),

Lyndsy Kail (Mephistopheles), Rachel Harker and Halsey Varady (above). Photo: Kirsten Brandt.

Figure 17.16a and b The good and bad angels, *The Tragical History of Dr. Faustus*, by Christopher Marlowe, at the San Jose Repertory Theatre. Actors: Halsey Varady (Good Angel/Bad Angel), Mark Anderson Phillips (Faustus). Photo: Kirsten Brandt/San Jose Repertory Theatre.

Figure 17.17 Mixing sound. East Stroudsburg University Students Michael Lloret and Destiny Washington. Photo: Yoshinori Tanokura.

Figure 17.18 Giving notes after a run of *A Christmas Carol* by Mavor Moore, based on the novel by Charles Dickens. Director Dr. Margaret Joyce Ball and Company. Photo: Yoshinori Tanokura.

Figure 17.19 Noel Coward's *Blithe Spirit* at East Stroudsburg University; student workers Tyler Adams and Robert McIntyre (up ladder). Photo: Stephanie Daventry French.

Figure 17.20 Circuiting strip lights. Lighting crew member Michael Llorett with lighting designer Dave Dougherty. Photo: Stephanie Daventry French.

Figure 17.21 Costume design concept. Photo: Charles Perry Hebard, courtesy of East Stroudsburg University, and Dave Dougherty.

Figure 17.22 Actor notes during tech. Director Stephanie Daventry French and cast on *Polaroid Stories* by Naomi Iizuka. Photo: Charles Perry Hebard, courtesy of East Stroudsburg University.

Chapter 18

Figure 18.1 Stanislavsky's Plan of Experiencing, 1935. Original diagram courtesy of the Moscow Arts Theatre Museum.

Figure 18.3 Jamil Joseph and Jannel Armstrong in *Spike Heels* by Teresa Rebeck. Photo: Luis Vidal.

Chapter 19

Figure 19.1 Samantha Crawn and Christopher Centrella in *Polaroid Stories* by Naomi Iizuka. Photo: Charles Perry Hebard, courtesy of East Stroudsburg University.

Figure 19.2 Joseph Bednarchik and Samantha Crawn in *Polaroid Stories* by Naomi Iizuka; Lighting Design by Pierre Clavel. Photo: Charles Perry Hebard, courtesy of East Stroudsburg University.

Figure 19.3 David Ausem and Angel Berlane in *A Streetcar Named Desire* by Tennessee Williams. Photo: Stephanie Daventry French.

Figure 19.4 *The Threepenny Opera* by Bertolt Brecht, San Diego Repertory Theatre, directed by Sam Woodhouse. Actors: Jeffrey Meek (MacHeath) and Amanda Kramer (Polly Peachum). Photo: Ken Jacques.

Figure 19.5 *Oedipus del Rey* by Luis Alfaro, at Borderlands Theatre in Tucson, Arizona. Director: Eva Tessler, Design—Scenic: Andres Volovsek Urisic, Costumes: Kathy Hurst, Lighting: Frank Calsbeek, Sound: Jim Klingensus. Actors: Alida Gunn (Jocasta), Bryant Enriques (Oedipus), Guillermo Jones (Laius), Julian Martinez (Orestes). Photo: Andres Volovsek.

Figure 19.6 Mask making. Photo and designer: Yoshi Tanokura.

Figure 19.7 Ariel Princeton Mota and Ian Owstrovski in *The Phantom Tollbooth*, by Susan Nanus, based on the novel by Norton Juster. Direction: Stephanie Daventry French. Costumes and make-up: Amanda Kalinowski. Photo: Stephanie Daventry French.

Chapter 20

Figure 20.1 Stanislavsky in the late 1800s, Moscow Art Theatre company. Photo: Fine Art Images/Heritage Images/Getty Images.
Figure 20.2 Stanislavsky and Nemirovich-Danchenko, circa 1935. Photo: ITAR-TASS/TopFoto/ArenaPAL.
Figure 20.3 First reading of *The Seagull*, Moscow Art Theatre company. Photo: ITAR-TASS/TopFoto/ArenaPAL.
Figure 20.4 Leopold Sulerzhitsky. Photo: Courtesy of the Moscow Arts Theatre Museum.
Figure 20.5 Vsevolod Meyerhold. Photo: Sovfoto/UIG via Getty Images.
Figure 20.6 Evgeny Vakhtangov. Photo: Courtesy of Arsis Design.
Figure 20.7 The Cubist set design for Vakhtangov's production of *Princess Turandot*, by Carlo Gozzi. Photo: Courtesy of Arsis Design.
Figure 20.8 Mikhail (Michael) Aleksandrovich Chekhov. Photo: Fine Art Images/Heritage Images/Getty Images.
Figure 20.9 Sonia Moore. Photo: Courtesy of Irene Moore-Jaglom.
Figure 20.10 Bertolt Brecht. Photo: © Fred Stein/dpa/Corbis.
Figure 20.11 Jerzy Grotowski. Photo: Mondadori Portfolio via Getty Images.

Acknowledgments

Our gratitude to: the many people in our lives, including family, friends, students, and colleagues who supported our writing and carried on with a lot less of our time and focus because of it, particularly Pierre A. Clavel, Elise D. Clavel, Pierre S. Clavel, Pierre "Senior" Clavel, Anne S. Clavel, Ruth Ballard, Rachel French de Mejia, Adrian French, Jessica Ryan, Christopher Centrella, Margaret Ball, Yoshi Tanokura, Michael Landman, Naomi Snyder, Sara O'Donnell, Cristopher J. Koval, Grant Bashore, Bob Ebert, Bob Byars, To-Ree-Nee Wolf, Dawn Sellers, and Juan Rodriguez.

Our gratitude to: Talia Rogers for seeing that we had a book in us and nudging us for a year and a half until we said yes to writing it; to Talia and Pierre for pushing us to do it even though we said we didn't have time, which proved to be almost true; to Ben Piggott for guiding us through our first book with publishing, academic, and artistic expertise and laser focus to see inside the concepts and details while maintaining an incredible commitment to our vision; and to Anna Callander for guiding the book through the production process like a master whitewater rafting guide.

Our gratitude to: Darlene Farris-Labar, our brilliant illustrator, who worked tirelessly until each drawing was right, wanting always to deeply understand what we were trying to convey and find better ways than we could have ever imagined to do so, always with warmth and grace.

Thank you to the actors who modelled for various illustrations: Ben Adami, Pedro Kalil, and Lauren Wynn.

We are grateful to Yoshi Tanokura who contributed many professional theatre photographs to the book and whose designs are featured in ESU productions throughout.

We appreciate the contributions of the many Stanislavsky scholars and teachers whose work has been referenced throughout this book—in particular, the leadership of Dr. Sharon Marie Carnicke, whose Stanislavsky scholarship has gone a long way to correcting many misunderstandings (and to Robin Miller who connected Phil and Sharon), Dr. Rose Whyman, Lecturer in Drama and Theatre Arts, University of Birmingham (whose in-depth analysis of Stanislavsky's Plan of Experiencing was a valuable resource), and to Robert Andrew "Andy" White, who has been a leader in researching Stanislavsky's sources in yoga. We appreciate translator Jean Benedetti and Russian-language consultant Katya Kamotskaia's massive undertaking on the 2008 Routledge translation of Stanislavsky's earlier acting books into the one volume *The Actor's Work*, as well as to Benedetti's work in translating a number of important exercises not published in Stanislavsky's own books.

ACKNOWLEDGMENTS

This interdisciplinary book could not have gone forward without the careful, and in many cases repeated, readings and correction of references by experts outside our primary areas of expertise. Our gratitude goes out to Dr. Richard Wesp and Dr. Joe Meile for their detailed feedback and suggestions on the psychology and brain anatomy; to Dr. Margaret Joyce Ball for her crucial redirection in the area of voice that prompted the much needed update of our voice and speech knowledge; to Shirley Daventry French for her lifetime of yoga experience, which not only corrected any errors but allowed us to offer the yogic insights with the appropriate and deep respect for this ancient wisdom tradition; to Derek French whose expertise in both Western and Eastern medical wisdom has added to our understanding of the human instrument; to Sara Romersberger and Judith Chaffee for their knowledge of movement for actors and how it interweaves into training, tradition, and startlingly new approaches to creating theatre; to Dr. Peter Pruim for his pithy, always humorous, and apt vetting of our few references to nonacting philosophy.

Our gratitude to: to the brilliant artists and teachers we have had the great fortune to work with and learn from, some of whom include Jerzy Grotowski, Irene Moore Jaglom, Kama Ginga, Suzanne M. Trauth, Elizabeth C. Stroppel, Joseph Chaikin, Whoopi Goldberg, Tina Landau, Anne Bogart, Peter Brook, William Peters, Ruth Zapora, Bert Houle, Sophie Wibaux, Valerie Reed, Don Rieder, Theodore Shank, Les Waters, Sam Woodhouse, Michael Grief, Robert Woodruff, James Howell, Herbert Rodriquez, and Julie Hebert (as well as the many playwrights whose art taught us even though we never met them); to the Association for Theatre in Higher Education (ATHE) and our many colleagues there who invited us to present (which led directly to this book), attended our workshops, and shared their vast collective knowledge over many years; to yoga teachers Judith Hanson Lasater, Ramanand Patel and Jenn J. Allen.

Most importantly, this book would not exist without the lifelong dedication to art of the master teachers in our acting legacy: Konstantin S. Stanislavksy, Evgeny Vahktangov, Sonia Moore, and for French – Philip G. Bennett.

Thank you all from the bottom of our hearts.

Text acknowledgments

Act II extract, from *The Crucible* by Arthur Miller, copyright 1952, 1953, 1954, renewed © 1980, 1981, 1982 by Arthur Miller. Used by permission of Viking Books, an imprint of Penguin Publishing Group, a division of Penguin Random House LLC (for the USA), and of the Wylie Agency (UK) Limited (for the World, excluding USA).

Extracts from *The Feeling of What Happens* by Antonio Damasio. Published by William Heinemann. Reprinted by permission of The Random House Group Limited.

CHAPTER 1

An Invitation to the Quest for Inspiration

"All growth is a leap in the dark,
a spontaneous unpremeditated act without benefit of experience."[1]

—Henry Miller

- Enter the Actor . . . You
- What Is Inspiration?
- The Actor's Creative Journal
- What Are Audiences Hoping for in a Performance?
- The Path to Peak Performance—Myths and Realities
- If You Have Talent, Why Do You Need Technique?
- The Actor's Palette—Stanislavsky and Beyond

Enter the Actor . . . You

You have taken a leap, entered an acting class, and opened this book. Exploring the terrain of acting requires curiosity and courage. If you apply yourself to this journey actively and with discipline, you will make amazing discoveries about yourself, human existence, and the art of acting. Every new class, new company, new play or screenplay, new performance is uncharted territory for continued investigation and discovery. If you can approach growing as an actor with **beginner's mind**, no matter your level of experience, and engage fully in each new opportunity, expansion and insight await.

> **Beginner's mind** is a Zen concept designed to increase our capacity for learning and growth. The practitioner empties his mind of preconceptions, releases preprogramed habits, and is ready to accept new ideas offered and consider the possibilities. This perspective can be helpful for openness to learning whether the student is a neophyte or more experienced in the area of study.

[1] Henry Miller, *The Wisdom of the Heart*, 2nd ed. (New York: New Directions, 1946, p. 90.)

Of course you could settle for the limiting alternative expressed by Shakespeare's character Macbeth, who describes human existence as "a poor player that struts and frets his hour upon the stage and then is heard no more" and offer merely "a tale told by an idiot, full of sound and fury, signifying nothing." (*Macbeth* V.v. lines 2381–2385). Acting need not be merely a clever bag of illusions, however, but can be a path to greater awareness, truth, and communication. The actor has the power to be like a shaman from an ancient culture, leading the audience into a deeper understanding of themselves, other human beings, our present world, and our history. While still critiquing bad acting in his speech to the players, Shakespeare, through Hamlet, nevertheless

Figure 1.1 Bamboo forest, Kyoto, Japan.
Photo: Stephanie Daventry French

expresses hope for theatre art "to hold as 'twere the mirror up to nature" (*Hamlet* III.ii. lines 17–24). By taking this class, by opening this book, you have taken the first step to becoming an inspired and inspiring artist.

What Is Inspiration?

Artists, inventors, scientists, and athletes all understand that in order to achieve anything worthwhile and to feel the keen sense of aliveness possible through their endeavor, they must find an entry point into a state of peak performance. This state is referred to in various fields by different terms, such as the *zone* (sports), *flow* (psychology and business), or inspiration. As artists, we most commonly use the term *inspiration*. *Inspiration* comes "from the Latin *inspirare:* 'to breathe' or 'blow into.' The word was originally used of a divine or supernatural being, in the sense of to 'impart a truth or idea to someone.'"[2] Inspiration is something very difficult to describe but very clear when one witnesses it or experiences it directly. Here are a number of ways we sought to describe this experience that may remind you of moments when you have been inspired.

Inspiration can be:

- a realization of great clarity—an "aha" moment when something that had been challenging is deeply understood;
- knowing without thinking (when the truth of something is known at a gut level

[2] *Oxford English Dictionary*, Oxford Dictionaries Online, Oxford University Press, 2014. oxforddictionaries.com (British and World English), *inspire*, origins.

1 THE QUEST FOR INSPIRATION

prior to thinking it through logically—perhaps only after this knowing are the facts and logical path shown to support it);
- an insight, answer, or solution that comes to us spontaneously from the subconscious mind;
- a heightened sense of aliveness (akin to being in love); or
- a sense of being touched by a profound collective experience, the **collective unconscious**, the divine, God, or however you perceive this vast body of wisdom greater than any one of us alone (this can happen, for example, at a religious ceremony where a part of the ritual is collectively experienced at a profound level, or at a concert when the musicians and audience are elevated through collective song or dance).

> ### The Collective Unconscious and Universality in Art
>
> The collective unconscious—so far as we can say anything about it at all—appears to consist of mythological motifs or primordial images, for which reason the myths of all nations are its real exponents. In fact, the whole of mythology could be taken as a sort of projection of the collective unconscious. … We can therefore study the collective unconscious in two ways, either in mythology or in the analysis of the individual.[3]
>
> When a work of art is considered **universal**, touching and inspiring people across time and cultures, the artist may be tapping into motifs from the collective unconscious.

In acting, inspiration can take many forms; some examples include:

- a clarity of mind whereby an actor knows instinctively what to do as the character (in a state of true inspiration everything we do is right for the character);
- a sudden insight that provides a creative solution to a particularly perplexing challenge in the script;
- a deep understanding of the human *psyche* (the conscious, subconscious, and unconscious mind) that can be accessed and conveyed;
- a production where all the disparate insights into the play coalesce into a unified *aesthetic* (a guiding artistic principle);
- a shared experience between performers and audience; or
- a *superconscious* state, an experience whereby life is breathed into an artistic creation, and real emotions and insights are triggered in artist and audience.

The Actor's Creative Journal

Developing more awareness of yourself, and of others, is a key to acting. One tool that can be very helpful in this process is a creative journal. In it, you can write down insights as you observe yourself and others in the process of acting, observe real human behavior, and consider other topics of relevance to acting. Engaging in

---

[3] Carl Jung, "The Concept of the Collective Unconscious," *Collected Works*, 9.1 (Princeton, NJ: Princeton University Press, 1936), 42.

this way will help you retain and understand the new concepts, as well as enhance your ability to use the new information. You can write notes for classes and rehearsals, creative observations, and details of interesting human behavior. If you write in enough detail, you can go back and draw on these resources later for various characters and plays. Throughout this book, we will suggest reflection journals on specific topics. Here is the first of these:

> **1.1** *Reflection Journal—Inspiration*
>
> Recall and jot down one or more moments in your own life when you have experienced or observed inspiration. Do you recall any specifics as to physical sensations, thoughts, or emotions?

What Are Audiences Hoping for in a Performance?

It is easiest to start with a clear goal and figure out the steps we need to take to achieve it. Theatre is a collaborative performing art presented to a public group, rather than a solitary art appreciated by solitary members of the public. Perhaps a good starting place is the question, What are audiences hoping for from an actor's performance?

Audience members come to the theatre for a variety of reasons. Some of them are similar to the reasons we go to a live sporting event or a live music concert even though the quality might be much better if we were to watch it on television or listen to a high-definition recording. There is a need for collective experience, for feeling part of a group. We get great joy in collective expression—cheering together or heckling our opponents. At a music concert we may sing or dance with others. At the theatre, we laugh together, cry together, applaud together, and sometimes listen intently in silent, collective awe with hundreds of other people, perhaps releasing a sigh at a moment of familiar human truth. Most of us have experienced release when we let out a deep, extended belly laugh, or sob as we identify with a character's plight. These experiences can be even more powerful when echoed by others in the audience. At a live performance, the audience's responses affect the performers as well; thus audience and performers are cocreators of the event.

> "In the theatre with a packed audience, with a thousand hearts beating in union with the actor's heart a wonderful resonant acoustic is created for our feelings. For every moment genuinely experienced onstage we get back a response from the audience, participation, empathy, invisible currents from a thousand living, emotionally stimulated people who create the performance with us."
>
> —Stanislavsky, 2009: 294

At other times a performance can help us gain insights into ourselves. We cannot always see clearly what to do as crises arise in our own lives; however, from aesthetic distance, observing similar dilemmas performed before us on stage or in a film, we can consider possible solutions and learn from the effective or ineffective choices attempted by characters in the story. Sometimes, an actor demonstrates an understanding, through the character's dilemma, of an issue that we thought was unique to us, perhaps a shameful secret we have hidden and been burdened by. When we realize, from observing it truthfully depicted on stage, that others have experienced this, too, this in itself can be profoundly healing and we may feel less isolated.

Many people go to see theatre or films for entertainment or escape. A great performance can transport us to another life and time, thereby broadening our understanding of others and the world. Sometimes our own problems seem small as we put them in a larger perspective. We may laugh in the comedies at the ridiculousness of the petty struggles of life and feel relief from life's burdens.

"The theatre infects the audience with its noble ecstasy."
—Stanislavsky quoted in Moore, 1978: 5.

We are also drawn to greatness—both in the level of accomplishment of the athletes, musicians, or actors, and in the mountain they are attempting to climb before us at the current event. Plays and films generally reveal characters in challenging circumstances and also demand great feats of artistry from the actor to express this struggle. If the actors are inspired, they can provide a bridge so that the audience moves through that engaging experience with the characters. Through a great actor, we can be moved to depths of emotion—the agonies and the ecstasies—that make us feel more alive.

We live a more expansive life through identifying with a good actor in a role: We fall in love; we are triumphant, or we get revenge unfettered for a moment by moral restraint and lawful behavior; we speed through a car chase in a hot car out of our price range; we find, through our heroes, power to triumph against unjust forces. To be in the presence of an inspired artist can be equally inspiring for the audience.

The Path to Peak Performance—Myths and Realities

Many people watch sports, most listen to music, many watch actors. While most people have played sports, even if just in physical education classes, and have had at least early music training, far fewer have actually tried acting. While most people realize that to be an Olympic athlete takes years of dedicated training, some people believe that being a top actor is just a matter of talent and luck. In his book *Training Camp: What the Best Do Better than Anyone Else*, Jon Gordon debunks the myth of overnight success and discusses that one of the most notable differences between the good and the great is simple: the great put in additional hours of dedication and practice on top of what those who are pretty good do.[4] In American soccer/world football one of the biggest factors that determines the skill level of the player is the number of touches on the ball over years of training and game play.

There are many similarities in the training and preparation of artists, musicians, and athletes. Talent, luck, and the right connections are important for success but are not enough to become great. Top athletes, musicians, and actors all need years of training and practice before they can hope to deliver truly inspired performances on the world stage. Skill development and practice in application are central in the development of athletes, musicians, and actors. Even after they are accomplished, actors, athletes, and musicians continue to practice regularly if they hope to remain

---

[4] Jon Gordon. *Training Camp: What the Best Do Better than Anyone Else* (unabridged audiobook, 2010).

on top of their respective fields. All of this requires determination, encouragement, and a great deal of discipline.

In order to invite this state of creativity/flow/peak performance for an important event, athletes, musicians, and actors train until the task becomes reflexive, intuitive. Just before the event they warm up physically and prepare mentally to make sure they are focused and alert; actors also warm up vocally. Many have other rituals of a religious, superstitious, or secular nature that they perform unfailingly to encourage forces from outside to assist them in their goals, to call good fortune upon themselves and their team. Soccer players will often cross themselves, kiss their fingers and gesture up to the sky before entering the field or after a goal. Baseball players often have lucky tokens and a pattern of physical, often quirky, rituals they perform before pitching or batting. Some actors also have such rituals to invite inspiration.

There need be no direct or proven cause and effect correlation between the superstitious ritual and the desired outcome; however, there seems to be a proven effect on the subject resulting from their *belief* in the ritual. Belief comes from coincidental reinforcement—especially if the times when the ritual does not correlate with success are dismissed. Psychologist B. F. Skinner in his 1948 study "Superstition in the Pigeon," found that "a few accidental connections between a ritual and favorable consequence suffice to set up and maintain the behavior in spite of many unreinforced instances."[5]

This belief in the ritual has shown some impact on the performer and thereby the performance, even if the ritual itself has no demonstrated impact. Damisch, Stoberock, and Mussweiler in their research journal article "Keep Your Fingers Crossed! How Superstition Improves Performance" found that "activating good-luck-related superstitions via a common saying or action (e.g. 'break a leg,' keeping one's fingers crossed) or a lucky charm improves subsequent performance in golfing, motor dexterity, memory, and anagram games." They go on to suggest that "activating a superstition boosts participants' confidence in mastering upcoming tasks, which in turn improves performance."[6]

> **Flow**
>
> Psychologist Mihaly Csikszentmihalyi defined peak performance as "flow." This state, which people describe as highly enjoyable, involves being focused in the present on the task at hand for its own sake rather than for a future reward. In his book *Flow: The Psychology of Optimal Experience*, Csikszentmihalyi describes flow as "The ego falls away. Time flies. Every action, movement, and thought follows inevitably from the previous one, like playing jazz. Your whole being is involved, and you're using your skills to the utmost." (Csikszentmihalyi 1991: 39)

---

[5] B. F. Skinner, "Superstition in the Pigeon," *Journal of Experimental Psychology* 38 (1948): 171.
[6] Lysann Damisch, Barbara Stoberock, and Thomas Mussweiler, "Keep Your Fingers Crossed! How Superstition Improves Performance," *Association for Psychological Science* 21, no. 7 (2010): 1014.

1 THE QUEST FOR INSPIRATION

> In *Creativity: Flow and the Psychology of Discovery and Invention*, Csikszentmihalyi relates the concept of flow to creativity through the study of famous artists, athletes, scientists such as Nobel Prize winners, as well as other working people. The experience was described similarly among people in very different disciplines, even though the path to the experience in terms of activities was entirely different. He found that the feeling of creative flow that did not come easily, nor could it be achieved through taking drugs or alcohol, or through privileges related to wealth or position. In most cases, the path to peak experience involved demanding, prolonged and sometimes even painful work, risk and new challenges in areas that the participants were unsure they could meet. Yet, they were motivated by the quality of the peak experience to push through these obstacles (Csikszentmihalyi 1997: 110; 111–14).

In ancient Greece, the birthplace of Western theatre, artists prayed to goddesses called the *Muses*, who were thought to have the power to infuse them with inspiration. After Spain defeated Germany in the 2010 soccer World Cup semifinal, an ABC TV announcer said, "Germany couldn't quite find the muse!" The team was clearly good enough to get to the semifinal and probably good enough to win, but that day they lacked the inspiration that Spain managed to channel. This quest for some kind of magical or spiritual extra ingredient was humorously played out with the Germans' employing Paul the Psychic Octopus to predict the winner of the 2010 World Cup. The octopus beat the odds and correctly predicted 11 out of 13 games, but when he correctly predicted that Germany would lose to Spain in the semifinal, some Germans threatened to eat him. I guess Germany found their muse in 2014, as they came back to win the World Cup. In any sport reporting you will frequently hear reporters saying a team, or specific players, were inspired or uninspired. The techniques in this book are designed to teach you to invite inspiration more consistently.

Figure 1.2 Sarcophagus of the Muses, white marble, Rome, 180–200 CE, Vienna Museum of Art History.
Photo: © Araldo de Luca/Corbis

Figure 1.3 Paul, Germany's Octopus Oracle. He correctly predicted 11 out of 13 games in the 2010 soccer World Cup. Photo: © Wolfgang Rattay/Reuters/Corbis

If You Have Talent, Why Do You Need Technique?

When we witness realistic acting, the most predominant style today in films and theatre, we see people behaving much as they do in real life. Thus, many of us think, "I could do that!" Yet while in life we respond automatically through many autonomic systems to real stimuli, on the stage everything is artificial. The actress playing Juliet is not really in love with the young man playing Romeo. The actor who is portraying Hamlet likely starts rehearsals with no filial feelings toward the actress playing his mother, Gertrude, and we don't want Othello to really strangle the actress playing Desdemona. Additionally, when the actor exits through the door of the set, instead of a snow-strewn landscape or whatever reality the play's world conveys, there are in fact unpainted flats on the other side with braces to hold up the walls and a stage crew member on headset with a flashlight to guide the actors safely into the wings. Most people find even walking naturally across a stage, when observed by others, to be difficult. How hard is it then to generate a peak emotion at a precise moment in the script for eight live shows per week, or eight *takes*[7] in a row on a film shoot?

Actors, to consistently deliver performances at this level, require technique. Additionally, even the most naturally talented actors will meet scripts that they do not immediately connect with or understand. How do you begin to approach work on such a film or play? How do you consistently deliver peak performances? Stanislavsky dedicated his life to trying to answer these questions. The answer that

---

[7] A *take* is each time a segment of a scene or a whole scene is filmed. There are often many takes of one small moment. Some of the many reasons for that include the need for different camera angles, to adjust to technical issues, or to bring out something different in the acting.

he came to, and that our years of experience validate, is that the actor must develop reliable technique. Good technique, in sport or music or acting, must be trained and then trusted so that it flows instinctively. This leads to insights in rehearsal and inspiration in performance.

The Actor's Palette—Stanislavsky and Beyond

Whether you are a novice or an experienced actor, it is our intention to enrich your experience. We offer you an Actor's Palette of approaches to training and application of practical and useful techniques for rehearsal and performance. These may be used to begin to develop your acting ability or to supplement acting skills you have already acquired. A good house, as you know, needs a solid foundation—and for that we have chosen Stanislavsky's System. The System is a reliable basis from which to grow and expand as an actor into any theatrical style and through which you can incorporate a wide array of other distinct techniques.

The quest for inspiration was at the center of Konstantin Stanislavsky's work as actor, director, and acting teacher. Stanislavsky developed a system of actor training that, supplemented by our own unique approaches, will be outlined in this book. In addition to being an effective technique, it is important to know about the System if you plan to act in the Western theatre, as directors will use Stanislavsky terminology and expect you to translate that on the stage. We found Stanislavsky's System at the core of actor training in top acting schools as far away as Shanghai, China.[8]

Training will begin with conditioning your psychophysical instrument and exploration of all the key Elements of Action through nonverbal and then verbal exercises and improvisations. Then, as you move on to scene work you will advance to Active Analysis of a Role. We will take you step-by-step through Stanislavsky's culminating technique that coalesced during his work on Molière's *Tartuffe*, in his final years after a lifetime of experimentation and discovery. This book is about your present training and future possibilities. Learning goes deeper and the skills are more at your command if you know the theory behind them, and thus some theory will be offered, but the primary focus of our book is on applying the theory in active exploration. After you have had a chance to develop as an actor through this work, you might like to understand and honor Stanislavsky's legacy, and thus Chapter 20 will give you some of the history of the development and dissemination of the System.

Stanislavsky's research was inspired by his experience as an actor, director, and teacher. He expanded that by culling ideas from the great artists and thinkers of the nineteenth and early twentieth centuries, as well as from ancient wisdom traditions such as yoga. Stanislavsky read widely, integrating ideas that might shed light on acting from science, philosophy, ancient wisdom, and the emerging psychology of his time. He continued to revise his System throughout his life based on his own applied experimentation.

---

[8] The Xiejin Television and Film Art College of Shanghai Normal University teaches a four-year conservatory training in the late Stanislavsky System. This was taught to them by Russian teachers of the System in a Communist cultural exchange long before China was reopened to Western cultural influences. Professor French went to China in 2010 to develop an exchange program between this college and East Stroudsburg University's Department of Theater where she teaches.

This book is the synthesis of our many years of teaching the Stanislavsky System as passed on to us in direct lineage through the oral tradition (From Konstantin Stanislavsky to Evgeny Vakhtangov to Sonia Moore to Philip G. Bennett to Stephanie Daventry French). Our applied technique has been enhanced by Stanislavsky's own writings as well as the writings of his protégés. We have also looked at revisions to his writings, as errors have been uncovered and corrected by the many excellent Stanislavsky scholars, including but not limited to Dr. Sharon M. Carnicke, Professor and Associate Dean, University of Southern California; Dr. R. Andrew White, Associate Professor of Theater, Valparaiso University; Dr. Rose Whyman, Lecturer in Drama and Theatre Arts, University of Birmingham; and the late Jean Benedetti, Principal of Rose Bruford College of Theatre and Performance in London. It is also the synthesis of our many years of exploring these techniques in acting classes and rehearsals, as well as our amalgamation of Stanislavsky's approach with other techniques developed by innovators in acting, movement, voice, improvisation, and experimental theatre.

Just as Stanislavsky did not want actors to offer a performance frozen in a past rehearsal, but rather a performance that was as alive and full of spirit as the present audience, he did not want a fixed, but rather a living acting system. Because of this, we believe he would have wanted future generations to build on the vital legacy he gave us and incorporate new discoveries in art and science that he could not have imagined. To this end, we have intentionally borrowed from an array of sources that shed light on the many challenges of the actor, in particular how to consciously activate subconscious and normally autonomic systems of our body, mind, and emotions. These techniques interweave to develop a consistently *creative state* most conducive to inviting what Stanislavsky described as the **superconscious**.

> **Superconscious**
>
> "Professor Jules-Bois of the Sorbonne said in 1928 that French psychologists have investigated and accorded recognition to the superconsciousness, which, in its grandeur 'is the exact opposite of the subconscious mind as conceived of by Freud, and which comprises the faculties that make man really man and not just a super-animal.' The French savant explained that the awakening of the higher consciousness is 'not to be confused with Coueism or hypnotism. The existence of a superconscious mind has long been recognized philosophically, being in reality the Over-Soul spoken of by Emerson; but only recently has it been recognized scientifically.'"
> —Yogananda 1946; 1981: note 7.3

Stanislavsky came to the ultimate conclusion that *psychophysical action* (action that unifies the mind, body, breath, emotions, and spirit) is at the center of acting and that actors must therefore be psychophysically trained to be able to fulfill psychophysical actions at will. Many sources examine and shed light on the connections between the mind and body, mind and emotions, and emotional expression through the face and body. Scientists have developed tools that can measure some of the experiences that artists and yogis have claimed for centuries and that we are familiar with in our creative work.

1 THE QUEST FOR INSPIRATION

Sprinkled throughout this book are references to contemporary scientific findings that measure human experiences relevant to acting. Neuroscience has confirmed, for example, the inseparable interconnectedness of the mind, the body, and the emotions. Contemporary scientific studies in relevant areas seem to verify Stanislavsky's insights, but occasionally they also offer us new tools for actor training. In this book, you will find references to yoga, neuroscience, biological science, psychology, and additional scientific insights that add to Stanislavsky's original yogic and late nineteenth- to early twentieth-century scientific inspirations for the System.

This technique need not limit actors to a specific style of theatre, as some mistakenly believe. Stanislavsky did work a lot in early realism, for a number of reasons particularly as dictated by survival in the politically charged atmosphere of Soviet Russia (as discussed in Chapter 20, The Evolving Stanislavsky System). He had experience as both an actor and director and interest in a wide array of theatrical styles. He supported laboratories to explore new forms of theatre at the Moscow Art Theatre. He chose Molière's nonrealistic verse text *Tartuffe*—a *farce* inspired by the broad physical comedy of the Italian Commedia Dell'Arte—to convey his ultimate technique. He worked closely with Vsevolod Meyerhold, Evgeny Vakhtangov, and Michael Chekhov and influenced Jerzy Grotowski and Bertolt Brecht, all extolled for their various styles of nonrealistic theatre (more information on these artists and their overlaps with Stanislavsky is found in Chapter 20). Studying Stanislavsky's System does not preclude your expanding your approach with other valuable performance techniques but only gives you a springboard to make even better use of them.

Good actors and acting teachers are capable of continual invention, and yet there is no need to invent an entire acting system from scratch. This book will offer an introduction to acting in a comprehensive system that can serve as a foundation. This technique cannot be fully assimilated, to a point of being instinctive, in one semester or even one year, but in only one semester students will develop an awareness of themselves in the processes of acting and learn a comprehensive approach to either improvisations or work on a role in a play. The work of beginning students who study this system, even for one semester, is consistently good—and often excellent—depending on how diligently the students apply themselves to both the preparation and the onstage exploration. This is true for both liberal arts theatre and theatre conservatory students, as well as students taking acting as a general education requirement prior to making any level of commitment to acting as an art.

As we update this most valuable technique, we hope that future generations will do the same with our offering. By means of this exploratory approach, we hope to instill in you, the artist, the driving need to break through boundaries, to investigate the important ideas of your time, and to contribute to society through the advancement of science and through the public expression of your art. We invite you to begin, or continue, as a student of acting and to develop into the artist you wish to be so that you might carry on the quest for inspiration.

"The teacher opens the door, but you must enter by yourself"
—Anonymous Buddhist proverb

Figure 1.4 Ancient meditation garden in Kyoto, Japan.
Photo: Stephanie Daventry French

New Theatre Terms, Concepts, and Artists

Terms used in the Stanislavsky System are in italics.

- Actor's Palette
- aesthetic
- Bertolt Brecht
- Michael Chekhov
- Commedia Dell'Arte
- *creative state*
- farce
- Jerzy Grotowski
- *inspiration*
- Vsevolod Meyerhold
- *psychophysical*
- *superconscious state*
- Evgeny Vakhtangov

Interdisciplinary Terms, Concepts and Experts

- beginner's mind
- collective unconscious
- Mihaly Csikszentmihalyi
- flow (flow of impulse)
- peak performance
- the zone

PART 1

PSYCHOPHYSICAL CONDITIONING

Chapters in Part 1
2. The Actor's Palette: Interconnected Elements of Action	15
3. The Creative State: Preparing for Inspiration	37
4. Yoga and Acting: Dedication to the Creative Space	62
5. The Psychophysical Instrument: Exploring the Mind-Body Connection	77

In Chapter 2, The Actor's Palette: Interconnected Elements of Action; Chapter 3, The Creative State: Preparing for Inspiration; Chapter 4, Yoga and Acting: Dedication to the Creative Space; and Chapter 5, The Psychophysical Instrument: Exploring the Mind-Body Connection, the focus will be on the investigation of your mind and your body as amazing tools for creating art in the theatre. You will explore how to develop the creative state most conducive to peak performance in acting, called inspiration. A variety of exercises in these chapters are designed to develop your conscious use of the communication and activation pathways between your mind and your body. Sprinkled throughout is information from contemporary science and from ancient yogic practices that will deepen your understanding of your psychophysical instrument. Stanislavsky's foundational techniques, that serve as building blocks for the System, he called the Elements of Action. In Part I: Psychophysical Conditioning you will start by exploring only a few Elements of Action at a time. Later, you will learn how they interweave and how to juggle all of the elements simultaneously.

CHAPTER 2

The Actor's Palette: Interconnected Elements of Action

"Acting is action. The basis of theatre is doing, dynamism. The word 'drama' itself in Ancient Greek means 'an action being performed.' In Latin the corresponding word is action, and the root of this same word has passed into our vocabulary, 'action', 'actor', 'act'. So drama is an action we can see being performed, and, when he comes on, the actor becomes an agent in that action."[1]

—Konstantin Stanislavsky

Elements of Action Actively Explored

Imagination, sensory evocation, tempo-rhythm, to treat as

Other Acting Concepts Explored

Mime, physical obstacle, objective, three *wheres*

Part I: The Artificial Environment of the Stage
- How Do You Create Life-like, Truthful Behavior Onstage When the Environment Is Artificial?
- How Does Science Relate to the Study of Acting?
- Actions: Stanislavsky's Key to Acting
- Through-Action
- How Does This Relate to Actor Training?
- An Important Note on Personal Mental and Physical Challenges Arising in Actor Training

Part II: Early Diagnostic Exercises
- Exercise 2.1: A Habitual Activity (Nonverbal)
- Exercise 2.2: The Burnt House (Nonverbal)

Part III: The Preliminary Elements of Action
- Elements of Action to Develop Awareness of Self and Other
- Elements of Action Applied to Imaginary Circumstances

---

[1] Stanislavsky, *An Actor's Work* (p. 40).

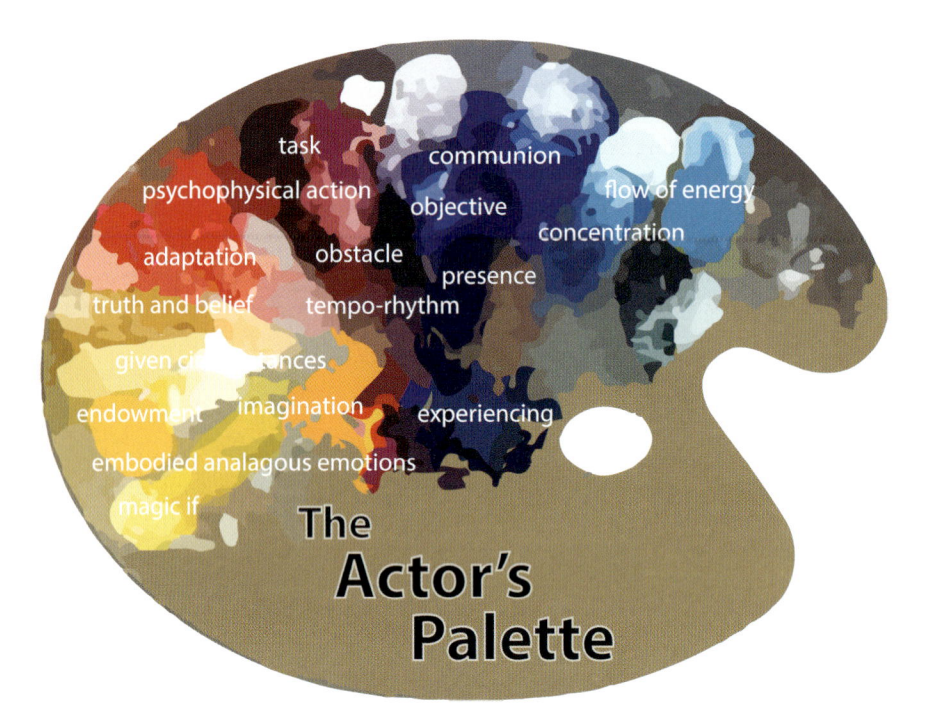

Figure 2.1 The Actor's Palette of colors from the Stanislavsky System.

PART I: THE ARTIFICIAL ENVIRONMENT OF THE STAGE

> **How Do You Create Life-like, Truthful Behavior Onstage When the Environment Is Artificial?**

In life, the circumstances of our birth, upbringing, and environment condition our behavior. While some physical behavior is instinctual from birth, such as a baby knowing how to suckle its mother's breast for milk, many physical movements, such as sitting up, standing, and walking, are learned through example and experimentation. Once initially learned, these physical behaviors become habits through repetition, embedded as neural pathways in our brains and connected to muscle memory in our bodies; we no longer have to think to fulfill them. They become *learned instinct* or *second nature*. We learn to use a knife and fork (or chopsticks), tie our shoelaces, read, ride a bicycle, and drive a car, and in a very short time we no longer have to consciously give thought to how to perform these actions. We can even be thinking about other things as we go through the motions of the behavior, and sometimes we can even fulfill habitual behavior without consciously realizing we are doing it.

Initially, when attempting to duplicate real-life actions in the artificial circumstances of the stage, however, they seem stilted and awkward. Sometimes this is because there is no natural trigger or motivation for the behavior, and sometimes because of the self-consciousness of knowing we are being observed. In order to repeat truthful human behavior on the stage, you will need to retrain consciously creating simple physical actions in this artificial environment until they become second nature. You can then perform them as you do when no one is watching. Stanislavsky often used the term *organic behavior* (derived from living organisms), as he tried to base his acting System on what he called "nature's laws,"[2] the principles that govern an actor's creativity as well as much of human behavior outside of acting.

During the course of training in the System you will gradually explore a wider and wider range of typical human behaviors, which we shall call *psychophysical actions*. You will start with simple physical behaviors, such as to sit in a chair or to open a door, and notice and respond to how they are conditioned by different types of imaginary circumstances. When *purpose* is added to *justify* (supply motivation for) these *physical actions* they become *psychophysical*. In other words the mind (thoughts, sensations, and emotions) and body (physical behavior as well as outward expression of the thoughts and emotions, and the physical feelings of emotions in the body) become integrated, and full of life, or as we say in the theatre: *justified*.

As the basics are assimilated, you will explore more-complex situations, such as the individual relationships within group dynamics in an imaged event. Examples might include a natural or man-made emergency, or a sophisticated spy intrigue where what is really going on in nonverbal communication often contradicts the obvious larger physical behaviors and the spoken words. Later, you will graduate to the imaginary circumstances given by a playwright, director, and design team and have to learn to reflect a character different from you while still triggering real emotional responses and expressing them through your psychophysical system.

How Does Science Relate to the Study of Acting?

It is not easy at first to have your mind, body and emotions respond as someone other than you, a character, would in the unfamiliar and artificial circumstances given by a playwright. You will need to become conscious of how all these mechanisms function within your own psychophysical system. Modern science offers you many insights to enhance your personal experience of your psychophysical instrument. In science, the study and understanding of the functions of living things or their parts is called *physiology*. The study of how the nervous system, including the brain, affects physical behavior is called *behavioral neuroscience*. An emerging field that combines psychology, philosophy, and biology is called *cognitive neuroscience*. Physiology's concept of *proprioception*, inner awareness of the body in space, balance and motion, and *kinesthetic awareness*, an external awareness of movement patterns and proximity to people and space, are also useful in actor training.

We will refer to the inseparable connection between the mind, body and spirit as *psychophysical*, a continuous multi-directional communication system. In books with a scientific basis the term *bodymind* is sometimes used; however, because Stanislavsky preferred the term *psychophysical*, we primarily use this term. To develop your psychophysical conditioning and responsiveness, we will draw on the above scientific fields along with new research on rewiring habits, as well as Stanislavsky's training, which relied partly on Ivan Pavlov's (1849–1936) *conditioned*

---

[2] David Allen, *Stanislavski for Beginners*. (New York: Writers and Readers, 1999), 141.

Figure 2.2 It's not easy at first to respond as someone other than yourself in unfamiliar and artificial circumstances. Jamil Joseph and Jannel Armstrong in *Spike Heels* by Theresa Rebeck.
Photo: Bob Weidner, courtesy of East Stroudsburg University

response. You will need to become conscious of how all these mechanisms function within your own psychophysical system.

Another field of wisdom on connecting the mind-body stretching back thousands of years is yoga. Yoga, you will see in Chapter 4: Yoga and Acting, is foundational to much of Stanislavsky's System.

Actions: Stanislavsky's Key to Acting

Stanislavsky found that psychophysical action is the central building block used in the creation of a character and a play. By subordinating all the elements of technique to psychophysical action, Stanislavsky answered several questions that had haunted him for decades: How does an actor honestly come from himself without pretending to be a character and at the same time project someone who is different in almost every way from himself? How does an actor perform in different styles and genres and execute different gestures, traits, and behaviors without repeating them from role to role? How can an actor safely stir feelings and emotions in an artistic and healthy manner? Through the truthful fulfillment of a purposeful, psychophysical action in concrete circumstances, he found, the actor can stir the entire inner complex of thoughts, feelings, sensations, and emotions that are appropriate for the given circumstances of the play and the character (or the improvisation).

Through-Action

After mastering single actions, you will need to practice a progressive pattern of *physical actions* until those patterns also become *organic* and *second nature*. When a young pianist begins practicing scales, she gradually progresses to more complex combinations of finger-patterns until the individual fingering of the keys becomes automatic, thereby allowing her, in the course of time, to master her instrument. In much the same way a dancer may learn a selected pattern of movements or an athlete a specialized task for their sport and be able to repeat the series as learned behavior while thinking of other things. As an actor, you too can explore and commit to *kinesthetic memory* (the *memory of the body*), patterns of physical and speech behaviors that can then be consciously recalled.

Remember that you already did this to learn patterns of behavior you use in life (such as daily grooming habits). You need to learn and use these patterns more consciously as an actor. In the same way, you will learn how a pattern of justified, and therefore psychophysical actions, lead as steps—a *through-line of action*—toward a character's larger purpose or *supertask*.

How Does This Relate to Actor Training?

As training in psychophysical action is at the core of the Stanislavsky System it will be a *leitmotif* (repeated theme) throughout this book and will be explored in detail in Chapter 8: Nonverbal Action: Communicating through Behavior. In Stanislavsky's training, the entire first semester—or, at one time, the entire first year—would be devoted to silent action. Today, most students work with scenes and monologues in the first semester. In preparation for successful scene work, training in silent actions allows students to experientially learn each Element of Action before applying these concepts in an integrated approach to a scene or monologue. This understanding also gives meaning to the teacher's or director's coaching when they refer to the elements in the scene that need to be strengthened. Ahead of our overview of the Elements of Action in this chapter, we offer two exercises. The first one is very simple. The second one more layered. An idea, which is foundational to learning the System, is that you have repeated actual experiences of every Element of Action. Reading the definitions and theory behind the elements then serves to deepen understanding of the experience.

> **An Important Note on Personal Mental and Physical Challenges Arising in Actor Training**
>
> Whether you approach acting though imaginary characters and situations or during exploratory and training improvisations where you come more from yourself, acting may tap into or reawaken strong personal feelings. This may make you feel more alive than you have felt for some time and be a wonderful, even cathartic, experience; however, if feelings arise that you would prefer not to awaken at this time, because of past trauma or other personal challenges, it is best to arrange to speak personally with your teacher outside of class to let him know. He can then bring understanding and work out with you whether to approach certain subjects, situations, or emotional stimuli or to put them aside (either forever or until you are ready at a later date). How much you choose to disclose is up to you. You need only say this exercise or this class is bringing up some challenging issues for me and I may need to pull back from that or sit out. Sometimes,

we choose as artists to work through personal challenges through our art, but this has to happen when an individual is ready and has the support to do this.

The teacher is not a therapist but may be able to point you toward a qualified professional should you need one. If you had a physical injury, you would not do the physical exercises without making adjustments that your physical therapist has told you to make and letting the teacher know of your restrictions. While some people feel there is more stigma around mental or emotional challenges, this is merely a limitation on the current evolution of society, not something wrong or shameful in you. Everyone has strengths and challenges. For the most part, artists, including your theatre teacher, will have more sensitivity to such issues and will try to make the acting class a safe space to express and explore more aspects of yourself.

While the ocean is calm we can have a relaxing day at the beach, but when it is stormy, we should treat it with caution and care. We need to have the same consideration for the emotional stirrings of ourselves and others and learn to stir our feelings in healthy ways as actors.

PART II: EARLY DIAGNOSTIC EXERCISES

Discover what comes naturally to you and what you will have to develop as an actor.

Exercise 2.1: A Habitual Activity (Nonverbal) (SDF)

Purpose: The focus is to explore a familiar human behavior in the artificial environment of the stage without using words. It is good to start with something familiar, as you can then recall and use the many details that circumscribe even the simplest behavior.

Guidelines:
- Select a simple physical task that you do every day, such as brushing your teeth, putting in your contact lenses, or making coffee or tea in the morning.
- Think about the room where you do this activity. Close your eyes and try to create this room in your mind using all of your senses:
  - **Sight:** What is the size and shape of the room? What pieces of furniture are in there? What are their sizes and shapes? Where are the closets, drawers, or cupboards, and how do they open? What are the colors in the room?
  - **Touch:** What do the surfaces feel like? What is the texture of the objects you are touching? Pay particular attention to the floor. Do you normally wear shoes or slippers or go barefoot when doing this task? How does your footwear or your bare feet feel against the floor?
  - **Smell:** What are the smells of this room? Try to recall each of them and the combined effect as they mix together.

- ☐ **Hearing:** What are the sounds of this room (most rooms have a buzz to them if you are quiet)? What sounds are associated with your activity in this room?
- ☐ **Taste:** Does your activity create any specific taste sensations?
- Think about what props you need to fulfill this task.
- Ask yourself, "If I were completing this task, what **steps** would I go through to complete it?" Then, picture yourself going through each step in detail.
- Now open your eyes but instead of seeing your acting studio and the other students, try to **see** this remembered location **(where)** around you with your **eyes open**.
- Once you have a clear picture of the location, begin to **mime each step of your task** (there is value to doing this exercise both without props, using only your imagination, and by bringing in and using all the items needed). Go through it a couple of times to make sure you have the exact sequence of small physical actions needed to complete it.
- Now imagine that **you are late** to get to a very important event such as an awards reception or a job interview. Make sure the task is important enough that you need to fulfill it before you leave for this event. Go through the task again, and notice how this affects how you fulfill it. Try to hold on to the room around you, the important event, and the details of the task.
- Lastly, add a **physical obstacle** that impedes you from completing this task. Remember that you are in a hurry to get to this important event. Try to make an adjustment that allows you to still complete the task, rather than giving up on it. Fulfill the task again with the obstacle and keeping in mind the urgency.

2.1 Reflection Journal—A Habitual Activity

Were you able to picture the room with your eyes closed? How well could you still picture it with your eyes open? Were you able to evoke any other senses to remember this room? Could you hold on to those sensations with your eyes open? Could you clearly picture yourself performing the task? Were you able to perform it accurately from memory? How did the way you fulfilled the task change when you added an important event that you were late for? How did it change when you added an obstacle? What did you notice about your outward choices? What did you notice about what was going on in your mind and body?

> "Onstage you shouldn't perform actions 'in general' for actions' sake. You should perform them in a way which is well-founded, apt and productive. … 'In general' is superficial and trivial."
>
> —Stanislavsky 2009: 42; 56

According to Sonia Moore in her recorded lectures, Stanislavsky would frequently say, "'In general' is the enemy of art."[3] What he was talking about is that to act *in*

---

[3] Sonia Moore, tape recordings of lectures on the Stanislavsky System (self-published and distributed through American Center for Stanislavski Theatre Art in New York, 1977).

Figure 2.3 Select a simple physical task that you do every day, such as making coffee or tea in the morning.
Gabryal Rabinowitz and Kirsten Walsh in *Blithe Spirit* by Noel Coward.
Photo: Bob Weidner, courtesy of East Stroudsburg University

general, to act out actions in general, such as to greet a friend in general or to make a dinner in general is not sufficiently clear, detailed, and interesting. Instead, you need to greet a specific friend or make a specific dinner for a specific reason, under very specific circumstances, and in a particular location. The more detailed you can be in your preparation and execution, the more clearly the specifics of the story of your improvisation will be relayed.

> ### Exercise 2.2: The Burnt House (Nonverbal): A Structured Improvisation (SDF)
>
> **Purpose:** The exercise introduces in an experiential way many Elements of Action as outlined by Stanislavsky.
>
> **Note to teachers and students:** This is a layered exercise, which works as a diagnostic for both you and your teacher as you enter this special technique of actor training. Please understand that most beginning actors will only get some of the many acting challenges required for this exercise, while those with more acting experience may be able to hold on to more at once. The goal is not to get all of them on the first try, but, more importantly, to notice which of the acting challenges come easier and which are harder. This will likely be different for some of your classmates. Throughout an acting class, you will observe and learn from others what they can do more easily, even as they gain insight from your strengths. Likewise, while at first you may not be able to clearly see your acting challenges, after they are pointed out to you by the teacher, you may be able to see these same struggles more clearly as you observe others.
>
> **Preparation:** For best results, actors are advised to do all the preparation exercises below but may do some in class and some ahead at home.

Exercise 2.2A: Imagination and Sensory Evocation Exercise: Create a House in Detail

Guidelines: In this entire exercise, don't rush, be as detailed and specific as possible.

- Do this first with your eyes closed. See the house from the outside. How do you approach it? Where do you enter it? Imagine walking up to and entering through the door. What kind of door is it? Does it swing in or out? What kind of handle does it have? Can you see inside through a window?
- Recall the specific details of the house using as many senses as possible for the most vivid impressions. When you enter the house, what kind of shoes do you have on, and on what kind of floor is there? What is the feel and sound of these specific shoes on this floor? Are there other sounds you hear in the house? Does the house have a particular smell—perhaps something recently cooked? Is there a foyer or a hallway, or are there stairs as soon as you enter? What are the colors and textures of the walls? Are there a lot of objects on them, or are they sparsely decorated? What does the wall feel like to your touch? Is it smooth or textured, painted, paneled, or wallpapered?
- Imagine walking through the house—opening doors, closets, and drawers where you find them, sitting in chairs, on couches, lying on beds. Notice the smells of everything, the textures of the fabrics, the shapes and colors of the furniture and the configuration of the rooms, the sounds of the doors and rooms. It is important to stimulate as many of your senses as possible, to create this place using more parts of your brain (as your brain maps different senses in different receptors).
- Open your eyes and see what you can still recall with your eyes wide open. Try to see some part of the house in front of you and around you. Let the images of the house replace the images of the acting studio.

Note to students and teachers: This will take some mental effort at first, but you used to be able to do this easily, as a child playing imaginary games, and it is a skill you can redevelop.

Exercise 2.2B: Imagination/Sensory Evocation Exercise: A Precious Object

Guidelines:
- Imagine an object of great sentimental and lasting value. It can be of great financial value, too, but does not need to be. It should not be an object of temporary or superficial importance (like a sandwich when you are hungry). You may have in mind a real or an imaginary object, but either way the important thing is that you invest it with deep personal meaning, or as we say in the theatre, *up the stakes*.

- Imagine holding the object in your hands (mime it). What is its weight, shape, and texture? If it has any functionality explore that. Think about the memories that are associated with the object as you investigate it.
- Take an 8.5 x 11 sheet of paper. It is important the paper used by each individual actor is the same size and color as the papers of the rest of the class. In the middle, write the name of your precious object. Then crumple the paper into a ball and give it to your teacher. If there are fewer than 15 students in the class, add some additional blank papers so you have a minimum of 20.

Exercise 2.2C: Before the Improvisation Have a Brief Discussion:

Have you ever been in or seen a burnt building? If not, ask someone who has, or research pictures and imagine it. What is it like? What happens when you touch things? What does it smell like? Is it safe? Is it light or dark? What are the sounds? What would you do if you had an important reason to enter the burnt house? How would you have to move through it?

Exercise 2.2D: The Burnt House Improvisation

Setup: Find objects in the studio such as tables, desks, and chairs and pile them up somewhat precariously (so they might fall and make noise but not fall and hurt anyone or be broken). If your studio only has chairs or acting blocks, they will work just fine. Then, while the students close their eyes or look away, the teacher hides the precious objects (collected crumpled pieces of paper) around the wreckage.

Guidelines:
- You must have **three** *wheres*.
  - **Where from (before time):** Be very clear as to where you are coming from. It helps if how you feel about this first *where* is quite different from the situation you will next encounter.
  - **Where now:** What is the location where the main scene takes place (in this case the burnt house)? Discover that the house has burnt down. The fire is out, and you knew that any people or pets were not at home, but you did not know until you see it now that there had been a fire. Take in this new information about this place you know.
  - **Where to (after time):** When you leave the house, where are you going, and what are you going to do?
- Once the *where from* is clear in your mind, **enter the stage area and discover the house is burnt** (where now). Make sure this discovery takes place in view of the audience.
- **Realize and take in the problem:** your house is burnt and your precious object is somewhere inside that wreckage and may be damaged. **Your task**

is to struggle with this problem mentally and figure out how to solve it physically. Consider, "How can I recover my precious object?"

- Perhaps your answer to the above question is to salvage your object from the wreckage. Any proposed solution is like an *objective* (or *goal*), which is a future event, but you need to focus your attention on the actions that you do actively and immediately in the present moment.
- In answer to your task and proposed solution (objective), ask, "**What action-steps might I take to recover my object?**" For example you might 1) enter the burnt house (decide how you will get in; the door may not be usable); 2) search for the object, *main action*; 3) discover your precious object (if you do actually find it); 4) assess if it is salvageable; and 5) decide to leave the building for the last time. In this case, you are actually trying to find your paper, so you don't have to pretend to be looking (in a play where you know where the object is hidden, you would have to re-create this action of looking, as though you didn't know). Open each piece of paper you find. If it is not what you are looking for, crumple it and go on to the next one. Allow not finding it to affect you.
- Through all the action-steps, try to hold onto the "where now," dealing with the specifics of the given circumstances *to treat the environment as* a burnt down house dealing with soot, smell, dangerous structures, etc.
- If you **find your object** (another discovery), take a moment to assess it and take it in. Try to *stay open* to the audience (don't have your back to them at this moment). Is your precious object salvageable or completely ruined? Don't rush this moment, as this is the climax of the scene. Then, decide where to go next, the *where to*, and leave this building for the last time.
- If you **don't find your object**, the teacher will act as the fire chief and say, "The building is unsafe and you must immediately exit the building!" Take into consideration not finding your object. Let that settle in on you.
- Whether you do or don't find your object, your last action is to **leave the building** for the last time.

Note: If you used a personal house or a personal object, after you leave the stage, **imagine them once more perfect, intact, and unburned.**

2.2A *Reflection Journal—Your Experience in the Burnt House Improvisation*

When were you able to see the imaginary circumstances? When did you forget about them? Were you invested in finding your object? Did you have any real emotional responses either to finding or not finding your object, or to taking in the burnt house? Was there anything that got in between you and full investment in the imaginary circumstances? Was there anything that helped? Were you self-conscious in front of the class? Did you have any moments when you forgot the class was watching? If so, when? In what moments did you have a discovery or make a decision? Were you open to the audience with your head up and eyes available at these times so that the audience could see these thoughts? It is important to write down some of these observations. You can then go back later to build on those things that helped you to be more present and responsive on stage, and to work to transform or eliminate those things that got in your way.

> **2.2B** *Reflection Journal—Burnt House and Acting Terminology*
> Select five of The Preliminary Elements of Action below. Identify how these elements came into play in either the Burnt House or Habitual Activity exercises above.

PART III: THE PRELIMINARY ELEMENTS OF ACTION

Please note that these Elements, as well as the other Stanislavsky terminology used in this book can also be found alphabetically in the glossary. They are listed here in order to introduce the concepts somewhat in the order you will learn them, with intersections on how they layer and overlap.

Elements of Action to Develop Awareness of Self and Other

To effectively use the more complex Elements of Action while acting in a play, first some basic elements must be developed: concentration, relaxation, imagination, and sensory evocation.

Concentration (Focus of Attention)

Definition: Concentration is the ability to focus all your attention on a specific object or task.

Explanation: Focus is placed on both inner objects (such as images) and outer objects (including physical actions). Concentration is an exercise of willpower, which generally takes some training and discipline.

Relaxation and Flow of Energy

Definitions: *Relaxation* in acting is freeing the body from unnecessary tension and the mind from anxiety, while moving the flow of energy to where it is needed. *Flow of Energy* is the movement and direction of energy throughout the muscles and organs of the body.

Explanation: The purpose of relaxation is to increase and learn to control the *flow of energy*. The free flow of energy leads to the creative state that invites inspiration. The flow of energy involves the circulation of mental energy, physical energy, and breath, as well as healthy movement and communication among the other psychophysical systems of your body, such as respiratory system, circulatory system, nervous system, and muscular system.

Imagination (Visualization) and Film of Images

Definitions: *Imagination* is your ability to create and see mental pictures at will. It is also called visualization and creative imagination. *Film of Images* is a continual flow of visual pictures, both those related to the given circumstances of the character and also relevant emotionally evocative images for the actor.

Explanation: Your mental images may be imaginary, personal, observed, or a combination of the three. Imagination acts as a strong stimulus to emotion and can lead you into the desired creative state for acting. One of the measures of the quality of your work as an actor will be your ability to attain a balance between physical action and evocative images to create the reality of the world of the play for you and the audience.

2 THE ACTOR'S PALETTE

Sensory Evocation (Sense Memory), Memory of the Body, Proprioception, Kinesthetic Awareness
Definition: *Sensory Evocation* involves not only seeing images but filling them out using the other senses by evoking smells, sounds, tastes, and textures stored in the memory of the body and the sensory centers of the brain. *Sense Memory* is the memory of sensations received by the sensory receptors of the body and registered in the sensory centers of the brain. *Memory of the Body* includes sense memory, and also the memory of emotions and actions that have imprinted in the body and brain. Related interdisciplinary terms: *Proprioception* is inner awareness of and communication between the central nervous system (including the brain) and the body regarding space, balance and motion. *Kinesthetic Awareness* is an external sense relating to the body's awareness of sequences of movement, movement in relationship to external objects or people, and movement in time and space.
Explanation: As *imagination* is a visual term, it does not quite capture the various tools you need to stimulate full psychophysical response. You will also learn to use sensory evocation, memory of the body and proprioception. Some in science consider proprioception (as described above) to be the sixth sense, others in theatre might consider kinesthetic awareness to have this role.

I Am, I Exist and Presence
Definition: *I am* or *I exist* is the ability to temporarily live in and respond to a situation imagined or evoked with other senses, as if it were real. *Presence* is focused attention on the here and now. Presence is also that exciting quality that makes an actor captivate our attention.
Explanation: You do not need to actually believe the imaginary circumstances are real (otherwise you would be insane) but only to behave and respond as you would if these given circumstances were taking place in real life. This is the first step towards your ability to come alive in imaginary circumstances as both yourself and the character. "I am, I exist" are prerequisites to presence onstage.

Dual Perspectives (Dual Consciousness) and Internal and External Monitors
Definitions: *Dual Perspectives* refers to the state of consciousness where 95 percent of your attention is on inhabiting the role as the character and 5 percent on awareness as an actor. *Dual Consciousness* is an interchangeable term. The *internal monitor* observes and senses internal processes and creates a character's internal life. The *external monitor* observes and senses the body's actions in time and space, in relationship to others and to everything in the environment. Through this you seem to be viewing yourself from the tenth row of the audience while fully engaged in the performance. This state of consciousness is highly desirable and allows you to *experience your experience*, thereby living the life of the character while simultaneously conveying this character's life artistically.

Public Solitude
Definition: Public solitude allows deep concentration, as though completely alone, experiencing the life of the character, while simultaneously inviting the audience into innermost thoughts and feelings.
Explanation: In public solitude you maintain dual consciousness as described above—a sense of being alone and yet that you are in public as well.

Communion (Communication)
Definition: Communion is defined as mutual influence between people.
Explanation: Communion and communication are terms used interchangeably. Communion begins with oneself, as in public solitude. The next step is communion between actors, and the larger circle extends beyond the footlights to engulf the audience. Communion goes beyond verbal communication to include the ways you influence another through nonverbal communication: thoughts, gestures, and body language. At the level that the essence of you contacts and affects another energetically it becomes what Stanislavsky called spiritual communion. Learning to be present with and aware of others in your class is the first step.

Psychophysical
Definition: *Psychophysical* is the inseparable body, mind and spirit (consciousness).
Explanation: A simple starting place with this concept in acting is that every thought or emotion has a physical expression, every physical act related thoughts and emotional responses. In acting you are always doing something physical, thinking something and feeling something.
Origins: Psycho is short for psychological and is derived from psyche, meaning an embodiment of the soul. According to the Oxford English Dictionary, Psyche was a character in Greek mythology considered the personification of the soul. She often took the form of a butterfly. She had a union with Eros, the god of passionate love. The preceding Greek word (psukhe) means breath, life and soul/spirit. The physical aspects include the body, its organic functions and movement, and the biological aspects of the brain.

Elements of Action Applied to Imaginary Circumstances

Throughout this section, examples from the play *A Streetcar Named Desire (Streetcar)* by Tennessee Williams will be used.

Circumstances (Givens) and First and Second Plan
Definition: The *given circumstances* consist of the entirety of the details of the imaginary world of the play as conceived by the playwright and given through the script (or conceived by the actors in the case of an improvisation).
Explanation: The given circumstances are often called the *givens*. In literary terms this is equivalent to both the exposition (background information or back story) as well as all the information that is revealed or referred to throughout the play. In production terms it also includes all the elements given to you by the director, the designers, the ensemble of actors and all the other artists and technicians working on the production. You arrive at an understanding of the play's given circumstances by a careful reading and rereading of the play and by asking the following questions at every step of work on a role: Who? What? When? Where? Why? With whom? What for? Where from? Where to? How? In working on a play we consider the *first plan* as the events and circumstances that we watch unfold and the *second plan* as the given circumstances that are referred to from the past or take place between the shown scenes.

> The given circumstances of *Streetcar* include a second-plan early-life tragic event that has disturbed Blanche's psyche and set her on a destructive course. Also before the start of the play, Blanche has lost her ancestral home, the plantation Belle Reve. She has been fired from her job for making sexual overtures to one of her young male students, and she has further ruined her reputation through numerous sexual liaisons so that she was basically run out of her hometown, Laurel, Mississippi. In the first plan, she arrives in the French Quarter of New Orleans in 1947, in the hope that she can stay with her sister Stella and Stella's husband Stanley who works as a parts salesman for a plant. She hopes to redeem her reputation, and rebuild her life. At first she hides her destitution from Stella and pretends it is just a visit, but later in the first scene Blanche reveals to Stella that the family plantation, Belle Reve, has been lost.

The "Magic If"

Definition: The "magic if" is an evocative question that stimulates imagination and leads to action.

Explanation: It is the key to activating the given circumstances by stimulating appropriate thoughts and behavioral responses. When building an improvisation or actively analyzing the actions and circumstances of a play, ask, "What would I do if today, here and now, for the first time, I were in these circumstances?"

As you move further from self and into character in the course of your training and rehearsals, you can add the phrase, "and if I were a person like this, in this character's shoes, in this time period, country, etc." The supposition "if" is used during conditioning exercises and training improvisations, as well as during rehearsals, in order to discover the character's behavior. It is also used moment-to-moment during a performance to keep you alive and present and responding to obstacles through inventive and appropriate adaptations.

> The actor playing Blanche might ask the magic-if question: "If I were ashamed of my past behavior and I wanted to rebuild my life, how might I conduct myself? How might I present myself to my sister and others?" Blanche lies and covers up her indiscretions in the hope of a clean start.
>
> In another example from scene one of *Streetcar*, the actor/Blanche might consider: "If I had to tell my sister I lost our family home but I didn't want to be blamed and disliked because I need her to take me in, how would I do it?" Blanche does a variety of things. Here are just a few examples: she blames Stella (to blame); she makes out that she slaved and sacrificed to try to save the plantation (to praise her own efforts); and she portrays herself like a victim (to incite pity).

To Treat As (Endowment)

Definition: To treat objects, the environment or other people as though they were something else.

Explanation: Through sensory evocation, specific actions and willpower you *treat* cheap props as objects of great value, the stage as *if* it were a variety of locations, and other actors as if they were specific characters in specific relationships with you. In other theatre traditions, such as comedy improvisation, this is called *Endowment*.

Problem and Task[4]

Definitions: *Problem* is an unwelcome or harmful internal or external situation, event, emotion, or other person, encountered in the given circumstances, that the character needs to resolve. *Task* is the active mental, emotional and physical struggle to overcome an obstacle and solve the problem.

Explanation: This struggle creates drama onstage and makes the scene active and interesting. The struggle with the task reveals the character moment-by-moment through the course of the play. To identify the problem ask, "What is my problem? What do I want to change?" To find the task ask, "How can I change it?" It is helpful for you to identify both a problem and a task. You will work intensively with problems and tasks in exercises and improvisations throughout the training. At times you encounter a problem that leads to a task as above but at other times you are given a task which presents a problem.

> In *Streetcar,* scene 2, while Blanche is bathing to calm her nerves, Stella tells Stanley that the plantation has been lost. Stanley takes an immediate dislike to Blanche, assuming that she has tried to swindle Stella and, thereby, him. Stanley and Stella fight about it, and this is likely overheard by Blanche because it is a cheap, small apartment with thin walls.
>
> Problem/Task: Blanche now has a problem that she desperately needs a place to stay. In figuring out her active task she might come up with: *How can I overcome Stanley's dislike and distrust of me so he will let me stay?*

Objective

Definition: *Objective* is the proposed solution to the problem (the aim).

Explanation: To discern the objective ask, "What do I want?" Objectives are not just internal motivations but have specific external outcomes. Generally you will want to focus on changing something in your scene partner. Try to make it something physical and specific that you can tell you have achieved.

---

[4] For this key element of the System, Stanislavsky used the Russian word *zadacha*, which has two English meanings: *problem* and *task*. In some contexts, Stanislavsky used this term to mean "problem" and in others he used it in ways that more closely relate to "task." Hercules' famous Tasks are also called Labors, tying tasking into both action and a struggle. In Active Analysis, Stanislavsky wrapped the objective into the problem. Actors focus on what they can get the other character to do or think to solve the immediate problem. This is then the task that the actor/character struggles with actively in rehearsal and performance, at this moment in the play. The original English translator of Stanislavsky's early books translated *zadacha* as objective, which does not capture the full possibility and complexity of this key technique of Active Analysis. However, *objective* is a term widely used by directors and actors in the profession so it is important you understand how it is used. Its common usage involves what the character wants (a goal).

> Blanche might imagine this solution to her problem: "If I can get Stanley to like me, he will let me stay, and I will not end up on the street." So her task is getting Stanley to like her.

Action-Steps, Through-Action (Through-Line), Score or Spine of the Role
Definitions: *Action-steps* are active means you employ to solve the problem and reach your objective. *Through-action*, also called the *through-line*, is the sequence of action-steps and threads that connect them in an unbroken line through the role. Collectively, the entire series of actions for a role is referred to as the *score of actions* or the *spine* of the role.
Explanation: To figure out your action steps, ask, "What must I do to solve the problem and get what I want (my objective)?" Make these steps have a clear physical component. As the actions are done towards a specific purpose, they will be inwardly justified.

Action
Definition: A purposeful act of human behavior.
Explanation: When you imbue an action with *purpose*, you involve your entire psychophysical instrument—mind, body, sensations, and emotions. An action is purposeful when it is inwardly *motivated*, and then we say the action has been *justified*. We call such a justified act that links the mind and body *psychophysical*.

After you have framed your objective, or desired outcome to the problem, then ask: How can I . . . ? to uncover a series of logical *actions* to carry out in order to solve the *problem*. Actions are written in the active, transitive verb form to accuse, to deny, to elevate, to squelch. You engage your partner through actions in moment-to-moment, initiating and responding, a give-and-take. The actions are active and thus bring the character and the play to life.

Explanation of the connection between problem, task, objective, action and action-steps: Problem, task, objective, action and action-steps can each be defined separately but they are so entwined they can only really be explained in relationship to one another. The situation poses a *problem* for the character/actor, something he doesn't like and wants to change. The *task* is the active struggle to find a solution to the problem. The hoped-for solution is the character's *objective*, which, if achieved, gives the character some sense of satisfaction or reward. The character attempts a variety of approaches called *actions* to try to solve the problem and reach the *objective*. The series of actions taken are called *action-steps* and they create a *through-line* of the scene or role.

> In our example from *Streetcar*, scene 2, actress/Blanche might consider: How can I get Stanley to like me so he will let me stay in his apartment? Blanche has a limited repertoire of behaviors to get what she wants from men and so despite Stanley's being her sister's husband, her actions are to interest, to entice, to flirt, etc. More specifically, coming out of the playwright's lines and circumstances, she tries to get him to smell her, to imagine her getting undressed behind the thin curtain, to touch her back by buttoning her buttons, to create intimacy by sharing the same cigarette.

Supertask
Definition: The ruling idea of the playwright that guides the action of the play and characters, as revealed by the director in collaboration with the designers and actors. Each character also has a character's supertask, which is the overarching struggle of the character.
Explanation: The director searches through preproduction and into rehearsal to discover and figure out how to artistically reveal the *supertask* of the play. The character's supertask reveals the essence of the character and the character's purpose in the play.

Obstacle (Object of Struggle) and Conflict
Definitions: An *obstacle* is anything that impedes the character's objective. *Conflict* is the struggle between two opposing forces.
Explanation: As you attempt to solve the character's problem and pursue his objective, obstacles arise that impede you. These obstacles can be external, such as a physical obstacle, or internal, which in literary terms we call a *complication*. In a play or scene, external obstacles often arise because another character has an opposing objective. The act of meeting an obstacle creates conflict and, if you are sufficiently invested in the character's imaginary circumstances, will stimulate emotion.

> In scene 2 Blanche encounters an obstacle: none of her tried and true methods of flirtation to get men to like her are working on Stanley.

Adaptation (Adjustment)
Definition: An *adaptation* is an *adjustment* that the character makes to an obstacle, or to a counteraction initiated against him by another character.
Explanation: Adjustments can also occur as a result of mishaps on the stage: lines and sections of scenes being dropped, blocking (stage movement) being off, props missing, an accident, etc. It is important to know how to make an adaptation. An adaptation must be sharp, clear, interesting, and fitting to the situation, character, and play. Adaptations are always improvised in the moment during performance and can be figured out using the *magic if*.

> Blanche's adaptation to the obstacle of Stanley's resistance to her feminine wiles is to change her approach. She still wants him to like her (same objective), but next she tries to achieve this objective by being straight with him about the loss of the plantation by laying her "cards on the table."

Tempo and Rhythm
Definitions: *Tempo* is the speed or timing of your actions. *Rhythm* is the inner intensity of an action.
Explanation: Tempo is primarily, but not exclusively, influenced by the external circumstances, whereas rhythm is primarily determined by our inner images, thoughts, and emotional responses. *Tempo-rhythm* serves as a bridge between

our inner experience and its physical expression. In life, anything important—for example, a decision, revelation, discovery, obstacle, or new idea—will change the tempo-rhythm. If on stage at such moments there is no change in tempo or rhythm—or more often, both—the behavior will seem false.

In comedy, until you achieve the correct tempo-rhythm, the piece will not be funny—timing and intensity is everything.

> "Choose tempo-rhythm properly and feelings and experiences arise naturally. But if the tempo-rhythm is wrong, inappropriate feelings and experiences will arise in precisely the same way, in the same passage, and you won't be able to put things right until you have replaced the wrong tempo-rhythm."
> —Stanislavsky 2009: 469

> At the moment Blanche realizes her flirtation approach is not working, this realization would affect both her internal rhythm and her tempo. She would be more concerned (affecting rhythm) because her usual tactics are not working, and she might slow down or pause until she comes up with another approach to get Stanley to like her. When she gets the idea to try being straight with him, she might get a burst of internal lightness with the relief of having a new plan, and as she begins to pursue it through her new through-line of action steps, the cards-on-the-table tactic might be pursued at a different tempo from the flirting one.

Measure of Truth (Truth and Belief)
Definition: The *measure of truth* means that we must fulfill a realistic action with the same degree of energy, tension, and tempo-rhythm as we would under similar circumstances in life.
Explanation: Even if you choose the most fitting action, if you do not apply these other elements, it will not be believable. The results may seem false to an audience if you unduly rush or retard time, or try to show (indicate) or force through extra physical effort or breath. Belief arises naturally when you can accept the possibility of the *given circumstances* because you have invested in them through research and imagination and now bring them to life by behaving truthfully in the circumstances.

Whether acting in a realistic drama or one that is completely fantastical or absurd, you only need to invest in the truth of your actions in order for the audience to accept even the most otherworldly or outrageous scenario.

> For example (not from *Streetcar*), if a person were shooting at you, would you most likely quickly or slowly get out of the line of fire?

Inner Monologue and Inner Dialogue
Definitions: *Inner monologue* is the character's private thoughts. *Inner dialogue* is an argument within the character's mind.
Explanation: You need to have continuous thoughts as the character in the situation. This is one of the key elements to keep the character alive and responsive on stage.

> In *Streetcar*, while Blanche is going about trying to hook Stanley with flirtation, and Stanley resists her overtures and says very little, he might have the following inner monologue, "I am on to her from the start. Who does she think she is to bamboozle me with this kinda crap? I am not taken in by any dame. Besides I'm married to her sister. What the hell is wrong with her?"

Analogous Emotions
Definition: *Analogous emotions* are emotions you have experienced that are similar to those the character is experiencing in the given circumstances.
Explanation: The stimulation of emotions in our audiences is often a primary goal of theatre and film artists, particularly evoking specific emotional responses in connection to the author's or director's supertask.

> **Common Misunderstandings about Stanislavsky and Emotions**
>
> The acting techniques that have been developed to try to impact our audiences emotionally are some of the most controversial aspects of actor training and the most misunderstood in Stanislavsky's legacy. (For more on the actor's stimulation of emotions, see Chapter 20: The Evolving Stanislavsky System and Chapter 12: Orchestrating Emotions.) Stanislavsky's early experiments during the 1920s were based on affective memory. As Sharon M. Carnicke quotes in her book *Stanislavsky in Focus*, affective memory is "a term, borrowed from French experimental psychologist Theodule Ribot (1839–1916), which refers to a human being's ability to recall previously experienced emotional states by recalling the accompanying physical sensations." (Sharon 1998: glossary.) Although Stanislavsky initially used a direct approach to emotions, he later realized that emotions needed to be coaxed to the surface. One cannot order his emotions through willpower without pushing and forcing. Also, using personal emotions too directly can result in self-indulgent acting that reveals the actor more than the character in the play and has been shown to lead to psychological issues. There are some actors who have used the older emotional methods to great effect because their talent trumped their technique; however, why take such risks with your emotional instrument for dubious artistic results, especially when it is unnecessary?

Experiencing (Living Through)
Definition: *Experiencing* or *living through* is your ability to come alive through the imaginary given circumstances of the character in a specific play.
Explanation: The entire System is designed to bring you into the *creative state* where you make a psychophysical *transformation* into character while simultaneously achieving the end result of *experiencing*. While the performance is carefully planned and rehearsed, at the moment of performance you are infused with the life of the character, and this immediacy and presence infects the audience. You must experience the life of the character afresh at every performance. Stanislavsky considered this to be the highest form of an actor's art. He called this form of acting the *School of Living Experience*.

Weaving the Elements of Action Together

Elements of these techniques will be outlined throughout this book and experienced in your classes. How these elements all fit together for the rehearsal of a play will be outlined in Stanislavsky's culminating technique of Active Analysis through Events and Actions, covered in chapters 13–16. There are additional Elements of Action, primarily used when working on plays, that will be introduced in Part III: Introduction to Active Analysis. Active Analysis can only be successfully applied when you have conditioned your psychophysical instrument's autonomic systems to respond to your will through conscious means. This is an essential acting skill for you to develop, but it will take some time (multiple semesters) to really master.

When you actively analyze a play on your feet, you begin to connect imaginatively to the inner world of the character. When psychophysical training exercises are combined with this form of Active Analysis through Events and Actions, you are led to appropriate behavior for the character that will also communicate the play clearly to an audience. Through the fulfillment of a purposeful action in concrete circumstances, an actor can project the character's intentions, the physical style of the play, and stir the entire inner complex of appropriate states of being, sensory feelings, and emotions. *Psychophysical actions* give an actor the means to perform in all styles and genres of plays, not only realism.

Summary

We started with a discussion of the need to reprogram human behavior for the artificial environment of the stage. This is achieved with a focus on re-creating human behaviors called actions, which then expands to include actions with a purpose, which are called psychophysical actions.

You then had the opportunity to personally experience a few of the many Elements of Action through two exercises: The Habitual Task and the many-layered Burnt House exercise. You began to exam yourself in the process of acting by making observations about your strengths and weaknesses, openings, and obstacles on the stage during these improvisations.

Finally we offered the Actor's Palette of Elements of an Action and alluded to the ever-evolving nature of the actor's art. We introduced some revised understandings regarding terminology for the Stanislavsky System and some of our own acting concepts and terminology for key Elements of Action.

Through your acting class and the supplemental reading of this text, we hope that you will come to appreciate the masterful achievement that is Stanislavsky's System of actor training, including the evocative technique of Active Analysis through Events and Actions.

New Theatre Terms and Concepts

We will not list all the new acting terminology of this chapter as it is an overview and a large percentage of the acting concepts are first introduced and defined but not yet explored. They will begin to be listed in the new terminology list at the end of each subsequent chapter. All concepts are also listed alphabetically and defined in the glossary at the end of the book.

Interdisciplinary Terms, Concepts and Experts

- behavioral neuroscience
- bodymind
- cognitive neuroscience
- conditioned response
- kinesthetic awareness
- kinesthetic memory
- learned instinct
- leitmotif (from Music and the System)
- Ivan Pavlov
- physiology
- proprioception
- second nature

CHAPTER 3

The Creative State: Preparing for Inspiration

"It is in this sense that creative individuals live exemplary lives. They show how joyful and interesting complex symbolic activity is. They have struggled through the marshes of ignorance, deserts of disinterest, and with the help of parents and a few visionary teachers they have found themselves on the other side of the known. They have become pioneers of culture, models for what men and women of the future will be."[1]

—Mihaly Csikszentmihalyi

Elements Actively Explored

"I am, I exist" (presence, awareness of self and other), dual perspectives, concentration, relaxation

Other Acting Concepts Explored

Internal and external monitors, flow of energy, visualization, soft focus, stage fright

Part I: The Creative State—Awareness of Self

- I Am—Presence (I Exist Today, Here and Now)
- Sources of Presence in Yoga and Science
- The Internal Critic
- Dual Perspectives—Developing Your Internal and External Monitors
- Concentration
- ☐ Exercise 3.1: Watching the Breath

Part II: Scientific Research on Creativity

- What Can We Learn from Science about the Factors That Help or Inhibit Creativity?
- Anatomy of the Creative Mind
- Factors That Help Generate Creativity

Part III: Awareness of Self in Front of an Audience

- Stage Fright
- "Fight or Flight": The Fear and Excitement Response
- ☐ Exercise 3.2: Observation of the Fear Response in You
- Feeling the Fear and Doing It Anyway
- Relaxation
- ☐ Exercise 3.3: Shifting the Breath
- Tips for Alleviating Stage Fright
- Exercise 3.4: Sunset on the Beach

[1] Mihaly Csikszentmihalyi, *Creativity: Flow and the Psychology of Discovery and Invention* (p. 125).

In Chapter 1, we discussed some kinds of inspiration—Aha! moments—that a person might experience and how these might translate to acting. We also looked at the goal of exceptional acting: to move or inspire an audience. Stanislavsky found, as many others in the field of research into creativity have since verified, that inspiration needs to be wooed, lured out indirectly, and does not respond well to force or demand. Stanislavsky and contemporary scientists have also uncovered many conditions that make inspiration more or less likely. We will make use of some of these scientific ideas, some of Stanislavsky's ideas, and some of our own discoveries to help you toward the creative state that will best invite insight and inspiration into your acting.

> "What I wanted to learn was how to create a favorable condition for the appearance of inspiration by means of the will, what condition in the presence of which inspiration was most likely to descend into the actor's soul. As I learned afterward, this creative mood is that spiritual and physical mood during which it is easiest for inspiration to be born."
> —Konstantin Stanislavsky, *My Life in Art*
> Theatre Arts Books, New York, 1924

While you cannot force inspiration you can strengthen the mind and body's pathways to the creative state that invites inspiration. You can also work in conditions most conducive to creative insights (as will be emphasized later in Chapter 4: Yoga and Acting: Dedication to the Creative Space). What does an actor need to do to reach the *creative state* on a consistent basis? As the creative state is one of a heightened consciousness, one of the things you can do is to develop and expand your awareness. Two important areas to develop are *awareness of self* and *awareness of others*.

PART I: THE CREATIVE STATE—AWARENESS OF SELF

> "There is a vitality, a life force, a quickening that is translated through you into action, and there is only one of you in all time; this expression is unique, and if you block it, it will never exist through any other medium, and be lost. The world will not have it. It is not your business to determine how good it is, nor how it compares with other expression. It is your business to keep it yours clearly and directly, to keep the channel open."
> —Martha Graham, dancer/choreographer
> considered the mother of modern dance

An actor communicates the internal life and external expression of a specific human being, a character. We know that the actor chosen for a role colors her performance of a character. Therefore, each actor must understand what she intrinsically brings. Only then can the actor decide what of herself to use for the character versus what is not correct and must be replaced with borrowed or created physicality, behavior, perspectives, thoughts, and emotions better suited for the character.

Some actors can get *typecast* (always cast close to first impressions based on obvious traits such as physical type, vocal quality, personality, race, age, etc.) or focused on some aspect of their personality such as their brand of humor. Although,

Figure 3.1 Benicio del Toro as Dr. Gonzo in *Fear and Loathing in Las Vegas* (1998).
© 1998 Universal City Studios, Inc. Courtesy of Universal Studios Licensing LLC.

according to casting director Cathy Reinking, "This is happening somewhat less than it used to, and the range of actors being cast is expanding."[2] Some actors have made names for themselves by creating an interesting *persona* that they play, with slight variations, for each role. Often these are successful, A-list actors who are box office draws because we love their persona and know we can count on enjoying them in a film. Like a favorite character anchoring a book series, we feel we know them and want to spend time with them. There are certainly actors that off camera or offstage are not considered particularly attractive whereas in a film we can't take our eyes off of them. Stanislavsky called this *charisma*, "the inexplicable attraction exercised by the actor's whole being in which even faults are turned to advantage and are copied by his admirers and imitators."[3] While good looks are often a part of charisma, they are not requisite. Some examples of actors with charisma and a similar persona in many of their movies are Jack Nicholson, Bruce Willis, Vince Vaughn, Kate Hudson, Jackie Chan, and Marilyn Monroe. Marilyn's persona was clearly a carefully constructed image focused on sex appeal (and quite different than the unhappy woman behind it), but audiences loved this image so much she was expected to play that persona in every film.

---

[2] Cathy Reinking is an independent casting director for film, television, theatre, commercials, and the web. She is the former Manager of Casting for NBC, where she oversaw the casting of *Frasier*, *Arrested Development*, and *According to Jim*, as well as the original casting of *The Office*, *Medium*, and *Hawaii*, to name only a few of her credits. Many actors seek her advice on auditioning through workshops and her book *How to Book Acting Jobs in TV and Film*. She is the cowriter, coproducer, and casting director of *The British Invasion*, a web series that follows, in *Tootsie* fashion, what would happen if an American actor pretended to be British in order to get work.

[3] Konstantin Stanislavsky, *An Actor's Work*, trans. Jean Benedetti (London: Routledge, 2009), p. 549.

Figure 3.2 Ziyi Zhang as Moon in *Hero* (2002). Photo: © Russel Wong/Corbis

On the other hand, many of the greatest actors of our day, transform themselves in versatile and intriguing ways to fit each new part—Meryl Streep, Annette Bening, Gary Oldman, Alan Rickman, Viola Davis, Cate Blanchett, Ziyi Zhang, John Leguizamo, Benedict Cumberbatch, Helen Mirren, David Tennant, Ken Watanabe, Hugh Jackman, John Lone, Ben Kingsley, Kevin Spacey, Chris Tucker, Daniel Day Lewis, and Jennifer Lawrence. Many of these actors do have an interesting mixture of a core power and presence we are drawn to (that makes them recognizable box office names) and also transformational ability. Some actors clearly can and do transform in some movies but are asked to play their familiar and popular persona in multiple films.

Early career actors often struggle to get cast because they are not aware of how they come across to others, of what is conveyed physically and emotionally just by their presence on the stage. Perhaps the actor slouches and sticks out her chin and is from a family that has poor table habits. She would likely not be cast as a highborn character, steeped in balletic postures and upper-class manners, as in much classical drama. Perhaps the actor is very physically imposing and athletic and thus would not be cast as someone who is sickly and dying. Perhaps the actor carries an emotional burden that makes him seem dark, and thus he would not be cast in a light comedy or musical theatre piece. Perhaps an actor jokes about everything and avoids difficult situations so that we cannot take him seriously as a dramatic character struggling with major human events or issues.

I Am—Presence (I Exist Today, Here and Now)

The prerequisite for achieving stage presence is to achieve what Stanislavsky called the state of *I am* or *I exist* in the situation. Presence can be developed through training and artistry. This is different from personal charisma, which seems to be a combination of an inborn trait and the taste of the times. Presence brings us into a powerful moment in the play captivated by what is stirring in the actor/character. In Chapter 2, we mentioned that the actor's immediate focus in the present moment is one key. In life and on stage, after all, you can only really fulfill an action in the present. Shakespeare understood this, and his characters are always struggling with an immediate challenge. If your attention is on the past, or future, or has otherwise wandered away from the stage, your onstage actions will not be sufficiently invested so as to evoke anything dynamic or meaningful. Your ability to be present while connecting and communicating with your scene partners and the audience is called communion and will be explored in more detail in chapters 6 and 17, respectively.

Sources of Presence in Yoga and Science

Presence is a higher state of consciousness. Stanislavsky researcher Dr. Sharon Carnicke of the University of Southern California addresses this in her book *Stanislavsky in Focus*. She references the original Russian word for the concept, and how that can be translated:

> I Am *(Ia esm)*
> The actor's sense of being fully present in the dramatic moment. A term that functions in the System as a synonym for "experiencing" and suggests Stanislavsky's interest in the spirituality of Yoga. Contemporary Russian does not use a present tense form for the verb "to be." Hence, "I am an actor" literally translates as "I actor."[4]

Carnicke cites this concept, along with many other references throughout Stanislavsky's publically available and previously censored writing to substantiate a key source for the System as yoga. (A more involved discussion of acting and yoga is in the next chapter.) The grounding of the System in yoga makes sense as one of the fundamental tenets to any practice of yoga is learning to exist in the present moment and quiet the busyness of our minds. Past or future concerns pull us out of being present in life as well as on stage.

The idea of presence and awareness of the one who is present, a kind of observer or watcher, was also prevalent in the science of the late nineteenth and early twentieth centuries. In the sixteenth century the father of modern philosophy, Frenchman René Descartes (1596–1650) is famous for the dictum frequently

---

[4] Sharon M. Carnicke, *Stanislavsky in Focus: Emotion and the Human Spirit of the Role* (Amsterdam: Harwood Academic, 1998), 175. In *Stanislavsky in Focus*, Carnicke outlines the numerous ways in which Stanislavsky's System was mistranslated, or misconstrued by people who only studied with him in early years of his development of the System. She also discussions information that was removed or changed in Stanislavsky's writings by Soviet censors who removed much of the references to yoga or to spiritual ideas. These sources have been painstakingly reconstructed by scholars in the last decade. Carnicke's work on this is impressive and outlined in the above cited book.

summarized as, "I think, therefore I am." He considered what is real and came to the conclusion, "I now know that even bodies are perceived not by the senses or by imagination but by the intellect alone, not through their being touched or seen but through their being understood."[5] He also writes, "After thoroughly thinking the matter through I conclude that this proposition, I am, I exist, must be true whenever I assert it or think it."[6]

American philosopher and psychologist William James (1842–1910) responds to Descartes: "The universal conscious fact is not 'feelings and thoughts exist' but 'I think' and 'I feel.' No psychology, at any rate, can question the existence of personal selves."[7] It turned out that for the next century James's ideas were in fact questioned by behavioral science, which somewhat took the person and consciousness out of the equation. Now contemporary science has returned to, while advancing with new measurement tools, some of James's ideas on the perspective of the one acting or perceiving as central to the equation and also on the importance of feelings in the process of cognition. James also grounded the mind firmly in the body.

Researcher and neuroscientist Dr. Antonio Damasio of the Brain and Creativity Institute, in outlining the construction of consciousness, also posits that consciousness involves both "something-to-be-known but also the mental patterns which convey, automatically and naturally, the sense of self in the act of knowing. Consciousness, as we commonly think of it, from its basic levels to its most complex, is the unified mental pattern that brings together the object and the self."[8] In studies of emotion, and of consciousness of our emotions and other bodily processes, the concept of "I am" is now being discussed and recorded in science.

In acting, there are two I's that you must come to eventually blend into one: 1) I as myself, the actor, and 2) I as the character. As you progress through your training this concept will eventually become clearer and you will be able to exist simultaneously as both yourself and character, which Stanislavsky called *experiencing the experience*. This penultimate goal and achievement of the System is explored throughout this book and discussed fully in Chapter 18: The Actor of Living Experience.

Even, when given a past or future action monologue, you, the actor, must decide on the present action of why the character is remembering or anticipating the event. Other scientific studies shed light on how we perceive past and future events, based on our vantage point from the present. This may be relevant when your character recalls a past event or is excited about or fearing a future event (as it is also very important to the playwright whose words prescribed how the event is recalled or anticipated). According to research psychologists Y. Trope and N. Liberman in their 2003 study "Temporal Construal," we think of the present in very concrete terms but the past and future in more abstract terms.[9] This finding was supported by a related 2009 study conducted at East Stroudsburg University

---

[5] René Descartes, *Meditations on First Philosophy in Which Are Demonstrated the Existence of God and the Distinction Between the Human Soul And Body* (1641). Available online at www.earlymoderntexts.com/pdfs/descartes1641_1.pdf. Accessed December 6, 2014.

[6] Ibid., 4.

[7] William James, *Principles of Psychology*, vol. 1 (New York: Henry Holt, 1890), 226.

[8] Antonio Damasio, *The Feeling of What Happens: Body and Emotion in the Making of Consciousness* (Orlando, FL: Harvest Books, 1990), 11.

[9] Y. Trope and N. Liberman, "Temporal Construal," *Psychological Review* 110 (2003): 403–421.

by research psychologists who found, among other things, that, "Bad decisions can be made based on erroneous expectations about the pleasure associated with future events."[10] More important to consider in your acting is that, according to Wesp et al., this happens because when we anticipate distant positive future events, we do it in a general, abstract way whereas with more immediate future events we imagine not just the general idea of the event but the practical details of steps required to achieve it.[11]

The Internal Critic

Have you been surprised when you have seen candid (not posed) pictures of yourself or when you have heard a recording of your voice? Were you quite critical? While you need to become conscious of these aspects of yourself, the danger is to induce a harshly critical self-consciousness. When we say about an actor, "He is too self-conscious on stage," we usually mean that he is too focused on himself as a person in a way that undermines his acting. Instead, embrace your external presentation, while developing the range of it, but do so with kindness.

If an actor has a constant stream of self-criticism (like a little devil on the shoulder), it will be hard for him to have any confidence on stage, and this issue must be addressed. This can be more devastating to an actor than any bad review in the *New York Times*. While many people seek outside recognition to try to compensate for poor self-appraisal, fame and success do not make the critic go away. In fact they may even amplify it. If harsh self-criticism is an issue, we encourage you to start working on it now.

Some actors are able to work past it simply by replacing their own undermining thoughts with the character's thoughts in the situation of the scene. Some actors can learn to replace the negative attacks with more positive and balanced views of self by using cognitive restructuring techniques developed independently by Dr. Aaron Beck and Dr. Albert Ellis, who both assume that many of our problems are a function of our interpretation of the world around us.[12, 13] Another approach mixes Buddhist philosophy with cognitive psychology (Tara Brach's *Radical Acceptance: Embracing Your Life with the Heart of a Buddha*). For others, the early experiences that instigated this barrage of negative self-talk may need to be addressed with the help of a psychologist. (If this applies to you, counseling services are offered at most universities for crisis intervention and can refer you to longer-term treatment if necessary.) Even if an actor doesn't want to work on this for personal reasons, it is vital that actors who are overly self-critical (critique themselves in a devastating

---

[10]Richard Wesp, Joshua Sandry, Anthony Prisco, and Pamela Sarte, "Affective Forecast of Future Positive Events Are Tempered by Consideration Of Details," *American Journal of Psychology* 122, no. 2 (2009): 167.

[11]Ibid., 167–174.

[12]Aaron T. Beck, Gary Emery, Ruth L. Greenberg, *Anxiety Disorders and Phobias: A Cognitive Perspective*, rev. ed. (Cambridge, MA: Basic Books, 2005).

[13]In speaking with research psychologist Dr. Rick Wesp at East Stroudsburg University, he stated, "Beck's primary therapeutic procedure is to give the client homework assignments in which they look for evidence to support/contradict their erroneous beliefs about themselves, such as 'Everyone hates me, I have no friends.' An assignment would be to note each person you spoke with during the week and characterize the interaction. The intent is to develop evidence of the fallacy of the belief."

rather than a discriminating and productive way) do address this issue as it manifests onstage. If they don't, they will appear uncomfortable onstage, causing the audience to be uncomfortable watching them. This takes both actor and audience out of the imaginary world of the character and the play. Depending on how entrenched your own mechanisms for self-criticism may be, this may take some time but is well worth the effort for both your acting and your sense of self.

During the process of studying acting, we hope that you will learn to observe yourself with the compassion that you likely show toward your loved ones. Don't say things to yourself that you wouldn't let others say about your closest friends.

Dual Perspectives—Developing Your Internal and External Monitors

Dual perspectives (also known as the *two perspectives*) is a concept that needs to be developed to the highest levels of both training and performance and thus will be addressed throughout this book. In later stages it involves simultaneously living as a character in a specific situation, while also watching yourself from outside and making creative choices. To do this, you immerse yourself in the thoughts, feelings/emotions, and behavior of a specific person in the world of the play with a specific history and style, while also keeping a small part of yourself as the external observer, fine-tuning the aesthetic impact of your performance. This is similar to a concept in psychology called *metacognition*, which is about consciously watching your own thought processes.

You guide the character and sculpt the role along the *spine* of the play, while keeping awareness of safety and logistical concerns. You must not lose control and artistic restraint while playing; otherwise you will forfeit the ability to exercise creative choices, or actually may do yourself or another harm—for example, in a fight scene. You rely on your *internal* and *external monitors* to ensure this balance.

For the purposes of developing awareness of self, you can start to develop the *internal monitor*. The internal monitor observes your own internal processes. While you must later try to use and adjust your internal processes to reflect the inner state of a character, first develop an awareness of how sensations, ideas, breath, and emotion move and stir your psychophysical instrument. After all it is very difficult to study the internal world of another, so start with yourself. This is important in beginning exercises when you are asked to come from yourself and need to observe your own internal mechanisms on stage.

Even in beginning exercises you must also develop your *external monitor*, which senses everyone and everything around you. Through the external monitor you seem to be viewing yourself from the tenth row of the audience while fully engaged in the performance. This state of consciousness is highly desirable and allows you to *experience your experience*, thereby living the life of the character while simultaneously conveying this character's life artistically.

Before you begin to develop characters different from you, you must first take some time to understand the self that is your building block by developing your internal and external monitors. This includes awareness of your internal landscape thoughts, emotions, and physical sensations (internal monitor) and awareness of your external expression and how others perceive you when they don't already know you (also through the external monitor).

How strangers perceive you may be quite different from how you see yourself or would like to be seen by others. This can be humbling or amusing when you are first becoming cognizant of it. How we are seen on first impression, after all, is such a small piece of the fullness of who we are. For some, investigating and looking consciously at who they are and how others see them is a new process. Some beginning actors, however, already have a strong sense of their own presentation and how they come across to others. Either way, studying acting will expand your perceptions.

Concentration

> "Every activity requires a certain amount of concentration, and no effective action can be performed without deep concentration."
>
> —Paramahansa Yogananda

Acting requires intense concentration. This is your ability to focus your attention and not get distracted. In acting, you can focus internally on images and thoughts that affect your psychophysical instrument, which will be explored more in Chapter 5: The Psychophysical Instrument: Exploring the Mind-Body Connection and Chapter 6: Communion: Deepening Communication and Mutual Influence or externally on objects, scene partners, or the fulfillment of actions, which will be focused on in Chapter 7: Discovering and Endowing Circumstances, Chapter 8: Nonverbal Action: Communicating through Behavior, and Chapter 11: Verbal Action: Communicating through Words and Subtext.

To develop concentration, Stanislavsky borrowed meditation techniques from raja yoga (considered the "royal path" of yoga because it incorporates all eight paths or limbs of yoga) and insisted, "My whole System is based on this."[14] There is more about the connections between the System and yoga in Chapter 4: Yoga and Acting: Dedication to Creative Space. Some related techniques that we will introduce for you to try include focus of attention and circles of attention.

3.1A *Reflection Journal—Observation of Self*

Before the next exercise, take a moment to observe yourself. What are you thinking? What physical sensations do you have? What feelings are stirring inside you, and do you connect these feelings to any specific emotion?

Exercise 3.1: Watching the Breath[15]

If you do not have a teacher leading you through this, we recommend you tape the instructions in a calm voice and play this for yourself as you do the exercise, so that you can just follow along receptively.

---

[14] Quoted in Carnicke, *Stanislavsky in Focus*, 143.
[15] This is adapted by the authors from an ancient yogic exercise. Exercises like this using the breath and various types of concentration and meditation are now widely used, even in the West. Meditation, for example, is now used in hospital cancer centers to fight disease and ease pain. It is also used to help with a variety of psychological conditions such as anxiety and depression.

Guidelines:

a. Sit in a chair with your feet planted on the floor (or you may sit cross-legged on the floor, or in the yoga pose of Verasana (see pictures for options and find the most comfortable position for you). See illustrations in Figure 3.3.
b. Clasp your hands on your lap easily and without grasping, or place them palms down on your knees.
c. Widen across the back to allow the spine to lengthen.
d. Allow the neck to be loose but long as though your head is floating on top of your spine.
e. You can release into the back of your chair so that you use less effort holding yourself up, but don't collapse into it.
f. Allow the eyes to close on the exhalation and open slowly on the inhalation. Do this three to four times, then gently allow the eyes to remain closed.
g. With your internal monitor, observe the exhalation of the breath.
h. If you notice anything else—physical sensations, sounds from outside, sounds from within your body, thoughts or emotions—just notice and release them, as though allowing a balloon to float up and away.
i. Remain in this posture watching the outgoing breath for five to ten minutes, depending on the length of your class.

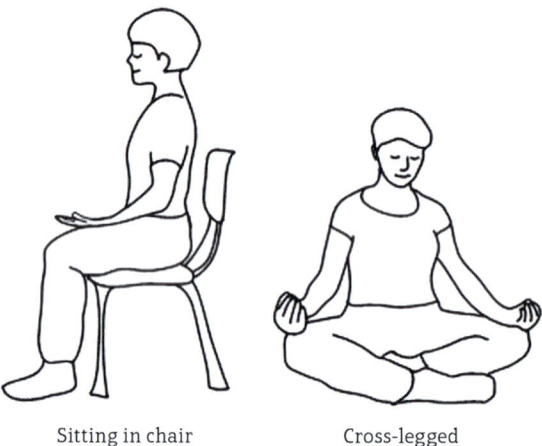

Figure 3.3 Positions for meditation—watching the breath.

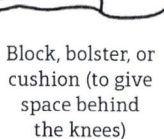

Sitting in chair

Cross-legged (or you can use the lotus position from yoga)

Block, bolster, or cushion (to give space behind the knees)

Note: In addition to the variation of the postures shown above, this exercise can also be done lying down, but you may then fall asleep if tired. As you get more comfortable with it, you can also do it with your eyes open and focused on nothing or focused on a simple object, or a special place, that brings you peace. This may help you to develop the ability to see images with your eyes open, a key skill for actors.

3 THE CREATIVE STATE

> **3.1B** *Reflection Journal—After Watching the Breath*
>
> Notice what you are thinking. What physical sensations do you have? What feelings are stirring inside you, and do you connect these feelings to any specific emotion? Did you notice any change from before the exercise, during, after? Were you able to focus on nothing but the outgoing breath? How might this exercise relate to acting?

PART II: SCIENTIFIC RESEARCH ON CREATIVITY

> **What Can We Learn from Science about the Factors That Help or Inhibit Creativity?**

A century ago, Stanislavsky set out to methodically study science and yoga to get hints about human possibility that might enhance the experience of the actor. His references to science were widely acknowledged, but his references to yoga were often obfuscated through Soviet censorship, misunderstanding, or mistranslation. Now, the tables have turned and instead of the artist studying the science, there is a field of research devoted to scientific study of creativity and creative people.

While understanding the processes of emotion and how to stimulate specific emotions on cue has long been the purview of actors, and studying emotion has also been a focus in psychology, scientists in other fields, such as biology and neuroscience, now have the tools to gain more understanding of the physiological underpinnings and processes of emotion and have made some surprising discoveries (some of which are discussed in Chapter 12: Orchestrating Emotions. Artists in all fields (musicians, painters, dancers, actors, writers) are among those studied, as well as inventors, Nobel Prize–winning scientists, and innovators in business and cultural systems such as government. What all of these people have in common is that they have immersed themselves in a discipline and then made leaps into previously unknown territory, thereby expanding their discipline and making cultural contributions.

> "We cannot do without men with the courage to think new things before they can prove them"[16]
>
> —Sigmund Freud

Society often considers scientists and artists on opposite ends of the spectrum. It turns out that regardless of the discipline, the human processes and mechanisms for breakthroughs—inspiration—in science and art have much in common. Some scientific findings in the areas of creativity, as well as mind-body connection and emotion, support concepts that have long been known by artists; other discoveries are more surprising and have challenged previously held convictions. By combining the insights of artists with the research of scientists, we can learn to enhance the creativity of people in all disciplines.

The famous American physicist Albert Einstein (1879–1955), considered one of the world's foremost geniuses, had an interesting perspective on creativity:

---

[16] Sigmund Freud, *The Origins of Psycho-Analysis: Letters to Wilhelm Flies*, ed. Marie Bonaparte, Anna Freud, and Ernst Kris (New York: Basic Books, 1954), 137.

I am enough of the artist to draw freely upon my imagination. Imagination is more important than knowledge. Knowledge is limited. Imagination encircles the world.[17]

Psychologist Mihaly Csikszentmihalyi, in his book *Creativity: Flow and the Psychology of Discovery and Invention*, cites some attributes of creativity: "Creativity involves the production of novelty. The process of discovery involved in creating something new appears to be one of the most enjoyable activities any human can be involved in."[18] Another common trait he cites is, "Many creative scientists say that the difference between them and their less creative peers is the ability to separate bad ideas from good ones, so that they don't waste much time exploring blind alleys."[19] Having a clear goal or problem to solve is important, but he noticed that "for artists the goal of the activity is not so easily found. In fact the more creative the problem, the less clear it is what needs to be done. . . . In such cases, the creative person somehow must develop an unconscious mechanism that tells him or her what to do. . . . The ancients called that voice the Muse."[20]

Anatomy of the Creative Mind

Developing more knowledge, as well as experiential understanding, of the way your mind works relative to the brain and body is paramount to your training. After all, your psychophysical system is your primary tool. Most of us know very little about this amazing instrument in which we have lived our entire lives. Mind is defined by Antonio Damasio as a series of conscious and unconscious processes, not an object such as the anatomical brain. He goes on to say:

What we know as mind, with the help of consciousness, is a continuous flow of mental patterns, many of which turn out to be logically interrelated. The flow moves forward in time, speedily or slowly, orderly or jumpily, and on occasion it moves along not just one sequence but several.[21]

Brain anatomy is complex, and brain functions are mapped in different parts of the brain, often simultaneously. Additionally, in speaking to psychologist Dr. Joe Miele, he intoned that with the amount of research and daily discoveries in brain sciences, "Writing about the brain is like buying electronics,"[22] as soon as you put an idea about the brain down on paper, a new discovery alters it. There are many good books on the subject footnoted in this chapter and in the bibliography, should you like to know more. For now, start with the fact that our brain is divided into regions, partly based on when this part of the brain evolved, called the *hindbrain*, *midbrain* and *forebrain* (see Figure 3.4).

The midbrain and hindbrain are both considered part of the brainstem (or more primitive brain. The brainstem controls many vital survival functions. One

---

[17] Jeff Nilsson, "Imagination is More Important than Knowledge," *Saturday Evening Post*, March 20, 2013 (based on a 1929 interview with Albert Einstein).
[18] Mihaly Csikszentmihalyi, *Creativity: Flow and the Psychology of Discovery and Invention* (New York: HarperPerennial, 1997), 113.
[19] Ibid., 116.
[20] Ibid., 114–115.
[21] Damasio, *The Feeling of What Happens*, 337.
[22] Joe Miele, in conversation with Stephanie Daventry French.

import aspect of the midbrain, which is the smallest region, is that it connects the cerebellum of the hindbrain with the cerebral cortex of the forebrain and coordinates vision and auditory processing and functions. The hindbrain connects the spinal column with the brain and includes the *medulla* oblongata (which controls involuntary functions such as heartbeat, breathing, blood pressure and swallowing), *pons* (sensory analysis and motor control), and *cerebellum* (coordinates responses of the muscles to sensory input—including balance and posture in response to input from the ears, coordination, and communication between the hindbrain and the cerebrum).

The forebrain is primarily made up of the cerebrum. It also includes the limbic system, which is very important to actors. The limbic system is also known as the emotional brain. It houses the amygdala (important for learning and memory storage, motivation, and controlling emotions), the thalamus (relays sensory information to the cortex for consideration), and the hypothalamus (important to acting as it regulates the display of emotion and also regulates eating, sleeping, temperature, and reproductive functions). The cerebrum is further divided into left and right hemispheres joined by the corpus callosum and covered by the cerebral cortex. Observes Dubuc, "Perhaps the most striking anatomical characteristic of the human brain is that it is divided into two hemispheres, so that it has two of almost every structure: one on the left side and one on the right. But these paired structures are not exactly symmetrical and often differ in their size, form, and function. This phenomenon is called **brain lateralization.**"[23] The cortex controls perception, including perception of arts such as theatre; high cognitive functions, including reasoning, abstract thought, and concentration; and also controls memory. Each hemisphere is symmetrically further organized into a *temporal lobe*, *occipital lobe*, *parietal lobe* and *frontal lobe*, some of the basic structures of which are identified in Figure 3.4.

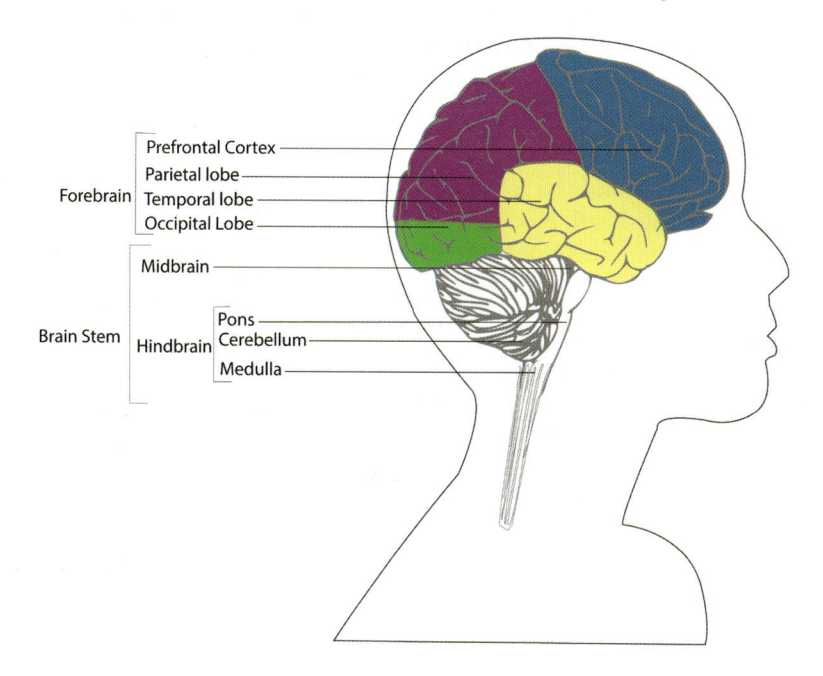

Figure 3.4 Primary brain regions.

[23]Bruno Dubuc, "Broca's Area, Wernicke's Area, and Other Language-Processing Areas in the Brain" accessed on-line on the website The Brain from Top to Bottom, May 17, 2015, http://thebrain.mcgill.ca/flash/i/i_10/i_10_cr/i_10_cr_lan/i_10_cr_lan.html, 3.

Originally it was thought that the left hemisphere, which primarily directs the right (generally the dominant) side of the body, was the more important, more human side, while the right hemisphere was the primitive and animal brain. The brainstem is now understood to handle the more primitive functions while the forebrain handles more-complex ones. *A Whole New Mind*, by Daniel H. Pink, sums up the common understanding in neuroscience: "The two hemispheres of our brains don't operate as on-off switches—one powering down as soon as the other starts lighting up. Both halves play a role in nearly everything we do."[24] He goes on to say, it is commonly understood that "both sides work together—but they have different specialties. The left hemisphere handles logic, sequence, literalness and analysis. The right takes care of synthesis, emotional expression, context, and the big picture." *Synthesis* (finding connections between different ideas, styles, disciplines) is considered a higher-order cognitive function and also is essential to invention and other forms of creativity and yet is handled by the right hemisphere. This certainly disputes left hemispheric superiority.

Language of the Hemispheres

Early correlations between behavior and specific areas of the brain were primarily based on patients with damaged brains who also demonstrated loss of specific behavioral functionality. In later autopsies, they were then found to have damage to a specific area of the brain, suggesting a link between the lost behavior or function and the damaged brain region. According to American neurologist Norman Geschwind, whose own work on the anatomy and physiology of behavior is fundamental to the development of cognitive neuroscience, "Paul Broca, . . . in 1861 published the first series of papers on language and the brain. Broca was the first to point out that damage to a specific portion of the brain results in disturbance of language output. The portion he identified lying in the third frontal gyrus of the cerebral cortex, is now called Broca's area." (see Figure 3.5)[25] Broca's area focuses on production of language and articulation of speech.

Ten years later in 1871, Polish-German neurologist Carl Wernicke identified an area associated with processing incoming language, giving context and meaning to the words we hear. Wernicke's area makes up a key component of our ability to comprehend language in speech or when read. Again Geschwind: "Wernicke made the natural assumption that Broca's area and Wernicke's area must be connected. We now know that the two areas are indeed connected, by a bundle of nerve fibers known as the *arcuate fasciculus*." Geschwind's research team in the 1960s was responsible for identifying the system of fibers that connects Wernicke's and Broca's areas, now called by some Geschwind's territory, and proposing the first map of a language system in the brain.

We know that the left hemisphere of the brain controls and receives information (such as visual stimuli) from the right side of the body just as the

---

[24] Daniel H. Pink, *A Whole New Mind: Why Right-Brainers Will Rule the Future* (New York: Riverhead Books, 2005; 2006), 17.
[25] Norman Geschwind, "Language and the Brain," *Scientific American* 226 (1972): 113.

3 THE CREATIVE STATE

right hemisphere does from the left side of the body. As Broca's and Wernicke's areas were both discovered in the left hemisphere of their patient's brains, and many subsequent patients with language problems showed damage to this area in the left hemisphere, language was thought to be only a function of the left brain. Dubuc clarifies this misconception: "The brain hemisphere in which the main language abilities reside has often been referred to as the "dominant" hemisphere for language. But since we now know that *the other hemisphere also contributes to language,* it would be more accurate to describe the two hemispheres as sharing responsibility for the many aspects of language, rather than one hemisphere somehow exercising dominance over the other."[26] Pink states, "To oversimplify just a bit, the left hemisphere handles what is said; the right hemisphere focuses on how it is said – the non-verbal, often emotional cues delivered through gaze, facial expression, and intonation."[27]

Brain imaging and other more advanced tools that allow scientists to observe the brain in living, thinking patients have shed further light on the attribution of the brain hemispheres and language. For example, "In the vast majority of right-handed people, language abilities are localized in the left hemisphere. But contrary to what you might expect, the opposite is not true among left-handed people, for whom the picture is less clear. Many "lefties" show a specialization for language in the left hemisphere, but some show one in the right, while for still others, both hemispheres contribute just about equally to language."[28]

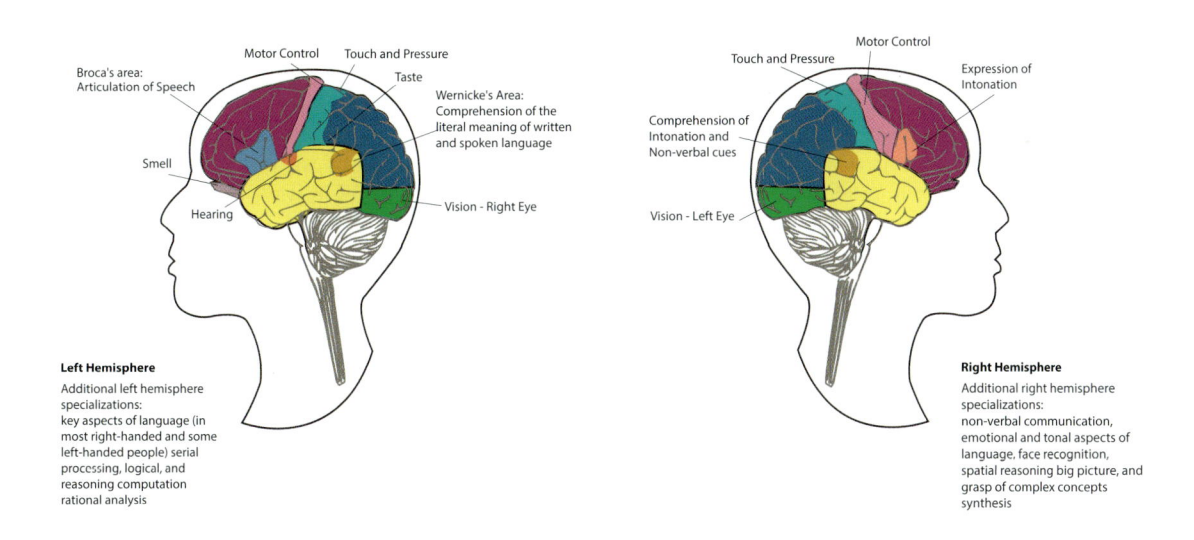

Left Hemisphere
Additional left hemisphere specializations:
key aspects of language (in most right-handed and some left-handed people) serial processing, logical, and reasoning computation rational analysis

Right Hemisphere
Additional right hemisphere specializations:
non-verbal communication, emotional and tonal aspects of language, face recognition, spatial reasoning big picture, and grasp of complex concepts synthesis

Figure 3.5 Selected and shared brain hemisphere functions.

[26] Dubuc "Broca's Area, Wernicke's Area, and Other Language-Processing Areas in the Brain," p. 3.
[27] Pink, 21.
[28] Bruno Dubuc, http://thebrain.mcgill.ca/flash/d/d_10/d_10_cr/d_10_cr_lan/d_10_cr_lan.html May 17, 2015, p. 5.

Most functions require aspects of both sides of the brain to a greater or lesser degree; for example, the basic grammatical sequencing of words is handled by the left brain, but interpreting their contextual meaning and any abstract concepts, such as metaphor or interplay between tone and word meaning such as in sarcasm and irony, are the territory primarily (but not exclusively) of the right brain. Additionally, as you will read more about in Chapter 12: Orchestrating Emotions, higher levels of cognition cannot happen without emotion, and emotion cannot happen without cognition. Another relevant finding for your acting training is that people are more stimulated when more parts of their brain are engaged; therefore your acting training will involve methods that stimulate both hemispheres.

Factors That Help Generate Creativity

In *The Age of Insight: The Quest to Understand the Unconscious in Art, Mind and Brain*, Nobel Prize–winning neuroscientist Eric R. Kandel reviews the work of Ernst Kris (1900–1957), an art historian who brought in elements of psychology and sociology to the analysis of art. On Kris's work with psychologist Nancy Andreasen, Kandel notes that "essential prerequisites for creativity are technical competence and a willingness to work hard. . . . They divided the creative process into four parts: (1) the types of personalities that are likely to be particularly creative; (2) the period of preparation and incubation, when a person works on a problem consciously and unconsciously; (3) the initial moments of creativity themselves; and (4) subsequent working through of the creative idea."[29]

These are important preparations for actors. While the process of studying and applying acting technique can be a great deal of fun, you must also work hard to make valuable progress. You must lay the groundwork for inspiration through preparation. First, steep yourself in everything you can consciously know about the subject, then allow new ideas to percolate by inviting input from your right brain—sleep, relax, dream, exercise. After you have an insight, the work does not stop; you will need to translate that insight into an expressive form, in ways that increase the likelihood that the wisdom gained, if not the moment of insight itself, will revisit you and impact your audience.

Also relevant to the creative state, Kandel observed that "personalities that lead to the creative mind-set are numerous and not centered entirely on the intellect: some highly creative people are slow readers or poor at arithmetic. In addition, the creative mind-set is most commonly not generalized but domain specific (relevant to a field of activity or research). It derives from a variety of features that are extremely important, including wonderment, independence, nonconformity, flexibility, and . . . the capability for relaxation."[30]

Each one of these features relate to training as an actor. Wonderment is a key ingredient of learning and growth. It is related to the idea of beginner's mind, introduced in Chapter 1. Csikszentmihalyi also uses the terms *awe* and *wonder*: "With age most of us lose the sense of wonder, the feeling of awe in confronting the majesty and variety of the world."[31] He related these concepts to the familiar

---

[29]Eric R. Kandel. *The Age of Insight: The Quest to Understand the Unconscious in Art, Mind and Brain* (New York: Random House, 2012), 456.
[30]Ibid., 457.
[31]Csikszentmihalyi, *Creativity*, 346.

3 THE CREATIVE STATE

human traits of curiosity and interest: "Creative individuals are childlike in that their curiosity remains fresh even at ninety years of age; they delight in the strange and the unknown."[32] Some people find the beginning exercises we do in acting childlike; this is because we need to reconnect with a sense of openness, imagination, and play that is a natural state of childhood and the natural state of creative individuals. Wonderment is also important for onstage discovery in improvisations or scenes. A technique that begins with wonder, called W.E.D.G.A.G. (which stands for Wonder, Evaluate, Decision, Gesture, Action, Gesture) will be introduced in Chapter 5: The Psychophysical Instrument.

Independence and nonconformity are important because you cannot offer new insights to an audience if you play it safe within what is already known and accepted. You must be willing, as in voyages of the starship *Enterprise*, "to explore strange new worlds, to seek out new life and new civilizations, to boldly go where no one has gone before,"[33] or in the words of poet Robert Frost, "Two roads diverged in a wood, and I—/ I took the one less traveled by/And that has made all the difference."[34] Theatre is a collaborative art, but you must find an independent spirit unfettered by the current cultural limitations. Find the focus to work independently outside of class and rehearsal in order to have the maximum to contribute when you are working with your company or class.

Flexibility is about the willingness to break out of the mold and entertain new paradigms. It is also the ability to adjust to obstacles and not get derailed by them. Instead of seeing change as a threat, see it is a dynamic opportunity, important for both the actor and actor as character.

Last, but certainly not least, of Kandel's observations above is the state of relaxation. This concept is intrinsic to both books on acting and books on creativity. Insight is much more likely to grace us when we are freed from tension and distractions. Stanislavsky recognized the importance of relaxation as a preparation for creative work. According to Kandel, "Relaxation is characterized by ready access to unconscious mental processes; in that sense it is somewhat analogous to dreaming. The recent discovery that, like much of our cognitive and affective life, even our decision-making is partially unconscious suggests that unconscious mental processes are necessary for creative thinking as well."[35] Csikszentmihalyi had similar findings that emphasized the importance of relaxation as well as reflection: "Constant busyness is not a good prescription for creativity. . . . Whether you intend it or not, new ideas and conclusions will emerge in your consciousness anyway. . . . Typical activities that facilitate subconscious creative processes are walking, showering, swimming, driving, gardening, weaving and carpentry. Neither stress nor monotony is a very good context for creativity."[36]

---

[32]Ibid., 346.
[33]From the opening voiceover, as to the purpose of the *Enterprise* in the *Star Trek* TV series and movies.
[34]Robert Frost, *"The Road Not Taken" and Other Poems* (Mineola, NY: Dover Thrift Editions, 1993), 1.
[35]Kandel, *The Age of Insight*, 459.
[36]Csikszentmihalyi. *Creativity*, 353.

PART III: AWARENESS OF SELF IN FRONT OF AN AUDIENCE

Stage Fright

Relaxation may help with creativity, but how can you relax when everyone is watching?

> "According to most studies, people's number-one fear is public speaking. Number two is death. *Death* is number two! Now, this means to the average person, if you have to go to a funeral, you're better off in the casket than doing the eulogy."
>
> —Jerry Seinfeld,[37] *Seinfeld*, Castle Rock Entertainment, 1992

The above is a famous, and toastmasters will say, overused quote about public speaking based on Bruskin-Goldring's 1973 and 1993 surveys, where people expressed a greater fear of speaking before a group than they expressed of death (which came in fifth in 1993). There are many challenges to this study, including that it was too small of a sample (1,000 people) and was administered to induce fear by using leading words such as *nightmare*, rather than more neutral ones. Supposedly, people fear public speaking more than they fear death (as found in a variety of surveys) although this has not been tested, as far as we know, in any actual life-or-death situations. This may be an exaggeration but still gives a glimpse of the high degree of fear associated with public speaking. Standing on stage as an actor, where you need to reveal deep and vulnerable aspects of your humanity can be even more frightening. So how can you overcome this?

The path to build confidence in the beginning actor, which eventually will lead to being able to perform for an audience of strangers, is slow and steady. In fact, professional actors also experience stage fright—some every time they perform, some only for really big auditions or opening nights for big shows, when the tough critics are coming. The difference is that experienced actors have learned that what goes on in the body as nervousness is very similar to what goes on during excitement and it generates energy that can be focused and used to enliven their performances.

In 1927, Harvard physiologist Walter B. Cannon discovered that physiologically this is in fact the case. According to Kandel, "Cannon found that the intense emotion caused by either a perceived threat or a perceived reward triggers an undifferentiated arousal—a primitive emergency response that mobilizes the body for action. In other words our body responds to the trigger whether it is real or imagined. Cannon coined the expression 'fight or flight' to describe this response."[38] We can change the thought that frames and interprets the physical feelings. To gain control of your thoughts, you must first become aware of what they are. Journal writing can be very effective in slowing down the thoughts enough to see them more clearly. To gain control of autonomic responses in the body and learn to dial them up or down as needed to fulfill the demands of the part, you will need to better

---

[37] Interestingly, Jerry Seinfeld studied the Stanislavsky System with Sonia Moore in New York City.
[38] Kandel, *Age of Insight*, 349.

understand how the "fight or flight" response works in your system. Learning to train your thoughts, as well as physical and emotional responses, is a key to what Stanislavsky called the "conscious means to the subconscious."[39] It is also a key goal of yogic training, as discussed in Chapter 4: Yoga and Acting: Dedication to the Creative Space.

"Fight or Flight": The Fear and Excitement Response

It is important to become conscious of how fear manifests in your psychophysical system so that you can counter it to ease the mental and physical restrictions that can accompany stage fright. First, there is a trigger, which can be an actual danger (external) or a perceived danger (internal). This signal is picked up by a primitive area of the brain called the amygdala (alarm). The amygdala then notifies the hypothalamus of the danger (much faster than the conscious mind can identify it). The hypothalamus is known as a communication center because it communicates with the rest of the brain and body to rally the whole system to respond to the threat through "fight or flight" via the autonomic nervous system. This activates the involuntary sympathetic nervous system, which causes the heart rate to speed up and direct blood to the heart, muscles, and other vital organs (thus extremities may turn white or feel cold); blood pressure increases to make more blood available to the muscles if flight is chosen; the pupils dilate to take in more light; the lungs open wide to receive more air; and a temporary flood of adrenaline increases mental alertness.

This entire response is meant to be short-term and is followed by a release of all these hyped-up systems as the parasympathetic nervous system returns the body to homeostasis (stability of internal systems). If the stress response gets stuck in the "on" position, chronic stress ensues. Chronic stress does not allow your body the replenishing of supplies and repair of systems that the parasympathetic system gives us if we allow sufficient breaks, rest, and sleep. Instead, try to balance moments of heightened response (as normal to living) with periods of more calm states, and stress will not build up. Thus, your body will not experience the accelerated deterioration and disease associated with chronic stress.

Exercise 3.2A: Observation of the Fear Response in You (SDF)

Guidelines: The next time you feel fear (you can use anxiety or worry if nothing truly fearful arises) and you have the option to step back from it, or to step into it (as long as you can do the latter without physical harm), choose to step in. The activity will be something you don't do often. This may be when a teacher asks a question to the class and you raise your hand to answer, you step up to go first in a solo exercise, you approach someone to ask them on a date, go on a job interview, etc. Within the next week either an opportunity will arise or you should create one. As you do the exercise, try to employ your internal monitor to notice the effects on your breath, heart rate, and mental alertness. Did you notice any increased muscular tension? If so, where? What thoughts accompanied this experience?

---

[39] Quoted in Jean Benedetti, *Stanislavski* (London: Methuen Drama, 1988), 217.

> **Exercise 3.2B: The Fear Response (Supplemental Exercise)**
>
> You may even wish to attempt, using one of the "Tips for Dealing with Stage Fright" in this chapter, to see whether they can modulate your "fight or flight" response.

Feeling the Fear and Doing It Anyway

French's motto on the impediment of fear is, "Feel the fear and do it anyway!" Think back to the experiences that have allowed you to grow the most, or even familiar life passages such as jumping into the deep end of the pool or riding a bike or driving a car for the first time. You probably experienced fear and yet by doing it anyway, taking a risk, you grew. In the box below are some techniques that help counter fear when it becomes so strong as to add too much tension and thus inhibit the flow of your creativity.

Inhibition in performance often has to do with fear of revealing ourselves to others who we believe will then judge us negatively. Yet, you are likely to find the opposite to be true. When we are willing to share the private and personal human aspects of ourselves with an audience, either as a speaker or an actor, most people respond supportively. There are many deep and powerful human experiences that people have never shared with anyone. Sometimes people feel ashamed and alone for having these experiences. When the actor reveals a similar human fallibility onstage, it can be liberating to audience members who realize that their private secret is in fact a part of shared human experience. The actor's personal experience need not be revealed openly but through practice during the rehearsal process becomes fused with the imaginary circumstances of the character. This is called *amalgamation*. During the performance the actor only need focus on the imaginary situation and his action, and new feelings and emotions appropriate for the character will emerge spontaneously and be felt by the audience.

Relaxation

Relaxation, or freeing the body from tension and the mind from anxiety, as in stage fright discussed above, is a key to creativity and a key to acting. It is also a key to freeing up the flow of your energy, leading to the creative state that invites inspiration. Increasing your flow of energy will be actively explored in Chapter 5: The Psychophysical Instrument. However, relaxation on stage is not a release of all physical energy, but a release of unnecessary tension to allow a targeted channeling of your flow of energy.

Willing oneself into a state of relaxation is equally as elusive as willing inspiration or crying on cue. You can learn to *release tension* and activate different parts of your body either in isolation or in groups. This will increase your ability to control the flow of energy and begin to allow you to direct it, thus creating a receptive, relaxed state of mind and body and an expressive physical instrument. As a starting place, you will need to become more conscious of the tension that blocks the flow of your energy. You may find that this not only helps you with acting but also reduces the negative impacts of stress.

3 THE CREATIVE STATE

To develop your ability to release tension a few tools will be explored below—shifting the breath and visualization.

> **Exercise 3.3: Shifting the Breath (Deep Breathing to Release Tension) (SDF)**
>
> **Purpose:** One of the simplest and most effective exercises for regaining control of your body in a fearful situation is to change the breath.
>
> **Guidelines:** When we are stressed, we breathe quickly and high in our chests.
>
> - Put your hand on your lower back or belly (you can even do this while sitting in a chair at a job interview or waiting to go on for an audition).
> - Breathe into your hand, feeling the expansion of your lower abdomen and the increased width of your back.
> - Now breathe out, counting 1-2-3-4-5-6, pause for 1-2, and breathe in, 1-2-3-4.
> - Allow the outgoing breath to release tension and the incoming breath to bring refreshed energy (if you need to perform) or to bring peace and restfulness (if you are trying to wind down).

3.3 Reflection Journal—Shifting the Breath

Did you notice any change in your body, thoughts, or emotions as you shifted your breath? If so, what was it?

> **Tips for Alleviating Stage Fright**
>
> - Relaxation (as outlined below).
> - Low and slow breathing: Regain control of your breath, which has likely gotten quick and shallow. Place your hand on your belly and allow the breath to fall deeply into your body and release out slowly. In, 1-2-3, out, 1-2-3; in, 1-2-3-4, out, 1-2-3-4; in, 1-2-3-4-5, out, 1-2-3-4-5. Even three deep breaths will begin to change your mind and body, moving it away from fear and toward calm and peace (although it might take more than three breaths to get far enough from fear to be more comfortable.
> - Calm the mind: You can try various forms of meditation and find the ones that work best for you. One simple example is the watching-the-breath exercise, 3.1 above. Try shifting your focus by placing your internal gaze on the third eye (between the eyebrows). This really helps to control the racing of the mind and allows you to focus on watching the breath while letting the crazy thoughts pass by. Another helpful tip for calming the mind is to sit quietly or lie down and open your eyes slowly as you breathe in and close your eyes slowly as you breath out.

- Reframing your thoughts: Some examples of reframing the thoughts that accompany fear might be to say to yourself, "This is excitement rather than fear," or, "This is just my body getting going for a big physical or mental push," rather than, "This is anxiety." Other helpful techniques will be releasing your fears through talking with friends who reassure you, or through picturing peaceful images.
- Inner Monologue of the Character: Replace undermining self-conscious talk with the thoughts of the character in the situation. If you are thinking as the character, and keeping the dual consciousness to be aware of the many artistic choices you and the director have made in designing the role, there is little room for undermining thoughts.
- Focus on how you are trying to affect others onstage (your objective), again rather than on self-critique or self-consciousness (which is another term for *nervousness*).
- Focus on the problem your character is struggling with.
- Focus on filling your action-steps one at a time.

Exercise 3.4: Sunset on the Beach (PGB) (a Progressive Exercise in Four Parts)

Guidelines: Sit comfortably on a chair or lie down with your eyes closed, practice dual consciousness as one part of you listens to the instruction and the other drifts into the images you are creating.

Exercise 3.4A: Releasing Tension through Guided Visualization

(Imaginary Creation of a Film of Moving Three-Dimensional, Detailed Images, Like Holographs or Virtual Reality):

- Imagine yourself on your favorite beach. It is just at sundown after a wonderfully warm and peaceful day. Watch the sun setting like an egg yolk on the horizon as it slowly flattens and expands before it plops into the sea.
- Take long, deep breaths and feel the sand under your body, its warmth drawing all tension from every nook and cranny. All thoughts fade into focus on your breath.
- Follow the breath into every organ and muscle of your body.
- Notice the beautiful clear, blue sky. Watch a seagull gliding effortlessly on the wind currents.
- Hear the sound of waves gently caressing the shore.
- As the sun disappears below the horizon, so do all your worries, fears, and nervousness.
- Take a period of complete silence for three minutes and just enjoy the serenity.

3 THE CREATIVE STATE

Exercise 3.4B: Feeling the Flow of Energy

- When you are ready, begin to rise from your prone position muscle by muscle, only engaging the necessary muscles. Move upward using circular movements (like a corkscrew coming up out of a bottle, rather than sitting up leading with head. Bring the head up last. Take a full two to four minutes to come to a standing position.
- Breathe into each muscle group before moving it, and begin all movements from the base of the spine. Observe the flow of muscular energy as it rises from the base of the spine into the appropriate muscle for movement.
- Keep your eyes closed, and remain interiorized and yet aware of all sounds and others around you.
- Do not engage your neck muscles until you are standing with both feet shoulder width apart. Let your head hang for a few moments before rolling up the neck vertebrae one at a time. Keep the neck floating easy on top of your spine.

Exercise 3.4C: Soft Focus with the Eyes Open

Guidelines:

- Open your eyes, but not too wide. Be aware of everything around you peripherally without any specific external visual focus. Allow your other senses to heighten but again without following specific stimuli, just noticing. Maintain some inner gaze and awareness of inner impulses. Take time to adjust to the external environment while maintaining your interiorized consciousness. With your eyes open, try to maintain pictures of the sunset on the beach.
- Walk slowly around the room, observing through dual consciousness, how the movement feels in your body and your associated thoughts and images (internal monitor) and also watching yourself move from the outside (external monitor).
- At first do not focus on others but rather sense them around you, keeping your eyes in soft focus and extending the use of your other senses to avoid bumping into anyone.

Exercise 3.4D: Extending Your Peace through Communion

- Next, gradually acknowledge each person as you pass.
- Look at everyone directly in the eye and share a positive, bright idea and image.

> **3.4** *Reflection Journal—Sunset Beach Reflection*
>
> Note your recollections of thoughts, physical sensations, and emotions at each stage of this exercise. Could you picture the beach and sunset in detail? Did the image change your level of tension? Could you bring awareness to different muscle groups? Which ones? Did you experience moving from the base of the spine? Could you continue to see your beach sunset with your eyes open? Were you able to sense your classmates moving around you without looking directly at them? When you did make contact, could you relay your images, or the feeling of them, just through looking into your classmates' eyes? Were you able to receive their images?

Summary

As with all human development, developing your potential as an actor involves both adding techniques and insights that are helpful, as well as diminishing those issues or behaviors that get in your way. In addition to Stanislavsky's sources in yoga and science, twenty-first-century cognitive neuroscience offers us many helpful insights. In Chapter 3: The Creative State: Preparing for Inspiration, you were introduced to the factors that are most conducive to entering the creative state that invites inspiration. Some of these include presence, increasing awareness of self and other through the internal and external monitors, developing a sense of curiosity or wonder, flexibility, nonconformity, and relaxation. Additionally, it helps to remove obstacles to creativity, such as stress, stage fright, self-criticism, tension, and distractions.

New Theatre Terms, Concepts, and Artists

Terms used in the Stanislavsky System are in italics.

- ☐ amalgamation
- ☐ awareness of other
- ☐ awareness of self
- ☐ Sharon M. Carnicke
- ☐ charisma
- ☐ *dual perspectives*
- ☐ *experiencing*
- ☐ experiencing the experience
- ☐ *"I am"/"I exist"*

- ☐ Naomi Iizuka
- ☐ internal and external monitors
- ☐ persona
- ☐ presence
- ☐ soft focus
- ☐ stage fright
- ☐ *visualization*
- ☐ W.E.D.G.A.G.
- ☐ R. Andrew White

3 THE CREATIVE STATE

Interdisciplinary Terms, Concepts, and Experts

- ☐ adrenaline
- ☐ amygdala
- ☐ Aaron Beck
- ☐ Tara Brach
- ☐ Paul Broca
- ☐ Broca's area
- ☐ Bruskin Goldring Research
- ☐ Walter B. Cannon
- ☐ cerebellum
- ☐ cerebral cortex
- ☐ cerebrum
- ☐ corpus callosum
- ☐ Antonio Damasio
- ☐ René Descartes
- ☐ Bruno Dubuc
- ☐ Albert Ellis
- ☐ "fight or flight"
- ☐ forebrain
- ☐ frontal lobe
- ☐ Norman Geschwind
- ☐ Martha Graham
- ☐ hindbrain
- ☐ homeostasis
- ☐ hypothalamus
- ☐ William James
- ☐ Eric R. Kandel
- ☐ Ernst Kris
- ☐ left/right hemispheres
- ☐ limbic system
- ☐ medulla oblongata
- ☐ metacognition
- ☐ midbrain
- ☐ Joe Miele
- ☐ occipital lobe
- ☐ parietal lobe
- ☐ Daniel Pink
- ☐ pons
- ☐ synthesis
- ☐ temporal lobe
- ☐ thalamus
- ☐ third eye
- ☐ Carl Wernicke
- ☐ Wernicke's area
- ☐ Richard Wesp
- ☐ Paramahansa Yogananda

CHAPTER 4

Yoga and Acting: Dedication to the Creative Space

"Inner creative work demands even greater order, organization and discipline. The mind is subtle, complex and extremely delicate. We must work in strict obedience to the laws of the human mind."[1]

—Konstantin Stanislavsky

- **Yoga and Acting**
- **The Origins of Yoga**
- **How Do the Sutras Relate to Training as an Actor?**
- **The Creative Space: Moving toward an Ethical Environment**
- **Communication Offstage**
- **Actor's Homework and Getting Off-Book**
- **Prejudice**
- **Dress**
- **Distractions**

While our characters often treat each other abominably, an atmosphere of support and trust is important in classes, rehearsals, and backstage at the theatre. The willingness to subjectively explore the secrets of the human psyche and share these findings with an audience in performance is a courageous act. It is very important that an environment is created in acting classes and rehearsals that supports this and encourages risk taking. A necessary ingredient for creating conditions most favorable for the creative state is a *creative space*. Here the actor can develop her acting skills and rehearse material for future performances in a supportive but challenging and stimulating environment. Everyone in the class or rehearsal room needs to get on board developing and maintaining the creative space. As psychologist Mihaly Csikszentmihalyi mentions, "Distractions disrupt flow, and it may take hours to recover the peace of mind one needs to get on with the work."[2]

---

[1] Konstantin Stanislavsky, *An Actor's Work*, trans. Jean Benedetti (London: Routledge, 2009), 554.
[2] Mihaly Csikszentmihalyi, *Creativity: Flow and the Psychology of Discovery and Invention* (New York: HarperPerennial, 1997), 120.

Experienced actors may still achieve amazing results in stressful and damaging environments that exist in some theatre, film, and television situations. (Some of these violations were shown in a TV show called *Smash* based on Broadway.) However, these harsh conditions can take a devastating toll on actors over the long term. (We see this as the substance abuse and other issues of famous actors are splashed so cruelly across the tabloids.) Because of the great emotional and physical demands placed on actors, we wish for a nurturing environment for all creative artists, but this is especially vital for the actor-in-training. The creative space of the acting class and rehearsal must be a safe space for the actor to take risks and explore.

In addition to its foundational influence on the development of the System, we can also look to the ancient wisdom tradition of yoga for guidance on establishing a creative community in which to work productively.

Yoga and Acting

For French and Bennett, who learned the oral tradition of the System, which was less censored by the Soviets, and also knew yoga, the overlaps between yoga and Stanislavsky's acting technique were evident. It was not until much later that scholars such as Dr. Sharon Carnike at the University of Southern California and Dr. R. Andrew White at Valaparaiso University provided us with written evidence of yoga as a primary source of Stanislavsky's psychophysical acting technique.[3]

Stanislavsky and Leopold Sulerzhitsky worked closely together for ten years from 1906 when they first met until Sulerzhitsky's death in 1916. They shared an interest in yoga and sought to bring techniques from it into acting. Sulerzhitsky worked closely with Stanislavsky as the director of the First Studio of the Moscow Art Theatre.

According to White, in his introduction to *The Routledge Companion to Stanislavsky*, Stanislavsky was particularly interested in how energy can be transferred from one person to another without words or touch. He was also fascinated by the state of heightened awareness observed in yogis that he felt was similar to the creative state he sought to establish as a basis for acting.[4] White writes more on this in his essay "The Spiritual Side of the System: Stanislavsky and Yoga," where he describes Stanislavsky's goal:

> Through his work and exploration of the acting process, Stanislavsky was not only seeking to activate an actor's subconscious but also her superconscious sphere of creativity through the exercises he borrowed from Yoga. Stanislavsky even wrote that in the superconscious realm exists "the wellspring of life, the main center of our nature—our innermost 'I,' inspiration itself." And if you pick up a copy of the English version of *My Life in Art*, translated by J. J. Robbins, you can see Stanislavsky's own bold assertion of the spiritual aims of the System when he affirms, "THE SUPERCONSCIOUS THROUGH THE CONSCIOUS! That is the meaning of the things to which I have devoted my life since the year 1906, to which I devote my life at present, and to

---

[3] The yoga sources were removed from Stanislavsky's writing by Soviet censors and not available to foreign scholars until after the collapse of the Soviet Union in 1991.
[4] R. Andrew White, ed., *The Routledge Companion to Stanislavsky* (New York: Routledge, 2014).

which I will devote my life while there is life in me." The capital letters are Stanislavsky's emphasis.[5]

Finding that tension was one of the obstacles to the creative state, Stanislavsky looked to yoga for relaxation techniques. Noticing that distractions impeded actors' ability to concentrate, he found resources in yoga for developing concentration skills and learning to focus the mind. The psychophysical (mind-body) basis of the System directly relates to the meaning of the word *yoga* (to yoke or join). Yoga seeks to create a union of mind and body, individual self and the universal self, and a connection through the universal with others. The familiar greeting you will hear yoga teachers say to students at the end of class, *Namaste*, basically means "the divine in me acknowledges the divine in you." The Stanislavsky System seeks to create a union of mind and body, self and others, onstage; as well as between performers, audience, and the greater society, an acting concept that Stanislavsky called *communion*. Stanislavsky sought to invite creative inspiration, which he considered a spiritual experience. When inspiration is a shared experience he called it *spiritual communion*. Spiritual communion is like namaste between actors and audience.

Stanislavsky was particularly influenced by Yogi Ramacharaka's books *Hatha Yoga: The Yoga of Philosophy and Well Being* and *Raja Yoga*. *Raja* means Royal Yoga and it incorporates the eight limbs of yoga, also known as Astanga (eight limbs or steps), as outlined in Patanjali's *Yoga Sutras*, with profound meditation at its head. Hatha yoga includes the more familiar *asanas* (the physical postures and related work) and *hatha yoga* is often used interchangeably with *asana*, but in fact it is a full discipline encompassing many aspects and levels of yoga (as are each of the eight limbs of yoga)."

Stanislavsky also saw connections between *pranayama* and acting. According to Yogananda, "The broadest meaning of the word *prana* [derived from the Sanskrit] is force or energy. In this sense, the universe is filled with *prana*; all creation is a manifestation of force, a play of force."[6] B. K. S. Iyengar describes prana as "the energizing force that is in the breath. The essence that we breathe in and out contains prana, which manifests itself as our life force. The moment breathing stops, the life force departs."[7] In scientific terms, prana would be energy and the body matter.

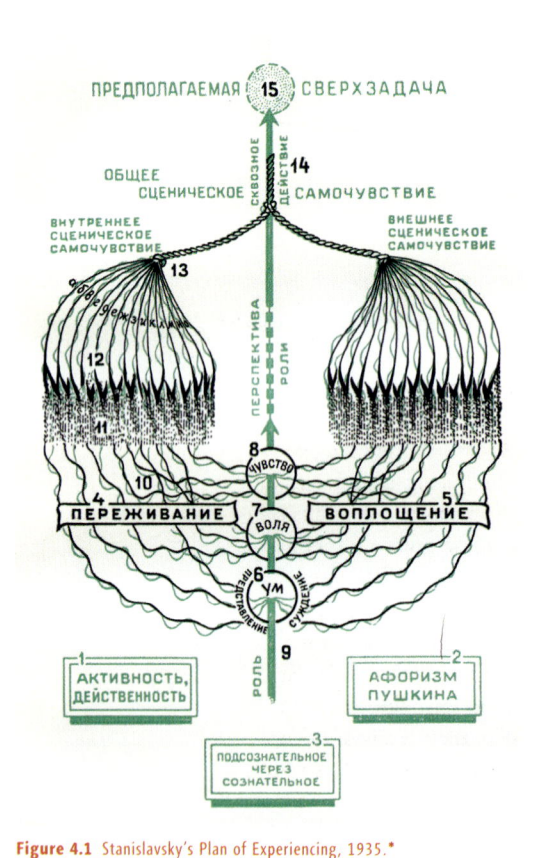

Figure 4.1 Stanislavsky's Plan of Experiencing, 1935.*
*See the translation from the original Russian by Philip G. Bennett in Chapter 18: The Actor of Living Experience.

[5] R. Andrew White, "The Spiritual Side of the System: Stanislavsky and Yoga." From an unpublished version sent to us by the author, 8–9.
[6] Paramahansa Yogananda, *God Talks with Arguna: The Bhagavad Gita* (Los Angeles: Self-Realization Fellowship, 1995), 497.
[7] B. K. S. Iyengar, *Yoga: The Path to Holistic Health* (London: DK, 2001), 252.

4 YOGA AND ACTING

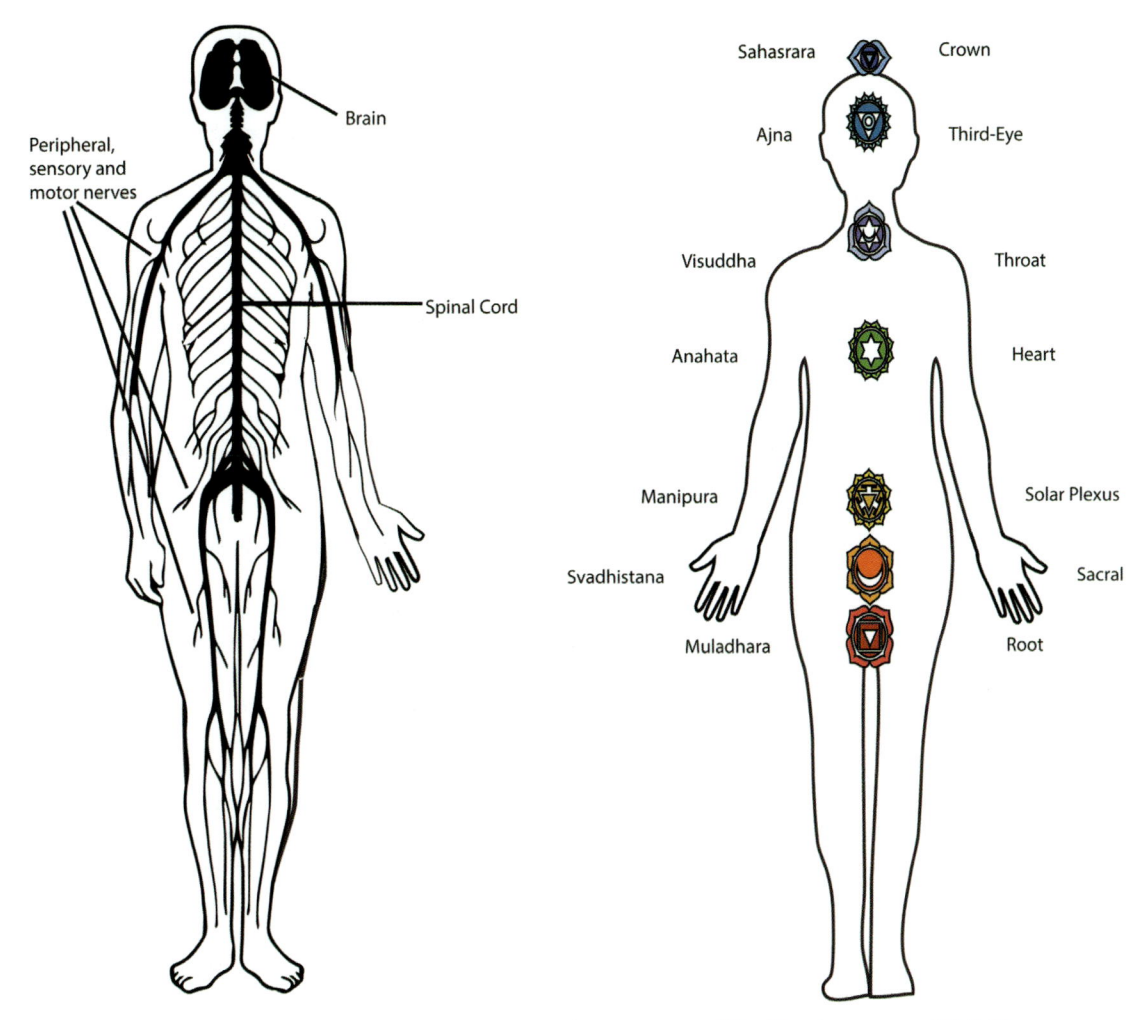

Figure 4.2 Communication pathways of the central nervous system (brain and spinal cord) and the peripheral nervous system.

Figure 4.3 Diagram of the chakras (energy centers of the body).

Pranayama is a technique for strengthening our vital life force and learning to direct it, primarily through a series of more and more-complex, conscious breathing exercises. Breath and mind are mutually influential.

Stanislavsky's yogic roots of the System can be seen in the famous diagram of the System he created. As you can see in Figure 4.1, he used the shape of a human torso with its many communication pathways, such as the nervous system (see Figure 4.2), and a series of centers along the spine taken from yogic science and known as the chakras (see Figure 4.3). In this diagram we also see Stanislavsky's interest in the life force energy the yogis call prana, which is facilitated through exercises called pranayama. Pranayama is very complex, but central to the exercises is deep and focused breathing, released from restrictive tensions or impediments. It is not surprising that Stanislavsky's central image for his diagram looks like a pair of lungs. After learning and experiencing all the aspects of the System, we will return to this diagram later in Chapter 19: The Creative Life: Communion with Audience and Society, for an explanation of how the diagram relates to the System.

According to Iyengar, "Chakra means 'wheel' or 'ring' in Sanskrit (the ancient Indian language) and our personal chakras have energy coiled within them." (Iyengar 2001: 36.) Through the practice of yoga and particularly pranayama we can learn to release and direct this energy. Stanislavsky was particularly interested in how this energy could enliven the performances of actors.

We will also borrow additional techniques from yoga (not directly related to Stanislavsky's sources) that we have found to most directly enhance the creative development of actors.

In recent years, yoga has grown in popularity in the Western world so that some aspect of it is probably familiar—in concept, if not in practice—with most actors reading this book. With the recent rapid growth, there has also been some watering down of the full potential and power of this ancient practice. Some exercise studios select the physical benefits of hatha yoga while tossing aside the rest of it and the other limbs of yoga. Yoga magazines often show only beautiful young people, rather than the full range of ages and abilities that yoga benefits.

As we reestablish the connection between actor training and yoga, there is much more we can gain from this ancient wisdom culture. Actors are encouraged to develop an ongoing yoga practice. You can start anywhere, even with only a physical asana practice, or with only a meditation practice, one limb will lead you to understand and value the others and to have more clarity in other aspects of your life outside of yoga. Additionally, a regular hatha yoga practice will strengthen your psychophysical instrument to make it capable and pliable for the demands of acting.

> **Is Yoga a Religion? What if I Belong to Another Religious Group or I Am an Atheist?**
>
> Throughout this book you will find references to yoga. Yoga originates in India and thus is often practiced and taught by people who also adhere to other Eastern religious practices, such as Vedanta, Hinduism, or Buddhism, common in that culture. Because of this, some yoga traditions have come to the West enmeshed in the symbology of these religions. However, many scholars believe that yogic practices actually predated these religions and were only later absorbed by them. There is more research to be done, as the origins of yoga seem to extend into the period of prehistory, prior to writing, which leaves us an ever-changing array of artifacts to try to piece together. Whatever, the truth of the origins of yoga, people of a variety of religions have found that the practice of yoga enhances their lives whether they believe in a monotheistic God, such as in Christianity, Judaism, and Islam, are of other spiritual beliefs, or are atheists. Yoga has great benefits for your mind and body. It is now being used in a variety of ways in Western medicine, such as to alleviate chronic pain or anxiety, curb the harmful effects of chronic stress, or to address or prevent physical limitations and injury.

The Origins of Yoga

The origins of yoga go back to prehistory, before writing, and therefore can only be gleaned through piecing together ancient artifacts. Statues showing yogis in meditative postures date back 5,000 years, to the Indus Valley Civilization.[8] Some people believe that yoga grew out of Hinduism, but in fact yoga predated Hinduism, and the Hindus adopted many aspects of ancient yoga as their religion emerged. The philosophical structure of yoga is often traced back to Patanjali's *Yoga Sutras*,[9] which codify the art and science of yoga. As described by contemporary yoga master B. K. S. Iyengar, the *Yoga Sutras* "outline the fundamental tenets of yoga, known as the eight limbs or astanga." Iyengar lays out a definition of Patanjali's sutras that will be helpful as we consider how the limbs of yoga relate directly to actor training.

Iyengar states, "The primary aim of yoga is to restore the mind to simplicity, peace and poise, to free it from confusion and distress. This simplicity, this sense of order and calm, comes from the practices of asanas and pranayama. Yoga asanas integrate the body, the mind, the intelligence, and, finally, the self, in four stages."[10] The stages are relevant to the stages of actor development: develop the body, then connect the mind and body, and then connect consciousness (which Iyengar calls *intelligence*). The final stage that Iyengar speaks of as the flow of spiritual awareness, Stanislavsky calls *spiritual communion*, as achieved through the acting practice of *experiencing*. We also refer to this final stage by the more commonly known concept of inspiration. There is a connection between the zone in sports, flow in psychology (as discussed in earlier chapters), spiritual awareness, and inspiration; all of these states are described in terms of a flow of energy and awareness. This peak state of human invention, insight, functioning, and awareness is also the ultimate goal of this acting technique.

> ### Patanjali's *Yoga Sutras* (The Eight Limbs of Yoga)
>
> *Sutra* literally means "thread" and was designed to offer guidelines toward a more meaningful life. Each of the eight limbs is considered its own path to awakening greater consciousness, but they overlap and interweave as well. The first three limbs are considered foundational practices necessary to prepare for the later practices. The idea is to prepare the channels of your mind and body and clean out some of the accumulated garbage (habits that hinder or harm) prior to activating the more powerful energy accessed through the other five limbs.
>
> The basic concepts in this summary are taken from Iyengar's *Yoga: The Path to Holistic Health*, supplemented by the oral tradition of yoga as passed down to

---

[8] The Indus Valley Civilization was centered in what is now modern-day Pakistan, Afghanistan, and northern India and is thought to have started as early as 3500 BCE (or over 5,500 years ago). It began slightly later than the ancient civilizations of Egypt and Mesopotamia but was much more extensive in geographic range.

[9] Patanjali lived somewhere between 400 BCE and 200 CE. His sutras are now in print in numerous versions; however, in the beginning and for generations afterward, they were memorized and transmitted orally as part of the practice, rather than written down, so precise dating of their origins is uncertain.

[10] Iyengar, *Yoga*, 37.

> French through years of reading and practice under the guidance of a number of experienced yoga teachers, beginning in her teenage years through her mother, Shirley Daventry French, a Canadian yoga master teacher of Iyengar Yoga and an expert in Patanjali's *Yoga Sutras*. Additional teachers included Swami Sivanda Radha (kundalini yoga), Judith Hanson Lasater and Ramanand Patel (Iyengar yoga) and Jennifer Allen (Iyengar, ashtanga, and vinyasa yoga).
>
> **yama**—ethical principles
> **niyama**—a current that helps with focus on the discipline and removes obstacles
> **asanas**—postures designed to develop strength and flexibility, balance and dynamism, relaxation and a sense of the mind-body continuum and that prepare the psychophysical instrument for other aspects of yoga, such as pranayama and meditation
> **pranayama**—a practice in directed breathing designed to develop control of mind and basic instincts and to revitalize the life force (prana)
> **(The three levels of meditation)**
> **pratyahara**—the ability to turn from focus on the senses of external perception and worldly pleasures to the rich interior landscape
> **dharana**—the rigorous focus of attention on one point
> **dhyana**—extended concentration to deepen consciousness beyond the boundaries of intellect and ego
> **(The ultimate goal of yoga: profound meditation)**
> **samadhi**—a release from the sense of being separate from others, replaced by a deep connection to our shared universal consciousness.[11]

How Do the Sutras Relate to Training as an Actor?

Asanas (and breath) and *dharana* (concentration) will be explored in Chapter 5: The Psychophysical Instrument. *Pranayama* relates directly to changing your breathing habits away from stress and toward deeper breathing that supports greater clarity, as already discussed in Chapter 3: The Creative State: Preparing for Inspiration under the heading "Stage fright," and further discussed in Chapter 9: Embodying Voice. *Pratyahara* (detachment from the external world) is not an ultimate goal for acting, but there are times when actors need to withdraw their senses from the externals of the artificial environment—such as lights, stage crew, and an audience member unwrapping a crinkly candy wrapper ever so slowly in the third row—and focus inwardly to the world of the play and the character. At the most heightened state of acting, we also feel our own ego, with all its issues, dissolve in the sense of *dhyana* (prolonged concentration), as we come alive in the experience of the character. In that "aha moment" of inspiration, which Patanjali called *samadhi*, we are connected to the shared source of all universal art and invention.

While the ethics we expect in the theatre today may vary slightly from those Patanjali put forward for spiritual aspirants in the Sutras, some of the *yamas* are

---

[11]Ibid.

apt for actors, too. Wisdom from the first two Sutras, *yama* (ethics) and *niyama* (a positive current of self-restraint) can help us develop the creative space. Relevant yamas include social responsibility (which will be discussed more fully in Chapter 19: The Creative Life: Communion with the Audience and Society, freedom from avarice (which could be translated for actors as generosity rather than selfishness), truthfulness, and nonviolence (which in theatre might mean replacing negative deeds and even thoughts such as anger, cruelty, or harassment toward classmates or company members with positive, constructive ones). Achieving each of these takes vigilance and discipline (niyama).

Setting New Year's resolutions is often similar to yama, as we try to redirect our energies toward a more ethical path in our treatment of ourselves or others. As we all know too well, making the resolution with words is not enough; we must also generate focused energy and behavioral changes to actually give shape to the resolution. That requires discipline (niyama). Perhaps it is better to think of yama as basic ethical principles to live by. Then set a New Year's goal (niyama) to live closer to your ethical principles. Unlike a resolution, which once broken is done until next year, a goal you can keep striving to meet noticing what helps and what hinders you.

A niyama that is very applicable to the aspect of creative state discussed in the previous chapter as *awareness of self,* is *svadhyaya.* Svadhyaya is defined by Iyengar as "the study of one's own self, which includes the body, mind, intellect and ego."[12]

There are a number of things you can do to help each other create a positive, ethical environment. It is not just for the teacher to create, but the class must become an ensemble of artists in support of each other's growth. The reward is that you will know your fellow students better than in any other class, and you are likely to form lasting friendships for future creative collaborations. The reward is certainly worth the effort.

The Creative Space: Moving toward an Ethical Environment

> "If you protect your theatre against 'all pollution', you will automatically establish a good atmosphere, which is favorable to the creative state."[13]
> —Konstantin Stanislavsky

Empathy and Compassion

In the class, remember that you will all be asked to get up and perform similar exercises with similar risks but that some exercises will be harder for you and some harder for other students. Some exercises you may find strange and uncomfortable because they will be very unfamiliar. Also, some students may be more private people that share intimacy only with their closest friends. Remember that you all will take risks, and thus you will sometimes miss the mark, or you may look awkward in the early stages of learning a more challenging technique. Be patient and compassionate toward yourself and have empathy for others, while you all struggle with the challenges of acting.

---

[12]Iyengar, *Yoga*, 53.
[13]Stanislavsky, *An Actor's Work*, 557.

Commitment, Generosity, Discipline

"If one person is late there's a muddle. If everyone is just a little late then working time is lost in waiting. That leads to a bad atmosphere in which no one can work."[14]

—Konstantin Stanislavsky

Commit to making consistently positive contributions to the class group. One easy thing to do is to be on time and prepared for each class meeting and rehearsal, including out-of-class rehearsals with your scene partner. If group members trickle in late, miss or interrupt the warm-up this does not just affect the focus of the actor guilty of the behavior but disrupts the teacher, who is trying to focus for the class, as well as the entire group. To be on time you must allow extra time to get there because obstacles frequently get in the way. Plan to arrive at least 15 minutes prior to class or rehearsal start time so that you can find parking, deal with traffic or weather, get organized, or use the restroom. Eat before rehearsal/class or on your breaks. Don't eat around others who are working on stage (and thus cannot eat), near theatre equipment, or when in costume.

If there is reading or other homework due in preparation for the active work onstage, make sure you have completed it so that you can make informed contributions to the discussion or rehearsal. Do not hold up the group or your partner in any exercises because you are unaware of the theory, having missed the day it was taught, or because you have not read the play. Not being prepared places extra demands on the rest of the class to be the ones to contribute while you detract from and impede the progress. In this case, you should change your behavior or choose to do something else that you can commit to more fully, as you are wasting

Figure 4.4 A supportive atmosphere in the dressing rooms is essential. Taneshia Davis (in mirror), Esther Joseph, and Mary Dennis prepare for a performance of *Sold!*
Photo: Bob Weidner, courtesy of East Stroudsburg University

[14]Ibid., 555.

Figure 4.5 Create a company as ensemble backstage and onstage. Stage management team, director, writers, cast, and crew of *Sold!* East Stroudsburg University, 2011.
Photo: Bob Weidner, courtesy of East Stroudsburg University

your time and everyone else's in the class. Acting is an ensemble experience, so your lack of discipline also detracts from others' experience.

Once on stage, be generous by being present with your scene partner and responding to what he does and says. When you are driving the scene, initiating the action, really force the other actor to respond to you as a human being. Often the harder you make it for the other character, the easier you make it for the actor.

Gossip and Personal Issues

It is important that if private things come out during exercises or in rehearsal that they are not gossiped about outside of rehearsal. This means that while you may choose or need to discuss something intense you experienced in acting class or rehearsal you do not reveal the identify of anyone who shared something personal outside of the class or rehearsal. (Do not discuss it with outsiders if you cannot do so without revealing the identity of this person). Give to your classmates or ensemble the consideration of their privacy that you would like for yours. If you are someone that shares your most private information on social media, still give others privacy consideration, which may be more than you need. Seek to create harmony in the group by not dividing members of the company or creating factions. Make those who are new to this particular group of people feel welcome and included.

> "We shouldn't come to the theatre with muddy feet. Clean off the dust and dirt outside, leave your galoshes, your petty cares, squabbles and the irritations, which complicate your life and distract you from your art, at the stage door."[15]
>
> —Konstantin Stanislavsky

[15]Ibid., 557.

Issues and problems will come up in your private life during the class period or rehearsal, but, as much as possible, **"Leave your problems at the door."** This is a very common saying in the theatre. All of us are constantly dealing with a barrage of issues in our personal lives, and some of these can be severe and intense. Talk to your teacher, director, or stage manager if you are, for some reason, unable to leave this problem at the door and it is impinging on the class or rehearsal process. Sometimes, in addition, deep issues may be revealed in class in relationship to the scene being worked on and may then have to be addressed; however, if everyone brought every issue into rehearsal it would end up as a group therapy session rather than a productive environment to work on a play or to learn acting technique. If you have a pressing issue, try to address it personally through counseling, journal writing, talking to friends or family, or whatever other methods work for you before entering the creative space. Try to use your warm-up or other preparation time to clear your head. As Stanislavsky said, "Don't spit in corners."[16]

Another common theatre saying, if you cannot get past the intensity of personal emotion moving through you, is "put it into the work." What that means is don't hijack rehearsal with side counseling sessions for you that may disrupt the work of others in the company. Then many people get focused around you instead of on the work onstage. Instead, stay focused on the scene being rehearsed and see if you can find a place to release some of the more relevant emotions and energy into the work. You may be able to release the emotion that has you in its grip; at best, you may find a new emotional path for what is going on with your character in the scene. In either case, you will have allowed the rehearsal to move forward productively and professionally.

Respect
You may not like and want to be friends with everyone in your class or everyone in your company, but be polite and respectful. Even if you are selfish and don't really care about others (which we hope is not the case), this is vital to your continued success in this business. Reports of bad behavior spread through a theatre department, theatre company, or the wider theatre community like a virus. Additionally, rudeness makes others feel unsafe around you, and therefore they cannot take the risks required to grow through class exercises or rehearsals. If someone trespasses against you, do not retaliate or you can create a vicious cycle that will destroy the creative space. Instead, assume that they didn't do it on purpose and respectfully bring the trespass to their attention. If they continue after this to knowingly hurt you, then bring up the issue with your teacher, stage manager, or director. Otherwise, it will quickly poison the working environment. Conversely, if someone is having a hard day in class or rehearsal, it is amazing how quickly that can be turned around by an empathetic (but not pitying) comment, a pat, hug, or smile. Even if your characters are cruel to each other onstage, you must work to create a supportive environment offstage.

---

[16] Ibid., 557.

4 YOGA AND ACTING

Got Your Back vs. Backbiting

At East Stroudsburg University, student Felicia Revero brought in a technique she learned as an orientation leader working with ESU's Assistant Vice President Patricia Kashner. It was applied in the theatre to have a positive backstage atmosphere. Each member of the company is given a person to support. So instead of backbiting backstage you feel like somebody really has your back. The primary method is a wall of envelopes where you can leave that person supportive messages. Some people also arrange, through the stage manager, to get that person simple little gifts (such as food, music, good luck charms) and other things to help him or her during the demanding rehearsal and performance time. On the closing performance, people try to guess their secret, and the secret is revealed.

Figure 4.6 Secret support wall; Tyler Adams checks his messages before a performance of *Sold!*.
Photo: Stephanie Daventry French

Communication Offstage

Communication on- and offstage is essential. Contact your teacher/director and any project partners if you are going to be late or miss for any reason. As theatre is a collaborative art, it is important that they know what is going on so that they can make decisions about how best to proceed when you are missing. Because of time constraints, it is important that work does not get delayed because of your personal obstacles. In the rehearsal process, you would always contact the stage manager.

Actors Giving Notes to Other Actors vs. Class Feedback

While as a learning tool some teachers may ask you to give feedback to the actors working onstage, this will usually be very structured, with the feedback coming in a specific and constructive way. You are not generally invited to make judgments about the quality of the work of other actors (this is for the teacher or director to make) or to give specific suggestions of how they should do it differently. It is important in scene rehearsals outside of class that you do not give notes to other actors or tell them how they should perform. In a professional rehearsal, actors must never give notes to other actors. It is considered offensive and undermining of the director, who may not hire you back and may even fire you if it continues.

Feedback

Whether you are asked to participate in giving feedback about other students' exercises or whether this is left solely to the teacher is a matter of personal style. If you are asked to participate, it is important to notice something that worked for you in the presentation or exercise, as well as something that you felt wasn't clear. One easy way to keep the discussion constructive is to serve as an audience member. You can address specific behavior the actor demonstrated onstage, and what that made you think or feel or believe. This way the actor gets feedback on whether or not his choices are having the effect he wanted and can consider if this works for the play and character, or in the case of early improvisations, to achieve the goals of the exercise.

Later, as you learn more acting concepts, you can try to articulate what you are seeing or what is missing using acting vocabulary. This is helpful in solidifying understanding of acting concepts for the speaker and others in the class. Also, any misunderstandings about the concepts and vocabulary can then be corrected for you and the entire class, as other students are probably unclear on many of the same points.

As you receive feedback, remember that discovering what doesn't work also leads you closer to what does—use both as opportunities to grow.

Actor's Homework and Getting Off-Book

> "Most actors seem to think you only have to work in rehearsal and that you can relax at home. That is not the way it is at all. All you learn from rehearsal (class) is what you have to work on at home."[17]
>
> —Konstantin Stanislavsky

One of the most obvious aspects of laziness that makes a poor impression in the theatre is being one of the last actors to get off-book, which means having your lines memorized. Get *off-book* by any class or rehearsal off-book deadline. In fact, do this ahead of the deadline, if possible, so you can really work on the play. (In professional theatre, most actors have done a lot of work prior to the first rehearsal. They start getting familiar with the script as soon as it is available, so that they are practically off-book in the first read-through. They do this so that they can use all the rehearsal time for other acting challenges.) If you are not off-book, you will be slowing down and disrupting the planned rehearsal for everyone, and you will be able to do very little with your part or give much to your scene partners. Beginning actors and audience members often consider getting off-book to be the most challenging part of acting. Invariably after a show someone in the audience will say, "I don't know how you could memorize all of those lines!" Really this is just an

---

[17]Ibid., 557.

early impediment to the real work of an actor. The good news is that memorization gets easier as you train your mind to do it.

Prejudice

Do not make hateful statements out loud, in writing, or on your clothing toward any specific group of people, including racial or ethnic slurs; rude comments about gender, age, or sexual orientation; body size; disability; religious put-downs; and the like. While we would hope these kinds of comments are not your practice in life (and they are not allowed on university campuses): freedom from prejudice must be the expectation of the class. The theatre has a history of being more tolerant than other environments. Let's keep it that way. Sometimes a play you are working on will have characters that are prejudiced, who will speak words that are horrible to hear, particularly if set in a historical time period. In this case a lot of sensitivity needs to be shown regarding how to handle the material. It may be that this perspective is merely one of the time period; this is certainly true with the status of women throughout history, but then what can you show by doing the piece right now? An excellent example of this is the early seasons of the TV show *Mad Men*, which was set in the 1960s but was created and filmed in the twenty-first century. The director and production team managed to accurately capture, with great effort and detail, the 1960s advertising world and the status of women. (The women are mostly secretaries that are regularly sexually harassed and treated as less capable or are housewives tucked away in suburbs while their husbands conduct separate, exciting, and often unfaithful lives in the city.) The show also depicts African Americans, who during this time period mainly held low-level positions such as the elevator operator, sandwich-cart man, and nanny/housekeeper. However, they also revealed, through the *subtext* and *inner monologue* in the acting, the cost of this inequality on the women and African Americans. In this way, a television show set in a historically problematic period was done with a more contemporary consciousness that revealed and critiqued, rather than reinforced, the prejudices of the time period in which it was set.

Dress

Acting class is active. It is better not to wear clothing that is too revealing of private body parts, as this is distracting to others in class and is not the appropriate focus for a working environment. For most acting classes and rehearsals the dress is casual but respectable. While letting it all hang out may bring you wanted attention, it is less likely to garner professional respect and, in fact, will be taken by many as disrespectful of them and the rehearsal environment, as well as a distraction from the work for you and/or others.

Distractions

During the time of the class or rehearsal turn all cell phones and other electronic devices completely off. It will distract even on vibrate if someone is in the middle of a focused exercise or performance. Do not hold side conversations during class or rehearsal. If you must speak with someone, then step outside, but make sure this is a rare occurrence. Plan to be in the room except when the group takes a break. Make sure to let the professor or stage manager know if you need to be out of the room for any reason during class or rehearsal. While others are working onstage, give them your full attention. If you want to work on your lines, read, or do anything else, you must ask to be excused and go to a separate space, as this is rude while others are performing or the teacher/director or classmates/actors are having a discussion. If you are preparing for your piece during another group's performance rather than paying attention, this is rude. In most instances, you are supposed to have prepared in advance of class. As well as disrupting the actors performing and the teacher or director who is trying to give them full attention, it also demonstrates that you didn't do your homework (certainly a terrible impression to make in either a class or a rehearsal situation).

Summary

Developing and maintaining a creative space in which to work is an essential ingredient to reach the creative state that invites inspiration. Stanislavsky infused his acting technique with insights and practice from yoga, and his ultimate goal for the higher possibilities of acting also aligns with many of the goals of yoga. There is much we can learn by expanding our understanding of yoga to enhance our acting technique. In this chapter, we looked at the *Yoga Sutras* as a model of ethical behavior to facilitate higher goals, and then outlined the expectations for ethical behavior in the theatre. Ethics in the theatre involve empathy, compassion, commitment, generosity, discipline, gossip, personal issues, respect, communication offstage, giving notes to other actors, feedback, getting off-book, prejudice, dress, and causing distractions.

New Theatre Terms and Concepts

Terms used in the Stanislavsky System are in italics.

- ☐ *communion*
- ☐ creative space
- ☐ "don't spit in the theatre"
- ☐ *ethics in the theatre*
- ☐ getting off-book
- ☐ giving notes
- ☐ "leave it at the door"
- ☐ offstage
- ☐ "put it into the work"

Interdisciplinary Terms, Concepts, and Experts

- ☐ asanas
- ☐ chakra
- ☐ dharana
- ☐ dhyana
- ☐ Shirley Daventry French
- ☐ hatha yoga
- ☐ B.K.S. Iyengar
- ☐ niyama
- ☐ Patanjali
- ☐ pranayama
- ☐ pratyahara
- ☐ raja yoga
- ☐ samadhi
- ☐ sutras
- ☐ svadhya
- ☐ yama

CHAPTER 5

The Psychophysical Instrument: Exploring the Mind-Body Connection

"The mind is 'embodied' in the sense that it exists within the body—specifically, in the three pounds of tofu-like tissue we call the brain—and engages in bidirectional communication with it, so that the state of mind influences the body, and the state of the body influences the mind"[1]
—Davidson and Begley

Primary Elements of Action Actively Explored in This Chapter
Psychophysical behavior, relaxation, concentration, imagination, inner monologue/dialogue
Related Acting Techniques Investigated
Alignment, flow of energy, language of the body, activating the spine, moving through the spine, film of images, W.E.D.G.A.G., anatomy of thought
Part I: Your Psychophysical Instrument
- The Mind-Body Connection in Acting
- Psychophysical Wisdom from Ancient Yoga
- The Primary Signal System: Language of the Body
- How Can You Bring Awareness to Your Natural Human Responses and Behavior and Train Your Instrument to Call Them Up at Will?
- Directing the Flow of Energy

Part II: Psychophysical Conditioning Exercises
- ☐ Exercise 5.1: Progressive Relaxation
- Observing Your Quirks and Energy Blocks
- ☐ Exercise 5.2: Mirroring Movement Patterns
- ☐ Exercise 5.3: Observing Your Alignment
- Optimal Physical Functioning
- Yoga and Alignment
- ☐ Exercise 5.4: Standing in Alignment: Tadasana
- ☐ Exercise 5.5: Articulating and Activating the Spine

---

[1] Richard J. Davidson and Sharon Begley, *The Emotional Life of Your Brain* (New York: Hudson Street Press /Penguin, 2012), 136.

- ■ Concentration
  - ☐ Exercise 5.6: Disobeying Hands
  - ☐ Exercise 5.7: Predator and Prey
- ■ The Anatomy of a Thought
- ■ Bidirectional Flow of Energy
  - ☐ Exercise 5.8: Simple Physical Action with W.E.D.G.A.G
- ■ The Inner Landscape
- ■ Creating a Film of Mental Images
- ■ Inner Monologue (Inner Dialogue)
  - ☐ Exercise 5.9: To Wait for the Jury's Verdict

Part III: Psychophysical Science
- ■ The Mind-Body Connection in Science
- ■ Brain Plasticity
- ■ Acting and the Science of Learning and Habit
- ■ Brain Cleaning and Maintenance

PART I: YOUR PSYCHOPHYSICAL INSTRUMENT

Of all the acting tools you can learn to employ, the most amazing are your own mind and body. To refer to the continual communication between mind and body, Stanislavsky used the term *psychophysical*. *Psychophysical* is a compound word—*psycho* is short for *psychological* and means "relating to the mind or emotions," and *physical* pertains to the body. The biological aspects of the brain also fall under *physical* whereas the attributes of emotion, will, memory, imagination, and consciousness are referred to as *mind*. The mind and body are inseparable, and with training you can learn to create better communication and more responsiveness between them. Like any tool, this can yield poor results and even be dangerous if used incorrectly, but with proper training, you can develop your mind and body and become an artisan in their use on the stage.

As an actor, you will need to harness the possibilities of your entire psychophysical instrument. An athlete must initially train in coordination, stamina, and specific skills associated with his sport until they become second nature. Even after that, in order to stay competitive, he must keep up his fitness and continually work on honing his technique. It is very similar for the actor. The Stanislavsky System involves conditioning exercises that develop your psychophysical instrument for the purpose of acting. Conditioning exercises prepare you for the complex synthesis of tasks required in the later technique of Active Analysis of a play, as outlined in chapters 13–16. Active Analysis, in turn, leads you to fully inhabit the life of your character in front of an audience, the goal of the System, which Stanislavsky called *experiencing*.

5 THE PSYCHOPHYSICAL INSTRUMENT

The Mind-Body Connection in Acting

Stanislavsky reveals in his *Collected Works* (*Sobranie Sochinenii*), 40 years of experimentation and development of exercises in the connections between movement, sensory stimuli, and the mind. The idea was to train actors to respond consciously and on cue, while using some aspects of the psychophysical instrument that normally only respond unconsciously.

Various students and contemporaries of Stanislavsky at the Moscow Art Theatre, including Vsevolod Meyerhold, Leopold Sulerzhitsky, Evgeny Vakhtangov, and Michael Chekhov, were instrumental in the development of Stanislavsky's System, and each developed his own unique approach to acting and staging theatre. All of these artists both learned from Stanislavsky and influenced his understanding of acting. One important area of experimentation was the role of the body in impacting the emotions.

After a long time of working closely with Stanislavsky as a student and collaborator, Meyerhold went in a very different direction. As Richard Brestoff describes in his book *The Great Acting Teachers and Their Methods*, "In realistic theatre, [Meyerhold] thought, the spectators were dreaming away their time. But he wanted the audience to be awake, excited and in the present. He wanted the audience to think about current political and social conditions and be aroused to action. He felt that properly presented physical action could arouse emotion in audience members through reflex."[2] This concept is often attributed to Bertolt Brecht, but Meyerhold was experimenting with it much earlier, developing his physically based system. (In fact, Meyerhold was one of Brecht's theatrical influences.) Again Brestoff: "The Meyerhold actor was freed from the prison of natural behavior, but he paid a high price. His body had to submit to rigorous training, and tremendous discipline. This training was accomplished through a technique that Meyerhold called *biomechanics*."[3]

Stanislavsky began with internal tools to arouse emotion in actors and, later, perhaps influenced by Meyerhold, turned to using action to arouse emotion. Meyerhold, at the end of his life, still claimed to be a student of Stanislavsky. Stanislavsky, in turn, tried to bequeath to Meyerhold the leadership of the Moscow Art Theatre, attempting to use his fame and status as an artist to protect Meyerhold. Despite that effort, Meyerhold was arrested, imprisoned, and executed by the government of Joseph Stalin. (More on the influential artists of the Moscow Art Theatre in Chapter 20: The Evolving Stanislavsky System.)

Psychophysical Wisdom from Ancient Yoga

> "The body and mind are in a state of constant interaction. Yogic science does not demarcate where the body ends and the mind begins, but approaches both as a single, integrated entity. The turmoil of daily life brings stress to the body and the mind. This creates anxiety, depression, restlessness, and rage. Yoga asanas, while appearing to deal with the physical body alone, actually

---

[2] Richard Brestoff, *The Great Acting Teachers and Their Methods* (Lyme, NH: Smith and Kraus, 1995), 71.
[3] Ibid., 71.

influence the chemical balance of the brain, which in turn improves one's mental state of being."[4]

—B. K. S. Iyengar (1918–2014), international yoga master

While scientists have started to measure how the brain and body communicate and coordinate, they are just beginning to delve into how we can consciously use the mind to affect the body, to improve physical health, and reverse the progress of disease. Some Western pioneers in alternative medicine have been trying to incorporate Eastern health and medical wisdom since the twentieth century, but until recently, massage, meditation, acupuncture, and even nutrition in mainstream Western medicine were not supported by medical insurance plans. Eastern medicine—Indian and Chinese medicine—on the other hand, has understood and made use of the mind's influence over the body as a healing technique for thousands of years. Slowly, there is more overlap between Eastern and Western medicine as cancer centers have adopted meditation for pain management, stress reduction workshops use relaxation techniques from yoga, and acupuncture is now more widely accepted, to name only a few adopted practices.

The yogis have understood the connection between the mind and body for over 2,500 years. Bringing awareness to the body is the first step in being able to consciously control physical responses that are subconscious for most people. Conscious control of the subconscious, remember, was a key goal of Stanislavsky and is a requirement of being able to call up, on cue, physical and emotional responses appropriate for specific moments in a play.

The Primary Signal System: Language of the Body

The *primary signal system* is that of the body. The architecture of the human body determines our fundamental movement patterns; for example, we creep, crawl, and walk upright. We are bipedal. We have four limbs and hands with opposable thumbs. Our senses are highly developed, and we have an advanced brain and nervous system. Our physical behaviors are determined primarily by our physiology. We reach, we examine, we evaluate, we observe, we sit, we feel, etc.

The primary signal system communicates our most fundamental impulses, thoughts, and feelings without words. It is universal and communicates to others regardless of social, ethnic, or cultural influences. Basic emotions such as fear, hate, jealousy, love, and anger are universally experienced and universally understood. This universal signal system we shall call the *language of the body*.

The popular notion of "body language," by comparison, is layered on top of the primal impulses and can be environmentally and culturally conditioned: a physical signal in one social setting might easily be inappropriate in another. A man and a woman meeting for the first time in a professional setting in the West would shake hands, but in some countries in the Middle East and Asia, it would be considered inappropriate for a woman to touch a man she has just met, and a slight bow of the head would instead be the professional greeting.

As an actor, you must be concerned with both body language and the language of the body. You need to learn to master and communicate the primal states as well as

---

[4] B. K. S. Iyengar. *Yoga: The Path to Holistic Health* (London: DK, 2001), 37.

5 THE PSYCHOPHYSICAL INSTRUMENT

the social and cultural behaviors relevant to your characters. No simple task, but it can be done.

The first means of artistic expression is the body, but it can also be your primary obstacle. All human beings have unique physical habits, stances, and ways of moving, but your habits must not automatically come into the expression of your characters. You can instead develop awareness of your own quirks and exchange them for those of the character. Additionally, you need to train your body to be extremely sensitive to stimuli, expressive, agile, and disciplined. Even if you have trained so as to achieve all of this, before every performance, as part of your warm-up, you must make sure to free the body of extraneous tension. Unnecessary tension inhibits the natural flow of energy in the body.

The body is our most controllable instrument; however, at the beginning of your training, it is often difficult to discipline. While in life the body responds automatically to natural stimuli, there is no reason to react naturally on stage. Nevertheless, your body can be trained to respond naturally to imaginary stimuli. We call this process *organic behavior*. Organic behavior means that our five senses and bodily organs are behaving just as they would in life.

At first, the body often offers physical resistance. You may feel like a fish out of water, not knowing how to move, when or where to sit, or what to do with your hands. Everyone has felt awkward on a first date or at a first dance; our feet don't seem to obey us, and we fear stepping on our partner's foot. Therefore, you train in order to learn to simulate consciously on stage physical responses that are automatic and often unconscious in life. This is why physical training is so important for the actor. Just as a gifted violinist must acquire great skill and technique to play a Stradivarius violin, greatly talented actors need the highest level of sensitivity, cultivation, and technical training to fully realize their gifts. Some valuable physical training techniques that can facilitate a suppler instrument for you include the following:

- ballet—to master classical acting forms and build the strength of long muscles and the core
- modern and jazz dance forms—for freedom of expression and understanding how to create abstract lines of physical communication in space
- fencing, to build quick responses and precision of hand and foot action, as well as to prepare for classical fight scenes
- yoga and/or martial arts—for balance, strength, flexibility, and mind/body/breath integration
- Suzuki[5]—to develop focus, stillness, grounding and a strong center;
- stage combat—to safely navigate fight scenes
- Viewpoints[6]—to develop a dynamic and instinctual awareness of the theatrical

---

[5] Tadashi Suzuki is the founder and artistic director of the Suzuki Company of Toga. His intense and powerful movement technique for actors draws from traditional Japanese and Greek theatre as well as martial arts, and ballet. Its focus is concentration, physical and emotional power, and intense commitment to being present in each moment on stage.

[6] The Six Viewpoints originally came to theatre through choreographer Mary Overlie at New York University's Experimental Theater School. Anne Bogart, Tina Landau and the SITI company later developed it into the Nine Viewpoints and focused them as training, devising and performance techniques for theatre artists. Viewpoints and Suzuki are two primary methodologies employed by Anne Bogart's SITI company to develop and perform original theatre pieces.

elements of time and space; to work kinesthetically and collaboratively with other performing artists; to increase flexibility, strength, and physical articulation of impulses and ideas. (More on the Viewpoints and the SITI company is presented in Chapter 17: Entering the Collaborative Process.)

Movement training must be done repeatedly over a long period of time in order to create new pathways of opportunity and expression in the body, new neurological pathways in the brain, and responsiveness between mind and body. It is at the point that the new physical training becomes "learned instinct" that it can become a responsive tool. The training of and communication using voice and speech is equally rigorous and will be explored in chapters 9 and 10.

How Can You Bring Awareness to Your Natural Human Responses and Behavior and Train Your Instrument to Call Them Up at Will? Communication Pathways Between the Brain and Body

It is helpful to become more aware of the many systems of communication between our minds and our bodies, including:

- the central nervous system—the primary communication pathway between the brain and spine, which communicates through electrical impulses;
- the peripheral nervous system—communicating between the spine and the body's exterior sensory input, muscles, and some organs;
- the somatic nervous system—sending signals between the skeletal muscles, heart, and brain;
- the autonomic nervous system—taking in stimuli and coordinating automatic responses through the motor nerves and the hormonal system to keep the body in balance (homeostasis);
- the circulatory system—distributing hormones (chemical messengers), nutrition, and oxygen, all of which affect the brain and the muscles; and
- the cranial nerves, which bypass the central nervous system to communicate between different parts of the brain or the brain and body. The most complex is the tenth cranial nerve, called the vagus nerve, which wanders through the face, chest, and abdomen. It is also very important to the perception of physical feelings that can influence or express emotions. (See a map of the vagus nerve in Figure 12.4 of Chapter 12: Orchestrating Emotions.)

As with the "fight or flight" system discussed in Chapter 3, in life all of these things function without our conscious thought or direction (*autonomic*). For acting you must develop the ability to activate aspects of your autonomic system at will and to suppress other aspects, such as the fear response. As a starting place, you will need to become more conscious of the tension that blocks the flow of your energy.

Directing the Flow of Energy

"In our course, naturally we teach alignment but not purely from a structural point of view. It is part of learning to refine seeing: to see skin and beyond as well as bones and joints. Where does energy flow freely? What effect has the structural adjustment had on the flow of energy? Where is energy blocked and why? Where is support lacking? Where do we see stress and strain? The science of yoga involves all this and much more."[7]

—Shirley Daventry French, Yoga Teacher

Acting requires stamina. Part of that is the ability to harness energy and release it in a directed way to impact an audience; however, before you can harness energy you must get the wellspring of your energy flowing.

Increasing the free flow of energy around the body is one of the goals of the Asian medical technique of acupuncture and the healing practice of massage. It is also an important goal of yoga to get the energy of the body flowing and connect it to universal energy.

Most of us operate at a level of physical and mental functioning well below our potential. Over time, bad habits in using our bodies, and in what we put into them, diminish the optimal functioning of our bodies and our minds. The flow of energy involves the circulation of mental energy, physical energy, and breath, as well as healthy movement and communication among the other psychophysical systems of your body, such as the respiratory, circulatory, nervous, and muscular systems. In life, all of these systems are autonomic, but for acting you must learn to influence them consciously. In addition to helping with acting and overall creativity, improving the flow of energy is a key to good health through the diminishing of the effects of stress.

Probably the biggest impediment to mental energy in acting is fear whereas to physical energy it is tension. Both of these certainly come into play in stage fright, as addressed in Chapter 3. You cannot ride your bike very efficiently if the brake is stuck or the chain falls off. There are other obstacles, as well: Improper alignment and usage of your body will impede the effective operation of your psychophysical instrument, even as chronic stress can derail and dismantle your cognitive abilities.

One avenue to expand your *flow of energy* is developing your *proprioception*, which is your internal awareness of the external place, position, and movement of your body. Through use of your *internal* and *external monitors*, as discussed Chapter 3, you will develop *kinesthetic awareness*—the ability to sense what you are feeling within and around your body—and *kinesthetic response*—your instinctual and creative response to stimuli. In this way you can see where you are running into blocks and limitations and learn to free up the energy of creative impulses. You will also watch the mind and see the busyness of thoughts and images that arise there in response to other thoughts or physical activity. Then you can learn to harness these as acting tools.

You can start by noticing when anxiety arises and learning to understand the physiological changes that accompany that and how they parallel those of excitement. You can then choose to harness this rising energy or consciously diminish it. Stanislavsky used the term *relaxation,* which is commonly known; however, willing oneself into a state of relaxation is equally as elusive as willing inspiration or crying on cue. You can learn to *release tension* and activate different parts of your body either in isolation or in groups. This will increase your flow of energy and

---

[7] Shirley Daventry French, "Reflections," *Iyengar Yoga Center of Victoria Newsletter,* Fall 2013.

begin to allow you to direct it, thus creating a receptive, relaxed state of mind and body and an expressive physical instrument.

PART II: PSYCHOPHYSICAL CONDITIONING EXERCISES

There are a variety of approaches to awaken the possibilities of your mind and body and remove obstacles to your full *flow of energy*.

> **A Note of Caution to the Student**
>
> Before beginning any course of exercise, including physical acting exercises, consult your doctor to ensure you are ready for physical activity. If you are new to physical activity, make sure to do it with the approval of your physician and in the presence of an experienced teacher. Let your teacher know of any special physical conditions that might affect your full participation in physical activity.
>
> Listen to the signs of your body and learn to tell the difference between sharp, dangerous pain, which means you should stop or pull back, and the "Wow! I haven't used this muscle in a while" tingling, alive sensations, which some people read as mild pain. This sensation generally suggests you should continue but with awareness, breathing into the sensation to help release, but not pushing.
>
> Gradually welcome the reawakening of your body to a more energized existence. The important thing is to use your internal monitor and not worry about how flexible or strong someone else next to you may be. Listen and respond to the needs of your own body.

"You cannot imagine how damaging muscular tension and physical tightness can be to the creative process."[8]

—Konstantin Stanislavsky

Stanislavsky advises that in order to begin to reduce tension the actor needs to develop an internal monitor. The monitor must "be tirelessly on the lookout lest excess tension, muscular constrictions appear. The monitor should eliminate these tensions as they emerge."[9] Bringing awareness to your psychophysical instrument is at the core of training in yoga; we believe, as Stanislavsky believed, that it must also be at the core of training the actor's instrument.

---

[8] Konstantin Stanislavsky, *An Actor's Work*, trans. Jean Benedetti (London: Routledge, 2009), 120.
[9] Ibid., 122.

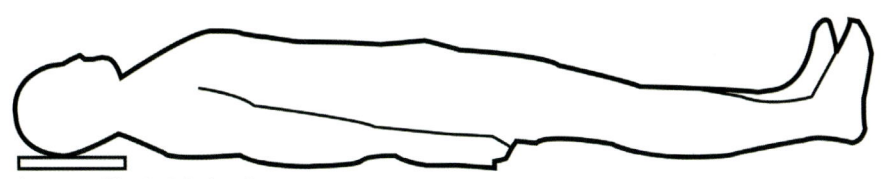

5 THE PSYCHOPHYSICAL INSTRUMENT

Place a small book 1" thick under your head. You may need a larger book if you have a larger and rounder back. Keep your neck in line with torso, not tilted back.

Figure 5.1 Prone position with a thin book under the head.

Alternate resting position

Knees up and falling together, feet flat on floor and slightly wider than hip width, should be still with book under head

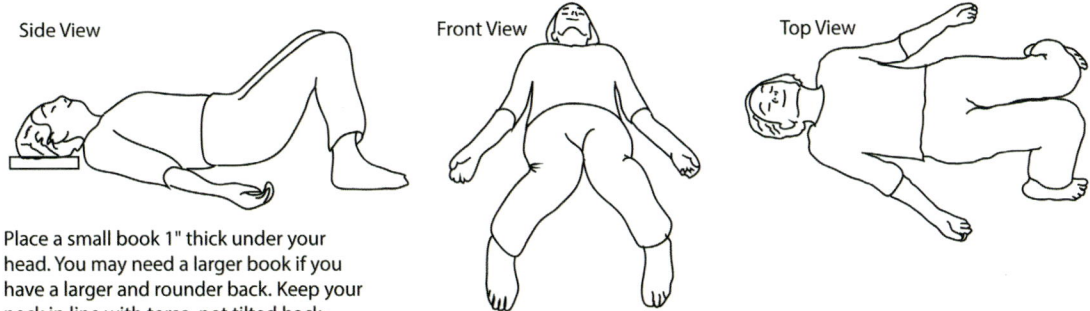

Side View   Front View   Top View

Place a small book 1" thick under your head. You may need a larger book if you have a larger and rounder back. Keep your neck in line with torso, not tilted back.

Figure 5.2 Alternate position for relaxation (often preferred by females).

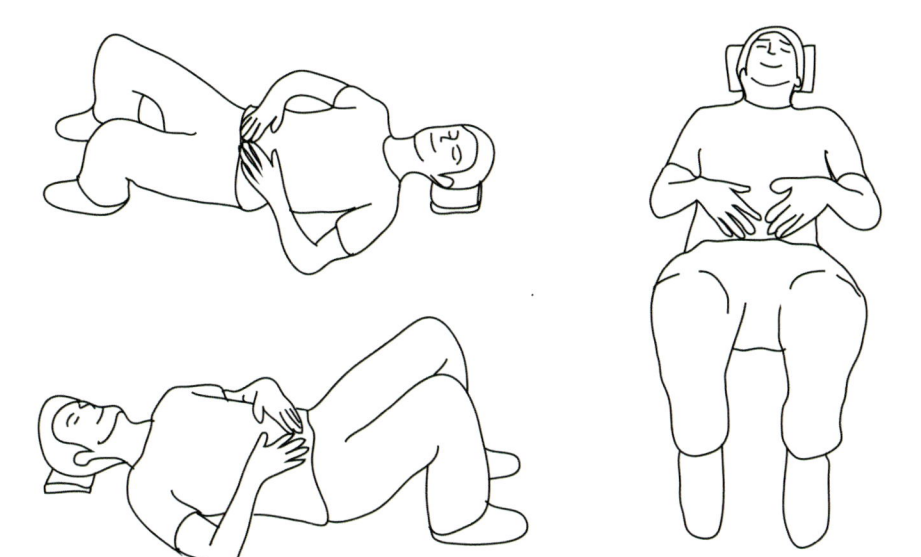

Figure 5.3 Alternate position for relaxation (often preferred by males).

Tools to Combat Chronic Stress

(See also Appendix II: 10 Yoga Poses.) At the end of each yoga practice, Savasana (corpse pose) is practiced, which is similar to the relaxation exercise in this chapter. You are still yet alert, which is a very important skill for actors. Also the yogic practice of activity followed by relaxation is much healthier than the go, go, go of our modern society. The lack of recharge time results in the chronic stress and related disease experienced by many in our society. In addition to sleep (which literally cleans out the buildup of harmful materials in our brains), finding time for relaxation or meditation periodically during the day is essential to combat the buildup of long-term stress. Physical busyness or stimulating mental activity without stopping, whether positive, such as intensive creative work, or negative, such as ongoing anxiety, can equally overtax our systems. We are designed to go intensively actively interspersed with pauses and rest such as naps, meditation, quiet reading, or relaxation techniques.

Exercise 5.1A: Progressive Relaxation (Jacobson/PY, SDF/PGB)[10]

Purpose: Learning to direct the mind to active muscle groups in isolation. This exercise also helps to release the tension that inhibits the flow of energy, thus invigorating the body and reducing stress. As discussed in Chapter 3, relaxation also enhances creativity.

Guidelines: Don't worry if you cannot immediately bring consciousness to any particular muscle group or tense and release it in isolation. This control will come in time in subsequent practices of this and other exercises.

- Lie on the floor (on a yoga or other mat if available) in the prone position (Figure 5.1, or if that is not comfortable for you, you may select the positions in Figure 5.2 or 5.3. To keep good alignment of your neck and head to your torso, place a book about 1-inch thick under your head (you may need a thicker book to ensure that your head is not tipped back). Make sure you are dressed warmly in clothing that does not constrict any part of your body, particularly on the torso. (Your temperature may drop during this exercise, so you might want to dress slightly warmer than you need for the present room temperature). Extend your arms to your sides, palms up, legs lengthening away from the torso in a slight V-shape. Roll the head

---

[10] This is our adaptation of American physician Edmund Jacobson's progressive relaxation exercise, developed in the 1920s. A famous Indian yoga teacher who came to America, Paramahansa Yogananda, developed and taught tense-and-release exercises, also in the 1920s, that he called "energization exercises." He had adapted these from yoga. Yoga has an asana called *Savasana*, which is a relaxation pose that is done at the end of asana practice. We have no knowledge of whether there was any connection between Jacobson and Yogananda, but it is interesting to note the overlap in their techniques. This exercise has long been passed down in the oral tradition of acting, but usually without attribution.

5 THE PSYCHOPHYSICAL INSTRUMENT

- gently side to side to release the neck, then lengthen the neck and spine along the floor.
- Bring your mental focus to your feet. On the inhalation, tense only your feet as much as possible holding your breath for a moment. Try to do this without adding tension to the legs (also check the jaw and release tension there). Then on the exhalation, release the tension, allowing your feet to be warm and heavy and relaxed.
- Bring your focus to your calves and shins. Inhale and hold your breath while tensing only the lower leg without tensing the feet or thighs. Then release the breath and the tension, allowing your shins to be warm and heavy and relaxed.
- Inhale and hold your breath; tense only your hamstrings and quadriceps (thighs). Try to do this without tensing the surrounding muscle groups. Then release the tension with the breath, allowing your thighs to be warm and heavy and relaxed.
- Continue with the breath in the same way as above for the next muscle groups breathing in and holding with the tension and releasing the breath as you release the tension.
- Tense your buttocks. Then release.
- Tense your stomach. Then release.
- Tense your chest, without tensing the stomach. Release.
- Tense the muscles of your lower and middle back. Release
- Tense your shoulders. Release. Tense your biceps and triceps. Release.
- Tense your forearms. Release. Tense only your hands. Release.
- You do not need to tense your neck but rather, again, roll it from side to side.
- Tense all the small muscles of your face by scrunching them together as tightly as possible then making them as wide as possible. Then release. Release any tension in the jaw, mouth, or behind the eyes. Imagine your ears releasing toward the floor. Release your tongue.
- Now feel your entire body washed with a magnetic, healing relaxation, wave after wave. Allow the breath to fall in and release out for about 10 more minutes.
- (Follow the instructions in Exercise 5.1b to come to standing.)

5.1A Reflection Journal—Tense and Release

Were you able to isolate the muscle groups? Into which muscle groups were you able to move some mental consciousness? Were you able to then release the tension? Did you feel more relaxed in that part of your body afterward? As you lay there for the last 10 minutes, what happened to your mind?

Exercise 5.1B: Rising without Tension (HR)[11]

Purpose: After the above exercises, which most people find relaxing, it is important that you do not suddenly jerk your head up, reintroducing the tension you just released. Instead, you want to come to standing in a movement sequence of ease that will help establish positive alignment of your muscles and support for your skeletal system.

Guidelines: (The following sequence of physical postures is also illustrated in Figures 5.4 and 5.5.)

- Roll over on your right side, staying aware of others in class around you, and gently open your eyes.
- After a breath, roll onto your stomach, and put your hands under your forehead, elbows bent.
- Press back with your hands, allowing your neck to remain released, head hanging down, until your buttocks come to rest on your heels. Breathe into your back, which feels open and wide in this position.
- Turn your toes under and, to get onto your feet, begin to straighten the legs as you push with your arms but remain hanging over in a standing forward bend with the knees slightly bent (depending on your flexibility). Again, breathe into your back.
- Imagine someone's fingers walking up each of the vertebrae in your spine, starting from the top of the tailbone and walking upward to the base of the neck. (Better yet, work in partners and take turns doing this for each other). Stack the vertebrae one on top of the next as you roll up slowly to standing.
- Make sure the neck is released and the head hanging down until you get all the other vertebrae stacked, then slowly roll the head up one vertebra at a time.

Rising with Resonance

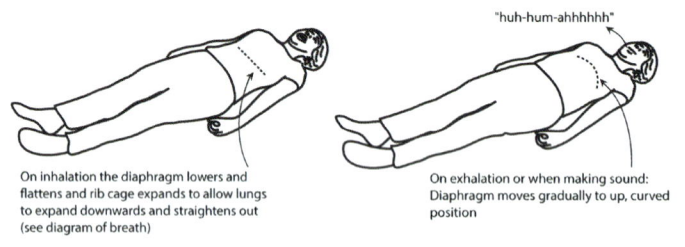

On inhalation the diaphragm lowers and flattens and rib cage expands to allow lungs to expand downwards and straightens out (see diagram of breath)

"huh-hum-ahhhhhh"
On exhalation or when making sound: Diaphragm moves gradually to up, curved position

Breath in and release sound into floor. Hands should be palms down on floor and under forehead.

"With each of these positions expand the rib cage as you breath in and feel the sound bouncing back to you from the floor as you breath out."

Figure 5.4 Rising without tension (you can do this with humming as part of a vocal warm-up as shown in Chapter 9). Continue with rolling up the spine as per Figure 5.5.

[11] This was originally taught to Bennett and French by Herbert Rodriguez as part of a Kristin Linklater–based voice class.

5 THE PSYCHOPHYSICAL INSTRUMENT

Fingers walking up spine. You can have a partner do this or just imagine it

Do not lead with the neck. Keep it released until you have rolled up the neck vertebrae

Okay to bend your knees slightly if you are not that flexible, or to hang down without your hands touching the floor. Release the back down towards the floor, and make sure your neck is also released with the head hanging down.

Stack the vertebrae one at a time as you roll up to standing

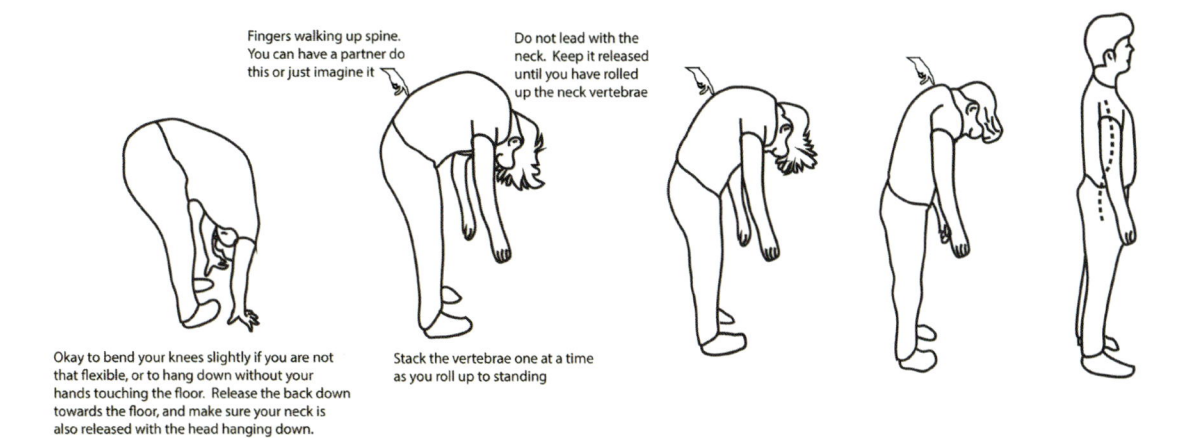

Figure 5.5 Rolling up the spine.

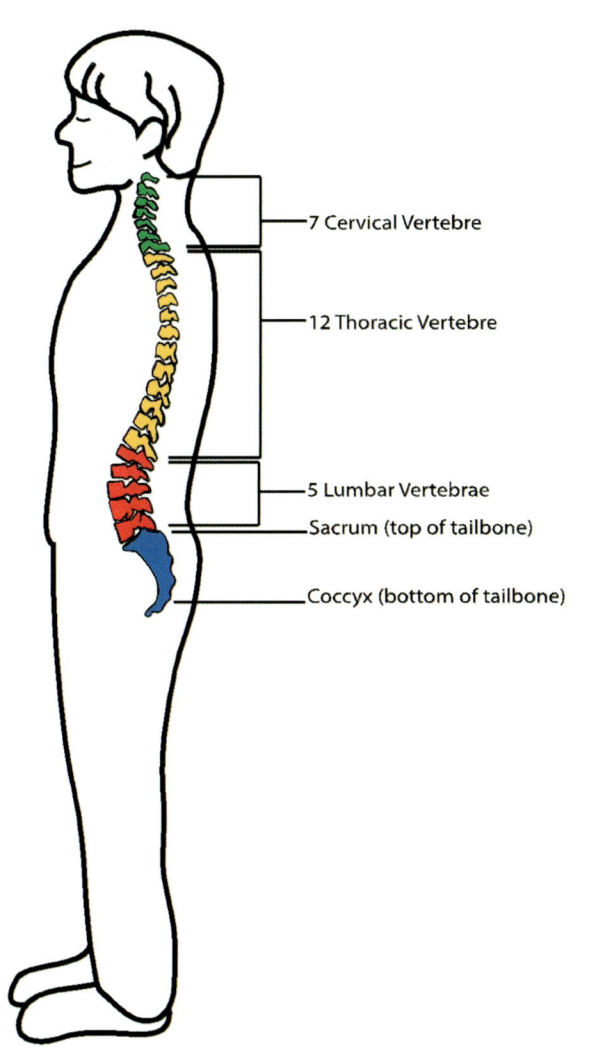

- 7 Cervical Vertebre
- 12 Thoracic Vertebre
- 5 Lumbar Vertebrae
- Sacrum (top of tailbone)
- Coccyx (bottom of tailbone)

Figure 5.6 Parts of the spine.

Observing Your Quirks and Energy Blocks

You have a lot to offer the stage and screen because you are unique. The goal in your acting, voice, and movement courses is not to train this out of you; however, it is important to become aware of and learn to release old habits and mind patterns, so they don't define every character you play in limiting ways. You do not want to discard them because 1) you may still need them for smooth functioning in your regular life; 2) they may also be right for a specific moment in a specific character's life; and 3) if you had to do everything consciously, without the use of habit, the simplest task of living would be all-consuming. What will be different is that you will develop consciousness of what your own patterns may be and learn to call them up or release them at will. As you begin to understand your psychophysical instrument more intimately, you can choose to imbue a character with some of your personal traits, to borrow traits of others through observation, to create new human behavior activated through your imagination, or combining these sources as best suits your characters.

Exercise 5.2: Mirroring Movement Patterns (JB)[12]

Purpose: Before you can effectively change your posture or movement, you need to become aware of ingrained patterns developed over years that are reflected in how you use your body now. Bringing awareness to the body is a first step.

Guidelines:
- Each person finds a partner and designates one as A and one as B.
- A moves about as B observes.
- Then B follows A, trying to approximate A's movement patterns. Try to notice where the person moves fluidly and where he carries tension.
- B demonstrates the movement and stance they observed in A, and the class, especially if they know A, gives feedback as to whether that is accurate.
- Repeat the exercises, reversing the roles so that each actor has both observed and been mirrored.

Exercise 5.3: Observing Your Alignment (Posture) (JH/SDF)[13]

Guidelines:
- While physicists have proved that the act of observing changes the object observed, do your best to do the first part of this exercise without changing anything. You can stop and write your observations after each body area or do the entire exercise and then try to recall your observations. As you

---

[12] Adapted from Jean Benedetti, *Stanislavski and the Actor* (New York: Routledge/Theatre Arts Books, 1998), 18.

[13] French adapted this exercise from James Howell (JH). Howell was for some time the music director of the Joffrey Ballet and later a teacher of ballet, yoga and Alexander Technique in San Francisco, California.

do this exercise, try to observe without judgment or criticism but just to gather the facts. If you are hard on yourself at any certain points, just notice that, too, but don't get caught up in it.

- **Stand in a circle** Notice your stance. Try to do this without adjusting anything. Where are your muscles tense? Where released? Is your spine long or rounded? Is the focus of your gaze outward on an object, person, or movement, or is it inward, on thoughts or feelings? Is your focus in the present moment or on past events or future anticipation? As much as you may not like some things, try to observe at first without changing. Also, the first time you do this exercise, keep the focus primarily on yourself, but do notice if any of the adjustments change how you feel in relationship to others.
- **Your feet** First bring awareness to how you stand on your feet. (An old pair of your shoes will show you which part of the sole you wear out first.) Are your feet together or apart? Are your feet pointed straight ahead or out to the side or one of each? Go up on your toes then lower your heels but keep the majority of the weight on your toes. Walk forward and backward. Next lift your toes off the floor. Put them down but without putting much weight on them at all. Walk forward and backward with most of the weight on your heels. One of these will feel more familiar, one more odd. This will tell you something about which of these you tend toward. Do the same with the inside and outside edges of your feet. Walk a few steps with the weight on the outside, then a few on the inside. While all of these exaggerations will feel weird, one will feel slightly less weird. This will give you a clue as to where you place your weight on your feet.
- **Your knees** Notice whether there is a lot or a little space between your knees as you stand and walk. When you rebalance your feet, that may change the alignment of your knees, but as you forget about your feet, your knees may revert to being slightly knock-kneed or bow-legged and may prefer to be overextended (straightened) or slightly bent.
- **Your pelvis** You will need to bend your knees slightly to explore a variety of positions for your hips. As you explore each, notice how it makes you think and feel. The hips can be an important center of movement, and changing their focus can shift how you feel as a person/character and also how you are perceived and how you feel in relation to others. First shift your weight to the left and push out your left hip. Then shift to the right. Come back to center. Now push the hips forward, walk forward a few steps. Now push the hips backward, slightly arching the lower back, and walk backward a few steps.
- **Your stomach** Allow the belly to fill with breath so that it looks as though you just ate Thanksgiving dinner. Move forward leading with the stomach. Now breathe in and pull the stomach up and back into your ribs. Let the breath out but not the muscles that hold the stomach there. Walk backwards to the outer circle.
- **Upper torso (chest)** Round the upper back so that you are hunched over. Let out the breath and walk forward and back in the circle. How does this make you feel in relationship to others? Notice how your head, neck, and

chin have to adjust. Now pull your shoulders back, lift the breastbone, open the chest, and breathe in. Walk forward and back.

- **Neck, head, chin, eyes** Move your neck forward of your body as far as possible. How do you need to adjust the head, chin, and/or eyes to see the person across from you? Walk forward and back. Now pull the neck as far backward as you can. Walk forward and back. Again, what do you need to adjust to be able to see?

5.2 & 5.3 Observation Journal—Movement Patterns and Alignment

What did your partner show you about your movement patterns in exercise 5.2? Were you aware prior to this that you carried your body in this way? In exercise 5.3, which of each type of alignment did you notice felt more and less familiar and comfortable? When you entered an alignment that was familiar, what were the physical sensations and emotional responses? Did you notice any changes to concepts of self that accompanied each adjustment (did any stances make you feel more like someone else you know or a different type of person)? In reality, you need to catch yourself throughout your day or in surprise pictures or videos (before you are aware of others watching you or bring your awareness to watching yourself) to garner what you really stand and move like. When you are stressed, where do you hold tension in your body?

Optimal Physical Functioning

Now you will have the chance to experience an alignment that is closer to how the body was designed for optimum functioning. What happens when the tires on your car are out of alignment? They wear more quickly and can even blow out. The same thing happens to our bodies. People whose feet are poorly aligned often experience knee problems. People with tight hamstrings often have sore lower backs. If one's back is overly extended one way or another, or a lot is demanded of back muscles when in poor alignment, that can lead to the all-too-common back pain. When you are out of alignment, the muscles have to engage in ways they were not designed to do for long periods. Just to sit or stand out of alignment, your muscles need to work harder to hold you in place. This increases tension in certain parts of the body and restricts the flow of your energy overall.

Neutral Alignment

Our skeletal system is designed such that if we align our bones, our muscles need to work only minimally to hold us up. One of the challenges of developing a more functional alignment is that our amazing *brain plasticity* (as discussed below) also helps us to adjust to the obstacles we give it, including poor alignment. If you tend to have your weight more forward then having your weight in a balanced alignment will feel to you like you are falling backward, until you make this your new normal (i.e., change the *habit* as discussed in Chapter 3). An extreme example of this is when someone is in an accident or has surgery that requires losing a limb. At first, after the physical limb is gone, the person will often sense a phantom limb, until the brain adjusts to the new state of affairs.

In retraining your alignment, one of the most helpful things is to have an outside person correct your stance until the adjusted alignment can be felt as normal. This

5 THE PSYCHOPHYSICAL INSTRUMENT

requires fairly regular reminders and hands-on adjustment from another person who can tell you from the outside what is balanced, before your internal balance centers have adjusted. One of the best methods for doing this is called the *Alexander Technique*, developed by Australian actor F. M. Alexander[14] (1869–1955) and taught by certified instructors around the world. Alexander Technique has been used to help optimize an assortment of physical and vocal techniques for actors, athletes, dancers, and opera singers. Of course a much older system of alignment, dating back to prehistory, comes from yoga. Yoga, which means union of mind, body, breath, and the divine or elevated consciousness (however you perceive this), is a key technique for unifying the mind and body for optimal use.

Yoga and Alignment

As discussed in earlier chapters, yoga was part of the fabric and foundation of the Stanislavsky System. Its concepts of the integration of mind, body, breath, and spirit are extremely helpful in advancing your acting skills. We recommend that you seek out an experienced yoga teacher in your area. Many universities now also offer regular yoga classes. Yoga, like the Alexander Technique, is a powerful practice that should be learned through an experienced teacher, but here are some simple beginning techniques that you can explore with great benefit.

> **Exercise 5.4: Standing in Alignment: Tadasana (Mountain Pose) (Iyengar)**
>
> **Purpose:** According to Iyengar, "This pose, the starting point of all standing asanas, lifts the sternum, which is the site of the anahat or 'heart' chakra (see diagram of chakras in Chapter 4). This helps reduce stress and boost your self-confidence, while the perfect balance of the final pose increases alertness."[15]
>
> **Guidelines:**
> - At each step of moving into the asana (pose), make sure you are not holding the breath. Allow the breath to fall in and release out to each of the parts of your body as you align.
> - **Feet and Ankles** (It helps to do this in bare feet or, at least, without shoes). Stand with your feet together, heels touching, toes spread (you may have your feet 2 inches apart to start, if this is easier). Center your weight over your arches while using your arches to distribute the weight to the surrounding parts of your foot that are touching the ground. Press the heels and mound of the toes firmly into the ground while stretching the toes forward but keeping them relaxed. Keep the ankles even with each other.
> - **Knees and Thighs** The kneecap should be pointing over the second toe

---

[14]F.M. Alexander was an Australian actor who continually lost his voice to laryngitis until he discovered that it was the excess tension he carried that was causing this dysfunction and created a system for releasing tension in the body and vocal instrument.

[15]Iyengar, *Yoga*, 186.

(next to the big toe) so that if you bent your knees they would move out toward this toe. Tighten your quadriceps (big muscles on the fronts of your thighs) to draw the kneecap up to make it strong and stable (back of the knees should remain soft). Do not straighten the knees by pushing them backward, as you may hyperextend and overstretch the tendons and ligaments). The thighs should be slightly turned in. Stretch both your legs upward while continuing to push the feet into the floor. Stretching in opposite directions from two or more points of the body energizes and expands the body and is widely used in yoga (and acting).

- **Hips and Stomach** Contract your hips and buttocks toward the center line of the buttocks. Pull the lower abdomen (part of the belly just below your belly button) in and up.
- **Arms and hands** Lengthen arms down along the sides of your body (but do not make them stiff), palms facing inward, fingers together and pointing toward the floor.
- **Upper torso** Lift your chest from the breastbone (bone between and just above your nipples) and widen your chest.
- **Head and eyes** Lift the back of the head up through the crown (the place where all your hair comes together). Make sure the neck is not jutting forward of the shoulders, but in alignment with the spine the neck floating the head. Let the chin rest without raising or lowering it or jutting it too far forward of the body. Release the jaw, so that your mouth opens very slightly. Release the shoulders, allowing them to fall away from the ears while imagining the ears drooping downwards. Soften the muscles of the face. Release the cheeks; again, release the jaw and tongue all the way through your mouth to where it connects to the base of your throat. Keep your gaze ahead at eye level, in soft focus, open but relaxed, seeing all around you but not fixed on anything.
- Consciously **shift most of your weight** to your heels for 20–30 seconds. As though the *plumb line* of your body (center line of your body from head to toe) was slightly further back.
- Then breathe into your body as a whole, noticing the movement of breath throughout your body.
- Feel the energy and vitality of your body in stillness. This alive stillness is vital for the stage. This is the potential from which action can spring.

5.4 *Reflection Journal—Observations in Tadasana*

You have stood every day for years. How did this alignment feel different for you? How did standing with this kind of conscious attention affect you? Did you notice any differences in your thoughts, physical sensations, and emotions before, during, and after this exercise? In your normal alignment, where might you need to add tension to hold your body upright because you are not usually in alignment there?

5 THE PSYCHOPHYSICAL INSTRUMENT

- Bottom of chin parallel to floor
- Ear above center of top of shoulder
- Lift the breastbone (center of chest)
- Shoulder blades not protruding from back (draw them down and in by lifting breastbone)
- Front of belt line slightly low than back Keep natural, but not over-arched, lumbar (lower back) curve
- Legs straight but knees not locked

Healthy
Natural lumbar curve

Problematic
Avoid removing the natural lumbar curve and locking the knees

Problematic
Avoid head and neck forward of shoulders

Problematic
Avoid hips thrust too far forward

Problematic
Avoid over exaggerating the lumbar curve

Exaggerated lumbar curve causes back problems later in life

Healthy
Weight balanced side to side and front to back

Avoid holding the head tilted to one side

Avoid one shoulder higher throws off other alignment

Weight on one side, not balanced

Problematic

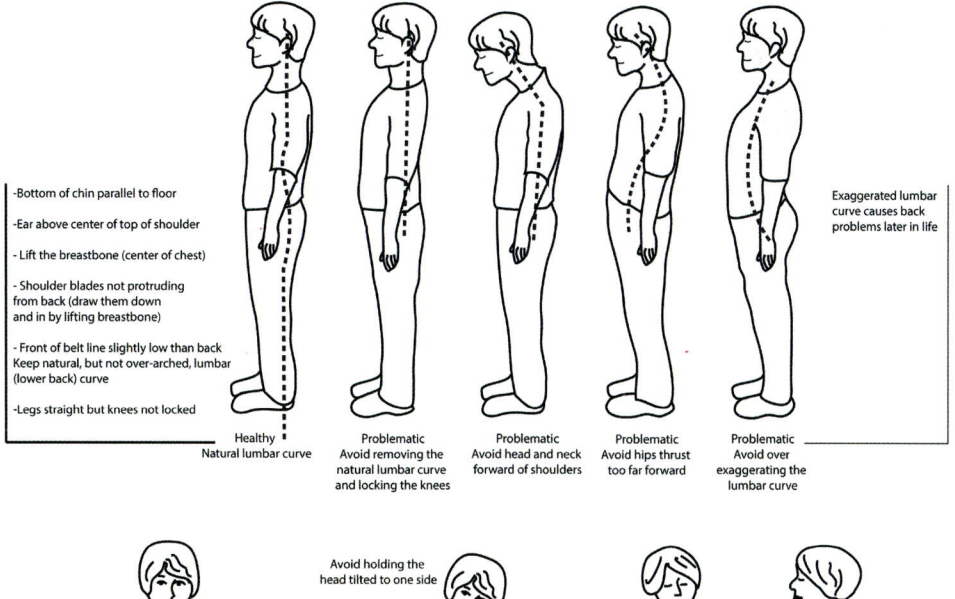

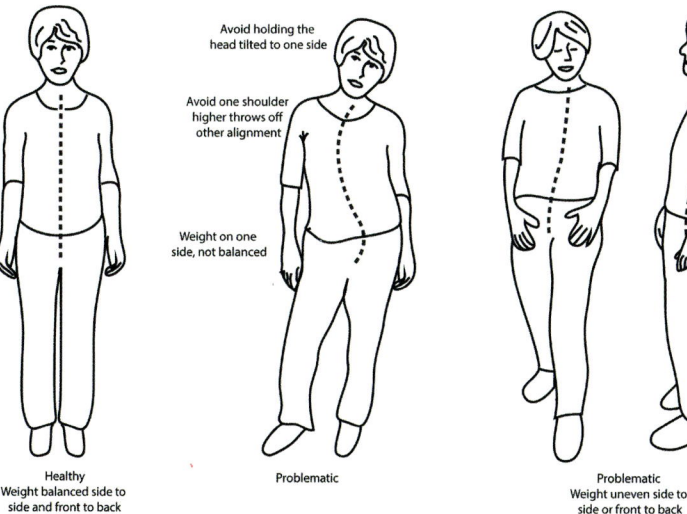

Problematic
Weight uneven side to side or front to back

Figure 5.7 Preferable and problematic alignment.

Exercise 5.5: Articulating and Activating the Spine (ZL/Ballet)[16]

Purpose: It is important to ensure that thoughts are reflected in the body (so they are communicated to the audience) and that actions that the body engages in or receives from others generate appropriate thoughts and feelings. The highway between the brain and body, of course, is the central nervous system that runs through your spine. To facilitate this communication, your spine needs to be supple and flexible and not held or caught at any points.

---

[16]Philip Bennett learned this from ballet teacher Zoya Laporska. It is also widely taught through the oral theatre tradition.

Exercise 5.5A: Rolling Up the Spine (see Figure 5.5)

Purpose: You began this process earlier by rolling up the spine from the prone position on the floor; however, if you do not have time for the entire sequence or enough floor space, doing just this part can be very helpful for bringing more movement and awareness to the spine.

Guidelines: Stand with feet shoulder-width apart, then

- fall over from the waist into a standing forward bend (bend your knees as necessary and don't worry about how far down your arms come);
- release the head, neck, back (check that your jaw and tongue are also released);
- roll up, stacking each vertebra one at a time.
- A helpful variation is to have a partner walk her fingers up the vertebrae as you stack them.

Exercise 5.5B: Rolling Down from the Plow Position (Halasana) (Iyengar/SDF)[17]

Purpose: The plow pose, according to Iyengar, "alleviates the effects of anxiety and fatigue. The chin lock in this pose soothes the nerves and relaxes the brain."[18] The second part, rolling down from the plow gives you a clear sense of the articulation of your spine and whether a part of your spine is too tight or jammed, thus restricting the flow of energy and impulses between the brain and body. A supple, flexible spine is the goal.

Guidelines:
- Lie on the floor.
- Bring your feet over your head legs straight, back off of the ground (see Figure 5.8, Rolling Down from Plow, below).
- Roll your back down onto the floor one vertebrae at a time, feeling each connect with the ground separately.
- Notice whether any vertebrae only move as a group rather than individually.

Figure 5.8 Rolling down from plow.

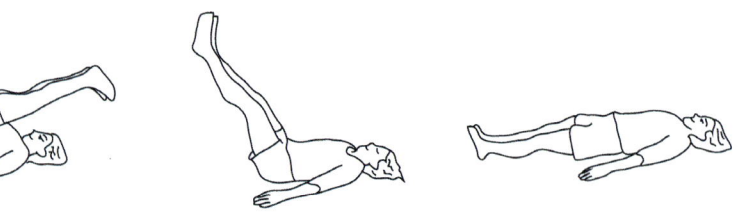

[17] Halasana is an ancient yogic pose that French learned through a variety of Iyengar yoga teachers, including Shirley Daventry French, Judith Hanson Lasater, and Ramanend Patel, and adapted for rolling down the spine.
[18] Iyengar, *Yoga*, 232.

5 THE PSYCHOPHYSICAL INSTRUMENT

Exercise 5.5C: Twists

Guidelines: Some of the best yogic exercises for increasing and maintaining suppleness in the spine and avoiding or alleviating pain and tension in the back are twists. One must turn into and release out of twists slowly and gently. Do not force your body. Before twisting always breathe in and lengthen the spine then twist as you release the breath. Twists should feel easy and good; if they do not, consult your teacher, and if you are having pain, consult your doctor. Even on days when you do not have time for a full warm-up, include some kind of twist to awaken the spine and facilitate psychophysical communication.

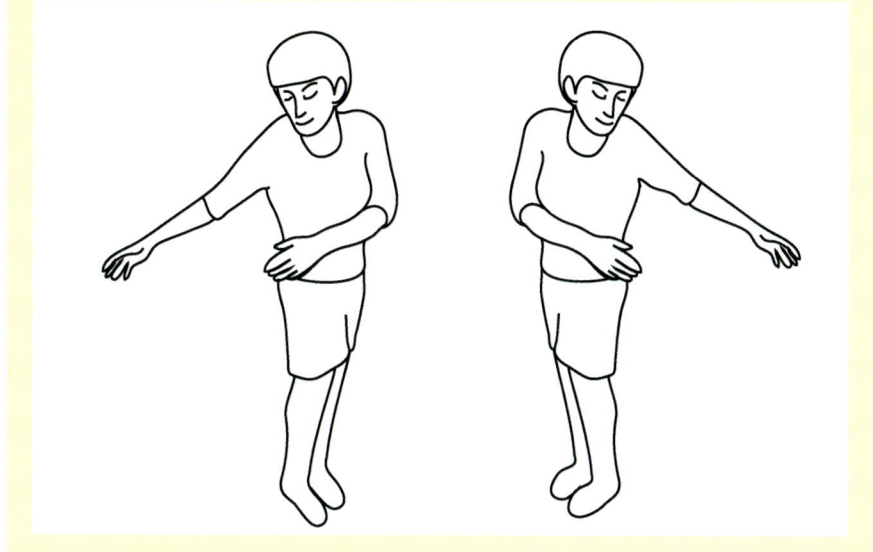

Figure 5.9 Swinging twist.

- **Swinging twist** (Figure 5.9) (SDF) Standing in Tadasana as shown above, swing your arms gently with your hands about hip height. For each height, swing the arms back and forth about three times. Allow the head and neck to follow and the feet and knees a little, too. Then swing the arms with the hands at waist height. Next swing the arms at chest height, and, finally, swing the arms at shoulder height. The idea is to gently warm up and release the spine.
- **Seated twist** (Figure 5.10) (Iyengar)[19] Sit in a chair extending the spine up out of your tailbone. Feel width across the shoulders. Inhale and extend the spine even longer. Exhale and begin to twist to the right, first from the hips. Inhale, lift, exhale turning from the waist. Inhale, lift, exhale, turn the chest, then shoulder, and finally the neck and head; look to the side or behind the chair, depending on your flexibility. Again, listen to your own body and where it is today. Unwind slowly and repeat to the left side.

---

[19]Bharadvajasana on a Chair (Torso Twist), in Iyengar, *Yoga*, 232.

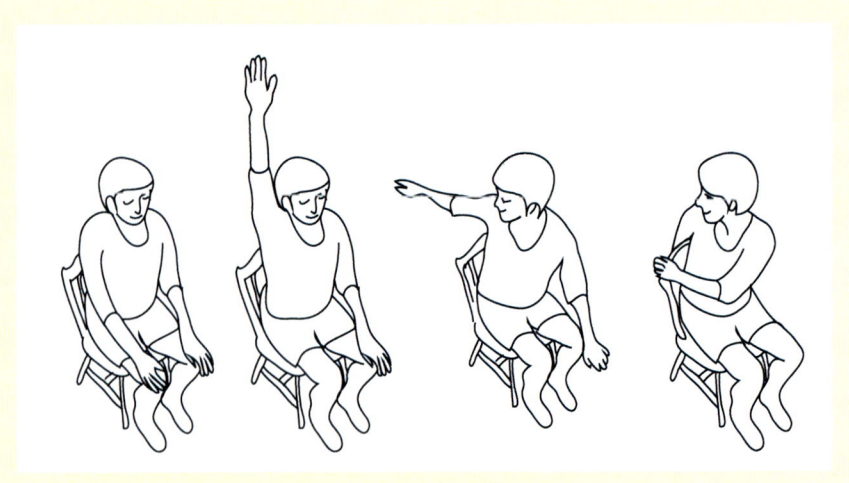

Figure 5.10 Seated twist.

- **Lying-down twist** (Figure 5.11) (Yoga/SDF)[20]—Lie down on your back, lengthening the spine along the floor. Place the arms out to the sides in line with the shoulders and perpendicular to the torso to make a T-shape. Lift the right leg perpendicular to the floor and place the right foot on the left knee. Inhale, lengthen the spine, and exhale while allowing the right knee to fall toward the floor to the left. Keep both shoulders on the floor (the shoulder on the opposite side will want to come up). You may place the left hand on top of the right knee to stretch a little farther, but don't force anything. Unwind slowly and repeat on the opposite side. Twists should feel good. If anything does not feel good in a twist, release and come back to center.

Figure 5.11 Lying-down twist.

Concentration (Focus of Attention)

Concentration is the ability to focus all of your attention to a specific point. The focus of attention is placed on both inner and outer objects and is an exercise of willpower. Ultimately the quality of an actor's work is judged by the ability to

---

[20] This is not a full asana but a modified one, frequently used and taught in yoga and excellent for gentle awakening of the spine or to gently loosen a jammed spine (remember always breathe into and out of twists and go in and out slowly without forcing anything). The full lying-down twist in Iyengar yoga would be Jataraparivatasana and would involve both legs bending and both falling over to the same side and is a more advanced pose that should be first attempted under supervision of a trained yoga teacher.

5 THE PSYCHOPHYSICAL INSTRUMENT

attain a balance between physical action and eidetic (vibrant and evocative) images. To develop concentration, Stanislavsky borrowed meditation techniques from raja yoga,[21] and insisted, "My whole System is based on this."[22]

> **Exercise 5.6: Disobeying Hands (A Psychophysical Concentration Exercise)(SM/PGB)**[23]
>
> **Purpose:** To develop concentration and begin to use the body in unfamiliar ways, developing new neural pathways in the brain, and to prepare for the mental acrobatics demanded later for more complex layers of acting. Learn the basics of this exercise now, as it will be used again with more layers in Chapter 7: Discovering and Endowing Circumstances. Sonia Moore told Bennett that this exercise was developed from *biomechanics* (a system of anatomy and physiology that looks at the body as a machine with specific usage and alignment, leading to optimum performance).
>
> When we build a character on stage, we have to create new behavior patterns—voice and speech, movement, breathing patterns, emotional responses and tendencies. Why do you think they have to be different than our own? It is because a playwright has written a character based on a type of person who is likely different from us in many ways—although possibly similar to us in some, as well. You have to be able to move and think in a way that is not your normal way of moving and thinking, a way that is unfamiliar, and then learn to justify why someone would move this way.
>
> For the following sequence of movements, follow this exact pattern, moving only one arm at a time with the second arm following the pattern of the first. Please see the photos in Figure 5.12 for a demonstration of the positions.
>
> **Guidelines:** Stand in neutral alignment with your arms falling comfortably along the sides of your body.
>
> 1. Lift your right hand and arm to the front, level with the shoulder and parallel to the floor. This is first position for this exercise (although not in ballet). The left arm remains at the left side.
> 2. Lift your right arm to pointing straight above your head.
> 3. Lift your left arm straight in front of the shoulder and parallel to the floor.
> 4. Lower your right arm to the right side, even with the shoulder and parallel to the floor.
> 5. Lift your left arm to pointing straight above your head.
> 6. Lower your right hand and arm to the side of your right leg.
> 7. Lower your left arm to the left side, even with the shoulder and parallel to the floor.

---

[21]Raja yoga is considered as the Royal Path of Yoga because it incorporates all eight paths (or limbs) of Yoga.
[22]Quoted in Sharon M. Carnicke, *Stanislavsky in Focus* (Amsterdam: Harwood Academic, 1998), 143.
[23]Sonia Moore, *Stanislavsky Revealed: The Actor's Guide to Spontaneity on Stage.* 2nd ed. (New York: Applause Books, 1968; 1998), 27. This exercise is adapted from Sonia more and expanded upon in years of teaching by Philip G. Bennett.

8. Lift your right hand and arm to the front, level with the shoulder and parallel to the floor as in #1 above, but this time the left arm is in position #7.
9. Lower your left hand and arm to the side of your left leg. Right arm is in position #1.
10. Continue through the sequence above with the right arm leading and the left following, only one arm moving at a time. Repeat three to four times, at first saying out loud, "left" and "right," and then saying only 1–8, and finally with no counting. At this time you need only learn the sequence. Later, in Chapter 7: Discovering and Endowing Circumstances, you will add context to each position.

Figure 5.12 Positions for disobeying hands.

Exercise 5.7: Predator and Prey (Another Concentration Exercise) (SDF)

Purpose: To expand your concentration and capacity for holding on to multiple points of focus simultaneously, thus challenging your mind and creating new neural pathways.

- Begin to move about the room and sit, stand, lie on the floor, greet others, and other simple movements. Don't try to be creative or inventive or leaping about; just normal, simple movement.
- Pick someone to stalk, as through you were a predator and the other your prey. Notice every movement and gesture, without that person knowing that you are stalking him.
- Try to observe and stalk a second person at the same time without missing anything that your first person is doing.
- Try to observe a third. How can you see all three at once even though they might be in different parts of the room?
- If you think you are being stalked, try to catch the predator watching you. If you catch him, he is out.

5.7 Reflection Journal—Predator and Prey

How did you keep an eye on your prey without them knowing? How many people were you able to track without losing them? How did you have to observe differently when you had three people?

The Anatomy of a Thought[24]

Have you ever tried to hide your thoughts only to have someone instinctively know what you were thinking? Your thoughts subtly reveal themselves through physical actions and gestures. A close examination of human behavior reveals that thoughts (electrical impulses and resulting chemical behavior) travel at 200 miles per hour between the brain and muscles,[25] expressing themselves as *neurophysiological impulses*. Impulses are responsible for your spontaneous movement and unconscious gestures. With diligent practice you will eventually be able to express the subtlest nuance of thought and feeling by means of a finely tuned instrument. This is a key goal in psychophysical conditioning.

Thought has an anatomy, a structure, that can be artistically expressed in a sequential order. Thought produces specific neurological signals that travel from the brain through the nervous system (see Figure 4.2) into the various organs and muscles of the body. When we learn a new skill, like driving a car, dancing, or playing a sport, the repetitive practice of our new behavior eventually becomes part of our nature.

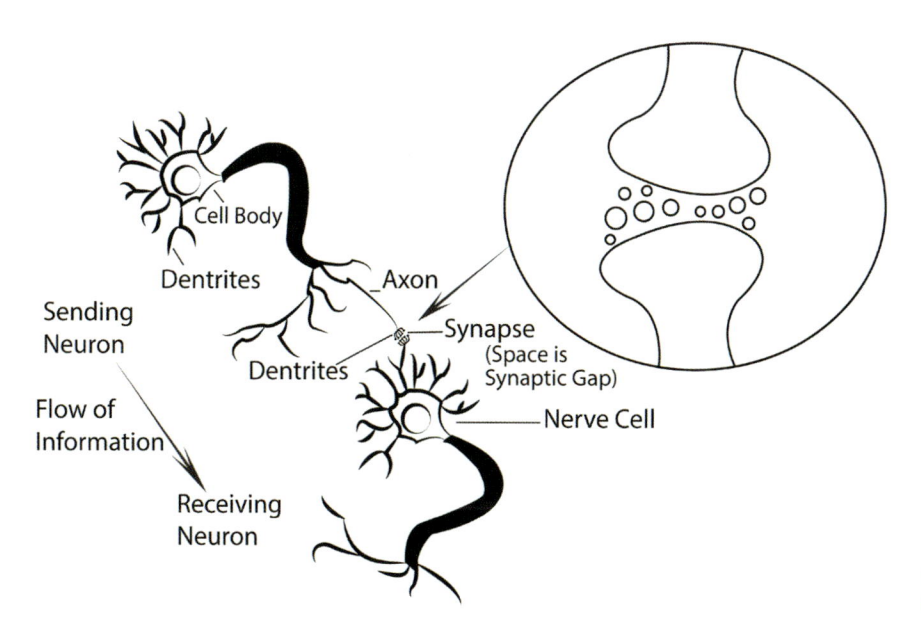

Figure 5.13 The synaptic gap.

---

[24] *Wonder, Evaluate, Decision, Gesture, Action, Gesture*, or W.E.D.G.A.G., was created by Sonia Moore. Philip G. Bennett coined the phrase *anatomy of a thought* in acting to further articulate and create exercises for W.E.D.G.A.G. French linked these acting techniques to relevant current understandings of the process of thought in cognitive neuroscience.

[25] This interesting fact supplied by psychologist Dr. Joseph Meile, East Stroudsburg University.

When doing a new mental or physical task, you are literally forging new pathways between the *neural synapses* (gaps between neurons) in your brain (see Figure 5.13). At first, this mental process requires great deal of energy for the chemical messenger (*neural transmitter*) to leap the *synaptic gap*. Then, as the behavior or thought process is repeated, it becomes familiar and takes less energy to make the mental leap. Neuroscientists talk about a *lower synaptic threshold* caused by physical changes to the synapse that increase the *long-term potentiation* (ability for it to more easily send this particular message). This is like a path through a field that has been worn by enough travelers that it is now easier to navigate. At this point the behavior becomes habit, and we no longer need to consciously focus on remembering each step. In fact, we can then often think about and even do other things at the same time.

Bidirectional Flow of Energy

When you can control your thoughts and direct the muscular energy to various parts of your body you will find that sensations and emotions arise of themselves and that they will be appropriate to the imaginary circumstances within which you are creating your character. This is because in addition to the brain providing signals to the body, the muscles provide signals back to the brain, and the brain relates those to previous feelings and thoughts. The psychophysical loop is thus said to be *bidirectional*. This is why physical movement training in various disciplines is essential: dance, tumbling, acrobatics, fencing, and stage combat are important and will give the actor confidence as well as an extended vocabulary for physical expression. Your physical instrument must become expressive, sensitive, and responsive to your every thought, impulse, and feeling. All of our muscles can provide feedback to our history of feeling or thought. On perceiving stimuli, the brain runs through a catalog of similar experiences and within this context generates our responses.

> **Exercise 5.8: Simple Physical Action with W.E.D.G.A.G (to sit in a chair) (PB)[26]**
>
> **Purpose:** Mental awareness of simple physical actions. A direction from the teacher leads to a mental impetus in you, and you decide to follow (or not) the teacher's directive. If you decide to move, this sends messages through the nervous system to certain muscle groups for physical activation. In the meantime, the muscles are sending sensations back to the brain and balance centers so that the brain can send out new signals to adjust at every phase of the movement until it is complete. All of this usually happens subconsciously, and the mechanisms for standing up are deeply programed into habit.

---

[26]Bennett created numerous exercises such as this to teach and experientially reinforce the *anatomy of thought* of W.E.D.G.A.G.

5 THE PSYCHOPHYSICAL INSTRUMENT

Exercise 5.8A: To Sit in a Chair

Guidelines:
- Sit in a chair and when directed, stand up.
- Now sit in a chair again and this time, try to notice some of the mechanisms at work.

5.8A *Reflection Journal—To Sit in a Chair*

How much did you notice the mechanisms that initiated the movements? Did you notice mental activity? Did you notice the impetus to move or a response to the movement?

Exercise 5.8B: To Sit in a Chair with W.E.D.G.A.G.

Purpose: This exercise is designed to awaken your awareness of the muscles that are engaged when you are thinking. It also develops your awareness of the anatomy of a thought that both initiates a physical action and registers thoughts in response to each phase of the action. A technique for actors to develop more consciousness about how these processes communicate in their psychophysical system is a series of action steps that Sonia Moore designated as W.E.D.G.A.G.

W.E.D.G.A.G. is an acronym for:

W—Wonder (awe, curiosity, astonishment, discovery)
E—Evaluate (consider, weigh up)
D—Decide
G—Gesture (expresses the decision)
A—Act (take action)
G—Gesture (expresses the result of this action)

Guidelines:
- Stand about 10 feet from your chair, turned away.
- Turn and notice the chair; let this stir your sense of **Wonder** or curiosity (don't *show* wonder but think thoughts about the chair).
- **Evaluate,** or weigh up, whether or not you should sit in it (these should be actual sentences of inner dialogue—your own thoughts arguing back and forth—about whether or not to sit).
- **Decide** to sit, again an actual thought must be said inside your head (like counting in your head instead of out loud).
- Allow the decision to move from a thought through your spine, resulting in a **Gesture** that expresses the decision. This gesture may only be a subtle move as the impulse moves through your spine and need not involve a hand or arm gesture.
- Take **Action**—in this case, go and sit in the chair.
- Think about sitting in the chair: is it satisfying or unsatisfying? Express this in a final **Gesture.**

Exercise 5.8C: To Treat a Chair as a Throne (using W.E.D.G.A.G. and "to treat as") (SM/PB[27])

Guidelines:
- Now imagine that the chair is a throne and you are a lowly servant. It is forbidden for anyone other than the king to sit in the throne, but you are going to evaluate and decide to sit in it anyway.
- Go through the series of steps in 5.8b and at each point express this situation.

Exercise 5.8D: To Treat a Chair as the Electric Chair (using W.E.D.G.A.G. and "to treat as") (SM/PB)

Guidelines:
- Now the chair is the electric chair, where you are to be executed. You cannot escape sitting in it. Go through W.E.D.G.A.G. again with this new circumstance.

5.8B, C and D *Reflection Journal—To Sit in a Chair and to Treat a Chair as, with W.E.D.G.A.G.*

Did you notice the impulses move through your body in response to the thoughts? Did each key point of thought—wonder, evaluate, decide, act—have a gestural expression (which need only be a subtle movement through the spine)?

The Inner Landscape

You will learn to use your creative imagination to build the *inner landscape* (internal life) of the character reflecting the character's world, time period, and predilections. This inner landscape will be composed of continuous thoughts as the character and a continuous film of images. First you must reconnect with and develop your imagination.

Imagination

In Chapter 2 we defined *imagination* as your ability to create and see *mental pictures* on demand. Stanislavsky insisted that actors must see a continuous *film of images* that are selected and composed from observation of imagined or personal experiences. You must learn to see images of the world of the play; these images can be in any style from realistic to fantastic or grotesque. You will also need images of any person, place, object, or event that the character speaks about.

---

[27]Sonia Moore created the "to treat as" exercises, but Bennett adapted them to include W.E.D.G.A.G.

5 THE PSYCHOPHYSICAL INSTRUMENT

Not everyone sees visual images when they close their eyes, but there is currently no better term for creating stimulating mental triggers. When scientists talk about mental images, they do not mean only visual images; they actually mean impressions. According to Dr. Kay Porter, a mental-athletics trainer for Olympic athletes, *visualization*, as she uses it with athletes, can be "any mental imagining, in pictures, words, feelings, or senses."[28] Later, you will learn more about using your senses to stimulate responses in you for acting; for now, whatever arises as impressions in your mind can be useful as long as they are vibrant and evocative and stimulate your mind and body as if they were real. Such evocative, or *eidetic*, images can be helpful if they stimulate you the actor in ways appropriate for the character at a specific moment in the play.

Imagination acts as a strong stimulus to emotion and can lead you into the desired creative state for acting. Remember that your mental images may be imaginary, personal, or a combination. The combination of real and imagined images is called *amalgamation* and creates new images unique to the role.

Creating a Film of Mental Images

In the following situation you will be asked to create a film of mental pictures. These images are an important aspect of human behavior and of stage action. Creating a continuous film of mental images that you see in your mind is essential to thinking continuously as the character. If at any point you stop seeing images or stop thinking in the situation, both you and the character die for the audience.

How do you find and create images? You can choose to borrow images from any source that has affected you. You may have personally experienced a real event that is similar to what your dramatic situation requires; however, observation is equally important, and you can use images of events you have witnessed, read about, or seen in film or on television. Use your imagination to create imaginary images. Imagination can be very powerful. What is important is that you use everything around you: personal associations, observations, and your imagination.

Sometimes a situation dictates that you do not move at all. This stillness can be a very powerful expression on stage, especially when it is full of thoughts, images, and emotion. You may appear to be physically immobile; however, that does not mean that you are inwardly immobile. Keep your breath and energy flowing through your body and notice how many thoughts and feelings arise.

Inner Monologue (Inner Dialogue)

Just as you have continuous thoughts in your real existence, you must have continuous thoughts as a character to bring the character to life. This is called *inner monologue* and must be relevant to the situation and the character's background and personality. Sometimes the character's private thoughts are more of an internal argument, in which case the term *inner dialogue* is used.

The more you can replace your own thoughts with those of the character, the more we see the character in place of you. This can also be very helpful

---

[28]Kay Porter and Judy Foster, *Visual Athletics: Visualizations for Peak Sports Performance* (Dubuque, IA: Wm. C. Brown, 1990), 23.

for overcoming self-consciousness onstage, which often involves thoughts of personal fears or self-criticism. The busier you are with the thoughts of the character and the situation, the less room you have for undermining or distracting thoughts that break the imaginary world you and your scene partners are working hard to create.

Inner monologue is reflected through the body and thus expressed to the audience. To enhance your ability to vividly reflect your thoughts you will need to continue your training to become a psychophysical actor. As a psychophysical actor you will easily be able to adjust your performance to the medium. Depending on the size of the theatre, or the size of the frame for film or television acting, the physical expression may be larger or it may be merely subtle movements of the spine or reflections in the eyes.

The audience will not know the exact words you are saying privately in your head, but they should get the gist of it. For example, if the play or film starts with a moment of the actor alone doing an activity but not speaking, we should get a sense of what is going on for the character but perhaps do not know exactly. Later, as more of the story is revealed, we should look back on that moment and say, "Of course, that is why the character was so conflicted in her thoughts," or, "that is why the character seemed to be carrying such a heavy burden," or, "that is why her thoughts seemed light and positive."

You must compose the inner monologue for a play in the language of the character, as revealed by the playwright. The inner monologue must relate to the lines you speak as the character and the actions you fulfill. Later inner monologue becomes vital to express important moments for the character, such as decisions, insights, and discoveries.

While the created and written inner monologue/inner dialogue may be of a similar vein at each rehearsal and performance, it is never exactly the same, as it must remain alive and fluid.[29] For beginning actors, this often answers the question, "What do I do while the other character is speaking?" The answer is that you think and allow those thoughts to be reflected through subtle reactions that you express with your thoughts and through your spine.

Exercise 5.9: To Wait for the Jury's Verdict (SM)

Purposes: This is an excellent exercise for acting for the camera; both inner life and subtlety are paramount. Inner monologue and images are also essential for the stage. The camera picks up and magnifies any false (unjustified) or exaggerated movements. The training goals are:

- to use imagination (images) and to affect the body;
- to think thoughts in response to a situation, inner monologue, and allow them to be reflected through the eyes and the body; and

---

[29] After you begin to generate character's inner monologue automatically and instantaneously onstage, you may no longer wish to write it down; however, many very experienced actors still choose to do so. Beginning actors generally must do this step to train themselves to think as the character continuously and in ways appropriate to the given circumstances.

- to keep a situation alive through a continual film of relevant images (to replace thoughts not relevant to the imaginary situation).

Preparation: A day or two ahead of this exercise, imagine in detail: a crime you were accused of committing, the arrest and the trial, re-creating the three events with as many senses as possible. You can be guilty or innocent. If innocent, you may only know what you have read in the papers and heard in the accusation and in the courtroom, but you should still have heard or seen pictures of the details of the crime. If guilty, you will have even more details of the crime. Where did it take place? Who were you with? What part did you play? Was it intentional or accidental? Did you get caught then or arrested later? Imagine the details of the arrest. What happened in court with the lawyers, witnesses, judge, and jury?

Guidelines for the improvisation: In the case of this exercise, less is more. Allow the inner life to be active and the body reflective.

- The trial is over. A bailiff will bring you, handcuffed, into a small room and seat you in a chair. He will remove the handcuffs. The bailiff is a supporting role and should help the accused focus, not distract or make a serious improvisation comic.
- You are waiting for the jury's return to the courtroom with its verdict. Keep your head up so you're observing classmates can see your eyes. If you look outward, see the walls of the small room rather than your classmates watching. Do not make eye contact with anyone watching but rather see the walls of the room or the images of your memory of the events.
- Your acting task is to create and see a constant film of mental images and to review the crime itself, the arrest (what were the police officers like, how were you treated, where and when did the arrest take place?) and the trial (lawyers, witnesses, the judge and jury). Be detailed and specific. What do you think about the crime itself? Did you commit it or not, and what do you think about that? Do you think you will be found guilty or innocent?
- Try not to show what you think your character would do. Do not plan an appropriate emotion to feel or a specific physical behavior to do; just see the images in your mind and allow them to affect you and express themselves subtly through the thoughts and visions in your eyes and the thought impulses along the spine.
- In large classes, three to four students may wait for the verdict at the same time.
- At a signal from the teacher, the bailiff will come and get you to bring you to hear the verdict. Before you rise, make sure to begin with wonder and evaluation. When you decide to get up let your impulses dictate a very subtle gesture. Prepare yourself for the verdict and make a final gesture that expresses your anticipation.

Class observation and feedback: After the exercise, the class votes on whether the accused was guilty or innocent and comments on what specific observed behavior, or perceived thoughts, led to that conclusion.

> **5.9** *Reflection Journal—To Wait for the Jury's Verdict*
>
> Were you able to see and hold on to your film of images? Did you achieve deep thought? Did you become so involved that you had a moment of public solitude, forgetting the audience was watching? Were any emotions triggered? If you were to do this exercise again what would you keep and what would you change?

PART III: PSYCHOPHYSICAL SCIENCE

The Mind-Body Connection in Science: What Are These Psychophysical Conditioning Exercises Actually Doing?

In learning this acting technique, we are asking you to become more conscious of your inner and outer processes through the use of your internal and external monitors. This understanding is important for you to create the internal processes and external behavior of a character.

Since the late nineteenth century, when psychology emerged from philosophy as discipline in its own right, it has struggled to reconcile, as University of Virginia research professor of psychiatry and neurobehavior Edward F. Kelly recounts in *The Irreducible Mind*, "the problem of relations between the inherently private, subjective, 'first-person' world of human mental life and the publicly observable, objective, 'third-person' world of physiological events and processes in the body and brain."[30]

> **Mind-Body Connections in Science (Nineteenth–Twentieth Centuries)**
>
> Some great thinkers of the late nineteenth and early twentieth centuries, along with Konstantin Stanislavsky, the primary inspiration for this book, recognized the interconnectedness of mind and body:
>
> - F. W. H. Myers (1843–1901) wrote about the mind-body connection in *Human Personality: And Its Survival of Bodily Death*. Ironically, Myers's book was published in 1903, after his death.
> - William James (1842–1910) was an American philosopher and psychologist who had trained as a physician. He was a great admirer of Myers. James is considered one of the fathers of psychology through his pivotal book *Principles of Psychology*, published in 1890. He theorized that emotion is the result of the mind's interpretation of stimuli perceived through the physical body.
> - Carl Lange (1834–1900), was a Danish physician who also posited that emotions involve physiological reactions to stimuli. He seemed to come, independently and through different means than James, to similar conclusions about the physiological basis for emotion. Their independently developed ideas are combined to form the James-Lange theory of emotion (addressed later in Chapter 12: Orchestrating Emotions).

[30]Edward F. Kelly, introduction to *Irreducible Mind*, by Edward F. Kelly et al. (Lanham, MD: Rowman and Littlefield, 2007), xvii.

> **Behavioral Science and the Temporary Move Away from the Integrated Body-Mind**
>
> A movement in psychology in the late nineteenth century and the early twentieth century sought to align the emerging field of psychology with the empirical processes then in place for physics. With his 1913 book *Psychology as the Behaviorist Views It*, J. B. Watson changed psychology from James's concept of it as the science of mental life, to a science of objectively observable behavior. According to Edward F. Kelly and colleagues in *Irreducible Mind*, Watson dismissed the terms "'consciousness, mental states, mind, content, introspectively verifiable, imagery and the like,'" saying that they had no place in psychological experiments. Winkielman and Schooler also reference this dismissal of introspection: "Behaviorism, and the ambition to make psychology 'objective' and equal to other natural sciences, brought disfavor to the methods of introspection and to mentalistic concepts like consciousness." (Winkielman and Schooler 2012: 55)
>
> While Watson turned to externally verifiable behavior, James, in his earlier observations, had noted both the external behavior and internal experiences of his subjects, even though instruments did not yet exist to measure the internal responses in living subjects.
>
> The view of Watson and others in *behaviorist psychology* dominated the realm of recognized and valued psychological science in the early to mid-twentieth century. In the 1930s and 1940s various scientist chipped away at behaviorism. As information-processing tools became more effective and accessible, they helped scientists to demonstrate viewpoints beyond mere external behaviorism, and such alternative views grew in the 1950s and 1960s. By the 1970s and 1980s, various studies using tools that could better measure the inner workings of the brain and body gave researchers additional ways to measure and demonstrate some of the internal functions of healthy living bodies and brains, and the more externally focused aspects of behaviorism finally lost dominance in psychology.

Any human being even slightly conscious of her own internal processes can recognize the existence and impact of internal experiences on external behavior. The scientific study of internal human processes and consciousness has exploded. This is in large part because there are now tools to measure the brain's response to the body, in addition to the previously existing tools to measure the body's external responses to the brain. Your body has its own internal/external monitors, such as *proprioception*—your internal awareness of surroundings, and the body within that space—as well as internal awareness of the relationship of the core of your body and the external components.

Utilizing these tools, scientists have demonstrated in a wide variety of experiments the inseparable interconnectedness of the mind and body. Neuroscientist Eric Kandel claims, for example, that

> mind and brain are inseparable. The brain is a complex biological organ of great computational capability that constructs our sensory experiences,

regulates our thoughts and emotions, and controls our actions. The brain is responsible not only for relatively simple motor behaviors, such as running and eating, but also for the complex acts that we consider quintessentially human, such as thinking, speaking and creating works of art.[31]

Brain Plasticity: How Do You Expand the Possibilities of Your Brain to Meet Acting Challenges?

As you train your physical body in new techniques, such as disobeying hands, in the exercise above, you are literally rewiring and expanding the pathways in your brain. In order for any physical activity to become second nature, this must happen. Our brains are much more pliable than originally thought. Research psychiatrist Dr. Norman Doidge in *The Brain that Changes Itself* writes about discovering experiments, done in the 60s and 70s, that shook his belief that the brain was fixed at a young age:

> They showed that the brain changed its very structure with each different activity it performed, perfecting its circuits so it was better suited to the task at hand. If certain "parts" failed, then other parts could sometimes take over. . . . They began to call this fundamental brain property "neuroplasticity." *Neuro* is for "neuron," the nerve cells in our brains and nervous systems. *Plastic* is for "changeable, malleable, modifiable."[32]

Joseph Chaikin (1935–2003)
Melodic Intonation Therapy

A therapeutic example of developing brain *plasticity*, the ability to adapt and create new neural pathways in the brain, is Melodic Intonation Therapy.

Joseph Chaikin, who was an experimental theatre performer, director, and intellectual with an excellent facility for language, suffered a stroke that damaged part of the processing mechanism for speech in the left hemisphere of his brain (Broca's aphasia). In order to regain language he had to reroute it through the right hemisphere. Therefore, the speech therapist took his left hand and moved it in a pattern from right to left while he chanted in a singsong tone simple phrases such as "cup-of-caaah-ffee [*coffee* extended]." Because music moves through the right hemisphere, the chanting acted as the needle pulling the thread of language into the right hemisphere. This reprograming eventually developed new circuitry, new neural pathways for language in a healthy part of his brain. Because our brains have plasticity, Chaikin regained his use of many aspects of language and speech (though not all).[33]

---

[31]Eric R. Kandel, *In Search of Memory: The Emergence of a New Science of Mind* (New York: Norton, 2006), xii.

[32]Norman Doidge, *The Brain That Changes Itself* (New York: Penguin, 2007), xix. This is also a term used in Russian movement and thereby acting to refer to a changeable and malleable body.

[33]This experience was transmitted to French and others in rehearsals for Chaikin's collaboratively created performance of *Utterance in the Firmament* at San Francisco State University in 1989.

Plasticity is also a term used in Russian movement (and thereby acting) to refer to a changeable and malleable body.

> **Acting and the Science of Learning and Habit: How Can We Change Our Psychophysical Responses to Respond as Someone Else Would in the Same Situation?**

Another interesting perspective on this rewiring of the brain through changes in physical behavior, relates to the rehearsal process. A relevant field is the science of habit, and changing habits. Stanislavsky was influenced early on by Pavlov's experiments on conditioned response (which is more of a behaviorist observation of external stimuli and responses as discussed above). Pavlov rang a bell every time he fed a dog. Eventually he only needed to ring the bell (but not put out food) and the dog would salivate. Duhigg, in his book *The Power of Habit: Why We Do What We Do in Life and Business*, reviews a wide array of more recent experiments on habit that connect the externally observed behavior to internal processes in our brains. He discusses the habit loop, in which a *trigger* (conscious or unconscious) sets in motion a *pattern of behaviors* that become linked in the brain (called *chunked*), and this is all reinforced by a *predictable reward*. This is great if you have triggered and performed a good habit such as brushing your teeth but less good if you have just smoked a cigarette.

Before we can understand how to train-in some habits we might need for acting a role, or train-out some bad habits that impede our acting, we must look at some relevant findings on habit from scientists at the Brain and Cognitive Sciences Department at the Massachusetts Institute of Technology as relayed by Duhigg and summarized here:

Habit Forming:
- When first figuring out a new activity, our brains are working hard and our physical response time is slow, but after the same sequence of actions is performed in the same way over and over, our brains group the mental sequence into something called a chunk, then the amount of brain power it takes to coordinate the sequence is much less but the reaction time much quicker.
- Once a series of behaviors becomes habit, such as the mechanisms for parallel parking your car, you can perform them with little brainpower and thus do or think of other things simultaneously.
- Our brains, when responding habitually without conscious thought, can't differentiate between good and bad habits but perform either automatically when exposed to the relevant triggers.
- This is great for good habits but also why it is hard to break bad habits. If we do something enough, we have literally made a fast track so that it can happen without us even consciously thinking about it, making it much harder to stop.[34]

Reprogramming New Habits:
- First, you need to observe all the triggers for the behavior you want to change. According to East Stroudsburg University psychology professor Dr. Joseph Miele, in conversation with French, "You can't remove or always avoid a trigger, which

---

[34]Charles Duhigg, *The Power of Habit: Why We Do What We Do in Life and Business* (New York: Random House, 2012), 12–16.

sets in motion a learned drive for a reward, but you can change the sequence of behaviors that follow."
- Second, you need to notice what reward you get for fulfilling this behavior.
- Third, you need to find a behavior or series of behaviors that results in a similar reward, without the negative effects you are trying to avoid.
- For quite some time, you will need to try to be conscious every time you are triggered to fulfill the undesired behavior and then to replace it with the desired or neutral behavior leading to the similar reward.
- It takes frequent repetition over a period of time to connect the new pattern of behavior to the trigger. According to research scientist Dr. Phillipa Lally and her colleagues at University College London, for the new, repeated pattern to become habit could take as long 245 days or as little as 18 (with an average of 66), depending on the person and the habit they are trying to imprint or change.[35] For example, say you walk into a mall and smell the cookie store; you then crave a cookie. After you eat it, you feel a reward: a temporary lift in energy from the chocolate chips (caffeine and sugar). Consider an alternative behavior that could give you a similar reward (lift in energy), such as a cup of tea or coffee, a brief exercise routine, or a meditation. Eventually, you will walk in, smell the cookie and desire that alternative reward, the cup of tea, meditation, or exercise.

How Does This Research on Habit Relate to Acting?

When the character is triggered, you can replace thoughts and behaviors personal to you with those more appropriate for the character and time period. It takes frequent repetition to create new physical and mental pathways of response, just as it takes repetition to learn a new physical or mental skill. Additionally, you can retrain your psychophysical instrument overall to be more responsive to stimuli.

Actors need to always keep dual consciousness and not confuse themselves with the character. They program specific behaviors in response to stimuli onstage when they frame responses with thoughts of the character. In their personal lives the actors' own thoughts, contexts, and personal backgrounds will frame the same stimuli differently. Thus when offstage, they continue to respond as themselves, not as the character.

Brain Cleaning and Maintenance

While involvement in theatre requires long hours, you must find time to sleep. If you don't, you will lose some of the functioning of your brain, which as we have seen above is essential to the functioning of your psychophysical instrument. Sleep deprivation is used as an interrogation technique because many of the functions of the brain that would give it strength to resist are vastly weakened by lack of sleep. Why? Maria Konnikova, author of *Mastermind: How to Think Like Sherlock Holmes*, reviewed some of the science on the brain and sleep:

> As your body sleeps, your brain is quite actively playing the part of mental janitor: It's clearing out all of the junk that has accumulated as a result of your daily thinking. The Veasey lab found that while our brains can recover quite

---

[35] P. Lally et al., "How Are Habits Formed: Modeling Habit Formation in the Real World," *European Journal of Social Psychology* 40: 998–1009. doi: 10.1002/ejsp.674.

5 THE PSYCHOPHYSICAL INSTRUMENT

readily from short-term sleep loss, chronic prolonged wakefulness and sleep disruption stresses the brain's metabolism. The result is the degeneration of key neurons involved in alertness and proper cortical function and a buildup of proteins associated with aging and neural degeneration.[36]

Summary

Your psychophysical instrument is your primary tool, the body your primal signal system to express the complex inner landscape of a character's experience. The mind and body are in constant communication, but much of this goes on subconsciously. As an actor, you need to become more conscious of the continual feedback loop between your mind and body. You also need to expand the possibilities of your psychophysical instrument by expanding your flow of energy through reducing tension, developing more physical and mental focus and concentration, cultivating your imagination, and expanding the capacity of your brain through exercises that lay down new neural pathways. Conditioning exercises prepare you for the more complex acting work of Active Analysis, which in turn prepares you for the ultimate acting technique of experiencing the life of the character in the role.

New Theatre Terms, Concepts, and Artists

Terms used in the Stanislavsky System are in italics.

- ☐ activating the spine
- ☐ Alexander Technique
- ☐ anatomy of a thought
- ☐ biomechanics
- ☐ body language
- ☐ Joseph Chaikin
- ☐ *concentration*
- ☐ creative imagination
- ☐ eidetic images
- ☐ film of images
- ☐ *flow of energy*
- ☐ focus of attention
- ☐ *inner dialogue*
- ☐ inner landscape
- ☐ *inner monologue*
- ☐ internal and external monitors
- ☐ kinesthetic awareness
- ☐ kinesthetic response
- ☐ *language of the body*
- ☐ mental images
- ☐ organic behavior
- ☐ patterns of behavior
- ☐ plastic (plastique)
- ☐ primal signal system
- ☐ *psychophysical instrument*
- ☐ relaxation
- ☐ *Sobranie Sochineni* (*Collected Works*)
- ☐ visualization
- ☐ W.E.D.G.A.G.

---

[36] Maria Konnikova, "Goodnight. Sleep Clean," *New York Times, Sunday Review*, Opinion, January 11, 2014.

Interdisciplinary Concepts, Terminology, and Experts

- ☐ F.M. Alexander
- ☐ autonomic
- ☐ Sharon Begley
- ☐ behaviorist psychology
- ☐ biodirectional
- ☐ Anne Bogart
- ☐ Richard Brestoff
- ☐ chunk, chunking
- ☐ Richard Davidson
- ☐ Norman Doidge
- ☐ Charles Duhigg
- ☐ Judy Foster
- ☐ habit (trigger, reward)
- ☐ Edmund Jacobson
- ☐ Maria Konnikova
- ☐ P. Lally
- ☐ Tina Landau
- ☐ Carl Lange
- ☐ Kristin Linklater
- ☐ long-term potentiation
- ☐ F.W. Myers
- ☐ neural synapses
- ☐ neural transmitter
- ☐ neurological impulse
- ☐ neuron
- ☐ neuroplasticity
- ☐ NYU Experimental Theatre School
- ☐ Mary Overlie
- ☐ plumb line
- ☐ Kay Porter
- ☐ SITI Company
- ☐ Tadashi Suzuki
- ☐ synaptic gap
- ☐ synaptic threshold
- ☐ tadasana

PART 2

PSYCHOPHYSICAL ACTION: ENGAGING OTHERS

Chapters in Part 2

6. Communion: Deepening Communication and Mutual Influence	117
7. Discovering and Endowing Circumstances	137
8. Nonverbal Action: Communicating through Behavior	155
9. Embodying Voice	193
10. Activating Speech	215
11. Verbal Action: Communicating with Words and Subtext	243
12. Orchestrating Emotions	267

The next phase of training is to learn to work with multiple Elements of Action simultaneously and to focus your actions on affecting your scene partners. In Chapter 6: Communion: Deepening Communication and Mutual Influence you will learn to focus your energy to affect others and to create and work collaboratively. In Chapter 7: Discovering and Endowing Circumstances, the techniques that you learned in Part I will become more detailed and specific by a multisensory approach to bringing to life Given Circumstances. Chapter 8: Nonverbal Action: Communicating through Behavior and Chapter 11: Verbal Action: Communicating with Words and Subtext form the heart of your training in Psychophysical Action, Stanislavsky's key for actors. Chapter 9: Embodying Voice will be an introduction to your vocal instrument, and Chapter 10: Activating Speech will introduce you to some basics of articulation and use of speech. Chapter 12: Orchestrating Emotions, respecting the wide variety of actors' emotional instruments, will offer you numerous tools to activate and focus your emotions, while respecting the wide variety of actors' emotional instruments.

CHAPTER 6

Communion: Deepening Communication and Mutual Influence

"The meeting of two personalities is like the contact of two chemical substances: if there is any reaction, both are transformed."[1]

—Carl Gustav Jung

Primary Elements of Action Actively Explored in This Chapter
Communion, mutual influence, imagination, images, public solitude

Related Acting Techniques Investigated
Spatial relationships, status

- What Is Communion?
- What Is Mutual Influence?
- Mental Action: Thoughts, Willpower, and Intention
- Improving Your Mental Game: Effective Use of Your Imagination
- How Can You Create Images That Impact You Most Strongly?
  - Exercise 6.1: Communicating Mental Imagery
  - Exercise 6.2: The Numbers Game
  - Exercise 6.3: "Row, Row, Row Your Boat..." Communion through Volume and Tempo
  - Exercise 6.4: Group Mirroring
- Spatial Relationship: Using Your Body to Communicate Relationships
  - Exercise 6.5: Communicating Relationships through the Language of the Body
  - Exercise 6.6: Communicating Attitude
  - Exercise 6.7: Exploring Space with Movement and Sound
  - Exercise 6.8: Endowing Imaginary Objects
  - Exercise 6.9: My Grandmother's Attic: A Silent Group Improvisation
  - Exercise 6.10: Sharing Images with Prana
  - Exercise 6.11: Communicating Relationships, Events, and Meaning
  - Exercise 6.12: The Rope Bridge: A Dynamic Exercise in Ensemble Communion
- A Note about Communication with Oneself: Public Solitude
  - Exercise 6.13 The Mystic Coin
  - Exercise 6.14 Patterns and Cues: An Ensemble Exercise

[1] Jung, C.G. *Modern Man in Search of a Soul*. Trans. W.S. Dell and Cary F. Baynes. London: Routledge ([1933] 2001).

While sitting in a train, bus, or car with the windows rolled up, have you ever had the sensation that someone outside of your vehicle was watching you, and when you look, there *is* someone looking at you? That is a confirmation of your *intuitive sense*. What is this feeling and how is it produced? How can you harness it to affect your scene partners and the audience? In this chapter we will attempt to answer this question, as well as examine concepts and communication exercises that will prepare you to experience communion.

What Is Communion?

Communion and *communication* are terms used interchangeably. Communion is mutual influence—the ability to affect another person through a variety of verbal and nonverbal forms of communication. In Chapter 4, you were introduced to some of the ideas from yoga that were foundational to Stanislavsky's System. Stanislavsky's use of communion most likely related to his interest in *yoga* and the radiating of prana, life-force energy (as introduced in Chapter 4). He sought to transmit prana through thought and action, without obvious visual signals.

In Chapter 3, you began to explore some breathing, meditation, and visualization techniques to create a more focused concentration. In this chapter you will investigate some of the ways that Stanislavsky sought to use meditation and visualization in an attempt to bring about communion. According to Dr. Sharon Carnicke, the actors were asked to concentrate deeply and then by means of strong inner intention, to send out rays of *prana*:

> [Stanislavsky] uses prana to ground his analysis of communication in theatre. In a successful performance, he explains, rays of Prana pass between actors and their partners and between actors and their audiences, thus prana becomes the vehicle for infecting the spectator with the artist's emotion.[2]

A few actors were able to achieve the desired result, but for others it remained too abstract. Stanislavsky was attempting to re-create a phenomenon he had witnessed and personally experienced while in performance: the seeming ability to know another actor's thoughts and feelings without any apparent visible sign of expression. When this did occur, Stanislavsky regarded it to be the highest level of communication, which he called *spiritual communion*. Spiritual communion goes beyond verbal communication to include the ways we influence one another through nonverbal communication: thought, gestures, body language, and exchanges of energy (see also "Flow of Energy" in Chapter 5).

Communion involves three primary *circles of attention*. The first is with oneself, as in *public solitude*. The next is communion between actors, and the final, larger circle extends beyond the footlights to engulf the audience. Later, we will discuss an even larger circle, which is the artists' embracing of their culture and society in their artistic expressions. In order to achieve communion, you must first focus on the practical elements of *communication* between people. Communication between you and another actor arises when you each successfully influence one another. This process is called, simply, *mutual influence*.

---

[2] Sharon M. Carnicke, *Stanislavsky in Focus* (Amsterdam: Harwood Academic, 1998), 141.

6 COMMUNION: DEEPENING COMMUNICATION

Figure 6.1 Mutual influence. Dave Ausem and Christi Berlane in *The Hobbit* based on the novel by J. R. R. Tolkien. Photo: Yoshinori Tanokura

"To be in communion with another person on stage means to be aware of that person's presence, to make sure that he hears and understands what you tell him and that you hear and understand what he tells you. That means mutual influence."[3]

—Sonia Moore

What Is Mutual Influence?

Just as in life, communion is established when you and your acting partners honestly strive to affect and influence one another in order to bring about a reaction. You may have heard of Isaac Newton's third law of motion that states that for every action, there must be an equal and opposite reaction. This is sometimes called the law of cause and effect, and it really holds true for acting. Because the circumstances of a play are imaginary, the reality must be created through interactions between you and your scene partners, as your characters. *Mutual influence* occurs when, together, actors strive to affect one another in order to bring about a desired reaction in the moment.

Observe how people relate to one another when they really need to communicate an important idea, or when they really want something from one another. Notice how they use their eyes to watch the reactions of the other person, how they look for a response and how they interpret the responses they observe. Pay attention to how their faces and gestures express understanding or misunderstanding, frustration or excitement. There are three means by which we can influence our partners: thoughts, physical actions, and words (voice and speech).

---

[3] Sonia Moore, *The Stanislavski System: The Professional Training of an Actor*, 2nd ed. (New York: Penguin, 1960; 1978), 41.

Mental Action: Thoughts, Willpower, and Intention

"We have the power to create our own reality with the thoughts and images in our minds. The images, feelings, and sound we have in our mind's eye have incredible power."[4]

—Kay Porter and Judy Foster

As an actor, you must master the ability to express your thoughts by means of subtle physical behaviors: a glance, a pause, or a gesture. Great *willpower* and strong *intention* are both needed to be able to concentrate and focus on the transmission of thoughts through *mental action*. When you have a strong desire to communicate, you find that you are able, by subtle actions, to transmit and receive thoughts and feelings. Your ultimate aim is to influence the audience, and this can be achieved when you actively influence your partners during a performance.

When you think deeply on stage, you can create an *inner environment* or *mood* that is felt by others. We all have the experience of being in the presence of someone who makes us feel good just to be with them; conversely, there are times a complete stranger enters our sphere and we get a deep gut-level feeling of unease. We influence one another by our moods and the inner environment we carry with us. In life, mutual influence occurs spontaneously and naturally; however, in the artificial environment of the theatre or soundstage of a motion picture company, you must intentionally strive to bring it about.

Improving Your Mental Game: Effective Use of Your Imagination

In any high-performance activity, such as sports or acting, artists and athletes know that reaching peak performance or inspiration requires getting your mind in the game. A big part of this for athletes and actors is visualization. You must work on mental focus and agility, even as you develop your physical instrument in terms of body and voice. You began to explore conscious use of images and imagination in chapters 2, 3, and 4. Now you will learn to focus your imagination through visualization to affect yourself and to affect others.

According to mental athletics trainer for the Olympics Dr. Kay Porter,

> The reason visualization/imagery works is that when you imagine yourself performing flawlessly and doing exactly what you want, you are physiologically creating neural patterns in your brain, just as if the body had done the activity. These patterns are like small tracks engraved in the brain cells. It has been demonstrated that athletes who have never performed a certain routine or move can after a few weeks of specific visualization practice perform the move. As in physical practice, mental 'practice makes perfect' too![5]

---

[4] Kay Porter and Judy Foster, *Visual Athletics: Visualizations for Peak Sports Performance* (Dubuque, IA: Wm. C. Brown, 1990), 17.
[5] Ibid.

Images seem to affect performance primarily in two ways:

1. Imagining yourself performing a task successfully seems to boost confidence and persistence (how diligently and long you pursue an activity to make it successful), and
2. Imagining yourself performing a task in detail seems to help with training your body to do that task; although it does not replace physical training it can enhance it.

How Can You Create Images That Impact You Most Strongly?

Shane Murphy, in an article titled "Models of Imagery in Sport Psychology," suggests that the most effective use of images has three parts:

> The first part is that the image itself must be a centrally arousing sensation so it is more like the real world. It has all the attributions of a sensation, the only difference is that it is internal. This image provides the imager with so much realism that it can enable him or her to interact with the image as if it were the real world. Secondly, there exists a somatic response. Therefore, the very act of imaging results in psychophysiological changes in the body. Finally, the third part of the image is the actual meaning of the image. Every image has a signification meaning and that specific meaning can imply something different to each individual. Since every person has a unique background and upbringing, the actual internal image can be quite different for each individual, even though the set of imagery instructions are the same.[6]

You have already been using images since the beginning of this training. In the following exercises, you will begin to learn to use your mind and mental imagery in more purposeful, directed, and specific ways.

Exercise 6.1: Communicating Mental Imagery (SM)

Purpose: This exercise helps actors both participating and observing to understand the level of detail needed to effectively communicate mental images (impressions made by any of the senses).

Guidelines: (Please refer to Chapter 5 for the introduction to working with Imagination, Visualization and a Film of Images) This exercise can be done with only one or two actors as an example or by the entire class if you have time.

- Picture someone you know very well.
- Then, sit facing the class and describe the person you see in your mind in every possible detail: height, age, ethnicity, coloring, facial features, physique, personality, dress, and manner.
- Those observing should notice the interplay between the image in the mind and the expression of that image to others. Where is the focus of the eyes, for example, in each instance?

---

[6] Shane M. Murphy, "Models of Imagery in Sport Psychology: A Review," *Journal of Mental Imagery* 14, nos. 3 & 4 (1990): 153–172.

6.1 Reflection Journal—Communicating Mental Imagery

The class reflects on the person described: Did you also see images of the person who was being described? What is your sense of this person? Does he or she seem like a good person? What kinds of feelings were conveyed? Did the description remind you of anyone you have seen or know? Notice how we are influenced on both conscious and subconscious levels the more clearly an image is described through details. Take some time to think about this and jot down your impressions in your creative journal. Time permitting, a brief discussion might follow. The person doing the exercise should reflect on where they were and were not able to see the person clearly. If time allows, assess how this lined up with what the class pictured clearly.

Exercise 6.2: The Numbers Game (Ensemble Exercise) (SM/Peter Brook)[7]

Purpose: This exercise is fun and develops several acting skills: concentration, focus, listening, cooperation, and teamwork.

Guidelines: Stand or sit in together in a very close circle. Hold the hands with the persons next to you and close your eyes.

- Keeping your eyes closed, count aloud from 1 to 15, with only one person speaking at a time. This is the goal. If there is any overlapping or interruption—that is, two or more people speak at the same time—then the group must start the exercise again from the beginning.
- Repeat the exercise reciting the alphabet.

6.2 Reflection Journal—Numbers Game

Were you able to get through the entire sequence of numbers or the alphabet without a mistake? What did you need to do in order to achieve the goal? How did the exercise affect your listening? Did you have a sense of everyone working together?

Exercise 6.3: "Row, Row, Row Your Boat..." Communion through Volume and Tempo (MK)[8]

Purpose: To control and influence the physical actions and decisions of one of your classmates and to create an awareness of a moment of spontaneous communication and inner realization by working together as a team.

---

[7] Bennett and French came to this exercise from different sources.
[8] MK stands for Marsha Kimmell of The Next Stage in San Francisco. She is primarily a Viola Spolin–based improvisation teacher who also draws on many other traditions and invents many of her own exercises.

6 COMMUNION: DEEPENING COMMUNICATION

Guidelines:
- One person, "the actor," leaves the room and waits to be called back in by the group, which we will call "the director."
- The group decides on three or four actions they wish the actor to accomplish on reentering the room. (Example: Enter and walk to the window, open the window, cross to the closet, take out a hat, and put it on the instructor's head.)
- The group quietly begins to sing, "Row, row, row your boat . . . " (or any other repetitive children's song or rhyme will do).
- The actor must attempt to figure out on his feet what he is to accomplish. As he moves closer to the desired action the director/group must work together to sing louder and more energetically, perhaps at a faster tempo, in order to control the actor's movements. If the actor moves away from the predetermined direction or task, the group must modulate their voices by singing more slowly and softly.
- It is the group's responsibility to work as an ensemble so as not to send mixed signals to the actor. When the actor accomplishes the desired series of simple actions the game may be repeated with another actor and new set of actions. (**Note:** Choose no more than four actions. It is great fun and more challenging to make them as illogical as possible.)

6.3 *Reflection Journal—"Row, Row, Row Your Boat"*

Were you able to work as a team to sing in unison and communicate to the actor the predetermined direction and necessary sequence of actions? As the actor, can you describe the moment you seemed to intuitively know what direction you were to move in and what action you were required to perform? Was this moment an "aha moment" of realization? (**Note:** Record that feeling of knowingness both in your journal and your memory.)

Exercise 6.4: Group Mirroring (VS)[9]

Purpose: Communion through unified movement and soft focus

Guidelines:
- Stand in a circle.
- Try to see each person without looking directly at anyone. It is best to use a "soft focus," as you might do to see the twinkling holiday lights that look slightly fuzzy and diffused, but be very alert to the slightest nuance of movement.
- Notice subtle movements of others and respond to them subtly at first, in

---

[9] Viola Spolin, creator of Theatre Games, about which she has written numerous books, but this one was passed on through the oral tradition and is widely used in theatre training.

your own way or by imitation. Try to follow the flow of the movements you sense but keep your focus on the entire group.
- As a group, see if you can get a sense of what movements you are doing together without looking directly at anyone.
- Eventually you may find that the movements of the group become unified.
- Try not to lead or follow but to stay tuned into the group.
- If your instructor can easily tell that someone is leading, release and start again.

6.4 *Reflection Journal—Group Mirroring*

What was your experience of this exercise? Were you able to resist the temptation of leading by staying in tune with the group?

Spatial Relationship: Using Your Body to Communicate Relationships

You can express relationships with other people with your body. Spatial relationships generate meaning to an audience regardless of the actor's intention. It is important to understand universal human expression, and also those expressions ascribed meaning based on cultural conditioning. Actors will be communicating with spatial relationship whether intending to or not. Some of the key factors affecting spatial relationships include: proximity to others; groupings; and differences in levels, gestures, and visual focus. The meaning of spatial relationships is also impacted by gender, age, race, culture and religion.

Spatial relationships can also be driven by intention: We can ignore someone by briskly walking past them and greeting another person whom we like more; we can

Figure 6.2 The opera *Sino alla Morte* at the University of California, San Diego.
Photo: Jim Carmody

6 COMMUNION: DEEPENING COMMUNICATION

keep a distance from someone we distrust; we can take sides with an ally by sitting next to her in an argument; or we can threaten an enemy by invading his space and looking him in the eye. There are innumerable possibilities for expressing emotions, allegiances, or status without saying a word.

You need to explore, use, and understand the impact of the silent *Language of the Body* (your unconscious physical and tonal actions that communicate universally to all people regardless of time, place, or culture), as well as culturally specific adaptations of common body-language communications.

As discussed above, emotions and states of being, intuitive feelings, and sensory sensations are also experienced and expressed through the body. We express our joy at seeing former classmates at a reunion, disappointment with someone, fear of an argument with a coworker, or longing to embrace a lover. How we stand, move, approach, retreat, and touch, or any physical action expresses to others our attitude, feelings, and relationships.

Exercise 6.5: Communicating Relationships through the Language of the Body (SM)

Purpose: To develop specificity in relationships and allow them to color simple actions.

Guidelines:
- Build in your mind an imaginary relationship with everyone else; deciding who that person is to you, whether or not you know her, what the status of that person is in relation to you, what you think and feel about the individual, and whether or not you like her.
- The action is to greet someone: One person at a time greets each individual in silence and must find typical behavior in the form of walking, gestures, and facial expressions to clearly express the circumstances you have selected.
- The class then gives feedback by sharing what relationships were clearly expressed and projected.

6.5 Reflection Journal—Communicating Relationships

In your observation, what relationships were you able to clearly express and project? What relationships did you get a clear picture of that others were communicating?

Exercise 6.6: Communicating Attitude (Ensemble) (PGB)

Purpose: To learn to endow relationships without words or sound

Guidelines:
- Begin to walk around the room, and as you pass one another make eye contact. Look directly into one another's eyes and pause a moment.

- At that moment make up an imaginary attitude toward that person and emit your thought while receiving theirs.
- Make no facial or physical gesture, just the thought.
- Continue to walk around the room until you have sent and received at least one thought to each person.

6.6 Reflection Journal—Communicating Attitude

Now, share with the group what you experienced: Did you pick up what was sent to you? How did that make you feel, and what sensations went through your body? Anything else?

Exercise 6.7: Exploring Space with Movement and Sound (Ensemble) (PGB)

Purpose: To create a group dynamic for ensemble communication: The first step of the exercise is to explore the space between people without making physical contact. The second step is to explore sound and movement in order to experience communion as an ensemble.

Guidelines:
- Begin to walk around the space and explore every area of the room while simultaneously exploring movements with your entire body: arms, legs, feet, chest, buttocks, torso, head and neck; for example, walk backward and sideways, run, skip, jump, creep, crawl, roll. Change tempo and rhythm with each new movement and exploration.
- Now continuously move toward the center of the space and begin to explore all the above combinations of movement while exploring the spaces between one another without any physical contact. Take your time and be aware of everyone around you. Continue to explore all possible elevations: Whenever someone near you goes down on the floor, you rise up; if someone crawls, you jump; and whenever there is an empty space near you, move into it.
- As the group becomes comfortable with this phase of the exercise, introduce sound into the mix. Begin to hum aloud together. No melody, just a humming sound. Allow the sound to affect your movements and listen to one another closely. Once you are all in tune together begin to use the vowel sounds of *ah, eh, ee, I, oh,* and *oo*. (See Appendix VIa for articulation and guidelines for vowel sounds.)
- Work as an ensemble and let the continuous flow of movement and sound take over the group for a sustained period of time until everyone gradually comes to a silent rest.

6.7 Reflection Journal—Space, Sound, and Movement

This exercise provides an opportunity to discuss the group dynamic of intuitive ensemble communication. Did you observe your partners and gradually come to feel that at times you were all working together as one unit? What was your experience of the exercise?

Exercise 6.8: Endowing Imaginary Objects (SM)

Purpose: to use *visualization* as a tool to explore relationships within an imaginary environment and with specific objects, creating sincerity and depth.

Guidelines: Create an imaginary situation in your mind.

- Sit back and relax, close your eyes, and take a few deep breaths. Imagine yourself to be searching an attic, basement, garage, or large closet where you once played as a child. Many of your old childhood toys, dolls, and games are there. Maybe some of your clothes, scrapbooks, or furniture still remain. How would you treat the space? This need not be a real space but can be entirely imagined or partly imagined and partly related to as a real place you know, or a real place you know but where you may never have had this experience. You are going to create a new experience in your imagination, but you may draw on things that you know as they arise spontaneously.
- How would you treat the objects within it? These objects need not be from your actual childhood but you do need to endow them with meaning and memories from your imagination. Imagine yourself picking up an old teddy bear, what feelings does it evoke? Perhaps there is a photo album. How does it feel under your touch? What sensations arise as you gently turn the pages and focus on the pictures of you as an infant, a young child? What events come to mind? Your graduation? Your prom? Are there things in your imaginary attic that you dislike or never saw before? See specific images, and as you focus your attention on them allow a relationship to develop.
- Do personal, analogous memories and feelings arise from your subconscious? If so, notice how your relationship to the attic room has expanded and become more real, more substantial. Become consciously aware of how you see your body in spatial relationship to everything around you.

6.8 Reflection Journal—Endowing Imaginary Objects

Now, open your eyes and record in your creative journal your personal reflections. As always, after the period of reflection and if time allows, discuss your observations.

Exercise 6.9: My Grandmother's Attic: A Silent Group Improvisation (PGB)

Purpose: Learning to endow objects with meaning and using them to communicate.

Guidelines: This exercise can be done individually or with the entire group, depending on the size of the group and time allotted. It can also be accomplished with a few students on stage at a time. The students are to set up the stage with props that they can then use to enact the previous imaginary exercise in the "Attic."

- "My grandmother's attic": Use the "magic if" and create specific circumstances about the location, time of day, time of year, who the other people are to you and what was your relationship to them and to your grandmother.
- Decide on where you are coming from, why you are there, and what it is you desire to accomplish in the attic.
- Justify and connect your treatment of the objects and make it clear to your classmates what your attitudes and feelings are in relationship to them.
- Set up your acting area as you see it in your mind and use real props. If you do not have a prop then treat another prop as if it were the object you need. (Avoid the use of imaginary objects for this stage of the exercise.)
- Your goal is to focus on the objects so truthfully that you begin to communicate your feelings with them and allow the objects to influence you as well. Send and receive imaginary currents of energy.

6.9 *Reflection Journal—My Grandmother's Attic*

Reflect on the exercise and then evaluate how effectively you were able to interact and actually commune with the objects. Did analogous feelings and memories from the past spontaneously arise? How did your physical behavior influence your thoughts and feelings?

Exercise 6.10: Sharing Images with Prana (Partners) (LS/KSS/PGB)

Purpose: Actors must become sensitive to one another's thoughts and feelings. This is an exercise in sending and receiving vibrational energy by means of strong intention. This is an exercise Stanislavsky and his collaborator in the first studio of the Moscow Art Theatre, Leopold Shulerzisky, developed to try to feel and communicate prana. It is important not to push or strain to send a thought, as tension defeats the purpose of the exercise. It is a mental discipline of will and intention that we are striving to cultivate, so never feel that you need to force it.

6 COMMUNION: DEEPENING COMMUNICATION

Guidelines:

- Bring your chairs into the acting arena and place them opposite one another about three feet apart. Sit down facing one another and decide who is A and who is B.
- Begin by taking a few deep breaths.
- Use your internal monitor to mentally scan your body for any points of tension or pain while continuing to breathe into those areas with long, deep breaths and slowly exhaling through your mouth.
- When you feel quite comfortable, place your consciousness (inner gaze), at the point between the eyebrows, but keep your eyes open. Imagine a place you lived, a house or apartment, it doesn't matter, and in your imagination take a tour of it, noticing every small detail. Take your time. Recall the people and events that took place. Sense the atmosphere and mood that arises from the environment.
- A, gaze into your partner B's eyes and, without any tension or effort, will yourself to open up and share your thoughts, sensations, and feelings of this memory with your partner. Make no conscious attempt to read your partner's mind, simply open up and send your energy while simultaneously receiving your partner's energy. Observe what you are experiencing.
- Reverse and have B communicate her images to A.

6.10 *Reflection Journal—Sharing Images*

After three minutes has passed, the instructor asks the students to share with their partners what they experienced, then asks who would like to share their experience with the group.

Exercise 6.11: Communicating Relationships, Events, and Meaning

Purpose: To use your eyes and body language to transmit thoughts and feelings to your partners. (Never force facial expressions, as that becomes indicative (fake) and creates tension.) The goal is to establish nonverbal communication through mental and physical action.

Guidelines for all 6.11 exercises: The improvisations are to be performed by three persons, and primarily in justified silence.

Exercise 6.11A: At the Theatre (SM)[10]

Guidelines:
- Three persons are sitting in a theatre at a live performance of a very serious play. Two of you are on a date.
- The third person is alone and finds that one person of the couple seems familiar to him. His task is to try to remember where he could have met this person.
- Think of real places, parties, or other situations where you may have met. Use personal images of people you know in real life.
- When you remember who the person is and where you met, your objective changes. You attempt to get the person's attention without alerting his/her date.
- Find subtle and truthful ways to accomplish your task.
- At the same time, be clear about the images you are seeing on the stage at the imaginary event you are attending.
- Be aware of each other's behavior and react to it psychophysically, as you would in life.

Note to Students: Spend two or three minutes with your scene partners prior to the improvisation deciding on what performance you are watching. Be specific: Where in the theatre are you seated? The couple may discuss their relationship; i.e., first date, married, etc. The "third party" must not reveal beforehand whom he or she is going to recognize or attempt to contact.

Exercise 6.11B: Two Spies and a Detective (SM)

Guidelines:
- Three persons are at a busy public place, such as an airport or bus terminal. Two are spies and one is a detective.
- One spy has a twofold task: try and assess who is the contact spy and pass a secret microchip to him.
- The contact spy who is to receive the chip must attempt to figure out who of the other two persons onstage is to pass the document to him.
- The detective's objective is to prevent the passing of the chip and make an arrest (but he can only make an arrest if he catches them in the act).

Note: The instructor will tell each actor who he is and what his task is privately. The students may decide where the action takes place but must not reveal themselves or their task to one another. The action ends with the arrest made by the detective who may say, "You are under arrest!" The improvisation may end if both spies succeed in passing the secret chip and exit before they are caught.

---

[10] Adapted and developed by PGB but based on improvisations outlined in Moore, Sonia and taught to Bennett at Moore's studio in New York. Sonia Moore, *The Stanislavski System: The Professional Training of an Actor*, 2nd ed. (New York: Penguin, 1978).

6 COMMUNION: DEEPENING COMMUNICATION

Exercise 6.11C: The Eleventh Hour (SM/PGB)

Guidelines: (3 relatives plus two guards)
- Three persons are closely related. One is in prison and is awaiting execution within the hour. The prisoner has appealed to the governor for a stay of execution and that two closely related friends or family members be allowed to convey the governor's decision.
- There is silence as he waits for the two to enter the visiting room or cell.
- As they enter the area they are too deeply moved to speak.
- Everything must be conveyed with the eyes and language of the body.
- Each actor may speak one time if he so chooses. He may say only, "I love you."

Note: The instructor informs the two visitors in secret whether or not the stay of execution has been granted. The task is to convey relationships, attitudes, and feelings without words, to transmit images and thoughts, and mutually influence one another.

6.11 Reflection Journal—Communicating Relationships, Events, and Meaning

In every exercise above that you had a chance to experience or observe, what did you discover about nonverbal communication? How were relationships communicated? What helped to give them depth and meaning? When did you feel most and least connected? For those observing, when did you see the most and least connection between the actors onstage?

Exercise 6.12: The Rope Bridge: A Dynamic Exercise in Ensemble Communion (PGB)

Purpose: To establish an Ensemble Communion; To truthfully use your imagination and to build circumstances, see images, use your memory of sensations, and express relationships.

Guidelines: The Given Circumstances:

- While seated or lying down on the floor, close your eyes and relax all of your muscles from head to toe. Take a few deep breaths and scan your body for tension, inhaling into the points of tension and releasing the tension with your exhalation.
- With closed eyes, use vivid imagination to build the following situation: You are on an expedition to search for the lost tomb of a Mayan king in the jungles of the Yucatán. Be specific as to your area of scientific interest, or your alternate role on the expedition.
- You and your comrades have been hiking through the jungle for days, and

have come to an impassable gorge, which is at least 1,000 feet deep. At the bottom of the gorge is a raging river. The only means of crossing the gorge is by an old rope bridge. The bridge is beginning to fall apart and has become unsafe. Its ropes are made of rotting twine, and the wooden planks are fragile, and many are missing.

- **The immediate problem:** How can I ensure that everyone crosses the bridge safely?
- Make sure that the imaginary wooden planks are in the same position as those whom you follow, and that the ropes you hold on to are at the same height. Observe one another carefully.
- The environment is also unsafe, with snakes, poisonous insects, and hostile natives. The atmosphere is unbearably hot, humid, and thick with flying insects. Although you have been traveling for two days, you are still far from the supposed location of the tomb as shown on your guide map. You are tired, exhausted, and you may be hungry, injured, or ill.
- Without discussion, in your mind build an imaginary relationship with each of the members of your party. See them clearly in your mind and decide whom you like and dislike and why. Why are you on this expedition? What do you hope to personally gain from it?
- You must establish silent communion with everyone by watching each person and making sure that you are all working together so that the movement of the bridge and crossing it is an ensemble effort.

6.12 Reflection Journal—The Rope Bridge

Were you able to observe others and work together as an ensemble, a team? If not, why? Were you able to be consistent with your sense memory and establish the circumstances clearly in your mind? Did you see images in your imagination? Did you have real emotional responses to the images, imaginary circumstances, or the other people? If you were to do it again, what would you choose to do differently?

A Note about Communication with Oneself: Public Solitude

Public solitude is the name given to the state where the actor/character behaves as if she is completely alone while acting in front of a live audience. In this state the actor deeply concentrates upon the inner life of the character while simultaneously inviting the audience into her innermost thoughts and feelings. In realistic acting there is the concept of the *fourth wall*, as though the fourth wall of the setting was just pulled up so the audience can peer in. Although the concept of the fourth wall is still popularly used, the System moved beyond this concept to allow the continual interchange of energy and communication between actor and audience during a performance, even if the character does not directly acknowledge the audience. Even in this style, you must be expressive and responsive to the audience, remembering to project ideas, voice, and emotions to them.

In early explorations it is enough that you seem to get lost in the situation of the improvisation and seem to forget the audience is even watching; however, as you progress in your studies, your consciousness begins to expand, you feel comfortable

6 COMMUNION: DEEPENING COMMUNICATION

with your audience and want to include them in your *circle of attention*. While in public solitude you must maintain a dual consciousness—a sense of being alone and yet aware that you are in public as well. (Refer to "Dual Perspectives," first explored in Chapter 3.)

The circle of attention is like a bubble of awareness that you can keep only on your internal monitor, expand to include your scene partner or partners, or expand even further to include the audience. You include the audience by *opening up*, which means allowing them to see your face and gestures (rather than hiding both by turning away), by *vocal projection*, speaking at a volume that can be heard at the back row even if your scene is intimate words of love to someone a few inches from you, and by *projecting your film of images* from your imagination onto a screen that is further from you and encompasses the audience.

Perhaps one of the most difficult stage actions to perform is the *soliloquy* (speaking aloud to oneself in public). Communication requires a subject and an object, but what is our subject and object when we are alone? Shakespeare often used the soliloquy as a device to inform the spectator of the character's inner landscape, his thoughts and conflicts. There are times when Hamlet alternately speaks to himself and to the audience, further complicating the task.

Figure 6.3 While in public solitude you must maintain a dual consciousness—a sense of being alone and yet aware that you are in public as well. Janel Martinez in *Polaroid Stories* by Naomi Iizuka.
Photo: Charles Perry Hebard, courtesy of East Stroudsburg University

Public solitude is not a private moment for the actor in which she may disregard the audience, that would be self-indulgent and break the line of communication; it is a moment when the character reveals her inner life to the audience in silent action or through a monologue. How can we communicate without being able to direct our words to someone else? Stanislavsky struggled with this same question and found a very sensible and simple solution. He had his mind speak to his solar plexus, or heart; that is, his rational, conscious self interacted with his emotional self: "I took the center in my head to represent consciousness and the solar plexus to represent emotion. . . So that my head was in communication with my heart. 'Well then,' I said to myself, 'Let them talk.' My subject and object have been found."[11]

It takes a bit of practice to become proficient with this device, but it is a valuable tool for the actor.

---

[11]Konstantin Stanislavsky, *An Actor's Work*, trans. Jean Benedetti (London: Routledge, 2009), 233.

Exercise 6.13: The Mystic Coin (PGB)

Purpose: To strengthen the power of *intention*, deepen *concentration and focus* upon an object in an attempt to influence the object through *mental action*.

Guidelines:

- Bring your chairs into the middle of the acting arena and place them in as round a circle as possible. Leave about ten inches of space between each chair.
- Let go of all muscular tension in your body as you've been practicing in the previous chapters. Clear your mind and breathe deeply several times with very slow exhalations. Stay still and silent for a few moments, focusing your attention on the point between your eyebrows in the frontal lobe of the brain.
- The instructor places a large coin in the middle of the circle. Everyone focuses on the coin without any tension. Imagine that you are sending your energy into the coin and that the coin's atomic and molecular structure is visible to you. Imagine the spaces between the molecules. There is energy produced by the coin as the atoms and molecules move about.
- Invite the coin's energy to come to you and affect your sensations. Send your energy and imagine that this interaction is actually taking place.
- (Note to Instructor:) Without any tension or effort, and in unison, the group is asked to direct its collective will to the coin and to ask it to move and rise up from the floor.
- After a few minutes ask someone to enter into the circle and do something with the coin. Let two or three persons touch and handle the coin.

6.13 *Reflection Journal—The Mystic Coin*

What was your experience? What thoughts, feelings, and physical sensations did you have? What mental images, pictures, personal associations came to mind? What did you feel when the coin was first touched by someone in the group, etc.?

Exercise 6.14: Patterns and Cues: An Ensemble Exercise[12] (San Francisco Mime Troupe)[13]

Purpose: To develop ensemble communication by remembering patterns of movement (similar to remembering blocking and choreography) and patterns of speech by careful listening (similar to line cues in a text) even when the two do not directly line up.

---

[12] Adapted from R. G. Davis, SF Mime Troupe Workshop Association for Theatre in Higher Education Conference, San Francisco, 2005.

[13] French learned this at a workshop at the Association for Theatre in Higher Education from R.G. Davis and other ensemble members of the San Francisco Mime Troupe. They have performed for general audiences—particularly working class people—for free in parks across the country since 1961.

Exercise 6.14A: Physical Pattern Sequence

Guidelines: Start with a ball (it can be from dodge ball up to American soccer/world football size).

- Stand in a circle.
- Person A with the ball crosses the circle and hands it to person B while A says his/her own name (if this is only the first or second class; otherwise, A can say person B's name instead).
- Person B does the same to person C, etc., until you have gone through the class.
- The actors need to remember whom they gave it to, as well as whom they received it from.
- Try to repeat the same pattern.
- Once the pattern is established, then the actors must anticipate their physical cue and arrive for the handoff while the ball is still in the center of the circle. Thus, the handoff now always happens in the center. Actors need to be aware of others' movement for their cues and avoid collisions.
- Increase the tempo until the exercise is really moving quickly.
- Try to remember this sequence while doing Exercise 6.14B below, as you will come back to it for Exercise 6.14C.

Exercise 6.14B: Verbal Sequence

- Person A starts a verbal sequence by stating the name of an animal. The actors to go second, third etc. in this pattern are not the same as in part A above. A different sequence of actors must ensue.
- Each subsequent actor also states his own animal.
- Again you must remember which animal is the cue to say your animal.
- Repeat the pattern a few times increasing the tempo each time.

Exercise 6.14C: Combining Physical and Verbal Patterns

- Start the physical pattern again keeping the ball always in the middle and anticipating it.
- A few actors into the physical pattern, actor A starts the verbal pattern.
- Now actors need to watch for the physical cue and listen for the verbal cue, which may come at a different point in the physical sequence each time.

Exercise 6.14D: More Complexity

- You can repeat this exercise at a later date, adding a third verbal sequence such as an additional verbal pattern of fruits or vegetables or any other familiar category.

Summary

In Chapter 6 you were introduced to the lofty goal of communion among people, and how by deepening your communication skills you could transmit to partners and an audience your thoughts and images. You delved into mutual influence and practiced exercises designed to increase your powers of will and intention. Spatial relationships were explored in order to increase the awareness of your body as a psychophysical instrument. Through the use of improvisational exercises you practiced with imaginary objects and learned how to apply the use of Prana, your life-force energy.

What is most important for you to remember is that the highest form of communication is spiritual communion, and that goal can only be accomplished within a safe and ethical creative space (as discussed in Chapter 4). In order for every individual actor to reach and reveal the inner workings of his own life and soul it is essential that everyone strive to keep the theatre free from negativity, gossip and other unprofessional behaviors that are the enemies of spiritual communion. The highest art can only be achieved through the highest desire for self-improvement. In her classes, Sonia Moore often said, "An actor needs a soldier's discipline … I consider good manners as part of an actor's creativity. When I was a young student at the Moscow Art Theatre, Stanislavsky often said to us, 'Ethics are simply good manners in the theatre.'"[14]

New Theatre Terms, Concepts, and Artists

Terms used in the Stanislavsky System are in italics.

- ☐ *communication*
- ☐ *communion*
- ☐ R.G. Davis
- ☐ *intention*
- ☐ intuitive sense
- ☐ Marsha Kimmell
- ☐ *mental action*
- ☐ mutual influence
- ☐ San Francisco Mime Troupe
- ☐ *spiritual communion*
- ☐ Viola Spolin
- ☐ *willpower (volition)*

Interdisciplinary Experts

- ☐ Shane Murphy

---

[14]Relayed by Moore to Bennett repeatedly in classes and rehearsals as he assisted her for seven years.

CHAPTER 7

Discovering and Endowing Circumstances

"'If' triggers off creative work. . . . 'If' is a spur to a dormant imagination, and the Given Circumstances provide the substance for it. Together and separately they help bring about the step forward."[1]
—Konstantin Stanislavsky

Primary Elements of Action Actively Explored in This Chapter

Given circumstances, "magic if," justification, inner monologue, endowment, status

- The "Magic If"
- Revisiting Justification
- Why Is It Difficult to Justify (Give Purpose to) Your Actions When First Studying Acting Technique?
- Inner Monologue (revisited)
- The Given Circumstances
- Who ("I Am" or "I Exist" Revisited)
- Status
- Endowment: To Treat As
- ☐ Exercise 7.1A: Assuming and Conveying Status
- ☐ Exercise 7.1B: Endowing and Receiving Status
- What (Action/Task)
- When
- Where
- With Whom (Relationships)
- Why and What For
- ☐ Exercise 7.2: Getting What You Want
- Where From and Where To (Two More Aspects of Where)
- Discovering the How
- Group Conditioning Exercises: Experiencing the Given Circumstances
- ☐ Exercise 7.3: Run, Stop, and Justify
- ☐ Exercise 7.4: Disobeying Hands with Images and W.E.D.G.A.G.
- ☐ Exercise 7.5: Three Separate Movements

---

[1] Konstantin Stanislavski, *An Actor's Work*, trans. Jean Benedetti (London: Routledge, 2009), 52–53.

Figure 7.1 Suppose you were at a baseball stadium ...
Photo: Karoline Culler

Suppose you were at a baseball stadium. It's the ninth inning, the bases are loaded, and the atmosphere is tense. Suddenly there is an announcement over the speaker system that the game is to be interrupted and the stadium is to be cleared in a calm and orderly manner. Armed riot police run into the stadium, the players clear the field, and the announcer continues to urge people to slowly move towards the exits. What would you think? What would be your first physical response? What would you imagine and feel?

Since we were young children, we have been imagining what we would do if something or other happened. All emergency planning involves suppositions. When we did a fire drill at school, we considered, "How would we exit the building if there were a fire?" All planning or anticipation involves suppositions: "What should I bring on that trip?" "Where will I live if I get into that college or get that job?" Many of us have been asked or considered, "What would I do if I won the lottery?" Or we have considered, "What would I do if he asked me out?" or "If I could afford a car or a house, what kind would I buy?" Life is full of such suppositions.

The "Magic If"

Within our own lives we respond habitually in the manner that is most *fitting and typical* for us in the circumstances that arise. We don't have to think much about it. It's spontaneous. Sometimes it is unconscious; such as evaluating how and when to cross a busy intersection. We may more consciously evaluate what to prepare for dinner or how to dress for the party this evening. We discover a challenge or an obstacle, and we wonder and evaluate how to solve the problem. However, that is not the case while acting. As we discussed earlier in this book, whether on a movie set or theatrical stage, we act in an artificial environment; there is no real stimulus to action, no real reason to habitually behave in a spontaneous manner. Stanislavsky found that the supposition "What would I do if?" ignited the imagination and stimulated thought, feelings, and emotions. He called this supposition the "magic if."

When you ask, "What would I do *if* I were in this situation, at this very moment, and for the first time?" you evoke a strong psychological stimulus to your imagination. In other words, you begin to see a flood of relevant images in your mind. You also feel an *impulse to act,* and you can develop the awareness of this impulse as you grow as an actor. This impulse to respond within imaginary circumstances is a key to solving the core challenge of acting: how do you respond truthfully in imaginary circumstances? This is why Stanislavsky called it the "magic if."

The "magic if" is one of the prime devices you have on the road to discovering and selecting the most *fitting and typical* actions needed to bring a character to life. It is one of the most valuable devices in your Actor's Palette.

Revisiting Justification

We have already stated that *justification* means that you must mentally motivate each physical choice with a definite purpose. This is why justified behaviors are psychophysical *actions*. An unjustified action where you outwardly show a physical behavior but do not motivate it internally is called *indication*. Indication is empty and thus will not be believable. It also will not stir you or an audience to think or feel deeply. A purposeful, *justified* action is the very essence of behavior both in life and onstage; that is why action brings life to your acting. Practice in justification will be more deeply covered in Chapter 8: Nonverbal Action: Communicating through Behavior.

Why Is It Difficult to Justify (Give Purpose to) Your Actions When First Studying Acting Technique?

The answer is that there is no reason to behave naturally on stage as we do in life. The artificial environment is unfamiliar, and when you first enter it, your attempts feel awkward and unnatural. Under these circumstances we forget how to perform the simplest of life's ordinary tasks. This is due to the partial breakdown of the psychophysical connection between the mind and body when we begin to act in front of people. We find ourselves pretending and indicating. Our hands move too much, our voice and speech seems to be inadequate and unprepared for projection. We don't know how to use a microphone correctly, or how to act at an appropriate level for the camera; an audience frightens us, and we become paralyzed, forgetting our lines and blocking. We may have worked very hard on learning our lines, but because we have not connected them to any motivation, action, thoughts or emotions of the character arising out of the circumstances, they fly out of our heads under the self-consciousness of performing.

Inner Monologue (revisited)

How Do We Overcome Self-Consciousness?
When you replace your own fearful thoughts with the vivid images and thoughts of the character—the *inner monologue*—your self-consciousness will disappear, and you

will feel natural and comfortable in front of people. (Other methods of dealing with nervousness are covered in Chapter 3: The Creative State: Preparing for Inspiration, under "Stage fright.") In Chapter 3, you also explored seeing the images of the situation and allowing your body to respond in the "Waiting for the jury" exercise. Your *inner monologue* is composed actively in rehearsal using the language of the character, as revealed by the playwright, or in the case of an improvisation, entirely using the "magic if" for the imaginary situation. When a debate is going on in the character's mind, we use instead the term *inner dialogue*.

The actor needs to have continuous thoughts as the character in the situation. This is one of the key elements to keeping the character alive and responsive onstage. When the character's thoughts cease, he seems dead onstage. When you think as yourself, rather than as the character, you break the reality of the scene for the audience. For beginning actors, inner monologue is the answer to the question, "What do I do while the other character is speaking?" You think and allow those thoughts to be reflected through your spine and thus externally in subtle ways through your body. Inner monologue is also one of the most important techniques in acting for the camera (film or television) where the experience of the character must be conveyed in even subtler ways.

How Do We Know What a Character Might Be Thinking?

Each of us was born in different circumstances. Perhaps you were born in a large seaport city, in the suburbs, or on a farm, at home or in a hospital. Although you may have had no control over the physical circumstances of your birth, the environment directly affected you. Perhaps the most important influence was your family, the people who cared for and raised you, shaping your beliefs, attitudes, and values, or perhaps it was the social environment of the neighborhood or your early schooling.

Just as your life's circumstances condition your behavior, thoughts, and feelings, every aspect of your psychophysical behavior, thoughts, and feeling as a character are colored by the background and current situations the playwright has created. Only through studying and activating the imaginary circumstances of the play using the "magic if" can you begin to know what your character might be thinking.

The Given Circumstances

The circumstances of the play and your character's background, as given to you by the playwright, are called the *given circumstances* (In the theatre some people abbreviate this as the *givens*). The given circumstances gradually condition and transform the actor's behavior into the character's behavior within the context of the play or improvised scenario. In this way we justify our actions. The given circumstances ask the following questions:

- Who? (always begin by coming from yourself and gradually moving toward the character step-by-step, as if you were tailoring a suit of clothes to fit)
- What? (event, action, task, activity, stage business)
- When? (specific time of day, season of the year, era, period, epic etc.)
- Where (place, location, environment, culture)
- Why? (purpose, in terms of motivating forces)
- *What for?* (purpose, in terms of aim, goal, objective)

- *With whom?* (relationships)
- *Where from?* (the *before time*)
- *Where to?* (the *after time*)
- How? (what must be done at each moment to solve the problem)

By thoroughly answering these questions you begin to justify your physical behavior, thus creating purposeful and specific actions. Consider each of the given circumstances in greater detail:

Who ("I Am" or "I Exist" Revisited)

Who am I? Stanislavsky always insisted that we begin with ourselves and later expand to character. This is why in many early improvisations you explore them as yourself and add the complications of a character's point of view and responses after you have mastered some of the earlier techniques. When you are ready to approach character, it is helpful early on to make a list of the character's traits and to identify which of these are like you and which unlike you. You must *come from yourself*; this isn't to be confused with *playing yourself*. Your primary goal as an actor is to build a unique and living human being—a character—and in so doing, serve the playwright's and director's vision. In the same way that an orchestra strives to bring to life the composer's music, the actor strives to create the inner spiritual world and the physical expression of another living human being as imagined first by the playwright and secondarily by the actor as guided by the director.

Through the revelation of the character's wants, needs, desires, dreams, struggles, and goals, you will gradually come to identify with and understand the character. Step-by-step you will bring from yourself, your own organic resources and experiences, and move gradually from yourself to the character. You may need to do research or *observations* of people who are more like your character than you are (more on this can be found in Chapter 14: Active Analysis: Reconaissance of the Character).

Of course a key tool is your *imagination*. Using the "magic if", you imagine and try to empathize with what it would be like to walk in the character's shoes, to look out from his eyes. Achieving the state of "I am" or "I exist" in the character's given circumstances is the first prerequisite for building a character.

> "There is only one way, as I have already told you: ceaselessly to fulfill the basic goal of our art, and that consists in the creation of the life of the human spirit of a role in a play and in giving that life physical embodiment in an aesthetic, theatrical form."
>
> —Konstantin Stanislavsky[2]

The given circumstances of a play arise from the playwright's imagination and are expressed through the plot, language, and story. The circumstances encompass the entire imaginary life of the character and are deeply influenced by the personality and physicality of the actor assigned to the role. Once a role is assigned, it is your responsibility to investigate and explore the character's background, family history,

---

[2] Konstantin Stanislavsky, *An Actor's Work*, trans. Jean Benedetti (London: Routledge, 2009), 36.

origin of birth, ethnicity, nationality, racial characteristics, education, religious beliefs, political viewpoints, customs, relationships, and perhaps most important, formative experiences. In fact, everything that surrounds you during the rehearsal process also influences the play's circumstances: the director's interpretation of the play, the world the designers have created through scenery, costumes and makeup, sound and lighting, the manner and length of rehearsals, the ensemble of the physical plant of the theatre and architecture of the stage, the backstage crew, the house crew, the administrative staff, and, during a performance, the audience.

Methods of extracting the character information from the play, expanding it through imagination and active exploration are covered in detail in Chapter 14. In order to fully create a living human being in performance, you will begin with a thorough investigation of the play, its *active facts* and the *events* within which the character struggles against opposing forces to achieve a concrete *objective*.

In a play, the active facts tell you what is happening moment by moment; for example: I open the door with my key and enter the living room. I step out of the night rain and into the house. I see that the upstairs bedroom light is on. I recall turning it off when I left for work this morning. There is an uneasy feeling and chill in the house. I hear an unexpected noise coming from upstairs, and I stop to evaluate it. Feelings of dread and fear arise. I wonder if it is an intruder. I must make a decision, etc.

> **Note:** In an improvised scenario, we create the circumstances and then improvise the facts while on our feet (as opposed to being given the facts by the playwright or director). In improvisation, we do not work out the physical actions prior to going onstage, as we do in rehearsals for a play.

Status

The concept of *who* involves both character and relationship and an important attribute of both is *status*. This is how high or low you are on the pecking order (or as we say on the West Coast of Canada: the totem pole). There is role status; for example, you might have high status as a parent, boss, or queen, or low status as a child, employee, or servant. But often times, plays and films are about the reversal of status roles so that the kids get one over on the parents, the employee is smarter than the boss, or the servants find a way to make fun of the queen.

Status can be assumed or endowed or be a combination of both. Assumed status is when someone behaves as if they are better or higher in the social order than others. Endowed status is when others treat you as though you were higher or better. Endowment is a particularly important tool when students of similar ages, who are peers (equal status), are cast in roles that have extremely unequal status. Below are a couple of exercises to begin to consider the many ways we convey and endow status.

7 DISCOVERING AND ENDOWING CIRCUMSTANCES

Endowment: To Treat As

Endowment is the actor's ability to endow the space, people and objects around him with personal life and meaning, derived from the given circumstances. The actor must not try to force the belief that he is the character, nor does he need to believe that the set, costumes, or props are real. A point of entry is *to treat* the character, partners, and properties *as if* they were real. Belief arises naturally when the actor can accept the possibility of the *given circumstances* because he has invested in them through research and imagination and now brings them to life by behaving truthfully in the circumstances. Whether acting in a realistic drama or one that is completely fantastical or absurd, the actor only needs to invest in the truth of his actions in order for the audience to accept even the most otherworldly or outrageous scenario. You have already been exploring endowment in previous exercises, but now you will enhance your ability to use this tool by being more detailed in your imagination and inner monologue and more specific in your behavioral choices.

Exercise 7.1A: Assuming and Conveying Status (Ensemble) (LW)[3] (Ensemble)

Main action: To greet

Figure 7.2 Assuming and conveying status.
Photo © François Guillot /AFP/Getty Images

---

[3] Director Les Waters taught this exercise to French at University of California, San Diego. At the time of this publication, Waters was the artistic director of the Actors Theatre of Louisville.

Guidelines:
- Each actor takes one card from a pile of playing cards (from which all face cards have been removed).
- The actor looks at the card secretly and then holds it to her chest so as not to let others in the class see it. This number is the actor's status, with the ace being lowest and the 10 highest.
- The actor then fulfills the action "to greet" using only the words "How do you do?" They can color the words and actions with any additional nonverbal cues to express status.
- After everyone has greeted everyone else, the class lines up from ace to 10 as best as possible. Then, all show their cards to see how well they assessed their status in relationship to others.

Exercise 7.1B: Endowing and Receiving Status (Ensemble)

- Take a new card from the pile but don't look at it.
- This time, holding the card with your left hand and facing out, place it on your third eye (the middle of your forehead between and just above the eyebrows).
- Fulfill the action to greet as in 7.1A, except that this time you must receive your status from how others treat *you*.
- Line up to assess how well you received the communication of your status.

Note: Both exercises can be repeated numerous times so that students get to explore assuming, conveying, and receiving different status levels. Also it is good to try different ways to communicate this as different types of people express high and low status in different ways.

7.1A & 7.1B *Reflection Journal—Status*

After these exercises, discuss the subtle signals you sent and picked up and how different actors conveyed high and low status nonverbally. Were you more comfortable conveying high, low or medium status? How did you feel when high or low statuses were endowed on you?

What (Action/Task)

What refers to the activity, called *stage business*, of your scene and what you do to reach the character's objective or to solve her problem, called *actions* or *tasks*. In this training process you will be given a concrete task to fulfill; for example, to open a door, to come home after a hard day's work in a mine and relax, to wait for an ambulance, etc. In a series of conditioning exercises later in this chapter and in subsequent chapters, you will be given a task and must decide on which *action steps* would be most typical and fitting to express your circumstances.

When

When does your action take place? What season and time of day or night? You must be specific as to hour. In our previous example of active facts we arrived home in a rainstorm at night, perhaps around six or seven in the evening; certainly we would behave differently if we arrived home at two or three in the morning than we would at two or three in the afternoon. Be specific! *When* also includes the era and epoch in which a character lives, including the sociopolitical and artistic influences. Art demands specificity.

Where

The place where our action is to take place is equally important. In most cases, *where* dictates your physical behavior. You will behave very differently at the home of your relatives during a holiday meal than at a train station, airport, or art gallery. While building your imaginary situations, look for interesting locations for your action and avoid placing every scenario in your living room while watching television, which limits your imagination and physical action. Investigate interesting locations and in that way you will explore many behaviors and stretch your imagination, which in turn will exercise your psychophysical responses to different environments.

With Whom (Relationships)

Our interaction with others is our primary stimulus for action onstage. The action is sparked into a dynamic force through our relationships. Determine what your character's relationship is to everyone. How we go about solving our problems or getting what we want is very different depending on whom we are trying to influence. This might include the consideration of whether you are with this person in private or in public; for example, most of us behave differently with significant others, close friends, or family when we are alone with them versus when we are in public. The *public/private* dichotomy becomes ever more extreme in classical plays where public behavior in many environments was expected to be much more formal. Even the passerby on the street can evoke some response. Perhaps you are in a bad neighborhood and an unsavory character is checking you out. How would the simple action of walking be different around this other person than with a lover in a beautiful garden on a summer's day?

Always, for *with whom* you ask yourself what kind of thoughts, feelings, and behavior do the other people evoke? How do they affect the *tempo* (speed) and *rhythm* (intensity) of your actions?

Relationships form the basis for conflict. Again, you must be specific, knowing exactly what happened between you and your scene partner within the imaginary circumstances that formed your attitudes toward one another. When discussing your relationship during the planning of an improvisation, decide together who you are to one another. Ask yourself, how will I need to treat my partner in order to express and project our relationship? Then look through your memory bank of experiences and recall how you may have treated someone like that in the past. You can then borrow from past behaviors, attitudes, and actions to more clearly express your behavior toward your partner's imaginary relationship in the present.

> **Note:** You do not need to try and see someone from your past while you are in this imaginary situation—that would be a bit crazy; simply borrow the actions you might do around someone you feel this way about. **Always communicate with and try to affect the person with whom you are working.** The personal images of *analogous situations* may arise spontaneously and can be *amalgamated* (combined) with the images you have created of the imaginary situation, but they don't need to be, as the relevant actions are likely to be sufficient triggers to evoke images with sufficient investment and detail.

Why and What For

Why and what for are closely interrelated. *Why* asks your motive for doing what you are doing, which may be prompted by a need you want to fill or a problem you want to solve. *Why* pushes you to do something. *What for* asks, toward what goal? *What for* is the hoped-for outcome that pulls you. What do you wish to gain or achieve through this action? What is your *objective*?

In your scenario, perhaps someone has lied to you the evening before (why/motivation) so you might choose to find out where they are this evening and plan to confront them to accuse them of having lied to you (action), in the hope that you can punish them, find out the truth, or get them to change their lying behavior (what for, or objective). There are unlimited possibilities with action.

> **Note:** In order to master your technique and instrument you must first master the selection and fulfillment of the most typical and fitting actions that answer the questions posed by the given circumstances. The action is the building block of character and acting. It is helpful to observe these actions transpiring in life.

Exercise 7.2: Getting What You Want (Observation) (SDF)

Purpose: To understand how people struggle with problems to get the outcomes they want (their objective, or *what for*). Plays are about issues and people struggling with those issues, and the ways that they try to get what they want reveal a lot about their characters. It is helpful to notice and break down the various components of two or more people locked in conflict so that you can invest in this kind of realistic struggle onstage.

Guidelines: Watch someone struggling with an issue he is invested in (why: need, problem task) and what he thinks will solve his problem (what for/objective/proposed solution) and how he goes about trying to get that (actions). For example, imagine this **problem**: Frank has tickets to a great concert by his favorite performer but also a 15-page research paper due that he hasn't even started to research. If Frank doesn't do well in his class, he'll be

7 DISCOVERING AND ENDOWING CIRCUMSTANCES

on academic suspension. His **objective/solution** is to get his roommate Dave to write the paper for him. (Of course, by even considering plagiarism we can see that Frank's academic problems run deeper than this one paper.) There are, however, a couple of major obstacles: 1) Dave is an honor student and values his integrity, so he won't cheat for Frank, and 2) Dave has a hot date with someone new.

Figure 7.3 Getting what you want.
Photo: © Photographee.eu/Shutterstock

> (Not that you would ever consider doing this, but **"magic if"**:) If you were Frank, a desperate student lacking any integrity, **what might you do** to reach the **objective/solution** of getting Dave to write your paper? When asked this question, students typically suggest things like request, beg, call in a favor, bribe, blackmail, or threaten. Your struggle with the problem is your task. You can see that if the obstacle is strong enough the lighter-intensity actions at the beginning of the list might not work, and Frank might have to move on to strong actions. Often in life we try stronger and stronger persuasive means until either we 1) get what we want, 2) change what we want, or 3) give up.
>
> - In the next few days, notice when somebody clearly wants something to go his or her way and tries many different things to get it.
> - What is the problem she is trying to fix?
> - What does she seem to think will resolve her problem in a way that works for her?
> - What specific action-steps, or tactics, does she use to get what she wants?

7.2 Observation Journal—Getting What You Want

Real-life observations are great research for improvisations and vital research for the roles you will work on later; however, you must take detailed notes in order for these observations to have any real value as fodder for your artistic creation of roles. Record all the different ways this person tries to get her way. What kind of obstacles does she encounter from the other person's opposing objective or the circumstances? Does she try different tactics when her first one doesn't work (*adaptation*)? Does she have an emotional response when she doesn't get her way? Does her tempo change when she encounters the obstacle? It is important to note the relationship between the people, where and when it takes place, and who else is present, etc.. as in the given circumstances above.

Where From and Where To (Two More Aspects of *Where*)

Simply put, *where from* asks, where are you coming from before you enter the stage? This is the first *where*: where *from*. You cannot just enter from backstage. Instead, the reality of the imaginary world and character must burst from offstage with every entrance. What has been the flow of your day before entering? What has just happened? How does this affect your entrance, and what behavior do you need to select prior to making your entrance so that the audience understands where it is you are coming from. Vladimir Nemirovich-Danchenko, cofounder with Stanislavsky of the Moscow Art Theatre, called what happens before the play begins, the *second plan*. The *first plan* is what the audience sees. The second plan also applies to what happens in the lives of the characters when they are offstage, between the acts and after the play. Stanislavsky also used the terms the *before time* and the *after time*. It is common today to say the *backstory, background*, or *exposition*.

The after time, or *where to*, is where you are headed when you leave the stage. This includes what you see in the imaginary circumstances when you open the door to leave. What you might actually see are the supports holding up the walls of the set, the blue running lights, the stage-crew person waiting on the rails to fly out the chandelier. What you must see is what would be outside the door in the world of the character and what they are exiting to go and do.

When working on a play using the System, we discuss and improvise the before time, the time between the acts, and the after time. When improvising we must create this also. Many actors and directors refer to these as the *three wheres*, with the *where* of the actual scene in the middle: (1) Where have you come from when you enter? (2) Where are you now in the scene? (3) Where do you go when you leave the stage?

Discovering the How

When preparing an improvised scene, do not think of how you'll perform it prior to going onstage. Work out the how while on your feet, otherwise you interfere with the creative process of discovery, and the observers do not get to discover with you. Even in a play with set blocking, the more subtle aspects of expressing each decision and discovery must be live and fluid each night so that the play does not seem stale and dead. Discovery allows us to be in the present moment, *the now*, and thus in an improvisational state. In fact, many books on awakening consciousness (very akin to inspiration) discuss the now, the present moment, as the key. However, when we are working on a script in rehearsal we are seeking the best possible way to express the character's actions, and once we choose and find the most fitting action, we then do very much need to ask *how*? What is the very best way to express this action at this very moment?—what Stanislavsky called "today, here and now, for the first time." This brings you to the next vital step in the preparation of your psychophysical instrument.

Group Conditioning Exercises: Experiencing the Given Circumstances

Physical exercises become *psycho*physical when we build our circumstances and thus justify our actions. The next level of psychophysical exercises will condition our instruments to behave truthfully, as we do in life.

Exercise 7.3: Run, Stop, and Justify (Group) (SM/PB)[4]

This was adapted by Philip G. Bennett from Sonia Moore, who learned it through the oral tradition and briefly outlined it in her book. The elaboration here is based on years of teaching and evolving it.

Guidelines:
- Observe with your *internal monitor* what is going on within you, and observe with your *external monitor* what you and those around you are doing. Enter into the acting space and at the instructor's prompt begin to

---

[4] Sonia Moore, *The Stanislavski System* (New York: Penguin, 1960; 1978). Adapted by Philip G. Bennett from Sonia Moore, who learned it through the oral tradition and briefly outlined it in her book. The elaboration here is based on years of teaching and evolving it.

run. When the instructor claps his hands, stop and hold the pose in which you find yourself.
- Do not freeze but continue to breathe into your entire body, keeping alive internally.
- Justify the pose psychophysically by building imaginary circumstances. You are yourself in this situation. Allow imaginary images to stir recalled images and for them to merge to create new images. Quickly answer all the questions: Who, What, Where, etc. Breathe and bring your energy to a peak and bring the pose to life. Repeat the exercise several times at the instructor's command, and each time you stop and hold, build new circumstances to a peak and at the instructors command bring the pose to life.
- Mentally direct the energy to the base of your spine, then up to the middle of your back and out to your arms and hands; simultaneously imagine that the energy is moving from the base of your spine up into your neck, throat, and head, down through the pelvic girdle to your legs, feet, and toes. With a little conscious practice you will be able to consciously direct the flow of muscular energy to any part of your body at will.
- When the instructor gives the signal "Action!" Bring your pose to life and fulfill your action with purpose.
- After a few moments in this situation, the instructor may clap his hands again and the process can be repeated, as time allows.

7.3 *Reflection Journal—Run, Stop, Justify*

Did you see mental images of your imaginary situation? Were you able to concentrate and focus your attention and direct your breath and energy into your spine and throughout your body? Did you experience any feelings or sensations?

Exercise 7.4: Disobeying Hands with Images and W.E.D.G.A.G. (group) (SM)[5]

Purpose: *Disobeying hands* is an excellent conditioning exercise designed to improve your concentration and coordination while simultaneously practicing what you have learned previously. You will learn to integrate some of the techniques (because they are combined in the reality of acting in production). The exercise will also develop connections between mind and body, forging new neural pathways in the brain. Practice disobeying hands often and you will soon become proficient at *mental acrobatics*, the ability to psychophysically juggle numerous thoughts and movement patterns at

---

[5] Adapted from Sonia Moore, *Training an Actor: The Stanislavsky System in Class* (New York: Penguin, 1974), 37, 48, 74.

7 DISCOVERING AND ENDOWING CIRCUMSTANCES

the same time. Mental acrobatics is a necessary skill to develop for more advanced character work and performance.

Guidelines: Take a moment to review the Disobeying Hands drawings and instructions outlined in Chapter 5. Each time you explore disobeying hands add some new elements to make it slightly more challenging. The next step is to practice transforming the stationary postures of this exercise into expressive psychophysical poses that express action.

Exercise 7.4A: Disobeying Hands with Images
- Review the eight steps of disobeying hands by reviewing the diagram and instructions for Exercise 5.6. Go through them two or three times ahead of this exercise.
- Stand in the first posture: right arm extended forward and left arm hanging down at your side.
- Ask yourself: "What could I be doing with my arms in this position?"
- Trust your first thoughts and impulses: as soon as you get an idea of where you are, go with it and build your imaginary circumstances, answering the questions: Who? What? When? Where? Why? With Whom? What for? etc.
- Select imaginary images to help you justify your action and bring it to life, or allow personal images to connect with the gesture spontaneously.
- Identify the action of your scenario, such as, waving to a friend, holding a bird in your hand, listening at a door, etc.
- When your circumstances are complete, breathe and direct your muscular energy from the base of the spine up and out to all the extremities of your body.
- Adjust your body from toes to the top of your head to express the action and image you have chosen.
- Adjust your body to fit the image of what you are doing.
- Where your thoughts go, that's where your breath and energy goes. As you bring the energy up through the base of your spine, allow it to build to a peak of intensity by investing more and more importance in your need to fulfill this action. Stay connected to the breath. Breathe in the circumstances and allow them to affect you. Allow the breath to respond to the growing intensity of your motivation.
- Fulfill the action.
- Now move your right arm straight up, (pointing toward the ceiling) and ask what you could be doing in that position for each pose; adjust your body to express the image and action, etc.
- Move your right arm straight out to the side.
- Move your right arm down to your side.
- Bring your right arm up to shoulder height and hold it straight out.
- Now you have completed the first cycle of the exercise.

Note: This exercise is very effective to repeat, justifying the poses in new ways each time, based on the neurophysiological impulses that arise.

Exercise 7.4B: Disobeying Hands with W.E.D.G.A.G.

Guidelines: Now repeat the sequence of disobeying hands, stopping to justify various poses within it using W.E.D.G.A.G ; for example, by imagining you have discovered a bird's nest close at hand in a tree. (Remember to express each thought with your spine and to go smoothly from each thought and movement to the next. In life, and as you advance in acting skill, this process happens quickly and continuously, but in training, you must first break it down and take time for each step.)

- Wonder (awe or initial reactions): "I wonder if there are little eggs in the nest."
- Evaluate: "I begin to evaluate the situation—should I look or stay away?"
- Decide: Make a decision and express it with an appropriate gesture. "I had better not touch or disturb the nest."
- Gesture: "I am moved by the life growing in the nest, and will protect this nest as best as I am able."
- Act: "I withdraw my hand and step back."
- Your final gesture sums up your whole experience with the bird's nest. It is where you can best express the feelings and emotions of the experience and project them outward to your audience. (Keep the gesture subtle at this point. Later you will be able to justify grand and stylized gestures but perhaps not yet.)

> **Note:** Continue the exercise creating a new situation with each new arm movement. Bring each to life using W.E.D.G.A.G. until the process is smooth and feels natural.

Additional ways of performing disobeying hands:
- While walking around the room.
- While singing a song in your head.
- Later, you can also do this exercise with a text in order to learn to justify as a character any kind of blocking a director might give you.

7.4 Reflection Journal—Disobeying Hands, with Images and W.E.D.G.A.G.

Were you able to coordinate the movements in the correct sequence? Were you able to bring the steps of W.E.D.G.A.G. together smoothly into one continuous action, and did new feelings and sensations arise spontaneously?

7 DISCOVERING AND ENDOWING CIRCUMSTANCES

Exercise 7.5: Three Separate Movements (SM)

Purpose: To justify and connect three random movements. Work on a role requires very specific choices of psychological and physical behavior. Every new character has a different pattern of physical actions than that of the actor. Additionally, when in rehearsal you will frequently be given specific physical actions that you must justify and fulfill. By learning how to connect and justify separate and sometimes illogical behavior, you will be able to find a sequence and pattern that is natural. Eventually you will be able to adapt that skill in order to find the varying patterns of different characters.

Guidelines:
- Go onstage one at a time and execute externally and justify internally a specific combination of actions for the class.
- The teacher might choose to use the examples below, invent his or her own sequence of physical actions, or ask the class for suggested sequences.

Note: It is important for this exercise that someone other than the actor performing them dictate the physical choices.

Exercise 7.5A: Three Separate Movements (Known and Planned in Advance)

- The sequence of actions is given to the actor in advance.
- Take a few moments to mentally select specific circumstances (answering the questions outlined above) to justify the sequences of actions you have been given by using the *"magic if"*: If I were in this circumstance, why would I be sitting, standing, etc.?
- Fulfill each physical action in the sequence fully justified within your circumstances.

Exercise 7.5B: Three Separate Movements (Responded to Spontaneously)

- Take a few moments before you know what the actions are to mentally select specific circumstances (answering the questions outlined above).
- After you have entered and are responding to your imaginary circumstances, the instructor will call out unplanned physical actions that you must execute, filling them with justification arising from your imaginary circumstances.

Make the combinations challenging (by adding some unusual movements or suggestions for changes in tempos):
- Sit down in a chair, stand up slowly, run off the stage.

- Stand on the chair, look up, look left, look right, look down, jump down and roll up into a ball.
- Run around the chair clockwise once and stop; turn around and run around the chair twice counterclockwise; jump up and down three times; stamp your feet and sit down.

Summary

Building concrete and imaginative circumstances is necessary in order to understand how to behave in each new situation. Always begin by asking What would I do if I were in this situation, today, here and now, for the first time? The "magic if" will act as a strong stimulus to your imagination and help you to justify your actions. Only when an action is purposeful can you say that it is justified truthfully. When you begin to work on improvisations and, eventually, text, a thorough analysis of the given circumstances will be necessary in order to choose the most fitting, typical and believable behavior for your characters. Mastery of the selection and execution of actions is a key to your training. This will lead you to becoming an independent and truly creative artist who can experience the life of a character, convey the character's supertask and find communion with your audience. This will be covered in the next chapter.

New Theatre Terms, Concepts, and Artists

Terms used in the Stanislavsky System are in italics.

- ☐ *active facts*
- ☐ *after time*
- ☐ *back story*
- ☐ *background*
- ☐ *before time*
- ☐ *come from yourself*
- ☐ *exposition*
- ☐ *first plan*
- ☐ *fitting and typical*
- ☐ *given circumstances (givens)*
- ☐ *"I am," or "I exist"*
- ☐ *impulse to act*
- ☐ *indications (indicating)*
- ☐ *inner monologue*
- ☐ *justification (justify)*
- ☐ *"magic if"*
- ☐ playing yourself
- ☐ public/private
- ☐ *rhythm (intensity)*
- ☐ *second plan*
- ☐ *stage business*
- ☐ *task*
- ☐ *tempo (speed)*
- ☐ *three wheres*
- ☐ Les Waters
- ☐ *what for?*
- ☐ *where from (before time)*
- ☐ *where to (after time)*
- ☐ *with whom?*

CHAPTER 8

Nonverbal Action: Communicating through Behavior

"Learn how to carry out simply and organically the simplest physical actions. The logic and consecutiveness of these actions will evoke in you the entire complicated, subtle scale of inner experiences. Carrying out the logic of a physical action will bring you to the logic of emotions, and this is everything for an actor."[1]

—Konstantin Stanislavsky

Focus of Active Exploration—Combining the Elements of Action

Named events, psychophysical actions, justification, logical and consecutive action steps, truth and belief, sensory evocation, dynamic conflict, objective, obstacle, adaptation, public solitude, dual perspectives, W.E.D.G.A.G, all leading to experiencing

- How Do You Select and Name Psychophysical Actions?
- How Do the Elements of Action Combine in Justification?
- What Is Meant by "Logical and Consecutive Action-Steps"?
- How Are the Components of Postmodern Plays Linked?
- How Can We Become Conscious of the Anatomy of a Thought through the Tool of W.E.D.G.A.G?

Part I: Active Explorations of W.E.D.G.A.G.
- ☐ Exercise 8.1: The Apple, or "Trespassers Beware!"
- ☐ Exercise 8.2: Run, Stop, Justify (with W.E.D.G.A.G.)
- ☐ Exercise 8.3: Improvisation: The Hospital Visit

Part II: Active Exploration of Nonverbal Action
- Observing Your Psychophysical Instrument in Action
- Public Solitude and the Internal and External Monitors
- The Named Event
- ☐ Exercise 8.4: Improvisation: Doors and Windows
- Beginning, Middle, and End

Part III: Exercises: Holding the Audience's Attention, Dynamic (Dramatic) Conflict, Dual Perspectives, and Experiencing
- Dynamic Conflict and Character Revealed

---

[1] Moore, *The Stanislavski System* (1960) 1978, p. 53.

- Objective
- Using Obstacles and Psychological Burdens
- Experiencing
  - Exercise 8.5: To Read

Part IV: Tempo-Rhythm: The Bridge between Inner Experience and Physical Expression
- How Do You Connect Inner Life with Outer Expression?
  - Exercise 8.6: Preparing for a Date
  - Exercise 8.7: Walking to Class
  - Exercise 8.8: Take a Walk!
- How Do You Decide What Adaptations or Adjustments to Make to Obstacles?
- Responding to Obstacles with Adaptations: General Guidelines
  - Exercise 8.9: Improvisation: Great News!
  - Exercise 8.10: Improvisation: the Job Interview
  - Exercise 8.11: Improvisation: Awards Banquet
  - Exercise 8.12: Improvisation: The Family Heirloom
  - Exercise 8.13: Additional Improvisation Actions for Practice
- How Do You Create Life in Artificial Circumstances? Endowment: To Treat As
- Truth and Belief
- Enemies of Truth
  - Exercise 8.14: Improvisation: My Precious Object
  - Exercise 8.15: Additional to Treat As Actions for Practice
- Sensory Evocation (Objectless Exercises)
  - Exercise 8.16: The Important Document
  - Exercise 8.17: Additional Sensory Evocation Actions for Practice

Part V: Zones of Silence: Two- and Three-Person Nonverbal Improvisations
- Exercise 8.18: Improvisation: The Silent Treatment
- Exercise 8.19: Improvisation: Secret Agent
- Exercise 8.20: Improvisation: The Elegant Performance

Of all the techniques in your Actor's Palette, psychophysical action is your primary tool for analyzing a script and building a character. It is the key that will later enable you to experience and share the life of the human spirit on stage or screen, the goal of Stanislavsky's System. Stanislavsky defined an action as a purposeful act of human behavior. In other words, action is motivated behavior, and action is also the basis of the art of acting.

In this chapter we will explore a progressive series of steps designed to experience simple-to-more-complex nonverbal action. Gradually, you will learn to combine more and more Elements of Action throughout this chapter.

How Do You Select and Name Psychophysical Actions?

All psychophysical actions used in this technique, whether nonverbal (without words) or verbal (spoken), are *transitive verbs* (an action verb with a direct object). Verbal actions will be covered and practiced in Chapter 11: Verbal Action: Communicating with Words and Subtext. An action is something specific done to affect another person or an object. In this technique, you will name these actions (literally write

8 NONVERBAL ACTION

the transitive verb on your script at the appropriate moment or plan them into an improvisation) to make your acting dynamic and specific. Learning how to use this primary color of your Actor's Palette will be explained fully throughout this chapter.

Begin by closely examining the use and practice of *nonverbal actions*. An example of a nonverbal action would be to hide, to search, to eavesdrop, to prepare a dinner for a friend, etc. If the action you have selected evokes in you an idea of how to fulfill it, then it is a strong choice. Some transitive verbs that are too general may be hard to clearly invest in; instead of "to question," for example, try "to hint," "to prompt," "to insist," "to interrogate," or "to threaten to get information." There are other types of verbs that do not activate a scene. Intransitive verbs are also active but they are not done with intention to make an impact on another person or thing or on oneself; for example, the bird sang, the boy fell.

Verbs of being, such as to be fatigued, to be upset, to be worried, or to be happy, are not *active* but *passive*. Verbs of being describe physical and emotional states. Emotional states are important to acting, of course, but are reactions not actions. *Passive verbs* are necessary in acting because out of these reactive emotional states we are motivated to respond with action. States of being color and give depth to our physical actions. If you find yourself writing them in your script as your action, however, you are more likely writing your character's reaction to people and events than an action trying to affect those people and events. To attempt to play a passive verb is to immediately go for the result (this is called playing the emotion). It is problematic because it bypasses the organic process of psychophysical behavior that connects and unites your mind and body, allowing you to respond at the moment in the scene when your character is triggered. Also, a passive state is less likely to trigger the other character and therefore does not activate the scene. On the other hand, a dynamic transitive verb, by its direction toward other characters, provokes them. Another trap is that often a particular emotional state will go on for a long period of the scene, and if you "wash" the scene (color the whole scene one emotional color) by playing the emotion you will miss all the interesting nuances happening between the characters. You may feel cathartic afterward, but you will not have taken the audience on a step-by-step journey through the character's experience so that they also are stirred to both their own emotional response and understanding of what just happened. We will explore applying physical and emotional states of being in Chapter 12: Orchestrating Emotions.

For now let us focus our attention on two aspects of nonverbal action:

1. How to physically express our thought processes and feelings when reacting and making a decision in silence; and
2. How to choose and fulfill active verbs in justified silence.

How Do the Elements of Action Combine in Justification?

> "When actions come to life spontaneously we have to use the principle of going from the outside in. We put the constituent Elements in logical, coherent sequence and create action out of them. The logic and coherence of the parts reminds us of the truth of life….Once the actor believes in them, he comes alive."
> —Konstantin Stanislavsky[2]

---

[2] Konstantin Stanislavsky, *An Actor's Work*. (trans. Jean Benedetti). (London: Routledge, 2009), 619.

When we first introduced the Elements of Action in Chapter 2: The Actor's Palette, we explained that a physical choice becomes a psychophysical action when this act of human behavior is *purposeful*. It is purposeful when it is *inwardly motivated* (taken toward a specific goal or to solve a specific problem) and *fulfilled* in concrete circumstances. This is called *justification*. In Chapter 7: Discovering and Endowing Circumstances, you practiced coloring physical choices through the context of specific created and imagined circumstances (of course, in a play these would be given by the playwright). In Chapter 5: The Psychophysical Instrument, you began to condition your instrument to respond in a fuller way, connecting your mind and body. All of the Elements of Action—the colors of your Actor's Palette—will begin to be combined in this chapter as you move from understanding and fulfilling simple actions to fulfilling more-complex ones. Experiments in selecting and fulfilling actions for specific plays by means of improvisations and études[3] form the basis and central focus of our acting technique. (This will be explored in detail in Chapter 13: Active Analysis: Reconnaissance of the Play, Chapter 14: Active Analysis: Reconnaissance of the Character, and Chapter 15, Active Analyis through Events and Actions.)

What Is Meant by "Logical And Consecutive Action-Steps"?

Imagine medieval stonemasons building a cathedral. After the ground has been leveled and prepared, stones must be selected and cut precisely into shape for the foundation to be laid and the supporting buttresses and walls to be built. Each block must fit perfectly into place, and the walls need to be sturdy enough to support the weight that the higher elevations of the structure will create. The entire building, when completed, must be sound and aesthetically pleasing. Perhaps our imaginary cathedral is of gothic style (the form of the structure) and adorned with paintings, sculptures, and statues (the content within the structure). All art forms, including theatre, have structure and form. A *recurrent theme* in the decorations of a Gothic cathedral might be depictions of the lives of the saints. This would be a *leitmotif*.[4] Plays and characters also have their leitmotifs.

In the same way, an actor, choosing and executing actions for his role, must cut and shape each moment of action. He too must see that the pieces or *bits*—"*bits of action*," as Stanislavsky called them—are perfectly proportioned and fit tightly together. Due to Stanislavsky's strong Russian accent *bits* was heard as *beats* and, so now *beats* is the more commonly used term in North America.[5]

The director guides the orchestration of the sequence of actions of the entire cast through the episodes and acts of a play. He may or may not work on this with the actors. If not, actors can do this work as preparation on their own to have something tangible to offer in the rehearsal process but should defer to the director's vision of the action for all actors and other elements of the production. The actions should also be carefully chosen in order to exploit the various themes and serve the

---

[3] An étude is a study, an improvisational sketch designed to explore a particular idea, subject, theme, or trait for the building of a character when using Active Analysis.
[4] A recurrent theme.
[5] French likes the term *beats*, even if a mistranslation for Stanislavsky, because, not only is it now commonly used in the American theatre but it implies rhythm: Carefully marked beats are not only helpful for rehearsing small moments in detail, but later in your rehearsals can be very helpful for rhythm and pacing of a scene.

8 NONVERBAL ACTION

overall intent of the playwright. Stanislavsky called the playwright's theme the *ruling idea*. The ruling idea, as interpreted in production by the director in collaboration with the designers, and enhanced and executed by the technical staff and actors, is what creates the *supertask*[6] of the production. This is what the artists want the audience to take away with them when they leave the theatre, generally referred to in professional theatre today as the *production concept*.

Just as the architecture of our cathedral must have a consistency of design that serves its function, the selection of actions in the form of human behavior must also be *logical, consecutive,* and *fitting*. When actions are correctly selected, connected, justified, and executed in the character's circumstances, they reveal the unique inner world of the character and contribute to creating and revealing the dynamic struggle and conflict of the play. Actions that are not logical and consecutive may confuse the spectator, detract from the direction in which the story is headed, and fail to communicate the supertask. Even within the most bizarre plays or films, familiar and logically executed acts of human behavior and revelations of familiar but profound human truths give us entrée into these strange new worlds and allow us to consider what it would be like to inhabit them.

How Are the Components of Postmodern Plays Linked?

There are some exceptions. Postmodern plays experiment with writing that may not have a consecutive through-line of action. They may be intentionally designed to confuse audiences by not having a clear narrative or emotional path. This challenges actors and audiences to receive and respond in new ways. While our logical and consecutive left-brains abdicate in confusion, the conceptual and big picture right-brain can delight in the images and symbolic language. These plays may link more through themes, characters, locations, or parallel situations, images, or abstract symbols rather than by a unifying plot. We will not deal extensively with such plays in this book, as they require more-advanced techniques. As you move forward in your career, this acting system can also be a foundational technique to empower the impact forms of theatre outside of realism. In fact, the System was a foundation and jumping-off place for some great innovators who created groundbreaking theatre, such as Evgeny Vakhtangov in his Fantastic Realism productions in the Third Studio of the Moscow Art Theatre, Jerzy Grotowski in his ritual-based Poor Theatre productions in Poland, and Bertolt Brecht in his Epic Theatre productions at the Berliner Ensemble in Germany.

Truthfully fulfilled, inwardly motivated actions can also stir your emotional involvement, but not just any action. The action must be *indispensable* and reveal the content of the given circumstances at each moment. We find the indispensable action by a thorough analysis of the circumstances, and then we test it on our feet by creating improvisations designed to explore the physical and spiritual life of the character.

You can compare logical and consecutive actions to the electrical wiring in your home that when properly connected will safely carry and distribute electricity. The same phenomenon occurs when your actions are connected. The life-force energy in

---

[6] The supertask is the play's main action. In the first English editions of Stanislavsky's books, it was translated by Elizabeth Reynolds Hapgood as "Superobjective."

your body begins to function at optimum levels, thereby making possible acting at peak performance ability.

> **How Can We Become Conscious of the Anatomy of a Thought through the Tool of W.E.D.G.A.G?**

In Chapter 5: The Psychophysical Instrument, you first experienced the technique called W.E.D.G.A.G. In Chapter 7: Discovering and Endowing Circumstances you began to contextualize W.E.D.G.A.G. The Anatomy of a Thought is a complex technique that must be repeated frequently in order to bring more consciousness to this normally automatic process and to retrain your psychophysical instrument. To achieve this, a more thorough exploration of W.E.D.G.A.G follows. This concept will be used from here on out as part of the fulfillment of every action. This will condition your instrument to be able to express and stir the most subtle thoughts and feelings. The exercises that follow are designed to awaken your awareness of the muscles that are engaged when you are thinking.

To review, W.E.D.G.A.G. is an initialism for:

W—Wonder (discovery, awe, curiosity, astonishment)
E—Evaluate (consider, weigh-up)
D—Decide
G—Gesture (expresses the decision)
A—Act (take action)
G—Gesture (expresses the final thought and feeling)

In life we are constantly reacting to external and internal stimuli. Close observation of ourselves and others will reveal that the above pattern is continuous and repeats itself over and over again, though not necessarily in the same sequence. The sequence here is for practice; however, it is the most common observable pattern. We will call this sequence the *Anatomy of a Thought*. The anatomy of a thought includes its structure and how the pattern of thought is expressed psychophysically in moments of reaction and decision.

Employ W.E.D.G.A.G to explore the following improvisational exercise and see what you might discover.

Through the training steps in this chapter, you will experience, first in exercises and later in nonverbal improvisations, the possibilities within nonverbal communication and interaction.

I. Active Exploration of W.E.D.G.A.G.
II. Active Exploration of Nonverbal Action
III. Holding the Audience's Attention through Dynamic Conflict, Dual Perspectives, and Experiencing
IV. Tempo-Rhythm: The Bridge between Inner Experience and Physical Expression
V. Zones of Silence: Two- and Three-Person Nonverbal Improvisations

8 NONVERBAL ACTION

PART I: ACTIVE EXPLORATIONS OF W.E.D.G.A.G.

Exercise 8.1A: The Apple, or "Trespassers Beware!" (PGB)
Guidelines:
- Imagine that you have been walking for some time down a country path and have sat down beside a beautiful brook that runs through an apple orchard (or you can substitute another fruit that you prefer).
- Where have you come from?
- Why are you taking this path? What time of day or evening is it?
- Use all the elements of your sensory awareness that might apply in this imaginary situation: temperature, weather conditions, sights, smells, textures, sounds, etc.
- You look up and spot a big, juicy, ripe apple. You long to taste it, but between you and the prize apple is a fence, and nailed to a post is a sign reading, "Trespassers Beware!"
- Before rising from your seated position use W.E.D.G.A.G:
  - **Wonder:** Look at the apple with wonderment and awe, maybe even surprise. Imagine how delicious it must be. Admire its size, shape, and color. Perhaps your mouth begins to water at the thought of biting into it. Are you hungry? If so, how much? With your *internal monitor* (mind's eye), observe your breathing, take air into your lungs and notice the natural movement of the torso while you breathe and how your head and the muscles around your spine physically express your awe and wonderment.
  - **Evaluate:** Begin to evaluate whether or not to ignore the warning sign and risk the danger of being caught. Ask yourself, "Should I crawl through or climb over the fence and steal the apple?" Express each thought with the muscles of your torso by imagining the breath filling your entire body. What feelings spontaneously arise? Breathe into the areas of your body where you feel these sensations. (You are controlling the flow of muscular energy with thought and breath, while at the same time permitting the energy to pass through your body as impulses.)
  - **Decide:** Finally the desire for the apple becomes overwhelming and you must have it. Notice if your breathing changes as your desire for the apple builds until it must be expressed in an action. At the moment of impulse, make a decision to steal the object of your desire.
  - **Gesture:** As soon as you make a definite decision, notice how your breathing changes, and a gesture will often appear of itself, or if you wish, you may choose to express your decision with an appropriate and fitting gesture (often the decision and gesture occur simultaneously). With very little practice you will be able to make good choices spontaneously. Breathe and allow the impulse to incite you to take action.
  - **Act:** Breathe and rise to your feet with the determination to ignore the warning, overcome the obstacles, and steal and eat the apple. (This nonverbal action happens in silence.)

- Final **Gesture:** Just as you are climbing or crawling under the fence you hear a number of fierce dogs barking. Notice what happens to your breath (Are you holding it? Is it faster and higher in your chest?) Evaluate the barking (Do the dogs sound fierce and dangerous? Weight the prize of the apple with the risk of getting mauled). As you hesitate in this weighing up, breathe in the danger of the dogs, and as you breathe out, express your emotional response to the barking dogs with a final gesture. Hold the gesture, keep breathing, and stay alive; do not freeze. Bring the improvisation to a conclusion by remaining quiet and still. Perhaps you are listening to hear whether the dogs are approaching or moving away.

Exercise 8.1B: The Apple, or "Trespassers Beware!" Reprise (PGB)

Guidelines:
- In order to make the exercise seamless and easy, repeat it once or even twice again.
- This time, practice moving through the six steps continuously, without any interruption.
- Keep your energy and breath flowing through your body.
- Feel completely free to express your thoughts and gestures impulsively.
- There is no need to repeat your gestures exactly as you did the first time.
- When you feel the psychophysical expression of your thoughts become easy and spontaneous, reflect upon the exercise and record your findings in your creative journal.

8.1 *Reflection Journal—"Trespassers Beware" with W.E.D.G.A.G.*

Discuss your experience. When could you clearly see the images? Where did you feel the impulses in your body? Could you feel the energy moving through your torso and along your spine? Were you able to experience wonderment? What must you focus on in order to have the exercise flow more consistently throughout?

Exercise 8.2: Run, Stop, Justify (with W.E.D.G.A.G.) (SM/PB)

Purpose: The goal is to eventually have each phase of W.E.D.G.A.G. flow easily and naturally into the next to form one unbroken stream of energy and physical expression; do not be impatient, for this will take repeated practice and repetition until it becomes new learned behavior. At first, to ensure that you touch on each point of the Anatomy of a Thought as described by the steps of W.E.D.G.A.G., it will be slower than the action happens in life. Eventually you will be able to get the actions up to pace while still filling them with this flow of the Anatomy of a Thought.

8 NONVERBAL ACTION

Guidelines:
- Run randomly around the stage, and when the teacher claps her hands, stop and hold, but do not freeze. Stay alive. Keep the breath moving through the body even in outer stillness.
- Inwardly justify your pose by asking yourself, "What would I be doing *if* I were in this position with my body?
- Trust your first impulses, there is no need to try to figure it out; keep it easy and fun.
- Using your imagination, build concrete circumstances, answering the questions, Who am I (remain yourself in this situation)? What am I doing here? When is it (what time of day or night)? Where am I? With whom (am I alone or with someone)? What for (what do I want to achieve)? Why am I doing this (what is my motivation and purpose)? Do not ask how to do it. Let the *how* take care of itself when you begin to bring the pose to life.
- Now that you have your imaginary circumstances and images in mind, place your mind's eye (internal monitor) at the base of the spine and will your energy to travel up the spine while simultaneously breathing in slowly. Feel the expansion of your lungs and the tingling that travels up your spine. Let this subtle sensation fill your whole torso and travel into your arms, legs, hands, feet, neck, and head.
- Sculpted pose: Sculpt every muscle group in your body to express fully each element of your imaginary situation, your feet, legs, torso, arms, hands, and head. (**Note:** your sculpture must be three-dimensional so that someone could view you from any angle and understand what you are thinking, feeling, and doing.)
- Now, you are ready to bring the pose to life by connecting the six steps of W.E.D.G.A.G., with thought and physical expression.
- Complete the exercise with a final gesture that expresses one or a combination of the following: your attitude, feeling sensations, and emotions that arise in response to the action you performed.
- Repeat the exercise several times, and each time the teacher claps her hands take a new pose.

8.2 *Reflection Journal—Run, Stop, Justify, with W.E.D.G.A.G.*

Were you able to picture clear circumstances? Were you able to imagine the sensations moving up the spine and torso? Were you able to find and connect with the muscles that expressed your thoughts? Did you become aware of spontaneous emotions and feelings? When repeating the exercise was it easier to accomplish?

> **Exercise 8.3: Improvisation: The Hospital Visit (SM/PGB)**
>
> **Guidelines:**
> - You are visiting someone you know very well who is seriously ill or injured and may die.
> - Decide upon the relationship and what your basic feeling is for this person.
> - The entire exercise is carried out at the entrance to the room.
> - You approach the doorway and stop.
> - There you are conflicted as to whether to enter. (Justify inwardly what psychologically is preventing you from entering.)
> - Now go through the six steps of W.E.D.G.A.G.
> - Your final gesture must project your thoughts, decision, and feelings clearly to the audience. Do you enter or not? What is your purpose? What are you feeling? What are you hiding? What does this person mean to you? etc.

> **Note:** If the use of your back muscles and torso felt unnatural and forced, keep practicing. In a very short time it will become second nature and simple. When you master the subtle movements of muscles, you become aware of creative impulses arising, and you will be able to express your thoughts and the feelings with absolute clarity. You will also be more attuned to muscular impulses that prompt actions. It is important to remember that your breathing and back muscles must be quietly and constantly engaged while acting, especially in silences and pauses.

8.3 Reflection Journal—The Hospital Visit

Take time to reflect and write your experiences in your creative journal. Have a discussion and share your reflections with the group. What did you find difficult and what easy to do?

PART II: ACTIVE EXPLORATION OF NONVERBAL ACTION

Observing Your Psychophysical Instrument in Action

There is no inner action without a corresponding physical response, nor is there a physical action without its inner component. Physical action can stimulate inner life just as inner life is able to stimulate physical action. There does not always need to be a visible movement to honestly reflect a physical action. Sometimes absolute stillness says much more, but in this case your eyes must remain visible to the audience so they can see the life of the character stirring behind them as you see the appropriate images and think the thoughts of the character's inner monologue. Continuous inner monologue and a continuous film of images are important for the stage and a key to film acting. While both the inner world and outer expression must

8 NONVERBAL ACTION

be part of the expression of the life of the human being in acting, for the purposes of clarity we often need to focus on one or another aspect of behavior, internal or external, psychological or physical (especially in training), before this link becomes second nature. Keep in mind that they are not separate.

For our immediate purpose we will need to focus primarily on your choice of logical and consecutive behavior; that is, physical actions that you choose to use to convey your imaginary situation.

Prior to going onstage, you will build an imaginary situation that answers the questions posed by the given circumstances: who, what, when, where, etc. The audience will naturally attach human stories to what it sees. Therefore, if you wish to tell a specific story and not an unintentional one, you will need to gain control over both your inner and outer means of expression, and that is why we begin by practicing actions alone and in silence.

Public Solitude and the Internal and External Monitors

There are many situations when you find yourself alone. Sometimes you are alone in the midst of a large crowd of strangers, Stanislavsky called this *public solitude*. Observe yourself while practicing. Observe your thoughts and images with your *internal monitor* and the world around you with your *external monitor*.

When you achieve profound thought and can express it physically, the audience will understand your behavior and identify with your feelings. Silent improvisations give you the opportunity to develop your creative imagination through the building of circumstances and the solving of creative problems. When you practice seeing pictures in your mind (*mental images*), you will increase your powers of concentration, improve your ability to focus on necessary tasks, and most important, establish communion with your partners and the audience. Diligent practice will lead you to the eventual mastery of your technique.

In the previous section, you practiced the basic steps of reaction and evaluation that naturally occur at the beginning of every new action: wonderment, evaluation, decision, gesture, action, and final gesture. Now we will practice using W.E.D.G.A.G. to express reactions and decisions you make in response to an imaginary situation: the improvisation takes place in justified silence. Follow the guidelines below and have fun with it.

The Named Event

The *named event* is an important Element of Action that will be used in subsequent improvisations and is very important to later chapters on Active Analysis. In the improvisations that follow, give the imaginary situation a title in the form of a noun or metaphor; for example, "Night Noises," or "Late Date." This is the *named event*. The event keeps you focused on a specific situation that suggests typical action steps to choose in order to fulfill the main action. While a main action may be specific to one character, the named event focuses the actions for all the characters involved in the improvisation or scene. It must have meaning for all the characters involved, although how they feel about it and whether they want it to happen and are helping it happen or stopping it from happening may be different for each.

Exercise 8.4: Improvisation: Doors and Windows (Main actions with Named Events) (SM/PGB)

Purpose: Every physical choice that you make as an actor or that is given to you by a director must be justified. Specific given circumstances change how you perform even the simplest physical behavior.

Main actions (SM/PGB)[7]:
- To open the door
- To look out the window

Guidelines:
- You have a choice of one or both of the main actions above.
- Named Event: When you have chosen your action give the imaginary situation a title in the form of a noun or metaphor as discussed above.
- Decide on your motivation and purpose.
- Choose behavior that is typical for you and fitting for the imaginary situation.
- Choose personal images of people, events, etc., and write them down in your creative journal prior to going onstage. (Your images can be from real people and events you have seen or completely imagined and will often be a combination of the two, especially later when you get into circumstances clearly described by a playwright. The important thing is that the images you select stir a response in you that is right for the situation.)
- You may choose to re-create an event similar to one in your own life or make one up.
- Do not attempt to play a character in these early improvisations (unless your instructor has designed a particular exercise where character traits are needed). In some cases, you will be in circumstances you have never been in before. A character is a complex human being with many intricate facets. Simply explore yourself using your internal monitor to increase awareness of your inner life and your external monitor to observe its physical expressions.
- Your improvisation must have a beginning, middle, and end; however, you must not decide beforehand how to act it out or how to bring it to a logical conclusion. Wait until you are on your feet, then let the *how* take care of itself.
- The Three Wheres: Remember, whenever you are onstage there are three questions to ask regarding *where*:

---

[7] These are relayed by Sonia Moore from Stanislavsky's oral teachings. Moore was dedicated to the accurate presentation of Stanislavsky's System. This sometimes involved directly translating what he or his disciple Vahktangov had taught her, whereas at other times she invented exercises in the spirit of earlier exercises of Stanislavsky that were designed to teach and develop the same element. All teachers of the System make the exercises their own in this way.

8 NONVERBAL ACTION

1. Where are you coming from when you enter the stage (where from)?
2. Where are you during the main part of the improvisation (where at)?
3. Where are you going when you exit the stage (where to)?

- Be specific about where you are going and what you are going to do when you leave the stage.
- Remember to use W.E.D.G.A.G. when encountering obstacles and making decisions.

8.4 Reflection Journal—Door and/or Window

Was the action clear, truthful, and interesting? Did the action steps project why you were opening the door or looking through the window? Did you see personal and imaginary mental images? What did you want to say with your final gesture? Did you experience involvement?

Beginning, Middle, and End

How Does the Structure of an Improvisation Relate to the Structure of a Scene?

In the last exercise (opening a door or looking out a window), did you notice that an action has a beginning, middle, and end (as described by W.E.D.G.A.G)? You have probably already realized that this is the same structure as a well-written story or play. Your improvisations are also short stories that are told as a kind of subtle *pantomime of the body*, and they must be acted out with what is called *true measure* or *the measure of truth*. This means that your actions must be executed with the same degree of tension, *tempo*, *rhythm*, and relaxation as you would use fulfilling the same action under similar circumstances in life.

PART III: EXERCISES: HOLDING THE AUDIENCE'S ATTENTION, DYNAMIC (DRAMATIC) CONFLICT, DUAL PERSPECTIVES, AND EXPERIENCING

Dynamic Conflict and Character Revealed

We are not interested in stories of life going on as usual. For a story to hold an audience's attention it must be *dynamic*, based on a struggle with a conflict. We want to see the protagonist of the story strive to overcome opposing forces. This is called an *object of struggle*. An object of struggle is a conflict that is either physical or psychological and that is difficult to overcome because it continuously requires battle with it in order to win.

We go to see recognizable human beings in extraordinary situations. When characters come up against large-scale public or important private challenges, by their responses we see what they are made of. Plays and films reveal profound truths about human beings represented as characters. They are often about the growth or demise of a human being in extraordinary circumstances. As we watch the lead characters get tested, we imagine ourselves in these situations. We may identify with the hero and for a time feel his strength or special powers flowing through our veins. We may experience the power of the villain and enter, fascinated, into the mind of a killer. We may understand the weakness of the victim that did not allow him to stand up and in this understanding forgive ourselves for the times we did not take a stand. Characters are tested in struggles called conflict; conflict is at the center of drama.

The Loma Prieta Earthquake: A Real-Life Event

The following story is an example of a major event that focuses everyone's attention. You may have already experienced a natural disaster in the earlier improvisations of the Burnt House and the Rope Bridge. A challenging event creates dynamic conflict by providing obstacles that test and reveal character. French and Bennett were in the 1989 7.0 Loma Prieta earthquake in San Francisco, California (although in separate locations). French relates her experience of this event:

Living in San Francisco we experienced many small earthquakes, as evidenced by the cracks in the walls of our homes. When one occurred, we would decide whether it was worth getting out of bed and moving to a more protected location, such as under a staircase or in a doorframe, depending on how strong the earthquake was and how long it was lasting.

Some people can hear sound frequencies that others cannot. On October 17, 1989, I was in a Capoeira culture and history class at San Francisco State University. I could hear the sound wave of the earthquake seconds before it actually hit and screamed out to my classmates, "Earthquake! Get under the desks! Find shelter!" We all did so, ahead of the actual earthquake arriving.

I knew intellectually from science class and reading that the things that seem solid, such as cement buildings, are actually made of moving molecules. It was another thing though to have a sensory experience of that phenomenon. I could feel the many-feet-thick concrete foundation of the building I was in at the university flow beneath our feet like a wave in the ocean. This was a mind-altering experience.

When we got outside, someone had a portable device where we could get the news. There were no cell phones yet—at least not for regular people (probably hard for you to imagine not having the world at your fingertips). Some people immediately started directing traffic at the large intersections where the traffic lights were dimmed due to a lack of electricity; other people looted the stores with malfunctioning (or unpowered) security systems, grabbing televisions and stereos and jewelry. We heard that a major bridge, the San Francisco Bay Bridge, had collapsed. This piece of news was overblown and led us to believe the quake was even more devastating than it was. We found out later, however, that the two-story freeway in an industrial neighborhood near Oakland, on the eastern side of the San Francisco Bay, had sandwiched together, trapping and killing many people in their cars.

Immediately after this catastrophic event, some people who lived near the collapsed freeway, most of them low-income, responded by risking their lives to go into this dangerous freeway that could collapse on their heads at any moment to try to rescue survivors. These heroes were widely celebrated, and the officials representing the cities around the freeway promised that when they rebuilt the freeway they would not put it through their neighborhoods this time. This was their reward because no one really wants a freeway running next to their home. However, the rich people in other neighborhoods didn't want the freeway by their houses, either (although they probably all used it more), and I assume they had more political clout. When it actually came time to rebuild, they reneged on this promise and built the freeway exactly where it had been: through the heroes' neighborhoods. All of these people revealed their characters.

Figure 8.1 Aftermath of the Loma Prieta earthquake. Workers carry materials to be used as reinforcement of Interstate 880 in the Bay Area. The 1989 earthquake killed an estimated 273 people and did $1 billion in damage. Photo: © Chris Wilkins/AFP/Getty Images

A few years later, another devastating incident impacted the Bay Area, started this time by human error (or malice). This was the 1991 fire that wiped out whole neighborhoods in the Oakland-Berkeley Hills, as seen in the picture below. But it was the human response that left a lasting impression on me. The media interviewed the victims, asking as always those invasive and mostly obvious questions, "How does it feel . . . " and finding ways to provoke people to break down on camera for our voyeuristic interest. One man responded, "I lost everything: my house, entertainment system, my new car." Another man whose house was also destroyed, said, "Everyone got out safely. I am so grateful." This revealed a lot about the characters of the people interviewed and, I suppose, about those of us gawking at the devastation on the news or by driving through to get a better look.

—Stephanie Daventry French

Figure 8.2 A burned-out car and blackened trees are all that remain on a hillside in the Berkeley/Oakland area after the wildfire of October 20–21, 1991.
Photo: Photo © Morton Beebe/Corbis

> **8.1** *Observation Journal—A Test of Character (SDF)*
>
> Have you ever observed (or been in) a real-life situation where a human being was tested? How did he or she respond? This might be an incident of violence or threatened violence (even on a smaller scale, such as an incident of bullying), a political or work situation where somebody had to take a risk and stick his neck out, or any other situation where someone was asked to step up and lead, do nothing, or make things worse.

Objective (Need, Problem, Character's Goal)

How Do We Re-Create Human Struggle on the Stage?

In observation exercise 7.2 in the last chapter, you watched someone go after something they wanted and the different actions, steps, or tactics they used to try to get it. We use a variety of tactics to get what we want from various people in our lives. You have probably figured out what different strategies and tactics work best to get what you want from a mother or father, boss, teacher, friend, or significant other. The way you get what you want reveals something about your character. Over the next few weeks of your training, it will help you to continue to observe this common human behavior in life.

Consider the situation where student A (lacking academic integrity or a commitment to his own learning) wants to get his roommate to write a paper for him so he can go to a concert. The roommate, student B, however, has a hot first date (and also thinks writing someone's paper violates his own academic integrity). What might be some ways that student A tries to persuade student B to write his paper?

- Brainstorm different ways (actions/tactics) that student A might try to get what he wants (objective) to try to solve his conflict (wanting to go to a concert but having a paper due). In this case, student A would be driving the action in pursuit of his objective, and student B would be responding. These types of dynamic situations will be explored in detail throughout this chapter and in Chapter 11: Verbal Action.

When trying to pinpoint a character's objective, ask yourself, What is the problem my character is struggling with? What does the character want that he believes will solve the problem or fill the need (objective)? An objective is like a goal, a direction that will focus all the other choices and behavior of the character (and thereby you, the actor, inhabiting the character). When, in the case of these improvisations, you are acting as yourself in a variety of situations, ask the "magic if" question, "If I were in this situation and had to deal with this problem, how could I get my roommate to write my paper for me?" You must fulfill moment–to-moment the action steps you take to reach the objective. In the above situation the action steps might progress from "requesting" to "calling in a favor," to "bribing," and finally to "blackmailing." The actions are active and thus bring the character and the play to life. The variety of tactics involve the actor in interesting nuances within the main dynamic. When working with a play, these action steps are referred to as the *through-line of action.*

Make the objective specific. If, in a scene with other characters, it helps to discern something specific you want them to do or say that will make you know your need is more likely to be met, then figure out what to do to get that response. Ask the questions "How can I get her to do or think this thing that will solve my problem? What can I do physically to make it happen? What do I need to get the other character specifically to do, and can I make that something clear and physical?" Objectives are not just internal motivations but have specific external expressions and manifestations.

Using Obstacles and Psychological Burdens

How Do We Gain and Hold an Audience's Attention?

As we watch a dynamic conflict unfold, we want to know who wins and who loses. All of your improvisations must have an *obstacle* with which to struggle: a conflict. In a play the conflict might arise due to an *external obstacle*, an opposing force or an opposing character. If the obstacle arises from within the character, in the form of doubts, fears, low self-esteem, or even the need to hide a headache, this is called a *psychological burden*. A psychological burden is an emotionally based worry that you must carry with you and often need to hide from others. (In dramatic or literary analysis of plot structure we also refer to this as a *complication*.) Perhaps there is no better example in all of literature than *Hamlet*. Hamlet's murdered father, the king, appears to him as a ghost and describes how he was murdered and who was to blame and demands vengeance. Hamlet allows doubt, conscience, and fear to cause him to hesitate to take revenge against the murderer: his uncle, Claudius, who is now king. As a result of his psychological burden Hamlet does not act until the final scene of the play, his indecision having led to the deaths of others along the way.

To begin, choose physical obstacles with which to struggle, then progress to psychological burdens. When you get proficient, then you may choose both physical obstacles and psychological burdens. For example: There may be an obstacle such as the door is locked and you don't have the key; there is an emergency, but you have lost your phone and none is nearby; or you are trying to sleep, and it is too hot and humid. In a verbal improvisation the opposing force could be another character or group of characters, society, an aspect of nature, or the supernatural. The most complex situations employ both psychological and physical objects of struggle.

Experiencing

How Does *Dual Perspectives* Relate to the Central Concept in the Acting Technique Called Experiencing?

Psychophysical actions bring you, the actor, and you as the character to life. This is called the *Dual Perspectives*. The Dual Perspectives is an important element of an action where the actor puts at least 95 percent of her attention on the creation of the character in performance but watches herself with the remaining 5 percent as the actor in order to practice artistic control and restraint.

The advanced aspects of this fine brush in your Actor's Palette will be thoroughly discussed later in Chapter 18: The Actor of Living Experience and Chapter 19: The Creative Life: Communion with Audience and Society.

When your actions are purposeful, logical, and consecutive, you and the imaginary character begin to merge. This is called achieving the state of "*I am*" or "*I exist*." Again, this is not that you believe you are the character, merely that you walk a mile in his shoes: you see the events through his eyes and experience what it is to be a human being like him in that situation. It is the first major step toward transformation into *experiencing* your character in the role, and what Stanislavsky called "living the life of the human soul."

> **A Breakthrough Discovery**
>
> The following is a real-life story of Philip Bennett's about Sonia Moore, who late in her career discovered a new psychophysical key to spontaneity for the actor. This discovery helps actors to fulfill Stanislavsky's ultimate goal of experiencing the role.
>
> When in my early twenties I went to New York in order to receive actor training, I was very fortunate to find a Russian émigré actress, teacher, and director by the name of Sonia Moore. Sonia had trained under Evgeny Vakhtangov, whom Stanislavsky had called his "greatest disciple." Vakhtangov was in charge of the Third Studio of the Moscow Art Theatre, and Sonia had studied there during the time of the Russian Revolution and civil war.
>
> Sonia had been cast as a member of the orchestra and played a comb in the studio's production of *Princess Turandot*, a highly stylized production staged on a cubist set. Sonia related to me on more than one occasion how Vakhtangov was never satisfied with his staging or the acting. She said that the actors would rehearse into the early hours of the morning, and finally when they thought they had found something that worked, he would return the next day to begin all over again with new ideas.

Constant experimentation and discovery is the key factor in the System, and Vakhtangov was absolutely dedicated to the principle. Sonia was, too.

Every summer she would pack up a large box of books, magazines, and theatrical articles from Germany, Poland, and Russia that she had received during the year and fly off to Capri in Italy, where she would read, study, and distill all she could about new developments that were occurring in European and Russian theatre. Each fall, Sonia returned to her studio in New York with a series of new exercises and a deeper understanding of how the System was being used by actors and directors.

In September 1969, I entered my second year of training at the studio. Sonia's research had led her to realize the importance of the movement of the back and torso in order to express and convey thoughts and feelings. Furthermore, she insisted that we move from the spine before we spoke. It was very confusing, but we tried it and found it uncomfortable and artificial. Nevertheless, she explained that in life, when we really listen and react, there is nearly always a slight movement of the spine. She explained that this occurs due to the great number of nerves along the spine and that we must become aware of these subtle energies and trust our body's first impulses. Although it was difficult, we continued to practice, and eventually we were able to do it.

The experiment was amazingly successful. In a few months I was able to express all of my thoughts and feelings with very little visible movement, but it was there, nevertheless. I noticed that gradually I became more comfortable in my body and that emotional involvement arose naturally and with greater spontaneity.

Sonia believed that her experiments grew out of the natural evolution of the System, and like Stanislavsky, she did not believe that the System should ever be fixed. It was to expand and develop as we learned more about human nature and the laws of physics that influence our creativity.

In the years that followed, Sonia came to realize that not just any movement of the spine was needed in order to do this but the movement of specific muscle groups. Exercises were invented to help the actor discover his own muscular movement with greater specificity. She theorized that there may be no universal pattern that worked for everyone and that each actor needed to find which muscles were connected to which thoughts, feelings, and impulses. She speculated that once an actor mastered his bodily impulses he could become emotionally involved as the character in the imaginary situation quite easily and that such an actor could easily go from moment to moment while performing a role and convey to an audience the most subtle of impressions.

For nearly forty years I have been using and teaching this process, which my students teasingly call W.E.D.G.A.G. As an actor, teacher, and director I can honestly testify that it works with great success. My students are capable of achieving involvement as the character in their roles every time they enter the stage. There is never any need to do "emotional memory preparation" prior to any scene or improvisation. All that is needed is to think deeply within the circumstances and fulfill a purposeful action with the whole body, mind, and soul.

—Philip G. Bennett

Exercise 8.5: To Read (Subtle Nonverbal Actions with Obstacles and Dual Perspectives) (SM/PGB)

Purpose: To practice dual consciousness by having a real activity—reading—that requires a high degree of internal focus while also being aware of an external obstacle to that focus. To achieve this you must employ the internal and external monitors.

Main actions:
1. To read at home.
2. To read at the library

Guidelines:
- The main action of reading should be primarily stillness, with subtle movements through the spine as you think and respond to what you are reading and the surrounding circumstances and obstacles. After you have decided to act on the obstacle, there may be a larger physical choice in that action.
- Truly read and do not only pretend.
- Choose a strong physical obstacle with which you need to struggle and attempt to overcome; for example, a very noisy neighbor who disturbs your concentration, etc. Remember that you are alone and must not try to interact with imaginary people at home or in the library.
- Part of you must really be reading and making sense of the book while the artistic part of you creates images (using whatever sense or senses are most apt) and also responds to them.
- Do not figure out beforehand how you will overcome the obstacle. Work that problem out on your feet.

8.5 Reflection Journal—To Read

Did you remember to use the "magic if"? Did you actually read part of the book? Did you see specific images of the obstacle (or hear specific sounds)? Did you use W.E.D.G.A.G. to respond to the obstacle? Were you able to control the flow of muscular energy by using the muscles of your torso? Did you struggle with the obstacle, or was the obstacle not that important? Who won, you or the obstacle? Did you get any physical feelings and/or emotional responses arising out of the situation? If yes, how did that change your internal intensity or your external speed?

PART IV: TEMPO-RHYTHM: THE BRIDGE BETWEEN INNER EXPERIENCE AND PHYSICAL EXPRESSION

How Do You Connect Inner Life with Outer Expression?

Remember the definition of *tempo-rhythm*. *Tempo* is defined as the timing and speed of your actions, and *rhythm* as the inner intensity. *Tempo-rhythm* is one of the most important Elements of Action as it creates a bridge between what the actor is experiencing inwardly and his ability to express it physically. An incorrect tempo *or* rhythm throws off your scene partners and can ruin a scene or even an entire play. For example, if the pace remains too much the same it can put the audience to sleep. If pauses are not in the right places, the audience will not laugh at a comedy.

Another issue about tempo-rhythm that is important to acting technique is that the correct tempo-rhythm can stir your emotions. If the connection between the inner rhythm and the external tempo is incorrect, though, it cannot bridge the necessary gap between mind and body. This interferes with psychophysical behavior, making organic emotional involvement nearly impossible and also the situation unbelievable to the audience. (This technique may be purposely employed in certain types of comedy or more absurd plays.)

The given circumstances of an improvisation or scene dictate the tempo (timing and speed of your actions); while the personal images, feelings, and emotional reactions of the actor dictate the inner rhythm. Of course, there is a strong overlap between external circumstances and inner images.

In this section we shall further explore exercises designed to work with several variations of tempo and rhythm.

Exercise 8.6: Preparing for a Date (Connecting Inner Rhythm with Outer Intensity) (PGB)

Purpose: Your task is to justify and connect the inner rhythms with the outer tempos spontaneously and truthfully. Directors often ask actors for a specific external movement tempo or rhythm for delivery of lines. The actor must be able to make this adjustment instantly and learn to justify it within the circumstances of the character and the play.

Exercise 8.6A: Preparing for a Date

It is best to try this at home and then bring in the props you need to re-create it in class. Really think about the steps you would take and the props you would need. However, it can also be done as a sensory evocation exercise miming the props (or using other items and treating them as if they were the specific tools of grooming).

Guidelines:
- In Chapter 2, Exercise 2.1 you performed a simple habit. Now you will re-create a sequence of habits that you might do when preparing for a date. Imagine the location with full sensory creation (using all your

senses). Think about the room where you do this activity. Close your eyes and try to create this room in your mind using all of your senses.

- **Sight:** What is the size and shape of the room? What pieces of furniture are in there? What are their sizes and shapes? Where are the closets, drawers, or cupboards, and how do they open? What are the colors in the room?
- **Touch:** What do the surfaces feel like? Pay particular attention to the floor. Are you normally wearing shoes or slippers or going barefoot when doing this task? How does your footwear or your bare feet feel against the floor?
- **Smell:** What are the smells of this room? Try to recall each of them and the combined effect as they mix together.
- **Hearing:** What are the sounds of this room (most rooms have a buzz to them if you are quiet)? What sounds are associated with your activity in this room?
- **Taste:** Does your activity create any specific taste sensations?
- Think about what props you need to fulfill this task.
- Ask yourself, "If I were completing this task, what steps would I go through to complete it?" Then picture yourself going through each step in detail.
- Now open your eyes but instead of seeing your acting studio and the other students, try to see this remembered location (the *where*) around you with your eyes open.
- Once you have a clear picture of the location, begin to mime each step of your task. (There is value to doing this exercise both without props, using only your imagination, and by bringing in and using all the items needed). Go through it a couple of times to make sure you have the exact sequence of small physical actions needed to complete it.

Exercise 8.6B: Preparing for a Date: External Tempo Directions (PGB)

Purpose: To notice how tempo affects circumstances and how tempo affects you.

Main Action: To groom yourself in preparation for . . .

Main Event: An exciting date.

Guidelines: During the following group exercise, the teacher will randomly call out additional circumstances and then numbers from one to ten that signify various tempos. *One* represents the absolute slowest tempo and *ten* the fastest speed of your action. Remember the number for the first exercise only dictates the speed. Allow yourself to respond to the changing tempos. Adaptations must be made for each individual circumstance. *Everyone is onstage at the same time.*

- You are grooming yourself for a date: brushing your teeth, combing your hair, etc. (The teacher calls out tempos.)

- Obstacle: You receive a text message that your date has had to cancel. (The instructor calls out a tempo. Take in the information and the new tempo.)
- Remember to direct the flow of energy from thought to your muscles and allow your body and specific physical actions to also affect your thoughts and emotions.

8.6 Reflection Journal—Preparing for a Date

How did this obstacle affect your tempo and rhythm? Did you see an image of a real person who canceled the date? How did your relationship with the person affect your inner rhythm? Are you disappointed, upset, angry, or relieved?

Exercise 8.7: Walking to Class (Leading with Internal Rhythm) (PGB)

Purpose: To notice how circumstances change your internal rhythm.
Main action: Walking to class.

Guidelines: Allow each of the circumstances below to change your inner intensity (rhythm). The teacher will suggest some possible circumstances that will color how you are walking. Allow each new circumstance to be from light to heavy intensity. This may also affect your tempo.

- When you get there, you will see the object of your current infatuation.
- When you get there, you will have to take a test you are not prepared for.
- When you get there, you will see your recent ex-lover with his or her new partner.

8.7 Reflection Journal—Walking to Class

Write a note about each circumstance and assign a number from one to ten for the depth of your internal response. *One* represents the lightest inner intensity (something of minimal concern requiring little attention) and *ten* something of deepest or gravest concern (which may require all your attention). What did you notice about how your tempo was affected by your inner intensity?

Exercise 8.8: Take a Walk! (Spontaneously Creating and Justifying Tempo-Rhythm) (PGB)

Purpose: To see how quickly you can put these elements together: building circumstances, creating an obstacle, reacting with a change of tempo and rhythm with truthful inner justification in the moment.

Guidelines:
- The tempo and rhythm may be different combinations than the more expected ones from the earlier exercise; for example, you may have a very heavy (*nine*) inner intensity but instead of slowing down may have to be moving at a tempo of *eight*. You could also be moving quickly (*seven*) doing something like skipping that requires only partial attention (*two*).
- You are walking: Begin!
- Decide where you are walking, including where you are coming from and going to (the three *wheres*).
- Quickly also decide who, what, when, and why.
- Name your event.
- Choose real images.
- Your tempo is *five*.
- You remember something important with an inner rhythm of *six*.
- Really think and allow the images to inform your tempo.
- It begins to rain.
- Use W.E.D.G.A.G. to encounter and evaluate what to do about the rain and go to tempo *eight*.
- Adapt your situation and your tempo-rhythm to express the obstacle of rain.
- A very pleasant memory comes to mind. Change your rhythm to *four* and your tempo to *six*.
- How does the memory in combination with the slower tempo affect your physical and emotional state?
- The rain stops.
- Justify gradually changing to a tempo of *three*.
- Justify bringing your inner rhythm up to *seven*.
- Gradually bring down your inner intensity to a *one* as you approach your destination.
- Justify coming to a complete stop and resting.
- End with a final gesture that expresses your feelings about the situation.

8.8 *Reflection Journal—Take a Walk!*

Did the internal rhythm (intensity) vary when you changed your external tempo? Were you able to keep up with the changes of thought and physical actions suggested by the commands? Did you see real and imaginary images? What feelings and emotions arose as a result of the combination of tempo and rhythm? Are you beginning to feel at ease using the muscles of your torso to express your thoughts and feelings?

8 NONVERBAL ACTION

How Do You Decide What Adaptations or Adjustments to Make to Obstacles?

Another very important element of an action is the *adaptation*. An adaptation is an adjustment to an obstacle. Obstacles, as we have previously discussed, come in many forms: psychological, physical, verbal. An adaptation is always improvised in the moment and is never fixed. Because adaptations are always improvised, it takes a bit of practice on the actor's part to develop the skill. There are a few points to remember in making a good adaptation: A well-executed adaptation must be *sharp, clear, interesting,* and *fitting. Fitting* means that an adaptation is aesthetically fitting to the given circumstances and appropriate for the character, period, and style of the play. An adaptation that is not fitting will draw the audience's attention away from the story and draw unnecessary attention to the actor. In those unfortunate moments, the actor as well as the spectator loses the character.

If an actor deliberately chooses an adaptation that is inappropriate for the character and executed for the sole purpose of drawing attention to himself, it is considered vulgar rather than fitting and disrespectful to the other members of the ensemble. (As with everything, there are always exceptions.)

Hello Dolly!

Although the following event was not a breach of ethics, and it was clearly selected by the artistic team, it serves to show how an adaptation might draw the audience's attention away from the story but still be entertaining and effective.

Many years ago, Bennett saw a Broadway musical that featured movie star Betty Grable, who had been a "pin-up" girl during the Second World War. She had her legs insured for $1 million, and was often called "the girl with the million-dollar legs." It so happened that she was cast as Dolly Levy in the road-show company of *Hello Dolly*.

The climactic act of the story takes place in a posh New York restaurant that Dolly used to frequent with her late husband. She had not been there for several years, and on her entrance, the waiters greet her with a song and dance.

In Thornton Wilder's original story, *The Matchmaker,* Dolly Levy was a turn-of-the-century Jewish widow who sustained herself as a matchmaker (someone who arranges marriages for lonely singles who needed a socially acceptable, proper introduction to someone of the opposite sex.) Remember now, that this is a polite society. Anyway, Dolly descends the grand staircase leading into the restaurant singing, dancing, and greeting all of her old friends. When the movie star actress playing Dolly reached the footlights, she suddenly ripped open her ankle-length skirt to reveal her still beautiful "million-dollar" legs. Now, this is supposed to be a middle-aged matron; she then walked out on the circular ramp that surrounded the orchestra pit and kicked her legs up in the air, intentionally enticing all of the gentlemen in the audience with whom she openly flirted.

It was great fun and and a big hit and very sexy. However, this behavior was an anachronism (something that does not fit the character in the circumstances)—especially in Wilder's nineteenth-century middle-aged,

> Jewish matron of polite society. It was effective, yes, but was it true to the story and character? Was it *fitting*? In the case of the musical genre and the star's reputation, perhaps it was a necessary commercial choice for the box office. In comedy, including musical comedy, directors may choose to include anachronism.
>
> —Philip G. Bennett

Adaptation, like every Element of Action, is a technical tool that when mastered will give you a greater range of colors on your artist's palette. The following list shows the four qualities that go into making a good adaptation (they need to be performed in the order presented here):

1. **Sharp:** The moment we encounter an obstacle there is an immediate reaction of awe or wonderment that changes the speed and timing of our actions. (This is when we need to use W.E.D.G.A.G.)
2. **Clear:** Your behavior must be clearly understood by the audience. Your reaction to an obstacle communicates what you think, feel, and do.
3. **Interesting:** Choices you make in the moment give you an opportunity to add a note of depth and interest to the character. It is important that you take the obstacles seriously and struggle to overcome them. When we see a character struggle with a problem, we can identify with what she is going through, and that is interesting—especially if the outcome is not predictable.
4. **Fitting:** The adaptation must aesthetically fit into the given circumstances and be typical for the character. Adaptations must not draw unjustified attention to an individual actor when it is not appropriate to do so.

Responding to Obstacles with Adaptations: General Guidelines

- In each of the following exercises you will encounter a physical obstacle that you must attempt to get around and overcome by making an adaptation.
- You must *not* decide how you will overcome the obstacle before going onstage but work out the problem "on your feet" and in the moment.
- Include as many elements of an action as possible that you have already learned and explored in previous chapters.
- Remember you may borrow situations from your own life and add your own imagination to adapt them to suit your purpose.
- Write down your images for all the planned aspects of the improvisation before going onstage, but try to see the images associated with the adaptation spontaneously (as you should not have planned ahead what it will be).
- Each obstacle must be addressed with W.E.D.G.A.G..
- Adaptations always require a change of tempo-rhythm.

8 NONVERBAL ACTION

Exercise 8.9: Improvisation: Great News! (SM/PGB)

Main action: You have come to tell a friend important and wonderful news when you discover your friend is not home.

- You have no phone on you (this may be a big "magic if" for some of you to imagine!). What do you do?
- Build your circumstances, but do *not* figure out how you will deal with the obstacle until you encounter it in the situation.
- Name your event.

8.9 Reflection Journal—Great News!

Did you remember to struggle with the obstacle? Did you make sure to have a sharp change of tempo-rhythm when you encountered the obstacle? Did you become emotionally involved in the imaginary situation? Did you see a real person for your friend? Was your news very important? How did you use W.E.D.G.A.G. when you realized that your friend was not at home?

Here are some other improvisations with an obstacle. Follow the guidelines and remember to reflect and record your experiments in your creative journal:

Exercise 8.10: Improvisation: the Job Interview (PGB)

Main Action: You are preparing to go to a very important job interview, and just as you are about to leave home, you cannot find your wallet or your keys. What do you do?

8.10 Reflection Journal—The Job Interview

If you decided to go to the interview, did you remember to turn out your lights and lock the door? The simplest of life's actions can be easily overlooked in the artificial environment of the stage. When your behavior is organic you will do exactly what you would do in life, only with artistic significance.

Exercise 8.11: Improvisation: Awards Banquet (SM/PGB)

Main Action: You are preparing to go to an awards banquet being held in your honor, but when you are about to leave, you discover a note under the door.

- The note expresses something urgent and of very high stakes that would pull the actor's attention away from the main action. The teacher or other students should write this so the actor must really discover it with no preconceived notions in the moment of the improvisation.
- What do you do?
- Do not attempt to figure out how you will respond to the note until you are in the situation.

> **8.11** *Reflection Journal—Awards Banquet*
>
> Did you pay attention to the details of preparation—i.e., dressing, grooming, polishing your shoes, etc.? Was each of your decisions accompanied by a corresponding gesture? What did you say with your final gesture? How important was the award as opposed to dealing with the note? How did these internal images affect your tempo-rhythm?

Exercise 8.12: Improvisation: The Family Heirloom (SM/PGB)

Guidelines: The following improvisation is slightly different for a man than for a woman.

The action for women is: to dress in order to attend a family reunion that celebrates the matriarch of your family, who has reached an advanced age. At the last minute you discover that the necklace, bracelet, or earrings she gave you, a family heirloom, is missing. What do you do?

The action for men is: to dress in order to attend a family reunion that celebrates the patriarch of your family, who has given you an antique pocket watch of great value (that you are expected to wear and show at this event). As you are preparing to leave you discover that it is missing. What do you do?

- It is important that you know what the lost item is worth to you both financially and personally. Does it have sentimental value?
- Use personal and/or imaginary images. The important thing is that the images are vivid and detailed and that they affect you.

> **8.12** *Reflection Journal—Family Heirloom*
>
> Did you express what the item meant to you? Was the item lost or stolen? Did you recover it? Did you think to call the authorities or decide not to go to the event? What feelings and emotions did the situation and action evoke in you?

Exercise 8.13: Additional Improvisation Actions for Practice (SM/PGB)

- You are asleep when you are awakened by a loud crash.
- You are studying late at night for a major examination, when the electricity goes off.
- You come home from working in a coal mine. You are filthy and covered with coal dust. Your body is aching and you are completely exhausted. You find a note from your spouse that reads: "I have taken the children and am leaving you, please don't try to contact us."

8 NONVERBAL ACTION

How Do You Create Life in Artificial Circumstances? Endowment: To Treat As

In the last chapter you explored how you endow the given circumstances with specifics that allow them to exist within the improvisation or production. In the following exercises you will take the concept of endowment into new territory. Endowment is a very important element of an action in your Actor's Palette that really addresses that fundamental question of the theatre we have already posed: How do you create life in artificial circumstances? While the actor, like the director and designers, is an interpretive playwright when responding to an already created play, bringing life to the stage is your generative power. *Endowment* is a term now common to acting and vital to improvisation, which was called by Stanislavsky *To Treat As*.

Endowment is a natural part of daily life. It means to give to someone or something qualities and values. We do this by means of treating another person or object as if they or it actually possessed the qualities we put on them. Some examples might be:

- to treat a stranger with kindness is to endow them with respect
- to treat someone dismissively in order to endow them with enemy status
- to treat a ring given to you by someone special (such as a wedding ring) with care is to endow it with love and value
- to treat a peer as if he were your lord and master

Endowment is essential for the stage because the environment of the stage is artificial but we must treat it as if it were the real thing. The other actors will likely not really be your lover or father or boss, and the wedding ring will be a fake one that was given to you by the props person, and the castle that your character lives in will be a set designed to represent a grand ancient castle.

When building a character, we need to ask ourselves, What is my relationship with the other characters? How shall I, as the character, treat them? How shall I use the tone of my voice and my body language to make this relationship clear? To make this specific, it helps to think about the behavior in similar relationships you have experienced or observed. If you have no experience of a specific kind of relationship for a play you may be doing, you would need to try to find people in relationships like this to observe, interview, or read about.

Props, sets, and costumes can also be endowed with special qualities. You have already treated a chair as if it were a throne or the electric chair. You have already treated piled up chairs or other objects as the rubble of a burnt house, and a crumpled up piece of paper as a precious object. Now you are going to practice this technique even more consciously, and through a variety of improvisational challenges, so that it can begin to be organic. To Treat As is also a good preparation for the sensory exercises that are to follow.

Truth and Belief

Dramatic truth, truth in acting, is similar but not exactly the same as in life. We are looking for what Stanislavsky called the true measure (or measure of truth). When you are acting you fulfill an action with the same degree of thought, tempo, and energy as you would under the same circumstances in life. When an actor rushes or goes too slowly or *tries* to show an emotion (indicating), or forces the emotion by more physical effort than is required or through pushing with the breath, the results seem false to an audience. You don't need to do more (overacting) or less (underacting) onstage than in life to fulfill an action or express an emotion (unless you are doing slapstick or farce or similar exaggerated style).

This is particularly true in film acting. One difference onstage is that while one part of you is fulfilling an important action or experiencing the important event, another part of you still needs to project to the back of the theatre and stay open to the audience so they can see your face and read the thoughts and images in your eyes (dual perspectives). As you develop your voice (which we will start working on in the next chapter) and as you get practice in dual consciousness on the stage, this will get easier to do.

Belief arises when you can fulfill an action truthfully enough to make it believable to an audience—but *you* don't have to believe that it is real. You, the actor as artist, will be working in an ensemble with a director and other artists, searching for the truth of human experience as written by the playwright and interpreted by the director. You are searching for two truths: the truth of the behavior of the character (who represents a human being), and the dramatic truth of the psychological and philosophical or spiritual ideas of the playwright.

When your actions succeed in convincing the spectator, they will also cause belief to arise in you. This has been observed as a phenomenon in the brain and described by Nobel Prize–winning neurobiologist Eric R. Kandel as when "both the artist and the viewer have Aha! Moments—sudden flashes of insight—that are thought to involve similar circuits of the brain."[8]

The behavior itself, as it psychophysically replaces behavior in the memory of your body and the neural patterns of your brain, will arouse related emotions that have flowed through these same paths. Cognitive science has now demonstrated that we respond psychophysically to imaginary or anticipated events similarly to how we respond to real events unfolding before us. For example, we can get scared in a horror film or feel anxious about an imagined future problem or feel joyous about the impending visit of a good friend. Note that none of these things has actually happened, yet we have a real emotional response.

Enemies of Truth

Some other choices that impede believability include:

- *indicating* (showing rather than telling) and, similarly, *telegraphing* (overblown choices)
- *grimacing* or *mugging* (overexaggerated facial expressions)
- *cliché*s (gestures repeated so often onstage by inexperienced actors as to diminish their meaning, so they become empty—crossing your arms, putting your hands in your pockets, hands on the hips, clasping and unclasping the hands, or leaning on the furniture.

Each of us as actors has habits that we fall back into when we don't know what else to do (some other common distracting fallback or nervous behaviors are rocking

---

[8] Eric R. Kandel, *The Age of Insight: The Quest to Understand the Unconscious in Art, Mind, and Brain, from Vienna 1900 to the Present* (New York: Random House, 2012), 449.

8 NONVERBAL ACTION

side to side or back to front, and pacing without purpose). When these are pointed out to you, know that you likely need to do more work on the scene to understand what the character is thinking and trying to do so that your choices are more apt and specific.

> **Exercise 8.14: Improvisation: My Precious Object (To Treat As) (PGB)**
>
> **Purpose:** To use images and specific thoughts of imaginary circumstances to imbue an object with great meaning.
>
> **Form/structure:** To practice the moment before, to reflect the important discoveries and decisions, to punctuate the improvisation with a clear final gesture.
>
> **Main action:** To treat a mundane object as if it held great personal and/or monetary value.
>
> **Guidelines:**
> - It is not necessary to *believe* that the chair is a throne (as in Chapter 5) or the glass a diamond; that would be delusional. What is important is that you treat the objects *as if* they were a throne and a diamond. What is needed is to make your actions believable and truthful.
> - Treat a small object as a precious item. It is helpful if you endow it with both personal and financial value, but it can work with only one or the other.
> - Give thorough thought to your improvisation.
> - Make certain to answer all the questions of the Given Circumstances.
> - Choose a strong obstacle.
> - Create a beginning, middle, and end: Allow the improvisation to begin by being in the circumstances and seeing the images of them clearly before your first discovery. Begin the action wondering about the object (discovery) and then following each of the other steps of W.E.D.G.A.G. Use W.E.D.G.A.G. as you meet the obstacle. Finally, make sure that your adaptation is sharp, clear, and interesting by using W.E.D.G.A.G. Allow the gesture after you make this adaptation to be a clear punctuation leaving a strong impact on the observing class.

8.14 *Reflection Journal—My Precious Object*

Did you find typical behavior to project that the object was both precious and valuable? (What is the difference between precious and valuable? How would you evaluate your adaptation? Did you succeed in finding the corresponding muscles that expressed your feelings?

> **Exercise 8.15: Additional to Treat As Actions for Practice (SM/PGB)**
>
> - To treat a pillow or large cloth as a cat
> - To treat a chair as a throne
> - To treat a chair as a vicious dog
> - To treat a liquid as poison
> - (and these from PGB):
> - to treat a stranger with kindness so as to endow them with respect
> - to treat someone dismissively in order to endow them with enemy status
> - to treat a ring given to you by someone special (such as a wedding ring) with care to endow it with love and value
> - to treat a peer as if he or she were your lord and master

Sensory Evocation (Objectless Exercises)

Sense memory is the recall of how a particular object, place, or situation looked, smelled, sounded, tasted, or felt through touch. *Sensory evocation* (or *re-creation*) is applying the "magic if," using all the senses through imagination: this object would look, smell, sound, taste, or feel this way, with this weight and functionality.

Use of the senses through sense memory or sensory evocation and *to treat as* are very closely connected; in fact, they are inseparable, as are all of the Elements of Psychophysical Action. Here you will practice sense memory exercises as part of an organic action but within imaginary circumstances. This next step builds on the Burnt House exercise in Chapter 2.

Sense memory and sensory re-creation, and their correlation with analogous emotions, will be developed further in Chapter 12, Orchestrating Emotions. In Chapter 12 we will explore the elements of *sensory evocation, analogous emotions,* and *memory of the body* in greater depth.

Using an imaginary object requires absolute physical clarity. An imaginary object must appear to the spectator as truly existing. The actor must endow the space with substance by giving the imaginary object weight, shape, and texture. The physical actions must be executed with exacting detail and consistency. Movements need to be precise. Sloppy actions will only confuse the onlooker and destroy the illusion.

> **Exercise 8.16: The Important Document (SM/PGB)**
>
> **Purpose:** To apply your understanding of the senses to an imaginary situation
>
> **Choose from the following actions:**
> - To burn a love letter
> - To burn the last will and testament of a rich relative
> - To burn a secret government document
>
> **Guidelines:**
> - Build your imaginary circumstances and name the event.

- If you have a similar situation in your own life, use it; if not, use the "magic if" and your imagination.
- See in your mind a real person or persons who may have sent you the letter, or who is connected with the will.
- Choose an obstacle that could easily prevent your burning the letter.
- Use a real piece of paper for your letter and know its exact contents.
- Express how you feel about the contents of the letter by controlling the flow of muscular energy and the use of muscles along the spine.
- You must not use real fire (as in most cases this will set off alarms and sprinklers in your building) but imagine the flame and recall its heat while holding the letter. You may use matches or a lighter; however, you must not ignite the lighter or matches. Instead, use sensory evocation to stimulate your senses as if there were a fire.
- Make each physical action simple, clean, and clear, thus allowing your classmates to believe in the illusion.

8.16 *Reflection Journal—To Burn an Important Document*

Did you have a strong reason for burning the letter or document? Were your physical movements precise and consistent? Did you succeed in convincing your classmates that there was a real flame? Did you remember to struggle with an obstacle that might have prevented you from achieving the objective? Did you get involved? What emotions arose spontaneously through the control of the flow of energy?

Exercise 8.17: Additional Sensory Evocation Actions for Practice (SM/JB/PGB)

- To toss a salad, make a sandwich, scramble eggs, or make coffee or tea
- To thread a needle and sew on a button
- To iron a shirt or thread a shoelace
- To clean and dress a wound
- To make someone else's bed

PART V: ZONES OF SILENCE: TWO- AND THREE-PERSON NONVERBAL IMPROVISATIONS

The impetus when onstage with others is to go immediately to speech. When speech is introduced, the trap is to become talking heads with unexpressive bodies. This does not reflect the life of a human being or real interpersonal communication. It is vital to be able to influence other actors (other human beings, for that matter) with nonverbal actions and also to receive and interpret the many nonverbal clues they are offering. In real life we are very much alive and in communication with others even when we are not speaking.

When words are added to your improvisations in the next chapter, they must be necessary and filled. You will need to practice with others in justified silence in order to see how much you can truthfully express toward others through nonverbal communication. Later these types of nonverbal communications will enrich the moments before and after you speak and when others are speaking, as well as adding the many required layers to your scenes and improvisations.

In the next improvisations, you will attempt to influence other actors through nonverbal actions. In the first improvisation your actions may be carried out primarily physically but, through justification, will be clearly connected to their psychological motivation. In the last two improvisations of this chapter, you will need to find appropriate physical behavior to justify the circumstances, but the main action will be carried out as *mental action*, with more-subtle physical expressions. Mental action involves concentrated focus to affect someone's senses through sending energy (such as the earlier-discussed idea that Stanislavsky explored of sending rays of prana, and the feeling someone is watching you while you are in a car with the windows rolled up). This is very similar to the scientific idea that all matter is affected by being observed.

Exercise 8.18: Improvisation: the Silent Treatment (Two Roommates Refuse to Speak to One Another after an Argument) (SM/PB)

Purpose: To convey as much information as needed in order to understand the situation and relationships between people without using words.

Main action (Partner A drives the action): To annoy

Counteraction: (partner B) responds to and challenges the main action: To ignore

Guidelines:
- The situation: You and your roommate have had quite a heated argument the night before, you each have vowed to yourself not to speak to the other until he or she apologizes. Meanwhile, you have another agenda, and now it is the next morning and you have no desire to repeat the row by speaking with one another. One of you has the action to annoy, and your partner has the action to ignore you. A quick review about building circumstances:
- Discuss the situation you wish to build and decide on: Who, What, When, Where, with Whom (your relationship), and Why (the purpose behind your action, its motivation).
- Where from and where to: If you are making an entrance or exit, decide where you are coming from and where you are going to (people don't just appear from nowhere). For example, if you are getting up after a night of partying you might be hung over, tired, and completely overwhelmed by the mess. So, how would you enter the kitchen under those circumstances? Choose behavior that is typical and will convey your entrance and physical state clearly to the audience.
- Do not think of how you will behave until you are on your feet and in the imaginary situation. Let the *how* take care of itself! This is a big part of what keeps any moment on stage alive.

8 NONVERBAL ACTION

- Discuss with your partner what the fight the night before was about and find behavior that makes your situation clear and, if possible, why you are not on speaking terms.
- Conflict on stage is about winning and losing. State your objective in active language. For example: I want my roommate to move out, or I'm going to ignore my roommate until she gets tired and gives up, to prove that I am the stronger.
- Write down action-steps. Action-steps are the smaller actions you choose before going onstage in order to accomplish your objective and win the conflict. Plan and write down your strategy but keep it to yourself.
- Borrow images from your daily life and use your imagination to create images, as well. Images will help you justify and believe in your actions.
- Keep in mind the measure of truth. Do not indicate (show us what you are doing in obvious ways), overact, or underact, as any of these choices will not be believable and thus will jar the audience out of experiencing the situation with you. Behave as you would in life.
- Do not try to be a character—yet. Remember, the way to transformation into character later will be to master selection and truthful fulfillment of typical actions of another human being, so practice this now, coming from yourself.
- When you have discussed and built the imaginary circumstances, go onstage and prepare your set, then begin the improvisation.

8.18 Reflection Journal—The Silent Treatment

If you made an entrance, were you able to clearly project where you were coming from? Did you achieve communion together? Were you able to affect your partner and react to one another spontaneously? Did your actions-steps assist you in achieving your objective? Did you find typical actions to annoy or ignore your partner, and did you project why you did not want to speak with one another? Did you make adaptations and adjustments to obstacles? Who won and who lost? What would you do differently?

Exercise 8.19: Improvisation: Secret Agent (Two Spies and a Detective) (SM/BGP)

Purpose: To establish and practice communication and observation while acting in a zone of silence.

Guidelines: The teacher assigns the individual roles in secret. It is important that the actors do not know who is their contact or the detective. Spy #1 is the spy whose mission it is to deliver a secret note. It can be in the form of a microchip or flash drive, whatever the student chooses. Spy #2 is the spy who must receive the secret information, and the third person is an undercover detective whose mission is to prevent the passing of the secret, to confiscate the information, and make an arrest.

- The actors may discuss where their event takes place but must not reveal to one another their roles. They need to imagine that they have never met and therefore must use their powers of observation to figure out on their feet who is who. The action takes place in a public setting: an airport, bus terminal, gallery, or museum. (Avoid setting the scene in a restaurant as that may require waiters and conversation.)
- Spy #1 must find his contact, pass the information, and speedily exit to avoid arrest.
- Spy #2, who is to receive the secret information, must also figure out who her contact is, get the information, and attempt to exit.
- The detective must hide his identity, prevent the transfer of the highly sensitive information, and make an arrest.
- The detective can speak only one line: when the arrest is made.

Note: At this point the teacher can decide to allow the actors to continue the improvisation with speech or to end it.

8.19 Reflection Journal—Secret Agent

Was the secret information successfully passed to the right person? What did you experience while you were trying to figure out who was your contact? Did you get it right, or were you arrested? What did you learn about observation from this improvisation in silence? Did you achieve communion with your partners?

Exercise 8.20: Improvisation: The Elegant Performance (SM/PGB)

Purpose: To fulfill the given action without disturbing the imaginary performance or those around you. It therefore requires you to develop more subtle means of communication. This is vital if you later choose to act on camera in films or television but is equally important for the stage.

Guidelines:
- Three persons are at a formal performance such as a play, symphony, opera, or ballet.
- Two of you are on a date. Discuss the details of your relationship. Is it a first date? How long have you known one another? What are your feelings toward one another? Choose images from your own life experience and observation.
- Use the magic if, asking, What would I do if I were in this situation, today, here and now, for the first time?
- Build the situation: The three of you must decide which type of performance you are attending: a play, opera, symphony, or ballet. Be specific and decide on the name of the production. Agree on the location of

8 NONVERBAL ACTION

> your seating and the location of the stage. Are you in a balcony, a box, or in the stalls on the main floor? Draw upon performances you have attended and/or use your imagination to create the performance.
> - The third person is alone. She (or he) arrives at the theatre and quickly recognizes one of the people on the date as someone with whom she has had a recent romantic entanglement. The first task of the solo person is to see a film of mental images in her mind to remember the details of the past encounter and try to figure out why this person is with someone else now.
> - **Note:** It is important that this not be discussed but improvised in the moment, in order that the actors on the date don't know which of them is the recognized person. The person who is alone must eventually remember where she has last seen the person she recognizes.
> - Here's the fun part: The person who is alone must do everything she can to get the recognized person's attention without the date seeing her.
> - What series of action-steps must you take to accomplish the task?
> - Everyone must improvise their reactions rather than planning them in advance.
> - Make entrances. Would you carry a program? What is fitting behavior for a theatrical performance? How would you dress, etc.?

8.20 Reflection Journal—The Elegant Performance

Were you able to accomplish your action? Were you able to see a film of images of the performance? Did you recall the music or speech of the performance? Write down your discoveries and thoughts.

Summary

In this chapter you have practiced many improvisations and exercises using nonverbal actions in silence. Nonverbal actions may focus on thought (*inner monologue* or *inner dialogue*, if you are struggling with your own thoughts) or actions directed at another without speech (*mental action*). They still must be conveyed physically so that the thoughts can be communicated to an audience. Other silent actions may be executed primarily physically (physical actions) but must also have associated thoughts: all actions need to be *psychophysical*. Selecting the most fitting and typical behavior is possible when you thoroughly study and understand the *given circumstances* as offered by a playwright or created by you and your scene partners in improvisations. You then fulfill the *actions* in a justified, logical, and consecutive sequence executed in the correct *tempo-rhythm*. As you struggle toward an objective through specific *action-steps*, you meet *obstacles* and respond with innovative and spontaneous *adaptations*, creating interest for the spectator. When executed truthfully, you will evoke both your senses and feelings. Try to practice some of the exercises at home to deepen your mastery of these elements. In the next chapter, try to bring all of the elements practiced in improvisations here as you begin to incorporate speech.

New Acting Terms and Concepts

Terms used in the Stanislavsky System are in italics.

- ☐ *études*
- ☐ *psychological burden*
- ☐ *sculpting*
- ☐ *supertask*

CHAPTER 9

Embodying Voice

"What is important is to find where our energy lies, and that is always with the breath"[1]

—Cicely Berry

- The Second Signal System: The Human Voice

Part I: The Components of Vocal Production
- The Anatomy of the Human Voice
- Alignment to Support Breath and Phonation
  - Exercise 9.1: Optimal Alignment
  - Exercise 9.2: Releasing Shoulders and Neck
- The Anatomy of Breath
- How Do These Parts of the Body Coordinate in Breathing and Vocal Production?
  - Exercise 9.3: Extending the Breath Cycle
  - Exercise 9.4: Tai Chi Breaths
- Onset, Phonation, and Pitch
- How do the Vocal Folds Create Sound?
  - Exercise 9.5: Pitch Trills (Lip Trills)

Part II: Caring for Your Unique Voice
- Developing Awareness of Your Unique Voice
  - Exercise 9.6: Personal Speech Habits
- Developing Healthy Habits of Voice and Effective Use of Speech

The advent of new scientific tools has increased our ability to understand the human voice in action, and actors can use this information to develop and sharpen this amazing tool in your Actor's Palette. The training and development of your vocal instrument is generally divided into voice, speech, and singing (also called *voice* for the sake of classes so this can be confusing). At higher levels of voice training, these are each taught in separate classes or private lessons.

Perhaps you've heard that acting is 80 percent voice and speech. When Stanislavsky played Othello as a young man, he asked the famous Italian actor Tomasso Salvini (whose performance of Othello was considered a work of genius) for his advice. Salvini repeated, "Voice, Voice and more Voice."[2] Shakespeare's advice to the players in *Hamlet*, and thereby to actors speaking his text, is:

---

[1] Berry, Cicely. *The Actor and the Text*. Revised edition. New York: Applause Books (1987) 1992, p. 25.
[2] Konstantin Stanislavsky, *An Actor's Work*, trans. Jean Benedetti (London: Routledge, 2009), 380.

> Speak the speech, I pray you, as I pronounce it to you, trippingly on the tongue; but if you mouth it, as many of our players do, I had as lief the town-crier spoke my lines. Nor do not saw the air too much with your hand, thus; but use all gently, for in the very torrent, tempest, and (as I may say) whirlwind of your passion, you must acquire and beget a temperance that may give it smoothness.[3]

In this chapter you will actively examine the following components of voice and speech: *Alignment, Breath, Onset, Phonation,* and *Pitch*. (Chapter 10 will cover a number of aspects of Activating Speech.) This will be accomplished in the following two sections:

- Part I: The components of vocal production
- Part II: Caring for your unique voice

> **Important note: Ongoing voice training is as important to the actor as fitness, conditioning, and skill training are to the athlete**
>
> This introduction to voice and speech is only to develop some beginning awareness about your vocal instrument ahead of your seeking the guidance of a certified voice teacher, or to supplement some basic information you may already have. Acting classes may provide basic technique, warm-ups, and a beginning framework for proper speech but do not take the place of formal voice, speech, and singing training. You will need an expert to give you feedback on your voice to ensure you are using it in healthy ways. You will also need a voice teacher to show you proper articulation of the sounds of English so that you can form the vowels and consonants clearly and precisely for maximum progress.
>
> The mechanisms of your vocal instrument are subtle, and most of us know little about them. If you do not have a good voice teacher available, you can acquire some important information from the books recommended at the end of this chapter. Even great books cannot replace the corrections of a voice expert, required to ensure the effective and healthy development of your voice, speech, and/or singing ability. Be patient. It takes years, even with excellent teachers, to develop the full capacity of your voice as a singer or professional actor or speaker.

The Second Signal System: The Human Voice

The human voice is a marvelous and unique instrument, combining properties relevant to both string and wind instruments. *You* are the instrument and the musician. To become a virtuoso in its use requires understanding and caring for the instrument and expanding your capacity to express through it.

---

[3] William Shakespeare, *Hamlet*, III.ii, 1–7, as punctuated in Wilbur L. Cross and Tucker Brooke, *The Yale Shakespeare: The Complete Works (*New York: Barnes and Noble/Yale University Press, 1993), 997.

9 EMBODYING VOICE

As an actor you must employ a wide range of sounds expressing a host of ideas and a range of subtexts and emotions. Your voice is superbly designed to reflect each nuance of human experience by means of infinite combinations of *pitch, volume, tempo,* and *rhythm,* all further shaped by *articulation.*

The voice is your *second signal system* as a person, and as an actor. When functioning organically, the voice emerges expressively from your *first signal system*, the body. Children use their voices freely and without strain enhanced by naturally fluid and supportive posture. They instinctively sit with long and free spines and open chests. For acting and singing you will want to regain some of this freedom while at the same time developing more capacity and control. In early voice training, these two things often seem to be at odds. Be patient but diligent.

PART I: THE COMPONENTS OF VOCAL PRODUCTION

The Anatomy of the Human Voice

How much do you know about your our own body and brain? Most of us learn the parts of the body that we can see on the outside but often know very little about the many aspects of our internal anatomy. It is good to first understand the anatomy and physiology of the voice and then to actively explore it through exercises. The exercises in this chapter can be learned a few each day. They are best done under the guidance of an acting teacher who has had significant voice training, or even better, a voice teacher. Repeat the already learned exercises while adding new ones.

We will start with the anatomical components of vocal production and in the next chapter discuss those involved with articulation. (They are shown together in Figure 9.1.)

The anatomical parts of vocal production include the *larynx (voice box),* its covering referred to as the Adam's apple, which can be felt externally on the throat (and easily seen in the necks of mature men). The larynx holds the all-important *vocal folds (*commonly called the *vocal cords).* While *vocal folds* is the medical term, many dynamic voice users prefer the commonly used term *vocal cords* because of the association it brings to musical chords, or the idea of "striking a chord," used to mean "hitting upon a truth." *Vocal folds* and *vocal cords* will be used interchangeably here.

The vocal folds are two tiny folds of flexible tissue made up of small muscles covered by a mucous membrane and framed on one side by a ligament. They are tiny, about the size of the tip of your index finger. According to Lynn K. Wells in *The Articulate Voice*, "By maturity the typical vocal fold length is about 23mm, or about 9/10 of an inch, for men and about 17mm, or about 3/5 of an inch, for women."[4] The vocal folds run across the top of the *trachea* (windpipe) and the bottom of the *pharynx* (air passage at the back of the throat), parallel to the floor when standing. The *glottis* is the opening between the vocal folds that allows air to pass through. The larynx (including the vocal folds and glottis) separates the *upper respiratory tract* (mouth, nose, and throat) from the *lower respiratory tract* (trachea and lungs).

---

[4] Lynn K. Wells, *The Articulate Voice*: *An Introduction to the Voice and Diction*, 4th ed. (Boston: Allyn and Bacon/Pearson Education, 2004), 52.

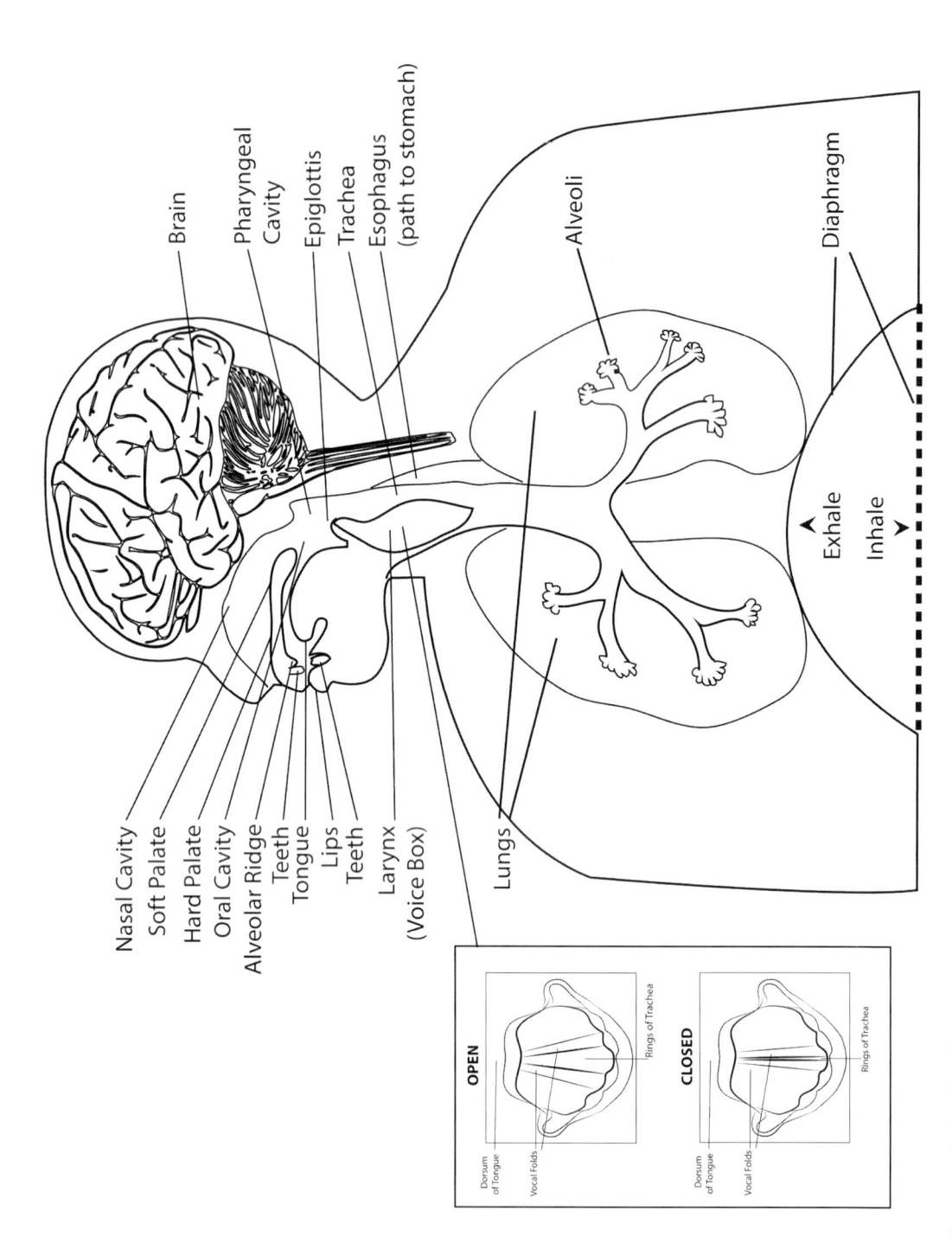

Figure 9.1 The anatomy of voice and speech.

9 EMBODYING VOICE

Another separate but important function of the larynx is to protect the lungs from materials that could be damaging. The vocal folds close when you swallow food so that you don't get any food in your trachea or lungs. According to Joanna Cazden in *Everyday Voice Care*,

> When the lungs need protection, the vocal folds squeeze together to close the glottis. This happens reflexively every time you swallow. Other reflexes can flicker the glottis open and closed, creating shifts in air pressure and flow to help clean the airway. The vocal folds clap together briefly to "clear your throat," and they bang together more vigorously in the cough that expels phlegm, smoke, or dust that your lungs need to get rid of.[5]

Alignment to Support Breath and Phonation

You may not be aware of it, but speaking involves the whole mind and body; it is a psychophysical action. Changing your posture takes constant awareness and some external feedback to correct postural issues. It is hard at first to do it with your own internal and external monitors. Much like the tree that grew leaning too far to one side, you have made physical and inner ear adaptations to your imbalances that make it hard for you to sense them.

Healthy voice and speech production begins with proper *alignment* of the body. For one thing, proper alignment is vital for full breath capacity. For another, if your head and neck are out of position, this may inhibit the ability of your vocal folds to vibrate and create the fullest range of sounds. Additionally, improper alignment causes added tensions that can inhibit full breath and restrict the fullness of the subsequent resonance. Exercise 9.3 will help to reduce tension in the neck and shoulders. Review the healthy and problematic alignments in Figure 9.2 (first introduced in Chapter 5). A type of good alignment from yoga was introduced as Tadasana (Mountain Pose) in Chapter 5. In addition to basic alignment to free up the body, there are some other things that are very important to alignment for voice covered in Exercise 9.2 below.

In training your voice, it is best to start with good alignment, standing or lying down, to support the breath and make room for the proper function of your vocal instrument. Then move to breathing exercises, to increase control and capacity; then on to creating and releasing sound, phonation, increasing your range of pitch, and resonance. Only after some proficiency in these areas should you seek to dramatically increase volume and projection.

Exercise 9.1: Optimal Alignment (F.M. Alexander/JH/SDF)

Purpose: As an actor you will need to be engaged in action onstage, which requires activation of muscles rather than complete relaxation; however, healthy alignment allows you to use your psychophysical instrument optimally, removing unnecessary tension and strain. Release of tension is

---

[5] Joanna Cazden, *Everyday Voice Care: The Lifestyle Guide for Singers and Talkers* (Milwaukee: Hal Leonard, 2012), 13.

vital to the flow of energy, as discussed in Chapter 5, and to the creative state, as discussed in Chapter 3. Additionally, alignment is vital to the healthy use of your voice and is the cornerstone of good vocal production.

Guidelines:
- Return to the standing pose of yoga called Tadasana (see Exercise 5.4).
- **Important note:** Firm the thighs drawing the kneecaps up to provide stability in the legs, but do not push the knees back to lock them. Many people mistakenly push the knees back to straighten the legs because this requires less muscular effort. This can result in locking the knees or in the extreme hyperextension of the knees. Locking the knees restricts the movement of the diaphragm and lower back, while giving stability to the knees through firming the thighs does not.
- When standing, the chin must be parallel to the floor, not tilted up or down. This allows for the opening at the back of the mouth and throat to be free of any obstruction, which in turn permits the free passage of air.
- Lengthen the neck, ensuring it is above the torso, not collapsed back or leaning into the front of the body. Feel as though your head is floating on top, lifting through the crown (see Figure 9.2).
- Release the shoulders, allowing them to drop away from the ears. Release the tongue, cheeks, and jaw. Allow the eyes to be in soft focus.
- Inhale and raise both arms up to the sides and over your head while pressing down into the floor with your feet. Feel how this activates your sides and begins to move energy through your entire body. (In yoga, you often extend parts of the body in opposite directions to begin activating the body and getting your energy moving.) Check that your shoulders have not crept up toward your ears; again check and release any tension creeping back into the tongue, jaw, or knees. Allow the breath to fall in and release out to the open and extended sides of your torso.
- Bring the arms back down alongside the torso, the palms of the hands in toward the body, arms still active. Release the arms but keep the length of torso and spine.

9.1 Reflection Journal—Your Alignment

What are some issues with your alignment that might inhibit the free flow of your breath and the optimal use of your vocal apparatus?

Note: It is important to become aware of these and start to correct them as soon as possible, as changing your alignment takes constant awareness and repeated correction over a long period of time.

9 EMBODYING VOICE

- Bottom of chin parallel to floor
- Ear above center of top of shoulder
- Lift the breastbone (center of chest)
- Shoulder blades not protruding from back (draw them down and in by lifting breastbone)
- Front of belt line slightly low than back Keep natural, but not over-arched, lumbar (lower back) curve
- Legs straight but knees not locked

Healthy — Natural lumbar curve

Problematic — Avoid removing the natural lumbar curve and locking the knees

Problematic — Avoid head and neck forward of shoulders

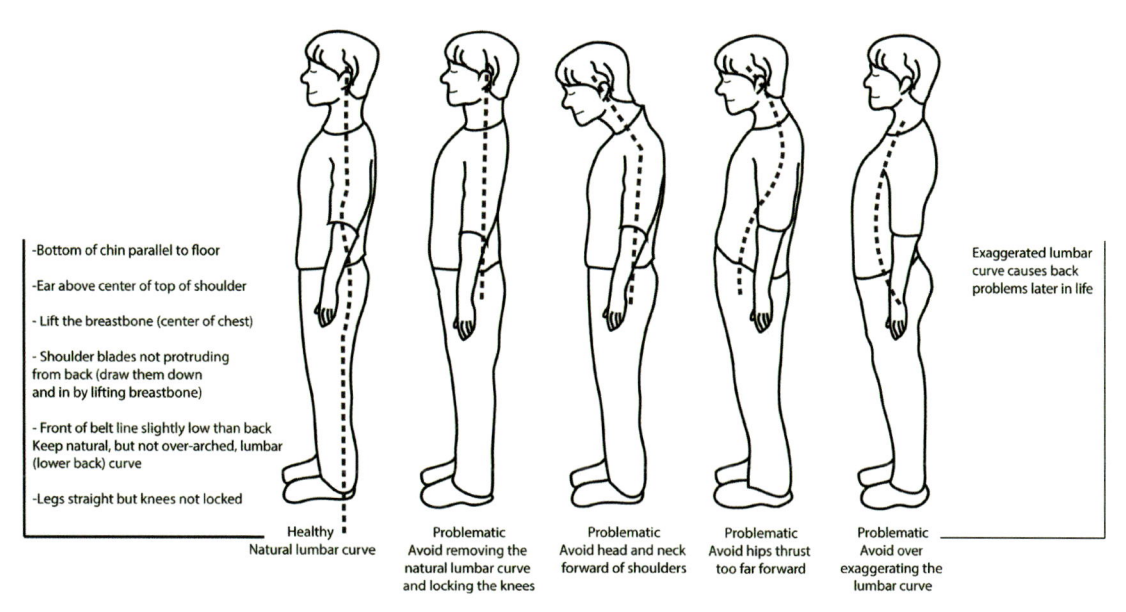

Problematic — Avoid hips thrust too far forward

Problematic — Avoid over exaggerating the lumbar curve

Exaggerated lumbar curve causes back problems later in life

Figure 9.2 Healthy and problematic alignment.

Exercise 9.2: Releasing Shoulders and Neck

Purpose: Muscular activity and "coordination between the breath source (the motor) and the larynx (the vibrator)"[6] is required. Unnecessary tension in the throat can diminish the full vibrational capacity of the vocal folds and inhibit the full resonance of sound in the pharynx. Prior to voice work you should do some exercises to help release tension in the shoulders and neck.

Note: Many people have lot of neck tension because of extensive time spent hunched over computer screens or smartphones. For others, stress may add tension to the shoulders, neck, mouth, tongue, and jaw.

Guidelines:
- Drop the head forward and do a half roll, ear to right shoulder, ear to left shoulder, back and forth a few times. Roll the head back up. (**WARNING:** Do not roll the head all the way around unless you are hanging the head down in a standing forward bend, as this can compress the neck vertebrae.)
- As you do these exercises, release any tension in the jaw, mouth, and tongue (many of us carry a lot of tension in these parts of the body). Continue to periodically say to yourself, or have the teacher say, "Release the jaw; release the tongue."[7] They do not need to be engaged during this sequence.

---

[6] Richard Miller, *The Structure of Singing: System and Art in Vocal Technique* (New York: Schirmer Books, 1986), 39.
[7] These incredible helpful reminders were the repeated mantra of yoga master Ramanand Patel (one of French's teachers).

- Roll your shoulder blades backward five times, trying to massage them with the movement. Roll them forward. For fun and more psychophysical control, try rolling one forward and one back. Reverse.
- Lift your shoulders up and then drop them. Do this three times.
- Now lift your shoulders up, squeeze them together at the back, and then clasp your hands behind your back, continuing to squeeze the shoulder blades together while straightening your arms behind your back. This may be enough of a stretch for you if you have very large or tight shoulders. If not, keep the shoulders squeezed together and the hands clasped behind the back and bend forward into a standing-forward bend. Check that you are releasing the neck and keeping the shoulder blades squeezed together while allowing the arms and hands to come forward over the head.
- Let your hands lead you back up, rolling up the spine. Release the hands.
- When finished, roll your head back up. Feel the head floating on top of the spine with as much ease in the neck and shoulders as possible. Make sure the head is directly above the shoulders (rather than forward) to allow the vertebrae to support the head through proper alignment and only minimal engagement of the neck muscles.
- While you want the neck and shoulders as relaxed as possible, you need to keep some control of the mechanisms of exhalation and of the articulators. This is one of the contradictions in voice work between complete relaxation and engaged physicality.

9.2 *Reflection Journal—Releasing Shoulders and Neck*

Where do you carry the most tension? If you were able to release some of the tension, did you notice any changes in the energy moving through your neck? Do you notice any change in how you feel now, or how your mind is working?

The Anatomy of Breath

No sound would be made without the movement of breath in exhalation from the lungs through the trachea and out the pharynx. On this journey, the breath passes through the space between the vocal folds, the glottis, and exits through the mouth and/or nose. If the vocal folds are lightly closed as air makes the exhalation passage, they vibrate, producing voiced sound. Breath involves the parts of the body you might expect, such as the mouth and nose, the throat (pharynx), windpipe (trachea), and lungs. The lungs include the bronchi (two branches off the trachea at the top of each lung), bronchioles (smaller branches off the bronchi), and alveoli (collections of air sacks at the end of each bronchiole that look like a cluster of grapes).

You may be less familiar with some other components in the anatomy of breath, such as the *diaphragm*. The diaphragm is the largest muscle in the body, a highly flexible muscle that separates the organs of the thorax, or upper torso, from those of the abdomen, or lower torso. The diaphragm is shaped like a dome, or like a falling parachute when relaxed and more flattened when engaged. It has openings to allow other parts of the body to pass through it. The diaphragm is attached on its edges to

9 EMBODYING VOICE

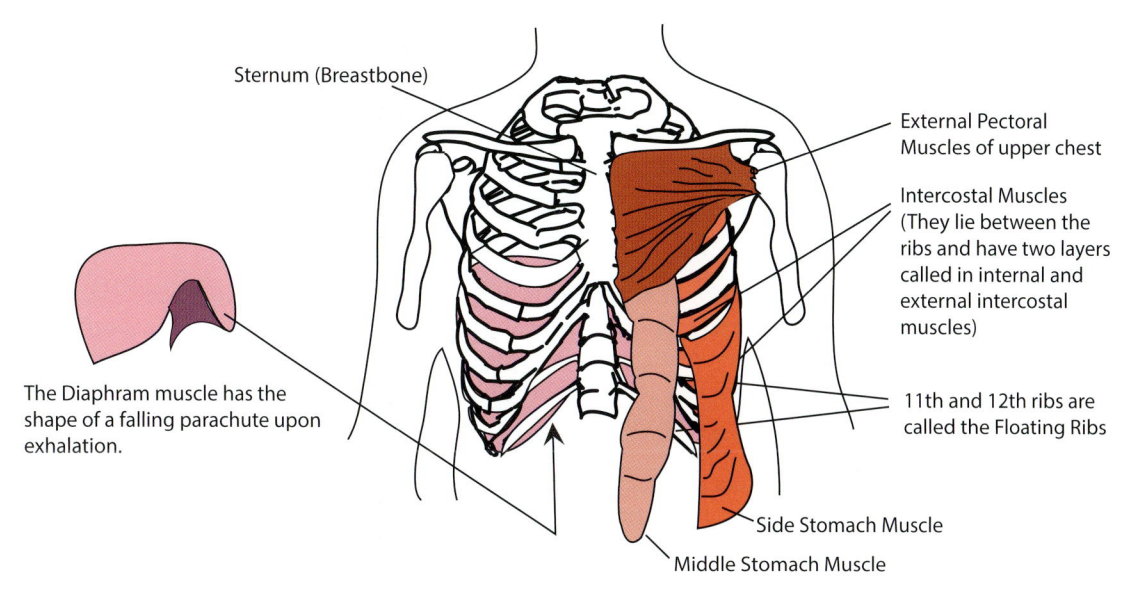

Figure labels:
- Sternum (Breastbone)
- External Pectoral Muscles of upper chest
- Intercostal Muscles (They lie between the ribs and have two layers called in internal and external intercostal muscles)
- 11th and 12th ribs are called the Floating Ribs
- The Diaphram muscle has the shape of a falling parachute upon exhalation.
- Side Stomach Muscle
- Middle Stomach Muscle

Figure 9.3 Additional components of breath.

Note: As the main parts of the lungs are shown in Figure 9.1, only the additional anatomical parts affecting breathing are shown here.

places all around the inside of the rib cage. Also important is that the bottom of each lung rests on the diaphragm. Other components that are involved with breathing and voice training are the rib cage (including the *sternum* (breastbone), the *intercostal muscles* (between the ribs), and the *floating ribs* (which are only attached to the spine but in front are unattached and thus have more flexibility to expand), and the muscles of the torso, including the *pectorals* (chest) and *abdominals* (stomach).

Breathing makes all of our bodily functions possible. The cells and organs, especially the brain, need to be oxygenated in order to stay alert, active, and healthy. The yogic practice of pranayama, a central aspect of which is guided breathing, can be very restorative of full functioning of the mind and body but takes years of guided practice to master. Many advanced yoga teachers can guide you in this practice, but you can read more about it in Iyengar's book *Light on Pranayama*, in which he states:

> Only recently have western savants become aware of the techniques developed in ancient India for examining the systems of breathing, blood-circulation, digestion, assimilation, nourishment, the endocrine glands and the nerves, the subtle forms of which are collectively known as the Conquest of Life Force (prāṇāmāya kosa).[8]

---

[8] B. K. S. Iyengar. *Light on Prāṇāyāma: The Definitive Guide to the Art of Breathing* (New York: HarperCollins, 2013), xxi.

> **Prana: Breath and the Life Force**
>
> Stanislavsky was very interested in prana and the ability of actors to transmit prana to one another and to an audience, which he called spiritual communion. According to B. K. S. Iyengar in his book *Light on Prāṇāyāma*, "'Prana' means breath, respiration, life, vitality, energy or strength. When used in the plural, it denotes certain vital breaths or currents of energy (prana-vayus)."*
>
> Developing your awareness of and ability to regulate prana is beneficial for your overall vibrancy and health. It can also be advantageous for your use of energy, breath, and voice in acting. The yogic technique for developing this awareness and control of breath and the related flow of energy is called *pranayama*. Again Iyengar:
>
>> Prāṇāyāma is a conscious prolongation of inhalation, retention and exhalation. Inhalation is the act of receiving the primeval energy in the form of breath, and retention is when the breath is held in order to savour that energy. In exhalation all thoughts and emotions are emptied with breath: then, while the lungs are empty, one surrenders the individual energy, 'I', to the primeval energy, the Atama.
>>
>> The practice of prāṇāyāma develops a steady mind, strong willpower and sound judgement.[+]
>
> As you will see in Chapter 19: The Creative Life, where you will review in more detail Stanislavsky's diagram of the System, willpower is essential to acting.
>
> A note of caution: Pranayama is an advanced technique of yoga and should not be practiced until the body and mind have been well prepared through regular asana practice. Just as in voice work, where you do not want to amplify the voice if you are using it improperly, in yoga you do not want to amplify your energy if you have many issues and blocks in the body or mind. This would only serve to amplify your mental issues and baggage. First you must work to create excellent alignment and ease in the body. When you can allow the breath to flow easily, even in demanding poses, this is the real beginning of pranayama. You will also want to grow in your awareness of other issues and your ability to unlock the different levels of your consciousness, as represented by the different chakras. Only then can you create a clear channel for intense flow of breath and energy that is pranayama.
>
> *B. K. S. Iyengar, *Light on Prāṇāyāma: The Definitive Guide to the Art of Breathing* (New York: HarperCollins, 2013), 16.
>
> [+] Ibid., 12.

Any Olympic athlete knows that to reach peak performance you must train the breath. Swimmers must time and pace their breathing with arm strokes; runners, skaters, skiers, all must learn to breathe deeply and rhythmically. Expanded breath capacity and control is also necessary for you as an actor. Acting requires great

Figure 9.4 Voice class with Dr. Margaret Joyce Ball.
Photo: Philip Stein, courtesy of East Stroudsburg University

athletic energy, strength, and stamina. A two-and-a-half-hour Shakespearean play with combat and fencing can be just as exhausting as any athletic game. A musical such as *West Side Story,* where actors are required to dance and act simultaneously, requires even more athletic coordination. During all of this, you must also have enough breath support to speak or sing.

How Do These Parts of the Body Coordinate in Breathing and Vocal Production?

According to Robert Caldwell and Joan Wall in *Excellence in Singing*, when a singer produces vocalization, her "nervous system excites a select set of neurons. The signals that travel down the axons of those neurons cause certain muscle fibers to contract to move parts of her body. And those parts of her body set the air inside her body in motion."[9] On inhalation the breastbone lifts; the intercostal muscles engage to expand the ribs to either side, particularly the floating ribs; and the diaphragm contracts, which means it descends and flattens out lowering in the torso (see Figure 9.1 for the positions of the diaphragm on inhalation and exhalation). The movement of the ribs and diaphragm create space for the lungs to descend and expand with the intake of air.

On exhalation, the reverse occurs. The intercostal muscles release, allowing the side ribs and floating ribs to draw in, the diaphragm relaxes and ascends into its dome-like shape up in the ribcage, forcing the lungs to compress and expel air.

Richard Miller, in *The Structure of Singing*, outlines the timing of a normal breath cycle compared to the timing of the cycle during singing. The demands are similar for an actor when speaking challenging passages onstage. Note also that in Miller's

---

[9] Robert Caldwell and Joan Wall, *Excellence in Singing: Multilevel Learning and Multilevel Teaching* (Redmond, WA: Caldwell, 2001), 148.

description of the breath cycle that follows, *onset* is the first instant of sound, *phrase duration* is how long you speak or sing, and *release* is finishing the sound:

> When the body is at rest, the normal inspiration-expiration cycle is brief, about 4 seconds. The inspiratory portion generally takes 1 second, or slightly more; the expiratory portion occupies the remainder. . . . In deep inspiration, as in preparation for singing, the diaphragm and the thoracic and abdominal muscles increase their activity. Phonation and physical effort modify the pace of the breath cycle. In singing, phrase upon phrase will occur in which the breath cycle is drastically prolonged, especially in the expiratory phase. To accomplish skillful control of breath management for singing, special coordination of the phases of the breath cycle (inhalation, onset, phrase duration, release) must be learned.[10]

Increased breath capacity allows increased volume and length of sound. Breath control provides a more sustained and even column of breath, which opens up a wider range of pitches for speech and singing and increases the length of time that actors can speak without pausing or that singers can hold a note. This is why development of breath capacity and control is so important to actors and singers.

To fully utilize the breath for vocal production and speech you will need to work on controlling the balance between p*honation* (making sound) and *airflow* (the coordination of air between the lower and upper respiratory tracts). Extending the breath requires that the pectoral and intercostal muscles resist the impulse of the sternum (breastbone) to collapse on exhalation. The abdominal muscles also come into play during inhalation for stage speech, resisting the impulse to push forward the abdomen, instead allowing the breath to expand laterally. This also helps to diminish the body's impulse to collapse inward in exhalation. Additionally, it is important not to overfill the lungs, as this will hasten the exhalation.

Exercise 9.3: Extending the Breath Cycle (Iyengar/SDF)

Purpose: To bring awareness to the movement of breath and to begin to learn to direct it.

Guidelines:
- Before beginning the exercise, and while still standing or sitting, count on the in-breath and again on the out-breath to get a timing baseline. For example, you might breathe in, counting *1 and 2 and*, and then breathe out, counting *1 and 2 and 3 and* (the *and* after the number just allows the count to be slower and more measured).
- Revisit the three positions for lying comfortably on the floor introduced in Chapter 5, Figures 5.1, 5.2, and 5.3 (p. 83). Select the position that is most comfortable for you.
- Place your fingertips on your lower abdomen.
- Place a book about 1-inch thick (or thicker if you have a very large or

---

[10]Richard Miller, *The Structure of Singing: System and Art in Vocal Technique* (New York: Schirmer Books, 1986), 20.

rounded back) under your head as a pillow. Your face needs to be parallel to the ceiling without your chin tilting back or forward. Avoid compressing your neck forward with your chin too close to your chest or compressing it back with your neck tilting down lower at the head than the shoulders.
- Rock your head gently from side to side to release any tension in the neck.
- Drop your shoulders down away from your ears and feel them spread out on the floor along with the muscles of your back.
- As your back widens, also scoot your buttocks down and notice the room that that gives your spine to lengthen along the floor.
- Close your eyes or focus on a spot on the ceiling.
- Notice how your breath enters the nostrils and flows down the back of your pharynx (throat). See if you can feel it go into your trachea (windpipe).
- Exhale through a slightly opened mouth. Notice the air returning through your trachea, then pharynx, feel it filling up your mouth behind the teeth and then passing out gently between your lips.
- Try inhaling through the mouth and see if you can feel a different level of openness in the throat.
- On the next breath, continue to notice the passage of air, and on the inhalation, notice the diaphragm engaging so that it moves from dome-shaped up inside the rib cage when relaxed, to a flat shape just at the bottom of the ribs when the muscle is engaged. You cannot consciously control the diaphragm muscle, although you can learn to control the muscles that it connects to. You may or may not be able to feel it moving, but if you can't, imagine it happening, to further your understanding.
- As the diaphragm lowers, also notice how the lower ribs expand and make room for the lungs to fill with air.
- Observe this process with your mind's eye (internal monitor) for a few minutes, noticing as much as possible where the breath is in your body at each point, even deep into your torso. Notice how a deep sense of relaxation comes over you as you oxygenate your body with fresh air and allow it to flow in and out at an easy pace.
- Notice the four phases of breath: 1) inhalation, 2) pause full with breath, 3) exhalation, 4) pause with lungs emptied before inhalation.
- Again count the inhalation and exhalation to see whether lying down and bringing awareness to the breath has changed the count of either inhalation or exhalation or both.
- Then, slow down the in-breath and the out-breath by one count in each breath cycle for three full cycles. For example, in: *1 and 2 and;* out: *1 and 2 and 3 and;* then, in: *1 and 2 and 3 and;* out: *1 and 2 and 3 and 4 and;* then, in: *1 and 2 and 3 and 4 and;* out: *1 and 2 and 3 and 4 and 5 and,* etc. Do this for at least three to four breath cycles to increase both inhalation and exhalation at the end by three to four counts above your baseline.
- Allow the breath to return to a natural, rather than extended, inhalation and exhalation pace and open your eyes slowly if you have closed them.
- Come to standing using the rising without tension sequence diagrammed and outlined in Chapter 5, Exercise 5.1B, pp. 85–6. *Do not jerk up your head and neck to sit up, as you need to minimize neck tension for successful voice work.*

Exercise 9.4: Tai Chi Breaths

Purpose: Connecting the breath with simple movements.

Guidelines: (See Figure 9.5)
- Allow the eyes to be in soft focus, open and aware of all shapes and movement around you but not focused on any things or people. The gaze (soft focus awareness) should be inwardly directed.
- Stand in a circle. Extend your right arm just slightly front of you and pointing towards the floor, a little out from your body, with your fingers slightly bent. Make sure there is a little space between your elbow and your body and your upper arm and your body.
- As you inhale, leading with your wrist, draw a line straight up in the air as high as your third eye, the space between and just above the eyebrows.
- When you exhale, leading with your wrist, draw the line down.
- Do this three times slowly.

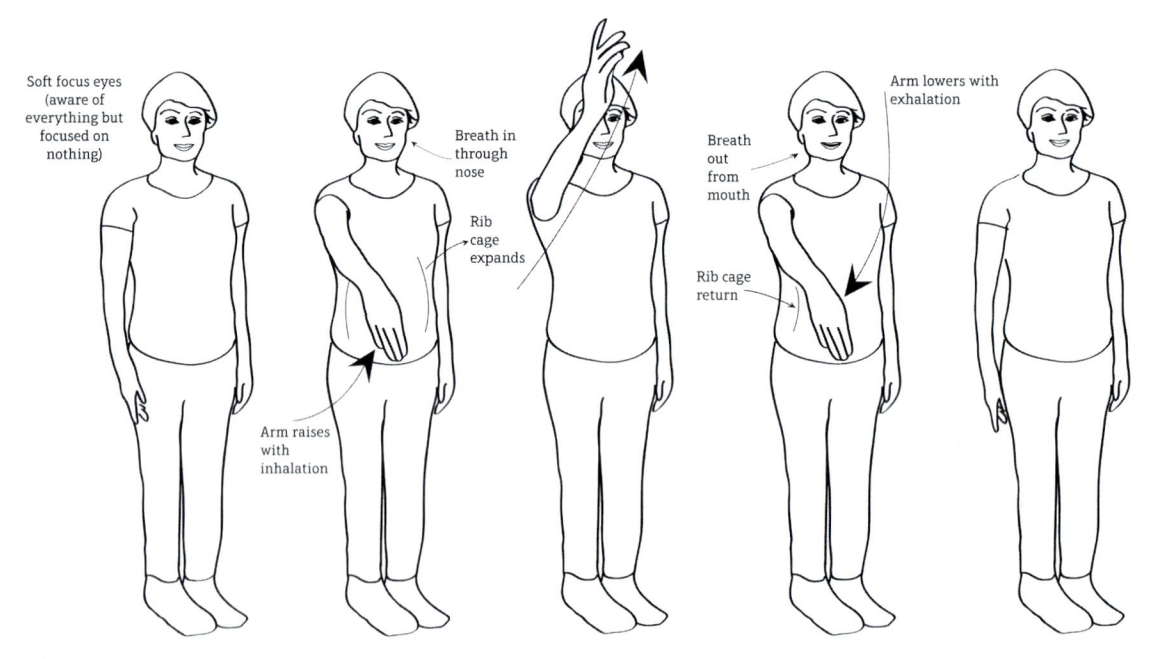

Figure 9.5 Physical movement for Tai Chi Breaths.

Onset, Phonation, and Pitch

Balanced Onset (Coordinated Onset)

Another area of balance that must be sought is in the *onset*, the first instant of *phonation* (making sound). If the vocal folds in onset are too tightly closed, the airflow builds up until it bursts through with a smack of the vocal folds, like popping the cork on a bottle of champagne, creating a sound called a glottal attack. This is known as the *hard onset* (like a catch in the throat or a cough) and causes you to release the air too quickly; in addition, the smack of the vocal folds may cause damage over time. Those with athletic ambitions or impatient personalities tend toward a hard onset.

The *soft onset* is where the vocal folds are prepared with too much of a gap and insufficient tension. This creates an inconsistent tone with a lot of breath (like a whisper). This may be the tendency of the more tentative, gentle, easygoing, or shy person. According to Miller, "Neither the hard attack nor the soft onset may be encouraged as pedagogical practices for standard use. They result from two opposing errors in phonation, and may be described simplistically as the 'grunt' and the 'whisper.'"[11]

For now, work on good alignment and breath support, which will help the most with achieving a balanced onset. If you need to correct habits of hard or soft onset this should be done under the one-on-one tutelage and feedback of a certified voice teacher.

How Do the Vocal Folds Create Sound?

The vocal folds open more toward the back of the throat and less at the front (Adam's apple and tongue), creating a V-shape when open (as pictured in the inset diagram in Figure 9.1), as if looking down the throat.

The vocal folds can be completely open, partially open, or closed through the action of muscles in the larynx. For deep breathing, including taking in a favorite smell, the folds are at their widest, with the largest opening of the glottis. For normal breathing, the opening is approximately a third as wide.[12] If the folds are mostly closed, but with a little open space for air to get through without vibrating the cords, sound comes out in the quality of a whisper. For the production of sound the vocal cords are close together, parallel, and barely touching, on the ligament side of the folds.

Studies looking at the voice in action through electromyographic instruments[13] have shown that after the intention to make sound but slightly ahead of the *onset* (the first instance of the sound itself) muscles in the larynx adjust the tension in the vocal cords in anticipation of making different *pitches*.[14] Pitches register in our ears as high or low sounds, depending on the frequency of vibration. As your minds anticipate the pitch, you adjust the length and tension of your vocal cords. If they are stretched longer and thinner, they create a higher pitch, and if shorter and thicker, the result is a lower pitch. If you close your mouth and hum, you can feel your lips vibrating in a similar way that the vocal folds vibrate, but the lips can only vibrate much more slowly because they are so much bigger and thicker.

As you cannot strum or pluck the vocal cords, you play them, instead, by passing air through them, similar to activating the reed on a wind instrument. When you move air through the vocal folds in the closed but barely touching position, they vibrate and produce a sound. In addition to the tension and length of the vocal folds, the tempo and amount of air passing through them affects pitch. The amount of air also affects the loudness.

---

[11] Miller, *The Structure of Singing*, 3.
[12] Miller, *Structure of Singing*, 6.
[13] Electromyographic instruments record and measure the electrical activity produced by the muscles.
[14] B. D. Wyke, "Laryngeal Neuromuscular Control Systems in Singing: A Review of Current Concepts," *Folia Phoniatrica* 26, no. 1 (1974): 296.

An individual sound is called a *phoneme*, and making sound is called *phonation*. Each phoneme can be made at higher or lower pitches and higher or lower loudness (volume). The mind tells the vocal cords to prepare by adjusting length and tension for a certain pitch, then an instant later tells the respiratory system to send air though the prepared shape. If the pitch you are about to make is at the extreme high or low end of your range, and you are fearful you cannot make it, you may add extra tension to the vocal folds that inhibits their vibration so that you are in fact incapable of making the sound, or you make it in a distorted way. This is similar to the discordant sound of a guitar when you do not have the fingers of your left hand pressed decidedly enough on the frets while you strum with your right hand.

The pitch you naturally start at is called your *basic pitch*. Your *optimal pitch* is the pitch at which you can make the most beautiful sound and can sustain it the longest. This may or may not be the pitch at which you naturally start speaking. Your cultural conditioning (for example gender expectations about voice) or native language (that may have a higher or lower basic pitch and different levels of intonation) may have influenced you to generally speak at a higher or lower pitch than is optimal for your anatomical voice.

An upward or downward change in pitch is call *inflection*, while the overall movement of the pitch is called *intonation*.

> **Note:** In all exercises where you explore a range of pitches, make sure that the pitches are natural and comfortable for your voice. Always start vocal exercises in your midrange and work up and down from there. Never start warming up in the extremes of your pitch range.

Exercise 9.5: Pitch Trills (Lip Trills) (MJB/SF)

Purpose: Warming up before active or demanding use of the voice helps to prevent injury and to ensure breath support on phonation. Pitch changes activate the vocal folds by lengthening and shortening them. Expanding your pitch range allows you to communicate and impact scene partners and the audience more effectively through verbal actions. You can also better bring out the meaning of your text and hold the audience's attention through vocal variety. Warming up and expanding your pitch range also ensures vocal safety and expressiveness for moments of heightened emotion.

Guidelines: Stand in alignment. Lift the breastbone and make sure the head and neck are directly above and not forward of the shoulders (as in Exercises 9.1 and 9.2 above).

- After a full (but not overly full) breath in through the open mouth (feeling great openness in the back of the mouth, through lifting the soft palate, and in the throat), on the exhalation blow the air through the lips to vibrate them, so that they flutter and make a sound like a motor on a small boat in the water. This is called a *lip trill*. Allow the lips to be as loose as possible (no matter how silly it looks!). Repeat.

- On another exhalation, continue to blow through the lips but now add sound. Do this twice to establish your basic pitch.
- On the next exhalation try with lip trills to sound out "Mary Had a Little Lamb," which has sufficiently small rises and falls in pitch for a warm-up. Any simple song with a limited pitch range will work as a warm-up. Later, to expand your range, you can try more-challenging songs, but if you run out of sound because you have run out of breath, or have trouble reaching pitches at the top or bottom, select instead a song with a better range for you.
- If you have a piano you can sound out a few notes above and below your base pitch and try to match them with lip trills. Start by going three steps above your base and three below, and if this is completely comfortable you can try going five. Later, you can work slowly on increasing to a full octave (eight steps) one exhalation and back down the same octave on the next breath, but only if the pitches feel comfortable for your voice.

PART II: CARING FOR YOUR UNIQUE VOICE

Developing Awareness of Your Unique Voice

Modern life, with its stresses and the resulting physical tension, interferes with the natural harmony and balance between mind, body, and spirit and their expression through the voice. Improper use of your voice diminishes its capacity and expression and may even cause you to lose it.

Like most people, as you get older, you will have used your body and voice in less than optimal ways. Even familiar behavior, such as repeatedly clearing your throat when you have a cold, can hurt your delicate vocal cords. An ongoing cough can be temporarily damaging, resulting in a hoarse voice or even laryngitis. You may do temporary damage to your voice if you are shouting at a sporting event, a political rally, or to gain the attention of an exuberant group of children. In these instances, damage is caused because the voice has not been warmed up, is being used improperly, or has not been trained to handle the demand. One of the worst things you can do to your vocal cords and lungs is to smoke. After many years of reinforcing, these habits you may find your vocal capacity limited.

Each person has a unique, personal vocal imprint involving both nature (your vocal anatomy and innate personality) and nurture (your cultural dialect, patterns of speech, and aspects of your psychology developed through your life experiences). Family and culture have shaped the sound of your voice and the way you use it. For example, you may have grown up speaking one language at home and another at school and with your friends. Even if surrounded by only one language, people from different parts of the country speak in different dialects, generally taking on the dialect of those they spend most time with in their formative years of speech.[15]

---

[15]Dialects are different speech patterns of people who speak the same language, for example British vs. American English. Even within these two general dialects there are different subdialects. If you spoke in a southern US dialect, as would someone, say, from Savannah,

(Although most of us think others have dialects while we speak normally.) You also grew up within a particular neighborhood, and within a particular social group, and even social class, within that neighborhood. All of this has shaped the way you speak.

Just as you do not want to bring your habits of posture and movement into every character you portray, you do not want to imbue every character with your unique habits of speech. You are encouraged to retain your dialect and native voice for use on some roles and in your community, while expanding your ability to speak in a variety of ways to meet the demands and increase the range of roles you can portray. Lately, there has been a move in television and film to mix a variety of English dialects into the same film or TV show without justifying the backgrounds or why people all speak with dialects from different countries, while supposedly growing up in the same region. Still, eventually it would be a good idea to develop a standard dialect for your country, and also to understand how to learn new dialects when needed. You need to develop vocal awareness and pursue voice training to effectively achieve this.

Psychological and cultural factors can also impact your voice and speech. You may have learned to always say what you think, even if your opinions are not in line with others'. On the other hand, you may have been made to feel you have no right to speak or that your opinions don't matter. You may have been encouraged to speak gently or expected to always sound tough. At the family dinner table, interruptions may have been the only way to get a word in, or you may have been taught to never interrupt. Perhaps you are from a passionate culture where speaking with emotion is familiar and accepted, or from a culture where emotions are expected to be more concealed. In your culture, physical expression and gestures may literally go hand in hand with speech, or more stoicism and containment may have been the expectation.

Whatever your family and cultural influences, it is important to be aware of them and how they are different from others'; else you risk bringing these to every character you portray, whether or not appropriate. Additionally, ingrained associations you have around the sound of your voice can affect your training. Most people are shocked when hearing a recording of their voice for the first time, asking, "Do I really sound like that?" For example, you may think you are being loud while being barely audible to those standing near you, because you come from a quiet family. You may think you are being subtle because your family is very loud and vibrant, and yet come across onstage as exaggerated. Also, because you are hearing your voice from the inside, as it moves through various tissues of the head, and outside at the same time, you hear your own voice differently than others hear it.

Georgia, your dialect would not sound the same as someone's from New Orleans, Louisiana. Someone from Brooklyn does not speak the same as someone from the Bronx (two of the five different boroughs of New York City). Even within one neighborhood there are often different dialects within different socioeconomic groups. Accents, on the other hand, are the speech patterns of people speaking a nonnative language—for example, a native Russian, Chinese, or French speaker speaking English—and are generally stronger at first but lessen somewhat after the speaker has lived in an English-speaking country and thus spoken and heard English for a few years.

9 EMBODYING VOICE

> **Exercise 9.6: Personal Speech Habits (SDF)**
>
> **Purpose:** It is important to know what cultural habits and aspects of your psychology have shaped your speech. Later, too, you will need to assess how those might be different for the different characters you will portray.
>
> **Guidelines:** Reread the section above—developing awareness of your unique voice to give yourself some ideas of what to watch out for.
>
> - Recall or observe a dinner, cultural holiday, or other event that involves your family or extended family speaking together. Consider how they interact(ed). Make a list of speech and conversation qualities and decide which of these you also have and whether there are some you do not have.
> - Within each of your groups, are you more of a listener or a talker?
> - What experiences with speaking up have shaped why you might or might not want to speak, as well as how and why you speak?
> - Consider your psychological makeup. How has your personality affected your voice and your speech?
> - If possible, observe communication in a cultural environment outside of your familiar group. Notice any differences and the unique speech and conversation patterns of this group.

9.6 *Reflection Journal—Personal Speech Habits*

What have you observed about your family's speech habits? What have you learned about your own? How are these different from those of people outside your family?

Developing Healthy Habits of Voice and Effective Use of Speech

General health is important for actors. While this chapter includes some ideas for what to do for your voice if you do get sick, it is far better to stay healthy. Many people take much better care of their cars than they do of their own bodies. They wouldn't put diesel in a car that takes gasoline, but they will eat all kinds of junk foods that drain them rather than giving them energy and don't allow their bodies to rebuild after exertion. As an actor, you need to care for your primary instrument, your mind and body, just as a musician would care for a valuable Stradivarius violin.

When he had a chance to play Othello, Stanislavsky realized that his vocal instrument was ill prepared to express the emotional qualities that the role required. He also realized that as a result of his poor breathing, his speech was incapable of conveying the subtleties of Shakespeare's poetic language. For a long time he was discouraged by this problem, but with a strong determination, he overcame his defects. No matter what your voice is capable of now, with training you can vastly improve your range and expressiveness. Sir Laurence Olivier, in a five-part interview with theatre critic Kenneth Tynan, expressed the same vocal challenge at climbing the mountain of a role that is Shakespeare's Othello. (You can hear this interview on YouTube at https://www.youtube.com/watch?v=Ug5xZjSOC0U)

Even in rehearsal you may find that voice, speech, and singing issues arise as you try to meet the vocal demands of a dramatic role. Perhaps your character must scream in a horror story, or express power and nuance as an exciting but evil villain, perhaps you too are scaling the mountain of Shakespeare. In performance in a large theatre, vocal problems are amplified with increased projection and use. You can develop better vocal habits and the stamina to use your voice safely and effectively all day. If you have allergies, you just have to work a little harder to keep your passages free of mucus and prevent inflammation to reduce wear on your vocal folds. (See Tips for Voice Care.)

> **Tips for Voice Care**[16]
>
> The voice is a phenomenally versatile instrument. Yet the amazing vocal folds are also delicate flaps of tissue that require great care. If you are in a demanding role or a performance in a large theatre requiring more volume and greater projection and you do not have good technique, the strain may cause you to lose your voice for a period of time and miss performances. In the worst case, you could do permanent damage to your vocal instrument. To take good care of your voice adhere to the following tips:
>
> - Make sure to get training under the guidance of a professional voice expert.
> - With advice from a knowledgeable instructor, and ahead of placing serious demand on your voice, correct any poor vocal habits that could lead to future problems.
> - Train your body so that proper alignment, freedom from excessive vocal tension, proper phonation, resonance, and projection are second nature for you.
> - Don't shout at any event, in or outside of the theatre, unless you have fully warmed up your voice and are using it properly.
> - Keep your vocal cords hydrated (drink plenty of noncaffeinated, nonalcoholic fluids). If you do drink caffeine or alcohol, drink extra water to compensate for the drying effects of these products.
> - Avoid milk products and sweets, particularly chocolate, before using your voice in performance as these can create excess mucus.
> - If you have a cold, avoid speaking, to rest your voice. Avoid clearing your throat and, instead, try to shower to free up and expel phlegm. Limit cough drops to only the most severe days, as ingredients in some cough drops, even natural ingredients such as menthol or echinacea, while temporarily alleviating pain, may paradoxically further irritate your vocal folds.
> - Stay hydrated by drinking a lot of water and herbal teas. If you are

---

[16] Voice care tips are adapted from Dr. Margaret Ball's advice to our shared students and recommendations in her voice classes (which French observes); from Joanna Cazden, *Everyday Voice Care: The Lifestyle Guide for Singers and Talkers* (Milwaukee: Hal Leonard Books, 2012); and from acupuncturist Jin Fang.

congested, add grated orange peel[17] (put it in a tea ball if you don't want it floating in your cup), to help your body clear mucus out of your nose and throat.
- If you have regular allergies, learn to use a noniodized saline spray or a neti pot[18] with a warm solution of water and noniodized salt (iodine may sting the delicate nasal passages). Be careful not to overmedicate, as most cold and allergy medications dry up the mucus but also dry out your vocal folds, which need moisture for safe and optimum functioning. (Avoid products with aspirin or any type of blood thinners.)[19]
- Take care of your hearing by using ear protection when exposed to loud sounds and by keeping the volume to a reasonable level on headphones. Good hearing is essential for making good sound.
- Cool down your voice after heavy use by gentle humming. This is an often overlooked but very important aspect of voice care.

Summary

You can develop a versatile and powerful voice capable of expressing a range of human experience. As with all aspects of this book, the starting place is developing your awareness. By understanding the anatomy of your voice and the proper physiology for creating sound, you can use your voice in the demanding environment of the stage in a healthy and effective way. Start with alignment that encourages good breathing and gives space to the vocal folds while minimizing strain in the head, throat, and shoulders. Learn and expand your pitch range so that you can keep the audience's attention with varied intonation. Then move on to the next chapter, "Activating Speech," to learn how to use your voice to clearly and dramatically express ideas and emotions through words and actions.

New Acting Term
- second signal system

---

[17] Orange peel is added to tea in Chinese herbal medicine to help expel phlegm.
[18] A neti pot allows you to pour a solution of warm water and non-iodized salt through nasal passages helping to clear the sinuses without having to use drying types of cold medication.
[19] A suggestion from voice expert, Dr. Margaret Ball.

New Voice Terms, Concepts, and Artists

- ☐ Adam's apple
- ☐ airflow
- ☐ alignment
- ☐ alveolar ridge
- ☐ alveoli
- ☐ articulation
- ☐ bronchi
- ☐ bronchioles
- ☐ Robert Caldwell
- ☐ Joanna Cazden
- ☐ dialects
- ☐ diaphragm
- ☐ floating ribs
- ☐ glottal attack
- ☐ glottis
- ☐ intercostal muscles
- ☐ larynx
- ☐ Richard Miller
- ☐ muscles
- ☐ onset (hard, soft, balanced)
- ☐ oral cavity
- ☐ pectoral muscles
- ☐ pharyngeal cavity
- ☐ pharynx
- ☐ phonation
- ☐ phrase duration
- ☐ pitch
- ☐ release
- ☐ respiratory tract, lower
- ☐ respiratory tract, upper
- ☐ William Shakespeare
- ☐ soft palate
- ☐ sternum
- ☐ Tai Chi Breath
- ☐ trachea
- ☐ vocal cords
- ☐ vocal folds
- ☐ Joan Wall
- ☐ Lynn Wells
- ☐ B.D. Wyke

CHAPTER 10

Activating Speech

"Speaking is one of the most intricately complex skills that we develop. Oral communication relies on the coordinated functioning of our organs for thinking, breathing, hearing, and speaking."[1]
—Lynn K. Wells, *The Articulate Voice*

Part I: The Components of Speech: Resonance, Articulation, Pronunciation
- **Resonance**
- ☐ Exercise 10.1: Exploring the Resonating Chambers
- **Articulation, Pronunciation, and Phonemes**
- ☐ Exercise 10.2: Warming Up the Articulators
- **International Phonetic Alphabet (IPA)**
- **What Are the Differences between Vowels and Consonants?**
- ☐ Exercise 10.3: Vowel Formation
- ☐ Exercise 10.4: Chanting the Vowels
- ☐ Exercise 10.5: Sound and Space
- ☐ Exercise 10.6: Consonant Articulation
- ☐ Exercise 10.7: Shifting Shape, Location, and Tempo
- ☐ Exercise 10.8: Combining Consonants and Vowels
- ☐ Exercise 10.9: Sounds with Tempo Variations

Part II: Communion through Voice and Speech: Timbre, Projection, Emphasis
- **Quality/Timbre and Tonal Subtext**
- ☐ Exercise 10.10: Vocal Qualities and Issues
- **Tonal Subtext**
- ☐ Exercise 10.11: Tonal Subtext
- **Emphasis: Rhythm, Intonation, and Stress**
- ☐ Exercise 10.12: Emphasis
- **Projection**
- ☐ Exercise 10.13: Projection by Intention
- ☐ Exercise 10.14: Projecting Intimacy
- ☐ Exercise 10.15: Vocal Actions
- ☐ Exercise 10.16: Sounding Out the Text
- ☐ Exercise 10.17: Guidelines for a Comprehensive Vocal Warm-Up

---

[1] Lynn K. Wells, *The Articulate Voice: An Introduction to the Voice and Diction* (fourth edition). Boston, MA: Allyn and Bacon/Pearson Education (1999), 2004, p. 132.

Psychophysical actions are the key catalysts for experiencing the life of a character on stage. They always have a mental component (purpose), reflected physically, and often are also expressed through speech. Ahead of effective use of verbal action, as outlined in Chapter 11: Verbal Action: Communicating with Words and Subtext, it is helpful to have some understanding of each component of speech: resonance, articulation, projection, timbre (quality), tempo-rhythm, and tonal subtext.

PART I: THE COMPONENTS OF SPEECH: RESONANCE, ARTICULATION, PRONUNCIATION

For the purposes of communication, the breath turned to vocal sound must be expanded and colored through resonance and shaped into speech through articulation. Even though resonance is vital to vocal production as introduced in the preceding chapter, it is introduced here with the beginning speech work because, according to Richard Miller, "No clear division exists between the latter two systems. Articulation, to some extent, controls resonance."[2]

Resonance

The vocal folds are tiny, and without further processes it would be hard to hear the sound they make. *Resonation* is the act of amplifying or adjusting the sound through reverberation to give it more volume, fullness, and other qualities. *Resonance* is the sound created once phonation has been initiated and the vibrations of your vocal folds have been amplified in the resonating chambers.

After sound is created by the passage of air through the vocal folds, those sound vibrations travel through the open spaces, or cavities, of our neck and head, allowing the sound to reverberate and expand. These spaces include the pharyngeal cavity (more commonly known as the throat), the oral cavity (space within the mouth), and the nasal cavity (spaces in and around the nose). Resonance is created by a combination of resonating chambers rather than by any one alone, although each can be more or less a part of the sound creation as directed by the *velum* and the articulators. The velum is the flexible *soft palate*. The part of the roof of your mouth that is softer and can move up to direct the airflow out the oral cavity (mouth) or down, to direct the airflow out of the nose. Also affecting resonance is the articulation of certain sounds that create more or less room in the oral cavity because of the shape the articulators need to make (the tongue to be high or flat, or the teeth and lips to be closed or open, the jaw to be dropped, etc.).

Many of us can feel vibrations in places other than the resonating chambers mentioned above, such as the chest, cheeks, or top of the head, but these are only *secondary vibrations*. The air with the sound wave does not actually move through these other places, but the vibrations do set other bones and tissues of our body to vibrating sympathetically.

To facilitate resonance, you will want to create a sense of openness in the throat on inhalation. While a yawn may be the most open our throats can be, this position is not only unnecessary for creating sound, it is undesirable. Certainly you can yawn and stretch as part of your warm-up, as a cat does upon first rising, but the cat does

---

[2] Richard Miller, *The Structure of Singing: System and Art in Vocal Technique* (New York: Schirmer Books, 1986), 48.

not stretch in the same way when engaging in more full activity, nor should you yawn while creating sound. The yawn has more tension than you will want for the best resonance. Instead, notice the openness you feel when you breathe in fully the scent of a favorite smell, such as of a flower, the ocean, or an appreciated food (even just imagining these smells can create this openness). Notice the space you feel when you think of a something or someone exciting. This is the active openness needed for optimum speech or singing.

> ### Exercise 10.1: Exploring the Resonating Chambers (Pharyngeal, Oral, and Nasal)
>
> **Purpose:** The amplification of your voice through resonance is imperative to reach and impact scene partners and the audience. This exercise helps to develop awareness of the reverberation of sound in the three resonating chambers—mouth, nose and throat. There are also times where you might want to redirect the voice to be, for example, more or less nasal to adjust your voice safely to reflect different characters. Some actors try to create character voices from the vocal folds and throat. This is not a good idea, as it generally adds harmful tension; instead, try creating characters by adjusting resonance, or with vocal qualities, as explored in Exercise 10.10.
>
> **Guidelines:**
> - First chant the humming sound *h-aaaaaaaaah* (*h* and *a*, extending the *ah* sound). Notice the resonance primarily in the pharynx but also where else it resonates.
> - Now start with the same sound but then close the lips to capture the sound vibration with an *mm* sound: *h-ah-mmmm* (*h*, *a*, and *m)*, extending the *mmmm* sound. Notice the resonance now building up in the oral cavity. Feel the vibration in your lips.
> - Now repeat this, holding the *mmm* to build up the resonance, and then release it again with an *ah* sound. Put the palm of your hand a couple of inches in front of your mouth to feel the air and vibration stream. (This is what further reverberates through the air particles and off objects and walls, to eventually vibrate in someone's ear, like a domino effect, one vibration setting the next in motion.)
> - Produce the humming sound *h-ah-mmmm* again, this time chewing the sound like a big wad of gum. Move it all around your oral cavity: forward, pursing your lips: sideways into each cheek; up into the soft and hard palates; and into the back of your mouth in the pharyngeal opening. You may feel some secondary vibrations in your chest, sinuses, or even the top of your head around the crown.
> - Using a *ng-ah* (ŋ-a-h) sound, focus the sound in your nose as best as you can. It helps to place two fingers of each hand on either side of your nose at first and then release them.

> **10.1** *Reflection Journal—Resonating Chambers*
>
> Were you able to feel the primary resonance? Were there any places you felt secondary resonance?

Articulation, Pronunciation, and Phonemes

We can communicate many things through only sound, as is shown through the complex sound communications of many animal species, and as you can explore in the tonal subtext gibberish exercise (Exercise 10.11) and vocal actions with a partner (Exercise 10.15) later in this chapter. As humans we often read more into the sound of the words than the words themselves. Most people agree that if there is a conflict between what is being said and *how* it is being said, we look for truth in the latter. However, for more sophisticated or specific details and for greater clarity in communication, we turn to words carved out through careful manipulation of "the tip of the teeth, the roof of the mouth, the jaw, lips and tongue."[3] This is our variation on a popular vocal chant and it would help you to chant it out loud privately or in your class to remind yourself of the many parts of the anatomy of speech that we use to create the forty plus *phonemes*, or individual sounds, that make up only one dialect of English, in this case General American English.[4]

Articulation is the careful manipulation of the anatomical mechanisms to create specific phonemes. When a series of phonemes are put together they create a word or sequence of words that we call speech. The anatomical articulators are the lips, teeth, tongue (comprising the tip, *blade* [just behind tip], sides, and back), roof of the mouth (including the *hard palate*, *soft palate* [called the velum], the *alveolar ridge* [a raised ridge on the roof of the mouth between the top teeth and the hard palate]), and the jaw. Some languages also involve the *uvula* (dangling tissue that looks like a mini-punching bag that you can see at the back of the mouth past the end of the soft palate).

A different but related concept is *pronunciation*. Pronunciation is the proper sequence of sounds with a strong emphasis (accent) on a designated syllable or syllables (and weaker emphasis on the others) in order to create a word recognizable within a specific dialect of a specific language.

Articulation is about making a huge variety of sounds clearly; pronunciation is about sounding out words correctly for a specific dialect. You may think that because you speak throughout the day in life that you are prepared to speak on the stage, but many of us are lazy speakers. In life, you can speak barely opening your mouth and be understood by most people if they are nearby. You can mumble through the expression of intense emotions, and others may get the gist of what you are expressing or not be paying that much attention. The stage demands clearer speech, clarity during emotional expression, and an ability to project the meaning of words to the back of a large theatre. Even on film, where a microphone is nearby, limited facility with voice and speech will limit the range of what you can express. Have you not heard the pathetic screeching of an untrained or poorly trained actor, attempting to be emotionally wrought or commanding?

---

[3] French's variation, inspired by Dr. Ball, of a popular vocal chant to encompass more of the articulators.

[4] Lynn K. Wells, *The Articulate Voice: An Introduction to the Voice and Diction*. 4th ed. (Boston: Allyn and Bacon/Pearson Education, 2004), 132.

10 ACTIVATING SPEECH

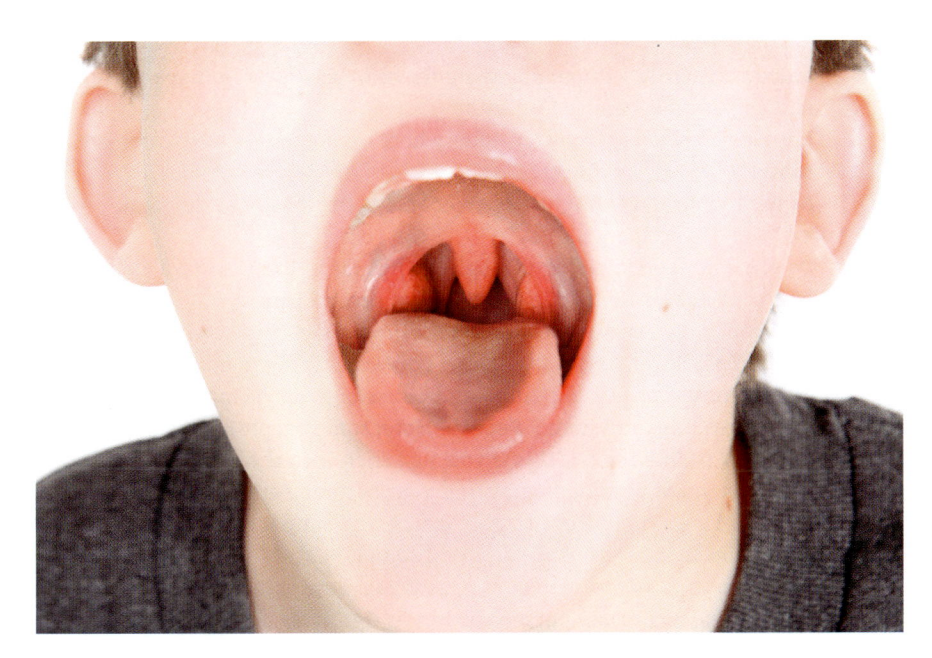

Figure 10.1 Swollen tonsils and the uvula (center).
Photo: © Suzanne Tucker/Shutterstock

Speech training is learning to consciously coordinate and strengthen the anatomical articulators to shape sound into the phonemes of a specific dialect of a specific language for specific effects.

> **Exercise 10.2: Warming Up the Articulators**
>
> **Purpose:** In order to produce the clearer and more vigorous speech the stage requires, you need to articulate clearly. This requires the agile manipulation of the various articulators. Facility of articulation is also important to launch verbal actions (as covered in depth in Chapter 11); for example, you shape and send the sound differently when threatening with words than when comforting with them.
>
> **Guidelines:** Identify all of the anatomical components of speech that you may be less familiar with on the diagram in Figure 9.1. Try to feel the external ones with your finger—the nose, lips, and jaw (and the muscle on either side where the jaw connects. Then, with the tip of your tongue trace the internal ones—teeth, alveolar ridge, hard and soft palates.
>
> - Stand in alignment (as in Exercise 9.1) and after releasing some neck and shoulder tension (as in Exercise 9.2):
>
> 1. Loosen the jaw
>   - Open your mouth and let your jaw hang loose.
>   - If your hands are cold, first rub them together vigorously to warm them up
>   - Take your bottom jaw in the fingers of one hand and try to move it up

and down gently without engaging the muscles (like a car's gearshift in neutral), until it hangs loose without tension.
- Imagine creating space at the joint where the upper jaw and lower jaw connect.
- As the mouth hangs slightly open, massage the muscle at the joint.
2. Loosen the lips and tongue
- Do some lip trills, blowing through the lips (as in Exercise 9.5 above); at first use only air then add sound. Repeat several times.
- Trill your tongue several times so that the tip hits your teeth and makes a sound as the air passes (as though you were trying to make the sound of a helicopter or fan whirring). At first use only air, as in a *hrrrrr* sound (h) (r-r-r-r) then add sound. Repeat. (**Note:** some people genetically have difficulty rolling the *r*. If this is you, just stick with the lip trills.)
- Tuck the end of your tongue behind your bottom teeth and stretch the middle of your tongue out of your mouth and snap it back and forth quickly. At first use only air, then add sound. Repeat.
- Open your lips as wide as you can, as if you were going to bite a triple-decker sandwich. Then purse your lips as tightly as possible, as if you just bit into a lemon. Repeat this in-and-out gesture, feeling the stretch in both directions.
3. Relax the soft palate (velum)
- Yawn to feel the soft palate rise and create space in the mouth.
- Try swallowing, as this pushes the soft palate down to aid the tongue in pushing saliva (or food) down the pharynx. (This action also causes the epiglottis to close off the windpipe so food does not go down there). When we speak we lift the soft palate to allow sound to come out through the oral cavity (except on nasal sounds), and we open the epiglottis so air can come into the lungs and back out as sound passing through the vocal folds.

International Phonetic Alphabet (IPA)

Because of the differences between written and spoken English, and the differences among different dialects of English, we will refer to the *International Phonetic Alphabet* (IPA) when discussing sounds.

There are only five to six vowels in written English (depending on whether you count *y* as a vowel. You may remember learning the vowels as a child (if English is your native language) by chanting, "a, e, i, o, u, and sometimes y." In spoken English there are many more sounds than there are letters. According to Wells, "There are over 40 sounds and only 26 letters of the alphabet,"[5] that we make in English. You cannot really understand all the sounds of English without learning IPA. In IPA, each phoneme is represented by a unique symbol that does not correspond to any other sound.

Note: Learning IPA can help you when you want to know the pronunciation of an unfamiliar word (essential for an actor). You can look it up in a good dictionary,

---

[5] Wells, *The Articulate Voice*, 146.

10 ACTIVATING SPEECH

which will spell out the phonemes of the word in IPA. It also can be very helpful in learning dialects or in learning other languages.

What Are the Differences between Vowels and Consonants?[6]

To a certain extent, the vowels carry the emotion and the consonants communicate meaning (this is an oversimplification but a useful place to begin your awareness of the affective possibilities of the sound of words). We will introduce some basic IPA here, but again, this is best learned in a formal voice class. Ahead of your formal voice training and ahead of learning IPA, you can start by increasing your awareness of the mechanical and anatomical parts of our bodies used to create different sounds, and where in the vocal instrument different sounds are placed. These are muscles and ligaments that need to be trained psychophysically to increase speed, strength, and agility.

Review the general properties of vowels and consonants below. Then practice the different IPA phonemes for different usage of the vowels outlined in the Vowel Articulation chart found in Appendix VIa.

> ### The Properties of Vowels
>
> **Vowels are**
> - *voiced* (the vocal folds vibrate to create sound)
> - supported by a constant, uninterrupted stream of air called *airflow* (which differentiates them from consonants). This is also why singers can release beautiful sustained sounds on the vowels.
> - differentiated by the shape and position of the tongue, lips, and jaw
> - differentiated by *location* in the mouth—forward, middle, or back
> - differentiated by *vertical location* in the mouth—low, middle, or high
> - differentiated by shorter or longer length of utterance
> - differentiated by more tension or less tension, called *lax*.
>
> **The properties of diphthongs**:
> - Two vowel sounds slide together to create a new single syllable sound called a *diphthong*. This can be true even if only one vowel is written, such as the *a* in *ate*. In terms of articulation, the tongue glides from one vowel position to another but the second sound has less tension. There is vibration of vocal folds through both articulator positions to create a blended sound.
> - **R coloration** (also called *rhotic*): If an *r* follows a vowel, it colors the vowel sound by either a bunching of the tongue in back or a turning up of the tip of the tongue. Generally in IPA, R coloration is shown by a little squiggle after the vowel symbol [ɚ] but some fonts also write it as $ə^r$.

---

[6] The information in this section on vowels and consonants is from our own vocal training and experimentation, supplemented by Wells's *The Articulate Voice*, pages 132–252, and Caldwell and Wall's *Excellence in Singing*, i–iv. IPA symbols come from online at http://ipa.typeit.org/ (accessed December 30, 2014). The exercises are created by French or Bennett to explore these vocal principles. Additional exercises required for vocal training were left out because we felt some should only be done under supervision of a trained voice and speech teacher (e.g. onset training).

Exercise 10.3: Vowel Formation (SDF)

Purpose: To bring consciousness to how you shape vowels sounds so that later you can learn to consciously adjust these sounds for specific dialects and specific vocal effects.

Guidelines:
- Take time, probably no more than one group at any practice, to study and create the shapes of the front vowels, then the central vowels, then the back vowels. How to manipulate your articulators for each vowel sound is outlined in detail in the Vowel Articulation Chart in Appendix VI. You may think because you are a native English speaker you do not need to do this, but actually you are probably less conscious of how you make sounds in English than a nonnative speaker because you haven't had to think about it for a long time.
    - Front [æ] æh (as in c<u>a</u>t), [e] ay, [ɛ] eh,[i] ee, [I] ih. Even though all these vowel sounds are created in the front of the mouth, each is shaped differently by the lips, teeth, jaw, and tongue.
    - Central ə (uh unstressed), ʌ (uh stressed), ɚ (ur unstressed), ɝ (ur stressed)
    - Back a (ah—long back a as in f<u>a</u>ther), o (oh), ɔ (aw), ʊ (oo lax), u (ooo more tension)
- Next take vowels sounds and words from different groups. Notice how you move the location of the sound from front to center, center to back, as you change from vowel to vowel, word to word. Here are a couple of examples, but you can use any vowel phonemes on the chart:
    - Front æ (ah) <u>a</u>s, to back a (ah) f<u>a</u>ther, to central ɚ (er), fath<u>er</u>, say "ask father"
    - Front E (ay) I (ee) L<u>a</u>t<u>e</u>, Back u (ooo) food, say "late food"
- After you have practiced the sounds looking at the chart, the next thing to do is to try them looking at the changes to your articulators in the mirror.

Exercise 10.4: Chanting the Vowels (PGB/SDF)

Purpose: To get a feeling for the uninterrupted flow of vowel sounds while gaining facility to adjust the articulators to shift from one to another. The flow of the vowel sounds is very important for the actor to vocally release the emotions.

Guidelines: Chant the following vowel sequences moving up and down a few pitches and trying to keep each different phoneme clear while moving seamlessly between them:
- Full breath in and then on the exhale whisper the most familiar vowel sequence: ah [æ], ay [e], ee [i] oh [o], ooo [u]. Full breath in then speak the sequence with full voice.
- Now chant: ah-ay-ee-oh-ooo [æ] [e],[i] [o] [u]. Full breath and repeat up in pitch two whole steps (whole notes on a piano, such as from A to C, or just

10 ACTIVATING SPEECH

- by ear). Full breath and repeat up another two steps. Full breath then back down two steps. Full breath then down to where you started pitch-wise. (Pitch pattern with full steps: 1, 3, 5, 3, 1).
- Try the same pitch pattern (1, 3, 5, 3, 1) on a new sound sequence: oo [ʊ], ee [i], oo [ʊ], ah [ɑ], oo [ʊ], ee [i] (the vowels-only sequence of "To be or not to be").
- Try the pitch pattern 1, 2, 3, 4, 5 while chanting the vowel sequence: ah [ɑ, ee [i], ur [ɝ] ay [e] (the vowel sequence in "Happy birthday"). If you are working in a group, go around the room and wish everyone a "ah-ee-ur-ay" [ɑ] [i], [ɝ] [e]. While making each sound, try different pitches, tempos, and volumes with each repetition to each new person.

Exercise 10.5: Sound and Space (Group Sound and Movement Exercise) (PGB)

Purpose: To explore space and physical relationships with movement and voice.

Guidelines: Throughout the exercise observe with your interior and exterior monitors simultaneously (as already introduced in previous chapters):

- Begin to walk around the space as a group.
- Walk in every conceivable manner: slow, fast, on your toes, backwards, raising legs, stretching out arms, explore all the space around you.
- Stretch and explore all spaces in the room and between your partners.
- Avoid physical contact with objects and other actors.
- Wherever there is a space, occupy it.
- Move closer and closer into the center of the room so that now everyone is close but never touching.
- Activate your sense of personal and group space as you turn, crawling under and over one another.
- Begin to release extended vowel sounds supported by breath. Do not try to extend past the support of the breath. Do not force it. Don't project unless you have warmed up to projection gradually.
- Let the exercise take over by sensing the group dynamic.
- Allow the vowels and your voice to take you wherever they go.
- Enjoy the pleasant sensation of ensemble communion, the "one mind" that seems to arise out of the exercise.

10.5 *Reflection Journal—Sound and Space*

Afterward, reflect on the exercise by writing down your experiences in your creative journal. Have a group discussion and share what has been discovered.

The Properties of Consonants

Consonants
- may be *voiced* (vocal folds are barely touching and vibrate as air passes through): (v) (b)
- may be *unvoiced/voiceless* (with a larger space in the glottis, air passes through without vibrating the vocal folds): (f) (p)
- may be *cognates*, pairs of sounds where the shape of the articulators is exactly the same but one is voiced and one is unvoiced: (b) (p)
- require an interruption of the stream of voiced sound vibration or unvoiced air vibration
- are produced through friction (f), explosion (p), or sending the sound out through the nose (n)
- are made by a particular combination of the movable articulators (one or both lips, the teeth, the tongue, velum) in various combinations with the fixed anatomy (alveolar ridge, hard palate).

The articulators shape the sound in different ways; namely, as a
- *continuant* (a prolonged sound without a change in quality; e.g., [m])
- *glide* (articulators change shape during the creation of the sound; e.g., [w])
- *fricative* (friction, and thus a kind of noisy turbulence, is caused by only a narrow amount of air getting through; examples are the cognates [f]—unvoiced, [v]—voiced, [s]—unvoiced, [z]—voiced)
- *plosive* (the air flow is interrupted completely and builds up to pop when released; examples are the cognates [p]—unvoiced, [b]—voiced, [k]—unvoiced, [g]—voiced, [t]—unvoiced, [d]—voiced)

The consonants are formed in a particular location in the mouth:
- *bilabial* (bi = two and labia = lips, so these are made with the two lips, which places the sound in the front of the mouth): [m]
- *labiodental* (lips and teeth): [v]
- *lingua-alveolar* (tongue and alveolar ridge, right behind top front teeth): [t]
- *lingua-dental* (tongue and teeth, made with the tongue between the teeth): [th]
- *lingua-palatal* (contact of the tongue against the hard palate (roof of the mouth)): [ʒ] zoom—voiced [ʃ] shine or motion
- *lingua-velar* (tongue and velum, the soft palate at the back of the roof of the mouth; thus made with the tongue touching the soft palate): [k]

Affricates
- Two consonant sounds that combine to make a new sound: [th], [cr], [gl], [ch]

Exercise 10.6: Consonant Articulation (SDF)

Purpose: To bring consciousness to how you shape the consonant sounds so that later you can learn to consciously adjust these sounds for specific dialects and specific vocal effects.

Guidelines:
- **Shape and location**: Take time to study the location and shape of the consonants in the IPA Consonant Articulation Chart in Appendix VI. Go through the phonemes, one group per practice; for example, you might move from the more forward consonants to those made in the back of the mouth following the progress of the chart from front: bilabial, labiodental, and lingua-dental; to middle: lingua-alveolar, lingua-palatal (hard palate); to back: velar (soft palate) and glottal. Notice the changes in location in the mouth. Notice the adjustments in the use of your articulators.
- **Seeing the shape:** After you have practiced the sounds looking at the chart, try them looking at the changes to your articulators in the mirror. Make sure that you are really articulating with your lips, adjusting your jaw, and moving your tongue quickly and cleanly from shape to shape. In other words, be more expressive with your mouth. Clearly shaped sounds are easier to understand and easier to project in a large theatre so they can be heard.
- **Cognates:** Take some time with the cognates, noticing the difference between unvoiced and voiced consonants (p and b), (t and d), (f and v), (s and z), (unvoiced th [θ], as in *with*, and voiced th [ð], as in *there*), (ch [t ʃ] and soft j/g [dʒ], as in *judge*).

Exercise 10.7: Shifting Shape, Location, and Tempo (SDF)

Purpose: After you have spent some time making sure that you form each consonant sound clearly, it is time to practice moving cleanly and then quickly between consonant sounds.

Guidelines: Before moving quickly between words, check the proper articulation of each IPA sound on Consonant Chart in Appendix VI.
- Using the chart below, go down the first column, articulating the front-placed sounds made with different articulators. Then go down the middle column to articulate centrally placed sounds, and then the last column for rear-placed consonant sounds. Go down the column and then try going back up. Do this three or four times. The first time, pronounce each word slowly and clearly (checking the articulation on the larger chart in Appendix VI). With each repetition of the list, gradually increase the pace without diminishing the clarity. **Note:** The symbol in the brackets (for example: [m]) represents the consonant phoneme and the capital letter or letters in italics after are short for the articulators primarily used to frame the sound (for example, BL).

- Using the chart below, move across the rows of the chart horizontally from front-placed sounds to central to rear-placed and then to central and front again. For example, mother, sings, cries, cries, sings, mother [m] [n] [k], [k] [n] [m]. Repeat each row at least three times, getting faster on each repetition while retaining clarity.
- Try a column or a row while changing pitches yet keeping the clarity of articulation.

Front **Focus bilabial (both lips)** BL **Labiodental (lips/teeth)** LBD **Lingua-dental (tongue/teeth)** LGD	Central **Lingua-alveolar (tongue-alveolar ridge)** LA **Lingua-palatal (tongue-hard palate)** LP	Back **Velar (soft palate)** V **Glottal** G
Mother [m] BL	Sings [s] LA	Cries [k] V
Fast [f] LBD	Risk [r] LP	Go [g] V
Thanks [θ] LGD	Gentle [dʒ] LP	Heart [h] G
Pop [p] BL	Zoom [z] LA	Crack [k] V
Voices [v] LBD	Laugh [l] LA	Growl [g] V
That [ð] LGD	Useful [j] LP	Lung [n] V
Best [b] BL	Dance [d] LA	Gown [g] V
Vast [v] LBD	Oceans [ʃ] LP	Harken [h] G
Weather [w] BL	Nasty [n] LA	England n] V
This [ð] LGD	Tastes [t] LA	Wrong [n] V
Famous [f] LBD	Chance [t ʃ] LP	Knight [k] V
Wow [w] BL	Jump [ʒ] LP	High h] G

Figure 10.2 Front, central, and back consonants.

Exercise 10.8: Combining Consonants and Vowels (PGB/SDF)

Purpose: To develop awareness of how the consonant sounds frame the vowels and how the vowels release a flow of sound.

Guidelines:
- Repeat each of the following consonant and long-vowel sequences with different types of vocal expression: a) whispered, b) spoken, and c) chanted.
- Then select different rows each time you do the exercise to move up and down in pitch.
- Make sure to have a full breath in-between the repetitions of each row.
- Try speaking and chanting down the columns switching quickly between consonants while remaining constant with the vowel sound.

10 ACTIVATING SPEECH

Mah [m][a]	May [m][e]	Mee, [m][i]	Moh [m][o]	Mooo [m][u]
Nah [n][a]	Nay [n][e]	Nee [n][i]	Noh [n][o]	Nooo [n][u]
Pah [p][a]	Pay [p][e]	Pee [p][i]	Poh [p][o]	Pooo [p][u]
Tah [t][a]	Tay [t][e]	Tee [t][i]	Toh [t][o]	Tooo [t][u]
Vah [v][a]	Vay [t][e]	Vee [v][i]	Voh [v][o]	Vooo [v][u]
Zah [z][a]	Zay [z][e]	Zee [z][i]	Zoh [z][o]	Zooo [z][u]
Lah [l][a]	Lay [l][e]	Lee [l][i]	Loh [l][o]	Looo [l][u]
Rah [r][a]	Ray [r][e]	Ree [r][i]	Roh [r][o]	Rooo [r][u]
Kah [k][a]	Kay [k][e]	Kee [k][i]	Koh [k][o]	Kooo [k][u]
Hah [h][a]	Hay [h][e]	Hee [h][i]	Hoh [h][o]	Hooo [h][u]

Figure 10.3 Combining consonants and vowels.

Exercise 10.9: Sounds with Tempo Variations

Purpose: To facilitate quicker and cleaner movement between sounds while adding tempo variation.

Guidelines: Speak the following in the manner prescribed. Make sure to fully move the articulators into each new position despite the speed:

A. Start lightly and rapidly but explore different tempo and rhythm variations:
   [w][i] "wee-wee-wee-wee-wee-wee-wee-wee-wee-wee-wee-wee-wee" etc.
   [w]][æ] "wah-wah-wah-wah-wah-wah-wah-wah-wah-wah-wah-wah" etc.
   "wee-wah-wee-wah-wee-wah-wee-wah-wee-wah-wee-wah-wee-wah" etc.
B. Start slowly and easily but explore different tempo and rhythm variations:
   [(*ee* as in *Lee* [i]—*oo* as in *loose* [u]—*aw* as in *saw* [ɔ]—*ah* as in *father* [a])
   "ee oo aw oo ee oo ah oo aw oo ee oo ah oo ee oo aw oo" etc.
C. With the jaw relaxed, open, and still, fix the tip of the tongue behind the lower front teeth while the middle of the tongue stretches in and out through your open mouth. Now continue this as you say easily, then more vigorously:
   [[j][ʌ] "Yuh-yuh-yuh-yuh-yuh-yuh-yuh-yuh-yuh-yuh-yuh-yuh-yuh-yuh" etc.

PART II: COMMUNION THROUGH VOICE AND SPEECH: TIMBRE, PROJECTION, EMPHASIS

Quality/Timbre and Tonal Subtext

Quality and *timbre* are used interchangeably. The timbre of your voice denotes the distinguishing *characteristics* of your voice that can be uniquely identified as yours. Some obvious and extreme examples of vocal quality might be the very nasal voice of Fran Drescher in *The Nanny*, the very breathy voice of Luna Lovegood in the later Harry Potter films, the guttural sounds of some German and some Scottish dialects, or the back of the throat *l* sound in *pull*. Other qualities are the strident voice caught in a high pitch and not adequately regulated through a variety of inflections; the voice lacking any nasal resonance, which sounds like you have a "code in da nose"; the raspy voice like you might sound after shouting over loud music at a concert or at a sporting event (or if you are a heavy smoker or have been coughing a lot), or the thin voice revealing too much tension and/or insufficient resonance.

When you listen to a recording of your voice, you may determine that you have some of these qualities. Changes in how you make the sounds can dramatically alter the timbre of your voice, but it takes years of practice and the help of an experienced voice teacher to really change the range of qualities you are able to convey or to change the personal quality of your speech, which may limit your casting possibilities.

As a start, you can become more conscious of the areas of resonance to create different sounds.

Exercise 10.10: Vocal Qualities and Issues (LW/SDF)

Note: Many of vocal issues take a lot of time and expert guidance to correct so be patient in developing good vocal habits.

Purpose: To sound out and listen to different vocal qualities or timbres so that you become more aware of the qualities in your voice and those you might like to employ for a character's voice.

Guidelines:

Your vocal quality:
- Using any passage of text, even reading a chapter from this book, record your voice.
- Describe in adjective form any particular qualities you notice (for example: *resonant, thin, guttural, soft, strident, nasal*, or *stuffed up*).

Nasal quality: Choose to add or omit nasal resonance. For nasal resonance, the velum (soft palate), is lowered and to remove it, the velum is raised. (Review Exercise 10.2: Warming up the articulators for ways to become more conscious of the movement of the velum.)

- Go back and forth between ng [ŋ] soft palate lowered, and [k], which raises it.
- There should only be nasality in the following sounds in General American English [n][m] and [ŋ].
- Lower the soft palate as you say *Now* [n] *moms* [m] *sing* [ŋ] *nicely nightly*. (Repeat a few times). These underlined phonemes all have nasal resonance.
- Raise the soft palate to say: *Kick the cuckoo carefully*[k]. This line has no nasal sounds and thus should have no nasal resonance.

- Try moving back and forth between the nasal and nonnasal lines above, moving the soft palate up or down as appropriate.

A common issue: Some people add nasality to sounds that should not have it and thus have a very nasal tone.

Breathiness:
- Try this sequence of unvoiced consonants that do not vibrate the vocal folds:
- [h] [f] [f]], ch [t ʃ] [f] soft th[θ] [s] th[θ] [h]
- Now try a sentence with the above consonant sequence: *Heath flies fast chasing Faith's silent myth home.* The vowels will be voiced, but all the consonants are unvoiced. See how you move between the unvoiced consonants and the voiced vowels. Hear the breathy sound of the voiceless consonants and the hiss of the [s] sound.
- **A common issue**: Some people add too much breath on sounds that should be voiced, to create a very light, breathy voice that will be hard to project.

Sibilant[s]:
A common issue: The sibilant (whistling) [s] sound is made as the air in the *s* is forced around the tongue tip (normal *s*, but in this case through the biting edges of teeth, which can happen if the teeth are either too close together or too far apart).

Adjustment: Remember when making the [s] as described in the chart: 1) to make sure the tongue tip is pointed toward the gum ridge, 2) not to touch the back of upper front teeth, 3) to lift the tongue, and 4) to press the tongue edges firmly against the sides of upper molars.

- Try saying these beginning [s] sounds without any whistle. Make an effort to end the natural [s] hiss clearly, quickly, and cleanly on each of the following sounds: *singing silly soppy songs.*
- Try some ending [s] sounds on *Pass the grass fast.*
- If you can master those with no whistle, try the tongue twister *The sixth sick sheik's sixth sheep's sick.*
- Your next challenge is to try to say these into a sensitive microphone. Microphones really pick up and amplify sibilance. If you want to work in film, radio, announcing, or voiceover, you really need to address any sibilance.

Popping plosives
Correct articulation of all plosives and affricatives requires a pop of air. Hold your hand in front of your mouth and feel the air pushed out explosively on the unvoiced plosives [p] [t] [k] and slightly less on the voiced plosives [b] [d] [g], because the vocal folds are more closed and slow down the air flow a little. There is also less of a force of air on the affricatives because the air is released more slowly in the fricative phase of the sound and thus does not build up

as much for the plosive, or popping, part of the sound. Try the affricatives ge [dʒ] and ch [t ʃ].

A common issue: When using a microphone, plosives can make an unpleasant popping sound that draws attention to the technology of the mic or the mechanics of speech and away from the content of the speech. This is generally not a problem in regular speech or on the stage.

Adjustment: The solution is to direct the flow of air so that it does not directly hit the microphone but rather goes just above, below, or to the side of it.

Guttural:
- Try this sequence of guttural consonants that do not vibrate the vocal folds:
- [g] [g] [k] [k] [g] [ŋ]
- Now try this sentence with the above consonant sequence: *Go get kinky gongs*. You will hear a very guttural quality, which is appropriate for such sounds. However, in General American English you will want to limit a back of the throat sound for most of the other phonemes. In other languages, such as German, the guttural sound is more prevalent.

A common error: Some people place sounds in the back of the throat that should be placed more in the middle or front of the mouth. This creates an overall guttural and harsh timbre, not appropriate for the majority of sounds in General American English.

If you have any of these common issues, you may need a vocal coach to work with you to help you make adjustments for employing effective speech for acting.

10.10 *Reflection Journal—Vocal Qualities and Issues*

Do you think that you have any of the vocal issues listed above? Were you able to hear the difference in quality and internally feel a different shape for the articulators in the exercises?

Tonal Subtext

Timbre along with pitch, inflection, tempo, rhythm, and volume combine to create the *tonal subtext* referred to by some people as the tone. Tonal subtext is different types of vocal sounds you use in different situations to communicate meaning outside the actual meaning and message of the words themselves. Tone or tonal subtext should not be confused with *intonation*, which refers instead to the overall movement of pitch. Tonal subtext can either support or work against the meaning of the words. It can communicate many things such as status, relationships, intentions, and underlying truths. For example, the tonal subtext might communicate the dismissiveness you actually feel in a situation where you are forced to use polite words. For example, consider when a parent or teacher might have said in a stern tone, "Don't take that tone with me," when they thought you disrespectful. It could also be a positive tone of love you have for someone that you are not allowed, or not yet ready, to overtly express.

Exercise 10.11: Tonal Subtext (Partners Exercise) (SF)

Purpose: To develop awareness of how the tone of your voice (including timbre, pitch, resonance, rhythm, tempo, and volume) with or without words, can communicate underlying meaning through the tonal subtext. In some cases, it can completely change the meaning you communicate.

Guidelines: Changing the Meaning with Tonal Subtext
- Choose a partner and designate one of you as A and one as B.
- Imagine you have the neutral line "Hello."
- A says "hello" out loud to B with the tonal subtext of "Do I know you?" B responds with the same subtextual meaning, but with B's own tonal way of conveying that. See how this colors the tone of the word.
- This time B begins with "hello" with the tonal subtext of "You're hot!"
- Try "hello" with the subtexts "Sorry, I really screwed up," and "I have a surprise for you."

Communicating Tonal Subtext with Gibberish
- Create a made-up language (gibberish). You can use as a model a language you have heard but don't speak, as long as you can do so without mocking people with other dialects, accents, or languages. Communicate with only tonal subtext and physical action (but without indicating): "Welcome to my home." Say this line again with a different-sounding language.
- Try the following lines with other gibberish languages: "Do you have any food?" and "You really shouldn't be here." Notice the color that the tones of each different made-up language place on the line.
- Say the actual words of the line in English, "You really shouldn't be here." Next try two different tonal subtexts: The first one is, "Get out of here quickly, or you will be killed." The second one is, "But I'm glad you are, because I want to have an affair with you."

10.11 Reflection Journal—Tonal Subtext

Jot down an example of a line and then a subtext that enhances the meaning, a subtext that changes the meaning, and a subtext that is opposite to the meaning.

Emphasis: Rhythm, Intonation, and Stress

In his excellent dialect series *Accents and Dialects for Stage and Screen*,[7] Paul Meier takes time to talk about the rhythm, intonation, and stress patterns of each dialect he coaches. In English we use variations in pitch, volume, and rhythm to create emphasis. He suggests, for example, that variations in rhythm and pitch are used much more in British Received Pronunciation than in Standard American English,

---

[7] Paul Meier, *Accents and Dialects for Stage and Screen* (Lawrence, KS: Paul Meier Dialect Services, 2012). Available online at www.paulmeier.com/product/accents-and-dialects-for-stage-and-screen/ (accessed December 27, 2014) or through other booksellers.

where volume is one of the predominant forms of emphasis. In American Southern English, however, rhythm variation is a much stronger emphasis factor, whereas New Yorkers are known for speaking more rapidly.

In one of the more familiar Canadian dialects (heard in the Prairies and in some West Coast speakers) an upward pitch inflection at the ends of sentences can frequently be heard. Some consider this to lack firmness or certainty, sounding like a question (because other dialects only rise at the end of sentences if they are questions). Others consider this to be a more inviting and friendly way of speaking. While for many the downward inflection implies closure, the upward one for some invites input. This demonstrates that the perspective of the speaker affects reception of the message.

Exercise 10.12: Emphasis (Key Words, Rhythm, Intonation, and Stress) (SDF inspired by the work of Paul Meier)

Purpose: To explore the effect of different emphases on meaning, and how to create emphasis through volume, tempo, and pitch.

Guidelines: For this exercise use the line, "I stole your dog."
- First notice how the meaning changes when the emphasis is on different *key words* in the sentence. Key words activate meaning and message. Say the line emphasizing a different key word each time, "*I* stole your dog. I *stole* your dog. I stole *your* dog. I stole your *dog*."
- Select one version and try to emphasize the key word by increasing the volume on that word.
- Try to emphasize the key word by raising or lowering your pitch.
- Try a few ways of emphasizing with tempo. Pause just before saying it. Pause just after saying it. Try slowing down and drawing out the emphasized word.
- Try various types of emphasis using other choices for the key word.

10.12 *Reflection Journal—Emphasis*

Jot down the tonal subtext for each line; for example, for the first emphasis, "*I* stole your dog," the subtext is "as opposed to someone else having stolen it." What differences did you notice about using volume for emphasis versus pitch versus tempo?

Projection

It is wonderful, and essential, for your vocal production to be free from strain, your articulation clear, and your pronunciation accurate, and you should work on all of these things first; however, none of it matters onstage if the audience cannot hear you. The term for expanding your voice to fill the theatre is *projection*.

Projection involves increased volume, better vocal production, clarity about what and to whom you are communicating, and your desire and intention to expand all of that to fill a large theatre. Lastly, your audience needs to actually want to listen

10 ACTIVATING SPEECH

Figure 10.4
Projection.
Photo: iStock © Alija

so that they can hear and receive what you are saying; in other words, you have to invest meaning in the words and to inflect and vary the tone enough to catch and keep the audience's attention. (The word *audience* comes from the Latin *audientia*, which means "hearing" or "listening.")

Volume is a key component of projection. Volume is achieved through increased amount and intensity of airflow; in other words, good breath support. Not being heard often comes down to not being loud enough, which can be a huge challenge for many beginning actors. You may not be able to increase your volume until you have developed healthy vocal production. This includes good alignment and solid breath support behind your speech, as outlined above.

Being able to understand you is partly a function of clear articulation, as covered above, and partly a function of understanding what you are saying. The latter is largely about text analysis, covered more fully in the upcoming Active Analysis chapters 13, 14, 15, and 16.

If you are not clear about what you are saying, as often happens with students working on Shakespeare or other challenging texts, the natural tendency is to not want to say it loud enough to be heard. If you don't understand the way that you want to affect others with your speech, it will lack the directionality required for projection. Additionally, if you are not making the meaning clear because you don't understand it or are not articulating clearly, the audience may stop listening.

All of the work in this chapter will help you with projection. If you are not supported by good alignment, if you don't breathe well, if you have not developed your resonance, if you do not articulate clearly, you will have difficulty projecting.

Another concept that is key for projection is your intention to be heard. This may seem obvious and yet so many beginning actors in their stage fright actually, on some level, don't want to be heard. Most of us can be quite loud if we really want to get someone's attention who is some distance away.

To create a sound across a space that someone else hears, we must generate vibrations (resonance) that displace air molecules and bounce off other actors and the architecture of the set and theatre, reverberating through other air molecules. These then vibrate the eardrum of the hearer. In this sense, sound leaves the inside of your body and moves to the inside of another's body. You are touching someone else across space with sound. Sound given and received is actually an act of connection between people.

Important note: Never work on projection if you have not properly warmed up all of the other components of voice and speech, as listed in the warm-up outline at the end of this chapter.

> ### Exercise 10.13: Projection by Intention (Solo or with a Partner) (SDF)
>
> **Purpose:** To remind you that you actually do project in life, when you have an important reason to do so, and therefore your mind and body already have programing for projection.
>
> **Guidelines:** Take a line from a play you are working on. If you have not yet started working on a play, then just use the line, "Hey, wait for me!" Remember to make sure you have warmed up your vocal instrument before working on projection (see the full vocal warm-up sequence at the end of this chapter).
>
> - First, put the palm of your hand a couple inches in front of your mouth. Say the line to your own hand: "Hey, wait for me!" Can you feel the air that is displaced by your breath as it brushes your hand?
> - Next, extend your arm out in front of you with the hand up, palm facing you. See if you can still feel the air flow at this distance when you repeat the line.
> - Then, work with a partner or the teacher (or just pick objects in the room and imagine them being a person you are trying to reach). Have your partner move 5 feet in front of you. Speak the line, trying to reach your partner. Then receive the vibrations of your partner's voice in your ears as the partner speaks the line.
> - Move to 10 feet, 20 feet, then 30 feet apart and repeat.
> - If at all possible, do this exercise in a large theatre or, if weather permits, outside.
>
> **Caution:** Don't try to project farther than 30–40 feet until you have worked with the exercise in this chapter repeatedly or have taken a voice class.
>
> - In subsequent repetitions of this exercise, after you have done the other vocal exercises a number of times, you can expand to 40 feet, 50 feet, and 70 feet. If you do not have the room, and weather or time do not permit going outside, you can imagine that you are outside and see a point in the distance and project to that.
> - For the farthest distance, imagine the person you are trying to reach is on the other side of a large field almost out of range (expand the walls of your

studio with your imagination). Perhaps you desperately need to reach him or her to give you a ride home so you are not stuck there in a dangerous neighborhood late at night, or because he is a stranger who forgot his wallet and you want to make sure he gets it back. Get his attention with, "Hey, wait for me!"

10.13 *Reflection Journal—Projection*

Did you find you were able to project better or worse than you expected in this exercise? What do you think inhibits your projection? What do you think will help your projection?

Exercise 10.14: Projecting Intimacy (With a Partner) (SDF)

Purpose: One of the biggest traps actors fall into with projection is speaking lines to a scene partner who is very close by, but forgetting that the audience is much farther away. We tend to project enough to reach that scene partner and thus he might hear us, but the audience might not. This is particularly a problem for more intimate or vulnerable moments, especially if we are already a little self-conscious about sharing a very private sentiment in the public sphere of the stage. Because a big part of projection is intention, there are a couple things that you can do.

Guidelines: Use the lines from an intimate moment in a scene you are working on. If you do not have a scene, then use the lines, "I have always loved you," and the response, "I always knew." (These lines are new to you and you may not have an intimate relationship with your partner. If you find yourself mocking them, it may be because you are afraid to reveal intimacy. See if you can get past the joking to find some truth here.)

- Go into a large space, the larger theatre where you are to perform, if possible, or another large space. First, do the scene so close together that you are touching some part of your bodies, such as knees, shoulders, or hands (or if you want to be more intimate, with the head of one of you in the lap of the other). Focus on really trying to reach and affect one another.
- Next, place one actor at one side of the space (for example, onstage) and the other as far away as possible (for example, at the back of the house (audience seating area). Try to maintain the sense of intimacy you found previously while being loud enough to hear your voices bounding back to you from the surrounding walls. This is how much volume you will need when doing the scene.
- Now return to sitting on the couch or standing near your partner. Imagine that you and your partner are in a bubble in which you will project images, sounds, and speech relevant to the situation and script. Now imagine expanding this bubble to include the audience to the very back row of the large space. Invite them into your intimate bubble. Speak at the same volume you did when speaking across the space, while revealing the intimacy between you, again trying to hear your voices bounding back to you from the surrounding walls.

10.14 Reflection Journal—Projecting Intimacy

Were you able to keep a sense of intimacy when adding volume across the space? Were you able to keep the volume when returning to close proximity with your partner? Did you feel you could allow people to witness the vulnerability of this intimacy?

Exercise 10.15: Vocal Actions (Partner Exercise) (PGB)

Purpose: Now that you have begun to learn and feel how to use your voice and to articulate sounds, it is time to explore using sound to affect another actor. We all know that words spoken with strong intention or emotion can impact us positively or negatively. It is important to learn how to do that more consciously for acting.

Guidelines: The *language* we will use for this exercise is the repeated sound "mee lah, mee lah, mee lah [m] [i] [l][a]." (You could use any gibberish phrase or any line, such as lines from your script, for this exercise.) You must convey your intentions with only these words while physically acting out the actions that the instructor dictates.

- Choose a partner and go into the practice space.
- Use your entire body to convey the given actions to your partner.
- Use only "Mee-Lah" with changes in pitch, volume, tempo, or quality to communicate vocally.
- Physical action is the basis for voice, so it is important to attempt to express your action psychophysically as well as vocally.
- *Actions:* to tease one another, to accuse, to mock, to plead and beg, to find out and cover up, to entice and ignore, to needle, to convince, to put down, to encourage.

Note: Take time with each action to be able to get a sense of truth. Don't exaggerate but execute each action as truthfully as possible.

10.15 Reflection Journal—Vocal Actions with a Partner

Could you communicate the message without words? Were you able to affect your partner? Did you feel affected by your partner when it was your turn to receive? How much meaning can be communicated without words, just by the quality of the sound?

Exercise 10.16: Sounding Out the Text[8] (CB/PGB)

Purpose: To keep the playfulness you found while exploring sounds and gibberish, as you move on to using actual text from your script or a sample text brought in by the teacher.

Guidelines: Make sure you have done a basic vocal warm-up, including alignment, breathing, pitch, and resonance. Place the written text near you in case you need to refer to it.

Exercise 10.16A: Sounding Out the Text

- Lie down in the most comfortable position for you on the floor as suggested in Chapter 5, Figures 5.1, 5.2, and 5.3 (p. 85).
- Slow down and deepen your breath (as in Exercise 9.3).
- Start with a few Lip Trills, exploring different pitches.
- Hum to awaken resonance in your resonating chambers.
- Recite a speech you know well, very slowly: ONE WORD AT A TIME!
- Feel the primary resonance of each word in parts of your pharynx, oral, and (depending on the sound) nasal cavity. Notice whether you have any secondary resonance in your chest or back. (You may not have a lot of secondary resonance here if your voice is naturally high; instead you may feel it more in other secondary vibratory places such as your cheeks or the top of your head.)
- Let the resonance of your voice excite images and feelings.
- Now repeat the exercise, reciting the speech phrase by phrase; that is, from punctuation mark to punctuation mark.
- Note the length of the phrases and how their length suggests changes of tempo and rhythm.
- Now recite from full stop to full stop (period, exclamation point, or question mark).
- Recite from thought group to thought group. (This may be quite long for complex writers such as Shakespeare, with many side thoughts like parenthetical tangents in the middle.)

Exercise 10.16B: Rock and Roll (To Break Any Fixed Patterns)

- Lie on the floor.
- Bring your knees to your chest and wrap your arms around them.
- Gently rock to and fro while reciting your lines.
- Notice how the words begin to come out in new ways.
- This exercise can help you discover new subtext and nuance of expression.

---

[8] This exercise is adapted from Cicely Berry. See her book *The Actor and the Text* (New York: Applause Books, 1992) for a series of excellent exercises for vocally bringing out the meaning and sound possibilities in your script.

> **10.16A & B** *Reflection Journal—Sounding Out the Text*
>
> Did you make any new discoveries about the meaning of your text? What did you observe about the possibilities of the different sounds of your text? Did you make any discoveries about rhythm?

Exercise 10.17: Guidelines for a Comprehensive Vocal Warm-Up

Purpose: We have filled in this outline with the exercises described in this chapter. You only need to select one to two exercises for each category of voice and speech each time. You do not have to do all the exercises in chapters 9 and 10 to cover a particular vocal attribute, but only to select one for each, during each warm-up session. Feel free to substitute helpful exercises that you have learned in voice classes, workshops, or rehearsals for any of the exercises in this chapter. Once you have had some formal training in voice, you can use the warm-up exercises from your voice teacher. Remember to never put a demand on your voice until you have warmed it up with this or another complete vocal warm-up.

Guidelines: Always start in your middle-pitch range and work up and down from there.

1. **Alignment:** Align your body, as outlined in Chapter 9, Exercises 9.1 and 9.2 and shown in Figure 9.2. Make sure that the spine is lengthened, and lift the breastbone to expand the chest. Ensure the neck is long and free (supported by a 1-inch-thick book if lying down), or above the shoulders rather than forward or back of them (if standing), and with the chin parallel to the floor.
2. **Breathe Slowly and Deeply:** Standing or lying down (as in Exercise 9.3), slow down and deepen the breath. To deepen the breath, try to encourage the expansion of the lower ribs and sides to make room for the lungs to fully descend and expand. Do not overfill the lungs so that they are too eager to quickly exhale and decrease the pressure, but allow them to fill to a comfortable, naturally satisfied level. Try to resist slightly the collapsing of the chest on exhalation, to develop control and to extend the exhalation. (Alternately, if you have less time, at a minimum do the Three Tai Chi Breaths in Exercise 9.4 and make sure to breathe fully before phonation in each subsequent exercise.)
3. **Releasing Tension:** Even while activating and engaging the necessary muscles for breath support and phonation, you will want to minimize unnecessary tension in your throat ahead of phonation to give your vocal folds the maximum range and flexibility while minimizing strain. Breathing exercises may serve to release sufficient tension; however, if you still feel tension, particularly in the neck and shoulders, you may want to add here some exercises to release tension, such as those offered as Exercise 9.2 Alternately, you can work in partners in the class to massage each other's shoulders (some teachers like to do this in a circle which

is fun and efficient but it may be hard to fully receive a massage and release tension when you are simultaneously using muscular tension to massage someone else). Some examples from other chapters of this book included the meditation in Exercise 3.1 Watching the Breath; the guided visualization Exercise 3.4 Sunset on the Beach; or Jacobson's Progressive Relaxation exercise outlined in Exercise 5.1A. If lying down you can roll your head side to side.

4. **Warm Up the Vocal Folds and Connect Voice to Breath**: Lip trills. If you have been lying down for the first exercises, come to standing with minimum tension as outlined in Exercise 5.1B Rising without Tension. Do some Lip Trills, first with only breath and then with sound. Trill "Mary Had a Little Lamb" and another simple song to add pitch variations connected to breath.

5. **Pitch**: Work pitch changes into most of the exercises you do. Try repeating quickly, "Mee Mee Mee [m] [i], May May May [m] [e], Nee Nee Nee [n] [i], Nay Nay Nay [n] [e]" while varying your pitch inflection on a five-level scale going down one full step with each repetition (5, 4, 3, 2, 1) or up one full step (1,2,3,4,5). Or, vary your pitch inflection by jumping two full steps up or down with each repetition (1,3,5,3,1). Alternately, use Exercise 9.5: Pitch trills (lip trills) or 10.4: Chanting the vowels. If you are not familiar with these musical patterns just hum a simple tune such as Mary Had a Little Lamb or Happy Birthday (the latter has a wider range so make sure it is comfortable in your pitch range).

6. **Resonance:** Once you have touched base with alignment, breath, and pitch, explore the reverberation of sound in your resonating chambers—mouth, nose, and throat (oral, nasal, and pharyngeal cavities)—by alternately humming with the mouth closed and releasing the stream of vibration with an open mouth on, "Hahmmm-ah [h][a] [m] [a]."
See Exercise 10.1.

7. **Articulation**: At a minimum, warm up the articulators as in Exercise 10.2 and speak some tongue twisters. Better yet, select one or more of the exercises involving articulation of vowels and consonants introduced above, such as Exercises 10.3: Vowel formation; 10.4: Chanting the vowels; 10.5: Sound and space (group exercise); 10.6: Consonant articulation; 10.7: Shifting shape, location, and tempo; 10.8: Combining consonants and vowels; or 10.9: Sounds with tempo variations. A simple alternative is to march in a circle while clearly articulating all the consonant sounds of the alphabet (omitting the vowels) such as b, c, d, f, etc. Continue to get familiar with the consonant articulation chart to reinforce correct articulation.

8. **Projection:** Just as an athlete includes sprinting or some other demanding exercise at the end of a warm-up, you must include projection, as in Exercises 10.13: Projection by intention or 10.14: Projecting intimacy.

9. **Connecting Voice to Text and Action:** Lastly, tie your voice work into the other techniques you are working with in the Stanislavsky System. It is helpful to connect words and sounds to action. Whereas Exercise 10.13 covers intention and projection together, for a more rigorous action, you can use Exercises 10.11 Tonal Subtext and 10.15 Vocal Actions.

Summary

Developing awareness of the anatomy of voice and speech and its use in clear vocal expression is essential for acting. First you must learn the components of good vocal production: good alignment, controlled and effective breathing, balanced onset, pitch variation, and full resonance. Then you can begin to expand what you can express through intonation and words as you further develop resonance through articulation. Learning proper placement and production of the sounds (phonemes) of speech will allow the meaning of the words you and your characters speak to be clearly understood. Developing your ability to project will allow you to share your experience of the character with the audience. Commit yourself to a daily practice of your voice and speech exercises so that voice and speech become additional colors in your artist's palette. This will allow you to bring the life of a role to an audience in a powerful, artistic, and meaningful way.

In Chapter 14, Active Analysis: Reconnaissance of the Character, you will learn additional methods of bringing a text to life. One of these is the Logic of Voice and Speech, a variety of methods to cull from a text more of the overt and covert meaning in the play that can be expressed through its language and your vocal instrument.

New Theatre Terms, Concepts, and Artists

- alveolar ridge
- affricates
- articulation
- audientia
- Cicely Berry
- bilablial
- cognates
- continuant
- diphthong
- dorsum of tongue
- fricative
- glide
- International Phonetic Alphabet (IPA)
- intonation
- labiodental
- lax
- lingua-alveolar
- lingua-dental
- lingua-velar
- lip trills
- Paul Meier
- phonemes
- plosive
- projection
- pronunciation
- quality
- R-coloration
- resonance
- resonation
- rhotic
- secondary vibrations
- soft palate
- speech training
- timbre
- tonal subtext
- tongue trills
- uvula
- velum
- voiced
- voiceless
- unvoiced

Additional Resources for Voice Training

For a spoken language you really must learn the proper formation of vowels and consonants through hearing them spoken by someone who has learned to shape the phonemes correctly. Then you will need to practice them over and over, receiving correction from a trained voice teacher. If you cannot find (or afford) a good voice teacher, however, there are available some excellent books and online resources by leading voice teachers. As several approaches to voice and speech training exist, we highly recommend that you explore the recommended list of books and websites that follow:

F. M. Alexander. The Complete Guide to the Alexander Technique website: http://alexandertechnique.com. A good book on the technique is *The Alexander Technique Workbook: The Complete Guide to Health, Poise and Fitness*, by Richard Brennan (London: Collins & Brown, 2011).

Cicely Berry. (See the Royal Shakespeare Company's website: www.rsc.org.uk.) Berry has been the vocal director of the Royal Shakespeare Company for many years. Her basic book is *Voice and the Actor* (New York: Macmillan, 1973). Her book *The Actor and the Text* (New York: Applause Books, 1992) focuses on Shakespeare but is extremely helpful to dissect any text and bring it alive vocally. The exercises are extremely helpful.

Catherine Fitzmaurice. www.fitzmauricevoice.com. Fitzmaurice's technique has been adapted by many graduate-school voice experts.

Roy Hart. www.roy-hart.com. The archives of the Roy Hart Theatre introduces the work of Alfred Wolfsohn as continued by Hart.

Arthur Lessac. *The Use and Training of the Human Voice* (New York: DBS, 1967) is a helpful sourcebook. The Lessac Institute trains in speech and movement (see www.lessacinstitute.com).

Kristin Linklater. See her website at www.linklatervoice.com. Linklater's *Freeing the Natural Voice* is a classic, but make sure to get the latest edition, which incorporates new scientific discoveries about the voice (Amazon lists the Kindle edition as published in 2014). To accompany her work or support her workshops in Scotland you can listen to audio files on-line at: www.linklatervoice.com/resources/audio-tips-and-exercises, but they won't make much sense until you have the book and have had an introduction to voice in a good voice class.

Paul Meier (International Dialects of English Archive). www.dialectsarchive.com. Paul Meier's system for learning dialects is extremely helpful. In addition to his collection of resources and CDs for learning dialects, the archive is an excellent source for listening to native speakers of a huge range of dialects of English. Meier and his associates continue to collect authentic dialects for you to listen to as you learn any English dialect.

Richard Miller. *The Structure of Singing: System and Art in Vocal Technique*. New York: Schirmer Book, 1986.

Patsy Rodenburg. Rodenburg is a master voice and Shakespeare teacher. Her website is www.patsyrodenburg.info.

Edith Skinner. *Speak with Distinction*. New York: Applause, 1990.

Konstantin Stanislavski. *An Actor's Work*. Edited by Jean Benedetti. London: Routledge, 2009. Chapter 19 is titled "Voice and Speech."

Lynn K. Wells. *The Articulate Voice*. Boston: Pearson, 2004. Contains a series of pictures showing the mouth positions for different phonemes and describing in detail the correct pronunciation of each sound.

Acknowledgments

We are particularly grateful to Professor Margaret Joyce Ball, DMA, who reviewed this chapter in two drafts and helped us update our vocal anatomy through her own knowledge and through providing some excellent reference books.

We are also indebted to the following master teachers for our voice training through the oral tradition. They have greatly influenced us, and we use a combination of techniques from these sources, as well as others that we have invented:

Alexander Technique (through James Howell, Music Director and choreographic assistant to Gerald Arpino at the Joffrey Ballet)
Cicely Berry (through Robert Taylor, Mary Corrigan, Ursula Meyer, Robby Ross, and Dan Milne of The Royal Shakespeare Company)
Alfred Dixon Speech Systems (through Mrs. Alfred Dixon on restoring the damaged voice)
Catherine Fitzmaurice (through Krista Scott workshops)
Carol Gill Royal Scottish Academy of Music and Drama
Kristin Linklater (through Herbert Rodriguez and Jessica Litwak)
Arthur Lessac (through Laurie Mufson and Kathy Dunn in workshops)
Voice for Singing (through Linda Vickerman, Wendy Grice, and Anna Coogan)

CHAPTER 11

Verbal Action: Communicating with Words and Subtext

"If you have a part which is witty and extravagant you will not make it funny by meddling with the inflections—that is, by telling the audience it is funny. The humor will come if you have found the necessity for those words. Similarly, if you have a part with great depth of feeling and the voice becomes romantic, what you are doing is telling the audience that you can feel but you do not convince them of the reason for that feeling; they do not, therefore totally believe it."[1]

—Cicely Berry

Primary Elements of Action Actively Explored in This Chapter

Verbal actions with one spoken line; verbal actions with three spoken lines; verbal actions with designated counteractions; selecting counteractions; problems, main actions, and objectives; verbal actions with hidden agendas; named-event improvisations; various ways to name an event

- What Is a Verbal Action?
- What Is *Subtext,* and How Does It Figure into the Equation?
- Avoid the Pitfalls
- Write It Down

Part I: Verbal Actions with Only One Spoken Line

☐ Exercise 11.1 The Eleventh Hour
☐ Exercise 11.2 A Wartime Farewell

Part II: Verbal Actions with Three Spoken Lines

☐ Exercise 11.3 Suspicion at the Doctor's Office
☐ Exercise 11.4 Black Market Border
☐ Exercise 11.5 The Two-Timer's Reward

Part III: Verbal Actions with Designated Counteractions

- What Is Counteraction?
- Agreement
☐ Exercise 11.6 "Neither a Borrower nor a Lender Be," or, the Big Mooch
☐ Exercise 11.7 The Cover-Up
☐ Exercise 11.8 The Accusation

---

[1] Cicely Berry, *Voice and the Actor*. (New York: Macmillan, 1973), 133.

> **Part IV: Selecting Counteractions and Negotiating Status**
> ☐ Exercise 11.9 Blackmail!
> ☐ Exercise 11.10 Cheer Up!
> ☐ Exercise 11.11 Forbidden Fruit
>
> **Part V: Improvisations—Problems, Main Actions, and Objectives**
> ☐ Exercise 11.12 The Interrogation
> ☐ Exercise 11.13 The Reluctant Hero
> ☐ Exercise 11.14 The Secret
> ☐ Exercise 11.15 Additional Actions: Practice with Counteractions and Naming Events
>
> **Part VI: Verbal Actions with Hidden Agendas**
> ☐ Exercise 11.16 Hidden Agendas
>
> **Part VII: Named-Event Improvisations**
> ■ What Is a Named Event and Why Is It So Important?
> ■ How to Name an Event
> ■ Three Types of Named Events
> ☐ Exercise 11.17 The Named Event

What Is a Verbal Action?

All psychophysical actions have a nonverbal component. Many also have a verbal aspect. *Verbal action* implies that we speak, using words to accomplish our aims and objectives. In Chapter 8, on nonverbal action, we defined action as an active transitive verb and an act of purposeful behavior. This holds true whether actions are fulfilled nonverbally or with speech. This is also true whether actions are fulfilled primarily through physical, psychological, or verbal means. Even if an action's primary vehicle is verbal, before, after, and during speech all of the nonverbal communication explored in the last chapter will still be active. All actions have a psychological component, and all have a physical expression, which may be obvious or subtle, but only some actions have a verbal component.

Verbal action flows from the mind and body simultaneously. It is both psychological and physical. Words are also physical actions. Verbal actions also have a nonverbal component (as you will experience while performing the improvisations in this chapter). Verbal action, like nonverbal action, is motivated by intention. Pursuing that intention is an act of *willpower* and must be driven by making the desired outcome very important, i.e., by *upping the stakes*. The power of will plus intention cannot be overestimated. Both are very important attributes for you to develop. It takes strong will and a clear intention in order to fulfill verbal actions. Action is the stimulus for speech onstage.

The playwright or screenwriter's primary vehicle for communicating his themes is words. The actor, director, and designer's art is in interpreting and communicating those themes through the playwright's words, using a variety of nonverbal and visual means to communicate to an audience. In film, large parts of the story may be told in images selected by the director and created and conveyed by a variety of visual artists. In the theatre, important parts of the story will also be conveyed nonverbally, and some of the images will be brought to life through design, but many of the important images of the play will be conveyed through the images the actor evokes with the words. In both mediums, the director's and actors' main task is to choose actions that will fulfill the characters' purpose, accomplish the characters' goals, and actively move the story ahead.

What Is *Subtext*, and How Does It Figure into the Equation?

All action springs from the subtext, the meaning under the text. The subtext is the character's subconscious mind at work. (Do not confuse that with your own subconscious, although that plays an important part in your creative process as well.) The actor creates the character's subtext on the basis of the information found in the play and the interpretation given by the director. You, the actor, must strive to express the subtext through your actions, body language, and voice and speech. Expressive behavior that reveals the underlying meaning, or subtext, will subtly convey your thoughts, feelings, and intentions to an audience, and that, in turn, will let them understand the purpose of your character in the story. Some key components of subtext are the *language of the body* and *tonal subtext*. Tonal subtext is the coloring of the line and the putting into it what you really mean to communicate with that line. This is very important, as the subtext often plays against the line. It is also very important in repeated lines that each must have its own flavor, and in ambiguous lines such as "hello" or "yes" that could mean many different things.

When working on a script, the director is the primary interpreter of the subtext, because only she has the responsibility for the overall artistic vision. In a mutually collaborative rehearsal situation the director incorporates the actor's ideas into her own. Such a true ensemble approach not only enhances the play, creating a positive atmosphere and dedication on the parts of the actors to do their best, but can also lead to artistic discoveries not otherwise possible for the director to find by herself.

Avoid the Pitfalls

One of the pitfalls for the novice actor is the tendency to jump right into character without adequate preparation. This sometimes occurs because actors are drawn to the idea of escaping from themselves into the world of another. Later, you will get to live by walking in the shoes of human beings very different from you, but first, you must bring all your understanding of the human experience to your roles. You must first work on the raising of your own awareness of what you do understand about the internal world as well as the external behavior of a human being. You can observe the behavior of others, but only you can observe your own internal mechanisms and the way that thoughts and feelings stir in you. To achieve this consciousness, every action and improvisation in the first months of training must be explored as if it were *you* in the situation. This is a key principle in psychophysical training and acting; it is designed in such a way that you may become conscious of how *you* behave, think, speak, move, and feel in each new situation. At first, expand yourself into situations you may have never been in; later, self-awareness will enhance your work on a role, and you will be able to explore a character's unique psychological and physical characteristics with greater depth and truth.

Creating a character who is a living and breathing human being cannot be achieved in just a few minutes. It takes some time to discover your role and explore actions that are *fitting* and *typical* for the character you are playing. When you fulfill an action with your mind and body working in unison—psychophysically—you will come to life, and when you begin to work on characters from a play, they will come to life because *you* are alive. If you go onstage in an improvisation and pretend to be some imaginary character that you have not developed and fleshed out, a dissonance (disconnection), occurs between the mind and body, thus obstructing the psychophysical connection. You will likely create a stereotype or will indicate rather than inhabit a character. You can avoid pretending by first learning how to fulfill actions truthfully as yourself.

The improvisational exercises in this chapter are designed to assist you in achieving the integration of the mind and body, which will not only benefit your acting but your personal life as well. You will notice a marked improvement in your mental agility and physical coordination, as well as your self-awareness. Practice on fulfilling actions truthfully by means of improvisation will provide the skills needed to build a living character.

Write It Down

Note: For these preliminary improvisations use the Basic Improvisation worksheet in Appendix IIIa. We hope that you have already begun to keep a creative journal where you can write down your reflections and chart your continued progress. The physical act of writing down your impressions and experiences during training creates a deep psychological impression and reinforces the learning process. A prominent voice teacher, Mrs. Alfred Dixon, had a sign on her door that read, "Create yourself, everything else has been done."[2] When you work to continually improve yourself, it reflects in your art and in your daily life. Charting your progress by writing down your reflections, successes, and setbacks gives you the power and confidence to keep moving ahead, to keep improving. It is important to be detailed about what helped you to achieve the goals of the exercise or improvisation or what inhibited you from achieving them. Write what you noticed about your thoughts, physical sensations, and emotions. Keep a personal record of what you discover within yourself and open up the wellspring of your unique artistic nature.

Bring all the steps you have learned in the previous lessons into each new improvisation. This is very important, as it will reinforce, by means of repetition, your assimilation of the System into one organic whole. Eventually the technique will become second nature, and soon you will be able to act organically. (*Organic* acting means that your mind and body will physiologically function on stage just as they do in life.) When that happens it really becomes fun!

In this chapter you will explore the following training steps designed to help you experience the ever greater complexities of verbal action:

I. Verbal Actions with One Spoken Line
II. Verbal Actions with Three Spoken Lines
III. Verbal Actions with Designated Verbal Counteractions
IV. Selecting Counteractions
V. Problems, Main Actions, and Objectives
VI. Verbal Actions with Hidden Agendas
VII. Named-Event Improvisations: Various Ways To Name an Event

---

[2] Philip Bennett studied voice and speech with Mrs. Dixon, of Alfred Dixon Speech Systems, New York, New York, from 1971 to 1975.

11 VERBAL ACTION

> **Important note:** In the appendices in this book you will find additional materials to assist you in the building of good improvisational scenes—a list of additional actions to use for your improvisations and scripted scenes (Appendix IV) and a worksheet providing an outline designed to assist you with the building of the following improvisations (Appendices IIIa and IIIb). It is highly recommended that you make copies of the worksheet and use them for each improvised scene, thus providing a valuable record of your work that can be added to your creative journal. For the first improvisation, we will go through the given circumstances in detail, as they relate to an improvisation, so you can see what might fit in which category.

PART I: VERBAL ACTIONS WITH ONLY ONE SPOKEN LINE

In life, much of the important interaction and communication goes on nonverbally, even with no restrictions on speech. Consider a situation in which you suspect that someone you trust might be lying (speech, verbal); in order to assess if this is so, do you pay more attention to the verbal or nonverbal clues? All the layers of action that you already explored in the nonverbal realm must still be present when you start to speak. The purpose of the next few exercises is to fill out all the human behavior that takes place before, after, and during any speech with the nonverbal behavior that you learned to truthfully re-create in previous chapters.

Purpose: Because we sometimes find ourselves in a situation where the emotions are so powerful we can hardly speak, the following two improvisations are designed to help you connect to your images, inner monologue, and emotions because the situation is serious and dynamic. The fact that you can only speak once will help you to build a lot of inner intensity; however, do not ever force your feelings. All scenes have moments of justified silence—at a minimum, before the first and after the last line but also often when decisions are being made or discoveries are occurring. In film acting, even more of the story is told nonverbally.

> **Exercise 11.1: The Eleventh Hour (Three people in the main roles, plus three from another group to serve as guards). (PGB)**
>
> **Structured Improvisation:** This means some circumstances are given and some filled in by you.
> **Name of Event:** *The Eleventh Hour*
> **Guidelines:** Divide the class into groups of three.
>
> **Given Circumstances:**
> - **Who?** Come from yourself instead of portraying character. What this means is, be yourself but perhaps in circumstances, roles, and relationships you have never before been in. Do not put on a different body or voice or persona and find actions that you might do were you in these circumstances. For this improvisation, decide which actor is A, B, and C. A is a prisoner who is imprisoned for a serious, violent crime. **Note:** *Only*

the prisoner knows for certain whether or not he or she is guilty or innocent and must not tell the partners. The prisoner must also decide how he feels about the crime now, after some years on death row.
- **With whom?** *(Relationship)* B and C are family members and/or very close friends. Decide by talking together your overt relational roles (e.g., father, brother, mother, wife, best friend, girlfriend). Decide and keep to yourself your actual relationship with each person as shaped by interaction (always hated him, he betrayed me, he took the fall for me, I'm in love with her, I worship him, etc.). Whether you think the prisoner is guilty or innocent and what you think about the crime that was committed will also color your relationship with the prisoner and the events of the improvisation. The guards should consider their own relationship, how they feel about the crime and this execution, and executions in general, but should just be observers to watch the prisoner and to escort the family in and the prisoner out. The guards must never upstage the main action or the characters in the scene or make comic choices that undermine the serious tone of the scene. As support characters they must instead give focus to and support the main actions and events.
- **Where? Where from and where to?** The improvisation takes place in the visitation room at the prison. If you enter or exit the scene decide where you are coming from and/or where you are going to if you leave.
- **When?** 11 PM (You can decide time of year. Make the *epoch* [time period] the current year.)
- **What?** The prisoner is facing execution at midnight. The lawyer has submitted an appeal for a stay of execution to the governor. The three actors fill in the additional circumstances beforehand: the nature of the crime, how long the prisoner has been incarcerated on death row, etc.
- **Why?** What motivated you to be there and encounter these other people?
- **What for?** What are you hoping to get out of this situation? *(Sometimes why and what are the same, the motivation and the objective.)* Know specifically what you want and how you will know that you got it.
- **How?** Let the *how* take care of itself. Instead of planning exactly what you are going to do, respond to what happens. Find truthful behavior within the circumstances arising from the magic if: What would I do if I were in this situation with these people in this place and this event unfolded this way?

Other Active Facts:
- The prisoner is brought into the visitation room to await the family and the answer to the appeal. How would you behave waiting for the answer to your appeal while believing you are to die within the hour? What would you be thinking? Say these thoughts, inner monologue, as sentences in your mind. For the purposes of this improvisation, the prisoner may not speak to the guards but may communicate nonverbally, as long as this is not miming or mouthing things either would like to say. Justify the silence.
- After a few moments the visitors are brought in by a guard and are handed a sealed envelope with the governor's decision. At first they cannot speak but must communicate everything with their eyes and bodies.

- You will not know until you open the envelope whether the appeal has been granted. The teacher must have two envelopes; one with *"Your stay has been granted,"* and one with *"Your stay has been denied. The execution will proceed as planned."* **Note:** There must be a zone of justified silence of at least a full minute or two before anyone says their one line. You may decide that the actors cannot speak until the teacher agrees that the justified zone of silence has been clearly inhabited and says, "Speak anytime now."
- Each actor can only speak once and can only say the following words: "I love you." Nothing else and nothing more. Each actor *must* say the line and is free to interpret it however they choose; for example, if you think the prisoner is guilty of something horrific or has shamed the family and ruined your life, you may want him or her to die. How would you behave and how would you say the one line you are permitted to speak? (This is an opportunity to use a *subtext* that is in direct contrast to the line you will speak.)

11.1 *Reflection Journal—The Eleventh Hour*

Were you able to communicate your thoughts and feelings without words? If you believed the prisoner was guilty even if the appeal was granted, how did you behave and how did you say your one line? What was the subtext communicated with the words *I love you*? Did you mean it, or did you have a contradictory feeling and meaning? Did you find actions to express and project your relationships? Did you become honestly emotionally involved in the imaginary situation? Make sure to record what you discovered and experienced.

Exercise 11.2: A Wartime Farewell (Three people with only one line each.) (PGB)

Name of the Event: *A Wartime Farewell*

Guidelines:

Note: In each subsequent improvisation, create the circumstances in as much detail as the prior improvisation, but it will not all be laid out for you as above. You can use the worksheet in the Appendices in your planning to organize the important information into the key components of the improvisation. In each improvisation, you will be given some circumstances and asked to fill in others.

- One of you has been ordered to go to war. The other two persons are close family.
- Decide where you are going and why? Do you know how long you will be gone? Do you want to go or not? These are final moments before you must leave. What would you have with you?

- Each of you may only speak once. The family members' line is, "Come home unharmed." The soldier's line is, "Don't worry. I will." You may interpret the subtext of the line any way you choose. Do you mean what you say or not? Why would you not mean what you would say?

> **11.2** *Reflection Journal—A Wartime Farewell*
>
> Did you become emotionally involved? Did the relationships feel real to you? If not, why? Think about it, and record your thoughts in your creative journal. Were you able to apply what you have learned in previous lessons?

PART II: VERBAL ACTIONS WITH THREE SPOKEN LINES

You are now asked to create your own lines; however, each person may only speak three lines. **Note:** What is most important here is that you not rely on words to give exposition to your audience. Only say what you cannot say without words. Try to say as much as you are able through your mental activity (images and inner monologue reflected through your eyes) and physical actions.

Part of the rehearsal process developed by Stanislavsky was to run a scene by saying a series of sounds to substitute for the lines, such as: La-la-la-ti. (This author uses me-la-me-la, but you can make up your own language, called *gibberish*, as well.) This *device*[3] is very helpful to the actor as you are forced to convey the action of the words through the intonation of the voice and the physicality of your actions alone. In the final rehearsals of a play, and once you know all of your actions, blocking, and lines, it is extremely useful to rehearse scenes in complete silence, requiring you to express every moment of action physically while remaining completely and solely focused on the text and subtext. This device helps you to get the physical actions entirely in your body, while demonstrating to the director whether the action is crystal clear. Remember that words are built upon the language of the body, so if you can express and project a thought or feeling physically in these improvisations, do so before speaking. Try to always begin every spoken action physically (subtly using the torso and spine of your body to express what you are about to say). Observe closely how people, especially when they are animated in conversation, often move from their spines before they speak. If you watch carefully, you might even be able to sense intuitively what they are about to say and do. Another great tip to use while actively listening to your partners is to think your inner monologue as specific sentences in your mind while allowing it to be subtly expressed only with your eyes and the subtle movements of the thought energy through your spine. Soon you will find that you can convey the most subtle thoughts and feelings mentally as well as physically.

---

[3] A device is a tool invented by the actors or director to assist in the analysis of an improvisation or play during rehearsal.

11 VERBAL ACTION

Exercise 11.3: Suspicion at the Doctor's Office (PGB)

Guidelines: This improvisation requires a minimum of four people (with the fourth being the receptionist); however, it works well with a larger group of, say, seven to ten. The actors must know whether they are a in a leading or a supporting role. If a supporting role, they must make choices to justify and help create the environment without upstaging the main action.

Name of the Event: *Suspicion at the Doctor's Office*

Main Action: The main action is *to suspect*.

- Three or more students go onstage and set up chairs and tables to resemble a waiting room at a doctor's office. One of the students may act as the receptionist who greets the patients.
- Each of you must make an entrance. Decide what type of doctor you are visiting and why. Make it specific and important. Sign a register with your name and the time of arrival. You are all waiting to be called in the order that you have signed into the office. What would you do if you were waiting? You may not be speaking on a cellphone as this would quickly use up your three lines. If you select reading a magazine, for example, make sure you are really reading and not indicating reading. Whatever activity you choose, fulfill it truthfully.
- While waiting, one patient (who has been secretly selected by the teacher) sees a person whom they suspect of having robbed them one evening while returning home late at night. You may speak if necessary but only three lines each.
- If you are the person selected as the victim, you may secretly choose at random anyone of the group for your thief. At first you are unsure, but as you begin to recall the incident you become convinced that this is the same person, because he or she is wearing a ring (watch, bracelet, or any other piece of jewelry you choose) that you recognize as yours. What would you do if you were in this situation?
- Evaluate and make decisions using W.E.D.G.A.G. before speaking out about your suspicion. How would you approach addressing the suspected thief?
- The suspected thief and the other patients must fulfill their tasks of waiting and then respond to any speech or behavior initiated by the actor *driving the action* (i.e., fulfilling the main action).

11.3 Reflection Journal—Suspicion at the Doctor's Office

What was your initial reaction on seeing your stolen item and realizing that this was the person who robbed you? If you were the victim of the robbery, did you use W.E.D.G.A.G. to make your discovery and assessment of the stolen goods? Did you attempt to express your thoughts and feelings physically before speaking? If you were the accused or a witness to this event in the doctor's office, what was your reaction, and did you choose to speak up? If so, why? If not, why not?

Exercise 11.4: Black Market Border (again a four-person scene, but works well with a few more nonspeaking roles to create the public space) (SDF)[4]

Main Action: To smuggle

Guidelines:
- You are in line at a customs and immigration border checkpoint.
- Three of you are passengers crossing the border, and one is a customs agent. Decide what country you are all coming from; what country you are entering; whether you came by rail, plane, or ship; and whether you are a native of the country you are entering or a foreigner.
- Each passenger will be given a slip of paper that will either say *passenger* or *smuggler*. Each passenger will then prepare three items (and write down what they are on a piece of paper; each passenger's piece of paper should be the same size) and hide them among the things in their bag. The smuggler has illegal goods he needs to get across the border, and this will be one of his three items, hidden in his bag (use whatever bag you brought to class). The smuggler must decide specifically what the illegal goods are and why he is smuggling them. The border agent must make it important that any smugglers not get black-market goods through. The others must create important reasons for why they are leaving one country or entering another to keep their own inner landscape active and engaged alongside the main action.
- The customs agent may only search one bag so he has to assess each passenger and choose carefully whose bag to search.
- The customs agent may say only one line to each person coming through, plus one additional line to the one she suspects. The passengers may speak up to two lines in response to the customs agent and one line to another passenger. Make sure to communicate as much as you can nonverbally and only use the lines if and when absolutely necessary.

11.4 *Reflection Journal—Black Market Border*

Were you able to clearly see the images of the customs area? Were you active with your inner monologue and images related to your circumstances? Did you notice a change in tempo or internal rhythm when your bag was searched? If you were the customs agent, what could you tell about the others from their nonverbal behavior, and what caused you to search that particular bag? If you were the smuggler, how did you behave in your attempt not to be selected? What got you through, or gave you away?

---

[4] The Black Market Border improvisation was invented by French to give you another opportunity to explore a situation where there would be a high level of intensity but also a justified zone of silence. We encourage teachers and students to invent their own improvisations for aspects of the System where the students need additional training. Repetition is key to assimilating the training and becoming psychophysical actors.

11 VERBAL ACTION

> **Exercise 11.5: The Two-Timer's Reward (three main roles but any extras to create the environment of the awards ceremony would be helpful, too). (SDF)**
>
> **Name of the Event:** *The Two Timer's Reward*
>
> **Roles:** One man, two women, and extras as others attending an awards ceremony (can be done with a women and two men or all same sexes in the different roles).
>
> **Action:** To claim your famous boyfriend/girlfriend.
> - A man is up for an important award. Decide beforehand what the award is for.
> - He has been dating two women at once, convincing each that she is the only one and that he is very serious about and committed to her. He didn't invite either to the ceremony, as it would be a very public event and would reveal his deceit. Each woman, thinking that he would really want her to be there and wanting to claim her association with this important man, has shown up and is sitting at his table.
> - The ceremony is going on and you really want to be seen as fitting into this esteemed event. You cannot speak until it builds up to a point where you don't care about interrupting the ceremony.

11.5 Reflection Journal—The Two-Timer's Reward

Were you able to reflect the issues through your inner monologue and subtle physical expressions? Were you able to move your agenda forward through nonverbal actions? What did you read in the others' nonverbal behavior? Was the situation clear before anyone spoke a word?

PART III: VERBAL ACTIONS WITH DESIGNATED COUNTERACTIONS

You may finally speak in the following two-person improvisations; however, make sure to always create a zone of silence to establish the circumstances before speaking. Pursue your action physically as well as verbally, and take in, think about, and express nonverbally your response to what the other is doing. While you are free to talk, do not feel the need to be constantly speaking. One actor chooses the *main action* and the other actor chooses the *counteraction*.

What Is Counteraction?

The word *counter* comes from the Latin *contra* and means "against" or "to oppose." So to have *counter*action means that two opposing forces must meet and clash on the stage. This battle between two forces is what creates *the dynamic conflict* explored in Chapter 8: Nonverbal Action. As you will read in Chapter 20: The Evolving Stanislavsky System, in the later years of his research and experimentation,

Stanislavsky further developed the concept of *the objective* and began to look at the objectives as a series of problems, asking questions such as, What is your problem in this episode? The actor was expected to respond with something like, How can I get him to do such and such? With this approach, Stanislavsky realized that more emphasis could be put on the immediate action and counteraction, thus making the conflict more dynamic. Using *counters* heightens the dramatic tension. When you as the character strive for your goals and objectives by having to fight at each moment for what you want, both you and the play come to life more, thus more intensely involving the audience through the dynamic conflict.

If you are an actor designated to fulfill the counteraction in an improvisation, you cannot come onstage without a conflict occurring until the main action is initiated. In that case, nothing will be happening, and the stage will be dead. You must have an initial action coming onto the stage, a purpose for being there and for being engaged, and this will have some level of conflict with other things going on. For example, if the main action is to break up a relationship, the counteraction might be to propose marriage. You can come in strongly with the counteraction before the main action is initiated.

Figure 11.1 You can come in strongly with the counteraction before the main action is initiated. Actors Kirsten Walsh as Ruth, Shannon Leigh Christmann as Elvira, and Gabryal Rabinowitz as Charles in *Blithe Spirit* by Noel Coward.
Photo: Bob Weidner, courtesy of East Stroudsburg University

Action steps are the smaller actions you choose beforehand as part of your strategy in order to fulfill your main action. However, you don't know what your partner is going to do and you both must make adaptations and adjustments to the obstacles that you toss at one another in the form of counteractions. Your strategy may not be effective, and then you will need to create a new one right on your feet in the moment.

Note: For many of the next improvisations you will be given very little information and must fill out the details of the given circumstances and other elements of a structured improvisation, some planned ahead (as outlined in the worksheet in Appendix IIIa) and some responded to spontaneously in response to surprises in the improvisation.

Agreement

In all improvisations, while the characters often disagree, there must be a sense of *agreement* between the scene partners. Onstage you must agree with offers made by the other actor, such as if he says, "Get out of the rain." You wouldn't respond, "It's not raining." If your scene partner says, "You have to do this, you're my brother" (thus endowing a relationship that you may not have planned on beforehand), you wouldn't say, "I'm not your brother; I'm your boss." Rather, you would go along with what your partner has invented in the moment—although you can redirect it; for example, you might reply, "I may be your brother, but at work I'm your boss, and I cannot treat you differently from any other employee."

Figure 11.2 In improvisation, "go along with what your partner invents in the moment." Douglas James Brehony as Tartuffe and Raj Shankar as Orgon in Molière's *Tartuffe*.
Photo: David Dougherty

Exercise 11.6: "Neither a Borrower nor a Lender Be," or, the Big Mooch (SM/PGB)

Main Action: to borrow money

Counteraction: to refuse to lend money

Guidelines:
- Really listen to one another and react truthfully.
- Choose a typical *activity (stage business)* and a specific location for your scene. For example: Perhaps you are preparing a meal or are in the middle of moving (stay active).
- Build a relationship that has a history. Your relationship to one another is vital here.
- Make it really important why you need the money or why you don't want to give the money.

- If you are the borrower, decide on specific early hints that the other might give that he is going to give you what you want and try to get those ahead of the main goal of getting the money. If you are the lender, what might you get the other to do or say that would lead you to believe he is more likely to stop asking and leave you alone, even prior to his actually stopping?

11.6 *Reflection Journal—"Neither a Borrower nor a Lender Be," or, the Big Mooch*

Was your action clearly fulfilled and projected? How did your activity help you fulfill your actions? Did you create a strong conflict? Did you remember to make adaptations to one another's counteractions? Who won and who lost?

Exercise 11.7: The Cover-Up (SM/PGB)

Main Action: To find out

Counteraction: to cover up (hide)

Guidelines:
- Sometimes in life we cannot directly go about revealing what we are doing. In this improvisation try fulfilling the actions in a *circumvented manner*; that is to say, gradually lead up to revealing your real intention to find out what is being hidden. How might you do this without being obvious?
- If you choose the counteraction of covering up, keep in mind the specific reason you do not want to reveal what you know. Perhaps some stage business or interesting activity might assist you in your cover-up.

Figure 11.3 "Stage business should always be detailed and specific to the given circumstances." Brandon Cabrera as Andrew, and Jamil Joseph as Edward, in *Spike Heels* by Theresa Rebeck. Photo: Bob Weidner, courtesy of East Stroudsburg University

11 VERBAL ACTION

> **11.7** *Reflection Journal—The Cover-Up*
> Were you able to find action steps leading to the accomplishment of your goal? Were you able to gradually go about revealing your intention? How did the relationship between you and your partner influence your behavior? Did you see both real and imaginary images?

> **Exercise 11.8: The Accusation (two persons) (SM/PGB)**
>
> **Purpose:** The actor with the counteraction does not know in advanced the circumstances and thus must practice making an adaptation in the moment.
>
> **Main Action**: to accuse
>
> **Counteraction**: to defend
>
> **Guidelines:**
> - Choose an environment for your scene that justifies moving about the space freely and decide on a clear relationship.
> - The accuser must decide in advance what she is going to accuse the other of and create specific images of the event so that she can give details. The accused responds to the accusation and can be either guilty and deny it or can be unjustly accused through a mistake or misunderstanding. The accused must decide whether he is guilty or not.
> - Choose a series of three or four action steps before you make your accusation. For example: to greet warmly, to pry, to find out, etc. See what you can come up with.
> - If you have the counteraction, you may wish to also choose a series of actions steps before you come out and defend yourself; for example: to play dumb, to deny, to shift the blame, etc.

> **11.8** *Reflection Journal—The Accusation*
> Are you using W.E.D.G.A.G. and evaluating with your body before you speak? Are you remembering to use your spine and torso to express your thoughts and feelings? Did you become emotionally involved in the imaginary situation?

PART IV: SELECTING COUNTERACTIONS AND NEGOTIATING STATUS

Raise the stakes in the next improvisations. This means that each actor has a stake in what they need and want in the situation and must make it very important—not getting it would create a crisis. As they struggle through opposing actions creating the dynamic conflict, sometimes one is winning, sometimes the other. It is much more interesting if the struggle could go either way than if the outcome is obvious.

Another aspect of any struggle onstage is *status*. This is a measure of who has more or less power and how high or low one is in the pecking order or on the totem pole. There is overt power that might be held, for example, by a boss over an employee, a king over his subjects, or a teacher over a student. There are also more covert power claims where the person without the overt power can still get the upper hand. The employees form a union to fight back, the subjects stage a rebellion, or the students disrupt or boycott the class. A classic example of this might be a certain kind of marriage where the husband is seen outwardly as the patriarch and head of the family but the wife really calls the shots.

Purpose: When you are working on a script, you will need to choose all of your main and counteractions, so this will be good practice. In this, and future improvisations, practice choosing your counteractions without telling your partner what they will be beforehand. Make sure that you select strong counteractions that are active, transitive verbs. Remember, you must always go into an improvised scene with your own action and objective.

Exercise 11.9: Blackmail! (two persons) (SM/PGB)

Main Action: to blackmail

Counter: (Select a strong counteraction)

Guidelines:
- **Note:** Reactions are always improvised in the moment. Have fun. Take turns choosing the main and counteractions. Use the list of actions in Appendix IV as a resource for selecting verbal actions.
- Throw obstacles at your partner in the form of unexpected information and actions in order to win. Any obstacles you create must fit into the agreed-upon circumstances and not be so wildly invented that they do not fit. Adaptations must be fitting to the action and situation, as well.

11.9 Reflection Journal—Blackmail!

Did you select a strong counteraction? Who won and who lost? Why? Did you think quickly on your feet and make adaptations to the obstacles? Did you strive to affect your partner and achieve communion? Was it successful? What would you correct if you were to perform the improvisation again?

Exercise 11.10: Cheer Up! (two persons) (SM/PGB)

Main Action: to cheer someone up

Counteraction: (You choose)

Guidelines:
- Build an imaginary situation where you are cheering someone up. You can choose someone whom you know well, like a good friend or family member, or someone you don't know at all.
- How would you cheer up someone whom you did not know, and what steps

would be needed to approach him/her? What obstacles would you need to surmount and how many different ways could you select? Explore all possibilities.
- If you are choosing the counteraction, what might be your initial reaction to someone who was trying to cheer you up against your will, or someone whom you did not know? What obstacles could you throw in your partner's way and why?

Figure 11.4 Cheer up! A positive backstage atmosphere contributes to success onstage. Selena and Shwanda Farber in *Sold!* by Stephanie Daventry French and Ahleea Zama (adapted from the novel *Day of Tears* by Julius Lester). Photo: Bob Weidner, courtesy of East Stroudsburg University

11.10 *Reflection Journal—Cheer up!*

If you had the counteraction, did it work? If not, why? Were you genuinely cheered up? If you had the main action, did you succeed in cheering up your partner? Did you achieve communion with one another? (Remember, *communion* means that you each affected the other; also called *mutual influence*.)

Exercise 11.11: Forbidden Fruit (Adding Status) (Two Persons) (PGB)

Main Action: to forbid

Counteraction: (you choose)

Guidelines: This improvisation deals with status.
- You need to ask yourself from where your authority derives to forbid another person to do something. What is your relationship? Build a relationship with a history that will justify your power to execute the action.

- How serious is the situation? How would you proceed if you did not have the authority to forbid but chose to do so anyway? How can you claim authority? If you have the counteraction, how can you undermine it?
- When choosing the counteraction, ask yourself what actions would best express your relationship and attitude? Make sure to agree as actors to a status imbalance based on relationship, roles, or other status, even if, as the character you, choose to challenge it. If it did not exist there would be no need to challenge it and thus not a very interesting improvisation. Always choose very strong and unexpected counters that will give your partner a run for his money. Never underestimate the power of surprise.

11.11 *Reflection Journal—Forbidden Fruit*

Did you write down the action steps needed to fulfill your action? Did you remember to make the stakes very high in order to create a dynamic conflict? How did the status between you play out, and did it change at any point?

PART V: IMPROVISATIONS—PROBLEMS, MAIN ACTIONS, AND OBJECTIVES

When we analyze a play, we look at each segment or episode and ask, What is my character's *problem* here? Identifying the problem first helps us then to select a *main action* and *action steps* that will help us move toward solving the problem. For example, let's say that you are interrogating a witness to a crime but suspect that the witness is actually the perpetrator of the crime. You would like to make an accusation but need the witness to give more information first, to incriminate himself. So you ask, How can I interrogate and find out the information, in order to accuse him? The moment we ask, "How can I?" we are well on our way to finding the correct actions and solving the problem. It is a great aid to look at each situation as a problem that needs to be solved.

Now, all actions have an objective built into them; that is to say, the purpose, motivation, and what you hope to achieve by each action naturally creates an objective.

Problem Improvisations

Guidelines: These improvisations can involve three people. Nevertheless, at this time, there must only be one counteraction. So, one person will have the main action and two will decide on the counteraction, or if you like, you may choose to have two persons with the main action and one person with the counter. In either case do not reveal your counteraction. Let it be a surprise. In the following improvisations you will be given a problem to solve and the main action. You will also be asked to choose action steps toward fulfillment of the stated objective in order to solve the problem. (Analyzing episodes and identifying problems will be thoroughly discussed in Chapter 15 on Active Analysis.) Use the improvisation worksheet in Appendices IIIa and IIIb to fill out the given circumstances.

11 VERBAL ACTION

Exercise 11.12: The Interrogation (three persons) (PGB)

Problem: How can you make an accusation?

Main action: To interrogate in order to accuse.

Action steps: To be considered ahead as a path to solve the problem. Do not reveal your action steps to your partner(s).

Counteraction: Select a main counteraction but do not reveal it to your partner(s). For your action steps, respond to each of the tactics of the actor(s) with the main action.

Exercise 11.13: The Reluctant Hero (PGB)

Problem: "How can I get him/her to commit a heroic act?"

Main Action: To push someone to commit a heroic act.

Exercise 11.14: The Secret (PGB)

Problem: "How can I cover up what has happened?"

Main Action: To avoid in order to cover up.

11.12–14 *Reflection Journal—The Interrogation, The Reluctant Hero, The Secret*

Were you able to choose logical and consecutive action steps to accomplish your objective? Did you choose strong counteractions and create a dynamic conflict? What images flashed through your mind as you were acting?

Exercise 11.15: Additional Actions: Practice with Counteractions and Naming Events (PGB)

Guidelines:
- Throughout the book a name has been given to each exercise and improvisation. When you can sum up a situation with just a word or short phrase, you will also have a clear idea of what to do in that situation. Soon you will be asked to name your improvisations and scenes. It is a good practice to name each improvisation, as it will assist you in naming events when analyzing the scenes from a play. If you would like to change the

names for these actions and find your own, that would be fine. We will work on *Named Event Improvisations* toward the end of this chapter.
- Choose strong counteractions and work to create dynamic conflicts.
- Use all of the applicable steps for building improvisations that you have learned so far.
- Give a descriptive name to each of the following improvisations:
  - to lie in order to defame someone
  - to denounce in order to destroy
  - to boast in order to make an impression
  - to persuade someone to commit a crime
  - Identify the problem by asking, How can I . . . ?

11.15 *Reflection Journal—Additional Actions for Practice*

Were the names you chose for the improvisations descriptive of what happened? Did you select fitting actions and images? If you were to do the improvisation again, which actions and images might have fit the circumstances better?

PART VI: VERBAL ACTIONS WITH HIDDEN AGENDAS

As you can see, the actions are getting more complex. Complex actions challenge your imagination and will help in building ever more interesting situations and characters. When you are working on a scene from a play, ask yourself, Is this a complex character in a complex situation? What would be the most fitting action steps to select in order to convey the important traits and behavior of my character? What actions could I choose to make the situation absolutely clear to my audience?" The more complex a character or situation, the greater skill you will need in selecting fitting actions.

The hidden agenda is an important element of an action because so many plays are written with characters who hide their true intentions. Also, a hidden agenda creates a very strong subtext.

Exercise 11.16: Hidden Agendas (PGB)

In these improvisations you will have a problem that requires you to hide what you really want to achieve. Figure out the problem and again ask, What can I do to solve it? Some possible main actions you would want to hide from the other character in the scene include:

1. To deceive
2. To befriend a stranger
3. To play a trick on someone
4. To mislead
5. To seduce
6. To cheat
7. To plan a surprise party
8. To swindle

Guidelines:

- The teacher places into a hat the following for each group: One piece of paper with the above hidden agendas listed, and two of pieces of paper with "select a main action (not a hidden agenda) based on the given circumstances." If you choose to do the exercise with additional people, make sure to have the same number of papers in the hat as the number of people in the group. This way, someone is sure to get the hidden agenda. You must not reveal it if you get the hidden agenda.
- Build an imaginary situation with your partner or partners filling out the action steps and other relevant parts of the improvisation guideline sheet (as in Appendix IIIa). Remember that you can base your situations on real-life events, either personal, observed, imaginary, or a combination thereof. You need not reveal to others whether they are real or completely imaginary events, unless you choose to.

11.16 Reflection Journal—Hidden Agendas

If you had the hidden agenda, were you able to express it through the subtext of your thoughts and behavior? Did you truly listen and react with evaluations and decisions prior to speaking? Were you able to move toward your objective without your scene partners figuring out what it was? If you did not have the main action, how did you respond to the pressure of the hidden agenda? Did you pick up on what the other was trying to do to you or get from you?

PART VII: NAMED-EVENT IMPROVISATIONS

Now you are preparing to take a very big step: When you finish this entire series of improvisations, you will be well prepared to choose actions for the analysis of a scene and then a play.

In the beginning of this chapter the improvisations were given simple titles. From this point on you will want to give every improvisation a name that best describes the event. For Named Events please refer to and use Appendix IIIb Advanced Improvisation Worksheets.

What Is a Named Event and Why Is It So Important?

Finding a name for each improvisation is crucially important, and more so when you are breaking down a play into its parts. (This will be thoroughly covered in Chapter 15: Active Analysis through Events and Actions.) A named event tells you exactly what the governing experience is all about.

According to *Webster's New World Dictionary*, the word *event* is defined as: (e-vent'). N. [OFr.; L. *eventus*, event, occurrence, pp. of *evenire*, to happen; *e-* out + *venire*, to come]. 1. a happening; occurrence, especially an important occurrence. 2. A result;

When you name an event correctly you will understand more clearly how to behave within it and which actions to choose and perform. This is extremely important, as your actions and objectives, and those of your scene partners, bring about the event. It often also evokes the type of dynamic conflict at the center of the scene.

How to Name an Event

It takes a little thought and time to come up with an evocative named event, but it is well worth it. The event must have importance for all the characters in the improvisation or scene in the play. Often one of the characters, usually the one who has the main action, is pushing for the event to happen, and other characters are either assisting with this effort or opposing it with counteractions.

Three Types of Named Events

The Title: You might choose something like, *Graduation Day* or *Lost in the Woods*. Right away you have an idea of what to do in order to make your event happen.

The Headline: *Mary Breaks Off Engagement with John*. Headlines are often a very good choice because they can give you the main action of the event and suggest something happening right now, in the present, between the characters.

The Metaphor: A metaphor is poetic and often describes the emotional mood and atmosphere of a scene. An example of a metaphor where people find themselves trapped by their own misdeeds might be named *Quicksand* or *Quagmire*. A business that has met with a disastrous obstacle might be called *Shipwreck* or *Crash*. I think you get the idea.

(**Note:** In Chapter 15, we will further outline how to use named events to stage a scene and a play.)

Exercise 11.17: The Named Event (PGB)

The following are two- and three-person improvisations. Below, you will find a list of six named events from which to choose for your improvisations:

1. *War* (A named event as a metaphor that expresses the dynamic of the conflict.) Not an actual war scene, but rather consider what kind of interpersonal interaction might seem like a war? Make this a verbal battle, not a physical one.
2. *Reunion* A simple title but one that can have many different possibilities. Each person must have opposing hopes for the event.
3. *Quicksand* A metaphor and a very challenging choice.
4. *The Vice* A metaphor that can be about a personal vice that holds someone in its grip or about a situation that is closing in on someone. It can also be one character metaphorically putting another in a vice, in which case it also represents the dynamic conflict.
5. *The Web* For this metaphorical named event, people can get caught in someone else's web or in one of their own making.
6. *Victory* This event suggests having battled through difficult obstacles in order to win.
7. *Tables Turned* (A named event as a metaphor that expresses the dynamic of the conflict.) This is an excellent named event to work on how interactions between characters often change the status quo of their relationship. For

example, one character might have been acting morally superior but then be caught in flagrante delicto (a legal phrase from the Latin meaning "while the crime is blazing,"; that is, in the very act of a misdeed). In fact, In Flagrante Delicto would itself be a great name for an event.

Guidelines:
- Create a structured (partly planned) improvisation based on one of the named events above.
- Each actor must choose a main action, objective, and action steps before going onstage. Actors with the counteraction do the same.
- You can later repeat this improvisation challenge using some of the other named events above, or invent named events of your own choosing.

11.17 *Reflection Journal—The Named Event*

How did having a specific event affect the scene? Were you able to select the best actions in order to bring about the event? If not, what actions worked and which did not? Was there a strong conflict, and did you remember to throw obstacles (weapons) in your opponent's way in order to win? Did you involve your body and move from your spine to evaluate what you were doing and about to say? Did you fulfill your actions and become honestly involved in the imaginary circumstances? Did you select and see both personal and imaginary images?

Summary

In this chapter, you integrated verbal and nonverbal action so that acting with words involved a fully fleshed out interaction between two or more people. You explored driving the main action of a scene or impeding it with surprise counteractions. You delved into getting active to solve a problem through action steps and pursuing and responding to hidden agendas. You began to work with named events that focus the action and often evoke specific kinds of dynamic conflict in a scene from a play or in an improvisation.

Now you are ready to name your own events and choose a variety of actions in order to bring your improvisations to life. With practice you will easily come to know how to excel in the art of dramatic improvisation. You will also become proficient at writing down all of your reflections, reinforcing your constant discovery and growth. Your imagination will expand, and soon you will psychophysically assimilate and know how to use this most important aspect of your technique, action! Your work in this chapter will prepare you to either break down a playwright's script through Active Analysis or invent your own plays through devised improvisations.

> **New Theatre Terms and Concepts**
>
> Terms used in the Stanislavsky System are in italics.
>
> - action steps
> - activity (stage business)
> - *atmosphere*
> - *circumvent manner* (see Appendix IIIb)
> - *counteractions* (weapons)
> - *device*
> - dynamic conflict
> - *environment*
> - fitting and typical
> - hidden agendas
> - *intention*
> - *mood*
> - *named-event improvisations*
> - raise the stakes
> - *subtext* (upping the stakes)
> - *verbal action*
> - willpower
> - zone of silence

(In Appendices IIIa and IIIb you will find worksheets for your use in building strong and fully fleshed-out improvised scenes. These scenes can engage your psychophysical instrument in organic response and behavior.)

CHAPTER 12

Orchestrating Emotions

"I've learned that people will forget what you said, people will forget what you did, but people will never forget how you made them feel."
—Maya Angelou

Primary Elements of Action Explored

Psychophysical sensory evocation; states of being: physical states of being, psychological (mental) states of being, emotional states of being; psychological burden; idée fixe; analogous emotions; emotional response through physical actions; music and emotion; obstacles and emotion.

Part I: Six Approaches to Emotions on the Stage

- How Can We Use the Mechanisms of Naturally Occurring Emotion to Generate Emotions on the Stage?
- How Can We Easily Stir Emotions that Fit the Character and Given Circumstances?
- **Approach I: Psychophysical Sensory Evocation**
  - Exercise 12.1 Sight
  - Exercise 12.2 Sound
  - Exercise 12.3 Smell
  - Exercise 12.4 Touch
  - Exercise 12.5 Taste
  - Exercise 12.6 Evoking the Sensory Hologram
- **Approach II: States of Being**
  - Exercise 12.7 Physical States of Being
  - Exercise 12.8 Psychological (Mental) States of Being
  - Exercise 12.9 Psychological Burden
  - Exercise 12.10 Idée Fixe
  - Exercise 12.11 Emotional States of Being
- **Approach III: Analogous Emotions**
  - Exercise 12.12 The Love Hologram
  - Exercise 12.13 Targeting Specific Emotions
  - Exercise 12.14 Targeting an Emotion to an Action
  - Exercise 12.15 Words and Analogous Emotions
- **Approach IV: Emotional Response through Physical Actions**
  - Exercise 12.16A Fulfilling Physical Actions
  - Exercise 12.16B Receiving Physical Actions
  - Exercise 12.17 Physical Actions Re-created from Observation
- **Approach V: Music and Emotions**
  - Exercise 12.18 Working with Music without a Text
  - Exercise 12.19 Working with Music with a Text
- **Approach VI: Obstacles and Emotion**

Part II: Scientific Insights on Emotion for Actors

- A Simplified Anatomy of Emotion

To feel more alive, many people seek out experiences that evoke high-intensity emotions—riding a roller coaster, sky diving, watching a scary movie, watching or playing the agony and ecstasy of competitive sports, attending the celebration of a music festival, or the release of laughter found with a stand-up comic. (Of course, there are also many people who avoid such experiences if at all possible.) We also turn to the arts to express aspects of the less outwardly obvious but more profound aspects of human experience—the stirrings in our hearts and souls. Emotions are the source of most creative work: poems speak of love and loss, pain and pleasure, as do songs, dances, and stories told through novels, plays, and films. Audiences go to the theatre or the cinema to be moved, to live vicariously through a broader range of experiences and emotions. In the words of neuroscientist Antonio Damasio, head of the University of Southern California's Brain and Creativity Institute:

> We cannot control emotions willfully. . . . We can control, in part, whether a would-be inducer image be allowed to remain as a target of our thoughts. . . . We can also control, in part, the expression of some emotions—suppress our anger, mask our sadness—but most of us are not very good at it and that is one reason why we pay a lot to see good actors who are skilled at controlling the expression of their emotions.[1]

Understanding emotions and emotional processes is vital to the actor for at least three reasons: 1) to be able to generate on cue emotions relevant to your character in a specific role, 2) to be able to release those emotions after the performance, and 3) to increase your understanding of audiences' emotional processing and responses to the art of the theatre, so that you can enhance their experience. This chapter is about how you, as an actor, can develop artistic control over your emotional instrument.

After learning and trying some techniques to stimulate your emotions, you will find it helpful to understand a little more about how emotions work in the human instrument.

PART I: SIX APPROACHES TO EMOTIONS ON THE STAGE

"Naturally anyone who improvises draws on his own memory, but that memory can also be imaginary."[2]

—Jacques Lecoq

> **How Can We Use the Mechanisms of Naturally Occurring Emotion to Generate Emotions on the Stage?**

As we have mentioned repeatedly, the stage is an artificial environment, so there are not the same real triggers for primary emotions. Stage emotions are quite different from those of real life. Stage emotions are *secondary emotions*. Secondary emotions are a *poetic reflection* of life's experiences rather than actual experiences. For the

---

[1] Antonio Damasio, *The Feeling of What Happens: Body and Emotion in the Making of Consciousness* (Orlando, FL: Harvest Books, Harcourt, 2000), 47–48.
[2] Lecoq, Jacques et al. *The Moving Body*. David Bradby trans. (New York: Routledge, 1997), 31.

artistry of the stage, it is necessary that you both experience them and observe yourself experiencing them, thus keeping some *aesthetic distance* through *dual consciousness*. You need to experience the correct emotions for your character, while maintaining consciousness of your actions and behavior. You still need to say the playwright's words rather than whatever you feel like saying and perform the specified behaviors worked out in rehearsals and approved by your director. It may seem enticing to tap into primary emotions on stage, but in reality you would not want to actually kill the actor playing Laertes when you play Hamlet, or really go insane every night if you are portraying Ophelia. In fact, if this happened, the audience would be thrown out of their artistic experience and into concern for the actors or their own safety. Additionally, this can often distance the actor from the role instead of bringing him closer to the character.

Stanislavsky observed that only the most gifted actors were able to behave onstage and respond emotionally as they did in life; however, even a genius does not always become emotionally involved and inspired. It is accidental at best. Inspiration and emotion need to be lured out by indirect means.

As Lecoq points out in the above quote, not just external stimuli but also internal mental patterns can stimulate emotions. This can take the form of remembered sensory stimuli, mental patterns created from thought, or visualization of events and situations that move us (whether we experienced them, observed them in life or art, imagined them, or some combination, as is much more common, even to our own *imperfect memories*).[3] You can tap into the emotions mapped in the neural pathways of your brain, and you can also tap the neural pathways of your body. To the emotional systems of the body it doesn't matter if the trigger is internal or external, real or imagined, the anatomy and physiology of our emotional system will still engage (which is why we can be so affected, for example, by nightmares). This is also why people can, in some circumstances, either amplify or diminish sickness or health on the basis, partly, of their emotions. We can, for instance, feel heartsick and physically disturbed to the point of mental or physical issues from a significant loss or completely physically rejuvenated and filled with energy from a new love.

> "Acting requires more than memories drawn from life. We must constantly go back to live observation: watching people as they walk down the street, or waiting in a queue, attention to the behavior of others in the queue."
> —Jacques Lecoq

We may not have been through the exact experience depicted in a play by a character, and we may not have experienced the exact degree of emotion this character goes through in the play. However, we have all experienced every human emotion to a greater or lesser degree. Each emotion has left patterns throughout our minds and bodies. For example, hopefully, you have never murdered someone, but you may have felt a murderous impulse toward, say, a mosquito buzzing around

---

[3] See Daniel L. Schacter, *The Seven Sins of Memory* (Boston: Houghton Mifflin, 2001), 4. Schacter proposes "that memory's malfunctions can be divided into seven fundamental transgressions or 'sins,' which I call transience, absent-mindedness, blocking, misattribution, suggestibility, bias, and persistence. Just like the ancient seven deadly sins, the memory sins occur frequently in everyday life and can have serious consequences for all of us." He goes on to demonstrate, however, that some of these are adaptive in a positive way for both our survival and our mental health.

your ear when you were trying to sleep. We can understand a character's response to situations through the *psychophysical patterning of analogous emotions* in ourselves. What Stanislavsky has given us is a means to evoke poetic, or secondary, emotions artistically reconstructed through a variety of triggers, including sense memory, images, thoughts, and relevant physical patterns generated through behavioral actions. To learn to consciously use them to generate specific emotions repeatedly on cue requires training and awareness of your psychophysical emotional instrument, as well as discipline and technique. This chapter will help you hone that technique.

> **How Can We Easily Stir Emotions that Fit the Character and Given Circumstances?**

Step-by-step we will prepare our instrument through a series of *psychophysical action* exercises, leading to the healthy use of *personal or imaginary images*, *sense memory*, *analogous emotions*, and *physical action* for work on the emotional demands of a role. Depending on your personal makeup, cultural and gender conditioning, and relationship with your emotions, different tools may be more or less effective. Perhaps you can put yourself in an entirely imaginary situation and generate emotion. Perhaps you can relate situations of the character to things you understand from your own experience. Perhaps re-creating the physical responses and behavior typical to the impactful situations will activate your emotional instrument. Most actors require some combination of these techniques.

Approach I: Psychophysical Sensory Evocation
- Sight
- Sound
- Smell
- Touch
- Taste
- Combinations of Senses

Approach II: States of Being
- Physical States of Being
- Psychological (Mental) States of Being
- Psychological Burden
- Idée Fixe (Obsession)
- Emotional State of Being

Approach III: Analogous Emotions
- The Hologram
- Targeting an Emotion
- Fusing an Emotion to an Action
- Verbal Improvisation with Analogous Emotions

Approach IV: Emotional Response through Physical Actions
- Fulfilling Physical Actions
- Receiving Physical Actions
- Physical Actions Re-created from Observation

12 ORCHESTRATING EMOTIONS

Approach V: Music and Emotion
- Working with Music without a Text
- Working with Music with a Text

Approach VI: Obstacles and Emotion (A Discussion)

Approach I: Psychophysical Sensory Evocation

Work with the senses used to be called *sense memory,* but as there are so many mistaken ideas about this technique and as we are using it in a different way, we will use the term *sensory re-creation*. Anyone who has walked by a bakery and felt a desire to taste one of its delicacies will understand how evocative our senses can be and how they can stimulate both emotions (in this case, desire) and action (to go in and purchase a croissant). Sensory re-creation is an important facet of your training, work on a role, and living through the life of a character. In Stanislavsky's early experiments he approached emotional memory directly through sense memory around specific emotionally charged personal experiences. He later came to abandon this approach, finding that it led to pushing and thus strain on the nervous system. Emotions generated in this way were about the actor and often distracted from rather than added to the character and play. He also found that some actors do not need real memories but only their imaginations to trigger the senses and the emotions. You can in fact work entirely from the imagination, from personal sense memory and images, or some *amalgamation* of the two. If you do use personal memories, there are safe and artistically more effective ways to do so.

By training your psychophysical instrument to a high degree of sensitivity and expression in prior exercises, you have already begun to prepare your system to be more emotionally responsive. Of course, you need more than a few weeks or even months to have a fully responsive instrument. Sense memory involves concentrating on the five sensory organs of sight, smell, hearing, taste and touch. Sense memory is a portal that can lead to organic emotional experience. Notice that to stir sensations you need only recall the memory of that sense in your sensory organs and mind but do not need to focus on an actual moment in your history when you experienced it. Sometimes personal memories associated with specific senses may arise, as they do in life, so you may observe these, too, but feel no need to dwell on any past personal experience.

Stanislavsky figured out what the science of emotion now confirms: the power of sensory images to stimulate emotion. While *images* is generally a visual word, in the brain all sensory input gets translated into mental patterns which are called images: According to Damasio, "By *image* I mean a mental pattern in any of the sensory modalities, e.g., a sound image, a tactile image, the image of a state of well-being."[4] Throughout your training you have been developing your ability to work with images. Now you will hone your ability to translate your body's memory of sensory perceptions into images in the brain that in turn affect psychophysical expression and generate emotion.

---

[4] Damasio, *Feeling of What Happens*, 9.

Exercise 12.1: Sight (KSS/PGB/SDF)

Guidelines:

- Always build specific circumstances with each exercise. Create a story in your mind and use both personal and imagined images. Adjust your body to what you see in your mind, paying attention to the placement of your feet and expression of your spine; this will assist you in making the exercise *psychophysical*.
- Remain aware of what feelings and sensations arise and travel through your body as a result of each image. Follow the movement of the image and adjust your body psychophysically in response.
- Build circumstances: why are you there? Consider how you are interacting with the image and act this out in each situation.
- Begin each new action with Wonder, Evaluation, Decision, Gesture, Action, and Gesture (W.E.D.G.A.G.).
- Never strain or push for a feeling or sensation, but simply allow the breath to respond naturally rather than trying to use it to drum up the emotion; if nothing happens, skip it and go to the next exercise.

Selected Images (These can each be done separately or in sequence, but it is preferable to do a number of them to increase your facility)

Imagine observing:
- a bird feeding its chicks
- a cat cleaning itself
- heavy traffic before crossing a street
- a child's toy in the corner of a room
- an array of vivid colors (on a painting, in a photograph, in a corner of a home, or a flower garden)
- a pet and its behavior
- a teacher doing an activity at the front of the class
- a large bird gliding on the air above you
- a small apartment or motel room
- a bully at school
- a falling star

12.1 *Reflection Journal—Sight*

What sensations arose with the images? Did you create circumstances and/or recall real situations? Did you find a psychophysical expression with each new visualization? What emotions sprang up spontaneously?

12 ORCHESTRATING EMOTIONS

Exercise 12.2: Sound (KSS/PGB/SDF)

Guidelines: Remember to involve your whole body.

Hear/listen to the following sounds:
- a speeding car passing by
- a bird singing its morning song
- an argument in the next room
- the scratching of a mouse in the corner
- footsteps on creaky floorboards
- a clock chiming at midnight
- a rooster crowing at dawn
- a faucet dripping at night
- a beautiful piece of music
- a lot of unpleasant noise in the apartment above you
- rude people talking behind you at the theatre
- a voice you find soothing
- a busy bowling alley
- coins dropping on a hardwood floor
- waves crashing on rocks
- wind rustling through autumn leaves
- sirens and car horns on a busy street
- the screeching of braking car wheels and then a crash

12.2 *Reflection Journal—Sound*

Did you notice how sound triggers mental images? What other aspects of sensory experiences did these exercises trigger?

Exercise 12.3: Smell (KSS/PGB/SDF)

Guidelines: Concentrate on the aroma until it is completely recalled. Allow it to bring up mental images both spontaneously created and from past memories. Allow recalled sensations to affect you physically.

Imagine smelling the following aromas:
- roses blooming
- incense burning
- rotten garbage
- your favorite fruit pie or cookies baking in the oven
- cigarette smoke
- a favorite perfume or cologne

- canned tuna or sardines
- fresh coffee brewing
- a ripe orange being peeled
- a forest after a light rainfall
- mint being muddled for a mojito

12.3 Reflection Journal—Smell

Did you think quickly on your feet and select given circumstances? How did the sense of smell influence your physicality?

Exercise 12.4: Touch (KSS/PGB/SDF)

Guidelines: Act out each of the following *physical actions* with exacting detail and in a *truthful measure*. Remember that *tactile sensory re-creation* demands mime-like precision. Take your time and avoid sloppy gestures. Get your audience to see the imaginary objects. Someone watching you thread an imaginary needle must believe that you are using real objects.

Imagine feeling the following sensations:
- velvet against your cheek
- holding an ice cube, then putting it in your mouth
- walking in deep snow, then making a snowball with your bare hands
- walking on slippery ice
- jumping over or into puddles in the rain
- walking through mud with bare feet
- washing your hands with soap and warm water
- rubbing your hands over rough sand paper
- holding a hot cup of tea or coffee in your bare hands
- walking or standing on cold tile in your bare feet
- walking barefoot on hot beach sand
- caressing the cheek of someone you love
- a gentle kiss on your lips
- jumping into a cool lake or pool on a hot day

12.4 Reflection Journal—Touch

Were you exacting in the execution of your physical actions? Did the situation evolve? Could you feel the different sensations?

Exercise 12.5: Taste (KSS/PGB/SDF)

Guidelines: All of the above guidelines apply.

Imagine the taste of:
- your favorite dessert
- peanut butter
- fresh strawberries
- salt
- bread and butter
- a cup of tea or coffee
- a lemon
- chicken soup
- cola
- garlic bread
- a fresh fall apple
- mint toothpaste

Exercise 12.6: Evoking the Sensory Hologram (PGB)

Guidelines: Now we will add new elements to the exercises. You are required to execute two or three contrasting sensory elements within the imaginary circumstances. Before you begin, as well as once you see the situation in your mind, imagine that you are projecting the picture three or four feet ahead of you as a three-dimensional hologram. (This may remind *Star Trek: The Next Generation* fans of the holodeck aboard the starship *Enterprise*.) When you see it clearly, then step into the picture. Glance around you before beginning and take in all of the details: ground/floor, walls, buildings, and people. Notice details. When the picture is *alive*, begin.

Sensory Evocations:
- Peel and eat a banana while walking down a busy avenue.
- Walk into a violent wind and rainstorm while holding a newborn kitten.
- Walk on a sidewalk covered with ice while holding a paper cup of hot coffee.
- Eat an ice cream cone in scorching summer heat while watching a baseball game.
- Listen to a phone call while the television is blasting an important news report that you want to watch.
- Comb your hair while chewing gum and driving.
- Listen to your favorite music while sipping an ice-cold lemonade.
- Watch a 3-D movie while eating buttered popcorn in a dark theatre.
- Lie on deep grass and take in the sights, sounds, and smells of the meadow.
- Lie on a hot, sandy beach and listen to the waves crashing against the shore while watching a gull glide on the warm air currents.

- Thread a needle while people in the apartment above you are dancing to loud music and stomping on the floor.
- While walking by a smelly drainage sewer, take a small bottle of cologne out of your pocket and smell it in order to block the foul odor.
- You are awakened in the middle of the night by the sound of a terrible automobile crash outside.
- People are loudly arguing in the apartment next to you when you hear a scream and a gun shot.
- Relax in a bubbling hot Jacuzzi while sipping an ice-cold drink.

12.6 Reflection Journal—Evoking the Sensory Hologram

How did combining sensory stimulations change your experience? Were you able to step into the holographic image? Did it evolve from the original stimulus?

Approach II: States of Being

Physical States of Being

Human beings are always in some form of a *physical state of being:* for example, we come home from work and are tired; a holiday comes, and we feel energetic and light; we have too much to drink and find it difficult to speak clearly and keep our balance. Correctly portraying a physical state is an important aspect of acting, but you must never play a state of being. States of being color and influence our actions, but when you are working on a role, ask yourself instead, What is my character's *action* and how does her physical state of being affect the execution of that action? Always fulfill the action, task, and objective; never make the focus of your scene the state of being. That would be going for the result and would wash the scene with a general state rather than bringing it alive with the moment-to-moment nuances of action and reaction.

Psychological (Mental) States of Being

Psychological states of being require deep and penetrating concentration and focus. The goal is to be so completely absorbed in the mental state that you affect yourself and others without any movement whatsoever. There are times while acting when absolute stillness is required yet your very presence must be felt by the audience. It is important that you not try to use your facial muscles to express your state of being. When you achieve profound thought, your face will reflect your inner state without consciously moving a single muscle.

Psychological Burden

A *psychological burden* is a mental state where something weighs heavily on your mind, but the circumstances dictate that you do not reveal it unless pressed to do so.

12 ORCHESTRATING EMOTIONS

Idée Fixe (Obsession)

Psychological burden is very closely associated with an *idée fixe*. An idée fixe (French for "fixed idea") is an obsessive thought that you cannot simply dismiss by willpower. Many characters suffer from such a psychological burden: Lady Macbeth continues to see blood on her hands that she cannot wash off; Richard III is obsessed with paranoia that compels him to kill in order to secure his throne. John Proctor in Arthur Miller's *The Crucible* carries a heavy guilt about his affair with Abigail; Blanche Dubois in Tennessee Williams's *A Streetcar Named Desire* is haunted by the suicide of her young husband.

Figure 12.1 Psychological burden: Merrill McGuinness in *Polaroid Stories* by Naomi Iizuka.
Photo: Charles Perry Hebard, courtesy of East Stroudsburg University

Emotional States of Being

An *emotional state of being* occurs when a character is affected by some emotion over a brief period of time. For example, when you are anxious about an upcoming event, or are joyful, exhilarated, terrified, or enraged. It may last for a certain period of time, but it is not constantly there as in an obsession. We use emotional states to color our actions, but we don't play the emotional state. Playing an emotional state makes our actions vague and unclear; again, it is going for the result and that must be avoided. Instead, find the correct and honest behavior that expresses your state, and then focus on your action and objective: what you want in the situation and how you want to affect the other characters. Emotional states are generally changeable, you may enter a scene excited and joyful, but that can change very quickly as the circumstances change. Your goal is to condition your instrument to be able to re-create sensations and emotions by means of your *imagination* and *physical actions*.

Exercise 12.7: Physical States of Being (SM/PGB)

Guidelines: Always build concrete circumstances and focus on imaginary and personal images. Project the images into the space and then, using all of your senses, step into the hologram you have created. Begin each action with W.E.D.G.A.G.

Physical States of Being:
- You have sprained your ankle while playing sports.
- You have a migraine headache and there is loud music playing.
- You come home from a very long day at work and are tired.
- You are driving home after a party and have had too much to drink. A policeman stops you and asks you to step out of the car and attempt to walk a straight line.
- You are blind and walking down a street in an unfamiliar part of town.

- You are nearly deaf and are attending a theatrical performance with a friend when your hearing aid stops working.
- You have a terrible cold or allergies and feel like you are about to sneeze.

12.7 Reflection Journal—Physical States of Being

How did your physical state of being affect your psychological and emotional state? What sensory sensations and feelings spontaneously appeared? Did you notice where in your body the sensations occurred?

Exercise 12.8: Psychological (Mental) States of Being (PGB)

Guidelines: Remember to put yourself in the picture prior to beginning. If one of the exercises requires you to make an entrance by walking into a room, then prepare the psychological state prior to making your entrance. Otherwise, stand or sit very still, but not frozen. Use W.E.D.G.A.G. and feel the muscular energy moving up and down your spine and throughout your body to assist you in initiating the action. (By this time images will probably be coming to you quite easily.)

Psychological States of Being:
- You are in a hospital, waiting to hear about the condition of a loved one who collapsed at home.
- You are at the cinema watching a touching love story.
- You are worried about how you are going to pay overdue bills.
- You are watching televised footage of the devastation of a natural disaster in your home state.
- You are in the peaceful environment of a meditation center sitting in silence.
- You have been presented a perplexing problem at work and asked to solve it.
- You are thinking about your beloved.

12.8 Reflection Journal—Psychological (Mental) States of Being

Were you able to focus deeply and remain very still? Did you notice how psychological states of being influence your physical and emotional states? What would you like to share with the group? How can you apply this exercise to a character and scene?

12 ORCHESTRATING EMOTIONS

Exercise 12.9: Psychological Burden (PGB)

Guidelines: Continue to employ all the elements of the previous exercises.

Psychological Burdens:
- You are standing in the wings of a theatre waiting to be called for your audition; you have a terrible toothache.
- You are working late with your boss trying to meet an important deadline; you have a headache and are worried about your unfed pet at home.
- You are hosting a party and have just received a very disturbing phone call in another room; you must hide the disturbing news as you reenter the party.
- It is very late at night; your child is out downtown and has not returned.
- You have just received disturbing news.
- Borrow from a personal experience and adapt it for your exercise.

12.9 Reflection Journal—Psychological Burden

Can you recall times in your life when you were weighted down with a psychological burden? Whom have you observed among your family and friends with psychological burdens? How does the burden express itself physically and emotionally?

Exercise 12.10: Idée Fixe (Obsession) (PGB)

Guidelines: In the following exercises you must build circumstances where you are driven to act as if you were obsessed. Stimulate your imagination by using the *magic if* continuously during the improvisation in order to explore the influence that your *idée fixe* has upon your physical, mental, and emotional state.

Idées Fixes (Obsessions):
- A relative who was unfairly cruel to you and you did not like has passed away. In the middle of the night you go into your relative's home to steal valuables. (Perhaps you have come to steal the will.)
- You are writing a letter to someone you cannot stop thinking about but who refuses to return your feelings.
- You are constantly worried about paying your rent and may be evicted from your home. You have not been able to sleep well for several days.
- Create an improvisation of your own based on a person with an obsession that you have observed or read about.

12.10 Reflection Journal—Idée Fixe (Obsession)

Can you think of other situations where you might use *idée fixe?* What films have you seen where a character portrays an obsession?

Exercise 12.11: Emotional States of Being (PBG/SDF)

Purpose: You will now perform a little experiment designed to condition your instrument to stir emotions through the use of imagination and physical action. Below is a list of *emotional states of being* that you might experience in the course of a typical day (you may wish to add more to the list).

Guidelines:
- Choose one of the following states that interests you, then closely follow the steps below:
  1. Ecstasy
  2. Love
  3. Joyfulness
  4. Cheerfulness
  5. Serenity
  6. Calmness
  7. Sadness
  8. Nervousness
  9. Fearfulness
  10. Aggressiveness
  11. Possessiveness
  12. Lustfulness
  13. Turmoil
  14. Torment
  15. Grief
  16. Disgust
  17. Tranquility
  18. Compassion
- Lie or sit down and relax your muscles. Breathe deeply and focus your inner eye at the point between the eyebrows so that you are looking at the *screen of you mind*. After a few moments of deep breathing create an imaginary situation where you might be in your chosen state. Use the *magic if* to build your circumstances. **Do not try to force or feel the state.** Observe the surroundings, people, atmosphere, sounds, etc., and use all of your senses. With your internal monitor watch the event and circumstances as they unfold in your imagination.
- As you envision yourself in the circumstances, pay close attention to your physical behavior as you gently allow the memory of sensations and the emotional state to arise of its own. After a few moments, open your eyes, get up, and step into the imaginary situation by assuming the physical posture or action you are doing in the moment.
- As you act in your imaginary situation, observe with your internal and external monitors the various sensations and feelings in your body. Now, dismiss the entire situation and shake out your body and run around the room to completely rid yourself of the experience.
- **Now perform a little experiment:** Without any forethought, immediately strike the pose or begin the activity you were doing in your imaginary situation. Recall the feelings and emotional state. Does the emotional state or one similar return spontaneously of its own? Once again shake it off!

> **Important note:** The point being made by this little experiment is that when you use your creative imagination combined with fitting and typical physical actions, you can effectively stir appropriate emotional states and feelings by simply repeating the physical side of the action truthfully. This is important and a key to Stanislavsky's final experiments. It is not necessary or advisable to dwell on personal experiences to create a role. Sometimes personal images and associations will spontaneously arise and merge with your imaginary images. This is fine but allow them to come and go without dwelling on them. You can make yourself ill by focusing on past traumas or forcing emotions. In any case, you may never have enough personal situations to cover the range of roles you might eventually play. Also, your personal issues may distract you from the supertask of the play and character.

12.11 Reflection Journal—Emotional States of Being

What was your experience of the exercise and experiment? Were you able to use your imagination to help you find both the images and physical pose or action? Did you become emotionally involved? How did it feel in your body? Write down your experience in your creative journal.

Approach III: Analogous Emotions

The *Theatre of Living Experience* requires that an actor build truthful human beings and live the life of the character, no matter how extraordinary or unrealistic the style and world of the play. Unfortunately, it is not always possible to live 100 percent at every moment during a performance. We can, however, approach a state of creativity that had been previously only reserved for the genius. Such great actors as Eleanora Duse, Tommaso Salvini, Alfre Woodard, Ian McKellen, Patrick Stewart, John Leguizamo, Michelle Yeoh, Judi Dench, Cate Blanchett, and Meryl Streep are the exception, not the rule. A few great actors possess the unique ability to stir appropriate emotions for the role and live the life of the character while also stirring the audience. Some of them can do it without technique or despite bad technique (although Meryl Streep, for example, has excellent Stanislavsky-based technique). Through training in solid technique and much disciplined practice, you can master your psychophysical instrument and activate your talent, releasing your own spark of genius.

As we mentioned earlier in this chapter, stage emotions are *secondary emotions* and therefore *poetic reflections* of our past experiences. Although it feels great to become emotionally involved as the character, we must always remember that we do so for the audience, not for ourselves, lest we become self-indulgent. It is not always necessary for the actor to feel what the character is feeling in order for the audience to feel it. Such is the great paradox of acting.

What Are Analogous Emotions?

Simply put, *analogous emotions* are personal experiences of emotions that are similar to the emotions required for a character you are building for a role. The situations do not need to be similar, just the emotions. You have already had a great deal of practice using personal and imaginary images and, as we're sure you have already realized, and scientific evidence has confirmed, that images contain powerful emotions themselves. Some actors may need to search their memory of past experiences and examine them to see whether they can be used to give characters nuance and depth, but even then the focus is on the physical response and behavior associated with the emotion rather than the event that triggered it. If on the other hand, you can see an imaginary person or situation, or recall something you haven't personally experienced but have observed, and this alone stirs your emotional instrument, by all means use your imaginary images or images recalled from the observation. Most artists create from both personal feeling and imagination and may start with one or the other, thereby activating both. The only question, as has been stated before, is how to do so artistically and in a healthy way. In the Active Analysis chapters to follow (13 to 15), we will explain how to apply the use of Analogous Emotional Experience to a text. First do a few more preparatory exercises.

Sometimes you will understand the emotions required in a scene but have difficulty finding and naming the transitive-verb actions needed to express them. The following exercises are designed to assist you in making the connection from emotion to action. **Remember:** *Our purpose is to stir emotions indirectly through imagination and actions; however, sometimes during the rehearsal process we must look at things from a different point of view and make adjustments to how we approach an acting task.*

Figure 12.2 Analogous emotions: Brandon L. Cabrera as Jeffrey, and Aaqilah Lewis as Dorcus, in *Sold!* by Stephanie Daventry French and Ahleea Zama.
Photo: Bob Weidner, courtesy of East Stroudsburg University

Exercise 12.12: The Love Hologram[5] (in Three Steps) (PGB)

Guideline: You are asked to recall a particular time in your life when you felt great *love*.

Important note: As with creating any strong emotion on stage, you may initially understand it through a personal experience, but never dwell on the personal situation after the initial investigation. Instead, as in sensory evocation, note the physical sensations, movements through the spine that arise, and any specific behavior you recall. It is these that you will use in later rehearsals and performances, not the specific memory.

All feelings of love are connected. Certainly the love you have for a pet can be very deep, but it is generally not quite the same as the love you might harbor for a parent, and that in turn is not the same as the love you have or have had for a lover. Most of the time you are not in love with the actor you are playing opposite, and often you have a love relationship with someone in the real world. How do you do it? Some actors use what is called *substitution*, where in their minds they substitute their acting partner for someone they have been in love with, or create a fantasy about their acting partner. We do **not** recommend using substitution in this way, as it blurs the line between professional artistic objectivity and mental health. It is not necessary to fall in love with your fellow actor in order to play a scene believably. All that is necessary is to borrow behavior (actions) and images from a past personal or even observed experience. Then with the use of your creative imagination transfer those behaviors to the scene and partner, using *to treat as*, as your primary means of expression.

If you had never fallen in love and had to play a scene where you were very much in love with someone, how would you do it? Anyone or anything that you have loved strongly can be used. You can also observe people in love and borrow physical postures and behavior from them.

Guidelines:
Step 1: The Sensory Hologram[6] (PGB)
- In your imagination reconstruct the physical circumstances and sense memory surrounding a time when you have felt great love. (It does not need to be romantic love.) Recall as many sensory details as possible: sight,

---

[5] This exercise was developed by Bennett at the San Francisco Theatre Academy in 1978–79 based on experiments he conducted with members of the repertory company while working on Arthur Miller's *The Crucible*. The intent was to create the imaginary world of Salem Village in 1692 in great detail by studying pictures that Bennett brought back from Salem Village, where he had visited and done research. The actors created the village in the large rehearsal studio and then improvised their tasks and daily routine. Each scene of the play was also rehearsed in this way. The production received acclaim and won the Hollywood DramaLogue Award for Best Direction and Best Production, 1979. More on rehearsals for production can be found in Chapter 16.

[6] The Sensory Hologram was developed at the San Francisco Theater Academy by Philip G. Bennett in 1977.

sounds, etc., and do not worry about what you cannot remember or the specifics of the person or events; focus on the sensory evocation. You can always fill in the blanks by using the *magic if.*
- The hologram: Now, once you have created your memory, project it like a motion picture into the classroom space or stage. Put yourself into the memory as you have been previously instructed for the *sense memory* exercises above, then *get up and physically step into the hologram picture.* Look and walk around the space and touch the objects you recall. With your internal monitor observe the images that flash through your mind and, most important, the sensations you feel in your body. Don't concern yourself with generating the emotion, or dwell on the details of the relationship, but allow the emotion to arise naturally in response to sensory recall and behavior. Never push your feelings.
- Now, begin to reenact what you were doing physically during that past event. If you cannot recall it in detail, don't worry, just use your *magic if* and improvise what you would do right now. Notice how your feelings intensify with the physical actions; how they seem to become more real. When this occurs, bring the exercise to a logical conclusion by gently stepping out of the projected hologram you have created. Dismiss it with some physical gesture, like clapping your hands or shaking your body.

Step 2: Create a Sculpture (PGB)
- Using the above exercise and circumstances sculpt your body into an expressive pose that depicts *Love*. Although still, your sculpture must be expressive, alive and breathing, as if you are suspended in a moment of time and space. As you sculpt each body part pay attention to how the feelings of your emotions arise spontaneously. **Note:** The more detailed your circumstances and sculpted pose, the more facility you will have in recalling the chosen emotion.

Step 3: Experiment with Muscle Memory (PGB)
- Shake off the pose and feeling then, at the clap of your teacher's hands, immediately strike the pose again and observe how the imaginary circumstances and feelings return of their own spontaneously through the conditioned reflex of muscle memory.

12.12 *Reflection Journal—The Love Hologram*

Reflect on the previous exercise and your experience of creating a three-dimentional holographic image and stepping into it. What did that feel like? Were you able to see images clearly, and were your senses stimulated? Did your personal memory of love come up also, or a related feeling of love? Most important, did you find physical behaviors and when you reactivated those physical behaviors, did the circumstances and feelings return easily and spontaneously? How could you apply this exercise to work on your character's emotional states and physical actions?

12 ORCHESTRATING EMOTIONS

Exercise 12.13: Targeting Specific Emotions (PGB)

Guidelines: Repeat the above three-part exercise using emotions from the following list: joy, desire, surprise, anger, frustration, grief, jealousy, dread, worry, disgust, rapture.

12.13 Reflection Journal—Targeting Specific Emotions

What is your experience of the exercise? Were you able to effortlessly recall emotions and dismiss them at ease? Did the selected emotion return with the repeated physical sculpture of your body? What did you have difficulty with, and what would you write down for future practice? What do you feel comfortable sharing with the group?

Figure 12.3 Targeting an emotion: Mary K. Dennis as Lydia, and Jannel Armstrong as Georgie, in *Spike Heels* by Theresa Rebeck.
Photo: Luis Vidal

Exercise 12.14: Targeting an Emotion to an Action (PGB)

Guidelines: Using your imagination and the *magic if*, build an imaginary situation and select a specific emotion and/or a state of being from the above list and exercises. Write down a specific emotion from your own experience that is analogous to what is required with the action.

Choose one of the physical actions below:
- *To read* a letter that grieves you (grief and sadness)
- *To receive a phone call* with wonderful news (joy and excitement)
- *To lose your way* at night in a strange foreign city (fear and apprehension)
- *To find* a great deal of money (wonder and surprise)
- *To search* for your car keys while you are late for work (anger and frustration)
- *To rescue* an abandoned cat or dog (pity and compassion)

> **12.14** *Reflection Journal—Targeting an Emotion to an Action*
>
> Did you remember to build concrete circumstances, and did you find that personal images of past experiences were evoked? If personal images triggered emotions from past experiences, how did they affect your behavior and actions in the present while performing the improvisation? Were you able to find physical expression for your feelings, and did you consciously use your spine and body to express them?

It took Stanislavsky forty years of constant research and experimentation to finally come to fully understand the true nature of action onstage. He realized that when an actor is trained to fulfill a psychophysical action, all the elements of the System can be stirred simultaneously: tempo and rhythm, concentration, relaxation, imagination, sense memory and emotional recall, etc. As you have now personally experienced, it is possible to trigger emotions spontaneously by the fulfillment of the physical action. And, when these emotions arise, they are fitting and appropriate for the character and circumstances. This is a great discovery.

Note: The following exercises should not be attempted until a high degree of comfort is experienced with the techniques in the previous exercises in this chapter.

> **Exercise 12.15: Words and Analogous Emotions (PGB)**
>
> **Guidelines:** Build a two-person verbal improvisation and follow all the guidelines you have learned in chapters 8 and 10: Name the Event, Create Given Circumstances, Counteraction, etc. (Use the worksheets that have been provided in Appendices IIIa and IIIb as a guide.) Here is a list of actions:
>
> **Main action:** To confess a deep, dark secret (Do not actually confess a personal secret—make one up!)
>
> **Counteraction:** Your partner will invest in a strong *counteraction* of his choosing that will make it difficult for the confession to take place; e.g., refusing to listen or insisting on discussing something else; whatever best suits the imaginary situation.
>
> **Remember:** The situation does not need to be analogous, just the emotions you wish to stir.
> - Prior to going onstage, decide on an *analogous emotion* that will fit the imaginary circumstances that you have built. You can use your body's memory of an emotion, or you can use an imaginary situation that you believe will trigger that emotion. To use your body's memory, think of when you felt that same way in the past and recall what was going on in your senses and body. What did you do physically when you felt that way? How did your body respond? What sensory responses were predominant? You do not need to dwell on the triggering event; merely notice the images and focus on the physical details surrounding the emotional response. If you are using your imagination, create the imaginary event in as much

12 ORCHESTRATING EMOTIONS

> detail as possible. Either way, amalgamate (fuse) the images for the upcoming improvisation with these stimulating images.
> - Review the experience in your mind and write down the details of your physical behavior, people, places, or senses. Recall what you were doing in the past experience and see if any of those actions are appropriate to bring into the improvisation. Do not reveal your personal past experience to your partner or anyone. *Keep it private.*

Note: Choose from your list of additional actions for practice provided in Appendix IV to build more improvisations using analogous embodied emotion.

12.15 *Reflection Journal—Words and Analogous Emotions*

Did you fulfill your action truthfully, and did your feelings and emotions arise naturally by means of your actions? What have you learned about your own emotional availability through the exercises in this chapter? What comes easily to you, and what do you still need to improve?

Note: Use analogous emotional pathways in all your future work.

Approach IV: Emotional Response through Physical Actions

Exercise 12.16A: Fulfilling Physical Actions (SDF/PGB)

Guidelines: Each of the following bullets is a separate but related exercise rather than a sequence of directions. Try some or all the physical actions below to see what, if any, emotions they evoke.

- Lay a flower on a grave and say good-bye (Let the images arise with the action, do not preplan how you will respond or what you will do other than the simple action, but do have a specific image of a person you are saying good-bye to, imaginary or real or a combination).
- Open a gift and discover what it is. Make sure to touch the object in great detail expressing its weight, texture, size, function, etc. You should not decide ahead what the object is but discover it as you open the package, go with whatever image comes to mind, and notice what it evokes.
- Think about what you do physically when you are really frustrated (most of us have experienced this enough to know such as throw down an object, kick a wall, raise one or both arms and hands quickly in a dismissive gesture while turning away, shaking your head, blowing a derisive "pfft") and repeat only the gesture, not trying to remember any specific event.
- Think about what you do physically when something astoundingly wonderful happens to surprise you. It could be a gesture or a sound or both (a shout of joy, a little or big jump, taking in a quick breath).

Exercise 12.16B: Receiving Physical Actions (SDF)

Guidelines: It is important not to undermine the exercise or the other people by mocking, side chatter, and the like. Practice your focus and concentration. If you are the receiver, allow any feelings or responses to arise spontaneously. The receiver must do nothing preplanned, and the others must only do the prescribed simple gestures. Do not plan any surrounding given circumstances but allow images and justifications to arise, or not. Try some or all of the bulleted exercises below separately.

- Divide the class into groups of three to four. One person acts as the receiver of the actions, and this should rotate.
- The Receiver is seated in a chair; the others come up and pat him on the shoulder, shake their heads, and walk by.
- The Receiver is sitting in a chair; others come up and lie on the ground, head toward the Receiver, face down with arms extended in a T, then make an offering, always keeping their heads below the head of the Receiver.
- The Receiver is in the middle of a circle of the others. They are all facing toward the center of the circle. The Receiver walks toward a member of the circle with palms facing the person, chest open; as he arrives, the person turns his back. He goes to each member of the circle and each turns her back.
- In pairs of A and B, B comes up and grabs A by the hands and swings her around a total of three times.

12.14 a & b *Reflection Journal—Initiating and Receiving Physical Actions*

Did you have any feelings stir as the Receiver? How about as one of the initiators of a gesture? What, if any, images came to mind?

Exercise 12.17: Physical Actions Re-created from Observation (SDF)

Guidelines: Each of the following bullets is a separate but related exercise, rather than a sequence of directions. Try one or both of the observation exercises to see what, if any, emotions they evoke.

- Observe someone experiencing a strong emotion and make notes of every detail of that person's interaction with objects, physical choices, subtle changes in the spine, head, hands, etc. Then, try to re-create these physical responses in as much physical detail as you can. Do not force or preplan any emotion but allow any physical sensations or emotions to arise.
- Practice the subtle microexpressions that accompany specific facial gestures of emotion re-created from photographs. Do a search on the internet for an Ekman Facial Expression chart or get his book *Unmasking the Face*, by Paul Ekman and Wallace Friesen. Take two different facial

expressions and try to replicate the subtle muscle changes in the face. Practice this numerous times, first just looking at the pictures and then checking in a mirror to see whether you got it right. Then, do the expression without looking in the mirror and notice whether it changes the way you feel. (The teacher could bring in the drawings.)

Note to actors and teachers: This experiment is only to notice how the physical can affect the emotional. Unless you are an expert at facial expressions, emotions created in the face first will tend to look fake, what we call a grimace, and will not move you or your audience. It is much better to allow the energy to move through the spine and let the face just respond.

12.17 *Reflection Journal—Observation Reflection*

For this exercise it would be particularly helpful for the observing class to reflect back what they perceived. This will let the actor know whether what he received from the originally observed action was being clearly communicated.

Approach V: Music and Emotions

Many of us turn to music to express something we are feeling that is harder to say in words. We use music to go along with a particular *mood* or pervasive emotional state or to alter our moods. We play music on our devices; we make music, or we go and listen to live music. Even if we are not feeling any particularly strong emotion, a piece of music can trigger it in us.

How can you use this relationship between music and emotions for your acting?

Exercise 12.18: Working with Music without a Text (SDF)

Advance Preparation: The teacher will compose a soundtrack with a variety of different pieces of music and bring in a device to play it.

Guidelines:
A. Moving to Music
- As each piece of music is played, the students listen and begin to move with the feeling of the music. This can be walking, running, dancing, doing an activity, or any type of expression. As the music shifts and a new piece of music plays, allow your spine, or whatever other part of your body responds first, to initiate movement (but make sure to move through the small muscles along the spine). Allow the changing tempo-rhythm of the music to affect you also.

B. Allowing Music to Move You
- In class or at home, select a piece of music that you find particularly stirring. Stand in good neutral alignment, or lie on the floor with your eyes closed (if you choose the latter, eventually get to standing). Allow the music to begin to move your body, even if just gently along the spine. Imagine that you can breathe the music into your body. Follow any movements or images as they arise, however subtly. Move in broader ways if you want to, but subtle movements are fine for this one.

Exercise 12.19: Working with Music with a Text (SDF)
- Using a monologue or scene you select or have previously worked on a little, find a piece of music that expresses to you what the character is experiencing. It is not important that the song have words, or if it does have words, that the words of the song are relevant to the topics of the play. All that matters is that the piece of music that you find or create captures something about the feeling of this piece of text for your character. Play the music and move to it as above.
- As an additional part, you can speak some words or the entire text with the music playing quietly in the background. You can work with the rhythm of the music or against it.
- If you have a scene partner, you can go through some of the action of the scene first with music you have chosen, second with music your scene partner has chosen, or, alternately, with a piece that you select together that expresses the dynamic between the characters.

12.18 & 12.19 *Reflection Journal—Working with Music*
How did different pieces of music affect the shape and quality of your movement? How did they affect your tempo-rhythm? Were any of the following stimulated: physical sensations, emotions, images, thoughts?

Approach VI: Obstacles and Emotion

As an actor in training, you will be encouraged to *up the stakes*, which means to invest in the character's needs and problems so that they become very important to you. If the situations your character is in or the way your character feels about them are not familiar to you, some research will be required before you can make this investment. The greater the understanding you have of your character's time period, psychology, and situations (achieved through numerous methods outlined in this book through techniques such as the *magic if*, Active Analysis, and reconnaissance) the greater you can relate to the character's experience and therefore invest more. The more invested you are, the more that achieving the character's goals or being thwarted will trigger emotions in you just as being rewarded or blocked in your own desires and goals will trigger emotions in life. No exercises are given here, as exercises on this are throughout the book. Obstacles are first introduced in-depth in Chapter 8: Nonverbal Action.

> **Important Reminder: Use Your Emotional Instrument Safely**
>
> Never force your emotions. Understand the nature and sequence of your character's actions, for it is through purposeful action and investment in the character's psyche and situation that appropriate emotions are triggered. Practice letting go of your feelings immediately after a rehearsal and performance. Achieving emotional involvement in a role is a success when the character really comes to life in a way that the emotion is both felt and communicated. This is a very positive experience, and it will reinforce your ability to do it better each time. If at any time you find yourself pushing, stop.
>
> If you do use personal images as an initial stimulus, use images that are not too raw and immediate but allow poetic reflection, not a psychodrama, which may be damaging or disruptive to you or your scene partners. You need to have some time and space between a past event and your use of it for a role, and, remember, you use it in rehearsal to find behavior and sensory evocation, but you never dwell on the actual past events in subsequent rehearsals or performance. If you have difficulty letting go of the painful emotions that are required for a scene, do not use personal experiences. Discuss any issues with your director or seek out professional counseling. Stay healthy!
>
> **Note to Students:** There are many interesting other approaches to work on emotions, and certainly you might try them and find what works for what you need to create artistically. One approach that can be very evocative is Michael Chekhov's work on *atmospheres*. In this book you begin to work on something akin to atmospheres when you make the three wheres that are a part of every scene or improvisation evocative places for your character to inhabit, and when you stepped into the sensory holograms above. He created this in part as an alternative to the earlier use of affective memory he learned from Stanislavsky. Stanislavsky also shifted his primary focus away from affective memory to physical action and memories of the body rather than specific personal memories. When you create the given circumstances in great detail and fully inhabit them, such as in the group disaster exercise, you are creating and responding to an atmosphere.

PART II: SCIENTIFIC INSIGHTS ON EMOTION FOR ACTORS

"Emotions, too, are embodied, and given their power to affect physiology outside the skull are arguably the most embodied form of mental activity."[7]
—Richard J. Davidson

---

[7] Richard J. Davidson and Sharon Begley, *The Emotional Life of Your Brain* (New York: Hudson Street/Penguin, 2012), p. 136.

Chapter 3 looked at some of the emerging science on inspiration and creativity. Chapter 5 introduced you to some of the current scientific ideas about mind-body connections. As mentioned in Chapter 5, leading twentieth-century behaviorists believed that mind-body connection, emotions, mental images, and consciousness were not suitable areas for scientific study. This impeded progress in scientific understanding of these areas during the mid-twentieth century.

In Stanislavsky's era, the late nineteenth and early twentieth centuries, some forward-thinking scientists had laid the groundwork. Philosopher/psychologist William James (already introduced in Chapter 5) and Danish physician Carl Lange (1834–1900) had very closely related findings. Their ideas came to be known as the *James-Lange Theory*, summarized thus by Eric Kandel: "Feeling is the direct consequence of specific information sent from the body to the cerebral cortex"[8] (a more advanced cognitive processing part of the brain). These great thinkers, along with Stanislavsky through his acting experiments, came to the conclusion that emotion is a mind-body experience. In 1890, William James, in *Principles of Psychology,* wrote: "A purely disembodied human emotion is a nonentity."[9]

More recently, in the mid- to late twentieth and early twenty-first centuries, vigorous scientific study resumed in these areas, largely prompted by better tools to more objectively measure internal landscapes. While some new ideas proposing different mind-body mechanisms to stimulate emotion are challenging a few aspects of the James-Lange Theory, the fact that the mind and body influence one another to create emotion is now being empirically proved. Many of Stanislavsky's insights, too, are now being validated and built upon as emerging scientific tools catch up to the insights of great thinkers of the past who came to these ideas through observation and more rudimentary tools and, in Stanislavsky's case, exceptional experiments with actors. Present-day neuroscientists and researchers into emotion in psychology and other fields, with much more sophisticated measurement tools, are affirming the mind-body interconnection in many areas, including the generation and processing of emotion.

Contemporary researchers have demonstrated the effect of emotion on thinking (which most of us have experienced) and the ability of thoughts to generate emotions (which some of us are becoming cognizant of). Another finding, still not widely known, is that higher levels of thought and reasoning involve aspects of emotion. Antonio Damasio works with people with damaged brains, as well as with healthy subjects. He states that "my laboratory has shown that emotion is integral to the processes of reasoning and decision making, for worse and better."[10] Kandel echoes this finding: "Despite the fact that emotion is mediated by neural systems that are partially independent of the perceptual, thinking and reasoning systems of the brain, we now realize that emotion is also a form of information processing and therefore a form of cognition."[11] While the popular notion that excessive emotion impedes or clouds thought may well still hold some validity, the most advanced cognitive processes require some emotional input to function.

---

[8] Eric R. Kandel, *The Age of Insight: The Quest to Understand the Unconscious in Art, Mind and Brain* (New York: Random House, 2012), 349.
[9] William James, *Principles of Psychology*, vol. 2 (Mineola, NY: Dover, 1890), 1066–1067.
[10] Damasio, *The Feeling of What Happens*, 41.
[11] Eric R. Kandel, *The Age of Insight: The Quest to Understand the Unconscious in Art, Mind, and Brain* (New York: Random House, 2012), 352.

I have a gut feeling about this!

How many times have you heard someone say this? During election cycles we hear that many people go with their gut when it comes to whom they vote for. We vote based on emotion. Advertisers know and target the fact that we often buy on the basis of emotion. Even for those of us that like to believe we do everything rationally, emotions are a big, often unconscious force in why we do what we do. The tenth of the twelve cranial nerves is called the *vagus nerve,* or wandering nerve, because it wanders through a number of places in the body and, according to Damasio, "bypasses the (spinal) cord altogether and aims directly at the brain stem."[12] One of the places from which the vagus nerve sends and receives signals that affect decision making is from the gut. In rats it was found that when the vagus nerve was cut, emotion no longer helped their performance, and they kept making the same mistakes over and over.[13]

> "It has been demonstrated, in both rats and humans, that recall of new facts is enhanced by the presence of certain degrees of emotion during learning."[14]
> —Antonio Damasio

What follows is an oversimplification of a very complex process to help you get a glimpse of how emotions are unconsciously generated within you, with the goal of being able to consciously generate emotions on cue in your acting. To understand the details of this process in terms of the multiple brain regions and bodily systems involved, please refer to some of our listed sources on the subject. Two of the most helpful were Antonio Damasio's *The Feeling of What Happens: Body and Emotion in the Making of Consciousness,* particularly Chapter 2: "Emotion and Feeling," and Eric R. Kandel's *The Age of Insight: The Quest to Understand the Unconscious in Art, Mind, and Brain,* particularly Chapter 21: "Unconscious Emotions, Conscious Feelings, and Their Bodily Expression."

While most of us use the terms *feeling* and *emotion* interchangeably, scientifically they are now separated. Damasio proposes that

> feeling should be reserved for the private, mental experience of an emotion, while the term *emotion* should be used to designate the collection of responses, many of which are publicly observable. In practical terms this means that you cannot observe a feeling in someone else although you can observe a feeling in yourself when, as a conscious being, you perceive your own emotional states. Likewise no one can observe your own feelings, but some aspects of the emotions that give rise to your feeling will be patently observable to others.[15]

---

[12]Damasio, *The Feeling of What Happens*, 152.
[13]Ibid., 295.
[14]Damasio, *The Feeling of What Happens*, 294.
[15]Ibid., 42.

The Vagus Nerve

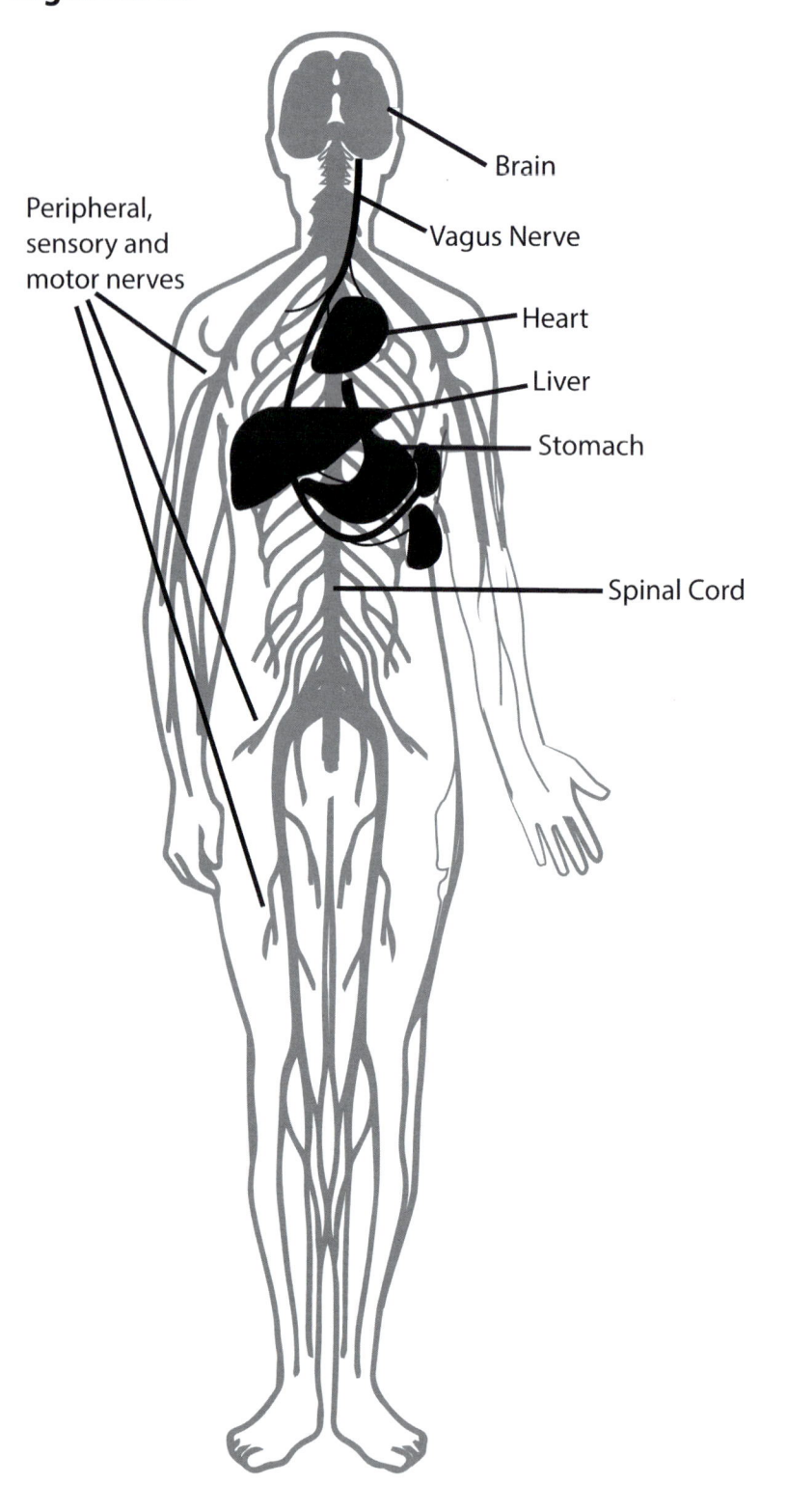

- Brain
- Vagus Nerve
- Peripheral, sensory and motor nerves
- Heart
- Liver
- Stomach
- Spinal Cord

Figure 12.4 The path of the vagus nerve.

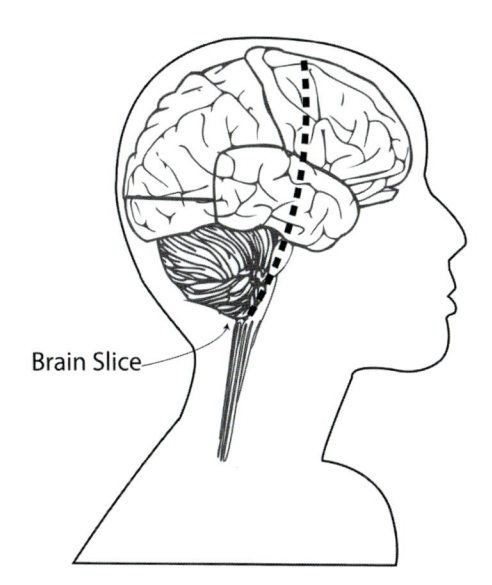

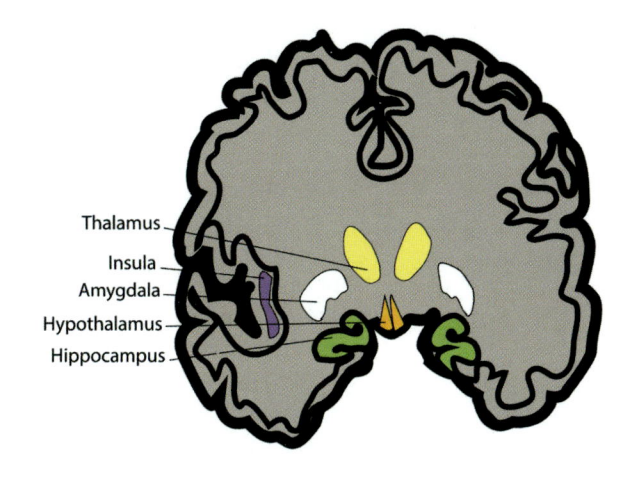

Figure 12.5 Key aspects of the limbic system for emotional response.

A Simplified Anatomy of Emotion

The mechanisms for emotion move in continuous feedback loops between the body and the brain. A number of systems of the body are engaged, such as the entire *nervous system* (central, peripheral, and cranial nerves, particularly as they combine as part of the autonomic nervous system), *cardiovascular system* (aka circulatory system: heart, blood, blood vessels), and many different regions of the brain are activated and working together, such as the areas of *limbic system*. The functions listed are by no means the only purposes of these anatomical areas or systems but rather those most relevant to the current (though oversimplified) understanding of the anatomy and physiology of emotion. Some of these are:

Sensory receptors: eyes, ears, nose, skin, taste buds

Nervous system (The pathways of the central and peripheral nervous system can be seen in grey behind the drawing of the vagus nerve in Figure 12.4): A communication pathway throughout the entire body and the body to the brain, that uses electrical currents generated by neurons to communicate with signals distinguished by tempos and patterns (our own internal tempo-rhythm). The central nervous system, peripheral nervous systems and vagus nerve are all key players in emotional response.

Cardiovascular system: Another communication pathway between the brain and body, which among other things carries hormones from the pituitary gland to the body, nutrients to the body and the brain, and distributes immune system cells to fight disease.

Brain: Particularly important is the limbic system. These structures exist symmetrically in both hemispheres although their functions may differ see Figure 12.5B:

- *Thalamus*—receives sensory input.
- *Hypothalamus*—located in the brain stem, the hypothalamus regulates feeding behavior, temperature, and the autonomic nervous system (fight/flight, aka approach/avoid) by controlling the heart rate and blood pressure and the release of hormones (from the *pituitary gland*). It is considered a primitive, instinctual part of the brain.
- *Amygdala*—orchestrates emotion, coordinates emotional states in the brain with the autonomic nervous system and hormonal responses, coordinates effect of emotion on thinking and of thought on emotion, signals the insula.
- *Insula*—the part of the brain that generates feeling: our consciousness of the emotional changes in our brains and bodies.

A simplified process of the current understanding of emotion follows (and omits many known details that would overcomplicate an initial understanding of this process). As research on emotion is exploding right now, by the time this book is printed, more will be known, and some of these things may be better understood. These responses all happen and amp up very quickly but are much slower to wind down.

1. **Trigger**: There is an external *or* internal trigger. An external trigger is perceived by one or more of our senses and communicated to the **thalamus,** which filters the input and translates the electrical signals into images (mental patterns), some of which activate the **hypothalamus**. An internal trigger, such as a memory or thought about an object, person, or situation, conjures images in the brain that stir the hypothalamus. The hypothalamus sends out messages of response to the body via **hormones** in the **bloodstream** and **electrical signals** through the **central nervous system**, and mental patterns to the **amygdala**.
2. **Emotion**: The **amygdala** evaluates stimuli. It is biologically predisposed to respond emotionally (usually for fear but sometimes rage) to some stimuli (found in nature). Additionally, the amygdala can learn to respond emotionally to stimuli on the basis of significant events that have occurred during prior encounters (conditioned emotional response). Either way, at this level the emotional response is still occurring automatically and subconsciously. Others can observe the response at this stage, but the one experiencing it may not yet be conscious of it.
3. **Feeling**: The brain receives signals back from the emotional response going on in the brain and body and creates a mental map that reaches a part of the cerebral cortex called the **insula**. At this point we observe the feeling of an emotion and have some ability, to a greater or lesser degree, depending on the emotion and the individual, to consciously regulate it.

According to Kandel, Bud Craig at Barrow Neurological Institute in Phoenix wrote that "consciousness of bodily states is a measure of our emotional awareness of self—the feeling that 'I am.'"[16] This ties directly into Stanislavsky's early concept of "I am" or "I exist" when the actor experiences living through the characters emotions of a situation.

Another thing that is important for our work in acting is that indirect triggers can also induce emotions in the form of obstacles that block an ongoing emotion. For

---

[16]Quoted in Kandel, *The Age of Insight*, 353.

example, if your car is sliding on the ice and you think you are going to ram into the back of another car, you begin to experience fear of anticipated pain, but if you somehow manage to brake just in time you experience relief from the anticipated pain. Thus the obstacle creates the relief. The inverse of that would be if you believe you are about to receive an award (anticipation of pleasure) and it instead goes to another, then the obstacle creates a sense of loss or disappointment. Again Damasio: "While pain is associated with negative emotions, such as anguish, fear, sadness, and disgust, whose combination commonly constitutes what is called suffering, pleasure is associated with many shades of happiness, pride and positive background emotions."[17] To put it another way, either actual pain (damage or dysfunction to your physiological instrument) or anticipation of pain can induce negative emotions, as well as can the withholding of something positive. While positive emotions can be the result of positive associations with stimuli based on context, such as a child's being happy or excited at the approach of its mother because it has associated her with food, comfort, and the like, positive emotions can also be the result of averting pain or discomfort to find balance in our mind and body. Some examples would be eating to avert or placate hunger, or drinking caffeine to counter tiredness.

In life, emotions and the corresponding feelings arise organically through external sensory triggers or internally through mental triggers. Our experiences are then stored as a *memory of emotion*, leaving their traces along the neural pathways in our brains and in our bodies. Both traumatic and pleasurable events are forever imprinted to help us learn what to avoid and what to approach, what is advantageous for survival or gives pleasure, and what is disadvantageous for survival or leads to pain. These experiences are called *primary experiences* because they are real and personal to us.

Some triggers are part of instinctual responses biologically preprogramed; others are experientially learned through our personal history, creating contexts that mitigate future responses. In other words, as with many physical behaviors, even our emotions are a mixture of nature and nurture.

Primary emotions can be either subtle or overpowering; they can also motivate us to action. Primary experiences can also trigger memories of *analogous emotions*— similar emotions but arising from different incidents—that amplify the current experience. When someone says a comment that hurts you, you might remember a time when you were rejected in some way. When you ride an ocean wave on a boogie board as an adult, perhaps you remember the exhilaration you felt in your childhood excitement of riding a bicycle down a steep hill or a ride at an amusement park.

Dr. Paul Ekman, researcher and professor emeritus in psychology at the University of California, San Francisco, is probably most known for the TV show inspired by his research, *Lie to Me*. Along with his colleagues, he discovered the microexpressions involved with emotion and set about to identify the facial gestures of key human emotions. He later did some experiments on which emotions are culturally based versus universal to all humans. He also set out to try to consciously replicate, using his own face and the faces of his colleagues and volunteer subjects, the subtle movements of the muscles of the face that create each human emotion, even the movements that most people do not control. In the process, he made an interesting discovery that was not part of the focus of his research. He and the other

---

[17]Damasio, *The Feeling of What Happens*, 76.

subjects in the experiment when making the face of a particular emotion with no thought of a specific trigger, actually started to have feelings related to the targeted emotion. In other words, as Stanislavsky and his colleagues at the Moscow Art Theatre discovered, specific physical action and movement of muscles alone can stimulate emotion.

Summary

To be alive and human is to feel emotion. Each of us has a different emotional capacity and makeup. What is important is to learn about yourself and your unique emotional life and to come to understand what tools work best for you. Observation is at least 50 percent of our creativity. You can learn so much about how people feel and behave in different situations by just going to a public square or mall and watching them. Anything you observe that affects you emotionally can be used as a resource for your creative work; it can be your own response to art or observation of another's experience rather an experience in your own life. You cannot always be expected to have experienced every possible situation or feeling in life; therefore, it is vital to expand your horizons by visiting museums, reading good novels, seeing artistic films, and observing how people around you behave in different settings. Develop empathy and compassion for others, also, for this will go a long way in your ability to convey the multiple facets of human feeling and emotion to an audience. Become aware of the world stage and develop informed views on topics that affect your community and society. Always keep in mind that we use our own experiences only to bring our characters to life for the audience. A true artist is never self-indulgent and brings personal experiences as an offering to others.

New Acting Terms, Concepts, and Artists

Terms used in the Stanislavsky System are in italics.

- *analogous emotions (AE)*
- *emotional memory*
- emotional state of being
- *experiencing*
- *idée fixe (obsession)*
- Arthur Miller
- *physical states of being*
- *poetic reflection*
- *primary experience*
- *psychological burden*
- psychological (mental) states of being
- *secondary experience*
- *sensory hologram*
- *sensory re-creation*
- *states of being*

New Interdisciplinary Terms and Experts

- cardiovascular system
- Richard Davidson
- feeling
- emotion
- hypothalamus
- insula
- James-Lange Theory
- limbic system
- nervous system
- Daniel Schachter
- thalamus
- vagus nerve

PART 3

ACTIVE ANALYSIS

> **Chapters in Part 3**
> 13. Active Analysis: Reconnaissance of the Play — 303
> 14. Active Analysis: Reconnaissance of the Character — 322
> 15. Active Analysis through Events and Actions — 346
> 16. Active Analysis in Rehearsal — 386
> 17. Entering the Collaborative Process — 406
> 18. The Actor of Living Experience — 450
> 19. The Creative Life: Communion with Audience and Society — 465

In Part I: Psychophysical Conditioning, you developed your internal and external awareness of how your mind, body, breath, and voice operate separately and in tandem. In Part II: Psychophysical Action you developed your ability to re-create believable human behavior in imaginary circumstances through the fulfillment of actions. You have now gained an experiential understanding of all of the important Elements of Action. Through this training, you have begun to condition your psychophysical instrument to create conscious pathways to the *superconscious* state. You have learned how to bring all your facilities to bear to evoke the creative state as an invitation to inspiration. Next, as you apply this work on a play, all the elements you have learned will coalesce.

Active Analysis includes two major aspects:

- *Reconnaissance of the Mind*, where you survey the landscape of the script through analysis and fill out your understanding through research
- *Reconnaissance of the Body*, where you move from objective ideas about the play and your character to a more subjective embodiment, stepping into the character's body and actively exploring the events of the role in the play within the given circumstances. You will flesh out all the layers and dynamics from the entire play, to the scene, to smaller episodes within the scene, to each action-step (beat).

In chapters 13, 14, and 15 you will be taken step-by-step through the process of Active Analysis of a role. Chapter 13 will focus on Reconnaissance of the Play. Chapter 14 will focus on Reconnaissance of the Character, and Chapter 15 will further develop the character and bring it to life through Active Analysis of Events and Actions, which will take you episode-by-episode, action-step by action-step, throughout a scene. In each chapter, you will move fluidly between Reconnaissance of the Mind and Reconnaissance of the Body, gathering active facts and then engaging in them on-your-feet. Through a deep understanding of the background information on the character, playwright and play you will invest in the motivations of the character so that fulfilling his actions moment-to-moment within the dynamics events of the scene, you will reveal truthful human experience and reveal the author and director's supertasks.

Chapter 16: Active Analysis in Rehearsal is a demonstration of how these techniques are actually used in the collaborative interplay between director and actor. In Chapter 17: Entering the Collaborative Process, you will gain an understanding of a typical professional rehearsal process for actors and learn some tips about how to apply Active Analysis within this structure, whether the director uses it or not. Chapter 18 outlines all the aspects of the Stanislavsky System as he brought them together in his Diagram of Experiencing. In Chapter 19 you are invited to investigate the leap from rehearsal to performance and to consider the possibilities of theatre art for a variety of social purposes.

Active Analysis Then and Now

Stanislavsky's Active Analysis through Events and Actions is a rehearsal technique. While improvisation is used by many directors as a rehearsal technique today, in the early twentieth century Stanislavsky's use of improvisation in rehearsal was a revolutionary and breakthrough technique. It was so unfamiliar to actors of his day that experienced actors who had already achieved praise using older methods resisted learning this new technique (actors not trained in an improvisational approach still often fear or resist it in rehearsal today). Stanislavsky had to turn to younger, more flexible actors to try it out as he developed this technique in rehearsals (more about this in Chapter 20: The Evolving Stanislavsky System). Active Analysis is now widely used in Russia and in many eastern European countries, even as far away as Shanghai, China.[1]

Many people associate Stanislavsky's rehearsal technique with sitting around a table talking about the play for months. This was an early rehearsal technique of Stanislavsky, but he abandoned it as intellectually stimulating but insufficient for activating the actor and the play. He moved on to active methods of rehearsal.

Active Analysis was developed by Stanislavsky in the last two to three years of his life, 1935–1938 (as outlined in Chapter 20: The Evolving Stanislavsky System). Some people translate it as Action Analysis. Stanislavsky began experimenting with this new approach by selecting a group of young actors to work on *Tartuffe*, by the seventeenth-century French playwright Molière. Stanislavsky died during final rehearsals of this production, and he did not get to write down all of his new ideas. Luckily, his rehearsal techniques were recorded and passed on by his students and colleagues, some of whom were present and participated in or observed the process and others who received the teachings from those present. Most notably of these are Maria O. Knebel, Mikhail Kedrov, and Vassili Toporkov. Knebel's work was adapted into a guide for directors by Georgy A. Tovstonogov.

Stanislavsky's early name for his active rehearsal process was the Method of Physical Actions, a term still used by some. There is still a lot of confusion between Stanislavsky's Method of Physical Actions and his Active Analysis through Events and Actions. The Soviet government lauded the Method of Physical Actions, especially aspects that were aligned with approved Soviet science, but they also discouraged some aspects of it that did not agree with their politics. For one thing, Soviet censors removed the System's origins in yoga from Stanislavsky's publications. The Soviets also pushed Stanislavsky's theatre, The Moscow Art Theatre (MAT), to keep producing in the style they claimed as Soviet Realism, even when MAT artists,

---

[1] Stanislavsky's Active Analysis is taught and used in rehearsal, for example, at the Xiejin Television and Film Art College of Shanghai Normal University, an actor training program considered among the top three in China. Russian teachers from the Moscow Art Theatre taught Xiejin teachers a four-year version of the System, including Active Analysis.

including Stanislavsky, were more interested in exploring other styles. The Soviet government also did not approve of experimental techniques in the theatre, including later approaches of two of Stanislavsky's top students: Vsevold Meyerhold's political and physically bold theatrical style, and Michael Chekhov's mystic and imaginative approach. This is one of the reasons why *Tartuffe* was rehearsed in Stanislavsky's home, away from the MAT Soviet watchdogs. Because of Soviet support, and perceived manipulation, of the Method of Physical Actions, many teachers and scholars dismiss it in favor of Active Analysis. Active Analysis is considered the ultimate technique created by Stanislavsky in his final years.

In actuality, The Method of Physical Actions and Active Analysis have much more overlap than divergence, and both approaches offer great tools for actors and directors, but there are a few important differences. One of the key differences is that The Method of Physical Actions focuses on finding the through-line of actions toward your character's objective, while Active Analysis asks you to identify the character's problem and engage in a struggle figuring out moment-to-moment tasks to try to solve it. The Method of Physical Actions is based in physical behavior that can evoke the emotional life, while Active Analysis, while still strongly tied to physical action to stir emotions, focuses more on finding the *dynamic conflict* through the action/counteraction exchange between scene partners.

Stanislavsky developed some of these active rehearsal techniques earlier and included them in his books, and thus these are more widely known. For just two examples, many people are familiar with speaking out loud the inner monologue and paraphrasing the text. However, his entire final technique of Active Analysis through Events and Actions is still not widely understood in the West (although that is gradually changing). The use of improvisational techniques in rehearsal, however, is now ubiquitous in Western theatre. Many of the subsequent directors who influenced active and experimental approaches, such as Vsevold Meyerhold, Jerzy Grotowski, Peter Brook, and Bertolt Brecht, were building on the legacy of Stanislavsky (as discussed in more detail in Chapter 20). Also, like Stanislavsky, these directors felt a strong need for theatre to have a social purpose, and some of them took this much further than Stanislavsky had.

Many directors have developed their own approaches to actively analyzing plays and using improvisation in rehearsal. Each director has a unique arrangement of borrowed and created rehearsal techniques. For such directors, Active Analysis offers additional tools that might supplement their techniques. For those not accustomed to improvisational rehearsal approaches, Active Analysis is an innovative approach that they can sample or learn and apply step-by-step through this book.

Active Analysis is not only for the director. For you as an actor, Active Analysis can help you flesh out the myriad layers of your script and bring your character to vivid life within the role of a particular production. If your directors, due to time limitations or preference or lack of familiarity, prefer a more traditional process, you will be able to use Active Analysis for your expected outside-of-rehearsal actor's preparation.

This System is *not* dogma. Stanislavsky did not believe his technique was set but was constantly improving it throughout his life, adding new ideas from science, from other contemporary theatre artists, and from his own continual experimentation. As teachers and experimenters ourselves, the authors, Bennett and French, have developed the process of Active Analysis in some ways that we have found to be productive for actors who are training in a variety of academic, conservatory, or studio or professional theatre settings. Therefore, we offer here a combination of Stanislavsky's techniques with those based on the solid foundation of the System that we have developed through experimentation. You may also recognize exercises from other theatre practitioners, and whenever possible we have given them credit.

Enough talking. It's time to rehearse a play.

CHAPTER 13

Active Analysis: Reconnaissance of the Play

"In order to grasp the genre and style of a play it is necessary to seek the emotional impulse that moved the author to write it."[1]
—Georgi Tovstonogov, Director

Surveying the Landscape of the Play through Analysis, Research, and Improvisational Études

Stanislavsky Techniques Actively Explored

Reconnaissance of the mind; reconnaissance of the body; supertask; telling the plot; tableau; second plan; main events; imagination (image landscapes)

Other Theatre Concepts Explored

Themes, climactic plot structure, mise-en-scène

- **Reconnaissance of the Mind and Body**
- **Selecting a Scene**
- **Aristotle's Components of Drama**
- **Beginning Active Analysis with Reconnaissance**
- ☐ Exercise 13.1: First Reading of the Play
- **Thought/Theme and Supertask**
- ☐ Worksheet 13.2A: Preliminary Theme Overview
- ☐ Worksheet 13.2B: Research the Playwright and the Playwright's Recurring Themes
- **The Plot: Analysis through Events**
- ☐ Exercise 13.3: Telling the Plot
- ☐ Worksheet 13.4: Climactic Plot Analysis
- **Spectacle, Composition, and the Mise-en-Scène**
- ☐ Exercise 13.5: Named Events Tableaux (Plot and Spectacle)
- ☐ Worksheet 13.6: Research on the Given Circumstances
- ☐ Exercise 13.7: Picture Compositions
- **Active Exploration of the Play's Events**
- ☐ Exercise 13.8: Second Plan Improvisation on Main Events
- ☐ Exercise 13.9: Floating Image Landscape

---

[1] Georgi Tovstonogov, *The Profession of the Stage Director* (Moscow: Progress, 1972), 168.

Reconnaissance of the Mind and Body

One of the many great gifts of a life in theatre, television, and film is delving into the wealth of worlds and characters offered by playwrights and screenwriters. Every play or film contains something new and interesting in terms of subject and often also artistic form. With most plays and films, there will be aspects of the subject matter that are immediately understood by the actor and others that are foreign, unfamiliar, but intriguing. It is this stretch between what you already understand and the perspectives and experiences of different people, worlds, or time periods that can offer much expansion of yourself as an artist and even as a person. Before you can fully inhabit these people and places you will need to survey the territory the playwright has mapped out and fill in, through research and observation, those areas beyond your current experience or understanding.

Even if you use the same approach to work on a play over and over (which is not necessarily ideal as each play has unique creative challenges) the source material—subject and form—is unique and offers to enrich you. As you gain acting experience, you will naturally develop your own approach to play analysis that will be influenced by each director, teacher, and play that you work with, as well as your own imaginative abilities.

Stanislavsky called the first part of this exploration of a play Reconnaissance of the Mind, which reflects the director's analysis and the actor's preliminary objective analysis of the play. He considered the focus of this work the search for the *supertask*, the idea or impression that the playwright wants to imprint on the audience. The second part is Reconnaissance of the Body, where the actor, working collaboratively with the director, moves from the objective analysis to subjective, active engagement in the role. Reconnaissance of the Mind is what is referred to in common theatre parlance as analysis, research, and imagination. Reconnaissance of the Body is the active embodiment of the play and the role: breathing life into the character through your psychophysical instrument. Stanislavsky designed the System to begin with psychophysical conditioning, advance to training in action leading to Active Analysis through Events and Actions (including Reconnaissance of the Mind, Reconnaissance of the Body), and ultimate artistic unfolding of experiencing the role in communion with the audience.

How does the actor begin to move from himself as sole source material in earlier investigations in acting to working on a play and a role with material provided by another artist, the playwright?

Where to start? **Read the play!** It shouldn't even need to be said, but it does. Yes, read the entire play even though you will only be working on a scene. This may be obvious to most of you, but you would be surprised how many students want to avoid having to read and believe they can achieve something meaningful intuitively without reading the play.

Why do I need to read and analyze the entire play when I am only working *on a scene*?

"A text comes to life only through detail, and detail is the fruit of understanding."[2]

—Peter Brook, Director

[2] Peter Brook, *The Open Door* (New York: Pantheon Books/Random House, 1993), 134.

13 RECONNAISSANCE OF THE PLAY

To do justice to any single scene an understanding of the entire play is vital. Throughout the play the playwright has embedded details about the given circumstances, unfolding sequences of events, and your character. Would you really want to work on a role without every gift the playwright has given you? Some actors would rather watch a film version of a play than read it themselves. Don't make this mistake. It robs you of the essential creative first step of allowing the play to come alive in your imagination, a vital creative source for acting. Before you are given other artists' interpretations, generate your own images of the people, places, and events.

Selecting a Scene

Perhaps your teacher has given you a scene to read and work on, or you may have chosen one along with your partner. It is best to begin practice with a contemporary scene, mid-to-late twentieth century or a relatively new twenty-first-century play. While the techniques you are learning through this book and your classes can be used on any *genre* and *style* of play, we suggest starting with a realistic play from an epoch not too far removed from your own and with characters of about your own age, gender, and race, if possible. The first step of your training process with text is to learn how to behave as would a real human being in similar circumstances. The elements of the System that you absorbed in the previous chapters will now be systematically applied to work on a text. That will take some time, and as you develop greater skill, you can expand to meet the challenges of foreign plays in translation, historical plays, plays written in verse, and a variety of styles.

Avoid the temptation to work on very long scenes, 5 to 10 minutes is a good general rule to follow. It is better to do thorough work on a shorter piece of text than to attempt a 15- or 20-minute scene and do shallow work due to time restraints both in and out of class. Put your mind on process, not results. Also, unless you are very adept and familiar with a foreign accent or regional dialect it is best not to attempt that at first. Accents sharply define character and must be done to perfection in order to be believable. A poorly spoken dialect will be more of a hindrance to your progress than a help. When the time comes to play a character with an accent, approach your acting teacher, voice and speech teacher, and director for advice and assistance.

A list of plays for beginning scene work that we have found is offered on the book's companion website. There are also many excellent scene books available at your local drama bookstores or at online bookstores.

Aristotle's Components of Drama

Ancient wisdom has valuable modern applications. The Greek theatrical epoch of the Golden Age of Greece from the fifth century BCE is considered one of the greatest theatrical periods and continues to have a resounding impact. Play analysis tools given to us by the Greek philosopher Aristotle in the fourth century BCE, as he looked back on the structure of plays in the Golden Age a hundred years earlier, are still used widely today. Aristotle noted that there are six basic components of drama: *Thought* (Theme), *Plot*, *Character*, *Diction* (Language), *Music* (Rhythm), and *Spectacle*. Every play combines these elements and, depending on the style of the play, highlights some more than others. Some great playwrights, like Shakespeare, are known for highlighting all of them. Students of theatre should study each of these elements and be able to identify their use by a variety of playwrights. Different theatrical artists, including directors and designers, draw from these components in unique ways to inspire their artistic responses to a play. For now the focus will be on how you can use some of these components to cull from the play information needed in order to perform it.

Below, your reconnaissance of the play will begin with Theme, Plot, and Spectacle. Although some questions of character will begin to arise here, character will be thoroughly addressed in Chapter 14. Although the structure of the plot does reveal the rhythm of the overall play, rhythm and language will primarily be covered in Chapter 15 through the full dissection and inhabiting of a scene.

A note on Interpretation: Every actor's version of a character is only one possible interpretation of that character. Every production of a play or film is only one of the many ways that text can be staged. The important thing for you at this point in your training is to dig deeply into what the playwright offers and then follow your own creative impulses for your character as they respond to the play. Notice your own imaginative vision as you consider many aspects of the play in the exercises and worksheets throughout this chapter. Developing your creativity and imagination is paramount to your development as an artist.

Beginning Active Analysis with Reconnaissance: Surveying the Landscape of the Play

Exercise 13.1: First Reading of the Play (Everyone in theatre has a first reading, but these directions are guided by SDF)

Purpose: Usually you will begin work on a play that has already been published; however, if it is a new play and the playwright is present, as often is the case in the premiere production of a new play, then there exists a wonderful opportunity for the playwright to read her own work aloud to the company. This used to be a standard practice in some theatres but is seldom done today, deferring to the reticence of writers. With or without the playwright, when you lift the words of the play from the page to actual voices, it is an important early step in the transformation of a play from page to stage.

Tip: Perhaps you are rehearsing on your own, as often happens with class projects, and will not have time to read the play out loud in class; ask your classmates to an out-loud read-through of the play outside of class. It can be a fun way to get to know the play and each other.

Guidelines:
- When you read aloud, allow the life in the words to jump off the page and into your character's voice.
- Read for sense and allow the words to affect you.

13 RECONNAISSANCE OF THE PLAY

- Keep in mind the basic meaning of what you are communicating, and consider to whom are you speaking.
- Listen attentively to your partners, and pay particular attention to what they are trying to communicate to you. Notice what thoughts and feelings their words stir in you.
- This is a great opportunity to get a sense of the power and impact of the words alone before all the other staging choices are added.

13.1 Reflection Journal—First Impressions: Why Write Down First Impressions?

Jotting down your first impressions is very valuable as we remember that most of our audiences will only have a first impression, as they come to see the play only once (The English still often use the term *hear a play*, and the Latin origins of the word *audience*—*audientia*—means a hearing, a listening). For beginning actors, sometimes they will only read the play once, which is unfortunate. Multiple readings are necessary to fully appreciate any great work and certainly to know it well enough to convey the essence of it to an audience. Whether the first reading is for all artists involved or is done quietly in private, each artist is encouraged to write down *first impressions*. First impressions are extremely important as they are often intuitive. Also they are in some ways closer to the experience of most of your audience members, who will only see and hear the play once.

Questions to Consider: What do you experience as your first impression of this story and how it unfolds? This is easier with some plays, while others are like a sophisticated wine or a challenging poem and require more investigation to be appreciated. What stands out to you or makes some sort of impact in your first impression? What impressions do you have of the world of the play, its characters, events, and ideas? What images and associations arise in your consciousness as you read? What emotions, if any, were stirred?

At a first reading, we might note, for example, the places in the script that made us laugh. This is a good hint to you that there are opportunities for humor to explore through a variety of comic techniques.

Thought/Theme and Supertask

Every play holds ideas the playwright is weighing and trying to get her audience to consider. They may be obvious, or they may be concealed and revealed in intriguing ways. The author may want the audience to ponder a question, and may or may not offer her own answer to that question. The author may have multiple points of view on the topic expressed through multiple characters, all of which help to round out the *theme*. Each character contributes to the *ruling idea* by expressing various *themes* through their *through-line of action*. The author and the audience will generally side with one character over the others in the end.

The theme is also referred to as the *thought* or *ruling idea*, and it runs through the whole play. The *theme* contributes to the development of the playwright's point of view and in a well-written play converges throughout the play, leading to the playwright's statement called the *supertask*. (It is always valuable for the director and the actors to read other works by the playwright and to learn about the personal life and social or political events that may have influenced the author's writing of a particular play.

This is how you begin to decipher the author's viewpoint. Unless the playwright is in residence and tells you the supertask, or has written about it elsewhere, you will never know for sure what her supertask was. Try to understand it to the best of your ability with all the material available in the play and from relevant research.

The director also will have a point of view based on his interpretation of the play's *supertask*, which is variously called the *super-supertask*, *production supertask*, or *director's supertask*. This may be arrived at independently through the director's reconnaissance of the mind, or it may be arrived at in collaboration with a dramaturg and design collaborators. In Active Analysis, where the director also works collaboratively with the actors, the rehearsal explorations further shape the production supertask. The production supertask will be expressed visually and aurally through the design elements (one aspect of *spectacle*). This may be very dominant in a supernatural film or play, such as a superhero movie or a science fiction one. As the playwright's and director's supertask are bound up with the characters in unfolding action and events, the actors communicate a large part of this to the audience under the director's guidance.

Worksheet 13.2A: Preliminary Theme Overview (SDF)

The theme will emerge in more depth as you work on the play, but to gain a starting picture it is helpful to try to figure out the following:

1. What is the **topic** of the play? Can you describe the subject of the play in one word or a short phrase?
2. What is the **playwright's point of view** on this subject? This is the **theme** of the play.
3. What is the author's **supertask** (overarching impression to leave on reader/audience)?
4. The actor also can have a **super-supertask**. What might be your **reason for doing this play**? What do you hope to contribute to your audience and/or the greater community? (This may have to do with content or form. You may wish to move them emotionally in some way, make them think about some big ideas, review a familiar topic in a new way, or help them find release from life's stresses, all in the form of entertainment.)
5. Are their **minor and major themes**? Do some of them repeat throughout building and reframing with each glimpse?
6. **Whose story** is this play?
7. How is your character important to the unfolding of the theme and supertask? What **dramatic device**[3] (or plot device) does your character fulfill, such as protagonist/hero, antagonist/villain, confidant, carrier of the subplot to express a parallel plot or theme, romantic interest, comic relief, bumbling messenger, etc.
8. What **dramatic question** focuses the action and keeps the reader/watcher in suspense? The dramatic question focuses the action of the play and thus is essential to plot; however, what the director focuses on as the dramatic question is a major element of his supertask, and thus it also relates to theme. This may be what you were wondering as you read the play. It should be a question that carries you through the whole play and is not answered under the final climax or resolution.

---

[3] Robert Benedetti, *The Actor at Work*, 9th ed. (Boston: Pearson/Allyn and Bacon, 1970; 2005). The idea of considering the character's dramatic device I got from Benedetti's consideration of the character's dramatic function on pp. 111–114.

13 RECONNAISSANCE OF THE PLAY

> **Worksheet 13.2B: Research the Playwright and the Playwright's Recurring Themes (SDF)**
>
> **Purpose:** Before you can fully grasp a playwright's theme, style, or even plot structure, you will need to know more about him and the period in which he was writing.
>
> **Research on the Playwright:**
> 1. Read biographies of the playwright. Does the playwright's life shed any light on the play or help you understand where he might be coming from?
> 2. Read other works by the playwright. Do you notice any reoccurring characters or themes? You will really see this, for example, in Tennessee Williams's plays. For example, in one of his lesser-known plays, Vieux Carré (which translates as the Old Quarter), you will meet fascinating characters based on his actual time of living in a boarding house in the French Quarter of New Orleans. Many of these characters form the seeds of characters in later plays, combined with other people he knew, aspects of himself, and his imagination.
> 3. Read about the conventions of theatrical time period in which the play was written (which might be different from the period in which the play was set). This influences the content, form of the play, and how it was originally designed to be staged. For example you need to know, if you work on a Greek play, that comedy and tragedy were kept separate and violence was shown offstage and delivered onstage. In Shakespeare, all female parts were played by men, and there was little in the way of scenery beyond the architecture of the theatre so, frequently, characters deliver descriptions of the where and when.
> 4. Does this research shed light that changes your first impressions of the themes in the play?
> 5. There is other research you do based on the subject of the play: time period, location, events, and people, but that is different for each play.

13.2 Journal Reflection/Discussion—Theme

Fill out your responses on worksheet 13.2 on theme and/or discuss them with other members of the company or your scene partner. If the teacher has selected a central play for the class, this could be a class discussion.

The Plot: Analysis through Events

While the *theme* represents the content, the *plot* is a key part of the structure of the play. The plot is the carefully selected and arranged events that the author uses to reveal the story of the play in an interesting and dramatic manner. For the purposes of beginning play analysis, we are going to assume that the plot is composed in the most common structure—a climactic (sometimes called dramatic) plot. Later in your work as an actor, you will need to learn to dissect plays in Epic and other play structures. For now, reread the play to understand the context of the scene you are going to work on in relationship to the entire play. When telling a story in the form of a play in a theatrical production, we must ensure we understand the key plot points so that we can help the author tell the story in a way that important parts of it are not missed by the audience. A quick way to get a picture of a play is to see how the author unveils the story through a series of events constructed into a plot.

The plot may move along through events shown onstage, called the *first plan*. The plot may also be enhanced through events that set the play in motion before it starts (revealed through background information, or *exposition*) or in events that are referred to but not seen by the audience, and may take place between the shown scenes. All of these referenced but not shown aspects of the story are called the *second plan*.[4]

Exercise 13.3: Telling the Plot (SM/PB/SDF)

Guidelines: With your group, tell the plot of the play in terms of key characters and events. Each actor may have already analyzed the main events of the plot as outlined on worksheet 13.4 (below), or this may be the first time you have to consider the important points of the plot. Speaking the *plot points* out loud allows a collective understanding of what is important and helps everyone to see the progression of the unfolding story in their imaginations.

When telling the plot, answer the questions: "What happens first?" "And then what?... And then what?... And then what?" This gives you a quick, clear snapshot of the entire play. This is vital even if you are only working on one scene from the play, because you must understand what has happened to the characters before your scene begins, and also what your scene sets in motion for the events that follow. When you tell the plot, feel free to fill in the blanks of the story with your imagination, but be sure to have all the given facts first. Later on, we will go back over what is called *Telling the Novel*. At that time you will have an opportunity to really embellish the story with great imaginative details.

Worksheet 13.4: Climactic Plot Analysis (SDF)

1. What **dramatic question** focuses the action and keeps the reader/watcher in suspense? (If you did the theme worksheet, you already answered this above, but it is good to also put it at the top of your plot worksheet.)
2. **Snapshot of the play**. Make a list of **key events** for each scene (see sample for *A Streetcar Named Desire* on the book's companion website). Ask yourself, what happens first in the play, and then what happens, and then what? There is usually at least one key event per scene but sometimes as many as three.

---

[4] The terms *first plan* and *second plan* came to Philip Bennett from Sonia Moore, who credited it to Vladimir Nemirovich-Danchenko.

13 RECONNAISSANCE OF THE PLAY

Figure 13.1 *A Streetcar Named Desire* by Tennessee Williams, at the Young Vic and broadcast through the National Theatre Live progam. Director Ben Andrews, Gillian Anderson as Blanche, Ben Foster as Stanley, Vanessa Kirby as Stella.
Photo: Nigel Norrington/ArenaPAL

3. **Name the events** on your event breakdown. This can be a preliminary name that changes as you get to know the scene better. It helps to get a clear overall picture to give a title to the main event in each scene (usually a noun or phrase). This is only essential if you are directing the piece or working on the entire play. At a minimum, name the events in the scene you are working on *(Examples of named events include the following:* tightrope, new life, abyss, the web, quagmire, celebration, swamp, on the rocks, devastation, aftermath, war, victory, dark victory, the betrayal, conflagration, reunion, surprise, revenge, reconciliation, seduction, destruction).
4. Which is the **event without which this play would not exist**? Does it happen during the play or before the play begins, as part of the *second plan*?
5. How does the scene you will work on fit into this series of events? What goes before and affects it? What does the scene lead to later in the play?
6. What is the **point of attack**? Where in the story does this author choose to start the play? What is the very first event?
7. What is the **main conflict**?
8. What **two or more forces are in opposition** to create this conflict?
9. What **type of conflict** is it? Woman/man vs. man/woman, man vs. nature, man vs. society, man vs. the supernatural, man vs. machine?

10. Which character(s) do you identify with on reading the play? Is this character the *protagonist* (character the play is about)? Is this character the *antagonist* (character opposing the main character)?
11. What is the **inciting incident**, the incident that sets the conflict in motion?
12. What **crises** happen (small but indecisive battles between the two opposing forces)?
13. What **foreshadowing** (hints about things to come) happens to help build suspense?
14. What are the major **obstacles** (external obstacles) for the protagonist? (**Note:** It is important to understand this even if you are not playing one of the main characters. These are things that impede the protagonist from achieving his objective.)
15. What **complications** (internal obstacles) arise?
16. What **discoveries** does the main character make?
17. What **revelations** are offered?
18. Is there a **reversal of fortune** (status change) or of purpose or of the main action of the protagonist, or a change of mind or point of view by any character?
19. What is the **climax**—the final, decisive battle between the two forces?
20. What event sets the end in motion?
21. What is the **denouement** (also known as *resolution*)? What is the final event of the play?
22. **Who wins** and who loses, or is it a draw?
23. What is the **supertask** that you believe the playwright wants to leave as the final impression on the audience? This is just a preliminary idea. It may take most of rehearsal for this to really crystalize for you.
24. Which events impact your character the most, and how?

13.4 Journal/Discussion—Plot Events and Your Scene/Role

It is important that each actor does his own analysis of the plot to gain more familiarity with the play, rather than only one member of the group doing it and reporting on it. Then, it is helpful to discuss your findings with your scene partner or the entire class or company, depending on how many of you are working on the same play. Where does the event of your scene fit in relationship to the other events of the play? What has happened before you walk in and after you leave this scene? What events have affected what you do and say in the scene? What in your scene sets in motion upcoming events?

See the companion website for a sample of a full Key Events chart for *A Streetcar Named Desire*.

Purpose: Doing a chart like this for your play will help you to clearly see the entire structure of the play and will assist you in creating the *tableaux vivants* (living pictures) for the following exercises. It also will make it easy to identify which events to improvise as études (studies). Note on the chart the key events for the overall play, such as:

- the event without which there would be no play

- the point of attack
  - inciting incident
  - climax
  - event that leads to the end (sometimes the same as the climax and sometimes different)
  - resolution
  - supertask (the issue or idea the playwright has wrestled with in writing the play)
  - production supertask (the director's expression of the supertask, arrived at in collaboration with designers and transformed with the passion for doing the play today, here, and now for a specific target audience)

Spectacle, Composition, and the Mise-en-Scène

> "It's that life in that house that determines that mise-en-scène."
> —Georgi Alexandrovich Tovstonogov, Russian theatre director (1915–1989)

Aristotle spoke of spectacle, and sometimes we think of spectacle as the larger, visual aspects of a production, which in Greek plays include the choral entrances, exits, parades, dances, and masks but also special events and effects such as revealing the dead body of Agamemnon, Oedipus with his eyes gouged out and bleeding, or Medea exiting on a golden chariot. In contemporary plays the spectacle might be ideas expressed through the scenic, costume, and lighting design, or big musical song and dance numbers. In *Hamlet*, an example of spectacle is the appearance of the ghost. In film, it might be car chases and things blowing up, a spaceship landing, or an alien crawling out of someone's stomach.

A more subtle aspect of spectacle is the *subtext of behavior* that reveals the story nonverbally, moment-by-moment, in a carefully selected orchestration of moving stage compositions, which is referred to in Russia and much of the rest of Europe as the *mise-en-scène*. The mise-en-scène in modern productions generally falls under the artistic guidance of the director, but may also be developed collaboratively between the director and designers. It may be preplanned to the minutest detail or evolve throughout the rehearsal process with the creativity and input of the actors.

In your readings of the play, inevitably pictures started forming in your mind about the location, the characters, and the unfolding of events. This is an important starting place for creating the spectacle aspect of a production. The director and designers will give you their vision, and you will also need to fill out your part of this collaborative vision. After research into the world of the play and gathering information about the people who inhabit it—the characters—you must imagine how these people would move in pathways through each other's most intimate lives. Finding this *subtext of behavior,* along with the revealing of the story through the key plot points, will lead the director and actors to most illuminating mise-en-scènes.

Tableau vivant is a French term meaning "living picture." It is used to describe an artfully composed image involving living people, often costumed and lit, but not speaking or moving. Tableau vivant brings together photography, theatre, and painting. Tableau in the theatre describes a series of *stage pictures* that tell a story by means of its artistic composition. Creating tableaux can be a very fun and informative way to capture key aspects of characters and relationships, important events, and other aspects of the given circumstances and can serve to clearly express the mise-en-scène. While perhaps initially working with tableau vivant, eventually, in the theatre, the artists must discover and express how one picture evolves into the next and what transpires in between.

Sometimes the subtext of behavior works against the text, or the inner life of the characters butts against the restrictive confines of the prescribed movement of the world. We may see how the characters present themselves externally while the truth bubbles up from underneath. If you speak to someone you suspect is lying, are you paying more attention to their words or their nonverbal behavior? There are certain styles that purposely juxtapose text and action, especially in some forms of comedy. Outside of only a few styles, generally you would not want the subtext of behavior to subvert the text so much that the imaginary reality of the world of the play is violated. However, it often plays against the text in a dynamic tension, the upshot of which is only revealed later in the play.

You have been working throughout this training on developing your internal and your external monitors. Your internal monitor helps you to find the inner monologue and emotional pathways of your character. Your external monitor helps you find the correct external expression in terms of physical character, movement, and behavior, but as you develop artistically, your external monitor also helps you to sculpt your acting choices for the role in artistic ways. You must have the dual consciousness of experiencing the character in the circumstances and also conveying key aspects of why this character and these events are in the play. The director will guide you in this important aspect of spectacle, but below are a few exercises to develop your dual consciousness and sense of spectacle further.

Figure 13.2 The stage picture must clearly depict the chosen named event. Molière's *Tartuffe*, East Stroudsburg University.
Photo: Dave Dougherty

13 RECONNAISSANCE OF THE PLAY

Exercise 13.5: Named Events Tableaux (Plot and Spectacle) (PGB)[5]

Here are some guidelines for creating expressive tableaux:

Selecting the Event: Once you have done your event breakdown and figured out which of the events of the play represent key events, select one of the key events to create a tableau. This might be selected from the event without which there would be no play, or from the point of attack, inciting incident, climax, setting the end in motion, resolution, or supertask. (We suggest you explore supertask early and often as your understanding of it will grow throughout rehearsal).

- **Composition:** The stage picture must clearly depict the chosen named event.
  - Everyone must be seen to be fulfilling a **purposeful action** with an objective by means of a psychophysical pose.
  - The picture must reveal the **relationships** between the characters and the conflict of the scene.

How to Proceed:
- After completing the plot analysis for the main events through the play, make sure that you have **named the events**.
- Come up with a brief description of each, using **main actions and counteractions** that reflect qualities in the struggle of each scene or that describe a major shift in the play. (Who is doing what to whom? What has someone discovered or realized?)
- Now have someone read out the named events and descriptions in the order they appear in the play. All the members of the company or class, regardless of the role they are cast in or whether they are cast or crew, can come up and **make a picture that expresses that idea.**

Note: Try to do this quickly without a great deal of discussion. It is better to just jump up, assume a role and take an active pose than to talk a lot about it. Trust your first impulses and have fun.

---

[5] Tableau has been used for composition in theatre, mime, ballet, and other performing arts, but this way of using it was developed by Philip G. Bennett. He also came across it in workshops with artists from the Royal Shakespeare Company, who used it as part of Active Analysis.

Worksheet 13.6: Research on the Given Circumstances (Play research is done by most dedicated theatre artists, but this is guided here by SDF)

Purpose: In order to be an informed creative artist and draw from a vast reservoir of sources, actors will greatly benefit from doing *research* for most plays. Look up everything in the play or referenced by the play that you do not already understand. All of this material will become fodder for your active, creative forays into the play.

Guidelines: Remember that the given circumstances are: who (and with whom), what (and what for), where (where from, where to), when, why, and how. Of these, who and with whom, character and relationships, will be primarily addressed in Chapter 14. Why, how, and what for will be primarily explored in Chapter 15.

- For now, begin to research and actively explore what, where, and when. You cannot fully put yourself in the *magic if* that the playwright has created if you know nothing about the culture and time period in which he has set the play and if you don't know about the events described.
- There are two important time periods: when the play was written that you may already have researched in Worksheet 13.2B, and when the play is set, which you can begin to investigate here. Just a few examples: You cannot begin to enter the world of *A Streetcar Named Desire* if you know nothing about New Orleans in the 1940s, World War II (that Stanley served in), or the declining plantations of the Old South. If you don't know the history of the US South, you might not even know that although Blanche and Stella's family home, Belle Reve, was a plantation, they were born long after the ending of slavery in 1865, so they were part of the declining plantation life after slavery, not the rich life gained off the backs of free slave labor (although their ancestors certainly were a part of this indecent economic system.) Nor can you understand the choices Stella and Blanche make if you do not know the options for married and unmarried women for work during this time period.

1. **When and Where:** Research the cultures and time periods in which the play is set or which are referred to as things the characters would know about or have experienced. What was life like then for men, women, children, poor, rich, those with power, and those without?
2. **What:** Research the events that are revealed or referred to.
3. **Visual Research:** Bring in pictures that represent the locations, time period, and events. These can feed into Exercise 13.7.

13 RECONNAISSANCE OF THE PLAY

Exercise 13.7: Picture Compositions (PGB/SDF, also used by other directors)

Note: You can do this exercise as well as or instead of 13.4 above. If there is not time to do this in class, make sure to gather these pictures for your character journal and to work with them outside of class rehearsals.

- **Bring in pictures** that represent each scene in the play. It is helpful if they are artistic works in painting or photography that use human bodies, but they can also be abstract if that better reflects the style of the play.
- **Create a set of tableaux** to reflect these compositions.
- Show the tableaux one after another (like a storyboard for a film), shifting between them with a clap of the hands in the order they arise in the play.
- When it comes time to work on the specific scene, you may return to any of these tableaux or the ones from 13.4 above and try to come to the tableau in the middle of an active exploration around the main event of a scene (as described in Chapter 15: Active Analysis through Events and Actions).

Active Exploration of the Play's Events

To begin to bring the play to life, lift it from the page to the stage; explore the play's pivotal events on your feet by getting up and doing *improvisational études* (structured and focused improvisational studies) of specific aspects of the play. These work best if they are planned and structured with the same care you took to prepare for the silent and verbal improvisations in earlier chapters using the improvisation worksheets in Appendix III.

Approaching the text without the script in hand at first can seem daunting, but it's the best way to start. For the moment you don't need to think about trying to become the character—in fact, that will just get in your way. There are two types of improvisational études: *second plan*, or *backstory*, improvisations and improvisations on *main and secondary events* in the *first plan*. It really doesn't matter which ones you do first. For our immediate purposes, let's say you are choosing to do Main Event #1 on the chart above, *the event without which there would be no play*: Blanche discovers her young husband's indiscretion and denounces him, which leads to his suicide. This act initiates many of her subsequent actions, leading to the play's opening exposition. As this event happens before the start of the play, it would be a second plan event.

Exercise 13.8: Second Plan Improvisation on Main Events (You can do this exercise on the play you are studying instead of on *A Streetcar Named Desire*, but *Streetcar* is offered as an example.) (KSS/SM/PGB/SDF)

Guidelines:
- Select a key event from your entire play, such as 1) The event without which there would be no play, or 2) the climatic event.

- Build an improvisational experiment based on this event by discussing with your partners the circumstances as related in the play by Blanche in her monologue in Scene 6. Select someone to play Blanche and someone her young husband. Discuss but don't try to stage Blanche's discovery of her husband in bed with another man. Begin the second plan improvisation after, as Blanche and her husband are dancing. The setting, time of evening, atmosphere, and mood of the event are all also given in the monologue.
- Choose the main action and counteraction for the event; decide where you are coming from and why, how each of you got into that situation, etc. That's really all you need to do to get started. Use the improvisational worksheets provided in Appendix IIIa Basic and Intermediate Improvisation Worksheets and Appendix IIIb Intermediate and Advanced Improvisation Worksheets to make sure you have considered all the relevant circumstances.
- For this first improvisation focus on the *magic if*: How would I really behave in these circumstances? Figure out what you would do. Just keep the circumstances in mind, as it is the circumstances that will dictate the boundaries of your action. Go onstage to find physical actions and examine your thoughts and feelings afterward. At first come entirely from yourself. (If you attempt to play the character this soon, you run the danger of going for the result and showing rather than experiencing.) If, for example, you are playing Blanche and you are not personally homophobic, then it may only be the issue of your husband's betraying you with another person that bothers you. If you were doing the entire play, you might need to do this event improvisation a second time, adding the circumstance "if I caught my husband in bed with another doing an activity that repulsed me, what would I do?" (Blanche *is* homophobic, and it is not just the betrayal of trust but also the act she saw that disturbs her.) Consider the many questions of the *magic if*. Here are a few: How would you behave toward someone you loved and married but are suddenly repulsed by? How would you respond if you know your wife knows, but she hasn't said anything yet?

13.8 *Reflection Journal—Second Plan Improvisation on Main Event #1*

Experimentation when you are improvising is a case of trial and error. There is really no right or wrong, as finding out what is not right for the play or character also steers you toward what is. After the improvisation, reread the source text. Then evaluate with your partners and teacher what you discovered that seemed relevant to the play, and what came out that was different from what is required. If you were in rehearsal for the full play, you might redo the same improvisation, moving closer and closer to the truth of the event for the characters, but if you are only working on a scene in the play, you will likely reserve this for event improvisations connected specifically to the first and second plan of your specific scene. Of course, if you are cast as Blanche, this event is at the core of your behavior in many of the other scenes.

Questions for Consideration: Were you able to find behavior? How did acting out this important event affect you? What did you experience in communion with your partner? And most importantly: What might you glean from the improvisation that will help you to understand your role in greater depth? Remember to write down your evaluations and findings for future reference.

13 RECONNAISSANCE OF THE PLAY

> **Important note:** Do as many improvisations as possible. If time permits, improvise on the events between the scenes and acts, or if time is limited, at least create them in your mind and discuss them with the other cast members. Be precise about entrances and exits. Know where you are coming from and where you are leaving to, and why. As you learn more about the character in the next chapter, you may realize some other events in the first or second plan that are important to your character and worthy of active exploration.

Figure 13.3 Christi Berlane as Stella, Dave Auseum as Stanley, and Angel Berlane as Blanche in *A Streetcar Named Desire* by Tennessee Williams.
Photo: Stephanie Daventry French

Exercise 13.9: Floating Image Landscape (SDF)

Purpose: To begin to see images of the world and circumstances of the play. To expand your own images by the input of other members of the company.

Guidelines:
- This can be done at any time but will be most vivid after the actors have done some research, including visual research of the location, time period, and related events.
- Have the company of actors lie down in a circle with their heads toward each other in the middle. Conduct a relation exercise as outlined in Chapter 3.

- Then begin to allow images from the play to float up and speak out loud something to name or describe them in one word or a short phrase.
- Allow the images floated by others to trigger further images.
- Make sure also to be listening to the others as in the listening exercise 6.2 when you tried to say numbers or the alphabet without overlapping.
- Do this as a brainstorming exercise.

Note on Brainstorming: One caveat: There are no wrong answers except those designed to intentionally undermine the exercise. Some of the things that arise may be funny, which is great, and you can laugh, but not if they pull everyone out of the imagination of the world of the play to think, Oh, Joe is really funny. Please try to know the difference and try not to distract others as they focus on the play. It doesn't even matter if what pops out is random or a repeat of what has been already said.

Summary

Moving fluidly between Reconnaissance of the Mind and Reconnaissance of the Body, you began to unearth and actively engage with important aspects of the play as a whole. You explored theme, supertask, key events of the plot, and vivid compositions, pictures, impressions of the play. In the next chapter, you will continue active exploration and begin to move from yourself toward the character's involvement with the events and struggles of the play.

New Theatre Terms, Concepts, and Artists

Terms used in the Stanislavsky System are in italics.

- ☐ climax
- ☐ *embodiment*
- ☐ *event without which the play would not exist*
- ☐ *first plan*
- ☐ key events
- ☐ main conflict
- ☐ *mise-en-scène*
- ☐ *reconnaissance of the body*
- ☐ *reconnaissance of the mind*
- ☐ recurring themes (leitmotif)
- ☐ *role*
- ☐ *second plan*
- ☐ *subtext of behavior*
- ☐ *supertask*
- ☐ *super-supertask*
- ☐ tableau (singular)
- ☐ tableaux (plural)
- ☐ *Telling the Novel (the story)*
- ☐ thought (theme)
- ☐ Georgi Alexandrovich Tovstonogov
- ☐ who loses?
- ☐ who wins?
- ☐ Tennessee Williams

13 RECONNAISSANCE OF THE PLAY

Interdisciplinary Terms and Concepts

- Agamemnon
- Aristotle
- *audientia:* (Latin for "audience")
- complications (internal obstacles)
- composition
- crisis
- denouement (resolution)
- diction (language)
- discoveries
- dramatic device (plot device)
- dramatic question
- dramaturg
- event that leads to the end
- exposition
- Hamlet
- inciting incident (inciting event)
- landscape of the play
- Medea
- music (rhythm)
- Oedipus
- parallel themes
- point of attack
- production concept
- revelations
- reversals of fortune
- spectacle

CHAPTER 14

Active Analysis: Reconnaissance of the Character

"To reach an understanding of a difficult role, an actor must go to the limits of his personality and intelligence—but sometimes great actors go further still if they rehearse the words and at the same time listen acutely to the echoes that arise in them."[1]

—Peter Brook

Stanislavsky Techniques Actively Explored

Reconnaissance of the mind; reconnaissance of the body; supertask; amalgamation; telling the character's story; embodying biography; seed, theme and supertask; character's second plan; relationships

Other Theatre Concepts Explored

Character embodiment; character dynamics; psychological gesture

Part I: Reconnaissance of the Mind: Objective Character Analysis

- **Unearthing Gifts from the Playwright**
  - Exercise 14.1: Reading the Play for Character
  - Worksheet 14.2: Objective Character Analysis
  - Worksheet 14.3: Subjective Character Analysis—Autobiography
  - Exercise 14.4: Autobiographical Character Diary and Artistic Scrapbook
  - Exercise 14.5: Finding Alternative Behavior

Part II: Reconnaissance of the Body: Improvisational Character Études

- **Amalgamation**
  - Exercise 14.6: Telling the Story of the Play from Your Character's Viewpoint
  - Exercise 14.7: Character Embodiment and Movement Dynamics
  - Exercise 14.8: A Beginning for Psychological Gesture
- **Three-Step Outline for the Embodiment of the Seed/Theme/Supertask**
- **Seed, Theme, and Supertask**
  - Exercise 14.9: Seed, Theme, and Supertask
  - Exercise 14.10: Activating the Seed, Theme, and Supertask in the Text
  - Exercise 14.11: Character Interviews
  - Exercise 14.12: Relationship Interviews
  - Exercise 14.13: Improvisation—Character Second Plan

[1] Peter Brook, *The Empty Space* (New York: Simon & Schuster, 1968), 110.

14 RECONNAISSANCE OF THE CHARACTER

The playwright is the original designer of the character. The director and costume designer work together on some visual ideas for the characters designed to express the production supertask. The director also influences the interpretation of character by casting a specific actor and by how he guides the actor in rehearsals. However, while speaking the words as the playwright wrote them and fulfilling the production concept, you, the actor, step into the character's shoes and bring him to life. You become the designer of the role for this production.

Directors know that you will come to understand that character much more intimately than they do. After initial forays to get to know the entire play, the actor must focus on seeing the world and events of the play from the point of view of his character. It is you who will invest the character's motivations and responses to events and other characters. You will focus your entire psychophysical instrument to fulfill the actions, meet the obstacles, engage in the relationships, and experience the thoughts and emotional responses of the character. You will experience the life of this human being as manifest on stage.

PART I: RECONNAISSANCE OF THE MIND: OBJECTIVE CHARACTER ANALYSIS

The purpose of these first forays into the script is to gather source material and stimulate possibilities for your active explorations soon to follow. The actor's initial approach to the character, reconnaissance of the mind, is an objective survey that shares similarities with literary analysis or the preliminary analysis you did for the play as a whole. The actor combs the play for references and clues to the character. This involves getting to know the landscape of the play through considerations of the components of drama, as outlined in the previous chapter, and getting to know the landscape of the character through specific analysis and research as outlined below.

Unearthing Gifts from the Playwright

Exercise 14.1: Reading the Play for Character (KSS/SM/PGB/SDF)

Purpose: Before you begin to interpret and create a character, it is essential to gather everything the playwright has given you about that character. Find quotes that reveal information about your character from the entire play, even if you are only working on one scene or even only one monologue. In each category, make note of specific lines that lead you to this information so that you keep relating interpretation back to the source text. In the rare case that the character is in a series of plays or that the play is based on a novel, you should gather all you can from those sources as well. The first part of character analysis is objective.

Guidelines: After an exploration of the overall play as outlined in Chapter 13, now reread the entire play paying more attention to your character specifically. Worksheet 14.2 will give you an overview of the types of information you want to be looking for in this reading. Glance at it ahead of reading for character and fill it out after this reading.

Worksheet 14.2: Objective Character Analysis (SDF; again, many teachers have some form of character worksheet to gather similar information)

Important note: This worksheet should be completed after Exercise 14.1. It is essential to use the entire play to answer these questions, not just your scene.

1. What **plot device**[2] does your character serve to further the plot? (e.g., protagonist-hero/heroine, love interest, confidant, antagonist-enemy, wise teacher, sidekick, authority figure, messenger, to name only a few)
2. **Gather biographical circumstances given by the playwright.** This step takes time, but do not skip or skim:
   a. Did he grow up in the country, suburbs, or city? Where does he live now?
   b. Was his early environment supportive or challenging? Describe the home and the neighborhood.
   c. How many siblings does he have? Where is he in the family order? Are his parents married, divorced, or never married?
   d. How was the family supported economically? How does he support himself now? What economic class is he in? Has that changed?
   e. Does the author let you know of any important formative events in the character's early years?
   f. Note any other biographical information given.
   g. What quotes by the playwright are most revealing of your character?
3. **Relationships: Draw a Relationship Map**[3] **(SDF)** This is like a map of the solar system (circles with names in them) showing which characters are closest to you).
   a. Put your character's name in the circle in the middle of a piece of paper with the other characters in circles around it.
   b. Draw a line between your character and the other characters.
   c. On top, put your character's role relationship to each (such as father, ex-wife, or boss).
   d. Below the line, write what the relationship is like (such as, We are close. We hate each other. There is a history of betrayal or a dangerous secret between us.)
   e. How do others see your character? Jot down things that other characters say about you. Make sure to note who said it, as that person's view may be colored by his relationship with you.

---

[2] Get from Chapter 13.
[3] The next three visual exercises were created by French: the Relationship Map 14.1; Like Me/Unlike Me Chart 14.2; and Character Dichotomy Figure 14.3.

14 RECONNAISSANCE OF THE CHARACTER

Character Relationship Map

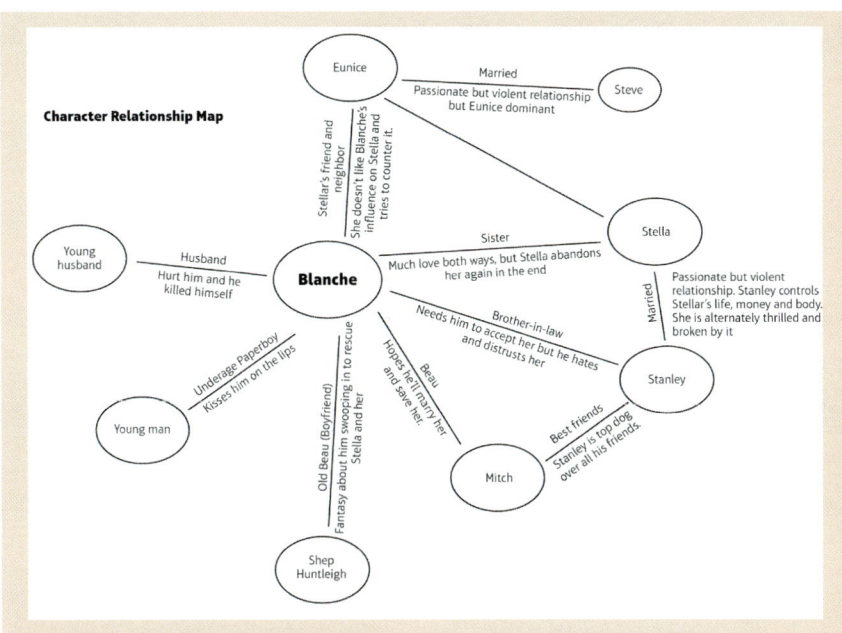

[Diagram: Character relationship map centered on Blanche, showing connections to:]
- **Eunice** — Stellar's friend and neighbor. She doesn't like Blanche's influence on Stella and tries to counter it.
- **Steve** — Married to Eunice. Passionate but violent relationship but Eunice dominant.
- **Stella** — Sister. Much love both ways, but Stella abandons her again in the end.
- **Stanley** — Brother-in-law. Needs him to accept her but he hates and distrusts her. Married to Stella: Passionate but violent relationship. Stanley controls Stellar's life, money and body. She is alternately thrilled and broken by it.
- **Mitch** — Beau. Hopes he'll marry her and save her. Best friends with Stanley; Stanley is top dog over all his friends.
- **Shep Huntleigh** — Old Beau (Boyfriend). Fantasy about him swooping in to rescue Stella and her.
- **Young man** — Underage Paperboy. Kisses him on the lips.
- **Young husband** — Husband. Hurt him and he killed himself.

Figure 14.1 Sample character/relationship map for Blanche in *Streetcar*.

4. **Character Dichotomy Figure: Perception and Projection of Character (SDF)**
   Guidelines: Draw the outline of a person (it can be a more human shape or as simple as a gingerbread man; the ideas matter more than the drawing art). Only the outline is necessary for this exercise, no features. On the inside of the shape, write how your character feels about himself. On the outside, how he tries to present himself to the world (this might be an interesting one to do for yourself, too).

[Figure: outline of a person with labels]

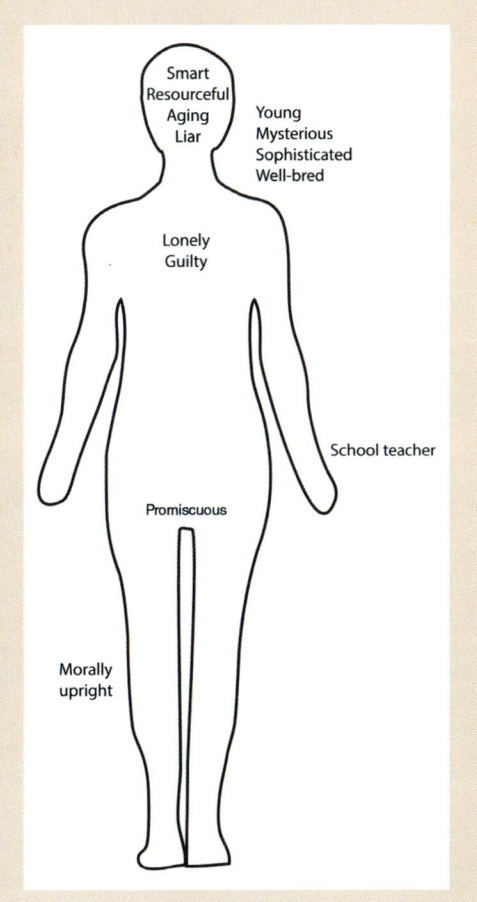

Outside (projection): Smart, Resourceful, Aging, Liar (head area); Young, Mysterious, Sophisticated, Well-bred; School teacher; Morally upright

Inside (perception): Lonely, Guilty; Promiscuous

Figure 14.2 Sample character dichotomy for Blanche in *Streetcar*.

5. **Like You/Unlike You Adjectives Chart (SDF):** Make a list with three columns. In column one, list adjectives to describe your character, then at the top of the next two columns, write **like you** in one and **unlike you** in the other. Place a checkmark or X to select the one that is more relevant.

Blanche Dubois	Like me	Unlike me
Flirtatious	X	
Smart	X	
Resourceful	X	
Liar		X
Alcoholic		X
Fragile	X	X
Beautiful		X
Aging	X	

Figure 14.3 Sample character adjectives chart from *Streetcar*.

6. **Character and Events and Character Arc**
   a. Which events of the play's first or second plan impact your character most? Why and how?
   b. Which events cause your character to evolve during the play? If so, in what way? Is this change gradual or sudden?
   c. In a few words, what is the journey of your character from beginning to end of the play?

7. **Imagining Your Character—Filling in the Gaps**
   Now, based on the facts offered by the playwright and the facts of the time period and location in which the play is set that you already researched as part of Chapter 12, fill out additional character information with your imagination:
   a. What is important to your character's generation?
   b. What would he put down in a social media profile?
   c. Is there a secret he holds that might shape this character?
   d. Does the character have a psychological burden, something that weighs on her mind and influences her behavior?
   e. What drives your character (seed)? Examples: love, lust, greed, power, revenge.
   f. If your character were an animal, what would it be?

   Supertask. What is your first impression of your character's supertask? What is the impression the playwright wants the audience to have about this character?

8. **Problem.** What is my character's problem in this situation, or with this person in this scene?

9. **Task/Objective.** What do I want to change about this situation or person?
   Important note: While some, in moving from Method of Physical Actions to Active Analysis, have abandoned the term *objective*, we find it a helpful tool, and it is commonly used in the theatre and in the larger culture. Although the struggle to solve the problem is the main thing to engage in during the present moment of acting, it still gives rise to the outcome your character wishes for in this struggle, which is an objective. How does your character want the problem to be solved? Answer it by saying, "How can I . . ." then fill in what you want.

10. **Typical Action Steps.** What do I do to try to change it? This may be through verbal or physical efforts or both. Try to list these in active, infinitive verb form: to accuse, to deny, to threaten. If you write "to be happy," that is passive, whereas "to convince him I am happy" would be active.
11. **Biggest Fear.** What is something your character is most afraid of doing or showing or encountering? Plays often push characters to this brink.
12. **Character Research** (In Chapter 12 you conducted research relevant to the play. Now do research specific to your character.)

    Time period: Note the time period your character grew up in and lives in now. What events of that period might feed into his outlook? One good source is that year's almanac, which will tell you major world events (e.g., the first man landed on the moon; the NYC World Trade Center was destroyed on 9/11/2001; World War II (1939–1945); the Great Depression of the 1930s; etc.). Print out articles, highlight them with notes, and put a summary of key findings relevant to the character and the play.

    Location: Do image research on all the locations of the play and of your character's history. Make a collage (or draw if you are so inclined).

    Research people: Find a collage of images of how you think you look and of how the people important to you might look. Look for people in the world around you who are more like your character than you are.

    Research circumstances and events: Find out your character's experiences in the play that are not familiar to you; for example, in *Streetcar* you might not know about the economics of declining plantations after the end of slavery, or about working in the Corps of Engineers during World War II. In the *Crucible*, you might not know about the historical Salem witch trials or the McCarthy hearings of the 1950s, both of which impact the supertask as played out through the characters and events.

    Find evocative images and objects: These may be of people or of other things, but they remind you of some aspect of your character. Create a scrapbook or collage of these images. Russian actor and teacher Michael Chekhov often had specific, metaphoric images of his characters in action that captured their essence. Director Jane Brody of Chicago works with research of heroes or gods from various cultures that might represent your character. Chekhov and others, such as Professor Lionel Walsh of the University of Windsor, work with archetypes. These options can be great, as they include both positive and negative attributes, thus fueling a more complex and interesting character.

Worksheet 14.3: Subjective Character Analysis— Autobiography (KSS/SM/PGB/SDF)

Purpose: Prepare to migrate from the objective analysis (looking at a character) to the subjective (looking at the world from the character's point of view). The first step is to try to think as the character about her situation, then, in the next chapter, you will learn techniques to step into the character's shoes and to embody the character while thinking on your feet.

Guidelines: Write a *one page* autobiography of thoughts in the character's own words using the first person "I." Focus on a central obsession or problem the character struggles with or a key past event. Try to capture the way the character would think and the way he uses language. (This is important in order to take the step from objective analysis to subjective experience of starting to think as the character.)

Exercise 14.4: Autobiographical Character Diary and Artistic Scrapbook (Ongoing) (PB; also done by other acting teachers)

Autobiographical Diary: As you begin active work on your role, you will want to keep a running record of your character's thoughts and experiences. Staying in the first person, "I," translate the facts of the play into a story of your life as the character. Include everything. Use your creative imagination to fill in the blanks that are not in the play.

Note: Over the years, Bennett has seen actors who have had relatively small roles and few, if any, lines be so present and alive on stage that we understand everything they are thinking, feeling, and reacting to without having to say a word! When I staged Anton Chekhov's *The Three Sisters*, one of our company's leading actresses was cast as a maid who had absolutely no lines whatsoever; yet, whenever she entered the stage, you felt that she brought her entire life with her. Remember, "There are no small roles only small actors."[4] As you learn more about your character, continue to write in your journal. If you are diligent, it will work wonders for you.

Artistic Scrapbook: Keeping in mind the dual perspectives of the actor, there are also notes you might want to make from the point of view of yourself as the artist creating this role, helpful observations from rehearsals and life, evocative research, odd things that remind you of the character even if you don't know why yet.

---

[4] This was one of the founding principles of the Moscow Art Theatre.

14 RECONNAISSANCE OF THE CHARACTER

> **Exercise 14.5: Finding Alternative Behavior (PGB/SDF; other acting teachers do it also)**
>
> **Purpose:** This will help you to expand from your own typical ways of moving, behaving, and talking to find those that may be more appropriate for your character. From this you can collect behaviors and responses to borrow for your character, but you must study them carefully so that you can connect the externally observed behavior to internal thoughts and responses.
>
> **Guidelines:** After you have a sense of the ways that the character is different from you and you have filled out some of that in research, it is particularly helpful to observe people who are more like the character than you are. The people you observe may only have one attribute like the character, and you may need to observe multiple people in multiple situations.
>
> - Think about places people like your character would go and find a way to be there and observe, without anyone knowing you are observing.
> - Find examples of people or even just behavior that reminds you of your character. Either at that moment, if you can do it without being noticed, or after you get to a separate location, write down in detail everything about the behavior and person you observed. You need enough detail to re-create it realistically.
> - It is particularly good if you can observe this source-person fulfilling a task or struggling with a problem.
> - Re-create the behavior in a private place or in your acting class if asked. Try to bring in as many details as possible so that the behavior stirs thoughts and feelings.
> - Bring the behavior to try in rehearsal where it seems most appropriate in exercises or scene work.

PART II: RECONNAISSANCE OF THE BODY: IMPROVISATIONAL CHARACTER ÉTUDES

It is reconnaissance of the body, the subjective exploration and inhabiting of a character, that distinguishes the actor from the critic and the actor of depth from the superficial actor. The director generally does not take this step himself, although when conducting rehearsals through the process of Active Analysis, will help to orchestrate this exploration.

   If you stay in the objective idea of your character, looking at him from the outside, you will show rather than experience the character. This is *indicating*. Indicating either character or behavior is not believable and does not invite the audience into the experience. When showing a preconceived idea rather than being alive with what is happening in the circumstances, you will not affect your scene partners, allow them to affect you, nor move your audience. You don't want to be this actor or act with this actor (although unfortunately sometimes you will have to be onstage with such actors). This is a trap for untrained or lazy actors, not the impression you want to make on directors. To avoid indicating, enter fully into the problems the play presents and fulfill detailed actions as you struggle in specific circumstances.

As discussed in the previous chapter, you must first gather all the facts given by the playwright and revealed by your character and by other characters. Then, through imagination and active explorations or études, connect the dots between the known points, thus catching glimpses of the vast unknown. These second plan improvisations can be solo, partner, or group. Generally, it is helpful to start with a solo nonverbal improvisation. A solo nonverbal improvisation will help you to focus on your physical behavior to ensure that your body is expressive, active, and alive. Once you have accomplished that, you may then proceed to verbal character improvisations with scene partners.

Amalgamation

The complete psychophysical merger of your inner life and body with the imaginary life of the character is called *amalgamation*. Amalgamation of your creative resources into a living work of art takes time and a lot of practice. Be patient, work consistently, and it will come. The first step is to experience that you exist, to step into the character's shoes. Not that you *are* the character, or believe you are, as that would mean you are crazy, but rather that you immerse yourself into the character's given circumstances, motivations, behavior, and ways of thinking. Allow yourself to respond as the character would in the situation. The more you can invest or *up the stakes* in what the character cares about, the more you see the clear images of the other characters and the world of the play, the more the events of the play will affect you.

The following *exploratory studies of your character* are generated to dig into the character's inner life in order to bring you into the state of "I exist," as mentioned in previous chapters, and prepare the way for experiencing, which is one of the main

Figure 14.4 The more you can invest in what the character cares about, the more the events of the play will affect you. Elyse Burnett as Gret, Eldee as Lady Nijo (and in background, Naomi Snyder as Pope Joan, and Michelle Jones as Griselda). *Top Girls* by Caryl Churchill. Photo: Bob Weidner, courtesy of East Stroudsburg University

14 RECONNAISSANCE OF THE CHARACTER

purposes for using Active Analysis. When active on stage, it is important to speak of the character in the first person, "I," rather than stepping outside and saying "he" or "she." This practice will help you to begin to merge with your character in order to bring to life the role. It will also ensure that you are able to bring a fully detailed, moving and speaking human being to artistic fruition rather than a generalized impression.

> **Exercise 14.6: Telling the Story of the Play from Your Character's Viewpoint (SM, influenced by studying Brecht in German from Berliner Ensemble Rehearsal Techniques and brought to PGB/This approach guided by PGB/SDF)**
>
> **Purpose:** Very often at the beginning of rehearsals some directors choose to tell the story of the play from their perspective, their director's concept. This exercise gives you, the actor, an opportunity to actively move from the playwright's and director's point of view on the whole play into the character's perspective.
>
> The actor **tells the story of the play** in the first person as the character might see and discuss the unfolding events and relevant characters. This character may not be involved in all events, may not have the whole picture, and certainly will have a unique perspective on each of them. Try to use this character's language and perspective as much as possible. If there is not time to do this in rehearsal or class, we suggest the actor either writes his story or dictates it into a recorder so as to complete this exercise for himself.
>
> **Note:** It's a very valuable rehearsal tool for the director/teacher to permit each actor to tell his story's viewpoint to the cast early on in the rehearsal process. If time does not permit that, then it is equally valuable to have one actor tell his story at each subsequent rehearsal. This tool keeps the actors engaged in the creative process throughout the rehearsal period and strengthens the ensemble goal of collective creativity.

> **Context and Perspective**
>
> "There is nothing either good or bad, but thinking makes it so."
> —William Shakespeare (*Hamlet*, Act 2, scene 2)
>
> An event unfolds and, as Shakespeare observes in the above quote from *Hamlet*, we give it meaning—ignore it, react to it, or embrace it. In life and in theatre, different characters' perspectives, as well as the culture and the time period, shape the interpretation of the event, give it context. A technique in cognitive psychology involves putting a familiar but disturbing event into a new cognitive frame in order to shift perspective from a stuck place to a place of possibilities. The unfolding event may not be either bad or good, except by our interpretation, which inevitably is colored by our life and cultural experience. Similarly, when three different people are asked to recount the

same event, each remembers it slightly differently. In marriage counseling, often each spouse has a divergent memory of events or interpretation of a recent event. The counselor tries to help each person see the event from the other's perspective in an attempt to remove the personally imposed clouded story and dissect the actual facts of the event. In a play, however, we want to bring out each character's unique point of view and response to the events. You must give the events context that is both relevant to your character and meaningful to you.

Exercise 14.7: Character Embodiment and Movement Dynamics (MC/JW/PGB/SDF)[5]

(These exercises can be done in sequence or separately)

Purpose: Character embodiment requires moving from thinking about the character (objective analysis) to thinking and responding as the character to embodying the character. Embodying the character means you are thinking deeply while simultaneously making physical choices that express her unique behavior moment-to-moment. Once you have composed your autobiography, it is time to start to stand, move, behave, and respond as the character. If you have not already completed preliminary character analysis outlined in worksheets 13.2A and 13.2B, for best results, complete this prior to embarking on the following active character études.

Guidelines: It helps to first do these exercises in comfortable clothing and shoes in order to safely explore the widest range of possibilities, and then to do the movement exercises again with rehearsal costumes. Costumes shape the body of the character. Start with the shoes, as we walk so differently in steel-toed boots, hard-soled dress shoes, heels, flip-flops, or sneakers. Consider which other costumes, aspects, or accessories might shape your character's stance and movement, such as fitted jackets, skirts, heavy coats, or accessories such as hats, purses, handkerchiefs (even if you don't have the correct items bring in mock-ups of your own to rehearsal (such as a shirt tied around your waist to represent an apron). In period play you want to work as early as possible with wigs, corsets, hoop skirts, fans, snuff boxes, walking sticks, and the like.

---

[5] Apparently the origins of the stepping into the character exercise are from Michael Chekhov, where Philip G. Bennett learned it, but French learned it through the oral tradition from Jessica Litwak, who credited it to Shakespeare and Company in Connecticut, USA. The active exploration of this exercise was created by French, pulling together some character embodiment observed working with Julie Hebert, some of Laban's ideas in his efforts, and French's version of how to actively approach Michael Chekhov's psychological gesture ideas from his book, *To the Actor*.

14 RECONNAISSANCE OF THE CHARACTER

Exercise 14.7A: Visualizing and Embodying Character (MC/JL/PGB/SDF)

Guidelines: Before beginning, place a few chairs around the space and leave a wide area open for movement.

- Stand in a circle.
- Come to a **neutral body** stance (As outlined in Chapter 5: The Psychophysical Instrument under "Tadasana") so that you do not begin to create a character with all your own unique physical quirks.
- Close your eyes and **picture your character** based on the adjectives and the picture you created from your character analysis in Chapter 13: Reconnaissance of the Play, and as you were reading through the play.
- See the character in a typical indoor or outdoor environment the equivalent of a block away. **Observe the character standing**. What kind of posture do you notice? What would his silhouette be?
- **Notice the character walking** toward you. What qualities of movement do you witness? Where does the character's movement stem from? This center might be any part of the body, but some common ones are head, chest, heart, shoulders, stomach, or groin. What kind of external tempo and internal rhythm does he demonstrate? What is the quality of his movement?
- **Hear the character talking** aloud or humming a little tune. What part of the body does his voice come from? What resonators or articulators shape it most strongly? What is the spirit of the talk or song?
- Now imagine the character is approaching your neutral body. Ask the character's permission to come up behind him and step into his body. Imagine that you could dissolve the front of your body and the back of the character's body, and then from behind **step into the character's body** so that you are looking out through the character's eyes. How does the presence of this person change your internal energy? How does he change the way you stand, where the weight of your body falls?
- Open your eyes but keep your focus soft and more internal so as not to bump into anyone but not to engage with them either.
- Begin to walk and explore the character's center—the part of the body the character moves from. For a while, exaggerate this part of the body just to ensure you have made a clear choice, and then move more naturally. If you are not sure, explore leading from different parts of the body. Some more common ones might be characters that lead from the head (eyes, or ears, or a jutting chin, mouth, lips, nose—each of these is different), from the chest (open heart or puffed from bravado or collapsed in fear), from the appetites (such as stomach or groin), or even the shoulders, hips, knees, legs.
- Go to the chairs and try sitting down motivated from this center, lying on the floor, and standing up and walking again.
- Explore walking in the character's circumstances and explore the length of your stride, the tempo of your gait.

Exercise 14.7B: Embodying Biography (PB)

- Create and act out a typical day in the life of your character. You are rising in the morning and preparing for the day through a series of morning tasks, or pick another typical task that your character spends a lot of time doing, such as a hobby, work-related activities, etc. Explore these behaviors in detail while observing how they are affected by the following considerations:
- What **height** am I? (The character may be a different height than you. While you will not actually be taller or shorter, except by high shoes, you can come across as taller or shorter just by imagining yourself so.)
- How much do I **weigh?** (Same as above.)
- What is my **age,** and how does that affect my movement, its flexibility and capacities to accomplish simple physical tasks?
- Do I have any **physical and/or psychological hindrances**?
    - If so, what are they, and how do they affect your body? How do they affect you psychologically?
    - Do you have weak knees, or a bad hip?
    - Do you have impairment to sight or hearing?
    - Am I in pain, where? How does pain affect my movement, mood and attitude? Place your hand on the part of the body that is in pain. Notice this gesture. When might it occur in the play where the character's pain is activated?
- What is my **attitude** toward the world? Express it in various poses?
- Begin to sculpt your body in a typical pose of the character by placing your feet in an asymmetrical position as if to be ready to walk.
- Then sculpt your torso to express what is in your mind at the moment of making a decision to walk.
- Adjust your arms and hands to carry the energy from the spine into the preparation for the action.
- Explore different static poses that express and project a variety of actions: To reach for an object, to inquire and find out something, to examine an object of interest, to evaluate a problem or dilemma.
- Activate the spine with thought, movement, and action in the character's circumstances; allow the changes to affect your feelings.
- Use wonderment and evaluation (as learned in W.E.D.G.A.G. in previous chapters) as you reach for objects and discover gestures that might be useful in the creation of your character's psychophysiology.

14 RECONNAISSANCE OF THE CHARACTER

Exercise 14.7C: Character Dynamics (Adapted by SDF from Laban's Efforts)[6]

- Stay (or return to) your character's stance and moving from his center. Explore each of the following movement qualities, and using your internal monitor, notice how they affect your internal landscape. Using your external monitor, consider what this quality conveys about your character. Which seem most in, and most out, of your character's comfort zone?
- Allow new circumstances, images, or thoughts to arise that might justify why your character is moving in this way. (Remember that plays are not about everything going on as usual for characters, but about unusual events; characters are challenged and tested by conflict, and it is their struggle to overcome obstacles that gives us the opportunity to see who they really are underneath the surface and, furthermore, to witness how they and the playwright might want us to see them.)
- **Explore tempo.** The natural pace you fell into for the moving from center exercise, and that you observed for your character, you can call 3. Now explore slower than that as 2, then very slow as 1. With each tempo consider why your character might be moving at this pace, what would prompt him to do so. Now return to medium and then move quicker than that at 4, so fast you are almost running. Bump up to 5 so that you are running and practically flying because you are moving so fast.
- **Explore feeling heavy and light.** First be as heavy as you can; most people slow down when they do this, but try moving heavily at various tempos. By counting up from 5 to 1 get lighter and lighter until at 1 you are walking on air. Again through each tempo consider what might lift or weigh on your character to evoke each of these.
- **Explore sustained or sudden.** Move steadily and evenly (sustained quality). Move in a series of bursts (staccato quality). Move in a sudden spurt.
- **Explore direct and indirect.** Again walking, sitting, lying, and even shaking hands with others. *Direct* means that you move in straight lines, right angles, with purpose. *Indirect* is lacking direction (aimless) or sneaky, like a cat or snake, or seductive, to name only a few qualities that often are indirect. Begin to consider the others around you and greet them directly or indirectly.
- **Explore the dynamics that shape your relationships to others.** Do you draw (pull) others to you, or come at them like a force (push), or avoid them? (Express these dynamics with physical gestures such as putting your arms out and pulling or pushing, lifting or pushing downward to crush.) Do you like to have attention or shy away from it? Do you put your sexuality out there or hide it? Do you like to be in control? Do you like to lead or follow? Do you play high or low status (as explored earlier in Chapter 7: Discovering and Endowing Circumstances)?
- Now select from each exploration above those that seem **most fitting for your character.** Choose from the five speeds from 1 (super slow) to 5 (super fast). Select from the scale of 5 = heavy to 1 = light. Select sudden or sustained. Select push or pull. Select direct or indirect. Select lift or crush.

---

[6] French learned this from Bert Houle and Sophie Wibaux Mime Theater (Decroux Mime) in San Francisco, California, but later discovered it was adapted from Laban's Efforts. She has adapted her version of Laban's Efforts for use as a character embodiment exercise.

> **14.7** *Reflection Journal—Character Études (Record in Your Character Diary)*
>
> After each exercise above or at the end of the full sequence if they are done all together, take some time right away to reflect on your discoveries. This is very important to consolidate the learning and discovery of the active process so that it can be carried into the next stages of Active Analysis. If you must rush off to another class or appointment, then do this as soon as possible, before the impressions fade from memory. Starting with the above exercises and moving forward into the moment-to-moment Active Analysis, jot down the mental images from your own life as they merge with imaginary images from the play. Images, as with all other notes on your script, must be written down in pencil and continuously changed, enhanced, and improved upon, or they will either disappear or go stale during the run of a play.

Exercise 14.8: A Beginning for Psychological Gesture[7]

Purpose: The creation of character is never fixed but always living, growing, evolving. This exercise trains you to respond spontaneously to all stimulation, including exploratory exercises, rehearsals, and what happens in performance.

Guidelines: Bring the character's body explored and created through the embodiment exercises into this next exploration.

- Walking around the room in this body, start to hum or talk you yourself as the character, noticing which of the resonators your character uses more, which of the articulators, such as teeth, lips, or gums, might be important. When creating a character voice it is much safer for your vocal instrument to create it by using in healthy ways, but with different emphasis, the articulators and resonators you learned about in Chapter 9: Embodying Voice and Chapter 10: Activating Speech. Most people not experienced in voice create voices from their throats, but with eight performances a week and projecting in a large theatre, you risk hurting or losing your voice if you do this.
- Consider what your character most wants. While fulfilling a related gesture that involves the whole body, speak out loud the following line, filling in the blank, "I want _____." Try at least three different ones, then settle on one.
- Select one of these desires and gestures and begin to expand it. Number 1 is the level you just completed, 2: a little larger, 3: larger, 4: larger than life, 5: like circus or grand opera, or the biggest happy dance you ever did, involving your entire body in an exaggerated way.
- Then adapt the gesture to a truthful size for your character, time-period, style of the play, and performance medium (live small theatre, large theatre, camera). Keep the same essence of the gesture, but adapt it to size.
- Then come back to a circle and in turn share your gestures. If your scene partner is in the circle and it fits, do the gesture toward her.

---

[7] This exercise was created by French based on reading Michael Chekhov's *To the Actor* on psychological gesture. It is a very simple preliminary exploration of this idea for first embodiment of character. It is not intended to replace more-involved explorations of psychological gesture or character supertask that may happen in later rehearsals.

14 RECONNAISSANCE OF THE CHARACTER

Three-Step Outline for the Embodiment of the Seed/Theme/Supertask

Best used during the early stage of rehearsals:

A. Know Thyself: A meditative and physical exploration of the student's personal seed—theme—supertask as he begins work on a role. (This stage is intended to help the student understand how his own personal seed expresses itself as themes, which motivate and energize actions leading to their dream and goal in life.

Can be immediately used with Part A or during the middle period of rehearsal when the actors begin to have a grasp of their verbal and physical actions:

B. Embody the Character's Perspective: A preliminary sculpting exploration where the actors place themselves into character and hypothesize about the seed—theme—supertask. (This is both an intellectual and intuitive experimental approach where ideas are allowed to emerge into consciousness without a preconceived outcome.)

Best used during the latter rehearsal period when physical actions need to be reviewed and refined, and/or even after the play opens in order to refresh performances. If used in combination with Parts A and B early in the rehearsal period, Part C can be used to motivate the students to research the play more thoroughly. Your choice.

C. Application—Put the Text in Action: The purpose of this exploration is to make choices from the text, then to find physical actions while on one's feet to express the seed—theme—supertask of the character for those moments selected from the script.

Seed, Theme, and Supertask

The *seed*, also called *kernel*, refers to the original idea that first entered the playwright's mind, germinated there, and took root, giving birth to the play and its characters. The germinating idea has power, a vital life-force (prana) of its own that pushes its way like a human embryo into physical existence. Sometimes a playwright gets an idea for a play from something he or she has read, heard about, or actually witnessed. Events that give rise to a germinating idea in an artist's mind can come from any source. Actors also have original and authentic creative ideas that germinate and take root in the subconscious regions of mind while working on a role. Think of the seed as a living organism that has the potential for life, growth, and fruition, just like the seed of a flower or tree that you might plant in your garden. When the conditions of the environment are right, the seed will send out its roots, develop stems, and grow. The blossom and seeds that our plant produces are its primary purpose for existence and are akin to the supertask of your character: "The act completed."[8]

---

[8] "The act completed"—a phrase used by Philip G. Bennett to describe the culmination of the Supertask of a play and character as it manifests in the form of a stage picture.

When working on a role, ask: What is the seed idea of the play and my character? How does my character's seed develop and contribute to the play? In other words, you need to identify the main idea and **name** it. Naming the seed identifies the character traits you will need to physically embody in your role.

When naming a seed idea, it is important to come up with the simplest one or two words possible. (Stanislavsky advises us to distill an entire idea into one or two words; and when we can do this, we have a full grasp of the concept.) Seed words need to be powerful because they will release the emotional energy that will drive your character's actions throughout the play. They also need to describe the very essence of your character, her traits.

The Greek philosophers Plato and Aristotle identified the most desirable human traits to be courage, wisdom, temperance, and justice. Words like *power, revenge, love, happiness, ambition* are excellent seed words because they are emotionally charged. You might want to look for motivating forces by examining the Seven Virtues: honesty, truth, duty, loyalty, compassion, humility, selflessness. Or, perhaps you might choose one of the Seven Deadly Sins: pride, greed, wrath, envy, slander, lust, or sloth. As an actor you can identify with these words because they excite your imagination and assist you in your exploration of the themes that will give power and meaning to your character's traits and behavior.

Sometimes a character has a hybrid seed, like honesty and wrath. In such cases the contrasting seeds will be expressed in the character's internal struggle. There are no real or absolute rules about choosing the seed. What is most important is that you search for it as you work on the character. If you have difficulty identifying the seed, then look to the main themes of your play. Well-written plays develop their themes through the characters, who, in turn, drive the play's action. In other words, the characters are the embodiment of the plays *thematic score and action*. Identify the play's themes and ask yourself which of them best describes your character.

Always identify your character's main theme; however, great classical and contemporary writers often have at least three themes for a well-defined character: *Primary, Secondary and Tertiary* themes. Search for the primary theme first and then when you feel it is correct, identify and name the other two as well.

So, we have established that the seed gives birth to the character's theme; and the theme develops along the through-line of action to eventually manifest as the character's *supertask*. The seeds, themes, and supertask of each character contributes to, and develops, the themes and supertask of the play.

Exercise 14.9: Seed, Theme, and Supertask (PGB)

Purpose: To actively search for the character's seed, theme, and supertask in order to create a vibrant, active character who fulfills the playwright's and the production's supertasks.

Note to students: Please think of the following series of exercises as explorations into your creative imagination, a place where you can freely observe your thoughts and feelings and thereby connect to your intuition. Trust your intuition; it is a deep reservoir for spiritual nourishment during the creative process.

Exercise 14.9A: Personal Seed, Theme, and Supertask (PGB)

Purpose: This stage is intended to help you understand how your own personal seed expresses itself as themes that motivate and energize actions leading to your personal dream and goal in life. This will help you understand how to choose vital themes for your character and role.

Guidelines: This is a meditative and physical exploration and requires strong internal focus, along with physical expression.

- Please remove your shoes and lie down on the floor on your back in the prone position. Take a few deep breaths and let go of any muscular tension with each exhalation. With your eyes closed, place your focus on the point between your eyebrows and look deeply into that space. Simply observe your breath, and when your mind wanders from the point of focus, gently remind yourself to bring your inner gaze back to that point.

Ask yourself the flowing questions and *pause* between each in order to allow your answer to come from a deeper place inside:

- What is my life's dream, my supertask? (Identify what you want most and use your imagination to visualize having it at this moment—not sometime in the future but right here and now. See how you would behave knowing that you had accomplished your life's dream. Notice the feelings and sensations that arise spontaneously in your body. Get excited about it!) (pause)
- What thoughts and feelings drive me to accomplish this goal? (Without judgment, be completely honest with yourself. As best as you can, observe and name the feelings. See if you can come up with one or two words that best describe the essence of what drives you, the *seed*.) (pause)
- Having now named your seed, roll up into a ball on the floor and imagine that the essence of your seed is a vital form of energy surging through your whole body. Wherever you feel the energy, move that part of your body. Perhaps it enters into your feet, and you wiggle your toes and stretch your legs, and the energy fills you.
- (You may now open your eyes to avoid accidentally bumping into a classmate, but stay in soft focus, aware of everything around you but focused on yourself.) Let your seed grow, and with your arms and legs reach out into the space around you. Imagine that you are growing and that rays of energy burst forth from your hands, head, chest, back, and feet, filling the room—bouncing off the ceiling and walls.
- Move around the room and send the energy out to your partners in the space. Let their energy fall on you, and take it in. Exchange energy as you keep moving and step into any open space.
- (After a few minutes, when the energy reaches a peak:) Come to a resting/standing position in the space, and pull the energy back into yourself.
- Using the energy, sculpt your body into a three-dimentional living pose that expresses your seed. Keep the pose alive inwardly; hold, but do not

freeze. Make sure that each part of your body expresses the seed you have chosen.
- Now transform the seed into your personal Supertask. Sculpt your body to express how you feel about achieving your dream. Although you may remain still, keep the energy flowing through your body. Keep it alive.
- Naming **Your Personal Theme.** (Please see Chapter 19: The Creative Life: Communion with Audience and Society for more information about how to use *Your Personal Theme* in the creation of a role.)
- Take your seed word and put it into a statement of what you want, and there you will have what is called *Your Own Theme*. So, let's say that your seed was *ambition* and your supertask was envisioning yourself winning an Oscar at the Academy Awards; your theme statement might be, *I want to be acknowledged* for *being a great actor. Write it down!*

Note: If time permits, the teacher may ask some of the students to demonstrate the transformation of their seed as a small ball on the floor, then growing into the sculpture of their seed and finally the supertask. See if the other students can identify and name the seed and supertask by their observation.

14.9A *Reflection Journal—Personal Seed, Theme, and Supertask*

The above exploration is designed to help you understand how important it is to find the seed (kernel) of your character by examining your own life's dream and seed. Reflect on the exercise and take a few minutes to record what you learned about yourself and the active use of your intuition. What was your seed and supertask? What feelings arose for you in the exercise? What did you learn about Your Personal Theme?

Exercise 14.9B: Embodying the Character's Seed, Theme and Supertask (PGB)

Purpose: This is a preliminary sculpting exploration where you place yourself into character and hypothesize about the seed, theme(s), and supertask. (This is both an intellectual and intuitive experimental approach where ideas are allowed to emerge into consciousness without a preconceived outcome.)

Guidelines: If immediately continuing the exploration from Exercise 14.9A, return to the bulleted guidelines above, only this time ask the questions of yourself by assuming the identity of your character. *Make the following adjustments in your questioning:*

- What do I (as the character) want most in the life of the play? What is my supertask? (Assume the character's point of view and even imagine

14 RECONNAISSANCE OF THE CHARACTER

stepping into his or her body as you did earlier in the chapter, Exercise 14.7.) What thoughts and feelings would drive you if you were in the character's situation? How would you identify and name your seed, theme, and supertask?
- **Note:** Not all characters achieve their goal; some win and some lose, but your character doesn't know that. So don't worry about that; just go for what you want by imagining you are in the character's shoes and must get what you are striving to achieve.
- Continue through the remainder of the steps in 14.9a, from the character's viewpoint.

14.9B *Reflection Journal—Embodying the Character's Seed, Theme, and Supertask*

When you wrote your analysis, you were asked to write down the main differences between you and your character. What do you now observe that is both different and the same? What additionally have you learned about yourself and the character from the above exploration? Did you experience any significant discoveries and/or realizations? Did the exploration bring up new ideas for the names of your seed, theme, and supertask?

Exercise 14.10 Activating the Seed, Theme, and Supertask in the Text (PGB)

Note: The following exploration is intended to be practiced once you have a grasp of the through-line of actions for your role. However, you might want to explore it at the beginning of the rehearsal when you are searching for actions, and then again later in the process when you know more about your character and are able to make more definitive choices.

Purpose: To interweave your discoveries of seed, theme, and supertask into key moments of the play as leitmotifs (threads).

Note: You do not need to be playing in a full-length play to apply this exploration to the full play. Begin with a short scene for class, and work at home or with a partner(s) on the active explorations of the other scenes of the play to inform and enrich the scene or monologue you will be performing.

Guidelines: It is important to have completed the exploration in 14.9b prior to embarking on this exercise. Then, while on your feet, find physical actions:

- Carefully **re-read your play** and mark in the script where your primary theme appears. If you are prepared, do the same for your secondary and tertiary themes. (You might want to choose a different color to underline or highlight these moments in the script.)
- **Primary themes** occur when there is a major event happening. Choose these first, and then find the most fitting and typical body language and

gesture for your character, in the form of living sculptures and gestures. If you have found a strong psychological gesture in the previous sections then use that. Never repeat the gestures exactly. Rather, allow spontaneous responses to the themes to bubble up from your subconscious and in response to your scene partners.

- **Practice the physical action** and gesture in silence at first, only thinking the line. As you repeat the thought and action, intensify it by recalling the seed, your motivating force, and with your willpower, send that energy throughout your body until the words of the text MUST be spoken aloud and burst forth.
- After you have repeated this process a few times and feel comfortable with it, then use your *Measure of Truth* and *Restraint and Control* to guide you so that you can execute the moment easily and truthfully.
- **Remember** that when you are actually in rehearsal or performance with your scene partners, these moments must always be improvised based on what you are given and experiencing at the moment. In other words, you might come to a moment where you will need to adapt what you have found in rehearsal practice at home, so that it remains alive and not rigidly fixed. Usually, at such moments, there is a kind of inner stillness that comes over a character, a moment of reflection where it is appropriate to react with a slight pause. These short or long pauses offer the astute actor an opportunity to focus on thinking profoundly. Deep thought, even in a split second, allows the theme(s) to emerge quite naturally. Never force or push.
- **A Rule of Thumb:** Use the same physical pose or gesture sparingly. When Bennett worked in American Stanislavsky Theatre, the Artistic Director, Sonia Moore, never allowed the same thematic gesture to appear more than three times in an entire play! So choose the three most important moments. The secondary and tertiary themes need to be even more subtle; perhaps only a certain movement of the head or eyes is needed.
- **Physicalize the supertask** by using the same process as you have for the seed and themes. You will need to make sure that your last moments of the role, those that appear at the end of the play, express the director's concept. Remember that it is the director who is responsible for the interpretation of the playwright's message and statement.

14.10 *Reflection Journal—Activating the Seed, Theme, and Supertask in Text*

Identifying, naming, and physicalizing actions is an art; an art that takes time and experience to master. As an actor, your mastery of the art of selection is a lifelong process. Be patient with yourself. Enjoy the search, and exhaust every avenue in hunting for the best and most aesthetically simple, clear, and truthful expressions for gestures and actions. Were you able to find at least three moments in your play where the themes were present? Were you able to use your body and gesture to express the emergence of your seed's generating force into a psychophysical action? What was your experience of this exercise? Did you find it helpful, and were you able to trust your intuition to guide you?

Exercise 14.11: Character Interviews (Commonly Used, but This Guided by PGB/SDF)

After any of the exercises above (or the full sequence of them), the teacher, director, or class can interview the actor as the character.

Purpose: This helps you to start thinking and responding as the character while also embodying the character.

Guidelines: Be as specific as possible in your answers to the questions you are asked. Based on what you already know about the play and character, use your creative imagination to respond spontaneously. While you are improvising your answers, practice seeing real and/or imaginary images (or a mixture of the two) of people, places, events, actions, and objects. Any questions that get the actors thinking and responding as the character are fine but here are a few examples:

- What is your name?
- Where are you from?
- What can you tell us about your education?
- What was your childhood like?
- What is your nationality, race, or ethnicity?
- What are your religious beliefs?
- What social class are you from, and which are you in now?
- How do you get your money? Do you have a lot or a little?
- What are your relationships like with the other characters in the play? How are you related to them? What do you think of them? What do they perceive and think of you?
- What do you love most, hate most, or fear? What excites you?
- What objects, events, or people are most important to you?
- What is something you really wish you could change? What can you do about that?
- What do you want most in your life, and how do you plan to achieve it?

Exercise 14.12: Relationship Interviews[9] (SDF)

Guidelines: An interesting variation on the character interview in Exercise 14.11 is to have other members of the cast, while also in character, interview the character with questions they want to ask him or her. They need to ask the questions as their characters, but only the character being interviewed needs to be onstage. This exercise will begin to activate the relationships between the characters. Use the language and dialogue from the play whenever possible. It is great to do this with an entire company rehearsing a play and works well after the director or teachers ask a few questions as in Exercise 14.9 first.

---

[9] We believe many people use interviews with early character work. . This addition of relationship interviews arose spontaneously in French's rehearsals, as other actors, instead of asking questions as another neutral person in the room, started to ask and react to the character on the spot from their characters' perspectives. . It deepened the interviews all around.

Exercise 14.13: Improvisation—Character Second Plan (KSS/SM/PGB)

Purpose: *Études with two or more people* are designed to both explore the essence of their relationships, the influence of past and present events, and the search for their individual *Supertasks* and the *Superobjective* of the play. It can be very helpful to explore key events that would have shaped the character but are not shown in the play. For example, if the play is about a breakup, it might be good to explore an event when the characters were most in love. If the play is about confronting someone about a past incident, it might be good to improvise that incident in order to understand and give substance to the moment in the play where the incident is referenced. (Some examples of second plan improvisations for Blanche in *A Streetcar Named Desire* are the day she was fired for having an affair with an underage student, or the day she was kicked out of the Tarantula Arms Motel, or the day Stella left Belle Reve for the last time).

Some things to remember before going onstage
- Continuously use the "magic if" in order to stay in the moment and make new discoveries. "What would I do today, here and now for the first time if I were really in this character's shoes?" Always begin your action the moment before entering the stage and keep your main action, counters, and objective in mind at all times.
- What psychological burden or problem is your character struggling with in this circumstance? What does he believe will fix it (objective)? In addition, what are some of the ways your character would try to get what she wants from the other characters (action steps)? Consider what images you need to generate in order to see the given circumstances clearly.

While onstage
- Follow the basic structure of an Action: Beginning, Middle, and Logical Conclusion. Just as in all your improvisational work in previous chapters, go onstage to gather information through W.E.D.G.A.G.—discover and evaluate.
- Explore the event and try to solve your problem, adjusting to the obstacles that arise. Finally, resolve, change, or abandon your objective. Never play the image of how you see the character in your mind, especially at this early stage of research and experimentation; rather discover things as you inhabit the circumstances.

14 RECONNAISSANCE OF THE CHARACTER

Summary

After plumbing all the given circumstances offered as gifts from the playwright you began to do some objective analysis and research to create a deeper creative source from which to draw inspiration for your character. You have now shifted from a view of the play as a whole to your character's viewpoint. You have begun to actively experience some of the thoughts, behaviors, and motivations of your character. These early improvisations are just the beginning, because you are ultimately not creating a stand alone character but a role within a play.

Through *second plan* improvisations you considered which events from the time before, between the scenes, or after the play significantly influenced you and the other characters. In the next chapter, Active Analysis through Events and Actions, you will fill out the many layers of the script with detailed scene work.

New Acting Terms and Concepts

Terms used in the Stanislavsky System are in italics.

- amalgamation
- *active facts*
- autobiographical diary
- character embodiment
- plot devices
- Laban's efforts
- movement dynamics
- plot and spectacle
- psychological gesture
- *reconnaissance of the mind*
- sculpting
- *seed (kernel)*
- telling the plot
- telling the story
- *theme(s) (primary, secondary, tertiary)*

CHAPTER 15

Active Analysis through Events and Actions

"The greater the artist, the more subtle his creative efforts, the more work and technique he requires."[1]

—Konstantin Stanislavsky

Stanislavsky Techniques Actively Explored

Tips for learning lines; reconnaissance of the mind; reconnaissance of the body; supertask; amalgamation; telling the character's story; embodying biography; seed, theme and supertask; character's second plan; relationships

Other Theatre Concepts Explored

Character embodiment; character dynamics; psychological gesture; listening to the script; articulating punctuation; line-by-line text analysis; the logic of speech

Part I: Reconnaissance of the Scene

- **Diction/Language**
- **Changes to the Script**
  - Exercise 15.1: Preparing Your Script for Active Analysis
  - Exercise 15.2: Listening to the Spoken Words
  - Exercise 15.3A: Articulating Punctuation
  - Exercise 15.3B: Moved by Punctuation
  - Worksheet 15.4: Initial Observations about Language
- **Preparing for Event Improvisations and Telling the Novel**
- **About Stage Directions**
  - Exercise 15.5: Script Analysis—Listing the Active Facts
  - Exercise 15.6: The "Three Wheres" and the Ground Plan
  - Worksheet 15.6A: Text Analysis—Identifying the "Three Wheres"
  - Worksheet 15.6B: Creating the Ground Plan
- **A Further Note about Characterization**
- **Episodes (Secondary Named Events)**
  - Exercise 15.7: Script Analysis—Marking and Naming Episodes
  - Exercise 15.8: Script Analysis—Identifying Your Character's Problem
- **Part II: Reconnaissance of the Body**
  - Exercise 15.9: Text and Subtext Improvisations
- **Selecting and Generating Evocative, Relevant Images**
  - Worksheet and Exercise 15.10: Finding Images in the Script

---

[1] Konstantin Stanislavsky, *An Actor's Work*, trans. Jean Benedetti (London: Routledge, 2009), 353.

15 ACTIVE ANALYSIS THROUGH EVENTS AND ACTIONS

- **Telling the Novel**
- **The Character's Inner Monologue and Inner Dialogue**
- ☐ Exercise 15.11: Telling the Inner Monologue/Dialogue
- **The Tonal Subtext**
- ☐ Exercise 15.12: Telling the Tonal Subtext
- ☐ Exercise 15.13: Naming Your Actions and Reactions Aloud
- **Part III: The Logic of Speech**
- **Phrasing of the Text, Pauses, and Punctuation**
- **Making a Graphic Analysis of the Text**
- **Determining Connecting and Dividing Connecting Pauses between Speech Measures**
- ☐ Exercise 15.14: Identifying Thought Groups and Types of Pauses
- ☐ Playwrights and Different Types of Pauses
- ☐ Purposes of Punctuation

PART I: RECONNAISSANCE OF THE SCENE

In the previous two chapters you examined reconnaissance of the mind and reconnaissance of the body in explorations of the overall play, and then some specific to your character. You may have explored using Tennessee Williams's *A Streetcar Named Desire*, as in the examples, or another common class text, or perhaps you started right away using a play related to the acting scene you are working on. You learned to use improvised *tableaux, études, (second plan structured improvisations)* and a series of exercises to initiate your development of character.

Now your exploration of character will be expanded throughout the rehearsal process of a scene or play as you select and develop *actions*. It is the actual work on actions with the text that builds the psychophysical life of a character. In life, a person's response to significant events reveals what that person is made of; so, too, is a character revealed by his response to key events in the play. Again you will go back and forth between reconnaissance of the mind and reconnaissance of the body. You will delve into the analysis of a role through improvisations specifically designed to plumb the depths of your script and discover the moment-to-moment psychophysical actions that will bring your character to life.

In order to experience the life of the character and ensure that you are able to repeat the process in subsequent performances, you will need to pay very careful attention to the active step-by-step process outlined here. This does not mean that there is a strict set of rules; on the contrary, you will be given many *devices* (improvisational colors of your palette) with which to paint and create. They can be used in a rehearsal process or as your actor's preparation for rehearsal. As you gain more confidence in improvisation, you may create devices of your own. What is important to remember is that the creative process must be the focus of your attention, not trying to achieve immediate results. Your script preparation at home and how you practice and conduct yourself during rehearsals will determine the quality of your performance.

As you move into using Active Analysis of events and actions on a specific scene from a play, you will move fluidly back and forth between the more objective reconnaissance of the mind and the experiential reconnaissance of the body. Just as you did when first reading the whole play, as you begin work on a specific scene, jot down your first impressions. Here are some areas where you might begin to pay more attention:

Diction/Language

Aristotle identified *diction* (spoken language), commonly translated today as *language*, as another of the six key elements of drama. One of the things that separates plays from other forms of fiction is that all the language is written as dialogue.

Modern plays are mostly in prose dialogue, language not bound by a set rhythmic pattern. However, each playwright has unique, if less structured, rhythmic patterns that he may use or vary within different plays and different characters. Language written in dialogue is what initially reveals the play to the director, designers, and actors and is part of what reveals it to the audience. The play is the author's original creation conveyed primarily through language written in dialogue. The many other aspects of a production are the interpretive creations of other artists as they respond to the play.

Language in Classical Theatre

Beginning with early Greek theatre, language was chanted (something between spoken and sung) in a rhythmic pattern called *verse* (most songs today are written in verse). It started as a long story monologue sung like a ballad. After the Greek actor Thespis stepped out of the chorus and responded to it, Greek theatre branched out into dialogue, but it was still chanted. In later theatrical periods, plays started to be spoken instead of sung or chanted, but for many centuries some of that musicality was continued by a structured use of language called verse. Verse structures are generally defined by a rhythm created by a specific pattern of stressed and unstressed syllables, and sometimes by an added specific rhyming pattern. In various periods of dramatic literature and in different languages, specific verse structures for plays were predominant. While not used in dramatic literature for the most part, an obvious, familiar verse form in our culture, for which most of us can hear an audible and familiar rhythm, is a limerick.[2]

> There once was a large man, could not think,
> His big head it got caught in a sink.
> He had tried for the spout,
> But when stuck, he did shout,
> "Someone help! Can you get me a drink?"[3]

When working with classical dramatic literature, one of the first things you need to assess regarding the language is the particular verse structure of this epoch and of this playwright. The verse will tell a lot about the rhythm

---

[2] A limerick is made up in a rhythmic pattern that is a form of anapestic trimeter. Each foot has two weak syllables followed by a strong one (da-da-DA). A limerick has three anapests each in lines 1 and 2, two anapests only in lines 3 and 4, and returns to three anapests in the final line. Additionally, a limerick has a specific rhyming pattern of AABBA, which means the first, second, and third lines have one type of true rhyme (A) and the third and fourth lines have their own true rhyme (B).

[3] Created by French as an example of rhythmic language in the verse style of limerick.

> of the play and the emphasis of words that the playwright intended. With Shakespeare, for example, who writes in a combination of verse and prose, it is important to assess when he is using verse (and what form, as even this changes within some plays) and when prose and how he uses each in that particular play. For example, sometimes the common people speak in prose and the noble-born characters in verse, but not always. In some Shakespeare plays, the characters in love speak in verse, while the rest speak in prose. In others, verse is the language of the public court, and characters speak less formally in prose in private. Many people learn in high school English that Shakespeare wrote in iambic pentameter,[4] but this is only the tip of Shakespeare's great iceberg. When you are learning to act Shakespeare, you must understand the basic verse and the many variations that point to something important for your character or the scene.

Changes to the Script

Beginning actors often ask if they can change the words. They want to say the lines in more familiar language. In fact, unless you are doing an adaptation and clearly presenting it to the public as such, actors are required to say the words of the play exactly as written by the playwright, in the version approved for production. One of the jobs of a professional stage manager is to watch the script as they are calling the technical cues of the show and to give actors daily notes if they veer from the script. If actors do not correct this, under actors equity rules (the actors' union), after the third offense they can be fired. Often, because of the shorter attention spans of modern audiences compared to their classical predecessors, classic plays that typically ran three to four hours are cut down to approximately two hours. Even if an older play is in the public domain and thus can be cut for a modern production, the actor is required to say the lines according to the script approved by the director, not their own sense of what the character should say. So, yes, actors must learn the script exactly as it is set down.

There are helpful hints for getting *off book* throughout this chapter, and they are summarized in the box that follows. If you work actively through the exercises in this chapter, you will find that not only are you mostly off book without much direct focus on memorization, but you will have connected the playwright's words to the characters thoughts, motivations, and actions, and therefore the words will come alive onstage.

---

[4] Iambic pentameter translates as: five (pent) feet (meter) that are in the structure of an iamb—a weak then strong (da DA) emphasis. Therefore the rhythm is da DA/da DA/da Da/da DA/da DA. All iambic pentameter lines are like this. Shakespears is also said to have written in blank verse, which means no specific rhyming pattern. However, he uses true and other types of rhymes all the time and will often include a rhyming couplet (two lines in a row that rhyme) either for emphasis, summation, or sometimes for comic effect. However, inside of a line that is otherwise iambic pentameter he seems to purposely substitute other types of feet to jar the rhythm and call attention to something important. Some of the more common examples are that he might use a trochee (DA da), sometimes at the start of a line. Or he might want to really give something a bang, so to make it stand out even more he weakens the foot before into a pyrrhic (da da) followed by the strongest two-syllable foot, a spondee (DA DA).

Getting Off Book: Tips for Learning Lines

Never memorize your lines mechanically by rote, as it will kill spontaneity. Instead, learn them organically through these active methods. Not only will you better remember your lines but you will bring to life many other important aspects of the scene and character at the same time:

- Do the exercises in this chapter, particularly all the exercises in the Telling the Novel section. You will find that you are mostly off book, and not only that, but you will understand what you are saying, why you are saying it, what you are trying to do with the words, what you are thinking, how you are responding physically, and a myriad of other aspects of the role.
- Learn the sequence of episodes. This will help you to know which group of your lines comes in what order.
- Understand your transitions—episode-to-episode and action-step to action-step (beat). That way you won't keep getting stuck on certain lines because you don't understand the transitions.
- If you have a long monologue, also make sure to break it into *units of action* (*beats*), and then to learn it by the beats. Then pay extra attention to the transitions and the inner monologue that takes you from one beat to the next. If you find you are *going up* (blanking out) on your lines at the same point in the script repeatedly, it is usually because you are not clear on the character's changes of mind or tactics.
- Understand the character's thoughts that lead to her speech.
- Learn your lines on your feet! Get up and work on your feet, with your attention on creating a logical and consecutive through-line of physical actions. If you are in a rehearsal process where the director has set blocking and the stage manager has recorded it, check her book and make sure you have it in pencil in your script. Then either on the rehearsal set or in a makeshift one of your own, walk through the blocking while working on the lines, actions, and images. See the other people there, see the images of things you describe, think the thoughts, moving from your spine.
- Say the lines quietly to yourself while acting on your feet, but not fully out loud. Saying the lines out loud can get you into the bad habit of listening to yourself, and this can kill any spontaneity in rehearsal and performance where you need to listen more to your partners response than to how you say it—focus on affecting the other.

Brain Stimulation Tricks for Memorization: Any strategies that engage more areas of your brain increase retention of ideas, or in this case, lines. Strategies that engage the mind and the body at the same time are helpful, especially if what you are doing physically is relevant or otherwise evocative.

- Work on your lines right before bed so your subconscious can help you learn them.
- Write out your lines. Type up your lines; always try to get other senses

involved, in this case touch, as well as hand-eye coordination to activate more parts of the brain.
- Learning lines: Make a recording (on your phone perhaps) of you and your partner reading the scene.
- Learning cues: Make a recording of your partner reading her part while you only mouth the words to what you say in response. This way you can listen and fill in the blanks.
- Make cue cards. Put the cue line on one side and the response line on the other.
- Run them regularly with your scene partner, but do it only one action-step (beat) at a time, building up to one episode at a time. If you don't get them right, start again at the beginning; always run them on your feet with physical actions and connect speech to the struggle and your desired outcome (objective).
- Make a game out of doing extreme literal gestures for parts of the text, such as a large pushing gesture with your entire body when Lady MacBeth says, "Out, out damned spot," to the blood of her victim on her hands, or playing and then eating a violin as the Duke Orsino says "If music be the food of love." This can serve another purpose as you learned with some active vocal work in Chapter 9: Embodying Voice by energizing the words of the text, even though the above gestures would be ridiculous in a real version of this Shakespeare play (unless it was a spoof of them).
- Language naturally follows the logical paths in your brain, but you can also appeal to other areas through seeing your images as you work on the line, or through connecting with emotions. Strategies that activate more senses are also good.

"Fortune favors only the prepared mind."
—Louis Pasteur, 1822–1895 (French scientist who discovered the principles of vaccination and pasteurization)

Exercise 15.1: Preparing Your Script for Active Analysis (KSS/PGB/SDF)

- Type up your script with your lines and those of the other characters and triple space it. Make sure you have a wide 1.5–2-inch margin on the right and a 1–1.5-inch margin on the left for notes.
- Alternatively, copy your script with one acting script page to one 8.5x11 paper. Place blank white pages around the book when photocopying so that you can create white (rather than black or gray) margins around the edges. Again, make sure you have room to write many notes.
- Highlight in a light color, like yellow, all *your lines only*.
- As you uncover them through the Active Analysis exercises in this chapter, **write at the top of the script**, in pencil, some key elements that will shape your role through the entire scene:
  ☐ The **main event** of the scene.

- The **main problem** your character is struggling with (often connected to the event).
- The **objective:** the outcome your character hopes for in the resolution of that problem.
- The "**magic if**": what would you do if you were this type of person in this situation?

Go on to do the active exercises below to fill in any gaps to the above questions that you cannot, at first, answer.

Exercise 15.2: Listening to the Spoken Words (ML)[5]

Purpose: In life, when we ask a question or make a statement, we do not know how the other person will answer. Onstage, you have to re-create this spontaneity, even though by the end of rehearsal you will know your partners lines almost as well a your own and will always know what you will say next. Nonetheless, you must re-create the sense that you are hearing these words for the first time. This exercise will help. It also helps to begin to generate the inner monologue.

Guidelines: For now just notice what comes to mind as you are listening to your partner. These types of thoughts will later form part of the character's inner monologue. While detailed work on a scene may happen after more comprehensive Active Analysis of the play, this exercise is very valuable to do early, before you have much familiarity with the scene. Follow the instructions below and with your internal and external monitors listen to your partner(s) and observe your first thoughts and impressions.

- Place two chairs facing each other.
- Sit facing your partner with your knees touching.
- Each actor puts a thumb on his first line and then looks up at the other actor.
- Lines must only be said directly to the face of the partner. To accomplish this, the actor with the first line looks down for an instant to grasp as much of the line as possible and then looks up and speaks the line while making eye contact with the scene partner (not the script). If you are delivering your line to the top of a head because the actor is not listening actively but looking ahead, stop, reset, and deliver the line again to her face.
- Your scene partner is not looking at his script but is waiting to receive your line. In this way, each of you hears a line spoken before you have any idea

---

[5] French observed this from Michael Landman, an actor, director, and teacher, and head of directing at East Stroudsburg University. He used a lot of Meisner, so may have learned it there. He was also influenced by Anne Bogart, as he studied at Columbia MFA program.

how you might respond, just as happens in life. This allows the responses, thoughts, and the wondering about what this person just said to be triggered before you find what to say in response. After you have allowed this wondering, only then look to the script to find what you say. Then look up and say the line to your partner's face.

Tip: When first learning this technique, you may need a director or teacher or fellow student to remind you when you revert to having your head stuck in the book. Also, in the case of longer passages look down as often as you need to, to get the entire passage in phrases or sentences. *However, for this exercise, never speak while your eyes are on the script.*

- If you do not already have your own scene, use the text section from *A Streetcar Named Desire* by Tennessee Williams.

15.2 Reflection Journal—The Spoken Words

Jot down on your script any responses that popped into your head before you knew what you were going to say back. This can form the basis of your *inner monologue*, thoughts as the character that you will compose later. Jot down any images or emotional or physical responses you had to what the other person said or to the words that you said. Did the meaning of any of the words, yours or your partner's, become clearer to you?

Note to students and teachers: The next two exercises actively exploring punctuation could both be done separately in sequence, or they could be done combined, or you could select one or the other.

Exercise 15.3A: Articulating Punctuation (PGB/SDF)

Purpose: Playwrights give punctuation to shape the actors delivery of the words. Some playwrights use punctuation more formally, as in writing, and others use it more to flavor how language is spoken. In any case, it is a given of the playwright that you need to consider when speaking the words. (For a better understanding, see the Purposes of Punctuation section later in the chapter.)

Guidelines: For this next out-loud reading of the scene with your partner, pay attention to ending punctuation, such as periods, semicolons, exclamation points, and question marks, that separates thoughts. Notice how your character phrases what she has to say as offset by commas, or lists or examples laid out by colons. Pay attention to when the author writes *pause, beat* and/or the symbol for ellipses (…) three or four dots in a row. As you work on your script you will need to interpret and fill these different types of pauses with connecting thoughts, actions, movement, and gestures. Do not underestimate the importance and power of the use of pauses. We will discuss pauses and the use of punctuation in great detail a bit later in this chapter. Also pay attention and make pencil notes where you notice major shifts in what is going on in the scene. This will help you with the next exercise. This can be done with the entire scene, but it is probably best to do A on no more than a page and then B on that same page and then go on to the next page.

- **A:** First read the script and speak aloud the name of each type of punctuation in your text. In an example from the character of "D" from *Polaroid Stories* by Naomi Iizuka, we might read her lines as: "i used to know this boy PERIOD this was a thousand years ago PERIOD he jumped off a bridge on the other side of town PERIOD he flew so fast PERIOD nobody saw him COMMA nobody heard him PERIOD he flew so fast COMMA he died before he hit the water PERIOD".[6]
- (You might notice, for example that the author uses lower case to start the sentence and uses punctuation to indicate the length of pauses rather than strictly for grammar.)
- **B:** Read the script again. This time, try to capture the vocal energy or redirection of the punctuation but without speaking the punctuation names out loud.

Exercise 15.3B: Moved by Punctuation (CB/PGB/SDF)[7]

Purpose: To get a sense of the redirection of punctuation on language and how the energy of language can also be experienced in the body.

Guidelines:
- Start with you and your scene partner sitting in chairs.
- Take one episode or one page of your script.
- At the beginning of a line get up and start moving.
- If you reach a comma, turn.
- If you reach a dash or dot-dot-dot, suspend your movement before continuing.
- If you reach a colon, pause while rising on your tiptoes, then jump from one place to another with each example (or item on the list) that follows.
- Sit again when you reach an ending punctuation mark and let the type of punctuation change how you sit—period, question mark, exclamation point each have different energy and make different statements.

---

[6] Iizuka, Naomi. *Polaroid Stories*. Woodstock, NY: Dramatic Publishing, 1999.
[7] Cicely Berry, *The Actor and the Text*, rev. ed. (New York: Applause Books, 1992), 82–90. Adapted from a variety of Cicely Berry's exercises for discovering the energy from line to line and movement of punctuation while working actively with a text.

15 ACTIVE ANALYSIS THROUGH EVENTS AND ACTIONS

> **15.3A & B** *Reflection Journal—Punctuation*
>
> It is helpful after the exercise, to jot down in pencil in the script on a side margin, if room, or a separate paper, the things you thought about, as this can be further basis for your inner monologue.

> **Worksheet 15.4: Initial Observations about Language (PGB/SDF)**
>
> **Guidelines:** After exercises 15.2 and 15.3, complete this worksheet to capture some initial observations about the playwright and your character's use of language:
>
> 1. What do you notice about how this author uses language?
> 2. Is it in verse (if so, what type?) or prose or some combination?
> 3. Does the language reflect a specific culture, subculture, part of the world, epoch in history, or social class?
> 4. Does the language set the play in a specific style?
> 5. Is the language formal or informal, or, if a mixture, when is it each?
> 6. Do all the characters use language in similar ways, or can you identify usage that distinguishes one character's language from another in terms of phrasing, vocabulary, dialect of English, expression or hiding of emotions, speaking a lot or a little, etc.?
> 7. Do any characters interrupt, trail off, use verbal fillers (such as *uh, you know, like*), or do they speak in full sentences?
> 8. Are certain phrases repeated in the play? If so, are they repeated by the same character or different characters?
>
> More details on how to dissect language are provided through the training in the Logic of Voice and Speech later in this chapter.

Preparing for Event Improvisations and Telling the Novel

There are a number of key components of Analysis through Events and Actions. Two very important ones are event improvisations (introduced in chapters 13 and 14, and also here) and Telling the Novel. In preparation for these two key components of Active Analysis, first you will need to identify the episodes within the scene, select the main event, name the rest of the events in each episode as secondary events, list the active facts, create a ground plan, note the initiator of action (who is driving and note when that changes), note action steps (also called tactics or beats), name the actions and counteractions, compose inner monologue and tonal subtext, and learn to express the subtext of the body.

Figure 15.1 "Exit, pursued by a bear," one of the most famous stage directions in dramatic literature. Actor: Philip G. Bennett (Antigonus) in Shakespeare's *The Winter's Tale* at the Rogue Theatre. Photo by Tim Fuller

About Stage Directions

As you begin to work on a scene, take note of the playwright's comments and any *stage directions* but with a caveat: In many older versions of plays the stage directions are not even suggestions from the playwright but rather were put in the script by editors to help readers picture the play more clearly. Often they were actually the subtext of behavior, blocking, and other physical choices made by the director and actors in the first professional productions. Sometimes they are put in a later edition of the play by the playwright, who was a part of this premiere production of the play and may have worked closely with the director. However, subsequent directors and actors do not feel beholden to these stage directions. Many directors and actors believe they must only follow those physical actions written in the actual lines. In fact, there is currently a big dispute about the creative solutions in the stage directions: Are they, in fact, the intellectual property of that director, just as the original scenic design is the intellectual property of the original scenic designer? Most directors would not want to copy the staging of an earlier production but would want to invent their own.

On the other hand, some playwrights, like Eugene O'Neill and Arthur Miller, have very detailed character notes and stage directions that do not come from earlier productions. Many directors also find that you need to follow Samuel Beckett's directions precisely, as they orchestrate the text like a complex piece of music (also if you stray too far from them you may be sued by his estate). Other playwrights, like Naomi Iizuka, have wonderfully evocative stage directions; Iizuka enjoys hers being interpreted differently by each creative team, such as in the *Polaroid Stories* stage direction, "She turns into a star." Some playwrights have few stage directions and expect the actors to find their own blocking and interpretation of the script without detailed character notes. Pinter, for example, writes in many pauses that create the rhythm of the text but does not indicate exactly what the actor does in them. Shakespeare and the French classical playwright Molière write key action and directions about time and place into the dialogue of the character's spoken lines.

Exercise 15.5: Script Analysis—Listing the Active Facts (SM, influenced by studying Brecht in German from Berliner Ensemble Rehearsal Techniques/PGB/this specific approach guided by SDF)

Purpose: To get a sense of what physical behavior is called for by the playwright.

Guidelines: Make a list of the *active facts* of the scene:
- What active facts, physical behaviors do the stage directions indicate (keep in mind the limitations of stage directions as discussed above)?
- What active facts do the lines suggest?

Examples:
In *Streetcar* Blanche says, "I keep my papers mostly in this tin box!" and the stage directions say, "[*She opens it*]." So the character's line suggests that she does something with the box. The actor could try to open it, as the stage directions suggest, or try something else. In any event, it is all about

15 ACTIVE ANALYSIS THROUGH EVENTS AND ACTIONS

you choosing, experimenting, selecting, and fulfilling a purposeful action, psychophysically.

In Anton Chekhov's *Three Sisters*, Olga says, "Enough, Masha. Enough, my darling." (*Kulygin enters.*) Kulygin. (*troubled*) "It's all right, let her cry."[8] In this case, the actress playing Masha has to uncover how to cry precisely on cue and the director had best give her all the help he can with staging choices and pacing.

Exercise 15.6: The "Three Wheres" and the Ground Plan (KSS/PGB/SDF)

Purpose: Before you get up on stage to rehearse, it is always a good idea to have some sense of the physical environment of the scene. You have probably already imagined it during your readings of the play. When you draw up your ground plan, you suddenly take the situation out of your intellect and by means of your imagination turn it into a physical reality. Using your imagination to solve artistic problems is the whole secret to making the very best choices as an actor.

Guidelines: First understand some basics of the "three wheres" of the scene for your character and any other characters involved, and then create the ground plan.

Worksheet 15.6A: Text Analysis—Identifying the "Three Wheres"[9] (SDF)

For your scene:
- Where #1 (Where from): Where do you come from when you enter?
- Where #2 Where does the scene take place?
- Where #3 (Where to): Where do you go when you exit?

For each of these you should identify:

1. Is it indoors or outdoors?
2. Is it public or private?
3. Whose space is it?
4. Write some adjectives to describe the location.
5. What is the mood and atmosphere of the place?
6. What is each character's comfort level in this space?

Then decide how these factors shape the layout of the stage or performance space.

---

[8] Anton Chekhov. *The Three Sisters*. Act Four, trans. Jean-Claude van Itallie, rev. ed. (New York: Dramatists Play Service, 1995), 65.
[9] Stanislavsky insisted on the actor being clear on where he was coming from, where he was, and where he was going to. It may have been Stella Adler that coined the term *the Three Wheres*. French created this worksheet to suss these things out.

> **Worksheet 15.6B: Creating the Ground Plan**
>
> 1. List all the needed entrances and exits, including those that go to the outside and those that go to other indoor spaces.
> 2. What other parts of the set are required (e.g., a window, balcony, stairs)?
> 3. What large furniture pieces are needed (e.g., a dining room table, a fridge, a cupboard, desk, bed with bedside tables, sofa, or a park bench and a trash can)?
> 4. Make a list of small properties (or hand props) that are required (e.g., stationery, a ring, a phone, a suitcase). Continue to update this list as you work on the scene and find need for additional objects. Do any of these small props need a piece of furniture, such as a telephone table or a desk for stationery?
> 5. Decide upon an initial diagram for the location of the doors, windows, furniture, and hand props. Draw it as though looking from above. For your acting purposes it need only be a rough hand-drawn sketch rather than a scale drawing.
> 6. Does your layout of the ground plan give you three to five distinct acting areas? If not adjust.
> 7. Does your layout of the ground plan give you opportunities to move up and down stage and side to side? It can be hard, but try to position something downstage near the audience to give you reason to move there.
> 8. If the location is your character's space ask yourself, "If this were my room, where would I as the character spend most of my time?" and "In what area would I not spend much time or avoid for any reason?"

A Further Note about Characterization

Periodically, review the exercises in Chapter 14 as you work through your script for actions. Piece by piece, the mosaic of your character will come together to form a whole picture that will be much more interesting and nuanced than if you just showed your initial image of a character. That would be akin to just going for the result. Instead, start from yourself and allow what you have learned and are learning to gradually seep into your muscles and find new paths through your neural circuitry that reflect another human being. When you have accomplished the script analysis and get up on your feet, put all of your attention on expressing and fulfilling your physical actions. Then, gradually sculpt the character traits you have discovered, where they apply, to the actions. Never, never act in general. Be specific.

> "By indirections find the directions out."
> —Polonius, from Shakespeare's *Hamlet* (Act 2, scene 1)

Episodes (Secondary Named Events)

Most well-written plays have scenes, and the scenes are composed of smaller units that Stanislavsky called episodes. You can identify an episode by closely examining the structure of a scene. A new episode can begin in several ways: the entrance or exit of a character, a major pause in the action, the introduction of a new topic or problem, or a major shift in a character's action or objective.

One character is the *initiator* of an action, who *drives* the scene, and there is always a *receiver* of the action who counters the initiator's action. The initiator is said to have the main action, and the receiver has the counteraction; this creates the conflict. However, these roles can, and often do, exchange during the course of the scene, and this is a *minor reversal*. (A *major reversal* in a play is when a character responds to an event, usually a key event, by completely changing his outlook, selecting an opposite objective to what he previously wanted, changing sides in a major struggle, a complete status shift [say, from beggar to king] or other such major switches.) In order to mark the episodes, it is important to look for the initiator and receiver of actions, as well as the minor reversals and other shifts.

Once you have decided upon the number of episodes within the scene, then you will need to title each as a named event within the scene. Select one of them as the main event of the scene; the others will be secondary named events. As we discussed in Chapter 11: Verbal Action, for naming events you can use a variety of impetuses; for example, title, metaphor, or headline. The title can also be the subject of the episode. Often you can find a word or simple phrase from the text of the episode itself that encapsulates or describes the event. In this case, just put a box around that, right within the text.

> **Note to Students:** The order of applying these exercises to your scene is not as important as doing all the steps. We have to teach it in a certain order, but that does not dictate that you must do these exercises in the exact order, although some exercises do prepare you for a following exercise. Most important is to follow your intuition. It is perfectly fine to do the exercises you find easiest first and move on to more difficult ones after you start to get some insights into the scene. This is different for each student.

Exercise 15.7: Script Analysis—Marking and Naming Episodes (Secondary Named Events) (KSS/SM/PGB/SDF)[10]

By now you are quite familiar with the naming of events and the choosing of actions for improvisations. The next step is to reexamine the events in your scene and give them names. Sometimes it takes time to come up with names, so just do your best and keep revising your ideas each time you return to the episode until the name seems right. Remember that the named event must be right for all the characters in the scene and that every character has actions and objectives that bring about or try to impede the event. (For those of you that have already worked with beats, episodes are larger sections of the scene than a beat. The two to three key events of the scene, for example, might each be an episode.)

Purpose: Naming each episode will sum up what is happening and really assist you in the subsequent exercise of selecting and naming the actions and objectives.

---

[10]The notation for marking the script here is French's.

It also is very important to understand the shifts in a scene. It is more effective to rehearse a scene an episode at a time in order to flush out all the nuance of the events and actions and how they impact the characters.

Rehearsal Tip: If you always run through the whole scene again and again you will not be looking closely enough at each moment. You need to work and rework the scene episode by episode to really make progress. It is also vital to understand minor as well as major shifts or transitions in a scene. Often when an actor forgets a line, it is at a moment in the script when he doesn't understand the character's transitions. Also it helps to understand the flow of the scene to see the sequence of named events. This also helps with remembering the order of your lines.

Guidelines: Do this on the copied-out script rather than a separate paper, and in pencil, because preliminary observations may shift with more knowledge and rehearsal:

- With your scene partner, tell the story of the scene event by event: "First this happens, and then this and then this . . . "
- Make a double slash mark (//) as you shift between one event and another. Take time to carefully decipher the first and last lines of each. They may come in the middle of one character's speech lines, rather than only at the end.
- Mark a // if a new problem is introduced.
- Mark a // whenever a character enters or exits.
- Mark a // if there is a major pause in the action.
- Mark a //if there is a major change in the focus of the conversation (and a / if there is a minor change in topic that may relate more to beats than episodes).
- Mark // if one or other character changes his objective.
- After you have done all these markings, then go through together with your scene partner and decide which are the major shifts of the scene and make the other markings slight shifts (dotted double slashes) rather than changes-in-episode solid double slashes as shown above.
- Name the major episodes with a headline, title, descriptive noun, or metaphor. Either find the episode name in the words of the text, and put a box around the word or phrase, or write it next to the start of the episode and put a box around that.

Exercise 15.8: Script Analysis—Identifying Your Character's Problem (KSS/SMC/PGB/SDF)[11]

Purpose: When you identify the main problem in the scene and the moment-to-moment problems in each episode, you will then be able to interpret the desired outcome or resolution of the problem that your character wants. This is your character's *objective*. You can then select action steps he might take to try to solve the problem in his favor.

Guidelines: Once you have decided upon the series of *episodes* and named each one as an event as in exercise 15.7 above, make sure you know what problem your character is struggling with in each. Then assess which of these is the main *problem* for your character in the scene. Depending upon how the play is written, a character has a main problem for each scene and a series of secondary problems to solve in the episodes.

Here are three *devices* to use for identifying the problem. Ask:
- What is the matter?
- Why won't he? (What am I struggling to change or shift in the other character?)
- What do I want to be different?

To identify your character's *objective* around that problem (ideal solution), ask:
- How can I change or fix this problem?
- What do I want to occur so that the problem is solved in my favor?
- How can I get him or her to . . . ?

To consider how to behave given this problem and this objective/solution, use the "magic if": "What would I do if I were in this situation, in my character's shoes, right now, here and for the first time?" Use this question throughout the entire process of rehearsal, at home when you are studying your script, and at times while on your feet in performance, such as when you need to make an adaptation to an obstacle. Questions to elicit the tactics or action steps you take might include:

- What would I do to achieve my desired outcome?
- What steps can I take to achieve my solution?

---

[11]Stanislavsky's idea of identifying the problem as opposed to the objectve came to us from Sharon Carnike. This key element of Active Analysis is very similar to many aspects of The Method of Physical Actions but has some subtle differences. Sonia Moore also passed on related ideas through her access to unpublished or untranslated Russian documents related to Stanislavsky's later experiments and the work of his disciples as part of her continual research into the latest Russian insights on Stanislavsky.

> **Note:** Prepare your script at home and come up with whatever names and action steps you think are best before meeting with your scene partner and teacher or director. Be prepared! When you meet with your partner, discuss and collaborate together to find the very best choices.

Example: Identifying Stanley's Problem and Response

In the segment of scene 2 of *A Streetcar Named Desire*, which Bennett names *The Exploding Trunk*, and French names *The Trial*, the actor playing Stanley might first ask himself:

- **Q: What is the matter?** A: Blanche has cheated me.
- **Q: What do I want to be different?** A: I want Stella to see I look out for her, not Blanche. I want our share of the money.

Finding the Desired Solution (Objective around the Problem)
- "**How can I** find out what happened to the money from Belle Reve?" "**How can I** prove that Blanche swindled Stella and me?"
- "**How can I** get our fair share of the inheritance?"

Finding the Behavior:
Once you have identified the problem then ask questions to find your character's ideal solution:

- **Q: What would I do to achieve my desired outcome?** A: I need to find evidence that Blanche swindled us.
- **Q: What steps can I take to achieve my solution?** A: I can search Blanche's belongings and interrogate her about the sale.

These are just suggestions; you can come up with much better ones. The point is to ask questions that make you probe into the depths of the character and play. As an exercise, you might consider how you would word Blanche's problem in this same segment of scene 2?

Figure 15.2 The Exploding Trunk episode in *A Streetcar Named Desire* by Tennessee Williams with Christi Berlane, Angel Berlane, and David Ausem, East Stroudsburg University, 2007.
Photo by Charles Perry Hebard

PART II: RECONNAISSANCE OF THE BODY

"A stage space has two rules: (1) Anything can happen and (2) Something must happen."

—Peter Brook, *The Empty Space*

Active Analysis is based on the principle that after only a brief discussion of the play, we search for the character and staging while actively engaging with the material of the play. This can be somewhat time consuming, and of course, we realize that in many theatrical endeavors there are the limitations of time and resources that may not always make it possible to find all the solutions in this manner. Nevertheless, the more active, on-your-feet steps you can use, both inside and outside of class, the better you can expect to learn and absorb this approach to a role. Once you have mastered the technique, your training will provide a shortcut to finding your character and staging a play.

During the initial stages of exploration, be patient; *do not memorize the script by rote*; memorization can kill any initial spontaneous discovery. The following steps will help you learn the role using your mind and body together, psychophysically. Once you have found your actions and have a better understanding of the character's subtext and behavior, you will find that most of the lines will come naturally with very little memorization.

Note: Your teacher/director may not have time to work through every one of the steps with all of the students while in class. Therefore it is your responsibility to meet and work with your partner(s) as often as possible and use these exercises as outside-of-class rehearsal guidelines.

Exercise 15.9A: Improvising an Episode of the Text (KSS/PGB)

Important: If you do not have the luxury of improvising each episode of your scene separately, then focus on the episode that contains the main event of the scene.

Purpose: To see what you understand of the situation coming from yourself and in your own words before you adapt to the words as the playwright has written them and the character speaks them, and before you stretch into those aspects of the character and situation that are less familiar to you.

Guidelines: Although you may have already learned a great deal about your character through various exercises, when approaching a script for the first time, it is best to do so entirely from yourself. Do not attempt to jump immediately into character. Allow the character to evolve at this phase based on the kinds of actions she pursues and how she struggles with the problems presented.

- **Paraphrasing and the Subtext:** After your initial discussion on the first episode of your scene, go onstage and improvise the main event in your *own words*; that is, *paraphrase* the text with your focus on finding the physical behavior. Explore the central problem as a struggle between the characters, with each of you focusing on pursuing the solution you desire. For example, when Blanche first comes out of the bathroom in scene 2, Williams's line for her is, "Hello, Stanley! Here I am, all freshly bathed and scented, and feeling like a brand new human being!" As Blanche you might paraphrase, "Hey, Stanley, don't I smell delicious? I'll appeal to your senses rather than your sense, you big brute. If you're attracted to me, maybe you will want me around and I'll have a place to live."
- Your focus must be on choosing actions that attempt to solve the problem as you have identified it above by asking, "How can I," etc.
- Paraphrasing is not about just mixing the words of the text around, it is about searching to say the meaning under the lines, the *subtext*. You may not be able to get the meaning the first time through, but if you keep practicing, you will be surprised just how much subtext you can uncover.

15.9A *Reflection Journal—Review Your Improvisation*

Once you have completed the improvisation, go back and reread the scene and discuss with your scene partner: What did we get and what did we miss? Which actions seemed to fit the circumstances, and which did not? Who is the initiator of the action, and who is the receiver? What is the conflict in the scene? Are there any reversals of the action? Where do they occur? Who and what drives the scene? How does the scene move the plot ahead? What themes are explored in the scene? Who is the winner in this event, and who is the loser? Make sure to write down what you have found in your rehearsal. Keep an ongoing record of your experiments and your findings.

15 ACTIVE ANALYSIS THROUGH EVENTS AND ACTIONS

> **Exercise 15.9B: Repeat the Subtext Improvisation**
>
> **Guidelines:** Return to the stage and repeat the improvisation using only subtext, making the corrections but still *using your own words*.
>
> - Keep the above points in mind with each successive improvisation and stay focused on engaging in the struggle.
> - Each time you re-read the script and return to improvise it, you may get closer and closer to the actual lines in the text until you start to use some of them in the improvisation. Use your own words as you need to, until you have a sense of your actions and your objectives, and then use the lines of the play.
>
> **Move Ahead:** Go through each episode of the scene this way until you are familiar with your main actions. When you reach this stage of progress, you will have begun to also find that you have a rough sketch of your blocking and movement through the scene.

> **15.9B** *Reflection Journal—Evaluate the Event and Supertask*
>
> Now evaluate once again the named event you have chosen, the supertask of the play, and the supertask of your character. Did the actions I chose bring about the event and lead to my character's objective in the scene? Would they lead to my supertask and help reveal the supertask of the play? What adaptations and adjustments do I need to make?

Selecting and Generating Evocative, Relevant Images

Transmitting mental pictures and the feelings associated with them is one of the primary goals of the actor. Once you have worked on your feet and begun to understand the flow of actions in an episode it is time for the next step: *examining the text for images*. As you have already experienced through improvisation, images arise from your inner world and reflect your environment.

Imagery is the term used for the playwright's language. In *A Streetcar Named Desire,* Tennessee Williams has written a great deal of poetic imagery; e.g., "The sky that shows around the dim white building is a peculiarly tender blue, almost a turquoise, which invests the scene with a kind of lyricism and gracefully attenuates the atmosphere of decay." Even the title of the play is a poetic metaphor. So, your first impression of the author's use of imagery is important. As we discussed in earlier chapters about the way our brains work, any sensory stimuli create mental images, so Williams's phrase "You can almost feel the warm breath of the brown river beyond the river warehouses with their faint redolence of bananas and coffee," even though it appeals more to smell than sight, still creates mental images.

Worksheet 15.10A: Finding Images in the Script (KSS/SM/PGB)

Purpose: Seeing mental images, whether imaginary, personal, or an amalgamation of both, creates depth in your acting.

Guidelines: Here are some preliminary steps as you comb the play for images:

- **Circle your image words** throughout the text. Image words are composed of nouns and pronouns: people, places, things, events, and circumstances, as well as descriptive verbs and phrases (example: stumbled down the stairs).
- As you study the script at home, pay particular attention to the language and choice of words used by your character. For example: If you are playing Blanche, make particular note of her descriptions of her family plantation, the hotel she lived in, and of her young husband.
- **To find images in the text** ask yourself:
  - What does the character see in her mind?
  - What is her feeling and attitude toward her mental images?
- Use your imagination to visualize these pictures as she might see them until you have a clear understanding of what they mean.
- What would these same images mean to Stanley? He would see them very differently than Blanche, wouldn't he?
- What are Stanley's images of the lost plantation?
- How does he think and feel about his wife, Stella, and how does he see her in his mind?
- Seeing the imaginary images of the character is only the beginning; it is also important to associate with them.
- Now search to find if you have any associations: images from your own experience and observation that may hold a similar meaning for you. Remember, the situations do not need to be the same, just what they mean to you. Having personal associations helps to deepen your work by connecting you even more deeply to the character.
- A good play is full of innumerable images, and once you find them, then you must practice seeing them in your mind as you say the words and phrases to which they are connected.
- You MUST get into the habit of writing down everything; otherwise your creation of the inner life of your character will always be accidental and weak. It's best to write down your images and actions in pencil, as you will need to keep changing and improving them during the course of rehearsals and performances.

Note: Images that seem to fit in the beginning of your exploration of the role, may later lose their effect upon you. Keep practicing until you find those that fit the character and playwright's imagery best.

- **Amalgamation:** You may use imaginary or personal images but will likely

15 ACTIVE ANALYSIS THROUGH EVENTS AND ACTIONS

use some combination, no matter what you intentionally aim for. At a certain point in rehearsals they will blend and merge into one and become what is called *amalgamation*. When this happens, you will spontaneously experience new imaginary images in performance. This is the beginning of transformation of your inner world into the inner world of the character. It also signals the beginning of your physical embodiment of the character, because the role is becoming psychophysical and second nature. At this point your thoughts and images will also be right for the character and powerfully communicate to your audience through your voice, speech, and physical actions.

Exercise 15.10B: Actively Finding and Creating Images (PGB)

Important note: It is important that you have completed worksheet 15.10a before attempting this exercise.

Guidelines: Now practice seeing the images. Here are a few possible exercises to assist with that:

- Speak your image word or phrases one at a time and take time to see each one, and allow it to affect you through your spine. You do not need to force anything, but allow them to come and respond.
- Either record your phrases around the words you circled or have your recording of all your lines, or have your partner read out parts of your script.
- Listen carefully, and as the image words or phrases arise, allow pictures to arise in your mind. As a new image phrase follows, allow the image to shift into the new one. This *flow of images* is really how it works during the course of a play or scene.

15.10A & B *Reflection Journal—Images and Imagery*

Which of the images did you have a clear picture of? For which ones did no picture arise? Were some of the pictures different than you expected? Were they primarily personal, imaginary, or did some start to amalgamate?

Figure 15.3 Yunzhou "Elldee" Gao recalls her lost child; from *Top Girls* by Caryl Churchill.
Photo: Bob Weidner, courtesy of East Stroudsburg University

Telling the Novel

"To play needs much work. But when we experience the work as play, then it is not work anymore. A play is play."

—Peter Brook

Pick up your favorite novel, but any novel will do. Read various sections of it, and you will have a good example of what we will be doing. Notice how the author describes the circumstances and immediate situation. A good writer not only provides the dialogue between the characters but enhances your visual picture of the story, the relationships, and conflicts by describing the character's thoughts, actions, and reactions; tone of voice; physical behavior; feelings; and emotions.

A play, however, is much different than a novel. The playwright may give us some descriptions of the setting, pauses, reactions, movements, but mostly gives us the dialogue. For the playwright, the dialogue must imply everything else. The actor's preparation and rehearsal must flesh out all the other layers of the novel or the play so that the actor can bring them vividly to life for the audience.

It is in Telling the Novel that the Elements of Action, already explored in previous chapters, are woven together to create the multifaceted layers of the character in the role. For now, we will focus on the preliminary levels of Telling the Novel, phase one. In the next chapter, you can get a glimpse of phase two, as well as how the director and actors might work together with Active Analysis in rehearsal, to tell the novel of the play. (A detailed example of a more complex form of Telling the Novel is outlined as part of the play rehearsal process demonstrated in detail in Chapter 16. However, most actors new to the process find it easier at first to start with one element at a time and build to Telling the Novel with all of them at once.)

Phase One: Telling the Novel
1. Inner monologue/dialogue: Composing the character's thoughts aloud
2. Tonal subtext: Saying what you are really communicating with the words
3. Saying your actions and reactions aloud

Phase Two: Telling the Novel
4. Subtext of the body: Physicalizing your subtext
5. Putting all the layers together

The Character's Inner Monologue and Inner Dialogue

Have you ever heard the expression "No two people think alike?" Well, it is true. One of the most interesting aspects of working on a role is finding out how your character thinks. As you have seen in the chapter on nonverbal communication, our thoughts can and often do speak louder than words.

You already explored inner monologue in a number of exercises going all the way back to Waiting for the Jury's Verdict. Now, however, instead of being you in the situation, you are moving toward how another person might think and behave. Now you are prepared to do a deeper exploration of your character. Saying your inner monologue aloud is a simple device developed by Stanislavsky early on in his exploration with the actors of the Moscow Art Theatre.

Exercises 15.11, 15.12, and 15.13 below represent the first phase of Telling the Novel on your feet!
Important note: Go through each of the Telling the Novel exercises below one episode at a time, and then discuss and evaluate together what you found that is useful and what was not. It is important that you don't try to do the whole scene at once. It is much more effective to do the two to three phases of each exercise one after another an episode at a time. It is easier to get very intimate with this episode if you do this.

Follow your script, but fold it up small and keep your thumb on your line so that you can make as much contact with your scene partner as possible during the process—giving and receiving. (Learning to be active and engage with others onstage while holding a script will not only help you in rehearsals but also later, when you get to *cold readings*.[12] (Cold readings are required at some point for most auditions.) *You will find by the end of this sequence of exercises that you are practically off book already!*

---

[12] A cold reading is reading from the script without much preparation and without having had time to memorize it and develop it to full performance level.

Exercise 15.11: Telling the Inner Monologue/Dialogue—Composing the Character's Thoughts (SM, influenced by studying Brecht in German from Berliner Ensemble Rehearsal Techniques/PGB/SDF)

You can see an example of a script with *inner monologue, images, and actions* noted in Figure 15.4.

Purpose: The aim of the exercise is to explore what your character is thinking in the moment by saying your thoughts aloud.

General Guidelines: Remember that an inner monologue is a stream of continuous self-talk, and differs slightly from inner dialogue, which is an argument or discussion within one person. The idea is to have continuous thoughts as your character when you are not speaking.

You must also listen carefully to your partner. Much of your inner monologue will be in reaction to what you hear, and by listening carefully, you can improvise your unspoken response to what your partner is saying to you. So, inner monologue is composed of your thoughts and reactions simultaneously while listening.

Exercise 15.11A

Guidelines:
- Say your character's thoughts aloud and then your line.
- Next, the other character says his thoughts and then his line.
- Go back and forth. Just as we do in life, think before speaking, but make sure to think as the character. Make sure to motivate and frame all action with thought. Weigh up with thought if your action is having the desired effect. Assess the other person's speech and behavior with thought. Think before you walk on the stage, or when onstage alone.
- Write down these thoughts in your script (as a guideline, although they will be slightly different each time). You will have continuous inner monologue written down one margin of your text (this is one reason you needed to type or copy it with wide margins). Designate what of your script notes you consider the inner monologue by writing "IM:" in front of them.

Exercise 15.11B

Guidelines:
- Now say only the lines, but make sure you are thinking the inner monologue.
- Whenever you are not clearly thinking, the teacher or director may stop you and ask you to mumble your inner monologue, even while the other character is speaking. Articulate specific sentences, words, and phrases in your head. Try to impact the other person and respond to everything going on in you and around you.

15 ACTIVE ANALYSIS THROUGH EVENTS AND ACTIONS

> **Exercise 15.11C**
>
> **Guidelines:**
> - Repeat the exercise and try to say your thoughts, barely mumbling them aloud so as not to distract your partner who is saying his lines.
> - Make a sincere attempt to listen to your scene partner and respond with your inner monologue at the same time. It only takes a little practice to get it.
> - Every *pause* must be filled with thought. There must be a connecting thought between your spoken lines during a pause. Often you will see written in the script, "Pause," "beat," or a series of dots (…) called an ellipsis. Each is of a different length, and very often your teacher or director will determine how long each should be.
> - Do not worry about "cue pick up"; say whatever you feel you would think *if* you were actually in the situation right now for the first time.
> - Again return to only saying the lines but keep that much thought of the character active in your mind at the same time.

Important note on pauses: Every pause is a decision made by the character. The audience will follow the logic of your actions by being able to understand the decisions you make in pauses. Pauses are usually, but not always, accompanied by W.E.D.G.A.G. (Too many pauses can ruin the soup, so don't allow yourself to drag out pauses or make unnecessary pauses.)

However, for the time being assume that a pause is whatever length of time it takes to connect what has just been said to what will be said next by either character. Some pauses last only a few seconds, and others are long and called psychological pauses. In either case, long pauses, whether active or still, make up a zone of silence. Through trial and error you will analyze the situation and choose a logical length of a pause.

A series of dots usually indicates that the character's words trail off into a short thought. Ellipses are best conveyed with an expressive gesture and hesitation in the dialogue.

When you see the word "beat," it is a very short pause and very often is used as a reaction to something that momentarily halts the action, a justified response.

> **15.11A, B & C** *Reflection Journal—Inner Monologue and Inner Dialogue*
>
> Return to your script and write down your inner monologue and any images you may have discovered during the exercise. The inner monologue must be composed and considered in detail, but it need not be exactly in same words each night. What was your experience of the exercise? Were you able to hold on to your continuous thoughts as the character? It takes time for your mind and body to adjust to creating the thoughts of another person, so stick with it, and think of it as a game.

For now, only focus on having the inner monologue while you are NOT speaking. However, in life you do think and assess with thought the impact of what you are saying on others, even before you are finished speaking, but that can come later. Images are continuous whether you are speaking or not.

Why Images and Inner Monologue? Anton Chekhov's Contribution to the Development of the System

(For more information about Anton Chekhov and his contribution to the development of the System, please refer to Chapter 20: The Evolving Stanislavsky System.)

Anton Chekhov's contribution to the development of the System cannot be overestimated. Chekhov's writing introduced for the first time characters whose inner spiritual lives dominated the action on stage. This concentration on the inner world in Chekhov's plays presented a monumental challenge to Stanislavsky during the preparations for the first season of the Moscow Art Theatre, and he realized that a new style of acting was required and a new technique created to address it.

Stanislavsky was the first to realize that the old style of external declamatory acting, so popular in the nineteenth century, had caused the failure of Chekhov's first play, *The Seagull*, by a group of Russian "stars" in a previous production. He surmised that the old, external acting style of acting would kill the delicate spiritual nature of the play and thus instructed the actors to focus on creating a film of mental image-pictures behind the spoken text and to have a continuous inner monologue going when they were not speaking. Today, with film and television dominating so much of our lives, it may seem obvious to us that actors need to think and stay in character while performing, but this was revolutionary during Stanislavsky's time. As a result, psychological realism was born, and it has changed our concept of acting to this day.

An Example of a Text Notated with Inner Monologue (IM) and Images (IMG)

The following excerpt is taken from the opening scene of Chekhov's masterpiece, *Three Sisters*.[13] It is intended to provide an example of one method for organizing and annotating your script for actions, images, and inner monologue. All three sisters appear onstage; however, Olga does not address them directly as she begins her speech, rather she is thinking aloud and includes them when needed. Give the scene a positive named event: *Building dreams on sand;* after all, the year of mourning is over, and Olga wishes to encourage herself and her sisters that a new life is beginning. In fact, we could also name it Beginning the New Life. (The interpretation of actions, images, and inner monologue here is based on Bennett's direction of the 1980 production of the play by his professional acting company, the Stanislavski Ensemble, and as taught in the classes at the conservatory. It is not intended to be definitive but offer suggestions and guidance for thorough script work. The example here focuses almost exclusively on Olga's actions, thoughts, and images. This is done for the sake of simplicity and clarity.)

---

[13]Sonia Moore, *Stanislavski Revealed, The Actor's Guide to Spontaneity on Stage*. Translated from the Russian by Sonia Moore (New York:Applause Theater Books, 1991), 32.

Act I

(The clock strikes twelve as the curtain rises. Olga, in a teacher's uniform, is pacing and correcting school papers. Irina, dressed in white, is daydreaming at the window. Masha, dressed in black, lying on the chaise, reading a book of poems.)

Olga: IM: *"Oh, the clock is striking twelve, I've got to hurry. I must finish correcting these papers as the guests are beginning to arrive. Sometimes I wonder if the students ever hear anything I say, these test papers are terrible!"*
Irena: IM: *"I can't wait to return home to Moscow!... All of the beautiful clothes to wear and balls to attend. I dream of marrying a handsome officer!"*
Masha: IM: *"This poem haunts me... 'and a golden chain about its bough....' I am chained here forever."*
(**Note:** Masha serves as a counterpoint to the other two sisters. Her reactions and inner monologue are very important to our understanding of the scene.)
Pause. Olga stops correcting papers, sets them on the table and sits.
(**Note to the actor:** If you are playing Olga, you must choose an image of someone you know, have known or perhaps create in your imagination; that you might feel about the same way as Olga feels about her father. If you create an imaginary image use exacting details. If you choose a real person they do not need to have died. The Main Action of the opening episode is to compare.)
Olga: IM: *"Oh, my God! With all of the preparations for the party I had completely put the memory of father's death out of mind. The clock brought the memory back to me. I must put this work on the table and sit down, just to remember him and contemplate how it was then compared to this beautiful day!"*
Olga: *(Action: To recall and compare.* **IMG:** *To me Uncle Joe is like Olga's father.)* **Father died exactly a year ago, on this very day, the fifth of May** (**IMG:** *My sister Mary's birthday party.*), **your saint's day, Irina.** *(Action: To compare the past to the present.* **IMG:** *The snow storm we had last Christmas in New York.)* **It was cold, and snow was falling.** *(***IMG:** *Finals week at the university)* **It seemed to me that I would never live through it, and you were lying unconscious as if you were dead.** *(***IMG:** *imaginary image of fainting here)* **IM:** *"How lovely Irina looks and she looks so happy."* **You are already wearing a white dress, your face glows.**
Pause. **IM:** *"I recall how the clock was striking twelve the moment father collapsed. I hope it isn't a bad omen that it is striking now as we begin our new life."* **And the clock was striking then, too.**
Pause.
(**Note to the actor: IMG:** *If you do not have a real image of a funeral in your own experience, create this image in your imagination by seeing a horse drawn hearse slowly progressing to the cemetery with soldiers and friends walking behind it.)* **It comes back to me that when father was carried away** (**IMG:** *Sound of a band playing music on the Fourth of July at Central Park.*), **music was playing and at the cemetery they fired a salute.**

> (**Note to the Actor:** Olga is not boasting here about her father being a brigadier general, instead she laments that there were only a handful of people attending and this makes her sad again.) *(Action: To lament.)* **He was a general, in command of a brigade, and yet there were only a few people.** *(Action: To excuse and forgive.* **IMG:** *The flood in St. Louis I saw on TV last year.)* **But it was raining then. Heavy rain and snowing.** *(To the Actor playing Irina: Why do you think Irina interrupts here? At what point in Olga's speech does she stop her daydreaming and listen to Olga?)*
> **Irina:** *(Action: To kindly stop her sister from dwelling on the past.)* **Why remember?** *(She returns to her daydreaming.)*

The Tonal Subtext

The *tonal subtext* is what you are really trying to communicate with the lines. This is only one aspect of the entire subtext of the play, which includes all aspects of Telling the Novel, including the subtext of the body explored in the next chapter. It also includes the design elements and the *mise-en-scene* (composition and movement of actors through the space).

Some lines are somewhat neutral. For example, if the line is, "Hello!" think of how you would say this with the tonal subtext, "Do I know you?" and how differently you might say it with the subtext of, "You're hot!" For some characters, like Blanche in *A Streetcar Named Desire,* what she is really saying can be quite different and juxtapose the line, creating a complex counterpoint. For example when she says in scene 2, as sampled in Appendix V, "Now the buttons!" what she is really communicating is "come and touch me." Other characters, like Stanley in the same play, are much more direct, and his subtext is closer to the text; however, you must still decide what he is communicating with neutral lines such as, "Yeah," which could mean many different things. There are also styles of comedy that use sarcasm so that when the character says, "Lovely dress," he really means that's hideous.

> ### Exercise 15.12: Telling the Tonal Subtext (KSS/SM/PGB/SDF)
>
> **15.12A: Purpose:** Discovering the tonal subtext adds nuance and meaning to your lines and also helps you uncover how to say them (as do the other Elements of Action).
>
> **Note:** Later in this chapter, in Part III: The Logic of Speech, you will learn some additional tools to add meaning and impact to your lines.
>
> **Guidelines:**
> - Say your character's tonal subtext aloud and then your line, trying to communicate that subtext through the sound and emphasis of the actual text.
> - Take turns going back and forth with your partner with both subtext and lines.
> - In your script, write down *TST:* under each line and then write down the tonal subtext you discovered (again, in pencil, as it might change).

- Now say only the lines. Make sure you are communicating the tonal subtext.
- **Gibberish:** If you find you are losing the subtext when you just say the words, try to communicate the tonal subtext through gibberish (made-up language) because then you are forced to communicate through pitch, volume, and tempo.

Exercise 15.13: Naming Your Actions and Reactions Aloud (KSS/SM/PGB/SDF)

Purpose: Actively engage with each other to bring out the dynamic energy of the scene.

Preparation:
- Break the scene into smaller action steps (beats). Beats (action steps) can be used later when you are ready to get the scene up to pace.
- Having a well-defined score of actions (i.e., listed in order) to test before you do the following exercise will give you confidence. Remember the actions are the steps you might take toward your desired solution (objective) of the problem (task). The actions are not written in stone. In the following "telling your actions" exercise, you are free to improvise in the moment and select actions that seem more fitting as you actively interact with your partner(s).
- You may choose to either use your script or not, depending on how familiar you are with your lines at this point. Go through your scene, but only do one episode at a time. Name the initiating action and then your reactions. Notice the thought that leads you from the response to the next action. Your reaction to your partner must be spontaneous and honestly related to what your partner has just said and/or done. It must not be pre-planned but improvised in the moment. Take time to take in what she says and does.
- There is a formula you can use for any play or character: Imagine that your partner has just accused you with his line; in response you would first say your reaction (which is improvised in the moment) and then name your action before saying your line. It might sound something like this: "When you *accuse* me I *defend* myself by saying . . . " (Here you can paraphrase or say your line.)
- **Remember**, as you did in previous improvisations, to name the actions as active verbs (to dismiss, to reproach, to apologize, to forgive etc.)

Telling Your Actions on Your Feet (PGB/SDF)
- **15.13A:** Say your action and then say the line trying to fulfill the action.
- **15.13B:** Once you have a score of actions written in for specific lines of the script, then go through and only say the actions and have your partner say his counteraction. Say it with the focus and energy of the action itself and trying to affect your partner with it.

- **15.13C:** Finally, only say your line but try to fulfill your action and affect your partner. Make sure to receive your partner's counteraction.
- **Write all your actions on your script in pencil in active-verb form: To protest.** The notation is **A** for *action*.

Important note: Each time your partner does it differently, you must respond differently.

Named Event	A phrase from the text, or your own name.
/	action step (beat shift)
//	transition between episodes
IM	Inner monologue
TST	Tonal subtext
A	Action
IMG	Image
^	A caesura to mark the phrasing
P	Problem
OBJ	Objective (character's goal or ideal solution)
Obst	Obstacle
=>	Initiator of the action (Who is driving the scene?)
EAE	Embodied Analogous Emotions

And from The Logic of Speech:

①②③	**Length of pauses**
<u>Underline</u>	Operative or key words in each phrase group

Speech Measures:
S = Group of the subject
V = Group of the verb
C = Group of the circumstances
Note: Sometimes you may see a symbol like SV or CV

At the top of your script you will also write:
Main Event
Main Problem
Main Objective
Magic If
Need

These do not need to be annotated and can just be written out in full, as they do not continually reoccur throughout the scene.

Important note: For scripts with more Elements of Action notated, sample text analysis charts, and for a worksheet in line-by-line text analysis, see Appendix V.

Figure 15.4 Symbols for Script Notation[14] (SDF/PGB)

[14]These are the script notation symbols for the Elements of Action that French has come to use. French got caesura (^) from the books of Royal Shakespeare Voice teacher Cicely Berry. It is a common symbol in Shakespearan script analysis.

> **15.13A, B & C** *Reflection Journal—Telling Your Actions*
>
> Did you notice that the novel is always told in the first person? This is to reinforce your ability to stay in the present moment and maintain the state of "I exist" in your character's circumstances. Did you notice how saying your reactions logically connects and leads to your counteraction? Always search for the logic and consecutiveness of actions. Keep in mind that you are free to react and say what you are doing physically in the moment. You can improvise and find the very best physical actions through these moment-to-moment improvisations. It's really all about finding typical and fitting physical actions through improvisation! If other Elements of Action occur spontaneously, such as images, thoughts, or emotions, so much the better. Make note of that, too.

PART III: THE LOGIC OF SPEECH

Phrasing of the Text, Pauses, and Punctuation

In Part I of this chapter, Reconnaissance of the Scene, you carefully analyzed the script to liberate creative opportunities. There you considered the importance and possibility of pauses. Now that you are familiar with the basic tools of Active Analysis through Events and Actions, look more closely at some ways of examining a text in greater detail.

When a musician goes to compose and create a written record for a piece of music, there is a standard procedure used widely throughout many countries (although different in some forms of music; Chinese, for example) for notation. In that way any artist can pick up the sheet music and with a bit of practice re-create the music as the composer intended. Unfortunately, however, there is no such notation for a play script. Perhaps that is just as well, as we actors are a very independent lot and like to come up with our own interpretations of the written word.

Stanislavsky was deeply concerned about how to approach scoring a text in such a way that the spoken word would emerge clearly and naturally from the script yet convey the many nuances of meaning between the layers. In Jean Benedetti's most recent translation of Stanislavsky's master work, *An Actor's Work*, the chapter on voice and speech cites several examples of the use of inflections and need to phrase speeches in such a way that they have an almost musical shape. We did not approach this area in this textbook, as the authors believed that there were plenty of fine voice and speech coaches with whom you could work who would be able to pay particular attention to the subject. However, what we would like you to recognize here is that it is important for speech clarity to be able to analyze your text line-by-line in order to properly phrase your words in such a way that your character's thoughts and actions are clearly expressed and projected to an audience.

The following few examples and exercises for the remainder of the chapter are based in Stanislavsky's theories as expanded upon by Russian speech teacher of the B. V. Schukin School at the Vakhtangov Theatre in Moscow, T. I. Zaporojetz in a booklet translated into English and adapted by Sonia Moore.[15]

---

[15] T. I. Zaporojetz, *The Logic of Speech on Stage*, trans. Sonia Moore (New York: American Center for Stanislavski Theatre Art, 1981), as adapted by Philip G. Bennett over many years for use in his classes and rehearsals.

"It is a mistake to think that actors must speak on stage as they do in life. In life people often speak poorly, fast, incomprehensibly, etc. Speech in daily life is often monotonous and dull which on stage irritates the spectators. To acquire good speech a great deal of practice is needed. Students, while practicing, should make a graphic analysis of the text."

—T. I. Zaporojetz

Making a Graphic Analysis of the Text (TIZ/PGB)

Our speech can be divided into three categories of thought, which we shall call *Speech Measures:*

S = Group of the subject
V = Group of the verb
C = Group of the circumstances

Note: Sometimes you may see a symbol like SV or CV. In these cases the speech measure might fit into either or both categories. The decision is yours.

A Scene from Arthur Miller's *The Crucible*

(Sample rehearsals for this play are offered in Chapter 16.)
Here is an example from the previous scene from *The Crucible*:

S = Subject and Verb   C = Circumstances   V = Verb
Elizabeth. No, she walked into the house ① this afternoon; ① I found her

C = Circumstances
sittin' ① in the corner like she come to visit.

Figure 15.5 Example: A graphic analysis of text.

We have four thought groups. The first introduces the subject of the rabbit and the verb, *walked*; the second tells when, circumstances; the third, verb; and the fourth describes the circumstances in greater detail.

Do not confuse breaking down the lines into patterns of thought with rules of grammar. The rules of English or even Russian grammar do not apply here because when people speak, their thoughts are random, they do not follow any particular grammar. Also, a speech can be composed of any variety of thought patterns. There does not need to be a subject, verb, and object, in the same sense as in regular English grammar. Here, subject can be a topic, an object, a person; it can vary. Not every verb is necessarily in the group of the verb, either. Think of the verbal group as describing an action or activity. Sometimes a verb will appear in the circumstances group. By the way, when the group of the circumstances falls at the end of the sentence, you will notice that it often takes the most emphasis in the sentence, but even this is not a hard and fast rule.

Determining Connecting and Dividing Connecting Pauses between Speech Measures

Thoughts move, and this affects the pattern, inflection, tempo-rhythm, and tone of our voice and speech. Between speech groups there is a slight *shift* of thought that is called a connecting and/or a dividing pause; they are:

- A connecting pause ①—two speech groups that are closely connected in meaning. There is very little shift of voice between speech groups with a connecting pause ①.
- A connecting/dividing pause ②—two speech groups that are not quite as closely connected in meaning. There is a noticeable shift of voice in a connecting/dividing pause ②. Depending on what is logical and consecutive, you may choose how you wish to express this, either by use of a change in inflection, tempo, pitch, volume, etc.
- A dividing pause ③—two speech groups that are not connected in meaning. A dividing pause is expressed as a slight beat or pause in action, such as an ellipsis (…). See the description below.
- Please remember that there are no hard and fast rules to any of these guidelines. The purpose is to give you, the actor, more techniques and brushes to use with your palette when creating the portrait of character.

Exercise 15.14: Identifying Thought Groups and Types of Pauses (TIZ/PGB)

Purpose: Just as music is notated in measures, so can your speech be notated in measures of logical and sequential thought patterns. Thought patterns determine speech patterns, and both lead to the patterns of your psychophysical behavior; i.e., your actions. Also, this simple tool will help you study your lines more deeply and learn them faster.

Guidelines:
- Identify each of the thought groups in your own scene.
- For notation to mark the space between the thought groups at first you can use a caesura ^.
- Next, determine whether or not they are closely connected in meaning, then choose and place the appropriate number pause between the groups, ①②③, and underline the operative or key word in each group.

Right away you will be able to see the value of examining each sentence of your script in this way.

A Further Note on Inflection: Placing numbers between thought groups gives you an opportunity to vary your tempo-rhythm and inflections. You don't need to do too much, but just become aware of the possibilities. Thoughts move and turn throughout a speech, especially when a speech is long, and this keeps your audiences alert and eager to hear more.

Figure 15.6 *Three Sisters* by Anton Chekhov. Director: Philip G. Bennett, The San Francisco Theatre Academy: Stanislavsky Ensemble.
Photo: Robbie Tucker

Please note that your choices are arbitrary. Different actors looking at the same line may make different choices. There is no single correct way. The best way is to phrase the line for understanding, to identify the operative words that will carry the meaning of the sentence, and to make choices!

The following sample is an example of how you may mark your script for actions, images, inner monologue, and numbered pauses. The excerpt is taken from Chekhov's *Three Sisters*,[16] Act 2, scene 2, Andrei and Ferapont.

In this scene Andrei has received a message from the chairman of the local district board via an old and illiterate messenger, Ferapont. The message requires Andrei to read a book and make a report at the board meeting on the following day. Ferapont is a kindly old man, and Andrei treats him gently in this scene. Andrei finds that his dreams of returning to Moscow and becoming a professor are fading away. He is a weak character, and in his depressed state makes the unfortunate decision to give up the struggle. This decision is in his subtext and not overtly stated. How would you as Andrei express such a subtext with your body?

---

[16] Sonia Moore, *Stanislavski Revealed, The Actor's Guide to Spontaneity on Stage* (New York: Applause Theatre Books, 1991), 61–62.

15 ACTIVE ANALYSIS THROUGH EVENTS AND ACTIONS

> **Three Sisters by Anton Chekhov, Act 2, Scene 2 (Andrei and Ferapont)**
>
>   c
> **Andrei: A:** *To dismiss:* **Nothing.** *(IM: "Why does Protopopov bother me at home?").* ③ **A:** *To evaluate:*
>   c   V
> **Tomorrow is Friday.** ② **A:** *To complain:* **I don't have to attend** ② *(IMG: Andrei does not want to go, do*
>   V   c
> *you have such a place in mind?)* **A:** *To decide:* **but I'll go** ① **anyway** … *(Notice the ellipsis, there must be a*
>   V
> *thought here.)* ① **A:** *To justify himself:* **to occupy myself.** ① *(IM: "I must get away from Natasha, and there*
>   c
> *is nothing to do here.")* **A:** *To complain:* **It's boring at home** …
> Pause.
> *(This is a major pause in the scene, and there is no need to rush it. Take your time to really achieve deep thought and logically come to a decision to continue speaking. Ask yourself what Andrei is thinking and feeling. What analogies do I have in my experience, either personal or observed, to use as a source of images in the following section. What do I need to create and see in my imagination to be able to justify Andrei's self-ridicule and state of loneliness. How did my life end up like this? Maybe Andrei thinks something like this: All the dreams I had when I was younger are fading away. I married to hastily and made a mistake, and now life has cheated me. Ferapont is deaf so I can quietly get this off my chest by speaking my deepest feelings aloud.)*
>
>   s   c   s   V   V
> **A:** *To quietly implore:* **Dear Grandpa!** ① **A:** *To ridicule:* **How strangely** ① **life** ① **changes and deceives**
>   c   c   V   V
> **us!** ① **A:** *To cite an example:* **Today,** ① **out of boredom,** ① **because I had nothing else to do,** ① **I picked up** ① *(IMG: Choose an image, either personal or imaginary, of something that has had a great meaning for you in the past and now it doesn't, so it seems ironic to you.)* **A:** *To treat the book as if it is a lost treasure:* **this**
>   s   s   V
> **book—old university lectures—A:** *To mock himself and Chairman:* **and I wanted to laugh** … *(Note the*
>   s
> *ellipsis.)* ① **A:** *To mock yourself:* **My God,** ① *(IMG: See an image of something menial that you look down upon.)*
>   s   s
> **I'm a secretary of the District Board,** ① **the Board** ① *where (IMG: Andrei dislikes and distrusts the*
>   s   V   s
> *Chairman intensely; what image would you choose here?)* **Protopopov** ① **is** ① **the chairman.** ③ **I'm the**
>   s   c   vc   s
> **secretary,** ① *(Andrei pictures himself as a nobody)* **and the most** ① **I can expect is to be** ① **a member of the** *(IMG: Andrei sees a place and occupation that is far beneath him and repulses him. What images do you*
>   s   s   s
> *have?)* **District Board!** ② **I,** ① **a member of the District Board,** ③ *(IMG: Take a slight pause here to capture the image of an analogous dream, savor it, and let it affect you before you speak the line. Use your*
>   V   c   s   s
> *voice to express your feelings.)* **who dreams** ① **every night** ① **that I am a professor** ① **at Moscow University,** *(IMG: Choose an analogous image of a wonderful place that you'd really like to be right now!)* ①
>   s   s   vc   V
> **a famous scholar** ① **whom all of Russia** ① **is** ① **proud of!** ① **Ferapont: I wouldn't know** … ① **I don't**
> V
> **hear well** … *(Up to now Andrei has been speaking aloud; however, mostly to himself. Ferapont is a device Chekhov uses to give Andrei a justification for speaking his private thoughts aloud. For further study please see Appendix V, p. 565.)*

Figure 15.7 A notated script.

Playwrights and Different Types of Pauses

Playwrights use different terms and notation for pauses in their scripts, and some use a variety of types of pauses within one script. Careful examination of a particular playwright's use and notation of the pause is required for each play you work on. Pauses are very helpful to bring out the subtext and inner life of the character.

Beats: As mentioned earlier, you will often see in a modern script the term *(beat)*. Some playwrights who may have some acting background may be trying to mark your beats (acting steps) for you. Instead, find your beats actively working with your scene partners and director. Others use this to denote a momentary pause. Sometimes a writer uses *beat* to indicate where the character needs to have a sharp reaction, or make a decision. Do not confuse the playwright's term with *beat* in the way that we are using it for actors—as a short exchange of action-counteraction on a specific topic prior to that topic shifting. However, both playwrights' marked beats and actors' found beats can and do often help you determine the variation of tempos and rhythms within a text. Pay close attention to them.

Ellipsis: Three or four dots in a row (....). When there are three dots it means that your voice trails off into thought, and when there are four it means that your voice trails off but comes to a full stop as the final dot is a period. In this case you would use W.E.D.G.A.G. as practiced in earlier chapters, and end the thought with a final gesture.

Pause: Pauses can be of any length but are most often longer than a "beat" and always filled with thought and often with action or stage business. All pauses are moments when the character makes important decisions. Sometimes pauses are used as transitions between episodes where the action begins to change or a character enters or exits the stage.

Psychological Pauses: Psychological pauses are just that. Usually they are moments of stillness where the character must relive a memory or come to grips with a serious question. The audience will follow the logic of your character's actions by the decisions you make throughout the performance. When you encounter a pause, work on making clear decisions using W.E.D.G.A.G. and consider that there may be also an adaptation needed.

Purposes of Punctuation

Use punctuation marks like musical notation. Punctuation will help you distribute your voice and speech expressively. Remember, however, that it is the action that dictates how you say your lines. Never get into a mechanical mode of saying your lines in a predetermined way. The best expression of your lines will come when you know your action, images, and subtext. Observing punctuation is simply a means for creating greater clarity.[17]

---

[17] As adapted by Philip G. Bennett from T. I. Zaporojetz, *The Logic of Speech on Stage*, trans. Sonia Moore (New York: American Center for Stanislavski Theatre Art, 1981).

Period: A period at the end of a sentence indicates the completion of a unit of thought. Identify the operative word(s) toward the end of the sentence and lower your voice to clearly express that you have arrived at the end of a thought. This could be followed by a slight pause when the next sentence is an entirely new thought.

Semicolon: A semicolon both unites and divides a thought. The voice may go down toward the end of the speech measure, but not as low as with a period.

Comma: The voice is usually raised slightly on the word before a comma. A comma means that there is a slight pause in the thought and that there is more to come, as the thought has not yet been completed. It is like raising your hand and saying, "Wait, I have more to say." The main thing to remember about a comma is that you must continue the energy of the line through to the final thought and period. If you do not, the audience will think you have ended the thought.

Colon: A colon is used to indicate that more information is coming. Sometimes a list of various ideas or items follows a colon. Raise your voice slightly to alert the ear of the audience that more is coming. There needs to be a slight pause after a colon so that the listener's ear has time to prepare for what is enumerated after it.

Dash: A dash indicates that a fact or theme opposes another fact or theme. Here the voice needs to make it clear that the two opposing facts are antithetical. (This is a common rhetorical device used in Shakespeare's poetry.) It also indicates that a sharp change of tempo-rhythm may be needed. When you see a series of dashes in a script, it is often a clue that the character's emotional state is irregular and agitated.

Question Mark: A question mark requires a strong accent on the operative word(s) within the sentence that accentuates the question. Interrogatives such as who, what, when where, to whom, why, and how are generally accentuated.

Exclamation Mark: An exclamation mark means that a strong emotion is present on the word or words that carry the most meaning in the sentence. The voice must raise sharply on operative word(s) that bring out the strong emotion; nevertheless, avoid prolonged or unnecessary shouting, as that will blot out the action and meaning of the sentence.

Parentheses: Parentheses denote a thought within a thought, or additional thoughts that may digress or add to the main subject. To make a parenthetical phrase clearly understood, there must be a change in voice, volume, and/or inflection. Raise your voice and take a slight pause before the parenthesis, then lower your voice slightly within the parenthetical phrase. When the phrase is complete, make a slight pause and raise your voice to the same level it was before lowering it. In this way the listener will clearly understand your intent behind the words.

Quotation Marks: Quotation marks indicate that a character is speaking as another person or referring to something that is well known. Always take a very slight pause before and after a quotation mark and change the inflection of your voice in order to make it clear that you are imitating or speaking as another person. You may also wish to color a phrase in quotation marks with your character's attitude toward the person or subject you are quoting.

The above list of types of pauses and various punctuation marks is intended to help you to become aware of how many possibilities there are for analyzing and interpreting your text. You will need to learn how a particular playwright is using these devices, often as hints to the actor, in a particular play. The more closely you study the text and its structure, the more choices you will have as an actor for the selection of actions and the infinite variety of verbal expressions you can master with your speech. A discovery of the character's logical thought patterns will help you find the character's patterns of logical and consecutive behavior as well.

Summary

You combed through your script to discover creative opportunities through listening to the sound of the spoken words, articulating and moving with punctuation, and making initial observations about language. You prepared for Active Analysis by listing the active facts, identifying the "three wheres," creating a ground plan, marking and naming episodes, and figuring out your character's problem and what he wants to do to solve it. Then you got active with your analysis by improvising the episodes, finding and creating images, and Telling the Novel. You then started to look at the script with an even finer comb by doing some beginning aspects of the logic-of-speech analysis.

This chapter gets at the very heart of Active Analysis. Within the chapter are sample texts for realistic plays, as it is best for students to begin in this style. However, the techniques outlined here can be used on any play. Some sample analyses of contemporary and plays using alternative plot structures, such as episodic plots, are included on the companion website.

While many Active Analysis techniques have been introduced in the last three chapters as separate techniques, it cannot be said too often that in practice they interweave inseparably. Different actors and directors will select from these tools and use them in the order that makes the most sense for the play, level of the actors, and length of rehearsal. For an outline of an exchange between an actor and director in an Active Analysis rehearsal, go to Chapter 16: Active Analysis in Rehearsal.

15 ACTIVE ANALYSIS THROUGH EVENTS AND ACTIONS

New Theatre Terms and Concepts

Terms used in the Stanislavsky System are in italics.

- ☐ Actor's Equity
- ☐ amalgamation
- ☐ *beat (a short pause)*
- ☐ caesura
- ☐ character's problem
- ☐ cold reading
- ☐ connecting and dividing pauses
- ☐ *devices*
- ☐ diction/language
- ☐ drives (the scene)
- ☐ ellipsis
- ☐ episodes (secondary named events)
- ☐ ground plan
- ☐ group of the subject, verb and circumstances
- ☐ iambic pentameter
- ☐ inflection
- ☐ initiator (of the action)
- ☐ limerick
- ☐ logic of speech
- ☐ major reversal
- ☐ operative (key word)
- ☐ paraphrasing the subtext
- ☐ pauses
- ☐ psychological pauses
- ☐ pyrrhic
- ☐ receiver (of the action)
- ☐ reconnaissance of the scene
- ☐ relevant images
- ☐ rhyming couplet
- ☐ speech measures (thought groups)
- ☐ spondee
- ☐ *Telling the Novel*
- ☐ tonal subtext
- ☐ trochee (trochaic)

CHAPTER 16

Active Analysis in Rehearsal

"Do you want to know who you are? Don't ask. Act! Action will delineate and define you."[1]

—Witold Gombrowicz (1904–1969)

Primary Elements of Action Actively Explored in This Chapter:

An étude—second plan improvisation; physicalizing your subtext: tonal and physical; Telling the Novel on your feet: flow of action; naming and drilling actions

- **How Do We Use Active Analysis in Rehearsal with a Director?**
- **Physicalizing Your Subtext**
- **A Brief Review**
- ***The Crucible* by Arthur Miller**
- **The Story**
  - Rehearsal 16.1: *The Crucible*: Act 2, First Episode
  - *The Crucible*: Act 2, an Étude—Second Plan Improvisation
  - Rehearsal 16.2: First Episode
  - Rehearsal 16.3: Act 2
  - Rehearsal 16.4: First Run-Through
- **A Final Note about Inspiration**

How Do We Use Active Analysis in Rehearsal with a Director?

In this chapter we will create an imaginary rehearsal scenario based on an actual series of rehearsals conducted at the San Francisco Theatre Academy's Repertory Company in 1978–1979 under the direction of Philip G. Bennett. The purpose here is to reinforce what you have read in this book and studied in the classroom through reenacting the rehearsal of a scene from a play. There is an active dialogue between actors and a director using Active Analysis. Other cast members are present at the rehearsal and may at times contribute to the collaborative process when invited by the director.

---

[1] Witold Gombrowicz, *Diary*, vol. 2 (1957–1961), ed. Jan Kott. Trans. Lillian Vallee. (Evanston, IL: Northwestern University Press, 1989), 130.
Since about 2003 this quote was falsely attributed to Thomas Jefferson. According to the Monticello.org website, "We currently have no evidence to confirm that Thomas Jefferson ever said or wrote, 'Do you want to know who you are? Don't ask. Act! Action will delineate and define you.' This can be unequivocally attributed to Witold Gombrowicz. How it came to be attributed to Thomas Jefferson is unclear." www.monticello.org/site/jefferson/do-you-want-know-who-you-arequotation.

16 ACTIVE ANALYSIS IN REHEARSAL

Note: The setting created here is ideal: one in which there is no time or deadline pressure, where all the actors are trained in the System, and where rehearsals can be conducted as learning opportunities for continual discovery and improvement of the technique. In this way we hope to make clear to you how you can apply and adapt what you have learned throughout the book for your use of Active Analysis through Psychophysical Actions. It is also intended to serve as a realistic example of what you may wish to strive for in your creative work.

Physicalizing Your Subtext

As has been mentioned in earlier chapters, subtext is simply the meaning under the text; however, since it springs forth from the imaginary subconscious mind of the character, we must analyze, create, and bring it to light. The previous steps you have been learning in chapters 13, 14, and 15 have prepared you for what you are about to experience here. If you have been working on a scene, most likely you have already discussed and discovered much of the subtext of whatever scene you may be rehearsing. Certainly, it is important to discuss the subtext with your partner, teacher, or director. If you haven't already done so, you may want to write down the subtext in your script, but if you do this, remember that during the early stages of rehearsal it is good not to fix things too soon. Write them down in pencil and then continue to search in order to find the best subtext and actions while on your feet.

The reason for this is simple: What happens in the moment of working with actions is spontaneous and can sometimes reveal a subtext you would never be able to find intellectually. Both intellect and physicality are needed. In other words, work like a scientist who first gets a hypothesis, writes it down, and then conducts the experiment to discover if it worked or not. Sometimes what you discover by so called "accident," is the best answer to a question, as well as the solution to the problem.

Figure 16.1 Forgiveness. Actors Kent Fillmore (John Proctor), Dolores Neese (Elizabeth Proctor). *The Crucible*, by Arthur Miller, performed at the San Francisco Theatre Academy Ensemble Company, 1979.
Photo: © Robbie Tucker

A Brief Review

There are two levels of subtext that we have discussed earlier in the book: *tonal* and *physical*. Here we will concentrate on finding the physical behavior that reveals the subtext; what is called the *language of the body (also subtext of the body)*, with some focus on how the physical influences your tonal subtext as well. Your body language will greatly affect your tonal subtext, as voice and speech arise out of mental and physical action. Your body language is largely unconscious; however, in the creation of a character we need to use conscious means to discover, express, and project it.

The Crucible, by Arthur Miller (October 17, 1915–February 10, 2005)

For our imaginary rehearsal we have selected Arthur Miller's *The Crucible* for three basic reasons: 1) it is a play with an important *social purpose*; 2) the story is full of dynamic conflict that lends itself to the need to choose strong verbal and physical actions; and 3) it offers wonderful opportunities to work on subtext.

The Story

The Crucible is based on a fictional retelling of actual historical events surrounding the witch-hunt of 1692 in Salem, Massachusetts. The story centers around three main characters, John and Elizabeth Proctor and their former young servant girl, Abigail Williams. Prior to the opening of the play, Elizabeth discovers that her husband and Abigail had an affair during the long period of Elizabeth's illness after giving birth to their youngest child. In a fit of righteous rage Elizabeth throws Abigail out of the house. (In this time period a servant losing a place would be disgraced and unable to find other work; however, due to the strict religious laws of the period, John and Elizabeth keep silent about the affair, but Abigail does not. She shares the event with her closest childhood friends.) Seven months have passed by the opening of Act 1.

The story takes place at a time of fear and superstition, when people believed that the devil was at work in New England, recruiting souls as witches in order to destroy the young Christian settlements.

Fear and hysteria take hold of Salem Village when the seventeen-year-old Abigail has been caught dancing naked in the woods with other young girls of the village. The terrified girls become hysterical for fear of punishment and begin to accuse the women of the village of being witches, who are afflicting them. Old grudges and hatreds are rekindled as neighbor turns against neighbor, sparking the consuming flames of hysteria and vengeance.

Abigail sees this as an opportunity to destroy Elizabeth Proctor and claim John for herself by accusing Elizabeth of witchcraft.

At Elizabeth's trial, prompted by Abigail, the girls fall on the floor of the courthouse and in their wild screams of hysteria claim that the accused Elizabeth is attacking and torturing them, by sending out her familiar spirit in the form of a yellow bird.

Figure 16.2 Dancing in the woods. Actors Joanne Lucich (Abigail Williams), Patricia Walker (Tituba). *The Crucible*, by Arthur Miller, performed at the San Francisco Theatre Academy Ensemble Company, 1979.
Photo: Philip G. Bennett

John finds that his defense of his wife's innocence has failed, and when he proclaims that "God is dead!" he also is accused by Abigail, and thus falls victim to the hysteria and is arrested and jailed.

Arthur Miller wrote *The Crucible* in 1953 in order to expose the hypocrisy behind the Red Scare[2] hysteria that

---

[2] Red Scare was a term used during the McCarthy era to denote a fear of a Communist takeover of the US.

16 ACTIVE ANALYSIS IN REHEARSAL

Figure 16.3 Hysteria. *The Crucible*, by Arthur Miller, performed at the San Francisco Theatre Academy Ensemble Company, 1979.
Photo: Philip G. Bennett

Figure 16.4 "God is dead!" Kent Fillmore (John Proctor). *The Crucible*, by Arthur Miller, performed at the San Francisco Theatre Academy Ensemble Company, 1979.
Photo: Philip G. Bennett

had swept the country during the early Cold War years. In 1952, Senator Joseph McCarthy of Wisconsin (1908–1957) became the chairman of the Government Operations Committee of the Senate and of its investigations subcommittee. McCarthy took inspiration from the House Un-American Activities Committee, originally created in 1938 to investigate private citizens, public employees, and particularly those suspected of having Communist ties, but he went even further. Witnesses were branded "red" with no evidence, just because they refused to name other supposed offenders without any real reason or evidence. Political opponents or those who dared to question the legality of the committee were often subsequently blacklisted with little to no evidence. In this post, McCarthy attacked the American Communist Party with the intention to purge all suspected Socialist activities from American society.

Hollywood artists, some of whom publicly challenged and questioned the ethics of these committees were particularly targeted. Many artists, particularly Hollywood screenwriters, actors, and directors were called before the committee and were accused of being "card-carrying" Communists; also, their associates were asked to provide lists of friends, family, or colleagues whom they knew or suspected to be Communists. A sense of fear permeated the country, and as a result of this modern witch-hunt many careers and lives were destroyed.

Previously in scene one, John has heard of the affliction that has fallen upon the girls who were caught dancing in the woods and he has decided to go to town, suspecting that Abigail Williams is up to some mischief. There, he has a short but secret conversation with Abigail, who confirms that the girls were only playing. Proctor has enemies, and soon an argument breaks out between him and Rev. Parris, whose daughter Betty lies unconscious. Proctor leaves in disgust. Suspicion and accusation now turns upon Rev. Parris's black house servant, Tituba, who was also with the girls in the woods. As the lowest member of their society, Tituba finds herself trapped, becomes hysterical, and confesses to witchcraft. Abigail sees this as an opportunity to turn all suspicion away from herself and leads the girls to call out the names of old women in the village whom they claim to have seen with the devil. The emotions and hysteria rise as the scene ends with demands for chains and arrests from the townsfolk.

Figure 16.5 Act 3: Mary confesses. Actors (L to R) Jim Peters (Judge Danforth), Cynthia Cristelli (Mary Warren), Kent Fillmore (John Proctor). *The Crucible*, by Arthur Miller, performed at the San Francisco Theatre Academy Ensemble Company, 1979.
Photo: Philip G. Bennett

The following is taken from Act 1, scene 2.[3] Several days have passed since the hysteria has broken out in Salem Village. Elizabeth has urged John to return to the village and tell the authorities what Abigail has told him in Rev. Parris's house: "that it had not to do with witchcraft." John has promised to go but has not, due to his feelings of guilt and fear to face Abigail. (He carries this subtext as a psychological burden in the scene, as it weighs on his mind, it is reflected throughout in his inner monologue.)

The Proctor's maid, Mary Warren, has become an official of the court and joined Abigail in the calling out of women's names in the newly established witch trials. Elizabeth now has every reason to fear for her life, believing that Abigail and Mary will call out her name as well. Elizabeth, still weak from her recent childbirth, has not been able to forgive John for his infidelity.

Tonight, however, John has stayed out quite late. He finally returns home. As the scene begins Elizabeth hopes that he has gone to Salem to expose Abigail and stop the madness before it is too late.

Rehearsal 16.1: *The Crucible*, Act 2, First Episode

Proctor's house [...]. On the rise, the common room is empty. From above Elizabeth is heard softly singing to the children. John Proctor enters D.R., carrying his gun, three seconds after curtain. He glances about the room. Crosses to wall U.C., leans gun against bench R. Crosses D.R. to wash stand, pours water into it from pitcher. As he is washing, Elizabeth's footsteps are heard. Elizabeth enters, D.L.

ELIZABETH. What keeps you so late? It's almost dark.
PROCTOR. I were planting far out to the forest edge.
ELIZABETH. Oh, you're done then.
PROCTOR. Aye, the farm is seeded. The boys asleep? *(Dips hands in water, wipes them.)*
ELIZABETH. *(Removes water and towel, goes out L., and returns with dish of stew.)* They will be soon. *(Serves stew in a dish.)*
PROCTOR. Pray now for a fair summer.
ELIZABETH. *(Goes out L., returns with another dish.)* Aye.
PROCTOR. Are you well today?
ELIZABETH. I am. It is a rabbit.
PROCTOR. Oh, it is! In Jonathan's trap?
Elizabeth. No, she walked into the house this afternoon; I found her sittin' in the corner like she come to visit.
PROCTOR. Oh, that's a good sign walkin' in.

---

[3] Arthur Miller, *The Crucible*, acting ed. (New York: Dramatists Play Service 1954), 27–28.

16 ACTIVE ANALYSIS IN REHEARSAL

> ELIZABETH. Pray God. It hurt my heart to strip her, poor rabbit.
> PROCTOR, Oh, it is well seasoned.
> ELIZABETH. I took great care. She's tender?
> PROCTOR. Aye. I think we'll see green fields soon. It's warm as blood beneath the clods.
> ELIZABETH. That's well.
> PROCTOR. If the crop is good I'll buy George Jacobs' heifer. How would that please you?
> ELIZABETH. Aye, it would.
> PROCTOR. I mean to please you, Elizabeth.
> ELIZABETH. *(It's hard to say.)* I know it, John.
> PROCTOR. *(As gently as he can.)* Cider?
> ELIZABETH. *(A sense of her reprimanding herself for having forgot.)* Aye! *(Gets jug from off L., pours drink into pewter mug, brings it to him.)*
> PROCTOR. This farm's a continent when you go foot by foot droppin' seeds in it.
> ELIZABETH. It must be.
> PROCTOR. On Sunday let you come with me and we'll walk the farm together; I never see such a load of flowers on the earth. Massachusetts is a beauty in the spring!
> ELIZABETH. Aye, it is.
> PROCTOR. I think you're sad again. Are you?
> ELIZABETH. You come so late I thought you'd gone to Salem this afternoon.
> PROCTOR. Why? I have no business in Salem.
>
> . . . and so the first episode concludes with the problem of Salem introduced.

What would you imagine to be the subtext of this episode? To understand the subtext you would first need to study the play very carefully, as you have been instructed. Then you and your partner would need to come up with a name for the event; for example, you might choose to give it a title, like *Salem*. Why *Salem*? Because what is happening in Salem is being avoided in this episode, and yet it is the unspoken subject and source of the problem and ensuing conflict in the scene. Or, you may choose to use a metaphor that describes the atmosphere and what is about to happen between John and Elizabeth Proctor: *Sparks Ignite!* Consider giving headline name to the Main Event for all of Act 2, such as *Smoke from Salem Engulfs Proctor Household!*

These are suggestions as to the thoughts and subtext that could be discussed before you get up on your feet, and then reevaluated after you have improvised the scene. Keep searching until you have found the most fitting names for the event.

The Crucible: Act 2, an Étude—Second Plan Improvisation

Note: In this situation the director has chosen to address the actors by their character names.

Director: *"I'd like to begin today's rehearsal with a nonverbal étude, or 'second plan improvisation,' where you each explore an important Event that occurs during the Flow of the Day, and prior to the opening of Act 2. . . . Elizabeth, what is important for you to improvise prior to the opening of the scene?"*

Elizabeth: *"I think that the killing of the rabbit for John's dinner is an important event, and I'd like to explore it."*

Director: *"That's an excellent idea."* John, what would you like to explore?"

John. *"I'm not sure. . . . I probably worked until dark and then came home for dinner."*

Director: *"Are you certain about that? Why does Elizabeth say, 'What keeps you so late? It's almost dark.'"*

John: *"That's right, I forgot. Maybe I struggled with the decision whether or not to finish plowing the field or to go to Salem earlier in the day."*

Director: *"I agree, that would be logical; so what would be your Main Action?"*

John: *"To struggle with making a decision."*

Director: *"Very good!"*

(The actors individually perform the improvisational études in turn.)

Director: *"What did you discover while executing the études?"*

John: *"I realized that I began the day with a determination to go to Salem but hesitated for two reasons."*

Director: *"What were those?"*

John: *"First, I thought, who would I go to speak to? Who would believe me if I told what Abigail said to me, that the girl's hysteria had nothing to do with witchcraft? Then I thought about Abigail and just couldn't face her."*

Elizabeth: *"Yes, I probably made him promise he would never see her again. Did I clearly project how difficult it was for me to kill and skin the rabbit?"*

Director: *"Yes, you did that well. Your decision to kill the rabbit rather than let it go was especially clear. You took time with the decision and struggled with it, giving it great importance."*

Elizabeth: *"Oh, good! I wanted to express that I did it out of appreciation and love for John."*

John: *"That came through to me."* How was my improvisation? Was it clear, too?"

Director: *"It was clear that you didn't want to face Abigail. It came through that you were struggling and felt guilty for your attraction to her."*

John: *"Oh, good. I don't think I could resist her!"*

(The cast laughs)

Director: *"You both did quite well; however, what is of most importance is that you use the second plan improvisational études to discover behavior and images in the imaginary circumstances that support and give life to specific moments in the scene."*

16 ACTIVE ANALYSIS IN REHEARSAL

Note: In the following examples, at times, the director may interrupt the actor to address specific moments in much the same way that a musical instructor will stop the singer or pianist when a wrong note is hit or not specifically interpreted. It is also recommended to "side-coach" the actors without necessarily stopping them, in order to avoid the actor having to step in and out of character. At this point in the process, however, it is too soon to "run through" the scene; the task is to work on moment-to-moment Elements of Action that explore the given circumstances. Once the actions have been found, then it is best to run through episodes[4] without interruption, in order to get a feeling of the tempo-rhythm and the flow of the action. At that time, the director may want to use quiet side-coaching to help the actors without breaking character or the flow of action.

> ### Rehearsal 16.2: First Episode
>
> This is an example of putting all the elements of *Telling the Novel* together: *actions* (including *nonverbal, verbal, and physical*), *inner monologue/dialogue*, *subtext*, etc. In this segment we are looking for physical behavior that is in contrast and, at times, a contradiction to what we are saying. (When you work on *tonal subtext* you will also be searching to express a tone of voice that may mean the direct opposite of what you are saying and/or doing.)
>
> *(The rehearsal begins:)*
>
> **Director:** *"At our previous rehearsal of the scene you both found a useful backstory for your character's flow of action prior to the scene's beginning. Today we want to work on putting all of the various elements of Telling the Novel together, working actively on your feet. You may put the elements together in any way that feels most comfortable to you. You really can't do it incorrectly. If it helps, may I suggest that you first say your reactions, and then actions (verbal and physical[5]) to one another; then add your thoughts and any emotional responses that come up spontaneously in the moment. Take your time, don't rush, and simply explore. It is not necessary to*
>
> **Figure 16.6** Avoiding Salem. Kent Fillmore (John Proctor). *The Crucible*, by Arthur Miller, performed at the San Francisco Theatre Academy Ensemble Company, 1979.
> Photo: Philip G. Bennett.

---

[4] Considerations for dividing a scene into episodes can be found in Chapter 15: Active Analysis through Events and Actions, Exercise 15.7.

[5] In training to Tell the Novel, you may have started with inner monologue, then subtext, and subsequently moved on to the greater challenge of naming actions. As you get more comfortable with all these elements, you may begin Telling the Novel by speaking out loud any of the elements of Telling the Novel that come to mind, and the next time through filling in others.

address me as the director when you are telling your novel. In fact, it is better if you stay in character and involved with your partner in the given circumstances. If I have questions, then you can address me directly. What did we decide to call this Event?"

John: *"I think we called it 'Salem,' because of what is happening there, and 'Smoke' that will soon affect John and Elizabeth. Maybe we should call it 'Dangerous Smoke from Salem?!'"*

Elizabeth: *"I agree with that, only it seems to me it is more about Elizabeth's fear. I would call it 'Fear.'"*

Director: *"You both make good suggestions. Certainly there is both danger and fear in the circumstances; however, remember that the Named Event must encapsulate the situation for all the characters in a scene. Let us keep in mind your suggestions as we work through the scene with a focus on the problems that both characters are struggling to overcome. Perhaps then we will arrive at the best name for the event."*

John: *"Shouldn't we review the Supertask of the play and characters?"*

Director: *"Okay, what are we searching to discover in this scene and how does it advance the Main Theme and Supertask of the play?"*

Elizabeth: *"I want John to protect me from being called out by Abigail and sentenced as a witch."*

Director: *"Is that your main goal in the play or in this scene?"*

Elizabeth: *"In this scene for sure (the actress stops and thinks for a moment); I want John to find himself and be honest with himself. I want him to forgive me for being a cold wife and to love me."*

John: *"Yes, I want Elizabeth to be warm and to know that I love her."*

Director: *"What both of you say is true. Their last scene together in Act 4 confirms their dedication and love for one another. It is a powerful scene of forgiveness, reconciliation, and love. But, what happens to 'danger' and 'fear'?"*

John: *"It disappears when they discover how much they really love one another— it is conquered by love!"*

Director: *"Elizabeth, what do you think about that?"*

Elizabeth: *(After a pause) "Love conquers Fear!" Maybe that is the Supertask of the play?*

Director: *(Excited) "That is brilliant! It puts a really human face on the play and the characters. Let's strive to bring that out in this scene by trying to express that you are two people who really love one another but cannot express it as openly as you would like, and that the fear and danger of the present situation is making it even more difficult to do so. Would anyone in the cast have a question or comment?"*

(A cast member raises her hand, and the Director acknowledges her.)

Cast Member #1: *"Is 'love conquers fear' then the Supertask of the play?"*

Director: *"For the present it seems to be the best that our collaborative process has come up with, so, what we want to do now is test it in this scene by exploring the subtext and expressing it through the tonal and physical subtext of the body. Remember that the search for the Supertask is an active process that continues throughout the entire rehearsal process and even during performances. It is the*

Reconnaissance of the Mind. To paraphrase Stanislavsky, he said that it often took him until the twelfth performance with an audience before he could fully realize and actualize the Supertask.

(*The actors go onstage and begin to tell their novel while acting out what they are saying.*)

Actor Playing John Proctor: *"I want to avoid Elizabeth and the whole topic of Salem. That is why I stayed away from home and did not go to Salem today. I take off my boots before entering the house so that she won't coldly reproach me for getting the floor muddy. I quietly open the door. I hear my wife singing a hymn to the children and to avoid her I tip-toe to the fireplace, lean my gun nearby and walk over to the wash basin. I pour the water from the pitcher into the basin and accidentally hit the side of the basin with the pitcher. Elizabeth hears this sound and abruptly stops singing. I know now I will have to face her, but don't want to. I keep my back to her as I hear her descending the stairs and entering the room and continue to wash my hands and face. Then I use the towel to dry myself off. There is a long pause and finally she speaks. . . ."*

Actor Playing Elizabeth Proctor: (*Before entering*) *"I felt certain that John would go to Salem today and tell the magistrate what Abigail told him at Rev. Parris's house last week, that it had not to do with witchcraft. If he really loved me he would have gone days ago. Mary Warren frightened me today when she defied me and said that she was an official of the court, then stormed out of the house. I believe that Abigail wants me dead and intends to take my place. In the hopes that John has gone to Salem today, I have killed a rabbit, something I dislike doing very much, and made a special meal of rabbit stew for him in gratitude. He is so late he must have gone to Salem. I hear a sound from downstairs so he must be home. I stop singing, tuck the children into bed, and with excitement and hope I come down stairs. . . . I see John, but he does not turn or look at me. Something is wrong, but I must push on and find out what he has learned in Salem. So, I stand waiting, and after what feels like an interminable pause, I decide to speak. . . ."*

Elizabeth. What keeps you so late?
Director. (*Interrupting*) *"Elizabeth, how would you use your voice here to express your hope that John has gone to Salem?"*
Elizabeth: *"Perhaps my voice would go up a little, as I would be nervous."* (*She repeats the line and continues.*)
Director: *"What is your problem here, and how would you express this with your body?"*
Elizabeth: *"How can I get John to acknowledge and answer me? I would take a short pause and lean forward with my spine because I am eager to get an answer."* (*She takes the pause and leans forward continuing with the following line:*)
It's almost dark.
Proctor: *"My problem and action is, how can I avoid the subject of Salem entirely, and so I decide to make an excuse. I do not turn around and look at my wife. I say this with my back to her. In order to emphasize this I raise the tone of my*

voice just a bit and make it sound final. My subtext here is that I don't want to talk about Salem!"

I were planting far out to the forest edge.

Elizabeth: *"John is clearly avoiding me, he won't even turn around to look at me; his voice is a bit harsh. I am deeply disappointed with him and very upset and angry. I will suppress my feelings, but he will get no warmth out of me tonight!" I will lower my voice here to express my displeasure."*

Oh,

"To communicate this I will raise my voice slightly and express my disapproval by emphasizing each word."

You're…done…then.

"Now, I will turn away and move toward the fireplace to dish out the stew."

Proctor: *"Well, I hear Elizabeth's disappointment and note of anger in her cold and unforgiving voice. I must insist that the farm is more important right now, so I state firmly:"*

Aye, the farm is seeded.

"I want to leave the room and go upstairs to see the boys in another attempt to avoid her, so I change the subject, turn, raise the pitch of my voice and begin to cross toward the staircase and say…"

The boys asleep?

Elizabeth: *"It has been a long and difficult day, and it took me an hour to settle the boys down. I don't want John disturbing them as he does, so I put my hand out and use a strong voice to stop him from going upstairs. With definite finality I order him not to proceed. He stops and looks, for the first time, directly at me. And, with sharp coldness I say…"*

They will be soon.

Proctor: *"Elizabeth stops me from seeing the boys. I don't want to fight with her, but I give her a look. I feel so guilty that I back down and try to find words that will lighten the tension between us. I look down to avoid her eyes and decide to cross to the table for supper, and say in a rather sheepish tone of voice and to change the subject…"*

Pray now for a fair summer.

Elizabeth: *"I feel badly that I have been so cold to John, but I just can't help myself. I'll dish out the stew into a wooden bowl and cross from the fireplace to the table and place it down where John has seated himself. He talks of a 'fair summer' as if there is nothing at all to worry about. I dislike responding, but I must say something, so I begrudgingly agree."*

Aye.

Proctor: *"She agrees, but begrudgingly. Maybe if I try to find out how she is feeling to show I do care about her and still love her. I say quite sincerely and kindly…"*

Are you well today?

"I look up at her and then down at the stew."

Elizabeth: *(For the sake of peace,* **I answer***, although* ***I'd prefer to leave*** *and coldly* ***say***…*)*

I am.

"I see that he is looking at the stew that I had made with such love for him. I say rather proudly…"

It is a rabbit.

> **Director:** *"That was a very good start, you both picked up the ball and communicated your actions and responses with a good sense of communication between you."*
>
> (The Director addresses the cast:) *"Were they able to tonally and physically express the subtext of love and fear we discussed?*
>
> (Cast member raises his hand.)
>
> **Cast Member #2:** *"I thought it came through in their inner monologue that they wanted to show love but couldn't.*
> **Cast Member #3:** *"What I saw was that they were both afraid to show their love. John tried, but Elizabeth kept shooting him down!"*
>
> (The cast laughs)
>
> **Director:** *"They did quite well with expressing their Novel and found interesting physical actions to cover up their true feelings; for example, John avoided Elizabeth's eyes as much as possible, and Elizabeth went about her tasks in an almost mechanical and very matter-of-fact manner, giving an impression of coldness and aloofness. (Addressing the actors:) Who won and who lost in this episode?"*
> **Elizabeth:** *"I believe that I'm winning at this point."*
> **Director:** *"Yes, John has not yet fully asserted himself, and Elizabeth still has the upper hand.*
> *Now, continue with the scene at the next class rehearsal, using Active Analysis by drilling the actions moment-to-moment. Make sure you are well prepared by knowing and having written down what we discovered today as well as your actions."*
>
> (End of rehearsal)

In the following rehearsal you will have a brief, but hopefully clear, picture of how you might work with a director who is using Active Analysis to discover the most fitting and typical actions for the scene. This is accomplished through a series of questions that we have listed and repeated throughout the book. The questions can be in any order; however, they are best when applied to each given moment so that if an actor is making an entrance, the first logical questions might be, "From where are you coming? Why are you coming here? What do you intend to accomplish? Then the director would ask the student actor(s)—addressed as "John and Elizabeth" here for clarity—to improvise the entrance. The entrance should be practiced until the actor has clearly found how he or she would honestly behave in the given circumstances.

Remember, it is the moment-to-moment circumstances that dictate the behavior and express what the character is doing and why. Therefore, you must be patient and try not to do a run-through of the scene prematurely, as that leads to acting in general, and art demands being specific.

During this phase of the work the director interacts repeatedly with the actors. It is a very intense and important collaborative step. Compare this process to working on a dance routine or a piano passage with a musical director. You must stop when major errors are made, or you may end up practicing the wrong steps and notes.

Rehearsal 16.3: Act 2

—Example of Director Dialogue with Actors Using Active Analysis
(Continuation of Work on the First Episode)

Director: *"John and Elizabeth, let's review just for a moment the first part of the episode. Who was the initiator of the main action?"*

Elizabeth: *"I think it is my character, Elizabeth, as she is trying to find out if John went to Salem today as he had promised.*

Director: *"John, do you agree with that, and if so, what is your counteraction?"*

John: *"I agree with Elizabeth because my counter is to avoid her and try to please her this evening. I am the receiver of the action, right?"*

Director: *"Right. You both seem to have a good understanding of that, and the reason why I ask is to remind you that action is composed of a dynamic conflict that is always passing back and forth between characters. Without that clash there is no drama and no play. Now, let's pick up the scene from where we left off last class when you were Telling the Novel, okay? John, Why do you think the rabbit was caught in Johnathan's trap?"*

John: *"Because Jonathan made the trap himself, with a little help from me. This would be his first catch and I'm excited for him."*

Director: *"Good response; let's do this moment again and see if you can project what you have just told us."*

(Actor says the following line, but it does not come across:)

Oh, it is! In Jonathan's trap?

Director: *"Let's repeat the line. What is your action here?"*

John: *"My action is to try and cheer up Elizabeth by saying something positive with a certain degree of excitement."*

Director. *"Good, do it again in your own words; paraphrase, but don't worry about trying to feel excitement. Just focus on honestly affecting her with your action."*

(The actor repeats the line and the action is clearly expressed.)

Director: *"Good! That worked. Now say the line as written and see the imaginary images that you described of Jonathan's trap and how excited he must have been catching the rabbit for his mother. Put all your attention on the action to try and cheer up Elizabeth."*

(The actor repeats the line and the action is projected. Actor playing Elizabeth responds with her line.)

No, she walked into the house this afternoon; I found her sittin' in the corner like she come to visit.
Director: *"What is your action here?"*
Elizabeth: *"To resent the fact that he thinks it was caught in Jonathan's trap when it was I who caught and killed the rabbit."*
Director: *"Is 'to resent' an action or an emotion?"*
Elizabeth: *"Isn't it both?... Well, I'm not sure. I guess it's more of an emotion. How do I choose an action when I know exactly what the subtext is and what I need to feel?"*
Director: *"It's very good that you know the subtext and how you might feel in Elizabeth's shoes at this moment; however, choosing the right action is your means to both convey to your partner and the audience the playwright's intention here while spontaneously stirring whatever emotion is evoked in the moment by the imaginary situation. Do you understand?"*
Elizabeth: *"I think so. So, maybe my action is to make John feel guilty."*
Director: *"That's an excellent choice! Let's try it again."*

(*Elizabeth repeats the line and the actor playing John is clearly affected by her trying to make him feel guilty. He responds defensively, and they continue with the next three lines of the scene.*)

Proctor. Oh, that's a good sign walkin' in.
Elizabeth. Pray God. It hurt my heart to strip her, poor rabbit.
Proctor. Oh, it is well seasoned.
Director: *"Why did you say it was 'well-seasoned'?"*
John: *I wanted to compliment her because I know she doesn't like to kill anything, yet she did it for me and that makes me feel even more... guilty!*

(*The class laughs*)

Director: *"Good. Continue."*
Elizabeth. I took great care. She's tender?
Proctor. Aye. I think we'll see green fields soon. It's warm as blood beneath the clods.
Elizabeth. That's well.
Proctor. If the crop is good I'll buy George Jacobs' heifer. How would that please you?
Elizabeth. Aye, it would.
Proctor. I mean to please you, Elizabeth.
Elizabeth. *(It's hard to say.)* I know it, John.
Proctor. *(As gently as he can.)* Cider?
Elizabeth. *(A sense of her reprimanding herself for having forgot.)* Aye! *(Gets jug from off L., pours drink into pewter mug, brings it to him.)*
Director: *"Let's discuss two points here: the subtext between both characters and the through-line of action. What is the subtext? What is not being said directly?"*
Elizabeth: *"As I see my character, Elizabeth can't forgive John for his infidelity, but more important than that, she says in the fourth act that she thought herself*

too plain and never worthy of his love. She says that it is her fault that he committed adultery because she was so cold."

Director: "That's exactly right! That's why Arthur Miller puts into the script that it is hard for her to say, "I know it John." Elizabeth is too proud to admit it at this time, and isn't even aware yet of how she really feels. She'll need to go through her own personal crucible before she can come to realize her faults. This is why you must constantly study the whole play and keep it all in mind while you work. John what do you think about the subtext and what is the through-line?"

John: I think my main action in this episode is to continue to try and please her. I am guilty and I have hurt her very badly. I love her; that is why I say, 'Cider?' so gently; then I see that she reprimands herself for not being a perfect wife. But, what I can't seem to get across to her is that she doesn't need to be perfect. I just want her to forgive me."

Director: "You both have a good grasp of the subtext and action. Let's repeat these few lines by saying your inner dialogue quietly to yourself in response to one another. Take your time, as you will both need to listen and evaluate one another's subtext using Wonder, Evaluation, Decision, Gesture, Act, and Gesture here. Then continue on with the scene."

(The actors repeat the segment and continue with the action.)

Proctor. This farm's a continent when you go foot by foot droppin' seeds in it.
Elizabeth. It must be.
Proctor. On Sunday let you come with me and we'll walk the farm together; I never see such a load of flowers on the earth. Massachusetts is a beauty in the spring!
Elizabeth. Aye, it is.

(Actor playing Elizabeth says line too angrily.)

Proctor. I think you're sad again. Are you?
Director: "John, what makes you think she is sad here?"
John: "I'm not sure; she seemed angry to me."
Elizabeth: "Well (in defense of herself), I am very angry here!"
Director: "Why?"
Elizabeth: "Because he promised to go to Salem and try to stop this madness and he did not go."
Director: "Then why does Arthur Miller have John choose the word 'sad' and not 'angry'?"
Elizabeth: (After a long pause) "Maybe because all I say is, 'Aye, it is.' But, aren't I still really angry with him?"
Director: "Yes, of course! However, there is always a need for balance between what is required by the playwright's intention in the text and your emotional response. The solution again is to be sure you are grounded in actions that are logical and consecutive, not in emotion. If you select the right action, the right emotional response will naturally follow. That is Stanislavsky's great discovery

16 ACTIVE ANALYSIS IN REHEARSAL

and what we are here to learn how to do. To select fitting actions that are logical and consecutive. Give a thought to a more fitting action and let's try it again."
Elizabeth: "May I use the 'Magic If'?"
Director: "I wish you would."

(Elizabeth repeats the line, "Aye, it is" and it is perfect; now John's response with 'sad' is justified too.)

Director: "What action did you choose?"
Elizabeth: "I asked myself what I would really do at this moment, and I realized that the best way to make John feel guilty was to let him see just how much I am hurt." *(The class laughs again.)*
Director: *(Laughing)* "Well, it worked! Continue."
Elizabeth. You come so late I thought you'd gone to Salem this afternoon.
Proctor. Why? I have no business in Salem.
Director: "Now these two last lines make sense. Elizabeth you accused John openly and he defended himself with a real touch of indignation. What happens next?"
Elizabeth: "I believe this is where the fight begins; they really argue to the climax."
John: "Isn't it the beginning of the next short action-episode?"
Director: "Correct. It is a reversal. In the previous segment Elizabeth is mostly the initiator of the action; now John becomes the initiator, and Elizabeth is the receiver with the counteraction.

That is enough for today. Be prepared for a run-through of the scene at our next rehearsal. We will run it without interruptions so that you can begin to work on temp-rhythm and come to feel the continuity of the piece as a whole. Continue working on the scene, and we'll pick it up from here at the next rehearsal. Very good work."

Figure 16.7 Act 4: final moments. Actors Dolores Neese (Elizabeth Proctor), Kent Fillmore (John Proctor). *The Crucible*, by Arthur Miller, performed at the San Francisco Theatre Academy Ensemble Company, 1979.
Photo: Philip G. Bennett

> ### Rehearsal 16.4: First Run-Through
>
> **Director:** *Today we will do a nonstop run-through of the scene. I promise not to interrupt you, no matter what. For this run-through, just let go and don't worry about making mistakes. Commit yourself to fulfilling the actions and trying to solve your problem. Work to genuinely affect your partner and achieve honest communion. Let's see what happens!"*
>
> *(The actors run through the scene and there are moments when they achieve living the experience of the characters. The scene ends and there is a long silence from the observing cast members then a burst of applause.)*
>
> **Director:** *"That was excellent. I believe you both had moments of true inspiration. What was your experience of the run-through?"*
> **Elizabeth:** *"I definitely felt something different that time."*
> **John:** *"So did I. (Addressing Elizabeth:) You seemed so hurt I couldn't look at you for feeling guilty."*
> **Elizabeth:** *"I **was** hurt and felt so helpless because I believed that you didn't really love me and were still in love with Abigail."*
> **Director:** *"Where was your focus during those moments in the scene?"*
> **John:** *"I was completely focused on my action, to avoid going to Salem, and at the same time very aware of my body, my inner feelings, and images."*
> **Elizabeth:** *"So was I. I wanted to get him to go, but I was also really aware that I had lots of new images and feelings."*
> **Director:** *"Then you both were experiencing your inner and outer monitors simultaneously, thereby using the dual perspectives. When you focus on your action and go about fulfilling it truthfully in a psychophysical manner, you will always stir new feelings and achieve communion with your partner. By the response of your fellow cast members, it is obvious that they were equally affected. You fulfilled your actions and achieved an honest communion; that is why you both began to live the experience of the character and became inspired. Very good. "*
>
> *(The rehearsal ends)*

A Final Note about Inspiration

At various times in rehearsal, especially during the final run-throughs of a scene, you may experience moments of genuine inspiration. During very emotional moments it is easy to confuse emotionality with inspiration. If this should happen bring your attention back to your action and your communication with your partner(s) in the scene. This way you will ensure that your emotion affects your scene partner, moves along the story of the play, and thus has a greater chance to affect an audience. It is not enough for you to be moved, in performance you must always ask, but did I move the audience?

Some scenes demand that you build gradually to an emotional peak; in other cases, a specific catalyst spurs a more sudden climax. Careful preparation in plotting out your actions before rehearsal is needed to allow freedom in rehearsal to follow impulses that arise, while keeping them connected to the source text.

When you are rehearsing the scene, always try to find the correct balance between your actions and strong emotions. Finding and maintaining a correct balance requires that you exercise a degree of restraint and control by using the dual perspectives.

Bennett was rehearsing with an actor who was so out of control that he threw a chair at his partner, barely missing her and destroying the chair. He said he was inspired; however, she would have none of it, and refused to continue working with him. (French has seen similar problems arise many times and always found them to be creatively destructive to the rest of the ensemble). Under these circumstances, there is no opportunity for the other actors to be alive in the circumstances as they and the audiences instead fear for their personal safety. In truth, that actor was not inspired but selfish and out of artistic control and just releasing his personal pent-up anger or frustration.[6] It is counterintuitive, because exercising a reasonable degree of restraint and control actually prepares the way for true inspiration rather than hindering it.

When true inspiration visits you in rehearsal, you and your partners will feel elated and very positive. You can use these momentary insights to bring life to your entire role. Sometimes, when inspired, the state is so strong that you may not remember much about it. If that should happen to you, there is no need to worry. Don't even fret about trying to repeat it. Just say, "thanks" and move on. However, if you do recall something of the experience, see if you can infuse it into the role. Reflect on the conditions that brought about the moment of inspiration and write down the experience in your creative journal in order to capture it. Recall your behavior to examine what you were doing physically, and attempt to review your images to see if some new images flashed through your mind. It is also valuable to recall any physical sensations you may have had. Inspired rehearsals are the most fertile ground for an inspired performance. Do not try to repeat everything exactly, as the role must never be frozen, only try to use some of the things that help the creative state, and remove those that hinder it, to invite inspiration more often.

Summary

In this chapter we have created an imaginary set of rehearsals based on actual rehearsals of *The Crucible*. Here you can get a glimpse of how what you have learned and practiced throughout this book can be applied toward work on a role. We have actively explored and reviewed major elements of an action: the given circumstances, nonverbal and verbal action, inner monologue, images, subtext of behavior, body language, communion, and other devices used with Active Analysis.

Here you have been given an example of an ideal rehearsal and working environment. Such an environment is only possible to create and maintain when artists are of a like mind and, with mutual respect, work with strong social purpose toward lofty goals. Such meaningful collaboration and the so-called rules of the road will be thoroughly explored in Chapter 17: Entering the Collaborative Process, and Chapter 19: The Creative Life: Communion with Audience and Society.

Should you wish to explore *The Crucible* further, here is a chart with a complete breakdown of the main and secondary events and episodes that you can study and use either as an example for other scenes or to create improvisational études and second plan improvisations.

[6] This incident refers to a class at the Bennett TheatreLab in San Francisco.

Figure 16.8 *The Crucible*—chart with main and secondary events and episodes.

The Crucible By Arthur Miller—A breakdown of Main and Secondary Events

SUPERTASK (Based on Bennett's initial analysis) Love and Courage Conquers Fear

Act One Metaphor – Sparks Ignite!	Act Two Metaphor – Foreboding Smoke – Salem!	Act Three	Act Four (Act Four Metaphor – Aftermath of Ashes)
Below: Breakdown of main events and secondary plot point events for creating Improvisational études	(Secondary Events) The Proctor house Relationship between Elizabeth and John Proctor	**MAIN EVENT #4** *The Climax–Central Event of the play as a result of the Through-Line of Actions.* (Act Three Metaphor – Fire and Conflagration) The Courtroom: John Proctor and Frances Nurse bring deposition to the court in Salem	(Secondary Events) Tituba and women in Prison
MAIN EVENT #1 *The Event without which there would be no play.* (Metaphor – Smoldering Woods) The Girls are discovered by Rev. Parris dancing naked in the woods.	Mary Warren arrives and threatens Elizabeth and John	Secondary Event: Judge Danforth calls court into session	Hale petitions Danforth to let him attempt to save Proctor from Execution by speaking to Elizabeth Proctor.
MAIN EVENT #2 *Initial Event of the Exposition* Betty Parris has fallen ill and tries to fly. Townsfolk on edge of panic.	Rev. Hale comes to examine John and Elizabeth Proctor. John fails examination of Ten Commandments	Frances Nurse is arrested for refusing to give names of those of the deposition. Giles Cory attacks Putnam.	Hale pleads with Elizabeth who asks to speak to her husband John.
MAIN EVENT #3 *The Inciting Event (Point of Attack) that introduces the source of the conflict and develops the subsequent Through-Line of Actions* Arrival of John Proctor and secret conversation with Abigail. Conflict with Rev. Parris and the Putnam's	Ezekiel Cheever arrives to arrest Elizabeth who is put in chains	Mary Warren recants her seeing of spirits and Abigail and the other girls are called into court for cross-examination. Abigail threatens Judge Danforth. Proctor calls Abigail a whore.	Elizabeth confesses to John her own weaknesses and flaws that led to his lechery. They forgive one another and their love is renewed.
(Secondary Events) Arrival of Rev. Hale, and Examination of Tituba	John Threatens Mary Warren	Proctor's confession and Cross-examination of Elizabeth	**MAIN EVENT #5** *The Event that ends the Conflict and brings about the denouement, (gradual resolution of the conflict).* (Metaphor – John's Catharsis) Although it is a lie, John confesses to being in league with the Devil to save his life, but will not allow his name to be in print, thus destroying the confession document.
Abigail and girls call out names of women as witches	Act Two, Scene 2 John meets Abigail in the woods to threaten Abigail	Girls go into hysterical fits and Mary condemns Proctor as a witch.	**MAIN EVENT #6** *The final event of the Supertask as conceived by the director's analysis and collaboration with the ensemble through Active Analysis.* **SUPERTASK:** Love and Courage conquers Fear John finds himself in the midst of a catharsis brought about by the purging Crucible. Elizabeth declares that he has found his honesty, and proclaims: "He have his goodness now. God forbid I take it from him!"
Hysterical Townsfolk call for chains and arrests		Proctor declares that "God is dead!" He is arrested as Hale denounces the proceedings.	

Note: Each play is written differently, and as a result the placement of the 6 main events and their secondary events, may differ from play to play and director to director.

16 ACTIVE ANALYSIS IN REHEARSAL

New Theatre Terms and Concepts
- ☐ flow of action
- ☐ naming and drilling actions

Interdisciplinary Figures
- ☐ Senator Joseph McCarthy
- ☐ Arthur Miller

CHAPTER 17

Entering the Collaborative Process

"They were nothing more than people, by themselves. Even paired, any pairing, they would have been nothing more than people by themselves. But all together, they have become the heart and muscles and mind of something perilous and new, something strange and growing and great. Together, all together, they are the instruments of change."[1]

Keri Hulme, *The Bone People*

Figure 17.1 The joy of collaboration. A curtain call for *Twelfth Night* at East Stroudsburg University. Costume design: Jennifer Tiranti Anderson.
Photo: Stephanie Daventry French

---

[1] Keri Hulme, *The Bone People* (New York: Penguin, 1983), 4.

17 ENTERING THE COLLABORATIVE PROCESS

> **Elements Actively Explored**
>
> This chapter has no exercises. A more traditional regional repertory production process, as it relates to actors, along with some alternative processes, are explained with suggestions of how to incorporate Active Analysis.
> - How Does the Actor Fit into This Process?
> - Producing a Play
> - The Artistic Team's Reconnaissance (Preproduction)
> - Casting in Theatre—Enter the Actors
> - The Rehearsals Begin
> - Early Rehearsals
> - Scene Rehearsals
> - Middle Rehearsals
> - Final Phase of Rehearsals
> - Technical Rehearsals (Commonly Called "Tech")
> - Rehearsal and Performance Dos and Don'ts

After completing sufficient training, you may wish to try for a part in a university production, an independent film or theatre production, and eventually a professional one. The following outlines some of the aspects of a theatre production process (often replicated in university theatre) that tie in most directly to the work of the actor. Even if you wish to eventually work in film, during your early years we recommend that you build up your acting résumé through theatre productions, where you can do many more shows a year than in most major film processes. At the same time, take every opportunity to get comfortable in front of a camera through student and independent films, a television club at your university, and on-camera acting classes. Actors can have versatile careers moving between mediums.

Theatre and film are *collaborative processes* involving the creative vision of many artists, the skill of many technicians, and the business acumen of administrative, fund-raising, and publicity people. Work in theatre and film involves intensive time commitment, focus, and discipline, but this is motivated by the passion of creativity and the fun of the camaraderie. As an artist in this process, it is vital that you understand and respect the work of others in your company. The creation of a theatre production is much like a recipe. Different ingredients are mixed separately and then added together during technical rehearsals.

How Does the Actor Fit into This Process?

In the last chapter you learned about the rehearsal technique of Active Analysis that Stanislavsky came to in his final rehearsals. This is a process to embody the text and explore the life of a character by actively inhabiting the circumstances of the play. This is an exciting approach, but is only one method of rehearsal. There are almost as many styles of rehearsal process as there are directors. In fact, Stanislavsky tried many approaches as a director before arriving at Active Analysis, and he worked as an actor in many more processes. Stanislavsky's fellow directors at the Moscow Art Theatre each created their own unique approach to rehearsal, even while incorporating many elements of the System. Today, directors often create different processes in response to the demands of different types of plays.

State-funded resident-acting companies, such as Stanislavsky's Moscow Art Theatre, have time to allow the interpretation to evolve as the work of the playwright, director, and designers intersects with the work of actors in rehearsal. This is one reason why Active Analysis has been more widely used in Russia and eastern Europe, where resident companies are more common. Professional theatres in the United States, on the other hand, have limited, if any, government funding.

When the theatre company is not a resident company and relies on ticket sales and corporate and benefactor donations, the actors are brought in for the shortest possible rehearsal period. Most professional theatres cannot afford to pay actors and directors during a lengthy rehearsal period or to keep them on salary between plays. This means that the actors come into the process very late. The concept for the production is already decided, and designs are already being built; therefore the actors' creative input has little effect on the design of the set or costumes. The schedule also hugely impacts what is possible in terms of the methods used in the rehearsal process.

In professional, and much amateur, theatre in the United States there is a fairly standard order of events for the production process. This serves a couple of purposes: it facilitates all aspects of a larger production coming together on schedule, and it gives freelance directors and actors moving from theatre to theatre an idea of what to expect and how to do their parts within that structure. It is important for you, as an actor, to understand how you fit into the big picture of a production. Also, once you understand and learn to work in this structure, you can make use of the many techniques in this book to design and experience the fullness of your role, within the structure of the collective rehearsals. If cast, you will need to do your own actor's preparation outside of rehearsal; Active Analysis offers great tools for this, and you can use all the Elements of Action to enrich your rehearsals. This way, directors will want to rehire you, as you will be an actor who can generate many creative ideas for every moment on stage—a smorgasbord of options the director can select from to best enhance the overall production.

Producing a Play

It is important to understand that there is an extensive part of the collaborative process that takes place somewhere between three months to a few years (depending on the scope of the production) prior to the play being cast and actors coming on board.

The Producer or Producing Organization

Long before the actor joins a production, much work by the *producer* and the director has already commenced. The producer is the person or organization who puts up the money for the production, finds or provides the rehearsal and performance space, coordinates the people to do the marketing, and hires and pays the artists and technicians. For a larger production, such as a Broadway or film company, the roles of fund-raiser and hands-on producer are often divided.

Play Selection

In regional repertory theatre, the theatre company generally picks a full season of plays, balancing more-risky new and experimental plays with well-known plays or playwrights, classics, and musicals that generate more certain ticket sales. A

17 ENTERING THE COLLABORATIVE PROCESS

professional theatre's next season is generally announced and marketed during the current season. Discussion of what plays will balance the season happens long before that. Many theatre companies have two or more performing spaces. Typical regional theatre architectural and *stage formats* might include a 400–700-seat *proscenium* (audience sees the play from one side), 300–400 seat *thrust* (audience on three sides), or a smaller *flexible theatre* or *black box* space (audience/performer relationship varies greatly and can be designed in new and inventive ways) that seats 100–200 (see Figure 17.2 for a picture of the different stage formats). Another popular format is the arena stage (with the audience on all sides). The theatre is often producing simultaneous productions, as well as new play workshops, and cabarets in the different spaces.

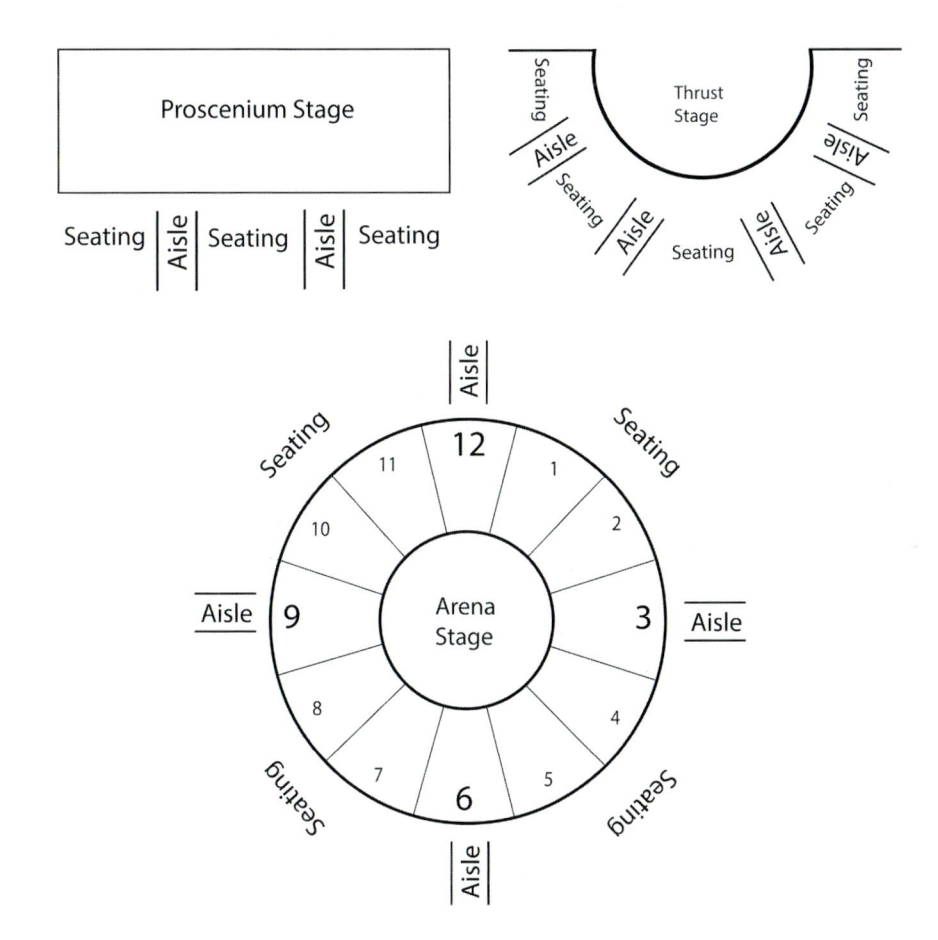

Figure 17.2 Primary theatre stage formats.

Obtaining the Rights

The theatre company, or individual director, in the case of an independently produced play, will need to write to the organization that owns the rights to the play to get permission to produce it and pay the required fees called *royalties*. The exception might be if the play is an older play and therefore in the *public domain* with expired copyright. With older plays in translation, the translation may be still under copyright, and thus royalties will be required unless the company undertakes a new translation (which will generally also cost additional money unless someone already on the company payroll is capable of doing it).

In the production presented in Figures 4.4–6 and 12.2, we obtained the rights to create a play adaptation—titled *Sold!*—of the historical novel *Day of Tears* by Julius Lester: the story of the largest slave auction in American history told from the point of view of the slaves.

Selecting the Director

For a regional professional theatre, generally the *artistic director* directs some set number of the season's plays and either has associate directors who direct the others, or brings in freelance directors, or some combination. For creative or financial reasons, two theatre companies may jointly produce a play. In this case, the *artistic team* (stage director, musical director (if any), scenic, lighting, costume, sound and multi-media designers, and choreographer) may all come from another theatre, or they may be variously connected with both theatres.

Selecting the Design Team

Sometimes designers come along as part of the producing organization, but more often the director gets to select the design team with approval from the producer. The team will include a scenic designer, lighting designer, costume designer, and sound designer (in the UK sometimes there is a combined scenic and costume designer whereas in the United States, more often the design areas are separate or lighting and scenic are combined). Sometimes there will also be a separate multimedia designer, hair and makeup designer (always working closely with the costume designer), or in the case of extremely technical shows a special-effects designer.

The Artistic Team's Reconnaissance (Preproduction)

Reconnaissance of the mind was Stanislavsky's term for the exciting and expanding work that the members of the artistic team in his productions undertook individually and collectively to undercover the supertask, or ruling idea, of the play. In professional theatrical processes, the search to express the themes and overall imprint the artistic team wants to make on the audience to express a particular playwright's work involves the combination of preproduction research, analysis, and design meetings. *Reconnaissance of the Mind* is a little misleading, as the exploration does not only take place in any artist's mind but involves the sharing of visual, aural, and sometimes textural research and the discussion of ideas about the play. It is a similar idea to the reconnaissance for the actor, as described in chapters 13–15, but far more exhaustive. This work is called *sourcing* by Anne Bogart of SITI Company and, due to her significant influence on contemporary theatre, you may hear this term used. A more standard but perhaps less evocative term is *preproduction*. This paves the way for Reconnaissance of the Body, which is the active search in rehearsal to express the play's supertask; although in most Western professional productions this term is not used, the work still aims for this kind of unity of purpose and expression.

Preparing the Script

The director will prepare the script for the production. In some theatres, this work will be done working with a *dramaturg* (a text-analysis and research expert), but the director has the final say on the script. (There may be an exception to this in a country such as Stanislavsky's Soviet Union, where government censors had the final say, or in big-budget productions or films where the producers have a lot of sway as they steer the production toward financial success). This may involve reading and selecting a translation (if the play was written in a different language). If the play is a longer classical script (three to four hours) and is in the public domain, the director may choose to cut it down to a length more palatable for today's theatre audiences (particularly for theatres outside the major theatre centers such as London or New York). If the production will be a *premiere* of new play, generally the director will work with the playwright (and dramaturg, if any), perhaps even doing early staged readings or workshops of the play to hone it for a full production.

Studying the Script

The director and designers reread the play often, taking notes and writing down questions, interesting *creative challenges*, ideas, and pictures that come to mind. It is important to write down first impressions of the play, remembering that the audience will generally only have one experience of the play. These early readings lead the artists toward some further investigations.

> **Important note:** This is yet another reason why theatre students must read plays and not just watch other people's interpretations of them on film. As you read a play it will generate your artistic ideas, rather than those selected by other directors, designers, and actors. This is important for the development of your artistic vision. Do not go on public media sites to see how others have done a play before original ideas have had a chance to germinate in you, as this inhibits rather than stimulates your imaginative response.

Reconnaissance and Sourcing

The director and designers will fill out their knowledge with research on the playwright, historical period, and location, based on both when the play was written and when it is set. They will investigate the cultural context as well as the literary, artistic, and theatrical style of each period. For costume, scenic, lighting, multimedia designers, and many directors, a big part of the research will be visual (painting, photography, sculpture, found objects), and for the sound designer and director, they may also start collecting sample sounds that interest them that are related to the play, genre, and period. The director will research all ideas, situations, or people about which she is not already well versed. All manner of sources that the artists intuitively or cognitively connect with the style or the themes of the play may become resources for concept and design. Figure 17.3 shows how the paintings of Salvador Dali influenced a director (Stephanie Daventry French and design team: Q. Brian Sickels [set and lighting], Jennifer Tiranti [costumes], David Docherty [sound]) to create a visual aesthetic for a production of Shakespeare's *Twelfth Night*.

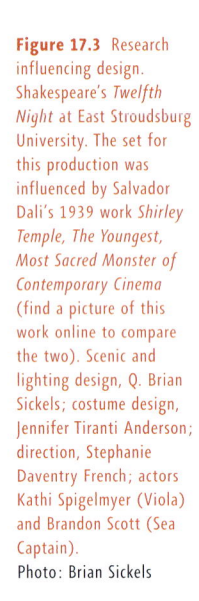

Figure 17.3 Research influencing design. Shakespeare's *Twelfth Night* at East Stroudsburg University. The set for this production was influenced by Salvador Dali's 1939 work *Shirley Temple, The Youngest, Most Sacred Monster of Contemporary Cinema* (find a picture of this work online to compare the two). Scenic and lighting design, Q. Brian Sickels; costume design, Jennifer Tiranti Anderson; direction, Stephanie Daventry French; actors Kathi Spigelmyer (Viola) and Brandon Scott (Sea Captain).
Photo: Brian Sickels

Analysis

Each member of the artistic team then conducts his own area-specific, in-depth text analysis on the play's theme, plot, characters, rhythm, use of language, and opportunities for spectacle.

Expanding

The director may then begin to imagine the play vividly and with as many senses as possible, drawing on or working directly with other artists. In the United States, often the artistic team members are scattered across the country for preproduction and thus must work with the various media to meet remotely and send each other source material for consideration and discussion (much easier now than it used to be but still more challenging than being in the same room). Any of the artists may find, draw, or describe from their artistic images, pieces of music, quotes, or other fodder to reflect on, or express, some obvious or indirect aspect of the play.

Interpretation

When collaborating in the theatre, including with the playwright, whether or not he is present, respect for another artist's work is paramount. Yet, there is not a right way to produce any play or a right way to interpret any character. Each production and each performance by an actor or a character is an interpretation. The particular attributes each artist brings to the interpretative arts of acting, directing, and design are what make any production of a play or screenplay a unique rendition. How closely aligned with the original or how great a leap off from it the company takes is a matter of *aesthetic* value and vision, usually guided by a director.

When a play is produced for the first time, the playwright is often in residence. The director and company generally try to adhere as closely as possible to the playwright's original vision for the characters and the play. At the same time, a natural expansion occurs in the move from page to stage, from concepts of characters to the voices and bodies of real people inhabiting the characters. The play usually goes through many rewrites in this process as the writer hears his written words spoken out loud and as the playwright works closely with the interpretive artists: the director, designers, and actors.

When the playwright's work has been produced many times, and especially when it is in the *public domain*[2] (so not subject to the same rights and restrictions), as often happens for example with Shakespeare, directors and actors may take great liberty with concept and interpretation. Directors may even do work that responds to or adapts a famous play rather than trying to achieve the playwright's original vision. *The Complete Works of William Shakespeare (Abridged)* by Adam Long, Daniel Singer, and Jess Winfield is a spoof of many Shakespeare plays at once. In *Rosencrantz and Guildenstern Are Dead*, Tom Stoppard takes two minor characters out of *Hamlet* and writes their story. The film *10 Things I Hate About You* adapts Shakespeare's *Taming of the Shrew* and *West Side Story* is a musical adaptation of *Romeo and Juliet*.

Foreign language productions of Shakespeare take particular liberties in interpretation as they are not as bound to the original text. *Translation* is already an interpretation and a different cultural lens, and use of language naturally impacts interpretation of material. When working on any play in translation you will want to read a number of translations to find one that is actable, even if it may not be as literally accurate.

A director may also approach a play with a strong *concept* that reframes the play but still uses the original text, as in Baz Luhrman's film of *Romeo and Juliet* (starring Claire Danes and Leonardo DiCaprio), which used a modern setting but classical language. Often a director's concept may be an attempt to get closer to a play that he feels others have missed in their productions. Sometimes this is okay with the playwright and/or whoever holds the rights to his work, and sometimes it is not.

Endgame

There is a well-known story in the theatre about a 1984 production of Samuel Beckett's *Endgame* at American Repertory Theatre (ART), directed by respected professional director JoAnne Akalaitis (one of the founders of experimental acting company Mabou Mines). First the publisher and then Beckett himself sued to try to shut down the production, originally without having seen it. Beckett did not like that Akalaitis set it in a different location and used incidental music, though these are common directorial responses for plays in production. Instead of Beckett's stage direction of "an empty room

---

[2] We encourage you as often as possible to support living playwrights by paying royalties to produce their plays. However, financially strapped theatre companies also sometimes look to plays they can produce for free. Royalties may not be owed if the play is in the public domain because the copyright has expired or because it comes from a historical period prior to the establishment of copyright laws. Copyright varies from country to country and for a production, it is the copyright law in the company where the play will be produced, not where it was written, that has jurisdiction. Plays in the public domain may be used in production without paying royalties, but be careful not use a new edition or translation that might be under copyright. Classical plays, except for those in more recent translations, often fall under public domain.

> with two windows" Akalaitis and her set designer Douglas Stein set it in an abandoned subway station layered with trash and an old, broken train.
>
> Beckett's plays have a very strong musicality to them so it is understandable that he would not want that to be altered by incidental music; however, most directors believe they have a right to respond creatively and interpretively to a play in their own unique ways, after the premiere production of it. Akalaitis had previously been an important director of Beckett plays, and the incidental music was by her ex-husband, the famous composer Philip Glass, who had also scored other Beckett plays. In the end, the play was allowed to continue with a statement by Beckett denouncing the changes inserted into the program. However, ART did not produce Beckett again for ten years. Other playwrights, such as Naomi Iizuka, love to see the variety of ways different artists respond to their plays.

In a further extension, an *auteur director* may create a new play that leaps far from the initial play source, leaving behind or merely sampling some lines, challenging or embellishing the original, and becoming a new creation. This can only be done if the play is in the public domain, only small samples of it are used, or with the playwright's permission. There is very similar to a phenomenon in some music; jazz for example is highly improvisational but often includes samples of very familiar musical themes. Most productions of plays are somewhere between these extremes. However, the best directors and comedians before taking a far-flung leap from a play generally seek to understand the source material deeply and intimately so as to make an informed and inspired leap that also respects the original.

In most plays, out of respect for a master playwright and because of requirements in the permission granted to produce the play, actors must speak the playwright's words exactly as written. The challenge for the actor, then, is to understand and internalize why this character is given these exact words at this exact moment and all the other impacting circumstances, events, and motivations that lead to needing to say exactly these words. There are many approaches to play and character analysis. Let's start with the identifying major components of the drama, as Greek philosopher and theatre critic Aristotle circumscribed as far back as the fourth century BCE.

Developing the Production Concept

All theatre is collaborative; however, the level of collaboration in the early design process in terms of arriving at *concept*, the unifying vision for the production, varies. The director, either independently or working with the design team, will develop a *concept* for this production of this play. Remember that every production of a play is only one interpretation; one of many ways it can be staged. The concept may be a metaphor or vision to focus the production, a particular twist on the interpretation; this may be a relocation of the play to a different time period or location to bring out a different aspect of it. This is frequently done with well-known plays and playwrights such as Shakespeare. Often, classical plays are set in contemporary times and places. It may be as close as possible to what the director believes was or is the *playwright's intention* (frequently done with premieres of plays or in more traditional companies) or it may be a re-envisioning of the play to evoke a particular spirit of the play. For example, Peter Brook, when he was director of the Royal Shakespeare Company in England, brought in toys and circus props to bring out the playfulness and danger of the fairies in Shakespeare's *A Midsummer Night's Dream*. (Since then, many productions have incorporated circus into theatre, including the exciting revival of *Pippin* on Broadway that opened in 2013).

After the concept begins to emerge, the director continually returns to the text to ensure that the concept works to bring out the play and that it works for the entire production and not just one scene or act. The concept is generally adapted and developed throughout the process.

Devising and Experimental Theatre
Rather than a playwright sitting down to write a play, some theatre companies generate material for a production through a collaborative creative process called *devising*. Generally, a playwright is still involved to pull all the material together cohesively. Often, a variety of improvisational forms are used in the process of generating a script so your training in the System with extensive improvisation is a good foundation for this type of work, too, although the type of improvisation may be quite different.

In the twentieth century, a movement called experimental theatre was at the forefront of this type of collaborative creation, even before the term *devising* was coined. Many great artists of the twentieth and twenty-first centuries have generated and continued to generate work collaboratively. Sometimes a script or movement score is fixed in performance, and sometimes it is loosely structured but still very improvisational in performance. Below is a list of only a few of the many great artists whose companies work in various forms of collaborative creation. Take some time to look them up and read about their fascinating work:

- **Joseph Chaikin** (New York), who was a member of the Living Theatre Company (founded by Judith Molina) and later founded the Open Theatre.
- **Jerzy Grotowski**'s Polish Theatre Laboratory of the 1960s and 1970s. Grotowski, one of the most widely influential experimental theatre artists, studied the Stanislavsky System, particularly the late work in physical actions and continually references the inspirations he got from all the artists at the Moscow Art Theatre. Grotowski later experimented with ritual and Eastern theatre techniques and breaking down actor/audience separation in an attempt to impact the soul of actor and audience.
- **Jacques Lecoq** of L'Ecole Internationale de Theatre, collaborative creation with a focus on physical play, and the many great companies inspired by his work (Complicité, Theatre du Soleil, Mabou Mines, to name only a few of the vibrant companies Lecoq's work inspired).
- **Peter Brook** (London and, later, Paris) was the artistic director of the Royal Shakespeare Company but later went on to found the International Center for Theatre Research in Paris, where he also worked extensively with Theatre des Bouffes.
- **Joint Stock Theatre Group** (David Hare, Max Stafford-Clark, David Aukin, Caryl Churchill, Howard Brenton, Les Waters, to name a few key members)—company collective research would inspire workshops as source material for playwrights to write their plays. One technique was to send people out to interview people in a community on a particular event or theme and bring back their stories and them as characters.
- **Blake Street Hawkeyes** (some founders and key members include Bob Ernst, David Schein, Whoopi Goldberg, Cynthia Moore)—a collective that trained, taught, and created collaborative work. They were extremely influential in the

vibrant San Francisco Bay Area Experimental Theatre Movement of the 1970s and 1980s in Berkeley, California. Most of the artists continue to create work on their own or in other groups.

- **Anne Bogart's SITI Company.** Their work is devised, collaboratively created, using the unifying theatrical tools of the Viewpoints. The *Viewpoints* are a series of training and rehearsal tools originally brought to theatre from dance by Mary Overlie in New York University's Experimental Theatre Wing and later developed for the theatre by Bogart, Tina Landau, and the members of the SITI Company and Wendell Beavers, who have largely been responsible for the teaching and proliferation of these techniques. The Viewpoints liberate traditional stage notions of time and space, keeping performers alive in the present and tuned in and responsive to collaborators.

Anne Bogart and the SITI Company

Anne Bogart, working collaboratively with members of her SITI Company, often creates work out of ideas or nondramatic material. When SITI does create a production in response to a play, the original play is only part of the source material for a very big leap into unknown artistic territory. SITI's *Small Lives/Big Dreams* is sampled from numerous plays by Russian playwright Anton Chekhov. SITI's *Going, Going, Gone* is about quantum mechanics, using the structure of Edward Albee's play *Who's Afraid of Virginia Woolf*. A 2008 production, *Who Do You Think You Are*, asked the question, How does the vast labyrinth, the systems and the layers of chemical, muscular and neuronal activity inform our tiniest interaction?"[3] SITI's productions are high concept and execution, but Bogart considers the concept a collaboratively created vision:

> I'm often told that there is a vision. I don't have visions and I don't have pictures in my head, or ways that something has to be. I think all of those three pieces [at Louisville—*The Medium, Small Lives/Big Dreams,* and *The Adding Machine*] and everything I've ever done is a highly, highly collective vision. I think there is a company vision that is emerging from the SITI Company because we've worked together for a while. But what I've tried to do is always work with people who aren't afraid of giving huge amounts of input.[4]

Part of the reason, Bogart and SITI are able to work so collaboratively on concept is because of years of trust and shared techniques. This process is much closer to Stanislavsky's ideal process of Active Analysis than most companies can afford to follow in the short rehearsal processes of most professional theatres today. This is because SITI is one of the few companies of actors and director that come together repeatedly to do productions. They have had to be extremely creative in fund-raising and figuring out how to survive financially as a company in a national artistic climate that is not generally willing to fund resident companies.

---

[3] From the SITI company's website description of their play at http://siti.org/content/production/who-do-you-think-you-are.

[4] Quoted in Daniel Mufson, "'I Don't Have Vision. I Have Values,': An Interview with Anne Bogart," Theatre 25, no. 3: 59–63.

Figure 17.4 The SITI Company's *Who Do You Think You Are?*
Photo: Michael Brosilow

Arriving at the Supertask through Active Analysis

Active Analysis is another process, like SITI's creative process, where the vision for the production emerges out of the exploratory rehearsals, not prior to them. Rehearsal is a long explore (as Pooh would say) to search for the supertask of the play. That is why Stanislavsky began his final project, *Tartuffe*, without any concept in mind, only the impetus to search. What is important for a Stanislavsky-trained director is to know how not to know what he/she is going to do, but only know *how* to find it in process.

The main idea of supertask is that it is the active statement made by the playwright as developed by the play's themes and the convergence of the individual supertask of each character that culminate in the *physical manifestation* of the playwright's statement during the final scenes of the play. The director trained and experienced in Stanislavsky's Active Analysis discovers the concept as a means to artistically express the supertask at each moment of the play's staging.

Design Concept

The director works with the designers to come up with the translation of the overarching production concept to visual and aural media through *design meetings* and the ongoing sharing of ideas and source material. In scenic design, for example, original pencil sketches lead to more-involved color drawings, which lead to models or other samples (see Figure 17.5 for a visual illustration of the steps in this process). The amount of autonomy each designer has depends on the director's style and often how much familiarity and trust already exists between the director and the designers. However, at some point the director is responsible to bring together all the different design elements with the work of the actors, and therefore she usually has the final creative say.

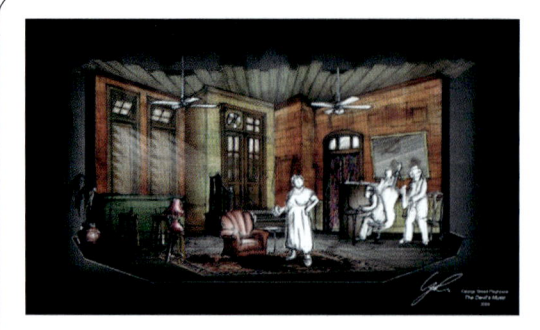

Scenic design color sketch for *The Devil's Music* at the George Street Playhouse

White model to scale (generally 1/4" on the model equals 1' on the stage)

Paint elevations for the charge artist (scenic painter)

The Devil's Music at the George Street Playhouse, production photo

Figure 17.5 Stages of design for *The Devil's Music* at the George Street Playhouse in New Brunswick, New Jersey. Scenic designer and photographer: Yoshinori Tanokura

Design Implementation

"Vision without execution is hallucination"
—Jon Gordon, *Training Camp: What the Best Do Better than Everyone Else*

The scenic construction drawings are submitted to the scene shop. The costume drawings are submitted to the costume shop. Plans are made for building (renting, purchasing, or some combination) of the costumes even before the specific actors have been cast and measurements are available. In professional theatre, designers do extensive work following along to ensure the designs are built to specifications and solving problems as they arise. In university theatre, designers also teach students how to implement designs and often do a lot of the hands-on work as well.

Figure 17.6
Consultation between charge artist (main scenic painter) and scenic designer. Designer Yoshinori Tanokura consulting with work-study students Chris Walters and Tyler Adams on scenic painting.
Photo: Stephanie Daventry French

Casting in Theatre—Enter the Actors

Casting* the Play

Usually only at this phase are the actors chosen. As an actor it is important to understand that months of work have gone into a production before you arrive. That is why when an actor shows up to a theatre rehearsal (or a film shoot) unprepared it is 1) annoying to the other artists and professionals who have already been working hard, and 2) gives a bad first impression of the actor as unprofessional.

***Note about the language of casting:** Please note that in theatre we say, "I am going to cast the play next week; I am casting the play now; I cast the play last week." (Some actors incorrectly use the past tense, "I was casted in a play last year," which reveals their lack of experience.)

Auditions

The most common method for selecting actors in the theatre is the audition. This is a demonstration of your abilities through a short, prepared dramatic or comedic performance, reading, and/or song. It may also involve seeing how you respond to a guided improvisation or how quickly you can learn and how well you can execute a short, instructed selection of dance choreography. As the focus of this book is the actor in training, rather than working as an actor, this is only a very quick overview of this process. For more information, you should refer to some of the many excellent books that can give you a better picture and that are updated with the latest resources on casting for actors. We recommend *How to Be a Working Actor: The Insider's Guide to Finding Jobs in Theatre, Film and Television,* by Mari Lyn Henry and Lynne Rogers, and *How to Book Acting Jobs in TV and Film: The Truth about the Acting Industry; Conversations with a Veteran Hollywood Casting Director,* by Cathy Reinking, CSA.

Auditioning is its own acting technique, which requires separate practice, and study on top of basic acting technique. Many good actors are terrible at auditioning and many mediocre actors can audition brilliantly. Unless you have some very powerful connections in the industry, to be a regularly working actor you must be able to audition well, in addition to fulfilling the challenges of the rehearsal and performance of the role when cast.

Headshots and Résumés

Headshots and *résumés*, along with prepared audition pieces, are the calling cards of the actor. The headshot is an 8x10 picture of the actor. The most important thing about the picture is that it looks like the actor who walks into the audition, your eyes are available and engaging, and you look like someone we'd want to work with. There are always trends on what is cool in terms of headshot style—fuller body poses, pictures going landscape direction, very serious half in shadow pictures for dramatic actors. If you stick with the more traditional picture—portrait direction and smiling—your picture will last you longer (and good headshots can be expensive). You will likely need some makeup, even just to look natural. If you do a glamor look with a professional makeup artist for the picture, but walk in with street makeup done only by you, you may not look like your picture. Glamor is only one look of many required and could limit you for other types of casting. The same goes for wearing a leather jacket or a punk look, tattoos and numerous or unusual piercings, or anything else really iconic. These are great for your personal expression but may actually block the director and costume designer from seeing you as they have visually created the role. Find a simple look that shows you at your best, shows a little of who you are without pigeonholing you and keeps the focus on your face rather than on clothing, makeup, or accessories. See the sample headshot and résumé in Figure 17.7.

Figure 17.7 Sample headshot and résumé, Carla Harting (as of 2014).
Photo: Laura Rose

Your résumé must be in a theatre résumé format with specific columns and categories. Make it look good but don't get too inventive, as the people looking at it have only seconds to find the information they want. Put your best work at the top and depending on the audition, put theatre at the top for theatre auditions and film or television at the top for those auditions. For contact information you should put a voicemail number (not your cell number) and an email you regularly check, rather than your street address. With your picture everywhere, including the Internet, you don't want to get stalked or spammed. Categories might include Theatre (in columns Play, Role, Director, Company (This should be the producing organization, not the theatre space), Film and Television (should put how you are billed: lead, supporting, guest star, etc.). Training and Education, put any college plus the key teachers you have worked with if you have studied voice, dance (put how many years; e.g., ballet (5 years), tap (2 Years), improvisation, acting.

Finding Audition Opportunities

It used to be that auditions were only posted in a particular city's theatre organization newsletter such as *Backstage* in New York, *Backstage West* in Los Angeles, Theatre Bay Area's *Callboard* in San Francisco, or in locations where actors gather, such as The Drama Bookshop in New York City or Limelight Books in San Francisco. However, in recent years online postings for auditions are much more common, and the above newsletters now have online notifications that you can sign up to receive. Actors may also post their headshots and résumés on a variety of websites that casting directors or directors can then peruse. However, not all sites that want actors to post are actually even seen by those casting, so it is best to do some research, such as current versions of the books mentioned above, to find out the websites most frequented by the people who might actually hire you.

Many auditions are not available to the general public but are only available through *breakdowns* (descriptions of the available parts) sent out by *casting directors* to *agents* and therefore only seen by those actors that that agency believes best fit the qualifications and are most likely to *book the job*. Other auditions are only posted on the websites of the unions, and only union actors are granted access. US unions would be Actor's Equity Association (AEA) commonly referred to as Equity for theatre roles, and for film and television, SAG-AFTRA—Screen Actors Guild (SAG) that merged with the American Federation of Television and Radio Artists (AFTRA).

Even if you have posted your materials on a good website and have an agent, you cannot sit back and wait to be cast. You must find out, by reading trade magazines and talking to your contacts, what is being cast right now and who is casting it, and then encourage your agent to submit you or try to figure out how to submit yourself.

Other auditions are available to non-Equity actors or to both. Many mid-sized regional theatres in the US have special contracts that allow them a predetermined ratio of Equity and non-Equity actors, and the initial auditions are likely to be separate.

Landing the Audition

Once you have found out that an audition has a part in your range, you will need to understand more about the company. One thing to investigate is the type of work they do, such as classical or new plays, and aimed at what kinds of audiences. Look at their production photos and past-seasons lists. If they do classical, are they more traditional or nontraditional? You also need to know how to sign up and whether you can call directly or need to go through an agent or casting director. Today this is much easier, as you can go to the company's website and find a host of information. Do not call the theatre company and pester them with a lot of questions before you have done your homework. In class, there is no such thing as a bad questions, as the teachers are there to help you learn (but even they always wish you were better prepared); in the profession, people are very busy, and often understaffed, and their purpose in life is not to take care of your every need but to take care of the needs of their company and production.

Many theatre companies have a resident casting director whose focus is to make sure a sufficient range of quality actors shows up to auditions and often to do initial screenings so that the director only sees actors that are 1) suitable in terms of age, gender, and other factors for the available part and 2) sufficiently experienced to fit in with the production levels of their theatre. Other companies may work through freelance casting directors or directly through online posting methods, advertising, and direct contact with agents (who represent actors). Even if there is no casting director, somebody at the company will be responsible for organizing the auditions, giving out slots, and making sure the actors have the information about where auditions are held and what will be expected. In university theatre, this is generally the stage manager.

Open Auditions

Many theatre companies hold *open or general auditions* at some point throughout the year. Sometimes a representative is sent to certain regional conferences to look for new talent. Casting directors may also go to general auditions such as the Strawhat auditions, the URTAs, or Theatre Bay Area or the Southeastern Theatre Conference general auditions. Often it is as simple as calling a number to request an audition slot or signing up online.

Courtesy

You never know to whom you are speaking when you call a theatre or arrive for an audition; even the receptionist may be the artistic director's son. Colleagues talk, so if you are rude, high maintenance, or otherwise disrespectful, this may get out to the people with the power to cast you.

First Auditions: Monologues

Once you have landed the audition make sure you know: where it is, what type of audition it is, how much time you have, and what if anything you should bring. For example, if part of the audition is a song, bring your sheet music in sheet protectors in a thin binder in the correct key and with start and stop points clearly marked. Even if you already submitted a headshot and résumé, either via the mail or as an online attachment, always bring extras to auditions in case yours was misplaced or there are additional auditors that could benefit from a copy. Sometimes the first auditions are in front of a casting director. The director then only sees you if the casting director selects you to move on to the second round. In other theatres, the director is involved from the beginning of auditions.

The first audition is generally a *monologue*, a part of a play spoken by one actor of generally one- to two-minutes long. You should have a range of prepared monologues kept in a fictional closet (serious, comic, classical, demonstrating movement, demonstrating use of complex language, contemporary (last five to ten years),

17 ENTERING THE COLLABORATIVE PROCESS

twentieth-century realism, etc.). Then you can pull out and dust off the appropriate one for each audition. You are generally given one to two minutes for your audition. If you are auditioning for graduate school, a resident company, or a general audition, you will often be asked for either two contrasting monologues or a monologue and a song with a set time slot of two to three minutes. As they usually have a full slate of actors, you will be cut off if you exceed the time. Exceeding the time is disrespectful of their time, and if you are cut off in the middle, it does not allow you to finish as strongly as you planned. Directors will generally know within seconds what you are going to offer for the entire one-minute piece and are rarely surprised by shifts later in the piece that change that impression. Therefore, shorter is generally better.

In union auditions, for the first audition with the actual script, the actor will often read a scene with the stage manager or casting director, rather than another actor who is auditioning. You are expected not merely to read but to be fully engaged in the scene and affecting the other person. This can be challenging to show what you can do with a stage manager if he doesn't have much acting training or experience.

Callbacks: Cold Readings

If you do a good first audition and you have something the director is considering for the part, you may be called back for a second audition. These are named *callbacks*: a misnomer as no one may actually call you; at universities you generally check a list posted on a board. Callbacks usually consist of *cold readings*, which involve reading a particular scene while holding the script (although again you should be as prepared as possible and get your head up out of the script to interact with the other person in the scene). If you can find out ahead of time what you are to read you can better prepare. If scripts are not available, then try to at least read the script out loud and do some preliminary Active Analysis in the hallway or waiting room, prior to going in to read it in front of the director. If the play was available through the company or in libraries or bookstores, you are expected to have found a copy and read the play. If you do not seem to have read the play, in addition to not being able to do your best on the reading, you will be perceived as lacking commitment, which no director wants to deal with later in rehearsals. This is a bad first impression to make.

Look through the script for creative opportunities such as transitions (by marking the beats), decisions, discoveries, or realizations for the character and make a light pencil note in the script. As you are working in Active Analysis, make sure you are engaged in the task of actively struggling to solve the problem, and living in the *magic if* through those moments. See images for the setting as well as any person, place, or event mentioned or in the scene. The reading may take place in a small empty room or a large bare stage, but the only props or furniture usually available are chairs. Often actors will use their script as a prop in a specific moment (while still keeping a thumb on their next line so as not to lose their place).

In a film audition, you may be reading with the casting director or an assistant or even another actor who doesn't give you much to work off of. You must activate the scene by fulfilling clear actions to solve a specific problem, and trying to get a specific response from the other person with whom you are reading. Fold the script so that you can hold it with one hand and gesture with the other as movement arises psychophysically through the spine. Keep the script from covering your face at all times. (If you need better glasses or contacts then wear them, as it doesn't matter how good you look if no one can see your face buried in the script.) Hold your thumb on your next line then get your head out of the paper and your eyes on your scene partner as much as possible.

Casting

Once you are cast—offered a part in a show—you will be given more specifics of when rehearsals are going to start. You will be given a script and expected to start doing your actor's preparation, such as the reconnaissance and Active Analysis outlined in chapters 13, 14, and 15.

The Rehearsals Begin

Who's Who in Rehearsal

The director generally conducts rehearsals and has final artistic say over the production. The stage manager handles most of the logistical aspects of rehearsal and throughout the rehearsal process is charged with learning every detail of what the director wants for the production so that he can orchestrate all the technical elements with the work of the actors during the actual performances of the show. Some rehearsal may be led by other artists in the collaboration—the musical director, choreographer, dialect coach, or occasionally an assistant director. The two people the actor interacts with most are the director and the stage manager. These two individuals have extensive responsibilities far beyond their interactions with you.

Director

The director has the final artistic say over all aspects of the production. Each director has his own way of working, and you must be flexible to learn the best way to work productively and professionally with each director. The director is the boss with the power to hire or fire you. In a professional production, actors generally have little say on the overarching vision for the production, which is well under way, in any case, before actors come on board. However, many directors will give you opportunities to have a lot of creative and interpretive input about your specific character and how specific moments might unfold in your scenes. There are also directors who do not want this input from actors and only want you to figure out how to deliver what they request without a lot of questions or exploration. This is more true the shorter the rehearsal period (such as commercials, some television formats, and even some theatre summer stock). In any of these situations, you must be well prepared and do your actor's homework.

Stage Manager

The stage manager is one of the most central and vital members of the company. Most directors are extremely grateful to their stage managers, who become organization and communication central for the production. The stage manager will eventually take over the running of the show, and his job in rehearsal is to a) help to run the rehearsals smoothly in terms of organization and logistics, b) learn the show in detail so that he can ensure that he can call it to unfold according to the director's vision each performance, and c) to help create a positive, professional working environment conducive to the highest levels of creativity. The stage manager may have one or two assistants in rehearsal, either called assistant stage managers or, more often in professional theatre and film, called production assistants.

Professional Conduct

As soon as you get an opportunity to be in a production, start training yourself to behave professionally, even if those around you or even those running the event are not. You want to make professional conduct a habit. As mentioned in Chapter 4, what is expected in a professional atmosphere whether theatre or other workplace is to, "leave your problems at the door." This is the time for you to enter into the joy, and sometimes difficulty, of working with others in a collaborative art. Leave your personal drama at home or in your personal relationships and be professional and easy to work with, whether or not you agree with what is going on in rehearsal. Shift your focus off yourself to the issues, events, people, and adventures that the playwright is trying to convey to the world. Problems come up in any group of people; try to make sure that you are part of the solution not part of the problem. You can always choose not to work with that company or director in the future, but you cannot, cannot, cannot risk getting a bad reputation. Unfortunately, **it takes a long time to build a great reputation and only a second to ruin it.** If you know what is expected, you are more likely to be prepared to meet the demands of a theatrical rehearsal. Study the dos and don'ts at the end of this chapter. If you don't adhere to these basic expectations of courtesy and conduct, you risk ruining your reputation, which no artist can afford to do.

Early Rehearsals

The common elements of the first rehearsal—company business, design presentations, first reading, or first sing-through—may happen in any order.

Company Business

The stage manager generally conducts *company business* before or after some kind of introduction by the director. The stage manager passes out *contact sheets* and has each member of the company check their information for needed corrections or updates. She hands out the rehearsal schedule, which may be only dates and times without details of what will be rehearsed each day. In this case, calls for each day's rehearsal are posted some amount of time in advance. In professional theatre, when this is the actor's current job, he is expected to be available during regular rehearsal times until the daily *rehearsal calls* are posted. In union shows, an Equity hotline will post calls a set amount of time in advance specific to a show and company. In college theatre, the call times may be posted on a company board or sent out by email or through some other agreed-upon method. All actors are expected to keep rehearsal times open until the call is posted.

Sometime in the first rehearsal, the Equity actors go off separately with the union stage manager to elect an *Equity representative* who represents the actors in any issues between actors and other production or artistic staff, including the director.

Production scripts are given to the actors, if they have not already been mailed ahead. (In the case of a new play, the script is in constant flux as it moves from page to stage. Actors are getting new scripts, new pages, or line changes almost daily, sometimes as late as through previews and right up to opening).

If the actors are from out of town, the *company manager,* or the stage manager acting as company manager, will make sure they get all the information about their housing, transport, gym access, and other perquisites (perks) associated with their casting in this company. They also get information on restaurants, grocery stores, and other things they may want access to in an unfamiliar town.

Design Presentations

The first rehearsal will often include a presentation of the designs. The actors get to see the unified vision of the director and designers. With color renderings and models, they see the world that the scenic designer has created. With sketches and fabric swatches the actors first see the costume designer's vision of their characters. The director may speak about her vision and approach to rehearsing this play. It is harder to present the lighting ideas, so they are often not included, sometimes the sound designer will already have some samples and sometimes not. Of course, if it is a musical, the score is available, and there may be a cast recording from an earlier production to give the actors/singers a feel for the music. All of this reminds the actor that he is being asked to fulfill a role as part of an overall production that must be unified by the director. After the design presentations, the actors may not see the designers, aside from the costume designer, whom they will see for fittings, until later in the process at *technical rehearsals*.

First Reading

Then there is the first reading. This is the first time for the company to hear the unique voices chosen to speak the words of each character. Often the director just wants everyone to read and listen and doesn't expect a lot of more invested acting yet. However, if the actors have been given the script ahead of time, they are often already so familiar with their part, having done the lion's share of their actor's homework in advance, that they are almost off book (have the lines committed to memory) and are getting their heads up and enjoying speaking for the first time to the other actors in the scene.

Getting Off Book

While beginning actors and those outside the theatre believe that learning the lines, called getting *off book*, is the hard part, professional actors know that this is only an important early step and the more challenging work on the role comes after memorization. Due to the short rehearsal time period in today's professional theatre, professional actors want to get off book as soon as possible so they have more time to explore other important considerations of the role in rehearsal. This is especially true in summer stock, where the rehearsal may be as short as two weeks, including technical rehearsals. In film and television, you are expected to come in to the rehearsal performance ready, having not just memorized all your lines but also having worked out many possibilities of what to do with them. Actors who are last or have trouble getting off book slow down rehearsals, make a poor impression on the company, and annoy the director—none of which is good for getting rehired. The techniques of reconnaissance and Active Analysis, outlined in earlier chapters, can really help you in learning your lines while you do your actor's homework to flesh out the creative opportunities in the script.

First Sing-Through

In a musical, there will also be a first sing-through of the music. This may or may not happen on the same day as the first reading of the book, depending on whether the rehearsals are full or half days. Generally, Equity rehearsals are eight-hour days, but not always.

Subsequent Read-Throughs, Table Work, and Active Analysis

At this point, the process begins to vary considerably. Some directors do a number of read-throughs, often incorporating table work (stopping to discuss scenes, themes, confusing aspects of the play, or many other elements). Some directors only do this for more challenging texts or when working with less experienced actors who need more help with text analysis. Some directors start to work with actions and objectives at the table before moving the scene to the stage. Other directors go from the first read-through directly to the *blocking*. Stanislavsky initially used extensive table work and discussion but later decided that this method helped the actors to intellectually understand the play but not to inhabit it. He later moved from the process of seated analysis to that of Active Analysis as outlined in chapters 13, 14, and 15.

Sourcing and Ensemble Work

This is not a step in rehearsal used by all directors. However, some directors looking to create a unified production style do their own unique forms of this work. *Sourcing* is part of preproduction but may also involve all members of the cast sharing research, inspirations, and artistic associations for the play. It may include bringing in people with direct experience of the circumstances of the play or expertise in the style or the playwright. The ensemble may train in a specific style of movement or performance to create a more focused or extreme style in the production. The director may wish to collaborate with the actors on the development or interpretation of the piece, inviting them into active conceptual explorations. Even if working with an established play, a director may use a variety of experimental techniques to upend the script, reframe it, or comment on it. Research may be conducted in a more hands-on way, such as going to meet and interview people, conducting observations of people or situations akin to those in the play, and a huge variety of other methods.

Scene Rehearsals

After a few full-company meetings, plays are generally rehearsed scene by scene. At this point, only the actors that are in that specific scene will be called to rehearse, and other actors have time to do more of their actor's preparation. Often, scene rehearsals will begin with a reading of the scene or section to be worked. The actors will then move to the stage.

Composition and Blocking

The director wants to create interesting stage pictures, called *compositions*, that tell the nonverbal story of the play, as you worked on in Active Analysis. When first working with movement in a scene, the methods again vary.

Traditional Blocking

In traditional *blocking* the director will have worked out the stage pictures and the movement of the actors in his mind, on paper, or perhaps using the model provided by the scenic designer. The director may give the actor only the major movements she would like to see at this point, such as where to enter or exit and major crosses, called *skeletal blocking*. Some directors orchestrate every movement of the actor, even down to the tilt of a head or the flick of a hand. Directors and stage managers will talk in blocking terms—upstage, downstage, center stage, stage left and stage right—when asking you to move yourself or objects around the stage. Coming from a historical time when the stage was raked (on a slanted ramp higher in back and lower toward the audience), *upstage* is farther away from the audience and *downstage* is closer. *Stage left* and *stage right* are from the actor's point of view when facing the audience (so the director and stage managers need to learn to reverse that when speaking to actors). A typical proscenium stage is thus laid out as follows:

U = upstage C – center D = downstage L = left and R = right
(so that DLC = downstage, left of center)

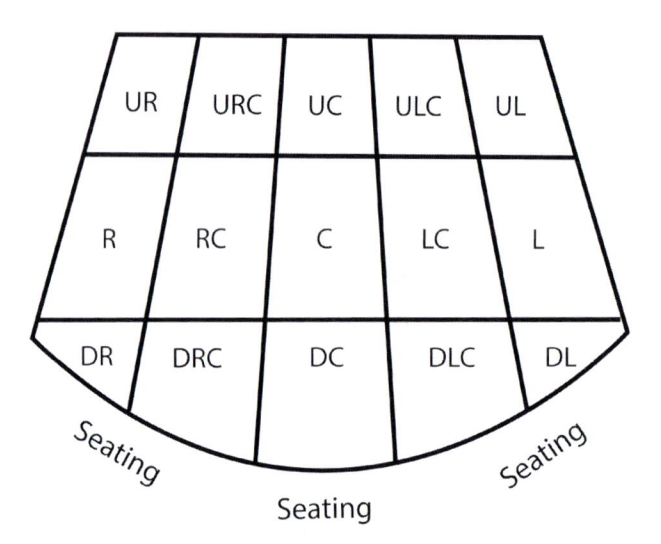

Figure 17.8 Stage area map—a proscenium with apron.

Organic Blocking

If the director only gives skeletal blocking, then he may allow the actors room to explore on their feet in a method called *organic blocking*. In this, the actors find some of their movement based on their active exploration of the text (although it may not be officially using Stanislavsky's Active Analysis, you will be well trained to create effectively in this way and give your director many evocative options if you have done your preparations for Active Analysis as outlined in chapters 13, 14, and 15. The director encourages actors to follow behavioral impulses arising in the moment prompted by the text, the circumstances, or the scene partner's actions. Again, as a psychophysically and improvisationally trained actor you will be more conscious of your arising impulses. At this point, the director observes and gives feedback as to what the different choices are communicating from the audience perspective and what she wants actors to develop further. The director also is looking for the specific choices that are most interesting and work best with the overarching goals of the production, which may be different from the most inventive ones you offered.

Tableau Blocking

The director works with certain stage pictures at certain points in the scene as you did in Active Analysis in Chapter 13. She then may have the actors explore how

17 ENTERING THE COLLABORATIVE PROCESS

they get into and out of these pictures relevant to the moving life of the events and dialogue.

Viewpoints Blocking

Many actors and directors are now trained in a theatrical style called *The Viewpoints*, as mentioned above. The Viewpoints provide an experiential investigation of the theatrical possibilities of time and space. They can be very effective tools to stage a play, develop a play, devise new work, and create a very alive and dynamic ensemble theatre. Some of the aspects that relate most to composition include the viewpoints of space, *spatial relationships, gestures, shape, topography* (which includes patterns of movement, textures of movement, and levels), and the *architecture* of the theatre and set. The aspects that relate to tempo-rhythm are *tempo, duration,* and *repetition*. The most connecting viewpoint, *kinesthetic response*, is about developing responsiveness to everything expected and unexpected that happens onstage and around the stage, which is very akin to the living experience of the Stanislavsky System.

Figure 17.9 Blocking created through Viewpoints in the SITI company's *bobrauschenbergamerica*.
Photo: Michael Brosilow

Blocking Responsibilities for Actors

Always bring a few pencils to rehearsals and write down all blocking given to you by the director. If the director does not allow you time to do this, then during the break get the blocking from the stage manager or assistant stage manager, who will be furiously writing it down in a special shorthand called *blocking notation*. You will seldom be working on the fully fleshed out set, so it is really important for you to look long and hard at the model in the first presentation (or again if it is left in rehearsal) to see the world and especially for blocking the layout of the world in your mind. The stage manager will tape the ground plan on the floor to give you an idea of the spatial relationship of different objects and where there are doors, stairs, platforms, etc. In regional repertory theatres you will be in a rehearsal studio and not the theatre, and this space may be much smaller than the stage, so you and the stage manager taping the set may have to adjust. (Today most of you have phones with cameras, so take a picture of the layout of each scene. However, do not take pictures while people are rehearsing, or post your images without asking. The director and publicity team will want to carefully control production and rehearsal photos, and there are also union rules protecting use of actors' images.

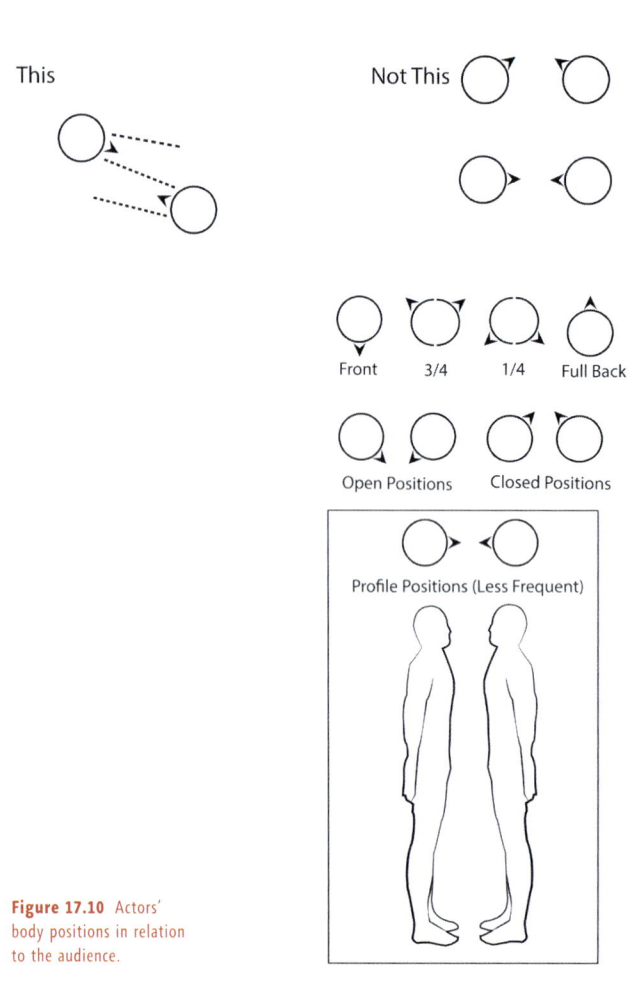

As you are working on your script, even if you are not able to be in the studio where the set is *taped out*, set up an approximate *ground plan* (map of where the furniture and set pieces will be). Then, walk around in the ground plan saying the lines and connecting them to the movement so that you learn both more easily. The next time you come in to work on the blocked scene, it is very important that you do not forget any blocking that the director gave you or you discovered and the director said she liked. Instead, show that you have not only learned it but have integrated it with other work you are doing on the character.

Figure 17.10 Actors' body positions in relation to the audience.

Incorporating Active Analysis in a More Traditional Rehearsal Process

Arrive early to rehearsal so that you can walk through your blocking on the taped out set. You can prepare for these and subsequent rehearsals by doing your own reconnaissance as described in Chapter 13. You can do Active Analysis as described in chapters 14 and 15. If time is not given in rehearsal, you can do Active Analysis on your own by setting up an approximation of the ground plan and imagining the other actors are there with their possible responses. Of course, it is better if you can do this work with the rest of the company, but the style of the director or the shortness of the rehearsal process often preclude this.

Write your autobiography to stimulate subjective thinking as the character. Do a few character études to explore the character's body and behavior. Highlight your lines, figure out your objective, and name your events. Actively explore your moment-to-moment actions, inner monologue, and tonal subtext. Work on developing and seeing your personal images as you speak the lines and move through the blocking created or dictated in earlier rehearsals.

Also, use the time you are backstage waiting to rehearse your scene to review and revise the work you did at home. Many actors see these periods of waiting as a time to goof off. Fooling around backstage is unprofessional and disturbs other actors who are seriously preparing to make their next entrance. Be quiet and courteous. Turn off personal computers and cellphones when you enter the theatre for both rehearsal and performance, as these can be a distraction for others as well. If you are called, do not leave the rehearsal area unless 1) the stage manager calls a break or 2) you check with the stage manager first.

TIP: You want to be the actor that offers the director a lot to work with. At all times, you must have many possibilities on how to create a beat of action in a play. Some directors have limited experience of acting and are more visually focused on the overall production (this is often especially the case in film or television acting). You are expected to deliver interesting stage business and emotions on cue without any coaching by the director. The director may just say, "I don't like that, give me something else." A good rule is to have at least five different ideas for how to fulfill an action. This entire book trains and prepares you to do that. As early as the run-stop-justify exercises, you have been training to justify and bring to life any physical choices the director requires. The need to get inventive with stage business and use it to express the *subtext of behavior* of the character and script you have uncovered is aided by always using props (or something to stand in for a prop) and working within the specific ground plan, even when working through the script on your own outside of the main rehearsal.

Stage Business

The actor is usually called upon to create his or her own *stage business* within the larger blocking picture of the scene. Stage business includes such things as lighting a cigarette, fixing your hair, putting on or taking off clothing, serving drinks, etc. Directors may prescribe specific stage business they want to see at specific points or just tell the actor which of the ideas offered by the actor she would like him to keep. Connect your stage business to your psychophysical actions and inner monologue in response to the given circumstances, whether they are realistic, dystopian, or supernatural. Action that is not psychophysical and in exacting detail often seems fake or uninteresting.

Rehearsals and Design

The production team will try to provide rehearsal furniture and platforms as much as possible. In the case of period pieces or other elaborate costumes, you may also be provided with rehearsal costumes, such as corsets, hats, snuff boxes, walking sticks, etc. If you are not, bring in accessories that help remind you of what you will be wearing, such as shoes similar to those you will wear as the character: a long skirt if you are a female in a period piece, or a jacket, tie, and hard-soled shoes if you are a male. (It does not matter so much what they look like but what they move like and how they function). If you are working without a costume designer, such as on a class scene project, you can discover what is appropriate by doing your own period research (which we would recommend anyway) to help you create images of the time and place and help you to imagine living in the circumstances of the play.

Middle Rehearsals

Actor Coaching

When the director works with the actors to find and express more layers and meaning of the script and to intensify the impact of the play, this is called *actor coaching*. Your training in the System will help you to more easily incorporate this feedback from the director. Before you enter the profession, you want to be able to receive direction and immediately incorporate it without a lot of explanation. Beginning actors will often need to be led through an idea step-by-step and may take many rehearsals until they can fully incorporate it, if at all.

In middle rehearsals, all the given and evolving circumstances must be made clear. The dynamics of the conflict between the characters' opposing objectives must be uncovered, intensified, and physically and vocally expressed. The unifying visual and movement style for the world of the play must be developed and incorporated. Important points of the plot or story must be clearly and interestingly revealed. Themes must be steeped out. The atmosphere and moods of various scenes must be evoked. The emotional depths must be plumbed. All of these elements need to be explored with an eye toward how to communicate them and create the desired response in the audience.

Figure 17.11 Actor coaching. Director Stephanie Daventry French coaching Merril McGuinness in Naomi Iizuka's *Polaroid Stories* at East Stroudsburg University.
Photo: Charles Perry Hebard (courtesy of East Stroudsburg University)

Note: If you find that you are unable to fulfill a direction or unable to understand it, work on it at home using the *magic if* and the other tools of your technique to help you justify what you've been asked to do. Never challenge a director's instructions in the rehearsal process or take up time with excuses and explanations; just accept the notes and work on them. Otherwise, you will interrupt the director's concentration as well as the concentration and focus of those around you. If you do not understand what is being asked of you, find a mutually convenient time to seek clarification. (This might be on a break or at the end of the notes section or after rehearsal or prior to the official start of rehearsals the next day. As notes usually happen at the end of a long day of focus for the director, she may not want to get into a discussion until she is fresh.)

Moment-to-Moment Work
Some directors will allow you to work in episodes (smaller segments of the script) and may call this phase *stop-start rehearsals*, *beat work* (which is really *drilling the actions*), or *moment-to-moment work*, or various other names. This is very important work that allows you to actively explore an important episode and hopefully experiment with your scene partner giving and receiving, working toward fulfilling actions and communion. Again, directors will give you more or less room to experiment, depending on their style. You may have the opportunity to run through your scene with your scene partner outside of the rehearsal with the director, but make sure that you do not direct the other actor in any way. Actors must never give other actors notes. If the actor is trained in a similar technique as you, he may wish to explore the scene through Active Analysis, but in suggesting this, you must be careful that you are not seen to be offering an alternative rehearsal method to that of the director.

Scene Runs with Notes
Some directors may not work moment-to-moment but may stick with running the full scene, giving notes and running the scene again expecting her notes be incorporated in each subsequent run. If you don't understand what the director wants in a note, depending on the style and flexibility of your director and your respectfully chosen timing as discussed above, you may ask for clarification, demonstration, or show her what you think she means. Some directors will give you room to try some of your own ideas, and others will want you to only follow their ideas.

Finding and Deepening Emotional Connections to the Material
Many actors find they cannot evoke full emotional connection until they are running longer sections of the scene or the entire play. It is the through-line of the character's journey through the play that gets them there. Some actors will not work on any emotional connection until the play is fully blocked. Based on what we know about the body's role in emotion this makes some sense, unless of course your director wants to block more organically, based on the actor's emotional response discovered in rehearsal and the *impulses* activated by it in the character's situation. This method does not work in film, however, as film is frequently shot out of event order of the story. (This is done to consolidate locations, limit moves and set-up of equipment and personnel, and contain costs.) An intense emotional scene for your character may be shot prior to filming the events that trigger that state for the character. Also

in film you will have to tap into that emotion over and over for subsequent takes and different camera angles. This is why whether you are working in theatre or film you must be well versed in your nonverbal and verbal actions and a variety of methods to stimulate your emotions as covered in Chapter 12: Orchestrating Emotions.

Some theatre actors state that they are saving their emotions for the performance and do not invest emotionally in any rehearsals. They mark out their movement and go over their lines and make sure to know where to stand to be in light or to be part of a specific stage picture the director is trying to create. While actors are often not able to connect emotionally during rehearsals where their throughlines are interrupted, such as stop-start rehearsals and cue to cues (discussed later), they understand they are expected to deliver emotionally in rehearsal during runs of scenes, sections, and full runs of the play. If they hold back waiting for the performance, this causes the director to expend far too much energy worrying about whether or not the actor will find it in performance and whether it will come out in a way that will override the overall production vision that the director has worked carefully to create. The director may choose to replace the actor or not work with him again, even if he eventually turns out an award-winning performance. It is also extremely hard on other actors in the scene. Constant giving and receiving is as essential to actors in a scene as it is to the human beings in life. If one actor is holding back, the others do not have a chance to develop their parts in a collaboratively responsive way. This can lead to a style of acting where one actor is turning out a great solo performance but not in response to the ensemble around him, or often even the story of the playwright as interpreted by the director. In a sports match, a team working together will outperform a team with individual superstar athletes who do not work collaboratively.

Holding back may also be devastating to the artistry of that actor's performance. If the actor taps into a deep emotional connection for the first time in performance it may be raw and more personal therapy than the appropriate and artistically evoked and crafted emotion needed. The actor doesn't have the opportunity to understand the mechanisms for how it was created and how to repeat it for every performance. It may not come at the right moment in the play. It may be so intense as to throw off the other actors and the overall unfolding of the scene as the director had planned, or even be dangerous in a fight scene. It may move the actor but may not move the audience. It may even disturb the actor so much that he afterward shuts down completely while the rest of the play unfolds. The most earth-shattering personal emotions may be triggered in rehearsal. The actor can observe the psychophysical patterning of the emotion. Then he can use technique to psychophysically stimulate and express the emotion required for the role on cue without ever having to dwell again on the personal event.

Additionally, I have been at a number of performances where the actors said, "I really felt it tonight," but they had not laid down a path of expression that led the audience to be moved at that moment as well. This type of acting is great for drama therapy but not appropriate for an audience who has paid to come to the theatre so that they may have a powerful experience.

For the most part, the work of connecting emotionally to the character and the situation is left entirely up to the actors. That is why it is so vital to learn and develop techniques that help you and your specific psychophysical instrument (body-mind) to activate appropriate emotions on cue repeatedly.

Note: Before every rehearsal review your action verbs, see the circumstances

17 ENTERING THE COLLABORATIVE PROCESS

in your mind, and experiment with your body and images. In other words, rehearse on your feet at home to make sure you really know what you want to bring to the next day's rehearsal. When you are rehearsing at home try to say the lines quietly to yourself, rather than aloud, at least at first. Otherwise you run the danger of listening to yourself and getting fixed in certain intonation. If you fall into the trap of fixing your intonations without a partner, you will most certainly kill any spontaneity at the rehearsal. This does not mean that you do not work on your lines for understanding and expression, it simply means that when you are alone pay attention to the physical expression of your actions, and when you are in rehearsal put your focus on their truthful execution while spontaneously responding vocally to what your partners give to you.

Getting Off Book

If you have done your actor's homework, you should have little trouble getting *off book* (memorizing your lines) given a sufficient rehearsal period. When it comes to film, television, or *summer stock*, you may have little *lead time* with the script and may need to employ some memorization tips. (Luckily in film you only have to memorize a few pages per day of shooting, not know the lines of a two hour play all at once, and films often show visually rather than having the high reliance on dialogue (in addition to visuals) there is in plays.) Also, if you are new to acting and have not yet trained the memorization pathways of the brain or are an actor who has memory loss or challenges or have a very lengthy part, extra work may be required to memorize. In this case, some additional tips might be helpful. Look to the Tips for Learning Lines box in Chapter 15.

Figure 17.12
Deepening the emotional connection. Maria Picon (Persephone) in *Polaroid Stories* at East Stroudsburg University.
Photo: Yoshinori Tanokura

Final Phase of Rehearsals

Run-Throughs

After the play has been blocked and work has been done on individual scenes, the director will call for sections of the play to be run through without stopping. Perhaps after rehearsing scenes in it, she would run Act 1 first. It is likely at this time that the transitions between scenes will first be blocked or otherwise addressed. You may not yet have a full crew, so any transitions that involve set changes are likely to require a little extra time for strike of the previous and setup of the next scene by the stage management team (or by one stage manager). The stage management team will be following you to ensure that you are saying the lines correctly and following the blocking dictated by the director and may give you line and blocking notes. The assistant stage manager (often called production assistant in professional theatre and film) will be tracking the movement of props to try to figure out where offstage you need a prop to be preset or handed to you by a crewmember or where you might have a quick costume change. In Equity productions, actors are not allowed to help move the set, and this may not matter if scenery can easily roll off or fly out, but again this smooth scenic movement will not happen in the rehearsal studio with rehearsal sets. In other company formats, and often in university productions, actors may be incorporated into choreographed set changes to make them more theatrical.

Character Arcs and Through-Line of Actions

Run-throughs are opportunities for the actor to work on the part with fewer interruptions from outside the world of the play. This is a chance to get clearer about the *through-line of actions* for your character, to start to live and respond more spontaneously in the imaginary circumstances and let this color your adaptations, to find a path within the time of the play and scenes to trigger and release the appropriate emotions, and to develop the expressions of all of this in the appropriate *tempo-rhythms* that will eventually convey the character's experience clearly to the audience.

Polish: Pacing, Punctuation, Buttons, and Nuance

The director will be working on ensuring that important plot points are clear; that the scenes are dynamic and *nuanced*; and that the ends of beats (units of action), scenes, and acts have strong punctuating compositions. In musicals and comedies, the director wants to make sure there is a *button* to cap songs or dances or laugh lines. This helps the audience know where to applaud or laugh so that they respond collectively rather than in sparse smatterings, which is less invigorating. On most television comedies they prompt this with laugh tracks. In the System we try to find final gestures to punctuate scenes or important moments by using the final gesture of W.E.D.G.A.G. as used throughout your training in the System.

This is also the time for actors and the director to work on *pacing*. The pacing includes the tempo and the rhythms. In climatic play structure, the director must

Figure 17.13
Polishing—the button at the end of a musical number. *The Threepenny Opera* at the San Diego Repertory Theatre.
Photo: Ken Jacques

orchestrate the rises and falls of the overall action to build tension to each *crisis*, release it, and build it again, rising to the *crescendo* of the *climax* of the play. Pace usually has to be picked up in many places, but also key pauses may be inserted that allow something important to be discovered, realized, or decided for the character (and therefore the audience).

There is usually different pacing for moments that are deep or wrenching versus the moments that are releases, light, or funny. Some playwrights purposely invert these natural tempo-rhythms for a specific, often comic, effect. Sometimes the tempo will be rapid as a character rattles off a list of things, prattles on about something light, or releases a tirade they have bottled up until now. At other times, the tempo will slow down so that something important can be delicately revealed. The rhythm includes the flow of key events, as mentioned above, as well as the rhythms of the characters. The director and actors, no longer thinking about lines or blocking, can explore more nuanced details of each scene and moment of the play, layering it even more richly and finding the flow of longer sections.

Designers in Rehearsal

Throughout the rehearsal process directors continue to meet with designers and other members of the production team in regular production meetings. Directors also visit the various shops to see the progress of the designs and discuss any issues with designers or shop heads prior to designs being loaded into the theatre. Additionally, the stage manager sends the designers and production team daily rehearsal reports on any aspects of the actors' work in rehearsal that the stage manager or director think might affect the design. Designers are generally welcome to rehearsals but usually speak with the director about the most important times for them to be there, where the director might show them things specific to their areas of design. If there is a dialect, vocal, or movement coach, he may be in rehearsals frequently and take his own notes for the actors. Choreographers and musical directors will generally have special rehearsals with specific groups of dancers or singers during the middle phase and later will be a part of larger rehearsals.

Figure 17.14 *Bruja*, by Luis Alfaro, at Borderlands Theatre Company, Tucson, Arizona.
Photo: Andres Volovsek

Run for Lights

At some point, usually far before the actors and director feel ready for it, a run-through that shows the basic stage pictures and patterns of movement must be offered for the lighting designer. Based on this, as well as lengthy discussions with the director, the lighting designer must come up with the lighting plot that shows the lighting crew where the instruments will be hung and where they are pointed, as well as what *circuits* in the electrical system they will be plugged into, and what *color media (gels)* and *frames*, if any, they require. A lot more goes into lighting design, but that is not the focus of this book. Actors need to know that they must follow their prescribed blocking for this rehearsal so the designer can get an actual picture and ensure the proper scene lighting and focus for the scene on the appropriate parts of the stage.

Working with Multimedia

The mechanisms to integrate media generally require the entire set, which requires being in the theatre, which usually happens just before or at tech. Therefore, media often cannot be integrated into rehearsal and often won't be unless the production is all about interactions with media. An example of this is the Wooster Group, who had a fresh live interpretation of *Hamlet* responding to an old film version of the same play and also interacting with live-feed video of other characters in the play streamed from other areas of the theatre or backstage. This would have required use of these elements from earlier in rehearsals. Even if this is not possible, frequently, the director and media designer will make an opportunity for the actors to see some of the visual images that are evolving so that they can at least have some of these imaginatively to respond to and consider in building their roles. Another example is special-effects in films. The actor must interact with his or her imagination of the supernatural images, as around them is only a *green screen* upon which the images are later added.

Figure 17.15 *The Tragical History of Dr. Faustus,* by Christopher Marlowe, at the San Jose Repertory Theatre, 2013. Direction/Photo: Kirsten Brandt

Figure 17.16 Quick, evocative transformation with projections. The good and bad angels, *The Tragical History of Dr. Faustus*, by Christopher Marlowe, at the San Jose Repertory Theatre.
Direction/Photo: Kirsten Brandt/San Jose Repertory Theatre

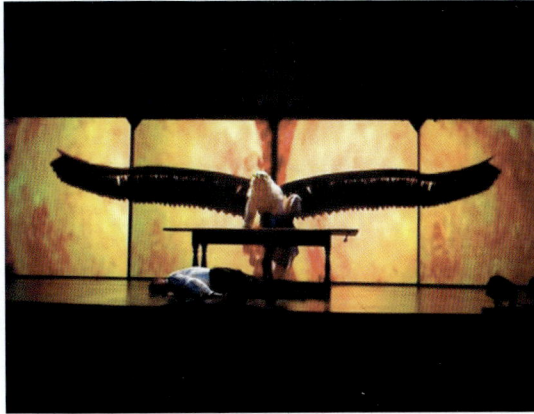

Working with Sound

Many directors like to work with elements of the sound design long before technical rehearsals. Of course with a musical or play with music, this will be an essential element right from the beginning. In a regular play, special rehearsals may be set up to try out different pieces of music or sound effects that are going to be used. The earlier in rehearsal sound effects and music can be introduced, the more integral they become to the work of the actors. Sound can inspire them to choices they might never have otherwise made and can be a very helpful tool for getting emotionally connected to a scene. (In fact even if there is no sound in your scene if you find a piece of music that captures the feeling of a scene, you can rehearse with it on your own anyway. Chances are it will affect you later in rehearsals and performances even without the music playing.) If a piece of music is integral to your scene, ask the stage manager to get it on a CD for you so that you can listen to it repeatedly and work with it in your private preparation.

Costume Designer

Of the design team, the actor generally works most intimately with the costume designer. The costume designer must measure and clothe the actor's body, which often requires seeing the actor partially or mostly naked. The actor will meet with the designer initially to be measured and later to be fitted for various costumes. The costume designer may also come into rehearsals of their own initiative or at the director's request to see what kinds of movement the actor is required to do in the costume. The costume designer might demonstrate for the actor how to handle functional costume pieces such as a boa, a fan, or a cape. If you feel positive about your costume, feel free to compliment the designer. If you have any issues about fit or your ability to do the prescribe movement, you should communicate these as well. However, if you don't like the overall design or any specific pieces, you need to keep quiet. The goal is not

Figure 17.17 Mixing sound. East Stroudsburg University students Destiny Washington (sound board operator) and Michael Lloret (sound designer).
Photo: Yoshinori Tanokura

to make you into a star or to look beautiful. The costume designer, working closely with the director, has come up with designs to fit into the overarching vision for the production. This may be for you to look ghastly, drab, dirty, or fat, and you do not have the right to criticize or refuse. It is considered very unprofessional, and if you do not wear the costume and makeup exactly as prescribed, you can be fired from the production.

Director's Notes

Generally, runs of parts or all of the production will be followed by notes from the director of things she would like to change or fix. Some actors take every note as a personal criticism and feel a need to defend themselves for every note they get. This is sometimes because directors focus primarily on what needs to be fixed and don't give as many notes for all the things that are working, possibly because the things that are working were pointed out in notes days ago. Most directors try to be sensitive, and succeed some of the time, perhaps flagging as the stress mounts and they feel more rushed. Whatever the case, as the director generally has many notes, it is important not to explain or justify yourself as she is giving them to the company, as this takes far too much of everyone's precious time and energy. It is also important not to argue because you have a different interpretation of the play. If you have a very good relationship with the director and are already a well-known actor, you may get input into the interpretation of your character. Also, some directors welcome input from actors, knowing that at some point in the process the actor knows more about the character than they do. However, it is the director that must hold the vision of the entire production, and what you believe is best for your character may not be best for the overall play or may not fit that director's interpretation. You must just file those ideas away for the future when you direct a version of this production. If occasionally you are very concerned by what the director says and need to speak

Figure 17.18 Giving notes after a run of *A Christmas Carol*. Director Dr. Margaret Joyce Ball and Company.
Photo: Yoshinori Tanokura

17 ENTERING THE COLLABORATIVE PROCESS

to her then find an opportunity in a more private setting to discuss the note. As was said earlier, never challenge the director or undermine her in front of the entire company. The director, who, after all, has the power to hire, fire, and recommend you to other directors, seldom appreciates this.

You are expected to incorporate the director's suggestions—additions, cuts, or changes—into the next run of that segment of the play. Therefore, if you do not understand a note, you should ask for clarification. If a director gives notes three times without you incorporating it, this is grounds for dismissal under Equity rules. Otherwise, just nod to show you have received it and write it down so that you can remember it and work on it later, either on your own or in subsequent rehearsals. The ability to quickly make adjustments based on the director's notes is the sign of an experienced professional, and these actors are those whom directors want to work with repeatedly. Your training in improvisation will give you the advantage of flexibility to engage with and justify whatever the director gives you.

Fixes

Even after you are into full run-throughs and previews, if the director has a note that is particularly complex she may arrange to work that moment with the actors involved. During preview week, actors routinely rehearse during the day and perform at night. Additionally, after opening, the stage manager may call and run a rehearsal if the play is diverting from the director's vision and blocking or the playwright's words. Hopefully, the actors will get some runs in the actual performance space prior to technical rehearsals, but not always.

Technical Rehearsals (Commonly Called "Tech")

At this point, a set date on the schedule, ready or not, the work of the actors with the director that has been moving along in rehearsals will be merged with the work of the designers that has been moving along simultaneously. This work has been developing in design studios, design meetings, and production meetings and has been built or prepared in the various shops—costume shop, scene shop, lighting shop, paint shop, sound studio. Technical rehearsals can take from days, to a week, to a month, to many months for a complicated show like *Spider-Man* on Broadway.

For the actor, the company seems to suddenly expand as all the creative team who were involved long before the actors are now all present in rehearsal, as well as the crew members who are being added in for the first time. Actors must understand that even though they are feeling the stress of moving toward opening and perhaps wish for more attention and input from their director to help them with this step, the director's focus is now split in rehearsal with all the collaborators needing input from the director to make or adjust artistic decisions. As most directors have worked repeatedly with the same designers, and as the director, designers, and tech team will probably leave the

Figure 17.19 Rigging a practical. Noel Coward's *Blithe Spirit* at East Stroudsburg University; student workers Tyler Adams and Robert McIntyre (up ladder).
Photo: Stephanie Daventry French

technical rehearsals after the actors, the director may also start interacting with them more socially, even if prior, she had been spending social time with the actors. All of these things can make the actors feel abandoned just when they need additional support; try not to take it personally. The director wants you to succeed and will help you and engage you as much as time, other demands, and her stamina allow.

Paper Tech (without actors)

Often about one week to a few days ahead of the rest of tech, there will be a paper tech with the director, stage manager, lighting, sound, and any multimedia designers to write the many cues for these designs into the stage manager's prompt book. This helps to move the rest of tech along. As the cues will change in tech, and new cues will be added, some time will need to be given in tech for the stage manager to rewrite his cues, even if paper tech is conducted ahead.

Dry Tech (also called Level Set, is without actors)

All technical cues are worked through without actors. The key participants are generally the stage manager, director, lighting and sound designers, any multimedia designers, and crew, as well as some people to walk the set and stand where actors will be standing. While sound will generally have already been introduced in rehearsal with a portable sound system it will now be played over the theatre's sound system. Sound levels are set, and timing is tentatively worked out for complicated changes to coordinate them with lighting and scene changes (this will be adjusted for timing with text and action later). The stage manager calls the lighting and sound cues, and the director looks at different lighting cues, often for the first time. The calling of cues may be stopped frequently for the lighting designer to adjust the look of the scene as the light board operator, assistant lighting designer, or master electrician programs the cue into the computer lighting board.

It is much better for dry tech to happen prior to cue-to-cue, but this is not always possible with the production schedule, as it requires the theatre to be dark (i.e., no set dressing or construction can safely be going on at the same time). Some levels are set if there are stand-ins to walk the blocking in place of the actors, but it is very hard to know whether lighting levels or timing are correct until there are people onstage in the correct positions. If there are complicated set changes, the production assistants may work with the crew to practice those. The crew will also change the scenery and props as needed to facilitate the lighting designer, although often only larger or certain key props will be required. The more that gets accomplished in dry tech, the more fluidly cue-to-cue will run.

Figure 17.20 Circuiting strip lights. Lighting crew member Michael Llorett with lighting designer Dave Dougherty.
Photo: Stephanie Daventry French

Cue-to-Cue (occasionally referred to as wet tech)

Actors are added into tech at this point. Typically, the stage manager runs this rehearsal, in coordination with the director, lighting designer, sound designer, and multimedia designer. This is a time-intensive process, often requiring longer rehearsals for a set period of time. In Equity productions, actors are allowed to rehearse for six days a week during tech with most of the days limited to eight hours, but for two of the tech days they may be called for ten out of twelve hours with prescribed breaks and time between calls. This is generally a very time-intensive process, but it is also very rewarding as the design ideas and drawings you saw in early rehearsals now come vividly to life. It always requires a lot of patience from all artists involved. Each cue is rehearsed so that all the elements that go into making that cue work are coordinated as the director and designers have envisioned.

Stop-and-Go Tech Runs

These are run-throughs with all technical cues, scene changes, and properties in their proper places. The actors run through large sequences of the play, practice costume quick changes, but stop as needed to make adjustments. Whenever possible, it's best for the director to avoid stopping the rehearsal and give notes afterward. The stage manager may stop the run to clarify and/or practice timing of cues and changes. Any personnel may stop the run if a potentially dangerous situation, or one that will permanently damage the set, arises.

Dress Rehearsals

These are full run-throughs of the show in costume, makeup, and hair as it is supposed to look in the show. The director will have generally already seen most of the costumes either in the shop, on the actors during fittings, or in a *costume parade*. Now the director and costume designer get to see these elements all together and with the action of the play and all the other design elements. If the production meetings went well, the costumes should work very well with the colors and styles on the set. The lighting designer will have seen palettes and fabric swatches so he will know what is coming and will have planned for it in his color choices. Dress runs only stop for critical problems or to work on the timing of any quick changes.

From the Director: Concept Affecting Costume Design in Molière's *Tartuffe*

In 2008 French directed Molière's *Tartuffe* at East Stroudsburg University. The play is about Tartuffe, the hypocrite who pretends to be extremely pious as a ruse to dupe the gullible father of the house of Orgon. Meanwhile Tartuffe steals Orgon's possessions, violates his wife, and eventually disposes the family of their home. I was captivated by a character that is never seen and has no lines in the play but is mentioned, Tartuffe's servant Laurent. One of the references to Laurent by a member of the family is, "He confiscates our ribbons and colognes." Scenic designer Sarah Lambert created a series of gilded frames leading to a door that was very elegant but also served as a mouth into which the family's belongings were slowly siphoned off. Costume designer Jennifer Tiranti Anderson and I came up with the following concept: we added a nonspeaking part of Laurent, who did confiscate pieces of the family's clothing throughout the play. Sometimes we'd see the theft, but more often we'd just see them having less and less clothing. The family starts the show overdressed, as was the style in upper-class families of seventeenth-century France, and ends the show in their period underwear. The two pictures in Figure 17.21 show three women of Orgon's family before and after.

Figure 17.21 Costume design concept.
Photo: Charles Perry Hebard, courtesy of East Stroudsburg University, and Dave Dougherty

Notes in Technical Rehearsals

After the various run-throughs, the director gives technical notes and actor notes. The order of these varies. Often the design and technical team will stay long after the actors have left to discuss tech notes and work together on any problems that overlap in different production areas. Sometimes the director gives quick notes to the actors first; at other times, actor notes are given in writing or the next day in a notes session while other tech areas are completing tech notes in the theatre. The notes after first dress runs may focus heavily on costume, makeup, and hair adjustments that either the director or the costume designer feel need to be made. Other elements of the production may be involved, such as some wire sticking out that is catching the actress's large hoopskirt on her entrance, or a slippery surface on the floor that when combined with his costume shoes is causing the actor to lose his footing, or the combination of the makeup and lighting angle causing the character to come across more or less menacing than required.

Figure 17.22 Actor notes during tech. Director Stephanie Daventry French and cast on *Polaroid Stories* by Naomi Iizuka. (Note the inattentive actor in the foreground on his cell phone; he regrets this poor behavior today.)
Photo: Charles Perry Hebard, courtesy of East Stroudsburg University

Conduct during Tech

It is very easy under the demands of tech and the mounting pressure of opening to an audience to feel stressed, under-appreciated, scared or tired, slighted, or many other intense emotions. Tech is a crucible that tests the best of us. Remember that most people involved are feeling some combination of these things—especially worn out—and that everyone's patience can wear a little thin. Try to resolve your own issues without further stressing anyone else, if at all possible. Try to show gratitude for the good work that people do all around you that usually far outweighs the issues that may still need to be resolved. This goes a long way toward giving people the energy to keep going until opening.

Patience is certainly a virtue in tech. Be patient about the things that are not yet working, understanding that not all can be fixed at once. Also, thank others for their patience with you. Try to forgive trespasses, but correct them if you can before they fester. If there is an issue that needs addressing, and you don't think anyone knows, it would be good to bring that to the attention of one of the production assistants. Safety is everyone's responsibility, as are issues that can derail a production, such as sexual harassment, other bullying, or prejudices.

Another really important thing leading up to and during tech and performance is to take care of your health: eat healthy food, take vitamins, sleep, and rest when you can. Socialize sometimes but not so much or so late that you are not sleeping sufficiently. Have a hiatus from screens so that you sleep instead of staying up all hours after rehearsal. If you get sick, you not only diminish your creative potential but you risk getting everyone else sick, and risk your understudy going on on opening night instead of you.

Rehearsal and Performance Dos and Don'ts

This list is by no means exhaustive but includes some of the most common pitfalls that befall early-career actors (some points are relevant for other artists and technicians). Not following these will tarnish your reputation in a professional or even an amateur setting. This may not only affect working with members of this company but everyone they know who might ask about you in the future (and they do ask, constantly), and may harm your chance of being rehired or recast.

Don'ts

- Don't *ever* give notes to another actor or artist on the production if you are an actor on it. (You can ask to try things that might involve another actor but don't use this to disguise telling them what to do.)
- Don't express your critique about the designs to the designers unless you are the director, and even then be aware that this is somebody's hard work and artistry you are talking about. You can design and direct your own production but don't try to do it if that is not your role on this one.
- Don't wear anything on stage in dress rehearsals or performances that the costume designer has not approved (unless you have been told a part of your costume is not done yet). Don't wear personal jewelry (including rings and watches) on stage during dress rehearsals.
- Don't smoke or eat in costume, or drink anything other than water that could stain the costume.
- Don't cut your hair, shave a beard or mustache or change your appearance from auditions until closing the show without first getting approval of the costume/hair designer and director.

- In rehearsals or warmups, don't wear clothing you can't move in or that is inappropriately revealing.
- Don't reprimand or otherwise discipline any crew member or other actors. You can make *polite* requests of people setting your costumes, props, doing your hair and makeup, etc. as long as they don't change anything their crew head or the stage manager/director has required them to do.
- Don't talk in the rehearsal room or theatre about anything other than what is the focus of rehearsal, unless it is a break. If there is a gap you can ask the stage managers if you can go to your dressing room and may chat there, but you would be far better using the time to work on your part.
- Don't text; use video or other computer devices; read magazines, books, or newspapers in the rehearsal room when other people are rehearsing. Show respect for and interest in the work onstage or go somewhere else until your call.
- Never leave the rehearsal space during your call, even to go to the bathroom, without letting the stage manager know. Try to only go to the bathroom on breaks—they are regular with professional companies.
- Don't take on additional commitments during the rehearsal period (not disclosed on your audition form) without discussing them with the director and letting the contact person for the new commitment know of your prior commitment to the play. Do this in person (or by phone) not by email or text, but you can email to set up a time to talk and say if it is important or urgent.
- Don't gossip or otherwise play one person off another in the company. If there is an issue that needs addressing, contact the appropriate person in a respectful, discreet, and direct way.
- Don't complain. If there is a problem, set about fixing it, if it is within the scope of your role in the company, or make the stage manager or an assistant aware of it. Do nothing to undermine the ensemble, or you will be labeled as a disruptive force.
- Don't play pranks on other actors onstage or backstage during a performance.
- Don't touch a prop that you do not use in the show or play around with a prop backstage, even if it is yours, unless you are working out business for the show.
- Don't make suggestive comments to anyone in the cast or crew. The theatre and any work place should be free from sexual harassment. In a sexy play, where intimacy or nudity are part of the artistic concept, this is particularly important for the sense of safety in rehearsal and performance for the actors that may be baring more than their souls or having to be otherwise intimate on stage.
- Don't give the director or stage manager any additional conflicts with rehearsal after you are cast. Work them out by letting the other parties know you are already booked at that time.

Dos
- Take care of your physical and mental health throughout the rehearsal and performance process. Find a way to exercise and eat well despite the demanding schedule (perhaps you will have to let go of exercising during tech).
- Call your stage manager immediately if anything interferes with your ability to do the dos (or avoid the don'ts). The stage manager may instruct you to call the director if it is critical.
- Respond promptly to messages from anyone on the artistic or stage management team. No matter how busy you feel, these people are busier, and waiting for you

17 ENTERING THE COLLABORATIVE PROCESS

may hold up what they need to accomplish. Make sure to regularly check the medium used for communicating in this company (for example, you may need to check email a few times a day even if you no longer use this tool personally).

- Read the entire play before auditions (no exceptions). Read it again, a few times, before the first read through. Look up every word and reference relevant to your part that you don't know before the first rehearsal. It is okay to ask about such things in auditions (unless you had the *sides* in advance or it is an easily available play), but at the first rehearsal it shows you didn't do your homework.
- Do get any cuts, if available, ahead and have them in your script.
- If the director has provided additional materials of any kind—dialect CDs/tapes, music, research—be thoroughly familiar with them prior to the first rehearsal.
- Arrive at least 15 minutes prior to your call times to allow for parking, traffic, and finishing your dinner. Be ready to go at the start time rather than arriving at the start time.
- Do lock up all your valuables with the stage manager, not in your dressing room that many people may need to go in and out of. Theft backstage happens and is very disruptive to you and the communion of the company.
- Prepare for rehearsals. If the scene to be rehearsed is posted in advance, you are expected to come prepared, having worked on the scene, including text analysis.
- Get off book as early as possible. Generally you will want to be off book by the time blocking is finished. Once you start more intensive scene work, the script gets in the way. Most actors will be off book well in advance of it. Trouble with lines is a sure sign that you are not spending enough time outside rehearsal working on your script in other ways. Many actors come to the first professional rehearsal almost off book. In film and television you come to the first rehearsal off book and performance-ready. An actor who doesn't get off book promptly is particularly annoying to the director and stage management staff, and it is the sure sign of an unprofessional actor.
- Incorporate every note your director gives you. Ask for clarification if you are not clear. Remember: Not incorporating the note three times is grounds for dismissal from an Equity contract.
- Treat everyone involved with the production with the greatest respect and politeness and thank them often.
- Leave your troubles at the door. Don't drag down the energy at rehearsal or around a performance. Be someone that everyone loves having in the company for your artistic and personal contributions.
- Do your hair, makeup, and costume exactly as the costume designer or designated assistants have instructed you for every dress rehearsal and performance.
- Make sure to see the performance of any production you work on in any way. This is limited if you are in the show, but if you are in a small role, see whether you can sit out front and watch early runs to see the work of the rest of your cast. Also, if the schedule allows, see other productions done at the theatre where you are working and say hello to the cast and crew after the show.
- Do report issues to the appropriate crew head and, if the problem continues, to the stage manager or director. This is particularly important for safety concerns; sexual or other harassment, as mentioned above; or if the problem prevents you from doing what the director has asked.
- Politely ask for anything you need from the crew, including something washed or ironed, or a prop not in the right place, even if they forgot or had too much other

work. Keep the backstage atmosphere positive and clean of gossip, rudeness, and other mental garbage.
- Dress respectably at all times if you want to be respected (for example, don't walk around outside your dressing room or warming up with barely any clothes on). This does not mean you need to dress formally. Clothing that helps you be the character is advised for rehearsal, especially shoes.
- Keep the backstage clean of physical garbage, too.
- Cover all tattoos with waterproof makeup and take out obvious piercings (tongue, nose, eyebrow).
- Say thank-you for notes from any members of the artistic or stage management team. Also, regularly thank the people who work around you supporting your performance. This is a small gesture that has a huge positive impact.

New Theatre Terms, Concepts, and Artists

Terms used in the Stanislavsky System are in italics.

☐ actor coaching	☐ dramaturg
☐ Luis Alfaro	☐ dress rehearsal
☐ David Aukin	☐ drilling actions (Ch 16)
☐ beat work	☐ dry tech
☐ Wendell Beavers	☐ L'Ecole Internationale de Theatre
☐ Blake Street Hawkeyes	☐ Bob Ernst
☐ *blocking*	☐ frames (for lighting instruments)
☐ blocking notation	☐ going up
☐ Borderlands Theatre Company	☐ Whoopi Goldberg
☐ Kirsten Brandt	☐ Jon Gordon
☐ Howard Brenton	☐ green screen
☐ Peter Brook	☐ ground plan
☐ callbacks	☐ David Hare
☐ character arts	☐ impulses
☐ Caryl Churchill	☐ International Center for Theatre Research
☐ climax	☐ Joint Stock Theatre Group
☐ cold readings	☐ lead time
☐ color media (gels)	☐ Jacques Lecoq
☐ company business	☐ lyricist
☐ company manager	☐ Molière
☐ composer	☐ *moment-to-moment work*
☐ composition	☐ monologues
☐ contact sheets	☐ Cynthia Moore
☐ costume parade	☐ no note concept introduced
☐ crescendo	☐ nuance
☐ crises	☐ off book
☐ cue-to-cue	☐ organic blocking
☐ David Cuthbert	☐ Mary Overlie
☐ dialects	☐ pacing

17 ENTERING THE COLLABORATIVE PROCESS

- paper tech
- perks (perquisites)
- polish
- Polish Theatre Laboratory
- public domain
- punctuation
- put-in
- read-through
- Royal Shakespeare Company
- royalties
- run-throughs (runs)
- San Diego Repertory Theatre
- San Jose Repertory
- David Schein
- sing-through
- skeletal blocking
- sourcing
- Max Stafford-Clark
- *stage business*
- stage manager
- standard dialect
- stop-and-go tech
- stop-start rehearsal
- *subtext of behavior*
- summer stock
- table work
- taped out
- technical rehearsals (tech)
- Tectonic Theatre Company
- Theatre des Bouffes
- understudy
- viewpoints: of space: architecture, gestures (behavioral and expressive), shapes, spatial relationships, topography; of time: duration, kinesthetic response, repetition, tempo
- wet tech
- Sam Woodhouse

CHAPTER 18

The Actor of Living Experience

"Only acting of this kind can fully capture an audience and bring them to a point where they not only comprehend but, more importantly, experience everything done onstage, and so enrich their own inner lives, leaving a mark that time will not erase."[1]

—Konstantin Stanislavsky

- Stanislavsky's Diagram: The Plan of Experiencing
- The Plan of Experiencing (translated)
- Stanislavsky's Diagram, the System and You
- The Three Bases of the System
- The Two Lungs that Breathe Life into the Dual Perspectives of the Role
- The Motivators of Psychophysical Action
- The Spine
- The Flow of Creative Energy
- The Interweaving of the Dual Perspectives
- The Crowning Achievement
- ☐ Exercise 18.1: Experiencing the Stanislavsky System

In Chapter 1, you began your quest for artistic inspiration, a journey to breathe life into a character and a role. The theme for this book has been to assist you, by means of the Stanislavsky System, to identify the artistic inspiration within yourself; then, through knowledge, exercises, games, and improvisations, give you the technical means and confidence to bring your talent and artistry to light for audiences. Step-by-step you have come to practice and assimilate the essential interconnected Elements of Action, as outlined in Chapter 2: The Actor's Palette. Through this conditioning you have begun to behave psychophysically onstage. This has allowed you to explore a play through the engaged techniques of Active Analysis. All of these steps will eventually lead to experiencing and incarnation of the character within the given circumstances. The last threshold is to establish communion with your audience so that you can impact them with your character's supertask as it serves the supertask of the play and production. How do you achieve this ultimate goal?

---

[1] Konstantin Stanislavsky, *An Actor's Work,* trans. Jean Benedetti (London: Routledge, 2009), 21.

Stanislavsky's Diagram: The Plan of Experiencing

Instead of a final word on the System, perhaps the most comprehensive and concise statement we have is Stanislavsky's own diagram of the System that he created in 1935, only three years before his death. It shows the relationship between the various elements and concepts behind the System both in training and in work on a role.

Philip G. Bennett has translated the diagram in this chapter from Stanislavsky's original Russian. Together we interpret its meaning based on both subjective experiences as actors and objective experiences as teachers and directors in the System. We are indebted to Dr. Sharon Carnicke (whose groundbreaking work in Stanislavsky scholarship is referenced throughout this book), who first brought this diagram to the attention of Bennett in 1994 (see personal story below) and first published it in English, in 1998, in her book *Stanislavsky in Focus*.[2]

For more information we also encourage you to review University of Birmingham professor Dr. Rose Whyman's, *The Stanislavsky System of Acting: Legacy and Influence in Modern Performance*. Here she wrote 100 pages about the left half of Stanislavsky's diagram (experiencing) and another 50 pages about the right (incarnation). In Carnicke's and Whyman's books you can also find references and critiques of the many scientific, yogic, and other influences that led to the formation of the System, drawn from margin notes in sourcebooks and entries in Stanislavsky's numerous notebooks.

According to Whyman, "The drawing by Stanislavsky of 'The Plan of Experiencing' . . . with its accompanying description, was included with manuscripts he was working on in 1935 and can be taken as the way he thought about the *System* in the last period of his life."[3] The diagram was not published, however for 20 years. It was first published posthumously, in Russian, in Stanislavsky's *Sobranie Sochinenie (Collected Works)*, volume 3, 1955, page 361.

Now that you have some knowledge and practical experience with the System, it would be good to once again examine Stanislavsky's diagram. It may be helpful to complete Reflection 18.1 for a more in-depth consideration. According to Whyman, when originally published, the editors called the diagram The Plan of the System, but she goes on to say, "It is in fact entitled 'The Plan of Experiencing' in [Stanislavsky's] notes, indicating the importance of this concept for him."[4] The diagram demonstrates the concept of experiencing as it arises organically through the interconnected components of the System, as applied psychophysically during an actor's training and in the course of Active Analysis and performance of a role.

Notice the resemblance of the diagram to the insides of a human torso. It is easy to see the branches as the two lungs, the connecting lines as the nervous system, and the center pole as the spine. It is not surprising he would connect these in his diagram of the System. Stanislavsky referred to the spine of the role as the arc,

---

[2] Sharon Carnicke, *Stanislavsky in Focus: Emotion and the Human Spirit of the Role* (Amsterdam: Harwood Academic, 1998), ix, plate #8.
[3] Bennett and French immediately saw a pair of lungs. Carnicke's first impression, as mentioned to Bennett and French orally, was also of a pair of lungs. Whyman corroborates this: "The diagram is in the shape of a pair of lungs, containing all the aspects of experiencing and incarnation, and a spine, which represents the role." Rose Whyman, *The Stanislavsky System of Acting: Legacy and Influence in Modern Performance* (New York: Cambridge University Press, 2008), 38–39.
[4] Whyman, *The Stanislavsky System of Acting*, p. 39.

or through-line, and understood the physical spine of the actor as the connection between the mind and body. Sonia Moore took this further, to encourage actors to move the muscles along the spine to increase the flow of energy. Interestingly, in place of the head, Stanislavsky has put the supertask of the role, thus visually representing the tenant of the Moscow Art Theatre that placed the artistic creation above the egos of individual star actors.

For the Russian diagram we keep what is considered to be Stanislavsky's title, "The Plan of Experiencing." However, because Stanislavsky places his diagram within the frame of a human body, and because throughout this book we have invited you to experience the embodiment of acting concepts, we call our English version of the diagram "The Anatomy of Experiencing."

Figure 18.1
Stanislavsky's Plan of Experiencing, 1935. Original diagram courtesy of the Moscow Arts Theatre Museum

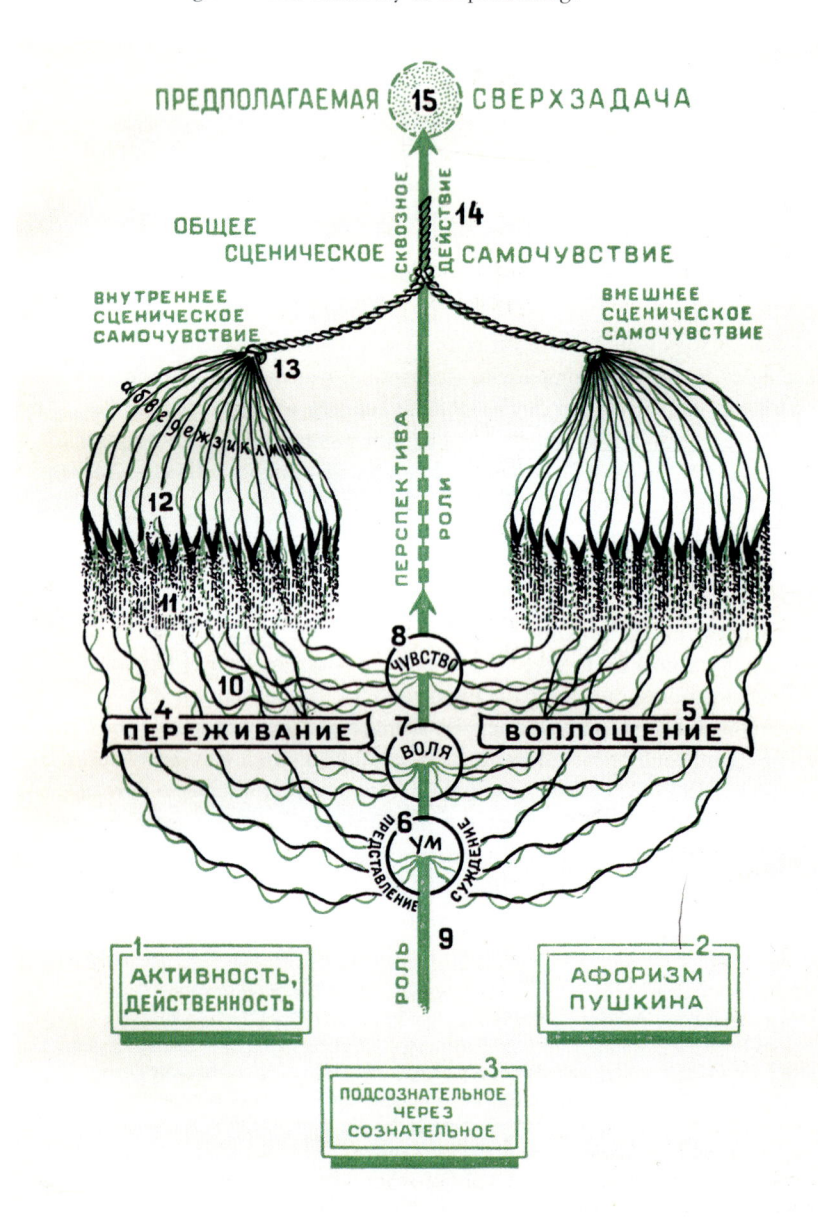

18 THE ACTOR OF LIVING EXPERIENCE

The Plan of Experiencing (translated)[5]

The Three Bases of the System
1. *Active Dynamics (Dynamism, Activeness)*
2. *Pushkin's Aphorism* (The *Truth of Passions* within specific Given Circumstances)
3. *Subconscious through the Conscious*

The Two Lungs That Breathe Life into the Dual Perspectives of the Role
4. *Experiencing, (Living Through)*
5. *Incarnation (Embodiment)*

The Motivators of Psychophysical Action
6. *Mind (Judgment)*
7. *Volition (Will)*
8. *Feeling/Sense (Sensation)*

The Spine
9. *The Role* (written vertically along the base of the pole): Also, between 8 and 14 vertically along the pole next to the image of beads strung together, *Perspective of the Role.*

The Flow of Creative Energy
10. Creative Challenges and Creative Impulses
11. The *Elements of Action—abcdefghijk*[6]
12. *Inspiration* and *Creative Solutions*

The Interweaving of the Dual Perspectives—*Amalgamation* and *Aesthetic Choices*
13. *Internal Theatrical Sense of Self* (woven rope on the left), *External Theatrical Sense of Self* (woven rope on the right)
14. *General Theatrical Sense of Self* (written horizontally on either side of the spine at #14) and Through Action (written vertically at the top along either side of the spine).

The Crowning Achievement
15. *Proposed Supertask*

Figure 18.2 The Anatomy of Experiencing (Philip G. Bennett's translation)

---

[5] Our translation from the Russian is by Philip G. Bennett.
[6] Stanislavsky did not put one Russian term or phrase for this area but the letters of the Cyrillic (Russian) alphabet.

Stanislavsky and Yoga
An Author's Story by Philip G. Bennett

Before examining Stanislavsky's Diagram in depth, I would like to relate a personal story of my early experience as a student of the System.

In September of 1968 I departed my native home of San Francisco, California, to pursue actor training in New York City and began studying the System at the Sonia Moore Studio of the Theatre. (You can read about Sonia Moore in greater detail in Chapter 20: The Evolving Stanislavsky System.) While reading Stanislavsky's first book, *An Actor Prepares*, I came across the word *prana* (discussed in previous chapters). As I had traveled to India and read about yoga, I decided to ask Sonia if Stanislavsky had used yoga in developing the System. Sonia replied that he had investigated Eastern philosophy in the beginning of his search for a system, but subsequently abandoned it as "idealistic."

I knew that Sonia was a devout atheist and adhered to the Soviet philosophy of dialectical materialism (a Marxist doctrine that denies the spirit or soul). Sonia's dismissal of Stanislavsky's interest in yoga only piqued my interest, and I vowed to investigate the matter further.

That same year a few of us young actors at the studio gathered at the home of Bill and Dolores Walker for Thanksgiving dinner. We began to discuss and compare our training experience at the Studio and discovered that we were mutually having enlightening experiences, both on- and offstage. Mostly we experienced an expansion of consciousness in our daily life, and many personal revelations. We agreed that it must be the effect of our training exercises with the System. I began to practice meditation and study Eastern philosophy and couldn't help but notice the similarities between these practices and many of Stanislavsky's Elements of Action—namely: concentration, communion, dual perspectives, and psychophysical action—and the exercises employed by meditation, yoga, and Buddhist philosophy.

In 1976, after having returned to my native home, I founded the San Francisco Theatre Academy with the express purpose of integrating the System with the spiritual principles I had learned as a practicing yogi Buddhist. In 1994, I received from a friend and colleague, Robin Miller, a package containing a audiotape and article entitled: *Stanislavsky's Eastern Self*, written by Dr. Sharon M. Carnicke, professor of directing at the University of Southern California. On the taped lecture and in the article, Dr. Carnicke described her experience of having discovered books in the basement of the Moscow Art Theatre, books on yoga and Buddhism annotated in Stanislavsky's own hand. This was a complete revelation!

Immediately I contacted Dr. Carnicke and set up an appointment to meet with her. We met at her office on the campus and she graciously showed me a draft of her forthcoming book, *Stanislavsky in Focus*. Then she handed me a drawing of Stanislavsky's Diagram and asked, "What do you think this is?" I studied it for a moment and replied, "It looks like Stanislavsky was drawing a comparison between the System and the chakras, the energy centers of the human body. Carnicke said that she was unfamiliar with their significance, and I promised to send her information about them, which I did. Along with the information I sent was a copy of *Autobiography of a Yogi*, the classic work on yoga written by Paramahansa Yogananda. I highlighted the passages related to the chakras, along with those describing prana and the psychophysical nature of yoga.

Experiencing the Connections between Stanislavsky and Yoga: A Personal Story of Stephanie Daventry French

My mother, Shirley Daventry French, is a Canadian master yoga teacher with 45 years experience. She is a direct student of yoga master B. K. S. Iyengar and also studied with Swami Sivananda Radha. Many advanced yoga teachers, including Mr. Iyengar and Swami Radha, stayed in our home. Through her influence, I began to study yoga, and through her introduction I was fortunate to study Iyengar yoga with advanced teachers Judith Hanson Lasater and Ramanand Patel, and kundalini yoga with Swami Radha. Later I also studied Iyengar and Vinyasa with Jennifer Allen.

In 1981, I began studying the System with Phil Bennett at the Theatre Academy in San Francisco. Immediately I noticed many similarities between yoga and this style of acting: the interconnectedness of mind, body, and spirit; the movement and conscious control of the breath; the flow of energy; improved concentration, and heightened states of awareness. There were also similarities in using a variety of techniques to consciously affect the emotions, and in communion with others, to name just a few.

I observed that I could begin with any aspect of the System (or of yoga) and find it to influence other aspects through an inseparable interconnectedness. For a few examples, I experienced the effect of the body upon my emotions; emotions and breath upon each other; the mind on emotions; concentration or meditation's effect on breath, body, and emotion, and the list goes on and on. As my studies expanded into dance (ballet, jazz, and a variety of African-influenced styles), corporal mime, and martial arts (capoeira), I also saw the connections between these systems of energetic awareness, focus, and transmission and the Stanislavsky System. Specifically, I observed the power of moving from a specific center in the body, focusing the arising energy and transmitting this energy outwardly. Yoga, dance, and martial arts also share with acting the need for a strong and flexible sense of balance and focus.

At first I thought that these connections were coincidental. Despite the obvious connections, I was influenced by the prevailing thought of the day, and I considered my performance arts in two camps: the physical theatre, mime, and dance theatre camp and the Stanislavsky acting camp. Nonetheless, finding they complemented each other, I continued to train, perform, and later teach, integrating these elements. It was only years later, through Dr. Sharon M. Carnicke's excellent research that the written documentation of the evidence of the System's roots in yoga came out of the previously closed and censored Stanislavsky archives. My intuitive understanding was shown to be correct. Those of us who learned the System from the final insights of Stanislavsky through the oral tradition were trained in an acting system whose roots in yoga were clear through experience. The Soviets had failed to censor the applied aspects of the System and through the exercises (though not the words of the training) the roots in yoga were transmitted, largely intact.

Stanislavsky's Diagram, the System, and You

15. Proposed Supertask

In Stanislavsky's Diagram of Experiencing, all the aspects of the System are rising toward the *supertask*. Even though it comes as #15, the last labeled, an understanding of the movement toward the supertask is vital to understand the other aspects of the drawing. As previously mentioned, Stanislavsky considered the prerehearsal *reconnaissance of the mind* and the rehearsal process of *Active Analysis* to be searches for the supertask of the play. This is also expressed through each character's supertask. For Stanislavsky, this search sometimes even went through the early performances.

The supertask of the play is the ruling or guiding idea that focuses other components, including the production concept and the actor's interpretation of the role. It is the impression that the author wants to leave on the audience, the director's concept of how to interpret it, and the creative team's vision of how to achieve it aesthetically. It is called the *proposed supertask* in the diagram, because during the process of Active Analysis the concept of the supertask may evolve and change.

What is it that sets a playwright, a play and its characters, the director and designers, and thereby you, the actor, in dynamic motion on the journey to achieve something through the writing and production of a play? The playwright has something that he wants to investigate—an idea, issue, or problem he chooses to explore. The playwright sets his characters in motion to grapple with a specific situation, or some writers claim the characters come alive in their imaginations (i.e., they write down what they see the characters do or hear the characters say). Some playwrights might begin with a more fixed dramatic structure; some reshape it along the way or after the inspiration of listening to the story unfolding in the imagination. In the process, the playwright uncovers or clarifies what he wants to convey about the idea, issue, or problem. This is the playwright's supertask.

In Active Analysis, the director and designers begin to excavate the supertask through *reconnaissance of the mind* in preproduction, and the director works with you as an actor to uncover your character's supertask and weave it into the production supertask.

The Three Bases of the System

It is interesting that in this diagram Stanislavsky put so many elements of the System ahead of work on the role, which doesn't come in until #9. This parallels the components of the System that include early conditioning and training in the Elements of Action and then intensive training in action as the unifying force for all the elements ahead of work on a role. This is also how we have laid it out in your training in this book.

The first three components of the diagram, which we can consider to be the bases of the System, are 1) *Active Dynamics*, 2) *Pushkin's Aphorism* (The *Truth of Passions* within specific Given Circumstances), and 3) *The Subconscious through the Conscious*. Once the actor is psychophysically trained and has increased his awareness sufficiently, he can then successfully approach the intuitive, creative work on a role in the process of Active Analysis.

18 THE ACTOR OF LIVING EXPERIENCE

1. *Active Dynamics*, *(Dynamism, Activeness)*
   One of the bases of the System is *active dynamics*. You train first in psychophysical solo action and then engage in dynamic action through working with a partner's counteractions. Only when you have gained proficiency at this are you ready to take full advantage of the Active Analysis of a role.

   Stanislavsky's final incarnation of his acting technique for work on a play was originally called The Method of Physical Actions, and later evolved slightly further to what we now call Active Analysis. Both of these final techniques have psychophysical action as their basis. This is why the psychophysical conditioning training is such vital preparation to this work. The playwright has given your character a problem, an object of struggle. The action arises as the characters perceive and grapple with these problems. Because of different motivators in the areas of mind, will, and feeling, your character will generally end up in opposition to another character in dynamic conflict.

   Dynamics also refers to the resulting polarities expressed through different tempos and rhythms, comic versus dramatic moments, crowd scenes versus private moments, and other variations.

   On the larger stage of theatre as a whole and for dramatic material specifically, according to Whyman, "In one of the appendices to AWHI, a slogan draws the students' attention to the derivation of the Russian word for action to the Greek word, δράση, to do, from which comes also 'drama'."[7] (AWHI is an acronym for Stanislavsky's acting book volume 2, *The Actor Works on Himself in the Creative Process of Incarnation*.[8]) The ancient Greeks put action at the center of their drama, as does Stanislavsky.

   Stanislavsky also read widely in philosophy and may have been influenced by the historical philosophical idea of dynamism—matter or mind are due to the action of forces. This supports the dramatic premise that a character is only really revealed when tested through great challenges, such as the central conflict of the dramatic action of the play.

2. *Pushkin's Aphorism* (The *Truth of Passions* within specific Given Circumstances)
   Another base of the System is the Truth of Passions within the imaginary given circumstances. Whyman:

   > Aleksander Pushkin (1799–1837), Russia's famous golden age poet, wrote part of an article in 1830 entitled, "Notes on popular drama and M.P. Pogodin's Martha, the Governor's Wife". Here he wrote of dramatic writing, "The truth concerning the passions, a verisimilitude in the feelings experienced in given situations—that is what our intelligence demands of a dramatist."[9]

   Throughout the training you have learned to adapt every action to reflect the given circumstances. In the System, you use the "magic if" to trigger your imagination and find the truthful behavior for the given circumstances. You

---

[7] Whyman, *The Stanislavsky System of Acting*, 39.
[8] This is a translation of the title of the Russian version. The English edition, first translated by Elizabeth Reynolds Hapgood, was called *The Actor's Work on a Role* and did not contain the diagram.
[9] Whyman, *The Stanislavsky System of Acting*, 44.

ensure that you fulfill this behavior with the measure of truth of the level that you might in such specific circumstances if you were in that character's shoes. Entering fully into the sensory world of the re-created given circumstances, and the truth of behavior, may trigger in your body the memory of emotions or trigger in your current experience the fitting emotion because you are living through the circumstances today, here and now. The emotions must be expressed at a level appropriate to the given circumstances or they will seem false. The School of Living Experience asks that the actor live through the truth of emotions in the given circumstances in each performance, rather than showing what has been created previously in rehearsal.

3. *Subconscious through the Conscious*
   As already discussed extensively, Stanislavsky developed the System in large part to find conscious lures for inspiration arising from the subconscious. You have begun training in exercises and improvisations that teach you to become conscious of things that most people are not conscious of, to learn to redirect aspects of your mind and body consciously, and to prepare the creative state that invites inspiration.

   As you get more involved in Active Analysis of a role, you will begin to consciously observe and learn to trust inspiration that arises in rehearsal and performance. As you trust it in yourself, you will be better able to sense and respond to it from other members of your company. This will further invite the deep wisdom and creativity of the subconscious into your collaborative creative process.

   Stanislavsky was interested in and read widely about the unconscious, subconscious, and superconscious, all with consideration of how actors could more consciously access each layer of consciousness in the service of art. Carnicke attributes Stanislavsky's interest in the subconscious to yoga. Whyman proposes that "Stanislavsky's ideas of the subconscious are rooted in the philosophy of the mid-nineteenth century, with an admixture of ideas from Sechenov and Ribot and confirmed by his readings on yoga."[10] She sees mid-nineteenth-century German philosopher Eduard von Hartmann (1842–1906) as an important influence on Stanislavsky's multilayered ideas of consciousness: "Stanislavsky's superconscious equates to von Hartmann's absolute unconscious; Stanislavsky's unconscious to von Hartmann's physiological unconscious; and Stanislavsky's subconscious to von Hartmann's psychological unconscious."[11] Our belief is that he had come to witness the power of these various levels of consciousness in his own creative work and that of others and found confirmation for his hypotheses in the ancient wisdom of yoga and the philosophy and emerging psychology available during his time.

The Two Lungs That Breathe Life into the Dual Perspectives of the Role

While in this diagram Stanislavsky has put the external aspect of embodiment in one lung and the internal aspect of experiencing in the other, and while sometimes they are approached separately for initial understanding and development in training,

---

[10] Ibid., 91.
[11] Ibid., 89.

in practice, in rehearsal and performance, mind and body, internal and external, function inseparably.

4. *Experiencing (Living Through)*
   Stanislavsky named this diagram the Plan of Experiencing, pointing to the importance of this concept in the System. He placed experiencing in the middle of one of the lungs. This placement may relate to Stanislavsky's interest in prana—individual life energy connected to universal energy every time we breathe in and out.

   #4 comes before #9, the role. In training, ahead of work on a role, you can develop your ability to enter into and experience imaginary situations and to allow them to trigger you emotionally. As you come to work on a role, the process of experiencing stems from the spine of the role, #9, moving away from it before coming back. This relates to your journey through Active Analysis, entering the given circumstances of the role by asking "What would I do if I were in this situation today, here and now, for the first time?" You first come from yourself, seeing ways in which the circumstances are familiar and the character and you are alike. Then you expand to meet the demands of the role that are less familiar through research, observations, and interviews, culling all the details of the given circumstances, and through new experiences of living the life of the role in rehearsals and performances.

5. *Incarnation (Embodiment)*
   The other lung represents incarnation. The first step of incarnation is embodiment. This started early in your psychophysical training where every thought must have a physical expression no matter how subtle, just as every physical movement triggers and/or is motivated by thought. As discussed in psychophysical science, even our minds are embodied in our brain and subject to the physiological forces of the body. This is why instead of representing an idea of a character, life is breathed into an incarnation of the character infused with the soul and beating with the life blood of the actor.

   Likewise, after gathering some initial information from the play, you move quickly to embodiment, exploring the given circumstances and facts and ideas about the character in active, physical ways. During the process of Active Analysis you continually move between onstage improvisatory explorations and reading and combining through the text until text and embodiment are entwined. You must engage in the character's purposeful (motivated) actions physically and vocally as well as internally. As you move toward performance, experiencing is not enough; you must find outward manifestations of the experience of the role and convey these to an audience. To have a psychophysical instrument capable of fully encompassing the demands of a role you must train your body and voice to be more expressive.

   Stanislavsky used the term *reincarnation* to express living as the character, but he never wanted the artist to believe he actually was the character but rather to walk the mile of the role in the character's shoes, maintaining the artistry of dual consciousness to aesthetically guide the performance (and ensure safety for the actor and his company).

The Motivators of Psychophysical Action

Look once again at the center pole. *Mind, volition (will), and feeling (sensation)* are at the center of the work on a role. Any one of them alone or in combination can motivate action, thus making the action psychophysical. Investing in the given circumstances enough to generate imagination and thought (mind), desires (volition), and/or feeling activate the process of *living through*, or *experiencing*, bringing life to the physical *embodiment* of the role.

It is not surprising, given the System's yogic influences, which we spoke about in greater detail in Chapter 4, that when trying to convey the movement of energy and awareness in the body, Stanislavsky chose to use circles placed along the spine, much like the yogic energy centers of the body called chakras (see Chapter 4). Chakras contain not just energy but layers of consciousness, just as Stanislavsky was trying to convey. Due to the psychophysical nature of the System and the body's importance in emotion, along with the mind's, Stanislavsky placed the mind, emotion, and the will to act deep in the middle of this model, deep in the middle of the body, rather than up at the top, where the head might be. At the head, where the crown chakra would be in yoga, he puts instead the supertask, the reason why a playwright has offered this character in this role. In other words, the mind, will, and emotions of the actor/character feed into, but are in service of, the larger social purpose of the supertask of the play.

6. *Mind (Judgment)*
   Mind does not only mean the brain in the head but also the thoughts, images, and consciousness as they reverberate through your body. In the diagram, the words written around the mind circle "**представление суждение**" literally translate to "representation of judgment." One important aspect is imagination, the representation of the given circumstances of the playwright in the mind. Representation also relates to how the characters' thoughts and beliefs frame the events and lead to decisions to speak and behave in specific ways. *Judgment* also relates to your artistic discernment, continually sculpting the role for aesthetic impact. The Stanislavsky System requires you to think as the character, while maintaining consciousness as the actor—the dual perspectives.

7. *Volition (Will)*
   Volition is a purposeful act of will that instigates action. Will plus physical action evokes physical sensations that are experienced as feelings and framed by thoughts. Will is the force that motivates behavior, the desires that prompt you and your character to action, whether they are conscious or not. Volition is the power of the mind over conscious or deliberate action (i.e., to effect a specific outcome). Will applied to any physical action imbues it with psychic life, gives it a psychological motivation, which energizes the action with conscious or unconscious thought and/or conscious or unconscious motivating needs or feelings. The purpose behind it makes the action psychophysical.

8. *Feeling/Sense (Sensation)*
   The meaning of the Russian includes the body's reactions to sensory stimuli, sensations aroused through emotions, and the emotions themselves. Stanislavsky used the words *feeling* and *emotions* interchangeably. (Earlier in the book we

18 THE ACTOR OF LIVING EXPERIENCE

talked about a contemporary twenty-first-century scientific distinction between feeling and emotion, but this is not what he had available). If the actor can fully invest in the imaginary situation using all his senses, and through the "magic if" select and fulfill truthful, appropriate actions, these sensory stimuli and psychophysical actions will stimulate real emotional responses. The emotions in turn will lead to the next actions and as the actor's actions and emotions impact other actors/characters, they will respond, generating further reactions in the initiating actor.

The Spine

9. *The Role* (written vertically along the base of the pole)
   After some conditioning in psychophysical action (#1), creating typical behavior within specific circumstances to stimulate truthful responses (#2), and working to activate the subconscious through becoming more conscious (#3), you begin to experience an imaginary situation (#4) and live in it through embodying its truth (#5). After also creating, through means 1–5, paths of energy that stir your own mind, will, and emotions, you are ready to embrace and inhabit a role (#9).

   Between #8 and #14, vertically along the pole next to the image of beads strung together, is *Perspective of the Role*. You enter the imaginary given circumstances of the role through the "magic if" to engage the mind, will, and feeling. A perspective on the role begins to take shape, focusing the character's aims and giving purpose to his actions, ultimately leading to and revealing his supertask.

   Grappling with the problem of the play leads to the supertask that you as character struggle to achieve throughout the play. Meantime the movement of sensations, thoughts, and motivations through the spine also activates the chakras (in the yogic sense) or the central and peripheral nervous system (in a biological sense), thus activating many systems of the body, changing the breathing patterns, and breathing the imaginary circumstances into the body of the actor, leading to experiencing and embodying the role.

The Flow of Creative Energy

Each of these motivating forces of mind, will, and feeling generate energy moving along your spine, connecting the mind and body through the peripheral nervous system, the vagus nerve, and other mind-body communication paths. This investment then gets applied to the active exploration of specific creative challenges of the role explored in rehearsal. These activate the internal world of experiencing and the external expression of incarnation simultaneously in a continual feedback loop. In addressing either internal life and motivations or external expression, the psychophysically trained actor always activates both.

10. *Creative Challenges and Creative Impulses*
    Each role has unique creative challenges. At first there are more questions than answers: What is going on for my character before he enters? What does he think, and how does he feel about this place, these people, these events? What is this event or encounter really about? How am I going to achieve this or that

important moment?, etc. When you actively inhabit the possibilities arising from the given circumstances, creative impulses arise that lead you to discover things you would not have discovered without engaging your full psychophysical system to uncover interesting and fitting creative solutions.

11. *Elements of Action*—abcdefghijk

    During your exploration in rehearsal, you investigate opportunities generated through the creative challenges using the colors of the Actor's Palette, the *Elements of Action*. *Relaxation* removes all excess tension, and *concentration* limits distractions. Both funnel the actor's resources toward the character and the role. Both facilitate the *flow of physical and creative energy* throughout your *psychophysical instrument*. *Imagination* brings the role to life in your mind as you project and inhabit a *film of images*. You enter the imaginary world by inviting and activating all your senses so that you, and thereby the audience, can see, hear, smell, taste, and touch it through *sensory evocation*. You use the "magic if" to decipher how to live and behave within the vividly projected *given circumstances*, *treating them as* if they were the actual world of the play. Through this you enter the state of *I am, I exist* in this world. Then applying

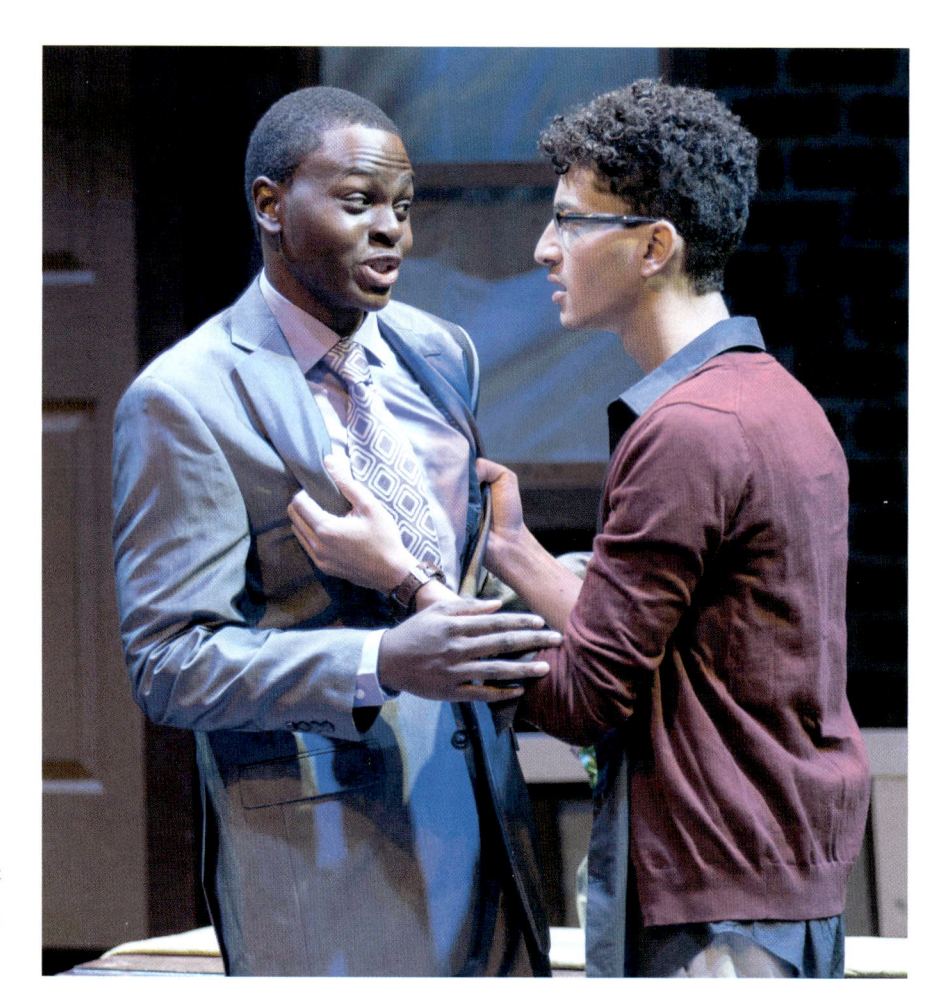

Figure 18.3 If you are sufficiently invested in the thoughts or desires arising out of the needs of the character, then upon meeting *obstacles* or counteractions, conflict arises. Jamil Joseph and Jannel Armstrong in *Spike Heels* by Teresa Rebeck. Photo: Luis Vidal

all your psychophysical resources to grapple with your character's *problem*, you engage in specific *tasks* to try to solve it, using a variety of *action steps* as tactics to chip away at the problem and achieve the desired outcome, or *objective*.

If you are sufficiently invested in the thoughts or *inner monologue* and desires arising out of needs of the character, then upon meeting *obstacles* or counteractions, conflict arises. This conflict squelches your desires, activating *analogous emotions* in the *memory of the body*. You find *adaptations* to try to get around the obstacles, initiating *counteractions* or sometimes giving up or changing your objective.

All of this is both internally activated, leading to experiencing, and externally expressed as an incarnation of the character. This incarnation is shaped by tempo-rhythm, voice and speech techniques that have been honed and trained, physically expressive tableaux, and gestures that arise spontaneously through your fit, trained, and responsive body. The final product must be executed with a *measure of truth* appropriate for the world, time period, and given circumstances.

12. *Inspiration and Creative Solutions*
    As the role is colored with the various *Elements of Action*, clarity slowly emerges as through a prism—in the white light of inspiration creative solutions are found for the creative challenges. Inspiration breathes life into the role through both Experiencing and Incarnation, which is why #4, #5, #10, #11, and #12 are all housed within images of the lungs.

The Interweaving of the Dual Perspectives—Amalgamation and Aesthetic Choices

13. *Internal Theatrical Sense of Self* (woven rope on the left), *External Theatrical Sense of Self* (woven rope on the right)
    The *Elements of Action* have generated an internal life of the character, which the actor breathes life into, *living through* the character's struggle. The character's struggle, when fully invested, is inherently theatrical, as dramatic action arises from conflict. Thus is crafted *the internal theatrical sense of self*. Simultaneously, you breathe life into the inseparable external expression of the soul of the character through your finely tuned psychophysical instrument, including a well-honed facility of voice and speech.[12] This gives shape to the *external theatrical sense of self*.

    Working with the director, you artistically select from all the possibilities generated in rehearsal, the most fitting, interesting, and aesthetically evocative choices to express the role. Eventually, a unified vision begins to emerge.

14. *General Theatrical Sense of Self* (written horizontally on either side of the spine at #14) and *through action* (written vertically at the top along either side of the line).
    Now the director must inextricably weave together the internal and external aesthetic expression as the actor/character drives through toward her proposed

---

[12] When you first read this, your psychophysical instrument may not be as toned and honed as you wish (and as it needs to be to create as the artist Stanislavsky, and we, envision), but if you want to emerge as the inspired actor you can be, we suggest this be one of your goals.

supertask. This forges the path of the journey, the through-line for the character's action, or *through-action*. This creates what in literature is often called the character's arc through the play.

The Crowning Achievement

15. *Proposed Supertask* (*Proposed* here means that during the process of Active Analysis the concept of the supertask may evolve and change.)
As you create and fully inhabit this role, your inspiration rises to express the character's supertask. The director also weaves this into the overall supertask of the play. Both must be transmitted to the audience in performance through *communion* between you and the other actors and the audience. When you connect to the audience through the high idea of the supertask of the character and play, you achieve Stanislavsky's dream of *spiritual communion*.

> ### Exercise 18.1: Experiencing the Stanislavsky System
>
> **Purpose:** To appreciate the overall System that Stanislavsky has offered through the training and communicated visually in this diagram
>
> **Guidelines:**
> - Glance at the diagram to gain your own first impressions.
> - Read through explanations by the numbers in order to grasp each of the individual concepts intellectually.
> - Refer back to the diagram and write about your experience with each Element of Action that you have studied and practiced throughout this training.
> - Consider and write about what you personally have noticed about how the different elements interweave.
> - Reflect on how this acting system has deepened your understanding and awareness of your own psychophysical processes.

CHAPTER 19

The Creative Life: Communion with Audience and Society

"Each of us has a spark of life inside us. Our highest endeavor ought to be to set off that spark in one another."

—Kenny Ausubel
(ecologist, writer, documentary filmmaker)

Part I: Communion with Audience
- **Collective Insight**
- **Preparing for Performance**
- Exercise 19.1: Preparing for Performance
- **Previews and Opening: Enter the Audience**
- **How Do You Achieve Communion with the Audience?**
- **A Personal Theme for Your Role**
- **Antithetical Themes**
- Exercise 19.2: Exploring Abhorrent Characters
- **The Actor of Living Experience**
- **Experiencing Performance**

Part II: Developing or Selecting Material That Matters
- Exercise 19.3: Personal Monologues

Part III: Social Purpose: Artistic Engagement with Society
- Exercise 19.4: Acting with Social Purpose
- Exercise 19.5: Investigating Other People's Perspectives
- **The Artist as Shaman: Catalyst for Change**
- **Experiencing the Creative Life**
- Exercise 19.6: Your Artist's Manifesto

PART I: COMMUNION WITH AUDIENCE

Collective Insight

Collective creation of theatre art is a powerful human experience. There is a reason why the ancient Greeks considered this process, and the offering of it in performance, one of the highest religious rituals. In India, too, theatre and dance have roots connecting them to the sacred stories and rituals of this ancient culture, and the artists who practice sacred dance and drama are highly respected. Like a shaman,[1] the actor can lead the audience to witness and experience the expansive scope of human existence, or the most intimate and personal.

In live theatre, the audience participates in the creation of that night's performance. In film, while there may be previews in which the creative team surveys the audience's responses and changes the film through cuts or even shooting additional scenes, the audience response will not affect the actors' performance.[2]

Figure 19.1 "In other arts the audience sees the result of a creative process. In theatre the audience is present during that process."[2] Samantha Crawn and Christopher Centrella in *Polaroid Stories* by Naomi Iizuka. Photo: Charles Perry Hebard, courtesy of East Stroudsburg University

Preparing for Performance

By the time you are preparing to show your artistic work as an actor to an audience, you have already prepared your psychophysical instrument through training and now through rehearsal. During the rehearsal and performance periods, take care of your health and fitness through exercise, rest, and good nutrition. This will fuel the optimum functioning of your mind and body. Remember that the creative state that invites inspiration is helped by relaxation. On performance days build in time to release the day's tension and worry through yoga postures and breathing, meditation, and other means. (See the Restorative Yoga practice in Appendix II for 10 simple yoga poses for stress release.) Also, just like any athlete, even if you are at the top of your game, you must warm up and prepare your instrument right before every performance to be as supple and responsive as possible and so as not to damage your body or voice.

---

[1] Shamans have been found in cultures from Siberia to South America (although under many different names). They are people with unusual insights that are thought to lead people through the most difficult passages, such as a journey from sickness to health or life to death. In some cultures they are thought to have special powers, but often it is just that they have had pivotal experiences, such as recovering unexpectedly from a terminal illness or having premonitions that came true, that mark them as understanding aspects of the world veiled from the general population. If you are interested in learning more, we recommend the book by the Romanian religious historian Mircea Eliade, *Shamanism: Archaic Techniques of Ecstasy*. In an example of how a play can expand your knowledge, French learned something about shamanism because a character in a play she directed was a shaman.

[2] Sonia Moore, *The Stanislavski System* (New York: Penguin, 1960; reprt., 1978), 20.

19 THE CREATIVE LIFE

From the outset, performance requires full use of your *internal* and *external monitors* to create the *dual consciousness* required. Invite the character in while putting on your makeup and costume. Ask others not to distract you in your dressing room, or if that is not possible, find a corner of backstage where you can focus.

Exercise 19.1: Preparing for Performance

Purpose: to bring your highest level of focus and concentration to your performance in order to impact your scene partners and the audience; to include the audience in your performance through communion.

Guidelines:
First, do one of the relaxations exercises from Chapter 3; make sure you have warmed up your body, as well as your voice and speech. Just before you go onstage:

- Use your imagination to fully enter into the *given circumstances* for your character, keeping in mind the *seed* that drives him and the *problems* he struggles to solve.
- Keep the focus of your thoughts on the character's images and inner monologue. When other thoughts or sensation intrude, let them float away (as you did in the watching-the-breath exercise in Chapter 3, Exercise 3.1)
- Clearly imagine the *where from* before walking on stage.
- Then, once onstage imagine a bubble, like the Holograph deck in the earlier improvisation, where your *film of images* can be projected all around you. Then, expand that projection bubble to include the entire theatre to the back rows.
- Remind yourself of the character's seed and objective. Make them very important.
- Focus on affecting the other characters through your *actions*, so that they help you solve your problem, change, or respond in some way that your character wants. The more strongly you try to affect the other characters, the more of a gift you give your fellow actors by forcing them to respond to *obstacles* that pull their focus away from themselves and any *stage fright* as they are forced to respond.
- At the same time, receive what the others say and do. Breathe it in. Breathe, in general; oxygen really helps with speech, fuels thought, and staves off fainting.

19.1 Reflection Journal—Preparing for Performance

Were you able to fully enter the given circumstances and have a continuous film of images? What percentage of your thoughts were the character's, versus yours as an actor (try to increase the percentage of thoughts onstage that are the character's until you get to about 95 percent). Did you invest in the character's objective? Did you have any real emotional responses to the imaginary situation or other characters? Were you able to include the audience by projecting your images, emotions, and voice and by opening up your face and body to them?

Previews and Opening: Enter the Audience

In professional theatre, the first experience of the audience is previews—lasting from a week to months for Broadway or London's West End. (In university theatre, there may be one preview night, if any.) Previews are the time for the company to adjust to the additional input of audience response. This is especially important for a comedy where the audience's laughter becomes part of the pacing of the show. At some point, those in rehearsal who have seen the show repeatedly no longer laugh at the comic lines and antic behavior. In fact, they will only laugh at novelty and mistakes, or not laugh, which is difficult for comic actors. If they play to the repeat audience in rehearsal they may diverge from the intention of the play, which is designed to impact the more common one-time audience member. It becomes really important to see what is and is not working, to hear the response of an audience seeing the show for the first time. In a drama, we want to sense the audience breathe with us, gasp in recognition, or hold their breath in suspense. As Stanislavsky put it, we want to feel "a thousand hearts beating as one."

A preview differs from an opening in the following ways:

- The press cannot review the show during previews.
- Rehearsals will likely continue for actors, director, and stage management during the afternoons.
- In a new play or musical, changes may still be made to the script, especially cuts, but even sometimes added lines or monologues, which is very challenging for actors. (In independent film you often don't get your final script for particular scenes until the night before, and even the day of shooting, you will receive changes.)
- The designers and director are at performances to review and discuss where they have and have not yet achieved the earlier production vision.
- The artistic team continues to tweak the design implementation to bring it closer to the production concept.

Opening night brings the press and the jitters. For a New York Broadway or Off-Broadway show or one opening on London's West End, a good review means the show will have a long run and recoup its expenses, but a bad review can prematurely close the show with the actors and crew out of work and the producers losing their investment. Thus opening night can be nerve-wracking for even the most-experienced company members. It also brings the excitement of sharing your art with the public and finding out if they respond. It is like the uncertainty of new love. On the moment of revealing your feelings, you are excited and scared, hopeful and fearful to find out if the other person will embrace or reject your offer of love. Performance is similar. You risk and reveal yourself by offering your creative work and await the audience's response.

How Do You Achieve Communion with the Audience?

As an actor, it is the very presence of this audience that you will want to engage and hold lovingly in your embrace. To feel you entered fully into the experience of your character in the situation of the play is satisfying. To feel that you affected your scene partners as characters and even as human beings is extremely rewarding. To move an

19 THE CREATIVE LIFE

audience and allow the presence and response of hundreds of people to move you is profound.

In addition to all of the in-depth and detailed preparation laid out in this book and in your subsequent rehearsals, there are some other ingredients needed for you to reach this final stage. Start with a willingness to be seen and heard. You need to be loud and articulate so that the audience can understand every word, without strain. Your thoughts must be psychophysically reflected so that they have both an inner life as well as an outward expression. Your actions need to be readable and understandable from the back row of the audience. These are just the basics and can be developed through the training in this book, supplemented by additional voice, speech, and movement training.

The next step is more challenging and requires the real courage of the actor. Are you willing to bare your heart and mind and sometimes your body? Are you willing, in the service of your art, to publicly reveal your very human soul? Are you willing to allow yourself to feel, while being watched, some of the most private and vulnerable aspects of what it means to be human? You must be prepared to donate yourself not only to your art but also to each audience. If you are not, and at some point you may realize you are not, then acting may not be your path (but there are many other ways you can fully participate in theatre). If you are, then you can experience that moment, like falling in love but amplified, when we forget that we live in separate bodies and feel momentarily united in spirit with our audience. This is the highest level of communion that Stanislavsky called spiritual communion.

A Personal Theme for Your Role

At some point in the process of working on a role in a particular play you may come to understand why you were drawn to this opportunity at this time. What is it about this play, character, situation, time period, or theatrical style that resonates with you as a reflection of something important to you or as an expansion from what you previously knew? This is your *personal theme* for the performance. Tovstonogov states in his book *The Profession of the Stage Director*, that a you as a director should not take on a project unless it is "the next step in the evolution of your consciousness."[3] The same principle can hold true for actors.

When you have studied and analyzed the themes of your role through the rehearsal process of Active Analysis, you gradually begin to identify with the innermost thoughts, feelings, and drives of your character. By doing your homework honestly, working on physical actions, images, and associations, you come to experience a deep emotional connection with your character. Even if you have already been performing the part for a while you may come to understand it in a new light, one that you may not have considered previously. Stanislavsky spoke of its sometimes taking through the twelfth performance before he'd find his own personal theme for a role.

There are many different ways that actors of different constitutions connect with their personal themes. For some actors, the personal theme might be an understanding of the character through recognizing parallels in their own lives. See the example in the Personal Theme: Anton Chekhov's *The Cherry Orchard* in the box in this chapter. However, Michael Chekhov, who Stanislavsky considered one of his best pupils, adapted the System in his own way and connected with his

---

[3] Georgi Tovstonogov, *The Profession of the Stage Director* (Moscow: Progress, 1972).

characters through a central visual image and/or a central *psychological gesture*. Mel Gordon in his book *The Stanislavsky Technique: Russia* gives a number of startling examples: In Berger's *The Deluge*, Chekhov saw his character, Frazer, as "a man who unconsciously wanted to break through the skin and clothes of his competitors in order to make the deepest human contact possible."[4] In Strindberg's *Erik XIV*, Gordon describes how Chekhov saw his character "trapped inside a circle. His arms dart out of the circle, attempting to touch something. But Erik finds nothing. His hands are left hopelessly dangling and empty."[5]

Unless you are creating an adaptation or a spoof, your personal theme should not be in contradiction to the playwright's play. Rather, it is a response to the playwright's conscious and subconscious themes and merges with them. The playwright need not be conscious of the seed of the play, but it is nevertheless embedded in the content and form of the play waiting to be uncovered. This does not mean there is only one appropriate response or interpretation. Each artist's perspective and personal themes interweave to create a unique production of a play or film.[6]

Personal Theme: Anton Chekhov's *The Cherry Orchard*

In the fall of 1968 Philip Bennett had begun his training in the Stanislavsky System at the Sonia Moore Studio of the Theatre in New York City. The following fall it was announced that a professional company of actors would be selected from the studio and that there would be a production mounted of Chekhov's *The Cherry Orchard* under the artistic direction of Sonia Moore. Phil was initially cast as Yermoli Lopakhin, the capitalist merchant who eventually buys and destroys the beautiful orchard in order to build summer cottages for profit. In the course of the play, the aristocratic Ranevskaya family is dispossessed of their ancestral estate, and through his uncontrollable greed, Lopakhin manages to destroy the lives of a family he has both envied and loved.

During the rehearsals Bennett observed the company's lead actress, Irene Moore-Jaglom.[6] Irene had already played other leading roles on Broadway. During the seven months of arduous rehearsals and three subsequent years of seasonal performances, Ms. Moore-Jaglom found some continuous source of nourishment for her role as Ranevskaya that permitted her to always transform into character and leave the audience dissolved in tears by the end of each performance. Bennett, mesmerized by the depth and breadth of her performances asked her how the actress was able to accomplish this. The answer was direct and simple:

It's no secret. I have found My Own Theme.... When I work on a role I always look for the kernel or seed of the character's actions, what the playwright is saying through my character. Eventually I find analogous experiences from my own life and the life of the world around me. At

---

[4] Mel Gordon, *The Stanislavsky Technique: Russia* (New York: Applause Theatre Books, 1987), 122.
[5] Ibid., 129.
[6] Irene Moore-Jaglom is Sonia Moore's daughter. She had studied with Sonia and at the Actor's Studio. Irene was also a teacher of the System at Moore's studio.

> some point they all come crashing together in a moment of revelation. It's as if all the little pieces of the part melt, fuse together and become one. It is usually such a profound emotional experience when that happens I break down and sob with tears of joy. After that I can always enter into the imaginary world of the character and live there. A role is just not complete for me until that happens.

As a young actor, Bennett had only experienced moments of such creative heights and usually when infected by the inspiration of the company as a whole; however, that did change. The following season Bennett was asked to switch roles with another actor in the company and play the role of Gaev, the fifty-year-old brother of Madam Ranevskaya who through his refusal to change and face reality loses the orchard to Lopakhin at auction.

Perhaps it was the fact that now he had completed his four-year course and had been acting in repertory for a few years, but something took hold of him while working on the role of Gaev. In the third act, Gaev returns from town after having lost the orchard, and although his sister, Ranevskaya, pleads with him to tell her what has happened, he cannot speak. Accompanied by his old servant, Firs, he weeps and exits. As Chekhov has written the scene, it is meant to be suspenseful and dramatic but during the long pause of Bennett's crossing the stage and exit one could hear audience members quietly weeping. This was followed by an even longer pause where you could always hear a pin drop until the drunken entrance of Lopakhin. The audience and performers were enwrapped in communion with each other and the inspiration of the playwright. After the first time this happened, Phil realized that he had found his own theme in communion with the actors of the ensemble. It was the sense of speechless profound loss of something of great beauty, not just the orchard but of a whole way of life. It was Chekhov's symbolic depiction of the death of a whole civilization that was prophetically about to sweep over czarist Russia in the early twentieth century.

Until that first moment, Phil Bennett had not realized that he had already experienced something very similar in his own life. The previous summer, he had returned to his home in the beautiful Santa Clara Valley of Northern California after several years of absence. The valley was completely transformed; gone were the orchards and vineyards, the magnificent seasonal blossoms and succulent fruit. The deep black soil was now paved over with freeways, the artesian wells of sweet water were polluted by toxic chemicals dumped in the ground by the dozens of electronics industry factories that had replaced the green fields and orchards. Gone were the magnificent pastoral estates and ranches of his childhood friends, the streams, ponds, and creek beds of childhood memories. In its place was a new and alien world that had destroyed some of the richest soil on earth. The valley was no longer dedicated to its patron, Saint Clare, and now it called itself—Silicon Valley![7]

After that he knew he had reached the depth of his own theme in the role and was always able to stir himself, his partners, and the audience during those moments.

---

[7] For those who don't know, Silicon Valley is the hotbed of the computer and tech industries. It is located near San Jose and south of San Francisco (although some companies are now relocating or having offices also in the city of San Francisco).

Figure 19.2 What do you do when your character is a bit of a mystery? Joseph Bednarchik and Samantha Crawn (behind) in *Polaroid Stories* by Naomi Iizuka; lighting design by Pierre Clavel.
Photo: Charles Perry Hebard, courtesy of East Stroudsburg University

Antithetical Themes

Sometimes when you are given a role, you will feel an immediate affinity to the character. This is good but not quite the same thing as discovering your personal theme. If you are fortunate enough to really associate with a character, by finding themes in your own experience that correlate to those of the character within the play, that, of course, can be very helpful. If you are assigned a role of a historic character whom you really admire, or you are working on a play with a strong social message that you agree with, finding *your own theme* may be easier. What do you do when the play's themes are not always that apparent, or when our character is a bit of a mystery? This requires all the Active Analysis tools at our disposal, as well as staying attuned to what arises in the creative state. However, you won't always like the character or agree with his or her traits. What is important to remember is that you can enjoy working on a role with its unique purpose within the context and themes of the larger play.

How do you create a character when you feel no empathy, let alone sympathy, for him? Even more challenging, how do you create a character who is anathema to you (represents feelings and behaviors deeply opposed to yours)? Actors love to play villains. The villains are often much more interesting than the romantic leads and have complex, if dark, personalities. However, these characters may represent things that abhor you. The following exercise offers some tips on how to approach such characters:

Figure 19.3 Exploring abhorrent characters. David Ausem and Angel Berlane in *A Streetcar Named Desire* by Tennessee Williams.
Photo: Stephanie Daventry French

19 THE CREATIVE LIFE

Exercise 19.2: Exploring Abhorrent Characters (SDF)[8]

Purpose: To expand beyond what you are comfortable representing; to find entree into the mind and behavior of someone you normally would judge and keep at a distance.

Guidelines:
- Select a character in a play or film (or even a person in the world) whose viewpoint is strongly opposed to your own.
- Conduct a character analysis of him, as you would do in normal reconnaissance, gathering all the facts available.
- Understand the device this character serves in the play. What does he need to do: serve as a catalyst for an event, or to test or sharpen the hero? Main characters are revealed when they are challenged and we see what they are really made of.
- Do research to fill out what you don't know. However, don't put yourself in danger by, for example, going and talking to a mafia boss. Dustin Hoffman, in preparing for his role in *Midnight Cowboy* actually lived on the streets for a few days. This was risky, as there is a lot of crime perpetrated against the homeless, including burnings, sexual violations, and battering, to name a few. When French did *Polaroid Stories*, we instead brought in a person who had been homeless to speak to us about her experience. Do read any biographies or, better, autobiographies you can find. You need to try to see how this person thinks and justifies what he does.
- Make notes of anything you can understand, or even relate to, even if a lot of him you cannot. For example, you might identify with a criminal mastermind's delight in being cleverer than those around him, even if you disagree with what he does with that. You might want to have the power to exact revenge on those that cross or hurt you, even if you would not carry it out through violent criminal acts.
- When you are ready to embody the character, step into his skin like you would put on a mask, an imaginary layer that separates what audiences see from who you really are.
- Make a clear demarcation internally that everything you do is the character doing it, and even though observers will see you this way, it is not you they are seeing. You can really enjoy acting onstage in ways you would never in a million years do in life.
- Let the character's thinking and behavior come into the foreground while yours are kept safe in a compartment that you can open like an air bag to reclaim the space at the end of each rehearsal and performance.
- Make sure to write the autobiography—a least a page—in the first person, as the character. It is helpful to do this focusing on a primary issue for the character.
- Create an étude as this character: Perform a typical activity that this character would do and at some point allow thoughts to arise. Use lines from your autobiography, lines or situations from the play, or your own

---

[8] This exercise was inspired in part by a directing exercise taught to French at UC San Diego by Robert Woodruff.

- imagination and research to figure out what to do and say. You need not speak continuously; the most important thing is to be present in the activity and thinking thoughts of the character in the activity.
- If time, the class or teacher could interview you, and you can respond as the character.
- When you are done, imagine peeling off the skin and sucking the thoughts out of you like a powerful vacuum, then expand your own compartmentalized thoughts back in to fill your mind and body.
- A helpful technique can be to have a peaceful real or imagined place that you can go to in your imagination to recharge.

19.2 Reflection Journal—Exploring Abhorrent Characters

How much did you find yourself inside the thoughts of the character versus outside observing yourself? If you succeeded, how did you feel about others seeing you this way? What was your experiencing of entering the point of view of someone so different? Were you able to identify with any aspects of him? Can you understand why he does what he does? Was it what you expected, or different?

If you play a character like Blanche Dubois or Hannibal Lecter (a mass murderer who ate his victims), it is not advisable to keep these characters' thoughts and emotions in you for the entire run of the play or film shoot without risking a great toll on your psyche. While some great actors do this and are exceptions, such as Dustin Hoffman, for those with different internal wiring it can be very damaging. The most famous example is the phenomenal performance of Heath Ledger as the Joker in the Batman movie called *The Dark Knight*. In this case the role took a toll on him, and he ended up not sleeping because his mind was spinning with the mentally ill thoughts of his character. Before the movie was even released, he, sadly, overdosed on prescription sleeping pills and died at the height of his career at the age of 28. (While he created an amazing performance that won him numerous awards, it was at a sad and unnecessary cost.) Another example is Michael Chekhov, mentioned above. Because he struggled with mental and emotional issues that at one point put him in the hospital, Chekhov needed to find a nonpersonal way to stir his emotions and chose imagination and physical embodiment. Each actor is different. The energy of creation can activate many things inside of us, which is why we recommend learning to stir your emotions in healthy ways, as we discuss in Chapter 12: Orchestrating Emotions.

You may hear in your pursuit of acting that you should not judge your character, as it keeps you outside looking at him rather than inside looking out from his point of view. There is truth to this, and yet being an artist often requires the discerning use of the hammer of judgment to sculpt your creation. You cannot think judging thoughts while you are performing and need to think the character's thoughts, but as you develop the role you can use your external monitor to make artistic choices that help the character better fulfill his purpose in the play. You can identify with fulfilling this purpose, and with the sources that cause this person to be evil, rather than hooking into the evil behavior or cruel thoughts and emotions. All roles require the dual consciousness of actor/character so that they are works of art and not just role-playing or therapy. It is advisable to keep connected to you as artist, you as a lifeline, while immersing yourself in the world of a damaged or dangerous character.

19 THE CREATIVE LIFE

> **Fulfilling a Dark Purpose of a Character in a Play: Shepard's *Curse of the Starving Class***
>
> French once worked with an actor on Sam Shepard's *Curse of the Starving Class*. The actor understood the character of an abusive, alcoholic father, but because of some past experiences he decided he did not want to get close to that type of person. Instead, this actor stayed in the part but changed it. He made the character funny and likeable—a relatively harmless and pathetic drunk. The character could have survived, at times being pathetic and at times being funny; however, for the rest of the play to work, the father needed to be also at times violent and dangerous. Instead of protecting his family, he was the worst threat to them. This character's destruction of his family was at the heart of the play.
>
> If you have a hateful character, you may need the audience to hate him. This is challenging. Keep in mind, they do not hate you personally; they hate the character. If you realize that a part is too close to aspects of your personal experience that you do not want to activate, speak to the director to see if together you can find a way to achieve the device of the role without damage to yourself. The director does not want to damage you but is tasked with achieving the play. Do not just change the purpose of the role without working with your director. Especially do not act like you are going to fulfill the dark aspect of the role in auditions and rehearsal and then change it in performance. Changing from what the director has clearly approved in rehearsal to something the director has not seen or approved will get you fired and will ruin your reputation. If you cannot fulfill the role, you may need to resign.
>
> In the case of an acting class, talk with your teacher about finding an alternate scene, which may take a little extra work at a later stage of rehearsals but is doable.

The Actor of Living Experience

In Chapter 1, you began your quest for artistic inspiration, on a journey to breathe life into a character and a role. This has been the theme of our book; to assist you by means of the Stanislavsky System to identify the art within yourself, and then, through knowledge, exercises, games, and improvisations, give you the technical means and confidence to bring your talent and artistry to light.

Step-by-step you have come to practice and assimilate the essential interconnected Elements of Action, as first outlined in Chapter 2: The Actor's Palette, that are needed in order to achieve psychophysical behavior onstage. The fundamental purpose of each step has been to prepare you for *experiencing*, the living through of the life of a character, before an audience or camera so that you might use your gifts to enlighten, educate, and uplift others. Experiencing the role, you become an actor of the School of Living Experience.

> **Experiencing Performance**

When you can live the life of the character onstage, feeling his emotions, thinking his thoughts, as though for the first time, while also fulfilling specific *blocking* that was set, saying specific lines written by the playwright, and pausing until the laughter peaks but before it dips, you have achieved dual consciousness. Pour your creative energy onto the stage and feel the energy of the life of the audience breathing, listening, and responding. When you are present with the audience and reveal real human truths onstage, the audience responds as it reverberates within them. This is experiencing the role and is one of the greatest feelings of being vibrantly alive and present. This is to be inspired and inspiring, in the superconscious state and enfolded in communion. As we introduced in Chapter 1: An Invitation to the Quest for Inspiration, this experience of acting is like the zone in sports or the flow described by Csikszentmihalyi. You know exactly what to do as though the character's life is flowing through you. This is the goal of our acting technique: experiencing.

PART II: DEVELOPING OR SELECTING MATERIAL THAT MATTERS

At the core of each artist lies a deep well full of insights, observations, and emotional treasure: some important sources for creation. Most people are drawn to create art, even before they study and develop technique, because they have something they want to express based on deep feelings inside or unique observations of the world around them. When your instrument has been well tuned and your technique approaches mastery, you will begin to experience deeper and deeper reservoirs of creativity and resourcefulness.

At this point, you have many insights about yourself and the others in your class, as you all have been investigating the process of acting. Once you have tapped into your creative well and forged pathways for your creativity to flow more freely, it is time to start asking yourself what you want to express through your art. This may be related to content—themes, stories you want to tell, characters you want to explore. In addition, it may relate to form—styles of theatre, uses of language, different forms of creating or rehearsing theatre, different performance spaces, or a variety of theatrical experiments.

Start keeping a list of plays you love as you read them on your own or in classes. Read novels and biographies and follow real-world people and stories to find material for plays and films. See great performances live and on film. Look to human creations and reflections of life in art museums, at live music concerts, by traveling to see the architecture and sculpture in Italy, Shanghai, or the magnificent human creations of Machu Picchu or the Egyptian Pyramids. Look to the small creative expressions in nature such as flowers in a garden or autumn leaves across the landscape or the grand scale of Yosemite or the Grand Canyon. Keep an artistic journal of what inspires you, interests you, aggravates, abhors, or frightens you. Continue to observe interesting moments played on life's stage before your eyes. Any of these things may fuel your future creations.

Exercise 19.3: Personal Monologues[9]

You and your classmates have come to know each other well during the intensive sharing and observation of an acting class. You have seen what the others' strengths are and perhaps what has challenged them. For this exercise you will work with a partner. You will interview your partner and then write a monologue for your partner to perform. She will interview you and write one for you to perform, but you will work together on strengthening the dramatic impact in the writing and rehearsal of the piece.

Purpose: The purpose of this exercise is to develop material using your own interests and passions as the source, to have the experience of performing a piece of theatre where the personal theme may be more easily accessible. The final monologues may be entirely true, entirely imaginary or a combination of the two. This is a chance to share some of the things you have learned, admired, or enjoyed about each other in the course of the class.

Guidelines:
- Divide the class into pairs who have not yet worked together on prior major projects. If there is an uneven number, then this assignment can work with a group of three. Select an A and B (and C, if necessary). It is vital that the sharing that is about to take place is in the strictest confidence and none of it is shared with anyone else in the class or outside the class.
- Either before or just after the interviews, the teacher or volunteers from the class will read out loud sample well-written monologues. This is to demonstrate dramatic and lyric forms, different uses of language, a variety of focuses, and ways to present content. (Alternately, for the sake of time, the sample monologues can be read ahead of the interviews or posted on an online classroom platform, but if they are read, they will prompt more ideas in the actor/writer's mind about how to craft these stories into a monologue.)
- Active Listening Interviews: Partner A then brainstorms out loud a list of issues or events that he feels strongly about, positively or negatively. For five to ten minutes, A speaks and B listens and may jot down a few notes but must not yet ask questions, agree or disagree, or make any kind of acknowledging sounds or responses. If A pauses, allow there to be silence, so the speaker can quietly sift and find what bubbles up out of himself without your prompting. Then reverse the roles so that B speaks and A listens and take notes.
- Now take turns telling each other stories of events that triggered these feelings. The partner will take notes on both the things you say and how you express yourself nonverbally while saying them.

---

[9] This exercise was developed by Todd Salovey, professor of theatre at the University of California, San Diego and associate artistic director of the San Diego Repertory Theatre. It is used here with his permission and has been used and developed by French for 20 years to become an adaptation of the original. The part of this exercise that involves observing how one actor actively tells the story is inspired by Joint Stock observations as mentioned earlier.

- Then, each partner goes away for a few days to write a one- to two-minute monologue for the other. The shared personal information is only the starting place. The monologue can be completely made up, or a true story, or a mixture. It can jump off of one issue or combine two or three. The writer should never disclose what came out of the personal stories and what was invented. The actor/performer can choose to disclose that to whomever he wishes as it relates to his personal information, but it is better to keep it a secret until after the performances. It can be in any dramatic style the writer chooses. The language should reflect spoken rather than written language and can be casual or more formal depending on the character and situation. The writer can choose to build on strengths he has seen the partner/actor achieve already, or push him to do something outside his comfort zone. (For example if the actor is naturally funny, the writer might give him a serious piece with depth. In another situation, the writer might gently prod the actor to laugh at himself or turn something upside down for examination.)
- While the writer is responding to personal information, the writer does not need to make the character in the piece the personality of the actor. The writer needs to consider all the given circumstances as outlined in Chapter 7 or in the improvisation worksheet in the appendix. Additionally consider: What is the character struggling with? Who is he talking to, if anyone? Does the character change his mind or behavior during the piece? Does he make any discoveries? Monologues (like plays and movies) are generally more interesting if there are surprising twists and turns.
- Each writer brings in a first draft and has the actor read it out loud. As scripts change a lot when they move from the writer's mind to the page, and again from the page to the actor's spoken voice, ideas for improvements are generated. If the teacher has time, she may help you with strengthening the dramatic structure.
- A final draft is brought in with copies for writer, actor, and teacher. The writer may make some slight changes to material to make it work better, but the actor should not change the writing without the writer's agreement. The script is then finalized.
- The actor prepares the final version of the script in actor's preparation rehearsals using various colors in his Actor's Palette and Active Analysis tools. It might be good at this point for the actor to first work on her own without a director/teacher, as this ability to prepare material on your own is a vital acting skill.
- The writer then directs the actor, giving feedback as to what is coming across and directions as to how to achieve the material as written as the writer conceived it. As it is one person's source material, revised, enhanced and written down by the writer, but performed by the source person as actor, there is usually a lot of collaboration between them.
- The actor announces the writer and then performs the monologue for the class.

19.3 Reflection Journal—Personal Monologues

How did you feel when you first found out you were to write a dramatic monologue? What is your observation of the process of writing it? What was your response to someone's performing what you had written? As the performer, what was your experience of developing and performing material written in response to what you are passionate about? Did you find you were more or less able to emotionally engage with this material versus material written without thought of you?

PART III: SOCIAL PURPOSE: ARTISTIC ENGAGEMENT WITH SOCIETY

If you speak with artists who have worked in the theatre for a while, each of them will have stories of productions where the communion between performers and audience was felt and acknowledged by all. This is amplified if the material presented has special meaning to the performer, audience, or, ideally, both.

Bertolt Brecht's *The Threepenny Opera* Echoing Financial Crises, 1928 and 2008

In March 2009, French worked with Sam Woodhouse on the San Diego Repertory's presentation of Bertolt Brecht's *The Threepenny Opera*. Brecht wrote the piece as an outcry against the greed and corruption that led to the financial collapse in Berlin in 1928, but it was equally relevant to the US banking collapse of fall 2008. In 2008-2009, people were angry with the greedy investment bankers who, through risky schemes, had gambled and lost working people's entire life savings while making millions for themselves. During performances, people in the audience were so moved they were shouting things out in agreement with expressions by the characters in the play, or against the actions of villains.

Figure 19.4 *The Threepenny Opera* by Bertolt Brecht, San Diego Repertory Theatre, directed by Sam Woodhouse. Actors: Jeffrey Meek (MacHeath) and Amanda Kramer (Polly Peachum).
Photo: Ken Jacques

> At many performances there were verbal agreements when MacHeath said:
>
> We don't want to keep the people waiting. Ladies and Gentlemen, you see before you a vanishing representative of a vanishing trade. We little handicraft workers and safe crackers, who toil with our humble tools upon the cash boxes of little businessmen—we are being swallowed up by big corporations backed by big banks. What is a crowbar in the hand compared with a handful of stocks and bonds? What is breaking into a bank compared to the founding of a bank? So now I take my leave of you and thank you for coming.[10]

Sociopolitical Engagement through Churchill's *Mad Forest*

In 1996, French directed Caryl Churchill's *Mad Forest* at San Francisco State University. The material had been researched out of a collaborative process developed by an English theatre collective called Joint Stock. Mark Wing-Davey and Churchill had taken a company of actors to Romania, just after the Romanian revolution of 1989 that resulted in the overthrow of cruel and corrupt dictator Nicolae Ceaușescu. The company lived with and interviewed regular citizens. The actors then brought stories back to rehearsals. They told each story taking on the characteristics of the person they had interviewed. Out of these characters and stories, as well as her own imagination, Churchill later crafted the play.

At San Francisco State, French's goal in restaging *Mad Forest*, was to uncover the human truths emerging from the historical incidents and reveal them through Churchill's nonrealistic play, which included vampires and talking dogs. She also wanted to bring awareness to Romanian elections that risked returning cronies of Ceaușescu's regime to power. Additionally, she felt the play was a warning about the dangers to human liberty involved when a government spies on its own people (now sadly a common practice even in supposedly civilized countries who claim to value human rights and a right to privacy).

The research and rehearsal process involved understanding the people, places, and events, using all available resources, to immerse ourselves in them, and lastly, to communicate the frustrations and joys of the Romanian people so that an audience could experience them, too. The challenge for the actors was to connect with material based on a time period they had not lived through as adults and a culture none of us knew enough about to accurately depict. In addition to massive reading on Romanian history—serial occupation by foreign powers and rich cultural heritage—we viewed footage on the revolution recovered from a variety of news sources. French contacted some members of the Romanian émigré community in the San Francisco

---

[10]Bertolt Brecht, *The Threepenny Opera*, trans. Brody (unpublished but used in production in 2009 at the San Diego Repertory Theatre), 109.

Bay Area. They were very generous with themselves, their community, and their time, inviting the *Mad Forest* company to attend their Orthodox church, have meals with them, and hear their stories of the revolution. The actors and director even attended an Orthodox wedding, which was very helpful, as French had to stage one in the play.

The day a large group of Romanians came to see our production, we were all a little nervous. We didn't want them to feel exploited or misrepresented. Historically this peaceful revolution started with a quiet chant of dissent at a carefully orchestrated government rally designed to pretend Ceaușescu had the people's support. The dissenters chanted the name of a town, Timișoara, where Ceaușescu's soldiers had brutally massacred unarmed demonstrators. As the actors began the chant, at first slowly and quietly but building in intensity, "Tim-i-soar-a, Tim-i-soar-a," the Romanians in the audience started to chant along. The audience was swept up in the cathartic moment that released the Romanian people from the grip of a suffocating regime. The Romanians felt that their story was heard and appreciated.

Exercise 19.4: Acting with Social Purpose

(It is helpful to repeat this exercise numerous times with different issues.)

Purposes: to develop your artistic connections to and reflections of society; to develop your ability to work with an ensemble to actively explore issues; to reinforce your ability to actively analyze the issues in a play; to emotionally engage in issues beyond domestic experiences.

Guidelines:
- Form groups of four to six.
- Starting place: Either a) brainstorm a list of issues in society (some examples to prompt you might be pollution, racism/prejudice, choices around unwanted/unexpected pregnancy, same-sex marriage, medical malpractice, drunk driving, drug use/abuse, domestic abuse or sexual abuse, immigration, capital punishment, etc.); you might consider what bothers you the most about our society today, or b) have each student bring in an article from the paper reflecting an issue that he felt strongly for or against.
- Select one or two topics to discuss in more detail and see which the majority of the group is most invested in. It helps if it is an issue for which there is a lot of passion.
- What are the negatives and positives of this issue? Break it into two main opposing factions within your group—choose sides. Those of you who want a challenge might take a position opposite to your own.
- In what kind of location would the issue arise?
- What kinds of people surround this issue? What kinds of events? For example, if the topic is drugs, is there crime involved, danger, or violence?
- How does it affect our society; how does it affect the world around you?
- This improvisation can be done on the spot or for more depth, detail, and nuance, the issue can be researched and presented at a later class.

- Build the improvisation according to the structures you have already learned (see the Advanced Improvisation Worksheet outline in Appendix IIIb).
- In creating your relationships, it is generally better to see the effect of the issue on a group of people that really care about each other.

19.4 Reflection Journal—Acting with Social Purpose

Were you able to invest in the subject and find specific actions to try to fulfill in order to convince others of your point of view? Were you able to do this if you picked a position opposite to your own? How did you respond when you met the strong counteraction? Did you see the issue differently during the exercise or now, upon reflection? Did you succeed in building and investing in honest and deep personal relationships that would allow you to experience genuine emotional reactions to the event?

Exercise 19.5: Investigating Other People's Perspectives[11]

(requires some research outside of class)

Purpose: to generate empathy for others and an ability step into their shoes; to develop characters through observation; to look at the beginnings of developing theatre through devised, collaborative means; this also develops your listening and observation skills.

Guidelines: This time pick an issue in your local community. For example, if you are a student at university you could pick an issue on campus, such as date rape, cheating, or financial issues, or, better, reach out to understand issues in the surrounding community.

- Each member of the group goes out and interviews 3–6 people on the issue. Ensure that at least two of the people are different from you in gender, age, race, educational background, or other ways. While you are interviewing the person, you might ask if you can make an audio recording of the discussion. Notice every detail about the tone of voice, gestures, movement of the spine, facial expression, use of language, and other details of the person telling the story or stating the opinion.
- Come back to the group and tell each story as the person who told it to you.
- Now, select one character each and put them in a situation that has a location where they might intersect, a central event, and opposing objectives.
- Do an improvisation together that brings in as many of the lines and character attributes that you can and brings out divergent points of view on the topic, as above.

---

[11] This technique was adapted from the Joint Stock process as taught to French at the University of California, San Diego, from Les Waters, who had been a member of the company.

The Artist as Shaman: Catalyst for Change

> "If we could change ourselves, the tendencies in the world would also change. As a man changes his own nature, so does the attitude of the world change towards him. . . .
>
> We need not wait to see what others do."[12]
>
> —Mahatma Gandhi, Indian nonviolent revolutionary[13]

Great artists sometimes use their art or their status in art to give back. Laurence Olivier's dream, which he achieved, was to create a National Theatre of Great Britain. Sonia Moore wanted to create art that uplifted society to thank America for having given her family refuge from Russian dictator Joseph Stalin. Angelina Jolie uses her status as a Hollywood star to work as an envoy for the United Nations to bring media attention to humanitarian issues around the world. Ask yourself, "What would I like to contribute to the advancement of art? What would I like to contribute to society through acting in theatre or film? Stanislavsky called this the actor's *supersupertask*.

Figure 19.5 Alida Gunn (Jocasta); Bryant Enriques (Oedipus); Guillermo Jones (Laius); Julian Martinez (Orestes) in *Edipo*, by Luis Alfaro, at Borderlands Theatre in Tucson, Arizona.
Photo: Andres Volovsek

---

[12] According to Waylon Lewis of the online *Elephant Journal*, the more well known and pithy version of this quote, "Be the change you wish to see in the world," cannot actually be attributed accurately to Gandhi. The quote used here is an actual quote, perhaps not as pithy, that represents a similar sentiment. http://www.elephantjournal.com/2011/08/*be-the-change-you-wish-to-see-in-the-world-not-gandhi/* (as of August 31, 2011).

[13] Mahatma Gandhi (1869–1948) led India to reject British rule and colonialism and create a national India through a widespread movement of nonviolent protest called civil disobedience. His techniques have since been employed in humanitarian uprisings around the world; for example, the Civil Rights Movement in the United States, the Antiapartheid Movement in South Africa, and the uprisings of the Arab Spring in the Middle East.

There is a strong worldwide theatrical movement made up of smaller local groups that in English is called Theatre for Social Change. There are many great artists that have used theatre to uplift society, and many who have directly tackled specific social, humanitarian, or political issues. Here are just a few notable examples: Augusto Boal developed theatre in the poorest, most oppressed communities in Brazil. You can learn about and emulate his methods through his book *Theatre of the Oppressed*; Luis Valdez and his El Teatro Campesino (Farmworkers Theatre) created theatre to uplift the migrant farmworkers during their California strike against inhumane and dangerous working conditions; Luis Alfaro, performer, playwright, and deviser, creates plays to address issues within communities and brings communities into the theatre; Norma Bowles's company, Fringe Benefits, goes into schools to collaboratively devise theatre pieces to counter racism, sexism, homophobia, and other issues; and, Eve Ensler wrote the widely performed *Vagina Monologues*, leading to a worldwide movement to liberate women and children from sexual violence, slavery, and oppression. Cirque du Soleil, which is one of most successful arts and entertainment companies in the world, has a division called Cirque du Monde. The focus is to bring circus workshops to impoverished parts of the world to build self-esteem, and a sense of belonging, among disenfranchised youth. They also built their headquarters on a reclaimed garbage dump in one of the poorest areas of Montreal and built a performance center nearby, staffed by locals.

The Romanians, and many other people today around the world, know what a privilege it is to, as the Quakers have said, "speak truth to power"[14] and to publish dissenting opinions in books and newspapers. In many countries, artistic and other expression is taken for granted. Even in the United States, which supposedly upholds free speech, censorship does occur. Luckily, it often backfires, catapulting the artist to fame. This was the case when the National Endowment of the Arts revoked funding for photographer Robert Mapplethorpe because his sexually provocative nude photographs depicted homosexual themes. Now he and his work are widely known and discussed. Tenure at universities is being challenged, threatening academic free speech, and public funding for education is being cut back, diminishing access to education regardless of income. Artistic voices are generally censored in oppressive societies for the very reason that artists can stir people to realize that others share their frustrations, and this can be a powerful recipe for change.

Experiencing the Creative Life

"Consciousness is, in effect, the key to a life examined, for better and for worse, our beginner's permit into knowing all about the hunger, the thirst, the sex, the tears, the laughter, the kicks, the punches, the flow of images we call thought, the feelings, the words, the stories, the beliefs, the music and the poetry, the happiness and the ecstasy. At its simplest and most basic level, consciousness lets us recognize an irresistible urge to stay alive and develop a concern for the self. At its most complex and elaborate level, consciousness helps us develop a concern for other selves and improve the art of life."[15]

—Antonio Damasio

---

[14]First coined in a Quaker pamphlet to stand firm against fascism in the 1950s, but now widely used by political activities working for social justice.
[15]Antonio Damasio, *The Feeling of What Happens* (Orlando: Harvest Books, 1990), 5.

19 THE CREATIVE LIFE

The creative life is a rich life. Perhaps, if you are at the top of our profession in theatre, film, or television, it will be a financially rich life. As long as you have a safe place to live, healthy food, clothing, and can pay your basic bills without too much worry, money (while quite nice to have) is not the real riches life has to offer. As an actor in the United States, it may take you a long time to make a living, even if you are talented and well trained, due to lack of public support of the arts, especially of developing artists, compared to other countries, such as Russia, England, or China. You may have to start out having a day job or working in other technical, educational, or literary aspects of theatre. However, to get to the top of any competitive and rewarding field it will take a lot of hard work and a determination to never give up.

> "The world is too much with us; late and soon,
> Getting and spending, we lay waste our powers"
> —William Wordsworth (1770–1850), English poet

Many people settle, because of fear and the need for security, or real responsibilities, into jobs and even lifelong careers that don't much interest or excite them. They don't feel valued or see the value they are giving others (the markers of job satisfaction). Many people are unhappy in their jobs, living for every evening and weekend, watching the clock. In the theatre or working on a film you will put in ridiculous hours to prepare a production, but you will love the majority of it. Don't spend your life saying, "I always wanted to…,"; say, "I do," or at a minimum, "I did follow my passion" for a part of my life. You can always do something more traditional later.

Figure 19.6 You can always do something more traditional later. Mask making.
Photo and designer: Yoshi Tanokura

Figure 19.7 "A life in the performing arts is a life fully inhabited, fully explored, fully lived." Ariel Princeton Mota and Ian Owstrovski in *The Phantom Tollbooth,* a play by Susan Nanus, based on the novel by Norton Juster.
Photo: Stephanie Daventry French

The jewels you will discover and the wealth you will inherit through a life in the theatre come from the creativity itself. Creative people are willing to work that hard because inspiration is a feeling of being alive and vibrant above all other temporary forms of excitement or sensual satisfaction.[16] If during a performance you can also stimulate that peak experience in your audience, you have offered a great gift. It is never the same dull workday; each new play or film offers a new journey of exploration into places, time periods, situations, and other people that expand your perceptions. We could not possibly actually live through all the circumstances we can explore through theatre productions and films (or even novels), but through these stories we expand our understanding and appreciation of the fullness of the human existence. A life in the performing arts is a life fully inhabited, fully explored, fully lived.

Just after retiring as a physician, a man said, "I realize how much of my life I missed out on because I was preparing mentally, physically, and materially for my work, or working so hard, or exhausted from working so hard. I didn't realize what a toll it took, always having people's lives in my hands."[17] Most of us are not independently wealthy and therefore have to work. One of the biggest criteria for employee job satisfaction is that employees are noticed and appreciated for their contributions. Beyond that, if you can find work you feel has value to others, that gives satisfaction. If you can get someone to pay you to do what makes you feel most vibrant and alive, even better, and if that also gives back to others or society, this is so much more than a job or even a career. It is an avocation.

Exercise 19.6: Your Artist's Manifesto

Purpose: A manifesto is a declaration of your passion for what you want to achieve through your art. They were very popular in the antirealistic modernist period of theatre that erupted as a response to realism but are also used today to help a company or artist gain focus, funding, and audiences. In a website today it may be called a mission statement.

Guidelines: Take some time first to reflect on a few key questions for a period of time. As your interests arise, figure out the format—written, visual, video, etc.—you would like to use to express your manifesto.

---

[16] As accounted by psychologist Mihaly Csikszentmihalyi in *Creativity: Flow and the Psychology of Discovery and Invention* (New York: HarperPerennial, 1997), 113.
[17] This person is very private and, we believe, would prefer to remain anonymous, but this was said directly to the writers.

- Look up artist's manifestos online to get an idea of some that have gone before.
- What is it that makes you passionate about theatre and art?
- What topics, issues, or situations do you want to explore through theatre?
- What genres (comedy, tragedy, drama, musicals) and styles of theatre (realism, absurd, Shakespearean, restoration comedy, farce, historical drama, fantasy) do you want to investigate?
- Which artists do you most admire? Which of these would you like to emulate?
- Whom would you like to reach? (For example, there have been theatres that sought to include the working class or Latino audiences or young people 16–25, etc. Peter Brook sought to create theatre pieces that told human truths that would transcend culture and speak to people from different cultures all over the world, including some of the most remote civilizations.)

Here is a sample of the SITI Company's mission statement, a modern-day manifesto on their website:

SITI Company is committed to providing a gymnasium-for-the-soul where the interaction of art, artists, audiences and ideas inspire the possibility for change, optimism and hope.

SITI Company was built on the bedrock of ensemble. We believe that through the practice of collaboration, a group of artists working together over time can have a significant impact upon both contemporary theatre and the world at large.

Through our performances, educational programs and collaborations with other artists and thinkers, SITI Company will continue to challenge the status quo, to train to achieve artistic excellence in every aspect of our work, and to offer new ways of seeing and of being as both artists and as global citizens.[18]

"The Road Not Taken"
by Robert Frost

Two roads diverged in a yellow wood,
And sorry I could not travel both
And be one traveler, long I stood
And looked down one as far as I could
To where it bent in the undergrowth;

Then took the other, as just as fair
And having perhaps the better claim

---

[18] http://siti.org/content/about-us.

Because it was grassy and wanted wear,
Though as for that the passing there
Had worn them really about the same,

And both that morning equally lay
In leaves no step had trodden black.
Oh, I kept the first for another day!
Yet knowing how way leads on to way
I doubted if I should ever come back.

I shall be telling this with a sigh
Some ages and ages hence:
Two roads diverged in a wood, and I—
I took the one less traveled by
And that has made all the difference.[19]

New Theatre Artists and Scholars
- ☐ Mel Gordon
- ☐ Todd Salovey
- ☐ Irene Moore-Jaqlum
- ☐ Georgi Tovstonogov

New Interdisciplinary Experts
- ☐ Mircea Eliade
- ☐ Mahatma Gandhi

---

[19]Robert Frost, *"The Road Not Taken" and Other Poems* (New York: Dover Thrift Editions, 1993), 1.

PART 4

HONORING OUR ACTING LEGACY

Chapters in Part 4
20. The Evolving Stanislavsky System — 489

In the following pages we outline the development of the Stanislavsky System through the collaborative creative crucible of the Moscow Art Theatre. Here we also reference many scholars and excellent books about Stanislavsky and his amazing contemporary artists.

CHAPTER 20

The Evolving Stanislavsky System

"Before attaining the beguiling heights of inspiration,
we have to deal with the conscious technique for achieving it."[1]
—Konstantin Stanislavsky

- Early Theatrical Impressions
- Amateur Theatrical Explorations
- The Moscow Art Theatre (MAT)
- The Actor Training Studios
- The Search for New Theatrical Forms
- A Reversal of Thought
- The Final Experiment: The Method of Physical Actions (Active Analysis)
- Summary of Key Events Shaping Stanislavsky and His Acting System

In Chapter 1: An Invitation to the Quest for Inspiration, you entered the world of actor training on the path to mastering acting technique. You have begun to experience and communicate artistic inspiration. Here we invite you to consider how Stanislavsky's lifelong search for an acting technique based on the very nature of the creative process relates to your own artistic quest. We hope that by understanding his dynamic struggle to develop the System, during 40 years of experimentation, you will more deeply appreciate its achievement and contribution as part of your own acting legacy. Many great artists at the Moscow Art Theatre (MAT) contributed to the development and, later, the dissemination of the Stanislavsky System. Some key figures are Leopold Sulerzhitsky, Vsevold Meyerhold, Evgeny Vakhtangov, Michael Chekhov, Richard Boleslavsky, and Maria Ouspenskaya (the last three of whom immigrated to and taught in the United States). All of them were inspired and nurtured in their artistic careers by Konstantin S. Stanislavsky, even as he was inspired by them, as well as other collaborators, students, and exceptional artists outside of MAT. (*MXT* is the Russian acronym).

---

[1] Konstantin Stanislavsky, *An Actor's Work*, trans. Jean Benedetti (London: Routledge, 2009), xxxvi.

Early Theatrical Impressions

> "If being a prodigy is not a requirement for later creativity, a more than usually keen curiosity about one's surroundings appears to be. Practically every individual who has made a novel contribution to a domain remembers feeling awe about the mysteries of life and has rich anecdotes to tell about efforts to solve them."[2]
>
> —Mihaly Csikszentmihalyi

Imagine that you are a young child and you and your friends love to put on shows for your parents and family. The world of make-believe, the costumes, the fantasies capture your imagination to such a point that one holiday evening while performing a little skit, you are suddenly briefly transported into the imaginary world of your story. During that moment, as if time had stopped, something indescribable had taken charge of your thoughts, body, and words. You experienced something magical. For a fleeting moment, while dozens of eyes were watching, you came to life as the character. In such a moment you were invigorated by the sweet nectar of inspiration.

It may be said that Stanislavsky's "quest for the System,"[3] as so aptly stated by Sharon Marie Carnicke in her groundbreaking book *Stanislavsky in Focus*, was motivated in much the same way by his personal quest for inspiration as an actor. He did have such moments at a very early age and within him arose a deep need to repeat the experience. Ceaselessly, with unwavering determination, even after he became a world-renowned figure, he searched for the key that would unlock an actor's creativity and simultaneously bring about a truthful transformation into character. He examined and experimented with so many approaches, that his many failures gave him insights for even greater later successes. Those who are motivated rather than devastated by obstacles, are able to turn failure into success.

> "Ninety-eight percent of genius is hard work. . . . As for genius being inspired, inspiration is in most cases another word for perspiration."[4]
> —Thomas Edison (1847–1931), inventor of the motion picture camera and a long-lasting lightbulb

Stanislavsky was such a man of genius; however, he was not born knowing the answers to complex problems. It is the persistence of the search for answers and the determination to succeed that transforms the talented actor into the great actor, the teacher into the creator of a worldwide actor training system.

---

[2] Mihaly Csikszentmihalyi, *Creativity: Flow and the Psychology of Discovery and Invention* (New York: HarperPerennial, 1997), 156.

[3] Sharon M. Carnicke, *Stanislavsky in Focus* (Amsterdam: Harwood Academic, 1998), 27.

[4] According to research by Dr. Garson Toole this quote is attributed to a publication referencing a speech of Thomas Edison, with this footnote: "1898 April 21,*The Youth's Companion*, Volume 72, Issue 16, Current Topics, Quote Page 194, Column 1, Perry Mason & Company, Boston, Massachusetts. (ProQuest American Periodicals)." This adage is commonly quoted as, "Genius is 1% inspiration and 99% perspiration." Toole found other resources for earlier versions of a similar idea in slightly different words, including a record of an 1893 Kate Sanborn speech on Genius. For more information go to Toole's fascinating website: http://quoteinvestigator.com/category/thomas-edison/ (our information from Toole was from a post dated December 14, 2012).

20 THE EVOLVING STANISLAVSKY SYSTEM

Who was this extraordinary man who many have come to appreciate and recognize as the very first to gather and systematize the objective laws of nature that govern an actor's creativity in performance? How did he develop a pathway to genius that the talented actor could follow and achieve?

> "An actor plays well only when his behavior is subordinated to natural organic laws of creativity which are rooted in human nature. Great actors achieved this spontaneously. This happened before the Stanislavski System. The System is the practical teaching of natural organic laws of creativity. Therefore whenever an actor plays well, convincingly, sincerely, he always plays according to the Stanislavski System—whether he did it consciously or unconsciously, acted intentionally or was subordinated to his talent, to the demands of Mother Nature herself."[5]
>
> —B. E. Zakhava

The Curtain Rises

Stanislavsky was born Konstantin (Kostya) Sergyevich Alexeyev on January 5, 1863, into one of the wealthiest families in Russia at that time. "As a nineteenth-century commentator testifies: 'so very rich were the Alexeyevs that their wealth became a by-word. Anyone wishing to accuse another of arrogance would say: 'Don't think you are an Alexeyev.'"[6] They were merchants who manufactured gold thread, but 100 years prior to Stanislavsky's birth, his family were serfs (peasant slaves to the landed gentry). This was Imperialist Russia, a monarchy, ruled by the Romanov family, at the time of his birth, Tsar Alexander II. Just before his birth, Alexander II emancipated the serfs.

At age 22 young Konstantin adopted the stage name Stanislavsky so as not to embarrass his family. Acting was not an acceptable preoccupation for a man of his social standing at that time. Nevertheless, the Alexeyevs loved attending the theatre and putting on amateur theatricals at their home on Great Alekseyevskaya Street as well as at their country estate outside of Moscow.

It was at one of the family theatricals, entitled *The Four Seasons*, when seven-year-old Kostya first appeared on the stage. He was given the part of Winter and told to pretend to put a stick in the fire of a burning candle. It seemed natural to him that he should really put the stick in the flame. A fire ensued. He created Konstanzo Alekseyev's Circus, composed of his brothers, sisters, and friends. Then a puppet theatre where in attempting to create realistic effects, he burned the scenery down. Luckily his parents did not discourage his theatrical interests, despite these two dangerous accidents. Unknowingly, each of these early experiences sowed the seeds that would become fertile ground for the development of his great search for an acting system. Many years later, upon reflection of the event, he came to realize that putting a stick in a candle taught him a valuable lesson of the great importance of truthfully fulfilling purposeful actions.

---

[5] Translated and quoted in Sonia Moore, *Stanislavski Revealed* (New York: Applause Theatre Books, 1991), unnumbered opening page.
[6] Elena Polyakova, *Stanislavsky* (Moscow: Progress, 1983), 5.

The Alexeyev Circle

The family's old country estate had a wing where the children played, but it was in need of great repair. Stanislavsky's father decided to tear it down. The children begged him not to, and due to their pleading he decided to put in its place a new building which could be used as a small theatre. The date of the opening, September 5, 1887, was in celebration of his mother's birthday. Under Stanislavsky's direction, at age 14, many plays were produced and performed there. Eventually it was decided to call the amateur group *The Alexeyev Circle*.

It was on that early training ground that he first began to keep what he called "artistic notes," a habit that would eventually become a hallmark of an actor's training in the System. The young actor kept an accurate record of his performances, where he meticulously noted his successes and failures. It was this lifelong note taking that would eventually lay the foundation for what would become his System.

At the opening performance, three one-act farces were performed. Stanislavsky appeared in two: *A Cup of Tea* and *The Old Mathematician*. In his notes he stated, "I played coldly and languidly, without a spark of talent, though I was not worse than the others. . . . It was Muzil (a popular actor at the time) who made their laughter, for I had copied even his voice."[7] He was brutally honest with himself, noting that he had poor voice and speech and that he spoke so fast that the audience could not understand him. (**Note:** Stanislavsky was always deeply self-critical. He did, however, manage to make the audience laugh in spite of his poor speech.)

The formation of his family's amateur acting troupe had taught Stanislavsky many subtle truths about the art of acting. In later years he would come to see that time as having contributed to what would be eventually called a feeling of *true measure* and the *inner life*.

Tomasso Salvini's *Othello*

In 1882, he observed the great Italian tragedian Tomasso Salvini, who was famous for playing the role of Othello. Upon the actor's entrance Stanislavsky was not impressed, he thought his costume made him look "almost fat," that his wig was obvious, and although Salvini had a good voice, his acting seemed no better than the actor who was playing Iago. Gradually and subtly, he found himself completely captivated by the great actor, as he describes below:

Figure 20.1 Stanislavsky in the late 1800s, Moscow Art Theatre company.
Photo: Fine Art Images/Heritage Images/Getty Images

---

[7] Quoted in Christine Edwards, *The Stanislavsky Heritage* (New York: New York University Press, 1965), 29.

Salvini approached the platform of the doges, thought a little while, concentrated himself and, unnoticed by any of us, took the entire audience of the Great Theatre into his hands. It seemed that he did this with a single gesture—that he stretched his hand without looking into the public, grasped all of us in his palm, and held us there as if we were ants or flies. He closed his fist, and we felt the breath of death; he opened it, and we knew the warmth of bliss. We were in his power, and we will remain in it all our lives, forever.[8]

The experience, however, also left Stanislavsky with a haunting question: What did Salvini and other great actors know, and what was the cause of their greatness? He determined to discover the secrets of the great actors.

Amateur Theatrical Explorations

Years of Trial and Error

The years that followed were filled with seeking to balance family and social obligations with pursuit of acting in amateur productions, during which time many valuable lessons were learned. One of Stanislavsky's great gifts was the ability to recognize his failures and by seeking their causes, realize underlying verities that would serve as the philosophical basis of his teachings. One such principle arose from his early desire to always appear handsome and dashing upon the stage. He wore thigh-length boots, a cloak, and carried a sword. He evaluated that this vain preoccupation had caused him to leave the true path of art. He came to believe "the first condition for creating this pre-work state [pre-creative state of mind] is expressed in the saying, *love the art in yourself, not yourself in art*. So let your major concern be the well-being of your art."[9]

Another such evaluation came from his habit of practicing for long hours in front of a mirror, eventually leading him to later state that it was dangerous to study your part in front of a mirror as it teaches the actor to look at himself from the outside and keeps him from looking inside. He also loved to imitate his favorite actors, and learned that while imitation created an external behavior, it led away from the soul. These early lessons became the philosophical foundation for his lifelong search for the secrets of great art.

The Society of Art and Literature

The dream of a society where artists, musicians, singers, and amateur actors could gather under one roof had been in Stanislavsky's mind for a while; however, when the famous stage director and actor Alexandr Fillipovich Fedotov[10] and his wife, the equally famous actress Fedotova, returned from Paris to Moscow, Stanislavsky seized the opportunity to put his plan into action. He had already spoken of the idea with the opera singer Fyodor Komissarjevsky, and when he brought the two men together, they became equally excited by the prospects of establishing such an artists' society.

The society opened its doors in the winter of 1888 with a gala event, and shortly thereafter presented two plays together, Pushkin's *Miser Knight*, with Stanislavsky

---

[8] Konstantin Stanislavsky, *My Life in Art*, (New York: Theatre Arts Books, 1952), 266.
[9] Stanislavsky, *An Actor's Work*, 558.
[10] Stanislavsky, *My Life in Art*, 148. (Fedotov was a director of what was called "the old French school" of acting.)

playing the leading role, and Molière's *Georges Dandin*. Stanislavsky had a preconceived image in his mind of how to play the Miser Knight, something he subsequently came to realize is always detrimental to true discovery of a character. When he told his idea to his new colleagues, Fedotov and Sollogub, a brilliant set designer, they laughed and poked fun at him. They informed him that he had brought all of his amateur *bag of tricks* with him, and promptly began to perform what Stanislavsky called a "surgical operation"[11] in an attempt to remove his bad acting habits. Although he tried to follow their demands to live the role, Stanislavsky was unable to do so. This experience taught him that it was necessary to search for a technical means to create the *inner spiritual life* of the character.

In the leading role in *Georges Dandin* by Molière, Stanislavsky began to live the role spontaneously, and he realized that emotions onstage could easily be mistaken for inspiration. His acting of the role came with ease, and everything he did felt right. He also noticed that when he lived the role simply and truthfully he was able to communicate the inner world of the character to the audience. He surmised that true inspiration is attained when the actor uses *restraint and control*.

The year 1889 proved to be a landmark for Stanislavsky: The first season of the new society had a series of successes; he began to come into his own as an actor of depth, and learned how to create more-profound characters. On July 5 of that year he married the actress Maria Lilina Perevoshchikova (Lilina), who had played opposite him in Schiller's *Kabale und Liebe*.

An Early Influence: The Duke of Saxe-Meiningen's Company

In the following year, the company of Georg II, the Duke of Saxe-Meiningen, traveled to Russia. The work of the troupe was highly disciplined and esthetically beautiful. There was an integrity to each element of production: scenery, lights, costuming, sound, etc. The director, Ludwig Chronegk, created shadowbox settings which depicted real settings with exquisite tableaux and engaging mise en scènes, (blocking and movement in the scenes). The company's repertoire was equally impressive, presenting such works as Schiller's *Maria Stuart* and Shakespeare's *Julius Caesar, Twelfth Night,* and *The Merchant of Venice*. Properties and costumes were real and authentic to the period.

The influence upon the young Stanislavsky was profound. Chronegk's directorial style intrigued him. Chronegk was cold, regimented, and dictatorial. His rehearsals were run like a military platoon: disciplined, precise, every moment timed and executed with rigid discipline. Stanislavsky copied Chronegk's manner and became a strict taskmaster, insisting that the actors imitate him exactly. He became known as a despot. The results, however, proved to bear fruit and, in terms of successful productions, that garnered positive attention. Soon Moscow became aware of a very gifted director. Under Stanislavsky's direction the society continued to thrive and produce more-challenging plays.

Since Stanislavsky had seen the great Italian actor Tomasso Salvini play Othello, he deeply wanted to play the role himself. He determined to stage the production with the amateur actors of the society, and in the summer of 1885 at his country estate at Liubimovka, he began outlining his rehearsal plan. He did deep research and wrote copious notes as to the design of the set, behavior of the characters, and the authenticity of the properties and costumes. In Paris he bought costume books

---

[11] Jean Benedetti, *Stanislavski* (London: Routledge, 1988), 29.

and fabric. He and his wife spent countless hours in Venice in museums, shopping for antiques, buying brocades and embroidery. In his artistic autobiography, *My Life in Art*, he wrote:

> I even found Othello himself. In one of the summer restaurants of Paris I met a handsome Arab in his national costume. . . . In another half hour I was already dining with my new friend in a private dining room. Finding that I was interested in his costume, the Arab, without saying a word, undressed to the skin. With the help of the waiter we made the designs of the costume. I learned several bodily poses which seemed to me to be characteristic. Then I studied the Arab's body, his movements and his outer anatomy. Returning to my hotel, I stood half the night before a mirror, putting on sheets and towels in order to make myself into a graceful Moore with quick turns of the head, movements of the hands and the body as graceful as those of a deer, a smooth, royal method of walking, and the narrow palms turned towards those who might speak to me.[12]

The production premiered on January 19, 1886, and received much acclaim and praise, as in the review written by Nicolai Efros[13] in *Novosti Dnia*:

> I do not offend against truth if I say that Moscow has never witnessed such a production of this Shakespeare play. The décor, props, costumes were distinguished by great taste, originality, living truth and, so experts in these matters tell me, absolute historical accuracy.[14]

Stanislavsky, however, was not satisfied with his performance. Years later he reflects in *My Life in Art* that he was not ready to play the more difficult scenes of the role; he strained his voice due to too much muscular tension. He was so completely exhausted after rehearsals that he was forced to lie in bed with his heart beating and his throat choking.

As always, his evaluation of the production and himself served to teach him yet another lesson that would later become a principle of his System in the training of actors: "Don't attempt to play those roles prematurely which God is kind enough to let you play at the end of your scenic career."[15]

The Moscow Art Theatre (MAT)

The years spent with the society had taught Stanislavsky many valuable lessons about the nature of an actor's and director's arts. He had both successes and failures, but the latter never detered him from his desire to find the secrets of great acting. On the contrary, his longing to eventually realize the creation of a professional acting company was only heightened.

---

[12]Stanislavsky, *My Life in Art*, 277.
[13]Nicolai Efros (1867–1923), Russian writer and critic who chronicled the development of Stanislavsky's work with the Society of Art and Literature and the Moscow Art Theatre for 25 years.
[14]Quoted in Jean Benedetti, *Stanislavski* (New York: Routledge, 1988), 52.
[15]Stanislavski, *My Life in Art*, 285.

Figure 20.2 Stanislavsky and Nemirovich-Danchenko, circa 1935.
Photo: ITAR-TASS/TopFoto/ArenaPAL

His business responsibilities with the family factory and time spent with the theatre, however, placed a constant strain on his home life. His wife, Lilina, fell ill, and Stanislavsky blamed it upon himself. After a brief separation they were able to come to an understanding and reunited. Upon this backdrop of overwork and personal issues, Stanislavsky did not hesitate to nurture his dream, and then an opportunity arose which would forever change the theatrical world.

Vladimir Nemirovich-Danchenko (December 1858–April 1943) was a well-known and highly respected director and playwright whom Stanislavsky knew by reputation and casual greetings. Danchenko was a playwright and pedagogue[16] of acting at the Philharmonic School in Moscow. On June 16, 1897, he wrote to Stanislavsky the following note, as Elena Polykova recounts:

> "I drafted a great long letter to you, but since I will shortly be in Moscow, I won't send it." On the same day he wrote on the back of a visiting card, "Did you receive my letter? I hear you'll be in Moscow tomorrow, Wednesday. I'll be at the Slav. Bazar at one o'clock. Can we meet? Or let me know at the address below where and when?"[17]

Nemirovich had a group of graduating students at the Philharmonic School who were extraordinarily talented, and Stanislavsky had a seasoned group of talented amateur actors from the Society of Art and Literature. Both men, writes Stanislavsky, were "poisoned by the same dream."[18]

On June 22, 1897, they met at the Slavianski Bazar and took lunch in a private room so as not to be disturbed. The landmark meeting lasted for 18 hours.

---

[16]*Pedagogue*: A teacher, or a person who follows a dull and strict approach.
[17]Polyakova, *Stanislavsky*, 88.
[18]Stanislavsky, *My Life in Art*, 292.

20 THE EVOLVING STANISLAVSKY SYSTEM

Nemirovich had earlier wondered what kind of actor Stanislavsky would be, suspecting that he might be egoistic and demonstrative. He found, however, a modest and quietspoken man of great dignity. As the meeting continued they seemed to agree upon everything that was essential. They were charged with energy and the spirit to create a new theatre at affordable prices for seats. They wanted a theatre of high ideals that would signal a reform from the other contemporary theatres in Russia at the time. They agreed to create an ensemble of like-minded artists who would place the artistic goals of the theatre above their vain individual interests. They would abolish the star system that had so plagued the Russian theatre. At their first meeting they seemed to agree upon everything.

In 1897, at this meeting, they founded the Moscow Art Theatre (MXT, as it is abbreviated in Cyrillic characters), originally called the Art and Publicly-Accessible Theatre. In 1901 the shorter name of the Moscow Art Theatre was adopted. They demanded the highest level of ethical behavior from their company and formulated the following principles:

1. There are no small roles, only small actors.
2. Today—Hamlet, tomorrow—an extra, but even as an extra, you must be an artist.
3. The playwright, the actor, the artist, the dresser, the stagehand all serve one goal: the idea, which is at the heart of the play.
4. Every violation of the creative life of the theatre is a crime.
5. Lateness, laziness, caprice, hysteria, bad behavior, ignorance of the role, the necessity of repeating things twice, are equally harmful to our enterprise and must be eradicated.[19]

They divided the directorship of the new company between them, based on their individual experience and talents. Danchenko would act as artistic director of dramaturgy and would have the last word on literature, while Stanislavsky took the role of artistic director and would have the last word on staging.

The summer following their meeting would place them at different ends of the country; nevertheless, they ironed out their differences through a continuous stream of letter writing. Danchenko had assumed that Stanislavsky would finance the enterprise. Stanislavsky was not in a position to do that and did not want to make the same mistake he had made by financing the Society of Art and Literature, which cost him dearly in financial losses. Money was always an issue. Stanislavsky wanted the company be a public trust but could not get the needed government subsidies to make ticket prices affordable to the working class. Instead the company was financed by shareholders from the merchant class (Stanislavsky's family's class). Their primary supporter was a wealthy Moscovite capitalist, Sawa Morozov, who financed the company for several years. MAT was primarily attended by the educated, upper-middle-class professionals. Danchenko wanted to open the theatre in the provinces but gave way to Stanislavsky's insistence for a Moscow opening. Most importantly the two men spent the year examining one another's actors (Stanislavsky's from the Society for Art and Literature and Danchenko's from the Moscow Philharmonic) and deciding upon which ones would be suitable, had sufficient talent, and were aligned

---

[19]Quoted in David Allen, *Stanislavsky for Beginners* (New York: Writers and Readers, 1999), 38.

with the ideals of the new company. Original company members included the actors Olga Knipper (who later married Anton Chekhov), Ivan Moskvin, and Vsevolod Meyerhold.

The following summer, on June 14, 1898, the company assembled for the first time. They lived commune-style on an estate where they were offered a barn in which to rehearse near the village of Pushkino, 50 miles from Moscow.

During their rehearsal period, new practices and techniques were employed. It had been the practice among "stars" during the period to "upstage" one another by standing behind the actor who was delivering a speech, dropping completely out of character and purposefully distracting attention from the other actor. Stanislavsky found such practices deplorable and had already set out to reform such behavior with the earlier society. They did away with footlights and the practice footlights were designed for: actors' coming downstage center to deliver important speeches directly to the audience rather than to other characters. They asked the audience not to applaud at actors' entrances (as was common in the star system) but kept the curtain calls at the end of each act.

Now, he had the opportunity to apply the principles he and Nemirovich-Danchenko had formulated. He could experiment further and search for new techniques that would put into practice a new realistic style of acting. Stanislavsky insisted that an actor must think continuously as the character and never break his concentration. This required new rehearsal techniques such as the actor's composition of an *inner monologue*. He also prepared a detailed outline of the *mise-en-scène* (literally, movement on stage, blocking) for each play, going to the extreme of writing down every gesture for each moment. In later years Stanislavsky would dispense with this method of dictating all aspects of the production.

It had been the custom for Russian theatres to use the same scenery, props, and costumes for different plays; for example, if there were a garden scene, a painted backdrop depicting a garden would be pulled from stock, or an actress would supply her own costumes, which might not have any relationship to the play, character, or circumstances. Although his direction at the society had already established the use of individual realistic settings, he wished to go further and ensure that the productions had a single-minded vision. He designed every detail: scenery, props, costumes, lighting; everything would be in line with the play's theme and the playwright's ruling idea. He would heighten the aesthetic values of the art.

Danchenko, who was a close friend of Anton Chekhov, wanted to stage *The Seagull*. Chekhov, however, refused to give his consent due to a previous production in St. Petersburg that he considered to have failed. The professional actors who were cast acted in the old style, the production was not thoroughly rehearsed, nor did they understand the gentle nuance of the characters. There is a scene in *The Seagull* where the protagonist, young Constantine, son of a famous actress, Arcadina, shows a play that he has written. When the actress playing Nina began her speech during the play-within-the-play written by the character Constantine, the real audience yelled and jeered at the performers. Chekhov fled in shame, vowing never to let the play be performed in Moscow. It took Nemirovich-Danchenko, who saw genius in Chekhov's work, a great deal of persuading to finally win his consent.

Stanislavsky was not excited about the play. He found it uninteresting and without any action; nevertheless, as he delved into the directorial planning of the text he fell in love with the play's simplicity, truthfulness, and poetic rhythms. He wrote a mise-en-scène describing in precise detail the characters, their appearance,

20 THE EVOLVING STANISLAVSKY SYSTEM

walk, expressions, and gestures. He found hidden within the play deep sentiment and wrote down every nuance of feeling, atmosphere, and mood. He added environmental sounds, such as a dog howling, birdsong, and a piano playing in the distance, with the intention to engulf the audience in the world of the play and give a realistic sense of country life.

It had been decided that the company would open its season at the Hermitage Theatre, October 14, 1898, with Aleksei Tolstoy's *Tsar Fyodor,* a historical drama depicting a weak tsar who fails his people. Rehearsals were well under way when the censors finally gave their permission to present the play. The second on the bill was to be Shakespeare's *The Merchant of Venice,* and after several setbacks with other plays they had considered, they eventually decided upon the third play in the season, *La Locandiera* (*The Mistress of the Inn*), by the Italian playwright Goldoni. *The Seagull* was to close the season (thus opening and closing the first season with contemporary Russian plays). As destiny would dictate, the choice of *The Seagull* would decide the fate of the new company. Stanislavsky writes in his account of the opening night,

> The next evening at eight o'clock, the curtain went up. The audience was a small one. I have no recollection of how the first act went, I only remember that all the actors smelled of valerian[20] drops. I also recall that it was terrible to sit in the dark with my back to the audience during Nina Zarechnaya's monologue, and that I had to hold down my leg which was shaking nervously. . . . It appeared that we were a complete failure. The curtain came down at the end of the first act, and there was a deadly silence in the theatre. The actors pressed close to one another and listened for a reaction from the audience. The theatre was as silent as a grave. The heads of the stagehands poked out from behind the scenes, and they listened as well. Silence.[21]
>
> Someone began to cry. Knipper[22] suppressed hysterical sobs. We silently began to leave the stage. At that moment the audience moaned and burst into applause. . . . Obviously we were all stunned and it took a while for the fact that we were a success to sink in.[23]

From that time on, the Art Theatre became known as The House of Chekhov, and provided a home for the birth of his other masterpieces: 1899, *Uncle Vanya*; 1901, *Three Sisters*; and 1904, *The Cherry Orchard.*

> It is equally mistaken to try and perform or *present* Chekhov's plays. You have to be, i.e live, exist, follow the deeply embedded, psychological artery of the role. It is there that Chekhov is powerful in the varied, partly subconscious way he works on us."[24]

---

[20] *Valerian*: A sedative in liquid or pill form taken to control nervousness and anxiety.
[21] Oksana Korneva, *Konstantin Stanislavsky, Selected Works* (Moscow: Raduga, 1984), 50.
[22] Olga Knipper played Mme. Arcadina in *The Seagull* and became the future wife of Anton Chekhov.
[23] Quoted in Korneva, *Konstantin Stanislavsky, Selected Works,* 50.
[24] Konstantin Stanislavsky, *My Life in Art*, trans. Jean Benedetti (New York: Routledge, 1924; 2008), 194.

Figure 20.3 First reading of *The Seagull* (Anton Chekhov seated center), Moscow Art Theatre company
Photo: ITAR-TASS/TopFoto/ArenaPAL

The Line of Intuition and Feelings

Anton Chekhov's contribution to the Art Theatre went far beyond the writing of plays. It was the very essence and spiritual nature of his characters that, perhaps, incited the deepest need for the eventual creation of an entirely new system of acting. Chekhov's characters were written with such simple human truth that all of the old staging tricks of actors and directors could not be used. Other theatres attempted to stage the plays, but they all failed due to the indicative and declamatory style of acting that was popular at the time. They did not understand the spiritual nature of Chekhov's writing. To play Chekhov, one must live subtly and truthfully in the character's circumstances. It must not be acted but experienced. Even contemporary productions that ignore this truth can only present the external shell, often relying upon a broad comic style. The comedy of Chekhov is in the simple human foibles, which we all possess, not in the broad strokes of the director's imposed interpretation. For an actor to bring to life and experience Chekhov's characters requires that the actor also examine his own soul and be willing to reveal his deepest feelings. In 1926, Stanislavsky expresses it best when he writes,

> While the period drama line brought us to external realism, the line of intuition and feelings showed us the way to inner realism. And thence we automatically proceeded to organic creation whose mysterious processes take place in the sphere of artistic superconsciousness. It begins where outer and inner realism ends. It is the path of intuition and feelings—from the external via the inner to the superconsciousness, a path that is not the most correct, but possible. In those days it was one of the basic paths, at least in my art.[25]

[25]Ibid., 87.

20 THE EVOLVING STANISLAVSKY SYSTEM

The Moscow Art Theatre came under attack by critics who claimed that the theatre was only interested in *naturalism*;[26] however, nothing could be further from the truth. Stanislavsky's object of direction was *spiritual realism*—a realistic style that expressed the inner life of the human soul, not merely the outer realities. Throughout his career he experimented with all manner of plays and styles: impressionism, realism, naturalism, broad farce, satire, fantasy, and classical plays in verse. In addition to Russian writers such as Chekhov, Gorky, Turgenev, and Tolstoy, the Moscow Art Theatre's repertory included works by Strindberg, Goldoni, Shakespeare, Molière, Maeterlinck, and Ibsen.

The notion that the System is limited to only naturalism and realism continues to persist particularly in North America. In 1923, MAT made its first tour to the United States and presented only its old repertoire of realistic works and thus created a lasting impression that the System was limited to just that. In defense of the System's application to all styles and genres, Stanislavsky later wrote,

> Those who think that we sought for naturalism on the stage are mistaken. We never leaned towards such a principle. Always, then as well as now, we sought for inner truth, for the truth of feeling and experience, but as spiritual technique was only in its embryo stage among the actors of our company, we, because of necessity and helplessness, and against our desires, fell now and then into an outward and coarse naturalism.[27]

Creating a Grammar for Acting
For some time Stanislavsky had been plagued with the problem of how to keep a role alive over a long period of time. He had become disappointed with his acting and felt that it had become habitual and mechanical. He felt that he had lost the spark of creativity that had initially given life to his roles. On July 15, 1904, at only age 44, Anton Chekhov succumbed to chronic tuberculoisis. His death was a great blow to the members of Moscow Art Theatre, and it was in this mood that Stanislavsky decided in 1906 to rest and take a summer holiday in Finland. As he sat on a cliff overlooking the sea, he pondered the question and asked where his creative joy had gone. He recalled that the great artists seemed to hold the secret. How were they able to perform the same role for years and never tire of it? He contemplated his role as Doctor Stockman in Ibsen's *The Enemy of the People*, and came to realize that he had lost touch with the original source of his inspiration; that the repetition of the role had dulled his feelings and passions. He had originally seen Stockman as a man with "pure intentions and sought only for the good in the souls of others, who was blind to all the evil feelings and passions of the little men who surrounded him."[28] A personal experience, wherein he had witnessed the destruction of a friend whose conscience would not allow him to submit to dishonest demands, had provided what Stanislavsky called "living memories."[29] Memories that undoubtedly provided the seeds that provoked the creative mood that had inspired his work on the role of Stockman. He continued to examine all of his other roles and with greater determination returned to Moscow.

Stanislavsky was now more determined than ever to discover the secrets that the

---

[26] *Naturalism:* A genre of theatre that depicts people and their social ills as primarily subject to the environment and the greater forces of power that control them.
[27] Stanislavsky, *My Life in Art,* 330.
[28] Ibid., 459.
[29] Ibid., 459.

most inspiried actors used to establish the creative mood and evoke their inspiration. When inspiration came to him onstage he compared it to a prisoner who had been freed from chains he had worn for years and now found that his movements were free. During the 1906–1907 season he continued his research and experiments in search of the theory and technique that would free the actor and serve the art. Gradually he began to uncover the hidden verities underlying the fundamental principles of the actor's creative state.

He observed that when the muscles are free from tension and in conjunction with concentration that he more easily found the creative state, thereby establishing that the first and primary state for the actor is complete concentration. (As we discussed in Chapter 3: Preparing for Inspiration: The Creative State, the relationship of relaxation to inspiration has now been verified through scientific studies.) Profound concentration led, he observed, to a rise in belief and a *feeling of truth*. The actor cannot believe that he is truly the character, but he can believe in the actions he is performing and in the inner feeling of human truth that arises from those actions. When the actor lives as the character through generating true human feelings in response to the imaginary circumstances, the spectator is stimulated to live through the experience also.

From these early theories and experiments both with himself and the actors of the company, Stanislavsky evolved the next important element of his System, the "magic if." Stanislavsky had established that the stage was an artificial environment, and therefore there was no organic stimulus for truthful behavior, or action. This often leaves the actor feeling disassociated from the environment and circumstances of the character, which in turn leads to pretending and purely external acting. However, when the actor asks himself, What would I really do if I were in this situation, doing this today, here and now for the first time? a strong impulse to act is evoked, and belief arises naturally. The "magic if" acts as a strong stimulus to the imagination while simultaneously giving rise to belief in one's behavior and the imaginary circumstances. As the fundamental elements of the System began to take shape, Stanislavsky always kept sight of his ultimate goal, the creation of a technique that would bring the actor into the creative state and allow him to live the life of a human soul.

Now it was time for Stanislavsky to clarify the aim of his research. He divided performance into three major approaches to acting: (1) craft (in this instance referring to what is called stock-in-trade), (2) representation, and (3) the living experience of the role.

1. Craft (stock-in-trade). The actor as a craftsman who has an established actor's bag of tricks from which he pulls to create certain effects. He makes no attempt to genuinely feel or believe anything but portrays the emotions through stock gestures and poses.
2. The art of representation. Actors of the School of Representation pay great attention to the external portrayal of the character, to the character's voice, speech, and movement. They examine the character's motivations, thoughts, feelings, and emotions during the rehearsal process but do not intentionally attempt to live through the role while in performance. The greatest actors of the School of Representation do become inspired and experience true feeling. The Comédie-Française, founded by the French playwright and actor Molière in the seventeenth century, is an example of the highest degree of the art of representation.
3. The art of living experience, or *living through* the role. Actors of the School of

Living Experience pay equal attention to both the external and internal lives of their roles, through meticulous analysis of both the psychology and behavior of the character they are to portray. But it is not enough to discover these details in an alive and creative rehearsal process and show the discoveries to the audience. Instead, the actor's artistic aim is to live through their character in the presence of each audience, each performance. By sharing a living human experience that resonates as a human truth, as offered by a playwright but understood live in that moment by both actor and spectator, *spiritual communion* unfolds. Stanislavsky considered this to be the highest form of acting.

> **Revolution and Theatre, Part I:**
> **Bloody Sunday and the Peasants' Revolt of 1905**
>
> In 1905 in St. Petersburg (at that time the Russian capital), 150,000 workers marched to demand better wages and conditions. They were unarmed and were gunned down by Nicholas II's security police; hundreds of people were killed. This only prompted more unrest—strikes, peasant uprisings, and military defections followed, and this became known as the Revolution of 1905 (or the Peasants Revolt). Tsar Nicholas agreed to created a Duma (parliament); however, further revolt was quashed in December when the Tsar's troops returned from the Russo-Japanese War.
>
> Life and theatre merged in the MAT's 1905 production of Gorky's *Children of the Sun*: when audiences heard a mob approaching, which was in fact part of the play, they feared it was a real riot outside and had to be reassured. The production was not well received by MAT directors or the public, and Gorky left MAT for another theatre taking with him the theatre's primary financial supporter, Sawa Morozov. The MAT struggled financially as it adjusted to this sudden turn of events.
>
> Even before the Peasants Revolt in 1905 the seeds of revolution had taken root in the soil of Russian consciousness. Chekhov's *Three Sisters* (1901) demonstrates how envious and vulgar forces represented by the characters of Natasha, Soliony, and Protopopoff, dispossess the noble but ineffectual Prozoroff sisters and brother of their home and dreams. *The Cherry Orchard* (1904), Chekhov's masterpiece, argues the need for change from the old, decadent life to the new, when in its ruling idea it asks, "Who is best suited to lead Russia into the future: Lopachin the capitalist merchant or Trofimov, the student who calls for a new life of social justice and change?"
>
> Certainly Stanislavsky was well aware of the need for social change. His life of privilege hadn't dulled his sensitivity to the realities of poverty and ignorance around him; indeed it had fueled his desire to reach the masses through theatre. Twenty years prior to the revolution he had set himself the task of bringing education and enlightenment to the common people through theatrical art. He called the revolution the "miraculous liberation of Russia. . . . Theatre for the starving! Starvation and theatre!"[30] He saw that there was no contradiction and declared that the theatre was not a luxury but a necessity in the life of the people.

---

[30] Jean Benedetti, *Stanislavski* (New York: Routledge, 1988), 226.

The Actor Training Studios

Adashev Studio in Moscow

Aleksandr Ivanovich Platonov (1871–1934), stage name Adashev, was a founding member of the Moscow Art Theatre who started in 1906 an acting school called the Adashev Studio where a number of prominent MAT members either taught or got their start. Evgeny Vakhtangov[31] joined MAT after much successful amateur directing and after completing the Adashev Drama School where he studied with Sulerzhitsky. Maria Ouspenskaya also graduated from this studio (1909–1911) before joining the Moscow Art Theatre's First Studio.

Studio on Povarskaya Street

The idea of having laboratories for artistic exploration and using improvisation to experiment came from Meyerhold. The actual first studio of the Moscow Art Theatre was created in 1905 and called the Studio on Povarskaya Street. Its goal was to experiment with emerging nonrealistic writing and theatrical styles, beginning with symbolism. Meyerhold was the artistic director with Stanislavsky as co-artistic director. This studio was not considered a success and was closed within a year, but in it Meyerhold initiated the practice of improvisatory exploration that later became a key tool in Stanislavsky's System for both training and rehearsal techniques.

The First Studio—Sulerzhitsky, Stanislavsky, and Yoga

Stanislavsky was disappointed by the seasoned actors performing in the company of the Art Theatre as most had rejected his theories and experimental methods. It was, however, to be expected. They had already achieved success and fame with the older methods, and it seemed unnecessary to change or give them up. On the brighter side, the younger generation were enthusiastic and eager to try the new approaches. In 1911, Stanislavsky decided to work with this younger generation in a lab called the Theatre Studio, which he created with Sulerzhitsky (after the creation of additional studios this was called the First Studio. Although technically it was the second laboratory to be created, the earlier studio had not lasted, and therefore this was the primary training studio at this time, thus the First Studio.)

Stanislavsky met Leopold Antonovich Sulerzhitsky (1872–1916) while on holiday in Finland. Sulerzhitsky, or "Suler," as he was called, was a friend of the playwright Maxim Gorky, who had introduced him to Stanislavsky. Suler was also a disciple of the novelist Leo Tolstoy and had assisted him with the resettlement of the Doukhobors[32] to Canada at the turn of the century. Sulerzhitsky was profoundly

---

[31] Other spellings of Vakhatangov's first name Yvgeny or even Evgeni.

[32] The Doukhobors were a small religious sect of Christian pacifists who practiced communism and who had been brutally persecuted by the czarist government. Even after their relocation to Canada, they were persecuted because they didn't believe the government had authority over them, particularly with regard to sending their members to war, or supporting war in any way, or sending their children to traditional schools. After their move to Canada, they protested government war measures with naked protests, taking off their clothes and burning them along with their possessions and even their homes. Much like the native people in both Canada and the United States, the Doukhobor children were taken away and put in special schools, where they were also purportedly abused. George Woodcock and Julie Rak. *Doukhobors. The Canadian Encyclopedia* online, www.thecanadianencyclopedia.ca/en/article/doukhobors/ (article published 8/22/13; last edited 12/17/13, accessed 6/13/14), 2tp://www.thecanadianencyclopedia.ca/en/article/doukhobors/.

influenced by the Doukhobors (a name meaning "spirit-wrestlers," which was slung at them as an insult and then adopted by them). They were known for being pacifists and living communally, a belief echoed by Suler and Tolstoy. They carried Bibles but favored psalms and songs as the transmission of its ideas. They also practiced yogic exercises such as meditation and pranayama.

> Every morning, Suler recalled, the Doukhobors performed a meditation on their daily activities. . . . These yogic exercise produced a calm and a certainty of purpose. The Doukhobors had become aware of Prana, a Hindu concept of the invisible life force that streams through all living things. Stanislavsky understood the importance of Suler's description. Prana was another name for the Creative State of Mind. A spring had been triggered in his imagination. Stanislavsky had found the beginnings of his System.[33]

Suler's influence upon Stanislavsky and the early development of the System was profound. Stanislavsky found in Suler a soul-companion in art and brought him to Moscow, financially supported him, and also made him his personal assistant for the 1906–1907 production of *The Drama of Life* by Knut Hamsun. Suler influenced Stanislavsky partly through his interest in Eastern philosophy, and in particular yoga. The period marking the turn of the nineteenth to the twentieth centuries was laden with interest in India, China, and Japan and their ancient cultural ideas and practices, which were considered mysticism. Madam Helena Blavatsky had founded the Theosophical Society in 1875 in New York with the expressed purpose to introduce and elucidate Western people in occultism. Many European intellectuals were investigating the subject, and Stanislavsky was no exception. In *Stanislavsky in Focus*, Carnicke states that "by 1911, at the First Studio, [Stanislavsky] and Sulerzhitsky were regularly using exercises based in Yoga."[34] Specific days were given over to focus on specific acting elements, and exercises were written in a book that was always laid out in the studio. After experiencing them, teachers and students could write comments in the book about the exercises.

Stanislavsky's interest in yoga may come as a surprise to many US actors and teachers; however, a close examination of the early period of his work will reveal that his experiments with hatha yoga, which includes but is not limited to the physical postures, or asanas; raja yoga, which translates as king yoga and includes all eight limbs of yoga, with particular emphasis on meditation; and pranayama, which has to do with the life force activated and strengthened through disciplined breathing techniques. These branches of yoga formed the basis for many of his acting exercises. Some of those with roots in yoga include

Figure 20.4 Leopold Sulerzhitsky.
Photo: Courtesy of the Moscow Arts Theatre Museum

---

[33] Mel Gordon, *The Stanislavsky Technique: Russia*. (New York: Applause, New York, 1987), 31–32.
[34] Carnicke, *Stanislavsky in Focus*, p. 141.

relaxation, concentration, controlling the flow of muscular energy, communication/communion, prana—willful sending of rays of energy between actors; and visualization—the creation of a film of mental image-pictures.

Nevertheless, Stanislavsky saw no division between the body, mind, and soul of the actor and continued to work toward the realization of a system that would bring together all of the actor's creative resources—material and spiritual. The period of experimentation at the First Studio added new exercises and elements to the developing System: *circles of attention* to improve concentration, *adaptation* to keep the actor alive in the moment and in honest communion with partners and surroundings, and the sending of rays of energy called *prana* to partners and the audience. As with any new theory and practice, strong opposition arose among the ranks of the Moscow Art Theatre actors and its codirector, Danchenko. At one point Stanislavsky threatened to resign unless his System was accepted.

Sulerzhitsky's untimely death on December 17, 1916, at age 44, completely shattered Stanislavsky, who felt he had not only lost a dear friend but the sole person who had completely understood and supported his quest for the System.

> "When Stanislavsky explains that his goal is 'to teach [the student] the laws of correct breathing, the correct position of the body, concentration and watchful discrimination,' he implicitly refers to major tenets of Yoga: . . . He further stresses that these ideas pervade every aspect of his practice when he follows the above list with the bald statement, 'My whole system is based on this.'"
> —Sharon Marie Carnicke[35]

Vakhtangov (1883–1922) was Sulerzhitsky's pick for his heir apparent. Upon Suler's death, in 1916 Stanislavsky appointed Vakhtangov director of the First Studio.

Théodule-Armand Ribot and Affective Memory

Théodule Ribot (1839–1916) was a French psychologist from whom Stanislavsky borrowed the term *affective memory*. Ribot had written (*Les Maladies de la Mémoire* and *Les Maladies de la Volonté*) that our experiences left traces of emotions upon our memories and that feelings of past experiences could be revived. Having read Ribot's books, Stanislavsky saw in the writings an opportunity to experiment. He developed exercises, first experimenting upon himself and then with his actors. The idea was to find emotional experiences analogous to those of the character and then to dwell upon the sensory images of the past experience—i.e., sounds, tastes, tactile sensations, etc.—thereby evoking emotions by revisiting specific past experiences. This method was a memory of experiences, not just a memory of emotions. Stanislavsky observed that although the technique worked, the actors were pushing their emotions, producing a state of inner hysteria that could prove to be dangerous. He further observed that some were walking around in a semitrance state attempting to hold on to their feelings, others became emotionally self-indulgent and began to neglect proper speech and characterization.

In time, Stanislavsky came to abandon this direct approach to evoking emotions and turned to more indirect means. Instead, he incorporated the use of imagination and physical actions that evoke memory of emotions in the body rather than the memory of a specific traumatic event that may have prompted

---

[35]Carnicke, *Stanislavsky in Focus*, 143.

a previous emotional experience. Great controversy still surrounds the use of emotional memory to this day. Emotions can be evoked through imagination and other indirect means related to investment in and response to human behavior, but they may still indirectly stir emotional memories. As each human emotion has carved a recorded path through our mind's neural pathways and imprinted in our body, the stirring of any specific emotion may stimulate other related emotional memories. Consider if you feel a loss how that may remind you of other losses you have experienced. Emotional memory remains an important element of the System because it is an important element of human psychology and behavior. The question of its use is not whether or not it *should* be used but *how* to use it while maintaining artistic integrity, as well as mental and physical health. Toward the end of his life, Stanislavsky would come to answer these questions with still further experiments and discoveries, but he first set about organizing the various elements into a cohesive system.

> "Speech is music. Dialogue in a play is the melody, an opera or a symphony. Diction on stage is no less as difficult an art than singing and demands preparation and technique at virtuoso level."[36]
>
> —Konstantin Stanislavsky

The Laws of Speech

Stanislavsky had been severely criticized for his poor speech in the role of Salieri in *Mozart*, by Pushkin. He realized that his physical and vocal technique were inadequate for the role. This pained him deeply and he determined to explore and develop the actor's external (physical) technique in as great a depth as he had the internal. Stanislavsky had extensive training as a singer in his youth and had performed in operettas; now he was determined to work simultaneously on singing and speech:

> How good it would be if teachers of singing could, at the same time, teach speech, and teachers of speech could teach singing. But since this cannot be, let both kinds of specialists work together hand in hand.[37]

In 1915, he began to create exercises in vocal production, support, articulation, and projection specifically for the actor. He paid particular attention to stage speech, working extensively with the actors so that they were able to phrase their thoughts in logical sequences and understand the shifts and pauses that make stage speech clear, articulate, and naturally expressive.

A Systematized Approach

With such great talents as Richard Boleslavsky, Michael Chekhov, Maria Ouspenskaya, and Evgeny Vakhtangov, Stanislavsky remained encouraged and determined to push on with his experiments. The young actors of the First Studio were beginning to absorb the elements that he called the *psycho-technique*: concentration, communication, communion, visualization, imagination, emotional memory, etc. The results were becoming impressive, and his critics were beginning to take notice; however, what was needed was a more systematized approach.

---

[36] Stanislavsky, *An Actor's Work*, 398.
[37] Stanislavsky, *An Actor's Work*, 385.

As was his habit, Stanislavsky used himself and his own work on a role as experimentation for the development of the System. During the period between 1916 and 1920 he delved even more deeply into his approach and process with the intention to formulate the next phase of training for the actors at the studio. While working on the role of Famusov in the Russian Verse Classic *Woe from Wit*, by Griboyedov, he decided to organize the work into three distinct stages.[38] The first stage he called *The Period of Study*; the second, *The Period of Emotional Experience, or Living Through*; and the third, *The Period of Physical Embodiment*. We cannot convey the full complexities of working artistically through this book, because each experience involves the nuances of each actor and teacher or director. So Stanislavsky struggled to convey simply the multifaceted art of professional actor training. It is important to note that during this early period of Stanislavsky's formulation of the System he was still primarily teaching how to work from the inner experience to the outer expression; although in his own acting he often found the character's external behavior first and only later was able to justify and connect it to an inner motive. In reference to this contradiction, Jean Benedetti writes,

> Stanislavsky the actor was not necessarily restricted to the System he taught. His own working method was more complex than his theories, and his response to his own needs as a performer inevitably pushed him beyond anything he had formulated as a teacher.[39]

1. **The Period of Study** consisted of an in-depth exploration of the *Given Circumstances* of the play and required that the actors sometimes sit around the table for many months. (An approach he later rejected as he came to realize that the actors understood everything, but when they went onstage they could do nothing.) During the initial period, the emphasis was on searching for the *inner spiritual life* of the character, its *soul*. Then the actor was to examine the play's plot and structure and write down the *active facts* of each event. The aim of this phase of the work was for the actor to arrive at the state of "*I am*," a state wherein the actor feels that she exists and is "*present*" in role; also called the state of "*I exist*" and "*I live*."
2. **The Period of Emotional Experience, Living Through** required that the actor begin to live in the role as the character, to become an actor of the School of Living Experience. This period was to be based entirely on *action*. At that time, Stanislavsky divided action into *internal and external action*, inner actions being composed of impulses, desires, wants, and needs. This came to be known as the psycho-technique. (Again, Stanislavsky later realized his mistake by dividing the inner, subjective experience of the actor from its physical expression and reversed his thinking to eventually unite the two halves into one organic whole, or psychophysical action.) The script was scored for actions and objectives based on the character's needs and desires; i.e., "I want to make him understand me," etc.
3. **The Period of Physical Embodiment** focused on the actor's creation of the inner life of the role to be expressed through voice, speech, and behavior (physical

---

[38] Konstantin Stanislavsky, *Creating a Role*, trans., Elizabeth Reynolds Hapgood (New York: Routledge/Theatre Arts Books, 1961, repr., 2003), v.
[39] Benedetti, *Stanislavski*, 201.

actions). All aspects of physical characterization were considered: walk, gait, movement, and gesture.

> "Alas for the actor if there is a split between body and soul, between feelings and words, between internal and external action and movements. . . . If the actor's physical instrument falsifies and distorts the expression of feelings, it is like a melody played on an instrument which is out of tune. Moreover, the more truthful the feeling, and the more spontaneous its expression, the more painful will be the dissonance and discord."[40]
> —Konstantin Stanislavsky

Richard Boleslavsky (February 4, 1889–January 17, 1937)

Richard Boleslavsky is the stage name for Polish-born Boleslaw Ryszard Srzednicki. He became an actor of the Moscow Art Theatre's First Studio under Stanislavsky in 1908 and later assistant to its director, Leopold Sulerzhitsky. He played Laertes in Gordon Craig's famous MAT production of *Hamlet*.

Boleslavsky immigrated to the United States in the 1920s and assisted the Moscow Art Theatre with their 1922 tour of America. Shortly after the MAT tour, he gave a series of lectures on Stanislavsky at the Princess Theatre. In 1923, he started the American Laboratory Theatre and is considered the first teacher of an early version of Stanislavsky's acting techniques in the United States.

Some students of the Lab that went on to teach acting include **Lee Strasberg** (founding member of the Group Theatre but best known as director of the Actor's Studio from 1951 to 1982 and creator of Method acting) and **Stella Adler** (an actor also in the Group Theatre, she created the Stella Adler Studio of Acting, which is now part of NYU's Tisch School of the Arts).

Boleslavsky left the Lab for Hollywood, where his film *Les Miserables* received an Oscar nomination for Best Picture. He is perhaps best known for his seminal book on acting, *Acting: The First Six Lessons*, published by Theatre Arts Books in 1933. He died of a heart attack in 1937 at age 48.

Maria Alekseyevna Ouspenskaya (July 29, 1876–December 3, 1949)

She was selected to be in the first group of actors of the First Studio of the Moscow Art Theatre and later taught there. In 1922 she toured Europe and the United States with MAT and shortly after, defected and immigrated to the U.S.

Her MAT contemporary **Richard Boleslavky** got her work on the faculty of the American Laboratory Theatre, but in 1929 she started her own theatre school, the School of Dramatic Art. She acted on Broadway and had a busy Hollywood career, finding a niche as a wise foreign woman in many films. She was a heavy smoker, fell asleep with a cigarette, and died three days later in 1949 from the burns.

---

[40]Quoted in Allen, *Stanislavsky for Beginners*, 89.

> ### Revolution and Theatre, Part II: Communisim and Civil War
>
> In February 1917, prompted by food shortages, inequality, corruption, and the failure and mismanagement of the Russian army during WWI, riots erupted. Tsar Nicholas II was forced to abdicate and put on house arrest in March. By October, the Bolshevik Party, headed by Vladimir Illich Lenin (flanked by Leon Trotsky) seized power.
>
> Following the tsar's abdication, the Moscow Art Theatre had scheduled to perform *The Cherry Orchard* on the twenty-sixth of that month. It was not at all certain how the play would be received, as it depicted the bourgeois life of the landed gentry that was now under attack by the Bolshevik uprising. The performance proceeded in spellbound silence as the audience respectively observed the poetic death of old Russia as symbolized with the death of Firs the old servant, and the chopping down of the beautiful orchard. The performance was followed by a thunderous ovation.
>
> Revolution was followed by five years of civil war between the Red Army loyal to the Bolsheviks and the counterrevolutionary Whites loyal to the tsar. The war did not abate even when in July 1918, Tsar Nicholas II, the last Romanov monarch, was executed along with his wife and five children. The economy collapsed, and the necessities of life became scarce. The times were full of hardship and loss.
>
> Stanislavsky did all he could to keep the company going, and there were rumors that the company might have to close. The civil war had split the company in two, as some of its lead actors had been on tour and were cut off from Moscow. For five years the company could only stage one new production. Many thought that the Art Theatre had become a relic from the past and should die; however, Lenin insisted, "If there is one theatre from the past, which we must save and preserve—it is, of course, the art theatre!"[41]
>
> In December 1919, Russian theatres were reorganized, and the Art Theatre was designated a state Academic theatre. As a state theatre, it acquired official status and therefore was fully independent and could receive state subsidy.

The Search for New Theatrical Forms

The immediate years that followed the revolution saw a resurgence of theatrical activity. Stanislavsky was busy with the development of new audiences and new studios, and many members of MAT were searching for new theatrical forms.

Stanislavsky and Vsevolod Meyerhold

Vsevolod Meyerhold (1874–1940) was born Karl Kasimir Theodor but also changed his name for the stage. Like Stanislavsky, he was from a wealthy merchant family in the liquor industry and was inspired by a production of *Othello*—only in this case it was Stanislavsky's famous performance and production. This inspired him to study

---

[41]Quoted in Allen, *Stanislavsky for Beginners*, 94.

20 THE EVOLVING STANISLAVSKY SYSTEM

acting and join the Moscow Philharmonic Society, studying acting under Nemirovich-Danchenko. He was one of the original actors hand-picked by Nemirovich-Danchenko and Stanislavsky to join the original company of the Moscow Art Theatre in 1898.

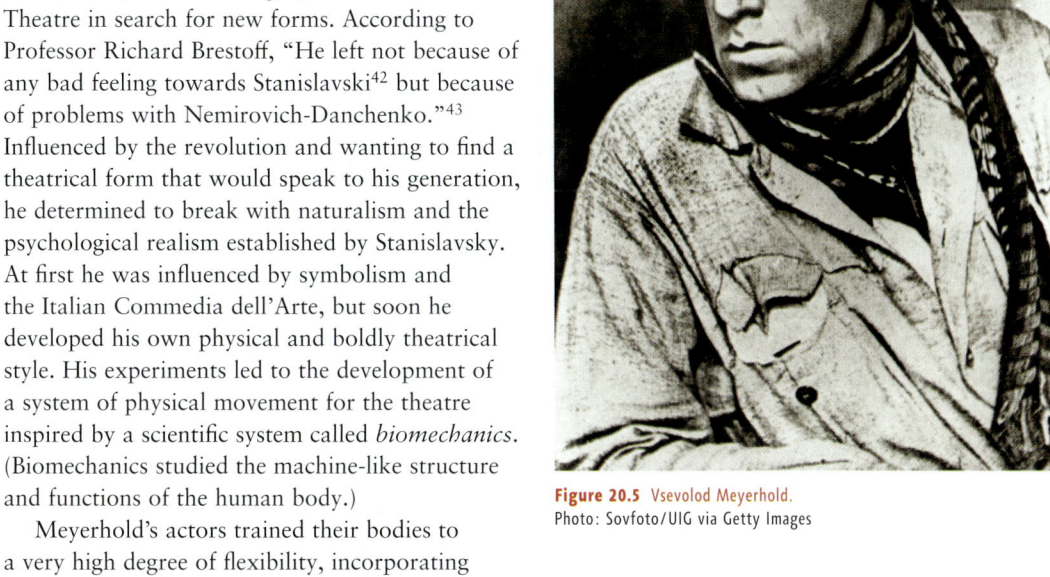

Meyerhold was Stanislavsky's assistant until 1902, when, like Vakhtangov, he left the Art Theatre in search for new forms. According to Professor Richard Brestoff, "He left not because of any bad feeling towards Stanislavski[42] but because of problems with Nemirovich-Danchenko."[43] Influenced by the revolution and wanting to find a theatrical form that would speak to his generation, he determined to break with naturalism and the psychological realism established by Stanislavsky. At first he was influenced by symbolism and the Italian Commedia dell'Arte, but soon he developed his own physical and boldly theatrical style. His experiments led to the development of a system of physical movement for the theatre inspired by a scientific system called *biomechanics*. (Biomechanics studied the machine-like structure and functions of the human body.)

Figure 20.5 Vsevolod Meyerhold.
Photo: Sovfoto/UIG via Getty Images

Meyerhold's actors trained their bodies to a very high degree of flexibility, incorporating acrobatics, mask, clown, Commedia dell'Arte, pantomime, Japanese Kabuki and Noh, and he created rhythmic movement in synchronized patterns called *plastique*. His 1922 production of the *Magnanimous Cuckold* was designed to express *plastique forms in space*, thus establishing him as the foremost avant-garde theatrical director of Russia in the 1920s and 1930s. His sets were unrealistic and designed to resemble giant machines. He was the first to bring this new artistic genre of *Constructivism* to the theatre. Meyerhold theorized that by working from the *outside in* (in direct opposition to Stanislavsky's *inside-out* approach at that time), content could be expressed through abstract movement and gestures. Gestures, he proposed, could evoke and convey emotions and made psychological introspection of the actor's personal experiences unnecessary.

Meyerhold's impact on the international avant-garde theatre is still present. Many of his theatrical inventions are misattributed to other artists, but his techniques of biomechanics are taught around the world.

Even in this new System of actor training and performance seemingly so different from Stanislavsky's System, the influence of Stanislavsky is still evident. Brestoff: "The influence of Stanislavski is clear. Meyerhold's 'intention' is like Stanislavsky's

---

[42](Authors' footnote, not Brestoff's) *Stanislavsky* is sometimes transliterated from the Russian alphabet using an *i* and sometimes ending in a *y*, so you will see it in English print spelled both ways.
[43]Richard Brestoff, *The Great Acting Teachers and Their Methods* (Lyme, NH: Smith and Kraus, 1995), 68.

'objective,' and his 'realization' is like Stanislavsky's 'action.'"[44] He remained connected to Stanislavsky. Again Brestoff: "While Meyerhold abandoned realistic theatre, he never renounced Stanislavki. Two years before his death, he proclaimed himself still a student of that great man."[45] Stanislavsky also remained dedicated to Meyerhold and learned from him as well. Stanislavsky and Meyerhold, who had similar roots at the Moscow Art Theatre but traveled in opposite artistic directions, came to value and incorporate many of each other's ideas in the latter part of their careers. Today at the Moscow Art Theatre School, students study both Stanislavsky's techniques and Meyerhold's in the same school.

Craig, Stanislavsky and Sulerzhitsky Symbolist's *Hamlet*
Stanislavsky had met English director/designer Gordon Craig through the famous modern dancer Isadora Duncan. In 1910, as part of his attempts to move his work and the System outside of realism, Stanislavsky engaged Gordon Craig to collaborate with him on a symbolist production of Shakespeare's *Hamlet*. Craig was the overall artistic director but collaborated with Stanislavsky and Sulerzhitsky (who were both listed as stage directors for the production, which in Russia involves significant work with the actors). The three men collaborated on blocking, and Stanislavsky contributed research to the production design concept, but Craig was responsible for the overarching vision.

Laurence Senelick, in his *Gordon Craig's Moscow "Hamlet": A Reconstruction*, references a conversation between Craig and Stanislavsky, in which Craig states: "I want between *Hamlet* and all the rest of the world that there should be not a single point of agreement, not the smallest hope as to the possibility of a reconciliation. I could see in *Hamlet* the history of theatre. In *Hamlet* all that is living in the theatre is struggling with those dead customs that want to crush the theatre."[46] According to the observation of Japanese director and critic Kaoru Osanai (1881–1928), Craig staged the entire play using only a series of screens that could be reconfigured to create different shapes for scenes such as corridors, barriers, and triangle pillars. They were painted differently on each side but within a similar hue—pale yellow or gilded gold. In scene 2, the marriage celebration of Claudius to Hamlet's mother, Gertrude, he staged as though it were all in Hamlet's mind,[47] a choice that later influenced Michael Chekhov's production of *Hamlet*. Stanislavsky worked on the acting through the application of his System.[48] In this world-renowned production, the System took flight through a symbolist style.

While Stanislavsky brought the System to Craig's work, Craig brought improvisational ideas into MAT. In the middle of rehearsals, Stanislavsky contracted typhoid fever and thus the opening was delayed until 1912. For the first time in the Moscow Art Theatre, they had closed rehearsals—members of MAT outside the *Hamlet* company were not allowed to observe, as they had been so critical of Stanislavsky's work. One of the reasons this production is so important to theatre

---

[44]Ibid., 74.
[45]Ibid., 75.
[46]Laurence Senelick. *Gordon Craig's Moscow "Hamlet": A Reconstruction* (London: Praeger, 1982), 69.
[47]Kaoru Osanai and Andrew T. Tsubaki, "Gordon Craig's Production of *Hamlet* at the Moscow Art Theatre," *Educational Theatre Journal* 20, no. 4 (December 1968): 586–593. Published by The Johns Hopkins University Press.
[48]Benedetti, *Stanislavski*, 179.

history is that Craig was able to realize very few of his designs, as most theatres could not afford the scale of his vision. The production was not immediately accepted in Russia but became renowned around the world as a hallmark production of the twentieth-century theatre; however, neither Craig nor Stanislavsky was satisfied. Some actors already mentioned that were involved with this production are Richard Boleslavsky as Laertes, Olga Knipper (Anton Chekhov's wife) as Gertrude, Vasili Kachalov was Hamlet. Vakhtangov had a small role. According to Franc Chamberlain, Michael "Chekhov's first role at the MAT was as a crowd member in the riot scene"[49] of Craig's *Hamlet*.

The Third Studio: Evgeny Vakhtangov, Fantastic Realism, Constructivism

Figure 20.6 Evgeny Vakhtangov.
Photo: Courtesy of Arsis Design

In 1920, The Third Studio was created and headed by Evgeny Vakhtangov (1883–1922) to explore his theatrical style of Fantastic Realism. That brought together the vivid theatricality of Meyerhold with the spiritually alive acting style of Stanislavsky.

Evgeny Vakhtangov and his Third Studio play an important role in the development of the Stanislavsky System. Vakhtangov, the leader of the Third Studio and a graduate of Stanislavsky's First Studio, was perhaps on the forefront of a search for new forms. After the revolution he wanted to depart from realism and search for a more vivid and intentional theatricality. He chose to stage *Eric XIV* by Strindberg with the intent of experimenting with the grotesque. Stanislavsky later wrote that the use of nonrealistic makeup and staging was not enough to create the grotesque, as there was no inner justification, no inner truth, on the part of the actors for the exaggerated style and that the best example of the grotesque that he had seen was in Salvini's Othello. His reproach, however, went on:

---

[49]Franc Chamberlain. *Michael Chekhov* (London: Routledge, 2004), 8.

Figure 20.7 The Cubist set design for Vakhtangov's production of *Princess Turandot*, by Carlo Gozzi.
Photo: Courtesy of Arsis Design

You do not even attempt to study the approach to the superconscious (wherein grotesque is concealed) through the conscious, a study that is especially imperative in the case of grotesque.

A grotesque, so what of it, you say? Surely it can't have become so degenerated, simplified, cheapened and demeaned that it is now nothing more than an outward exaggeration devoid of an inner justification?

No, a real grotesque is the outward, most vivid and bold justification of an enormous inner content, exhaustive to the point of overstatement. Not only must the human passions in all their embracing component elements be felt and lived through, they must be condensed and their manifestation made visible, irresistibly expressive, daring and bold, verging almost on caricature. A grotesque cannot be vague and difficult to understand. It must be definite and clear to the point of brazenness."[50]

Vakhtangov must have taken Stanislavsky's words to heart; his next and most famous production of Gozzi's *Princess Turandot*, staged in 1922, won wide theatrical acclaim from audiences, critics, and Stanislavsky. Vakhtangov had worked meticulously on every detail of the production. He insisted that the actors live the inner spiritual life of the characters in the most vivid artistic, scenic form. He created a completely fantastic world. The set was of a cubist design, and the actors had to master moving among a world of odd shapes and forms. Every gesture, thought, and expression was rehearsed exactingly.

Vakhtangov was too ill to attend the final dress rehearsal, and during one of the intermissions Stanislavsky telephoned a message to him:

> There was an outburst of delight. The curtain was raised. People called out: "We don't want to go!" . . . Congratulations! Well done![51]

Bertolt Brecht, a great admirer of Meyerhold, was also particularly inspired by this production, considering it a merger of the techniques of Stanislavsky and Meyerhold in terms of powerful acting within a vivid and politically charged form:

> In this regard it is very important to consider the influence of Meyerhold

---

[50]Quoted in Korneva, *Konstantin Stanislavsky, Selected Works*, 235.
[51]Ibid., 232–234.

on Brecht, and not only of Meyerhold but also of Vakhtangov and his "Princess Turandot," of which Brecht thought very highly. . . . Without this improvisation theatre, one could scarcely imagine either Piscator[52] or Brecht."[53]

Vakhtangov's search for a new and vivid theatrical form that still encompassed the deep spiritual inner life of the System resulted in the theatrical style of Fantastic Realism. The Third Studio of the Moscow Art Theatre was renamed the Vakhtangov Theatre and continues to this day to produce plays in the form of Fantastic Realism.

The members of Habima Theatre came to Moscow from all over Russia but wanted to established a Jewish Theatre in Palestine. They wanted only the best teachers and sought out the Moscow Art Theatre. Stanislavsky appointed Vakhtangov to the project. For Habima he directed *The Dybbuk* in 1922 and then taught in their studio in Moscow. Their goal was always Palestine, where they eventually moved to set up a national Jewish theatre.[54]

> ### A Story of Vakhtangov and Michael Chekhov: Master and Slave
>
> Michael Chekhov (1891–1955) and Evgeny Vakhtangov were the two leading actors of the First Studio, and they were rivals and friends. At times, they were even cast to share the same role, as in *The Deluge*. Even in the games they played as roommates on tour, they gleaned understanding that fed back into their action.
>
> In his book *Michael Chekhov*, Franc Chamberlain recounts a well-known story: Chekhov and Vakhtangov played a version of Master and Slave where the slave was an ape.
>
> They took it in turns to play the ape, which had to carry out all of the household chores and
>
> **Figure 20.8** Mikhail (Michael) Aleksandrovich Chekhov.
> Photo: Fine Art Images/Heritage Images/Getty Images

---

[52]Erwin Piscator was a German director who sought to use theatre to politically educate audiences and call them to political action. Many of his techniques were later incorporated into the work of Bertolt Brecht and commonly misattributed as being invented by Brecht.
[53]Nance Weber and Hubert Heinen, *Bertolt Brecht: Political Theory and Literary Practice* (Atlanta: University of Georgia Press, 2010), 84.
[54]Andrei Malaev-Babel, *Yevgeny Vakhtangov: A Critical Portrait* (New York: Routledge, 2013), 195–197.

> whatever else the master wanted him to do. The ape was to do most things on all fours. If the master was displeased with the ape, then he could beat him. One day, however, they took it too far, and the game ended in a fight in which Chekhov lost a tooth! Chekhov was later to be critical of how actors at the Studio believed it was necessary to lose themselves in the part, and this is a good example of two of the company's leading actors playing it "for real." Both Chekhov and Vakhtangov were to become concerned in their work to find an appropriate physical, emotional, and psychological balance in the performance without losing the sense that they were making theatre.[55]

The Second Moscow Art Theatre: Michael Chekhov

Michael Chekhov was a successful comic actor at the Maly Theatre in Moscow when invited by Stanislavsky to audition for the First Studio of MAT. He began to study the System under Evgeny Vakhtangov. He also worked closely with Stanislavsky. Stanislavsky considered Michael Chekhov, the nephew of the playwright Anton Chekhov, to be "his most brilliant student."[56] As any top student, he absorbed all of Stanislavsky's early ideas on the System but also evolved them and developed his own unique approaches. His presence at the studio led to some important developments in Stanislavsky's System.

During Michael Chekhov's tenure with the Moscow Art Theatre he was one of its principal and most popular actors and was also a leading actor for the First Studio, rivaling Vakhtangov, his first MAT teacher. His first role at MAT was as a crowd member in a riot scene in Craig and Stanislavsky's *Hamlet*, and after that he went on to have many acclaimed leading and smaller roles.

Two of Chekhov's greatest artistic strengths, his imagination and his sense of humor, also presented challenges. He was criticized when his imagination led him to create vivid characters beyond the original bounds of the play. While this often won him personal praise, it did not necessarily fit the role of that character in the overall play or production created by the rest of the company. The Moscow Art Theatre was committed to working with contemporary playwrights, most of whom were in residence during their productions, and respect for the playwright was paramount. In the improvisatory techniques employed at the studio, he often went in directions so far from the character's objective that it no longer made sense for the play or the other characters. As a teacher, he later developed structures around such improvisations that would mitigate this issue.[57] Additionally, while working on MAT's production of Molière's comedy *The Imaginary Invalid*, "Chekhov was criticized for having too much fun with the role and Chekhov himself describes how the fun, which started out as creative exploration, ended by undermining the performance."[58]

While Stanislavsky recognized his great talent and often praised his performances, during his participation in the First Studio he and Stanislavsky also differed on

---

[55]Chamberlain, *Michael Chekhov*, 11.
[56]Quoted in Mel Gordon's introduction to *On the Technique of Acting*, by Michael Chekhov, revised by Mala Powers. (New York: HarperPerennial, 1991), x.
[57]Chamberlain, *Michael Chekhov*, 11–12.
[58]Ibid.

20 THE EVOLVING STANISLAVSKY SYSTEM

several points. One important point of disagreement was the use of *affective memory*. Early on in Chekhov's training at the First Studio, Stanislavsky gave an assignment to re-create an event from his personal life. Chekhov reenacted the death and funeral of his father. Stanislavsky praised him only to find out later that Chekhov's father, although ill was still very much alive. Stanislavsky was initially very angry, and Chekhov was reprimanded and asked to leave the class because of his "overheated imagination."[59] He objected to Stanislavsky's use of an actor's personal experiences in the creation of the role. Chekhov felt that the key to characterization lay in the development of imagination. However, Stanislavsky learned from every positive and negative experience. This incident may have been a factor, along with other issues he encountered with affective memory, because Stanislavsky later abandoned the direct affective memory approach to emotions in favor of imagination and physical actions.

In 1915 Chekhov, like Meyerhold, founded his own studio outside the Moscow Art Theatre and auditioned and selected actors to experiment with using a collective unconscious means in an attempt to achieve a "reincarnation" into character. Stanislavsky was not without his interest and investigation into the spiritual source of yoga; however, his approach to actor training was primarily based in logical and practical means of application. By contrast, Chekhov's approach was more mystical. He believed that the actor must "go beyond the playwright or play"[60] in the creation of character.

In 1918, Chekhov's wife had divorced him and took his daughter. He had a nervous breakdown. He became increasingly distraught and paranoid, prompting a deeply concerned Stanislavsky to send psychologists and doctors to his aid. According to Mel Gordon's introduction to the second release of Chekhov's book *To the Actor*, under the title *On the Technique of Acting*, by Mala Powers:

> It was his encounter with Hindu philosophy and especially with Rudolf Steiner's Anthroposophy that altered Chekhov's psychic condition. In fact, Chekhov's passionate investigation of Steiner's "spiritual science" filled a dangerous void in his creative world. It unblocked his choking emotional life.[61]

Chekhov's many criticisms and open defiance of Stanislavsky, who had requested that his work at the First Studio be kept secret, led to Chekhov's publishing of some of Stanislavsky's techniques without permission. He thus angered the master and his fellow actors. Yet, in spite of this serious breach of ethics, Stanislavsky was able to forgive him. Shortly after the death of Vakhtangov in 1922, Stanislavsky offered him directorship of the First Studio, which under his leadership evolved into the Second Moscow Art Theatre in 1924.

During the 1924–1925 season of the Second Moscow Art Theatre, Michael Chekhov directed and acted the leading role in an acclaimed production of *Hamlet*. According to Franc Chamberlain in his book *Michael Chekhov*, "Chekhov chose not to have another actor play the ghost but to use his imagination to project the ghost outside of himself and then respond to it. This was so successful that some members of the audience claimed to be able to see the ghost. . . . In this way, Chekhov was attempting to solve one of the key problems of non-naturalistic theatre of the late

---

[59]Quoted in Gordon, introduction to *On the Technique of Acting*, xiii.
[60]Ibid., xii.
[61]Ibid., xv.

nineteenth and early twentieth centuries: how to stage the supernatural."[62] Franc goes he goes on to say,

> Despite the acclaim Chekhov received for *Hamlet*, however, it was the method of staging the ghost and his innovative rehearsal practices that attributed to his reputation as someone with "mystical tendencies," a dangerous charge in the Soviet Union. In 1927, there was a conflict with the Second MAT and 16 members of the company quit in protest at Chekhov's approach. What were the kinds of things that upset them? That Chekhov had them juggle balls while rehearsing in order to get a sense of rhythm and ensemble, and also that he was conducting experiments with archetypical images in order to approach the character's ego.[63]

When his experiments fell under the all-watchful eye of the Marxist revisionists, he was denounced in 1927 and branded as idealistic, alien, and reactionary; all very dangerous accusations, which indicated that he was slated for liquidation. In 1928, he left the Moscow Art Theatre and exiled himself to Germany.

He continued to teach and perform for seven years all over Europe, where he founded a studio in Devon, England. He moved to the United States, when tensions in Europe started to mount leading up to WWII, and created a studio in Connecticut. Chekhov borrowed heavily from the Stanislavsky System in developing his own unique actor training system. He sometimes used Stanislavsky's techniques as originally taught to him, sometimes adapted them, and at other times developed original approaches focused on acting elements he thought the Stanislavsky System did not cover. However, actors learning what is now called the Chekhov technique are still learning many of the basics of the Stanislavsky System as part of their foundation technique.

A Story of Vakhtangov and Michael Chekhov: Pool Shark

Another great story that relates to the shaping of acting technique through their playful relationships comes from Mel Gordon in *The Stanislavsky Technique: Russia*. He describes Michael Chekhov and Vakhtangov on a First Studio summer tour:

> The two of them were playing billiards. Each unable to sink even one pool ball in the pocket, they grew frustrated and agreed to call it a night. Suddenly, Vakhtangov announced, "Watch this!" Changing his entire physical stance and attitude, Vakhtangov sank ball after ball while Chekhov watched in amazement. After Vakhtangov finally missed a shot, a startled Chekhov asked how such prowess was possible. Vakhtangov replied that he decided to imagine that he was the greatest pool player ever, taking on his posture, movements and way of thinking. Vakhtangov explained that he himself could never play billiards as brilliantly as his character.[64]

---

[62]Chamberlain, *Michael Chekhov*, 18.
[63]Ibid., 19.
[64]Mel Gordon, *The Stanislavsky Technique: Russia* (New York: Applause Theatre Books, 1987), 77.

> This story demonstrates something that Vakhtangov, Chekhov, and Stanislavsky were all searching for: the complete commitment of mind, body, emotions to an action. Grotowsky calls this a total act of theatre.

1916—Stanislavsky's Self-Proclaimed Tragedy: The Village of Stepanchikovo

Stanislavsky wanted to restage an adaptation of Dostoevsky's story "The Village of Stepanchikovo," which he had staged in 1891. His critics had proclaimed that the Art Theatre was no longer relevant, and he desperately desired to answer the criticism by interpreting the story as a contemporary microcosm of Russia. He also saw the production as an excellent opportunity to use the System in the re-creation of the role of Colonel Rostanev. The work on the role went poorly. He could not seem to find the character within himself, nor could he intuitively experience the living of the character's inner life as he had done before. The rehearsal period became interminable, and the production costs were exceeding budget. When 156 rehearsals were reached, an unprecedented number, even for the Moscow Art Theatre, which was known for its long rehearsal periods, Nemirovich-Danchenko had reached the end of his patience, stepped in, and took over the rehearsals. Danchenko's interpretation of the character of Rostanev was at complete odds to Stanislavsky's ideas. Stanislavsky, the consummate professional, did not openly protest with Danchenko but painfully attempted to adapt to the new direction; however, he could not. Finally, confused and deeply depressed over his inability to rework the role and find the character after so many subsequent rehearsals, he was removed from the part, Danchenko replacing him with the actor Massalitinov at a dress rehearsal. Stanislavsky was so deeply hurt that he vowed to never act in a new play with the Art Theatre again, and he remained true to his word, calling this episode his personal tragedy. Under the new direction by Danchenko, the play was not a success and did not achieve the desired result of updating the theatre's repertoire.

A Reversal of Thought

Life and its disappointments, no matter how bleak, can also at times leave a glimmer of hope and open new doors. During the seemingly unfortunate period while working on *Stepanchikovo*, Stanislavsky came to a reversal of his thinking concerning the use of emotional memory. Previously he had assumed that stage action, like human action, must arise first from an emotional state, thus the emphasis on the use of the actor's personal emotional experiences as a prerequisite to action had been practiced. Instead, now the analysis period of rehearsal placed emphasis on finding the creative objectives of the role through conscious means and the use of actions; i.e., active verbs to evoke and bring about the unconscious storehouse of the actor's personal memories that were analogous to the role:

> Only the creative objectives of a role should be conscious, the means by which they are attained unconscious. The unconscious through the conscious. That is the watchword which should guide our coming work. (K.S. Archive, No. 1353.)[65]

---

[65] Quoted in Benedetti, *Stanislavski*, 217.

> Put yourself in the circumstances of the character as portrayed and put the questions: what should I do in such a circumstance, what do I want, where am I going; stimulate your will. Answer them with verbs which express actions not with nouns which express ideas and concepts. (K.S. Archive No. 1388/1.)[66]

In his account of the events of Stanislavsky's reversal of thinking, Jean Benedetti in his biography of Stanislavsky states that the cast was given exercises to help them with the synthesis of the personal and the textual. He goes on to say that there is no suggestion of the premeditated use of emotional memory and that the personal experience is brought into play unconsciously. "Here," he states, "in embryo, is the System in its final form, the Method of Physical Action, which Stanislavski was to evolve in the last years of his life."[67]

Then another opportunity presented itself that was to have a strong impact on the development of the System, the creation and directorship of a new Opera Studio.

The Opera Studio
In his youth Stanislavsky had entertained the idea of becoming an opera singer, but his voice did not have the required strength. He did, however, for a time play in operettas and loved the genre. In the autumn of 1918 the Moscow Art Theatre was approached with a proposal to create a collaboration with the Bolshoi Opera. The idea was to train a new generation of singers in the System through the formation of an opera studio as proposed by Maria Malinovskaya, who was in charge of the Academic Theatres of Moscow. Stanislavsky cautiously agreed to take on the project.

His first observation was that the singers had no sense of the theatrical nor how to involve their movement and gesture in connection with the music. He saw this as a great opportunity to experiment further with the System and work to create a synthesis between the three. Stanislavsky worked slowly, and carefully chose characters and scenes from the Alexander Pushkin opera *Onegin* that he felt were best suited for the training. The singers worked on acting exercises and singing technique, and this had a profound influence on Stanislavsky's theories of *"tempo and rhythm."* Music is measured with numerous variations, which provide impetus for feelings and action. From his work with the Opera Studio he applied the new exercises to the actor training at the other studios.

> "Rhythm is the bridge between the inner experience and its physical expression."[68]
>
> —Sonia Moore

On March 5, 1921, Stanislavsky was given a new home at Number 6, Leontyevski Lane (in Soviet Russia, even housing was controlled and distributed). Adjacent to the family living quarters there was a ballroom with four sets of pillars. He had decided

---

[66]Ibid.
[67]Ibid., 217–218.
[68]Sonia Moore, *The Stanislavski System: The Professional Training of an Actor* (New York: Viking, 1965), 48.

to stage the entire opera with the students, and the ballroom provided a perfect setting. From that time on it became known as the Onegin Room.

Moscow Art Theatre and the System Abroad

The revolution and civil war that followed devoured the world of the Russian bourgeoisie. The intelligentsia that had made it possible for the Art Theatre to exist had all but been swept away by the tumult of change. Stanislavsky and Nemirovich had to face the fact that their repertoire of plays by Chekhov, Tolstoy, and others were no longer considered relevant to the new Russia. The Art Theatre came under considerable attack not only from its critics but also from some of its former leading actors like Vakhtangov and Meyerhold. But, what was there to do? New plays and playwrights could not be plucked off the trees. Government funding had ceased, and even with full houses the Theatre could only earn half of what its annual budget required. During this period of abrupt change and transition time and income was needed to deeply reflect upon its future. The directors decided that a tour abroad to Europe and the United States, should it prove financially successful, might provide a solution.

In 1922 Stanislavsky and his family boarded a train for Petrograd as the first leg of their journey to Berlin in order to make arrangements prior to the company's arrival. There he was greeted by Morris Gest, a Russian-born American émigré, who was making arrangements for the US tour. The repertoire would consist of the old productions, at this point much in need of rehearsal: *Tsar Fyodor*, *The Cherry Orchard*, *The Lower Depths*, and *Three Sisters*.

The tour included Prague and Paris and was beset with turmoil and obstacles. Stanislavsky was losing his voice due to stress and fatigue, sets and costumes were lost en route only to be recovered hours before the Paris performance; nevertheless, the company received overwhelming acclaim. Stanislavsky sent a telegram to Nemirovich from Paris: "Colossal success, general acclaim, fantastic press."[69] The Company of the Art Theatre departed France on December 27 and arrived in New York Harbor on January 3, 1923.

Upon Stanislavsky's arrival in the United States, a news reporter asked, "Why did you choose these particular plays for inclusion in the repertoire? I mean, *Tsar Fyodor, the Lower Depth* and Chekhov?" Stanislavsky later commented,

> I understood right away what was behind the question, recalling what had been said and written in Europe, that we had chosen *Tsar Fyodor* to show a weak Tsar, the *Lower Depths* to demonstrate the strength of the proletariat and Chekhov to illustrate the feebleness of the intelligentsia and the bourgeoisie.
>
> We've brought precisely the plays that were precisely asked for and no others, I answered firmly. And they were asked for because they are typical of an earlier period of the Art Theatre and because we performed them in Europe in 1906 and just recently. America wants to see what Europe already knows.[70]

The New York season opened on the eighth of January with *Tsar Fyodor* followed by the *Lower Depths*, *The Cherry Orchard*, and *Three Sisters*. It was a resounding

---

[69]Benedetti, *Stanislavsky*, 256.
[70]Ibid., 257.

artistic success. The impact of the Art Theatre upon audiences and the American theatrical profession was profound. Richard Boleslavsky had immigrated to the United States four years earlier, and he had been engaged to assist Stanislavsky with the tour. Boleslavsky had been given permission by Stanislavsky to give a series of lectures on the System that were published as *Acting, the First Six Lessons* in the October issue of *Theatre Arts Monthly*, later to be published in book form by Theatre Arts Books. Boleslavsky was an advocate of affective memory to stir emotions and had developed the technique beyond what he had previously learned from Stanislavsky. Stanislavsky, however, had abandoned his earlier use of direct emotional recall as unhealthy and was now experimenting with *physical actions* as the means for evoking emotions.

American theatre artists were deeply inspired by the high degree of ensemble playing and transformation into character achieved by the Moscow Art Theatre actors, and they wanted to learn the techniques of the System. Boleslavsky and Maria Ouspenskaya formed the American Laboratory Theatre, of which Lee Strasberg, Stella Adler, and Harold Clurman were founding members, and in 1931 Clurman, Strasberg, and Cheryl Crawford formed the Group Theatre. Although some objected to the use of affective memory as a primary tool, actors dredged up their personal experiences sometimes to excess. Phoebe Brand, an actress with the Group, said,

> I lent myself to it for a while—it is valuable for a young actor to go through it, but it is too subjective. It makes for a moody, personal, self-indulgent acting style. It assumes an actor is an emotional mechanism that can just be turned on. Emotion can't be worked for in that way—it is rather a result of truthful action in given circumstances. Lee [Strasberg] insisted on working each little moment of affective memory; we were always going backwards into our lives. It was painful to dig back. . . . Lee crippled a lot of people.[71]

In 1934 Stella Adler, who vehemently disagreed with Strasberg's approach, met with Stanislavsky in Paris. There she learned from the master his approach based on action and objectives and imagination. Upon her return to New York, Strasberg refused to listen, and this led to a split. About Strasberg's Method acting she wrote:

> It's polluted water, and yet Americans, typically, continue to drink it. Stanislavsky himself went beyond it. He was like a scientist conducting experiments in a lab; and his new research superseded his earlier ideas: the affective memory belonged to the older, worn-out ideas. But Lee always thought it was the cornerstone of the Method, and in this way he became a laughingstock.[72]

Such vehement criticism is not entirely fair, nor is it without basis, as Strasberg had studied with Boleslavsky and Ouspenskaya, both advocates of affective memory. Also, there was, during the Stalinist period, very little knowledge in America of the developments with the System in Russia. In his own defense Strasberg justifiably wrote:

---

[71]Quoted in Allen, *Stanislavsky for Beginners*, 107.
[72]Ibid.

20 THE EVOLVING STANISLAVSKY SYSTEM

> I do not believe that anyone has a right to talk of the Stanislavsky System. I have to therefore stress the use of the word "Method" as against "System" to suggest that while we obviously are influenced by Stanislavsky's ideas and practices, we used it within the limitations of our own knowledge and experience. . . . By saying that the Group Theatre used an adaptation of the Stanislavsky Method, we mean that we emphasized elements that he had not emphasized and disregarded elements which he might have considered of greater importance. Also, that in experimenting with some of the ideas propounded by Stanislavsky, we came to conclusions and practices of our own which he might not have agreed with. Personally, I am critical of the way in which Stanislavsky used his own work in some of his own productions, and therefore, I could not subscribe to many of the basic essentials of the ideas which he made use of. . . . In other words, while it would be true to say that we try to make use of the basic ideas of the Stanislavsky System, we do not feel it necessary to be limited just to those ideas or procedures that Stanislavsky himself used, nor would he necessarily agree with whatever is done in his name. I therefore think it theoretically wise and practically sound to talk of the work done by the Group Theatre and the Actors Studio as being an "Adaptation of the Stanislavsky System. The *Method*" is therefore our version of the System.[73]

Strasburg's disclaimer makes great sense. This book is our version of the System inspired by Stanislavsky and true to what we believed was his final offering and yet updated with new ideas from science, art, other theatre techniques, and other wisdom traditions that Stanislavsky could not have known. While we have tried to keep what Stanislavsky offered intact, we have also expanded some of his ideas through our own long careers of experimentation in acting. None of us can hope to create a living art form that does not grow and evolve with each new generation.

Still, for all of the claims and disclaimers, the fact remains that until this very day Strasberg's "Method" is still thought of by many, incorrectly, as the Stanislavsky System. While Strasburg considers the Method an adaptation, it is widely misconstrued as Stanislavsky's legacy. In the late 1950s eminent Russian director Georgi Tovstonogov visited New York. Tovstonogov was a student of Stanislavsky's during his final period of work with the Method of Physical Actions. In the company of a friend and former classmate of the third studio of the Moscow Art Theatre, émigré actress, director, and teacher, Sonia Moore, the two paid a visit to the Actor's Studio where her daughter Irene Moore-Jaglom was studying. In response to what the Russian director saw, he said,

> [Strasberg] is considered a famous pupil of Stanislavsky and I would have believed that if I hadn't seen those lessons myself. But in actuality everything he did was in complete opposition to Stanislavsky: building on mood and atmosphere, demanding an emotional state all the time. That's just what Stanislavsky fought against. Strasberg took all of Stanislavsky's terminology . . . but he didn't possess the essence of Stanislavsky at all.[74]

---

[73]Quoted in Edwards, *The Stanislavsky Heritage*, 261–262.
[74]Quoted in Allen, *Stanislavsky for Beginners*, 110.

In spite of the controversy, it is an undeniable fact that numerous brilliant talents passed through the Actor's Studio or were deeply influenced by other great American teachers of the Method: Dustin Hoffman, James Dean, Marilyn Monroe, Rod Steiger, Shelly Winters, Kim Stanley, Al Pacino, Robert De Niro, Jack Nicholson, Heath Ledger, Christian Bale, Johnny Depp, etc., a virtual Who's Who of American stage and film acting.

The Method's hegemony over the System made it difficult for the later teachings of Stanislavsky to get a firm footing in the United States, but not impossible. The fall of the Iron Curtain in the 1990s and the increased cultural exchange between East and West has brought new ideas from eastern European directors. In Great Britain, where the Method did not take hold, the use of the System's emphasis on action, imagination, and speech could be readily absorbed into the already fertile cultural soil that has given birth to British actors who continually find themselves in Hollywood playing American roles.

A Dedicated Life in Art

Sonia Moore was born Sophie Evzarovna Shatzov on December 4, 1902, in Gomel, Russia. In 1920 she won admission to the Moscow Art Theatre's Third Studio under the direction of Evgeny Vakhtangov, Stanislavsky's greatest disciple. She auditioned with a monologue from Oscar Wilde's *Salomé*. Of her audition, Vakhtangov said that he could build a theatre based on her talent alone. Sonia's husband, Lev Borisovich Helfand, was appointed Soviet ambassador to Italy during Mussolini's Fascist regime.

Figure 20.9 Sonia Moore.
Photo: Courtesy of Irene Moore-Jaglom

In June of 1940 they received orders to return to Russia. Suspecting that they would be "purged" by Stalin as many of their friends, family, and associates had been, they decided to defect. With the help of the American ambassador, who provided exit visas, they managed to escape with their daughter, Irene, and arrived safely in New York City where the family adopted the surname Moore. After her husband's passing in 1957, Sonia decided to open a school of acting in order to bring to light the updated and revised teachings of Stanislavsky to America. She founded the Sonia Moore Studio of the Theatre in 1961 in New York City.

Moore dedicated herself to constant research in hopes of clarifying the many misunderstandings and distortions surrounding Stanislavsky's theories that had occurred during the early transition of Stanislavsky's teachings to America. As a result of her forty-year research and personal communication with former colleagues in Russia, she was able to uncover many additional facets of Stanislavsky's final experiments with the Method of Physical Actions and Active Analysis that had not yet been communicated in the

West. She would often say, "It is indisputable that there is a great deal of dilettantism in the theatre, and Stanislavsky fought it through the System." These revelations are succinctly and lucidly explored in Moore's first book, *The Stanislavski Method*, which was released in 1960 and later revised under the title *The Stanislavski System*. In the fall of 1968, her third book, *Training an Actor*, based on taped sessions in class, was released. It was eventually revised as *Stanislavski Revealed: An Actors Guide to Spontaneity on Stage*. The revised edition included updated research based on her discoveries concerning the movement of spinal muscles to trigger spontaneous emotional states (introduced in this book as W.E.D.G.A.G.). A fourth book, *Stanislavski Today*, was published privately and documented supportive material by Russian teachers, directors, and scientists (see box), giving further credence to Sonia Moore's teaching methods.

In order to further disseminate the final deductions of Stanislavsky, Sonia founded the American Centre for Stanislavski Theatre Art, (ACSTA), a research institute, in 1964. In 1970, she formed the center's professional acting ensemble, ACSTA-1, later renamed American Stanislavski Theatre (AST). The company had the unique distinction of consisting of advanced actors trained in the System. It made its debut in New York City with Anton Chekhov's *Cherry Orchard*, in an original translation by Moore and her daughter, Irene Moore-Jaglom, who played the leading role of Madam Ranevskaya. Following Stanislavsky's principles to the letter, rehearsals for *Cherry Orchard* covered a period of seven months, sometimes working seven days a week. Subsequent productions were rehearsed over a period of five months, always rehearsing several plays simultaneously and then presenting them in true repertory fashion. Actors played small and leading roles, often exchanging roles from season to season. Bennett, the company's first assistant artistic director, recalls:

> Because several of the actors had part-time day jobs we would meet for rehearsal at 1:00 pm until 6:30. Evening classes, which we were expected to attend, began at 7:00 pm and went until 11:00. We rehearsed from 10:00 am to 5:00 pm both Saturday and most Sundays, even when the heat was not on during the cold New York winters. We believed in what we were doing. We wanted to prove the value of our training in Physical Actions. There were times when the entire company would become spontaneously inspired during the final moments of *Cherry Orchard;* then we would hear the quiet weeping of the audience who remained silent until bursting into applause for the curtain call.

Sonia toured with her company throughout the United States and Canada to promote the System. She was a regular presenter and speaker at the annual Association for Theatre in Higher Education (ATHE) conventions. Throughout the remainder of Sonia Moore's life she continued her research into advancements being made in theatre and science. She received many honors and awards for her contribution and can be found in Who's Who of American Women. Sonia Moore passed away in 1995 at the age of 93 and is survived by her daughter, Irene Moore-Jaglom, and her two grandchildren, Andrew and Leona. Sonia's artistic life was one of complete dedication. She often stated that her work was her way of thanking the people of America for their kindness and generosity for having welcomed her family to its shores in a time of personal crisis.

She believed that the Stanislavsky System got to the core of actor training and often said, "Why discover an already discovered America? Stanislavsky has already given us the key to an actor's work."[75]

Bertolt Brecht (1898–1956), a German playwright and director, was extremely prolific and artistically and politically provocative in his short 58 years of life. Brecht's artistic style also owes something to Stanislavsky. He was an outspoken critic and critical writer challenging his society through Marxist ideology and challenging the theatre to be more provocative and political. He borrowed heavily from earlier directors, including Stanislavsky's Moscow Art Theatre contemporaries, the Russians Meyerhold and Vakhtangov, and German director Erwin Piscator to create his highly political and vividly theatrical style known as Epic Theatre.

According Carl Weber (former Director at Brecht's Berliner Ensemble, actor in Brecht's company and assistant director to Brecht himself), Brecht understood that in order to get the impact of the alienation, the actors had to first develop in rehearsal connections to their roles in a Stanislavskian methodology. Brecht's actors were then expected to step outside and comment on their own work through a rehearsal practice often referred to in English as distancing (which involved a variety of techniques such as the actor mocking his role, narrating his own action, doing the action in an incorrect tempo, having actor's switch roles, etc.). Alienation was the impact that Brecht sought to have on the audience, to first suck them into the story and have them identify with a character's plight and suffering and then to throw them out of it to intellectually and critically observe their thoughts and feelings. In performance he used some additional techniques. He forecast through titles, projections, and other methods what was about to happen so the audience could more critically watch it unfold (much like in comedy when the audience is invited to be smarter than the comic fool: we know what is about to happen to him so we can enjoy the details of how it happens). In his case he often used comic techniques to bring consciousness of oppression to

Figure 20.10 Bertolt Brecht.
Photo: © Fred Stein/dpa/Corbis

---

[75]Quotes are from notes by Bennett on her oral teachings from his many years of study and apprenticeship with Ms. Moore.

events and social relationships in our everyday lives. He also used comedy to hold the audience's attention long enough to deliver his political message. He didn't resolve the problems in his plays through the familiar dramatic cathartic release, where the hero triumphs over the opposing force, because he wanted the audience to stay in sufficient discomfort about the themes of the play to want to leave the theatre and take political action to resolve the issues raised by his plays in the real world. He wanted the audience to have the metacognition, to experience what is happening and think critically about it at the same time, thus have a chance of changing it. For Brecht, dual consciousness for the actor was not enough; he wanted dual consciousness for the audience. His idea that consciousness can liberate us is expressed in his poem:

The most beautiful of all doubts
Is when the downtrodden and despondent raise their heads
And
Stop believing in the strength
Of their oppressors.[76]

A Polish theatre director and innovator, Grotowski (1933–1999) was a leader in the experimental theatre movement in the 1960s and 1970s. Not since Stanislavsky had any theatre practitioner delved as deeply into the actor's nature in an attempt to find new answers to questions of technique and performance. Grotowski's primary aim was to create a theatre that would offer spiritual nourishment to the spectator through what he called a "total act," an actor's total donation of self. He used the term *holy actor* to describe an actor capable of making such a donation. To achieve his aim he developed a series of psychophysical exercises borrowed from Eastern as well as Western traditions: yoga, Japanese Noh Theatre, Brecht and Artaud and Stanislavsky. Grotowski studied acting and directing at the State Theatre School in Kraków and in Moscow.

Figure 20.11 Jerzy Grotowski.
Photo: Mondadori Portfolio via Getty Images

While his staging was unusual, including a variety of experimental audience-actor-set configurations, the acting in his company, called the Laboratory Theatre, was heavily Stanislavsky-influenced but colored by his Polish Catholic experience. He is author of the book *Towards a Poor Theatre*, which focuses on stripping away what he thought were the superficial trappings of elaborate costumes and sets in order to reconnect to theatre's powerful roots in ritual.

---

[76]Bertolt Brecht, "In Praise of Doubt," in *Poems, 1913–1956* (London: Methuen, 1976).

> In his writing he states:
>
> Stanislavsky was compromised by his disciples. He was the first great creator of a method of acting in the theatre, and all those of us who are involved with theatre problems can do no more than give personal answers to the questions he raised. When, in numerous European theatres we watch performances inspired by the "Brecht theory," and are obliged to fight against utter boredom because the lack of conviction of both actors and producers takes the place of the so-called "Verfremdungseffekt," we think back to Brecht's own productions. They were perhaps less true to his theory but, on the other hand, very personal and subversive as they were, they showed a deep professional knowledge and never left us in a state of lassitude.[77]

The Theatre of the Post-revolution, Censorship, and Stalin[77]

Stanislavsky's two years abroad on tour with the company vastly increased the Art Theatre's fame but not its bank account. Some of the actors had chosen to remain in the United States, and the company remaining in Moscow was in serious need of reorganization.

Stanislavsky faced a very changed Russia upon his return. Lenin was dead, and the newly created Soviet Union was constructing a post-revolutionary social and cultural philosophical foundation upon which to build its Marxist society. The Art Theatre had come under vicious attack by the press at home for its bourgeois repertory abroad. New plays and playwrights of the revolution had to be found and developed. Nemirovich-Danchenko decided to bolster the company and moved students from the Second Studio into the main company. Now the problem of how to unify the two generations into an ensemble arose.

It was decided to produce *The Days of the Turbins* by Mikhail Bulgakov,[78] a play about a White Russian family's decline at the time of the civil war. The choice of *Turbins* gave an opportunity for the company to reorganize and present a play set during the revolution. The state-established play-reviewing board, the Repertkom, had voiced strong official objection to the play's original title, *The White Guard*; it seems that using the word *white* (referring to White Russians, who supported the tsar, as opposed to Red Russians, Communist revolutionaries) was not a wise ideological choice. Also, the play depicted a White Russian family's resistance to the eventual takeover of the Red Guard in a sympathetic light. The title was changed, and the revised version opened on October 5, 1925, with great box office success and brought the company out of the red in spite of overwhelming philosophically negative critical reviews. *The Days of the Turbins* spoke to the new generation in much the same way that Chekhov's plays *Seagull* and *Cherry Orchard* had spoken to the prerevolutionary generation. In 1929 the play was banned, but three years later, in 1932, it was discovered that Stalin had seen the production fifteen times and wanted to see it again. By Saturday of the same week the play was on the boards again and played for the next nine years. It is said that Stalin saw the play an additional fourteen times.

---

[77] Jerzy Grotowsky, *Towards a Poor Theatre*. (New York: Simon & Schuster, 1968), 85.
[78] Bulgakov (May 15, 1891–March 10, 1940): Russian novelist, playwright, physician.

20 THE EVOLVING STANISLAVSKY SYSTEM

The Art Theatre had managed to cross the great divide between the previous period of intelligentsia theatre and the post-revolutionary theatre for the people. Stanislavsky was determined to include classical repertory among the new works of Socialist Realism. His idea was to present a prerevolutionary production with post-revolutionary social values. He wanted a spectacle. He chose Beaumarchais's *Le Mariage de Figaro*. Work on the production proceeded continuously from the end of 1925 to the spring of 1927 with a record 300 rehearsals. Through his work on *Figaro*, Stanislavsky began working on what Jean Benedetti calls:

> two important developments to the System. . . . Broad physical objectives and . . . Flow of the Day . . . a series of logically-connected actions, justifiable in terms of probability.[79]

Although Stanislavsky was deeply opposed to the imposition of plays for the sole purpose of propaganda, it remained necessary, for professional as well as personal survival, to prove to the powerful critics of the Art Theatre that it was ideologically in support of revolutionary ideals. His fear was that there were few if any worthy post-revolutionary playwrights available, and that the new playwrights and plays were hastily produced and full of clichés and hackwork.

Ever in search of new material, the Art Theatre needed a new production in order to celebrate the tenth anniversary of the October Revolution. Stanislavsky decided upon an adaptation of a short story by Vsevolod Ivanov, "The Armored Train No. 14-69." The story is about a simple peasant farmer, Vershinin, who by the capture of an armored train from counterrevolutionary troops becomes a hero of the Bolshevik Revolution. The production had great difficulty with the Repertkom, which banned several of the scenes. It was rather a rush job for the Art Theatre, with only 76 rehearsals. The production was well received, and the Art Theatre was praised for its ideological progress.

> "Through the revelation of the psychology of character it leads to the revelation of the social nature of that character. It reveals the period through man."
> —P. Markov, "Aktior Oktobriaski Revolutsii," *Sovremeni Teatr* 12 (1927): 179[80]

The jubilee celebration of the revolution was a great success. Stanislavsky was to perform his famous role of Vershinin in the first act of *Three Sisters*; however, during the performance Stanislavsky suffered an attack of angina pectoris and was confined to bed. Unfortunately, it was the last time he was to appear on the stage. After months of bed rest and convalescence at the Badenweller Sanatorium in Germany, he recovered, returning to Moscow in 1930.

The Publications in Translation

As early as 1906 Stanislavsky had attempted to compile his notes into some type of cohesive order. He wanted to create a grammar for acting, an "ABC" approach, but not being a natural writer he found the task daunting. Nevertheless, over the years he kept copious notes of his acting experiments with the thought that eventually he would get around to it.

---

[79] Benedetti, *Stanislavski*, 277.
[80] Quoted in Benedetti, *Stanislavski*, 283.

His first book was to be an autobiographical account of his theatrical journey. *My Life in Art* was written during the 1923–1924 foreign tour to America. It had been written in such haste to meet the publisher's deadline that Stanislavsky considered the binding to be better than the contents.[81]

Stanislavsky wrote his first book on acting in two parts over a period of thirteen years.

Part One: The Actor's Work on the Self in the Creative Process of Living Through was published by Theatre Arts Books 1935 in the United States and the United Kingdom under the title *An Actor Prepares*. However, there was a three-year gap prior to the publication in Russia of *The Actor's Work on the Self —Part One*. It did not appear until 1938. There were several points of translation that differed between the Russian and English versions.

The second book, *Part Two: The Actor's Work on the Self in the Creative Process of Physical Embodiment*, was published in the West under the title *Building a Character* in 1948. The thirteen-year gap between the writing and publication of the two halves of the book led to several misunderstandings about the System and gave the impression that the first book was the complete System. The third book in the trilogy, *Creating a Role*, deals with the three stages of character development: first, to study the role; second, to establish the life of the role; and third, to bring the role to physical form. The book had its first release in the United States in 1961.

The American translator, Elizabeth Reynolds Hapgood (1894–1974), had served as translator for Stanislavsky when he visited the White House and met President Calvin Coolidge during the Moscow Art Theatre's tour of 1924. Stanislavsky gave Hapgood power-of-attorney over the publication of all his books. Hapgood was a strong advocate for Stanislavsky and was responsible for the books being published in several languages throughout the world. There were, however, difficulties. Stanislavsky's writing style reflected how he actually taught classes with students and in printed form appeared repetitious. The American publishers wanted the books deeply edited. The Russian version of Part One has 575 pages, and the English version 295!

More serious were the mistranslations of several Russian words that were key terms of the System. Sharon Carnicke describes the confusion surrounding the mistranslations when she writes:

> In both Russian texts, Stanislavsky clearly outlines a logical process of analysis for each segment of the play: the actor first examines the *"given circumstances"* in order to describe the character's situation. The situation poses a *"problem"* (*zadacha*, in Hapgood's translation, "objective") that the character must solve through the choice of an *"action."* By carefully defining the *"problem,"* the actor discovers the character's specific "action" for that segment of the play.[82]

Finding the correct action to solve the problem within each episode of a play is crucial for the actor in order to bring the character to life. The logic and sequence of the actions lead to the logic and sequence of a character's emotions, arising naturally from the actor in the given circumstances through the struggle to overcome the stated problem. Although we may still use the term *objective*, there is a marked distinction between striving for a specific goal and struggling to surmount an obstacle by solving a problem.

[81] Benedetti, *Stanislavski*, 265.
[82] Carnicke, *Stanislavsky in Focus*, 85.

20 THE EVOLVING STANISLAVSKY SYSTEM

> **Theatre and Revolution, Part III: Joseph Stalin**
>
> In 1924, Lenin died, and Joseph Stalin maneuvered his way to power. He banished Trotsky (Lenin's heir apparent) and later sent an assassin to murder Trotsky, which he did in Mexico with an ice pick. To subdue a separatist movement, Stalin caused a famine in the Ukraine by exporting all their food, and 7 million people died. He started a liquidation program to imprison, torture, and kill all enemies. Despite Russia's bloody past under the tsars, Stalin's reign is considered one of the most brutal dictatorships in world history. Fearful oppression and censorship were keys to Stalin's iron grip on the country.

Stanislavsky and the Red Director
After his tour to the West, Stanislavsky returned to Moscow on November 3, 1930, to discover that Stalin's Central Executive Committee had assigned a watch-dog called a Red Director to oversee all rehearsals and productions of the company. To make matters worse, Stalin's new Five-Year Plan placed emphasis on quantity rather than quality. During the 1929–1930 season the Theatre produced 795 performances, and in 1930–1931, 751!

Stanislavsky became fearful that the Theatre's high artistic standards were being severely compromised, and in a letter to Stalin, expressed his protest and suggestions. The Red Director was dismissed and the company placed under direct governmental control. The company was renamed The Moscow Art and Academic Theatre of the USSR. For a time there was a bit more artistic freedom, and conditions improved. In 1934, Stalin instituted a new artistic directive stating that all writers and theatres were only permitted to write and perform realistic works of art. Socialist Realism became the required standard; all other styles and forms were banned and labeled Formalism. The Moscow Art Theatre survived in this period by producing Socialist Realism; this combined with the European and American tour, for which only realistic productions were requested by promoters, ensured that Stanislavsky was pegged as a realistic director and his technique diminished to only useful for realism. In fact, prior to the Soviet restrictions, Stanislavsky directed, acted, and applied his technique in all styles of theatre. When he wanted to produce something that wasn't Socialist Realism, he produced it in his home, partly to avoid the censors, partly because his health demanded it. For his final experiment, Stanislavsky chose the nonrealistic farce Molière's *Tartuffe*.

Meyerhold's company, based on constructivist sets and biomechanics, did not survive this censorship. It was condemned and closed in 1938. These were extremely dangerous times, as Stalin had begun his liquidation (targeted killing) program in 1936, and the show trials were well under way. (Show trials were mock trials intentionally set up for public display in order to create fear and control public opinion. These trials were a great injustice and abuse to the judicial system, as the accused were already presumed guilty.) Stanislavsky was either oblivious to the danger or showed great moral courage by publically inviting Meyerhold to rejoin Moscow Art Theatre and angering Stalin by declaring, "Take care of Meyerhold, he is my sole heir in the theatre."[83]

[83]Quoted in Allen, *Stanislavsky for Beginners*, 159.

Stanislavsky's efforts to pass on his legacy to Meyerhold failed, however, one year after Stanislavsky's passing in 1938; Meyerhold was arrested in Leningrad June 20, 1939, and tortured; on February 2, 1940, he was executed by gunshot.

> ### A Note on Soviet Science and the System
>
> In recent years, some of the articles published by Soviet scientists in support of the Method of Physical Actions have come under scrutiny by Western scholars. Academic criticism arose because the Soviet government influenced some scientists to adjust their findings in support of Marxist theories of dialectical materialism, and findings that challenged it were censored. Because of this, some scholars discarded all Soviet science related to actor training, and with it those people who built anything based on the science. In today's terms, this would be like throwing out all climate science because some scientists have succumbed to corporate and political pressure to downplay it. The fact remains that many great discoveries were made during the Soviet period (if you take the time to sift through them), just as in climate science, global warming has in fact turned out to be a serious problem.

However, the theories and practices in science employed by Stanislavsky, and later Sonia Moore and Philip Bennett, were tested through years of practical hands-on work with actors. The science that influenced the System came from a plethora of sources, not only Soviet science. Now much of it has been well substantiated by modern scientific studies, as you have read about throughout this book.

The Final Experiment: The Method of Physical Actions (Active Analysis)

Stanislavsky's health, due to serious heart problems and overwork, had been declining for some time, and he desperately wanted to ensure that his most recent deductions on the actor's training and rehearsal process would be deeply understood. He had been developing his theories about physical actions for some years, but now in 1936 he wanted to confirm and pass on his legacy by selecting a group of young actors from the Moscow Art Theatre to work with him in his home.

Perhaps chief among these disciples was the 43-year-old Mikhail Nikolayevich Kedrov (1893–1972). Kedrov had played the character of Molière in Bulgakov's play entitled *Molière*. Stanislavsky was not satisfied with the script, and when the production closed he cast Kedrov in the title role of *Tartuffe* by Molière,[84] which he wished to use for his experimental work with the young actors. Kedrov was also appointed as one of Stanislavsky's assistant directors, along with Nikolai Gorcharkov. Serving as dramaturgs were Grigori Kristi; L.P. Novitskaya, who also took notes on the training process (outlined by Jean Benedetti in *Stanislavsky & the Actor*, Routledge); and Vassily Toporkov, who left an account of the rehearsals. Some of the actors included Ivan Moskvin and Maria Osipovna Knebel (1898–1985), who also wrote about the process and later immigrated to the UK. Some were

---

[84] Born Jean-Baptiste Poquelin (January 15, 1622–February 17, 1673): French playwright and actor who adopted the stage name Molière.

experienced MAT actors; the younger actors had been studying under Stanislavsky's sister, Zanaïda, and were familiar with his new approach, the Method of Physical Actions. Now they would work in greater depth and apply the technique to a classic play. Stanislavsky wanted to demonstrate that the System was based on objective laws of nature that governed the creative process. He wanted to dispel the idea that the System was only applicable to naturalistic plays. The choice of a classic play in verse seemed ideal. The lessons and rehearsals in Stanislavsky's home continued for two years. In December of 1939, one year after Stanislavsky's passing, Mikhail Nikolaevich Kedrov sought permission from the Moscow Art Theatre to stage the entire play. Benedetti writes:

> A demonstration performance was arranged in the Art Theatre foyer. Kedrov gave the actors a single instruction before they went on: no concern for feelings, no displays of personality and emotion, only concentration on action. The months of painstaking work paid off. The management and the other members of the company acknowledged the advance in acting technique. What they had seen had been truthful in terms of human behavior and viable in terms of theatre.[85]

Stanislavsky began the *Tartuffe* project by openly stating that he had no intention of staging a production: "Laurels for directing do not interest me now. Whether I stage one production more or less does not matter. It is important to me to hand on to you everything I have accumulated throughout my life."

In previous years the actors would sit around the table, sometimes for months, analyzing a play. Stanislavsky observed that when they finally did get up on stage they understood everything but could do very little. The new rehearsal process would get actors up on their feet immediately without reading the play and with no discussions. To implement the process the director would need to create a preliminary analysis of the play's main events and smaller episodes. The play would then be actively analyzed by improvising a series of main psychophysical actions, eventually broken down into smaller psychophysical actions, bit by bit, by the actors during the rehearsals. The actors would also design and improvise events surrounding the play: the before and after time, where they are going and coming from each time they enter and exit, and what happens in between the scenes and acts.

In order to prepare for the process the actors would be trained to fulfill a series of *organic actions* through improvisations, like those presented throughout this book. The goal of the training rehearsal process was to completely unite the entire System of his past forty years' search into one cohesive whole. The actor could analyze the role, build the character, and without damaging their psyches or instruments stir the appropriate feelings and emotions through the logic and consecutiveness of a series of psychophysical actions. Stanislavsky considered the Method of Physical Actions to be the culmination of his entire life's work.

Under Stalin, Marxist revisionists required that all education, science, and art come into line with a philosophy called dialectical materialism. Dialectical materialism is based on the theories and writings of Karl Marx and Frederick Engels that asserts the primacy of the material world and the evolution of nature from lower to higher species solely as a result of materialistic interactions. The

---

[85]Benedetti, *Stanislavski*, 318.

official atheistic philosophy of dialectical materialism meant that all references to anything spiritual was labeled "idealistic" and had to be eliminated. Needless to say, Stanislavsky's emphasis on yoga and the soul fell under scrutiny and was sharply criticized and censored from his writings. Russian theatrical directors B. E. Zakhava, Georgy Tovstonogov, as well as scientist P. V. Simonov, fell in line with the official thinking, making particular note of the materialistic basis of *physical actions*, thus dismissing the spiritual side of human nature and Stanislavsky's System.

Exploring psychophysical actions, however, is only the beginning of the process. Discovering typical and fitting actions comprises about one-third of work on the role; however, it opens up an in-depth exploration by the actor in the character's given circumstances. As the actor explores the circumstances he then begins to focus on the inner, spiritual life of the character, building on what he understands from his own experience and expanding through research and observation to stretch toward a character and situation beyond his personal understanding. Eventually the actor fuses his own experiences with those imagined and created for the character by the playwright, actor, director, and design team. He then, within the style of the production, no matter how extreme, lives through these experiences afresh each performance to become an actor of the School of Living Experience.

The Final Bow

On the second of August 1938, Stanislavsky and his wife, Lilina, were preparing to go on his annual retreat to a a sanitarium for rest and recuperation in Barvika, some 30 kilometers outside of Moscow. He had seemed well enough and cheerful when suddenly he took a turn for the worse. His attending physician, Dr. Shelagurov, examined him and found that he had a very high temperature and his pulse was arrhythmic, indicating that he had had another heart attack. There was no question of travel.

On the seventh, he spoke briefly of Nemirovich, whose wife had recently died. The two men had not spoken for years and Nemirovich had sent a letter of reconciliation. Now in Stanislavsky's last moments he thought of his codirector and friend: "Who's looking after Nemirovich? Perhaps he's ill. Is he short of money?"[86]

His nurse, Dukovska, asked him if he would like to dictate something to his sister, Zanaïda. "Not something but a whole world of things. But I can't now, I get things muddled up so."[87] When the nurse returned at 3:45 in the afternoon she discovered that his face had turned pale, in death his head had dropped forward, as if for his final bow.

Stanislavsky's Legacy to You

Throughout this book we have presented an introduction to your beginning actor training based on the ever-evolving legacy of the Stanislavsky System. Stanislavsky's 40-year search for the objective laws that govern an actor's creativity was as much of a personal exploration as it was an investigation into the art. He believed that we could not, nor should we, divide the mind, body, and soul. We have seen how his courage in asking difficult questions, struggling with obstacles, and humbly charting both his failures and successes has led to our deepened knowledge of theatre and acting. Despite the incredible obstacles of the country and time in which he lived and the numerous obstacles that might derail an ordinary person's drive, Stanislavsky

---

[86]Quoted in Benedetti, *Stanislavski*, 322, from an account taken from Stanislavsky's nurse, Dukovska in *O Stanislavskom* (about Stanislavsky), Moscow, 1948, 523.
[87]Ibid., 322.

fought through all of it to find human truths that can become artistic truths in the field of acting.

Acting is a journey of self-discovery; that is why it is such an all-engrossing and wonderful path to follow, but it must not be self-indulgent. Your improvement as an actor depends on your constant improvement as a person. Exploring your humanity gives you access to the greater humanity of which we are all a part.

Training as an actor is also life training. What you learn about yourself, you learn about others as well. It is your humanity that is revealed through the creation of the characters you portray, and it is by means of the mastery of your technique, and the expressiveness of your instrument that you will bring out your individualized talents and gifts, gifts that you can use to educate and uplift others.

We, the authors, hope that you have been inspired by Stanislavsky's great legacy and know from our experience that if you apply the techniques offered in this book, they will serve you well. We also want to encourage and challenge you to continue to explore, refine, invent, break rules, and make new discoveries of your own. Who knows what you might contribute to the ever-evolving content and forms of our art? Stanislavsky's autobiography, *My Life in Art*, best captures his humble spirit and dedication:

> When I look back over the roads that I have traveled during my long life in art, I want to compare myself to a gold-seeker who must first make his way through almost impassable jungles in order to find a place where he may discover a streak of gold, and later wash hundreds of tons of the sand and stones in order to find at least several grains of the noble metal. And, like the gold-seeker, I cannot will to my heirs my labors, my quests, my losses, my joys and my disappointments, but only the few grains of gold that it has taken me all my life to find.[88]

Summary of Key Events Shaping Stanislavsky and His Acting System

1855–1881	Tsar Alexander II reigns as tsar of Russia until his assassination.
1861	Emancipation of the Serfs by Alexander II. (The peasants had been owned by the landowners of the land they lived and worked on in a kind of feudal slave system.)
1863	Birth of Konstantin (Kostya) Sergyevich Alexeyev (a.k.a. Stanislavsky).
1870–1876	Kostya's first role onstage as Winter at age seven (first stage fire). Konstanzo Alekseyev's Circus (a family circus). The Puppet Theatre (second stage fire).
1877	(Age 14) Stanislavsky founds The Alexeyev Circle in a theatre built on his parents' estate.
1881	Tsar Alexander III inherits the throne in Russia. He brutally represses opposition, tries to reverse his father's reforms, and implements a Russification (removing European influences).
1882	Stanislavsky sees Tomasso Salvini perform Othello.
1888	Founds The Society of Art and Literature, combining amateur and professional artists.
1889	Marries Maria Lilina Perevoshchikova.

[88]Stanislavsky, *My Life in Art*, 572.

1890	Stanislavsky sees the company of Georg II, Duke of Saxe-Meiningen, and gleans the value of an aesthetically and visually unified production.
1894–1917	Reign of the last tsar of Russia—Nicholas II.
1896	Stanislavsky directs and stars in the Society's *Othello*, to much acclaim. Meyerhold sees and is inspired by this production.
1897	Eighteen-hour meeting with Nemirovich-Danchenko to found MAT.
1898	Summer—MAT's hand-picked company lives communally to rehearse their first season.
	Fall—MAT opens its first season including Chekhov's *The Seagull*.
1898–1905	Considered MAT's realistic period, with a focus on Chekhov and Gorky, although they continue to produce plays in other styles as well.
1902	MAT moves into a better facility on Kammerherr Lane.
	Meyerhold leaves MAT to form his own company.
1904	Death of Anton Chekhov.
	Stanislavsky and Nemirovich-Danchenko seek to expand MAT's production style to include Leonid Andreyev's expressionist writing and Maurice Maeterlinck's symbolist plays with mystic influences.
1905	Bloody Sunday Massacre followed by Peasants Revolt.
	MAT's produces Gorky's *Children of the Sun*.
	Meyerhold and Stanislavsky started the Studio on Povarskaya Street (aka Theatre-Studio)
1906	Meets Sulerzhitsky in Finland.
1906–1907	Stanislavsky makes Sulerzhitsky his personal assistant.
	Stanislavsky divides performance into craft (stock-in-trade), representation, and living experience.
1909	He explores *subtext* and *through-action* in Turgenev's *A Month in the Country*.
1910–1913	Nemirovich-Danchenko explores mysticism, adapting novels by Dostoevsky.
1911	First Studio Created by Stanislavsky and Sulerzhitsky to develop a psycho-technique (Stanislavsky's early inside-out approach) to aid actors in performance.
1911	Sulerzhitsky and Stanislavsky use exercises in hatha yoga, raja yoga, and pranayama (*relaxation, concentration, flow of energy, communication/communion*).
	Experiments with Ribot's affective memory (sense memory, analogous emotional experience).
	Evgeny Vakhtangov joins MAT after much successful amateur directing and after completing the Adashev Drama School, where he studied with Sulerzhitsky.
	English director/designer Gordon Craig, Sulerzhitsky, and Stanislavsky collaborate on *Hamlet*.
1913	Season—Michael Chekhov performs with main company of MAT. Sulerzhitsky assigned to manage the First Studio.
	Vakhtangov directs his first MAT production for the First Studio, considered hyperrealism; the audience is moved to weeping.
1914	Vakhtangov starts the Drama Studio outside of MAT, but its first production fails and he learns the importance of unified content and form.
	Vakhtangov stars in Suhler's production of Dickens's *Cricket on*

20 THE EVOLVING STANISLAVSKY SYSTEM

the Hearth to great acclaim. Many designate him the First Studio's leading actor, much to the chagrin of his friend and rival Michael Chekhov.

1915 Stanislavsky develops laws of speech for actors, using exercises in vocal production, articulation, projection, logical phrasing of thoughts, shifts and pauses, clarity, and expression.

Michael Chekhov forms his own studio outside MAT, experimenting with collective unconscious and reincarnation into character. Chekhov publishes some of Stanislavsky's techniques that Stanislavsky was attempting to keep secret in their developmental phase.

Vakhtangov's production of *The Deluge* is a success at the First Studio.

1916 Death of Sulerzhitsky from tuberculosis at age 44.

Stanislavsky makes Vakhtangov director of the First Studio.

Stanislavsky starts the Second Studio to focus on pedagogical methods of teaching the System; part of its purpose is to develop the material for Stanislavsky's acting manual, *An Actor's Work* (Maria Knebel is among the first group of students).

1916–1920 Stanislavsky begins to organize his own work as an actor into phases (study, emotional experience/living through, and physical embodiment).

1917 Two Russian revolutions (prompted by food shortages, long-standing in-equality and corruption). The failure and mismanagement of the Russian army during WWI leads to riots in February and the ousting of Tsar Nicholas II in March. In October, the Bolshevik Party, headed by Vladimir Illich Lenin, seizes power.

1917–1922 Civil war begins between the Red Army loyal to the Communists and the White Army loyal to the tsar.

1918 Stanislavsky creates the Opera Studio with the Bolshoi Theatre to train the new generation of opera singers in the System.

July—Tsar Nicholas II, the last Romanov monarch, is executed along with his wife and five children.

1919 Nemirovich-Danchenko creates the MAT Music Studio.

1920 Third Studio created and headed by Evgeny Vakhtangov to explore his theatrical style of Fantastic Realism designed to bring together the vivid theatricality of Meyerhold with the spiritually alive, acting style of Stanislavsky.

1922 Evgeny Vakhtangov dies of tuberculosis and stomach cancer.

MAT Tour of Europe.

1923 Michael Chekhov returns for another season at MAT.

First tour of MAT to the United States.

Richard Boleslavsky and Maria Ouspenskaya of the First Studio open the American Laboratory Theatre with Harold Clurman.

1924 Lenin dies, and Stalin maneuvers his way to power.

First Studio becomes the Second Moscow Art Theatre, and Stanislavsky appoints Michael Chekhov to lead it. He remains the director from 1924 to 1927. It is closed by Stalin in 1936.

1927 Michael Chekhov's experiments denounced by Marxist revisionists.

1928 Michael Chekhov goes into exile in order to avoid liquidation.

1929 School of Dramatic Art started by former First Studio actors.

1931	Fourth Studio opens.
1932	MAT renamed the Gorky Academic Theatre (MH).
1938	Stanislavsky has a heart attack while performing *Three Sisters* and withdraws from MAT but continues his theatrical experiments.
1987	The Moscow Art Theatre splits into two performance groups: the Chekhov Moscow Art Theatre and the Gorky Moscow Art Theatre.

New Theatre Terms, Concepts and Artists

- broad farce
- Constructivism
- craft (stock-in-trade)
- dialectical materialism
- Fantastic Realism
- Marxist revisionists
- the Method
- naturalism
- Peasants' Revolt of 1905
- plastique
- realism
- School of Living Experience
- School of Representation
- spiritual realism

Companies:

- Actor's Studio
- Adashev Drama Studio
- Alekseyev's Circle
- American Laboratory Theatre
- Comédie Française
- First Studio
- Group Theatre
- Konstanzo Alekseyev's Circus
- Second Moscow Art Theatre
- Second Studio
- Theosophical Society
- Third Studio

Artists/Scholars/Historical Figures:

- Stella Adler
- Tsar Alexander II
- Madam Henena Blavadsky
- Richard Boleslavsky
- Phoebe Brand
- Mikhael Bulgakov
- Ludwig Chronegk
- Gordon Craig
- Georges Dandin
- Doukhobers
- Isadora Duncan
- Nicolai Efros
- Alexander Fillipovich Fedotov
- Fedotova (actress)
- Morris Gest
- Carlo Goldoni
- Carlo Gozzi
- Georg II, Duke of Saxe-Meiningen
- Maxim Gorky
- Elizabeth Reynolds Hapgood
- Henrik Ibsen
- Adashev Ivanovich
- Mikhael Nicholaevich Kedrov
- Maria Osipovna Knebel
- Olga Knipper
- Fyodor Komissarjevsky
- Maria Malinovskaya
- Ivan Moskvin
- Vladimir Nemirovich-Denchenko
- Tsar Nicholas I
- Kaoru Osanai
- Maria Alekseyevna Ouspenskaya
- Platanov
- Alexander Pushkin
- Théodule-Armand Ribot
- Lee Strasberg
- August Strindberg
- Leopold Antonovich Sulerzhitsky
- Alexsei Tolstoy
- Leo Tolstoy
- Turgenev
- B.E. Zakhava
- Zanaïda

Appendix I

A Selected Glossary: Terminology of the Stanislavsky System with Supplemental Terms

Vocabulary that directly relates to the System is italicized. In addition to the terminology of the Stanislavsky System we have included some terms used in the professional and academic theatres, yoga, science, and psychology that may have been adopted into the System. Wherever such terms appear they are denoted by an asterisk (*).

Action (To Act, Take Action, To Fulfill an Action): A purposeful act of human behavior. It is articulated by using a transitive, active verb (to accuse, to deny). What the actor does to solve the *Problem* (arising from the *Given Circumstances* and discovered through script analysis) is called *Action*. An *Action* is purposeful when it is inwardly *Motivated*, and then we say the *Action* has been *Justified*. We call such a *Justified* act that links the mind and body *Psychophysical*. *Psychophysical Action* is central to the creation of a character and a play. *Actions* are at the core of the entire System and serve as the building blocks by which a character is both created and revealed in performance. An *Action* can be both *Nonverbal* (silent) *and Verbal* (spoken). *Action* is also the primary means for the analysis of a play through *Active Analysis*. (See *Task and Objective; Given Circumstances*. For a further explanation please refer to Chapter 2 under Primary Elements of a Psychophysical Action; for training in actions see Chapter 8 under Nonverbal Action, and Chapter 10 under Verbal Action.)

Active Analysis: The final rehearsal process developed by Stanislavsky during the last years of his life (1935–1938), used to analyze the main events of the play. The process explores a play and its conflict, actively and dynamically, in two stages: The director's analysis (*Reconnaissance of the Mind*) and the director/actor collaboration (*Embodiment of the Role*). Actors are on their feet from the beginning of the rehearsal process and prepare improvisational studies (*Études*) in order to discover the *Actions* of their characters. These are then used to both solve the *Problem* and accomplish the character's *Task* or *Objective* in the scene. (See also the *Method of Physical Actions.)*

Active Facts: The fixed facts of both play and character to be found in the text comprise the *Plot* and *Story*. *Active Facts* are gathered by the actor and director during the initial stages of investigation and research into the play in order to give understanding to the various aspects of the *Given Circumstances*. (See *Given Circumstances*.)

Adaptation (Adjustment): An *Adjustment* that the character makes to an *Obstacle* or to a *Counteraction* initiated against him by another character. Can also occur as a result of mishaps on the stage: lines and sections of scenes being dropped, blocking being off, props missing, etc. An *Adaptation* must be sharp, clear, interesting, and fitting to the situation, play, and character. *Adaptations* are always improvised in the moment during performance and can be figured out using the *Magic If*.

Affective Memory: Based on the premise that an actor can experience previously experienced emotions by consciously evoking their associated physical, sensory states. Stanislavsky eventually turned away from direct *Sensory Recall* but continued to use the senses through *Sensory Evocation*. *Affective Memory* or *Emotional Memory* was adopted as the primary acting technique by Lee Strasberg, founder of the American Method. (See *Emotional Memory/Sense Memory*.)

After Time: The continuation of the life of a character after he or she leaves the stage. It also refers to the events that may follow after the conclusion of a play. Knowing and improvising the *After Time* of a scene and play gives the audience the feeling of continuity of scenic action and life.

Analogous Emotions: Emotions of the actor that are similar to those that the character is experiencing in the *Given Circumstances*. The stimulation of emotions in the audience is often a primary goal of theatre and film artists, particularly evoking specific emotional responses in connection to the author's or director's *Supertask*. Emotions need to be similar and relevant to those of the character in the situation but alive and responsive in the present moment to the play's events and to other characters.

Atmosphere: The surrounding *Air* of an *Environment* and closely associated with the *Mood* of a scene and/or character. The *Atmosphere* is brought about by a combination of factors, including the characters' moods, emotional states, physical locations, the setting, costumes, sounds, and lighting.

*Beat (Bit): A small segment of a scene akin to one topic or *Action-Step*. The length of the *Beats*, and which character initiates each, sets up a *Rhythm* for the scene that can be used in later pacing rehearsals. A *Bit* is smaller than an *Episode*. The *Beat* changes when something shifts in the scene. An actor can use the marked *Bit/Beats* to find the dynamic *Rhythm* and tension of the scene and to recognize the *Through-Line* of a scene or monologue. (See *Named Events, Episodes, and Units*.)

Before Time (Exposition, *Backstory): The *Before Time* is anything that has occurred in the world of the play or film prior to the start of the *Action* seen by the audience. The *Before Time* includes each character's biography, as well as historic, social, and political events that may influence the behavior and attitudes of the character. *Before Time* and *After Time* also apply to events that occur between scenes not seen by the audience. In literary analysis, when these facts are revealed during the course of the *Action* of the play the term *Exposition* is used. *Backstory* is a modern term used in film and sometimes in theatre for the *Before Time*.

*Blocking: The movement of the actor around the stage, such as entrances, exits, crosses, standing, sitting, and other movement. The blocking may be initiated by the actor or given by the director and is recorded by the stage manager. In some cases it is prescribed by the playwright in dialogue or suggested in stage directions. (See Mise-en-scène and Stage Business.)

Communion/Communication: *Communion* and *Communication* are terms used interchangeably; however, Stanislavsky preferred *Communion*. *Communion* is defined here as mutual influence between people. It begins with oneself, as in the states of "*I Am*" and "*I Exist*" and *Public Solitude*. The next step is *Communion* between actors, and the larger circle extends beyond the footlights to engulf the audience. Stanislavsky called this seemingly invisible connection between people *Spiritual Communion*. (See also *Flow of Energy*.)

Concentration (Focus of Attention, Circles of Attention): *Concentration* is the ability to *Focus* all of your attention to a specific point. *Focus* is placed on both inner objects (such as *Images*) and outer objects (including *Physical Actions*). *Concentration* requires that the actor's mind, body, and spirit be completely focused on the *Given Circumstances* of a play, toward the fulfillment of a *Purposeful Action*. *Concentration* is an exercise of *Willpower (Volition)*, which generally takes some training and discipline. One of the measures of the quality of an actor's work is his ability to attain a balance between *Physical Action* and *Evocative Images*. (See *Public Solitude* and *Dual Perspectives*.)

Control and Restraint: The ability of the actor to act within the *Measure of Truth* as well as distributing his physical, vocal, and emotional energy appropriately throughout the role. In the beginning of the work on a role, this helps the actor to focus on the inner life of the character. During performance *Control and Restraint* allows the actor to distribute his energy along the *Through-Line of Action*. (See *Dual Perspectives*.)

Counteraction: A clash between the *Main Action* of one character and the opposed *Action* of another, bringing about a dynamic conflict, is called *Counteraction*. It produces a struggle between characters that reveals the playwright's main idea as it progresses to the climax and resolution of the *Problem* of the play. (See *Through-action*.)

Creative Idea: An inspired potential creative solution that arises in response to a creative challenge posed to the company by the play or production. This may include any idea or *Device* that will help the actor and or director to stimulate the imagination and lead to the *Creative State*.

Creative State: A state of subconscious creativity leading toward artistic *Inspiration* (i.e., *Superconscious State*). A simple *Purposeful Action* truthfully fulfilled in concrete circumstances proved to be the best means to bring an actor into the *Creative State*, as it could trigger all of the subordinate *Elements of Action* simultaneously.

Device: An exercise, improvisation, game, or technique specifically designed to assist in the analysis and creation of a role or staging of a production. Each *Element of an Action, Imagination, Concentration, Tempo-Rhythm*, etc., is considered to be a *Device*. Many *Devices* may be used in rehearsal; however, those that are kept for the actual performance must be imbued with inner meaning and integrated with the other *Elements of Action*, aspects of the play, and the production.

Dual Perspectives (Metacognition, Dual Consciousness, Internal and External Monitors): A technique employed by the actor when he places 95 percent of his attention on inhabiting the role as the character and 5 percent on awareness as an actor. It requires the ability to maintain *Dual Consciousness*, awareness of multiple aspects of the self simultaneously. The actor guides the character, sculpting the role along the *Spine* of the play while keeping awareness of safety and logistical concerns. The actor must not allow himself to lose *Control* and artistic *Restraint* while rehearsing and performing, otherwise he will forfeit the ability to exercise creative choices and may even do himself or another harm (for example, in a fight scene). The actor develops and relies on *Internal* and *External Monitors* to ensure this balance. Another related concept in psychology is *Metacognition*; that is, the state of awareness of consciously watching one's own thought processes. (See *Restraint and Control*.)

Dynamic Action/Dynamism/Activeness: In performance the actor/character is always in *Psychophysical Action* made *Dynamic* by the struggle with a *Problem*, such as an internal or external *Obstacle* either presented by the *Given Circumstances* or deriving from another character. *Dynamic Action* is discovered through *Active Analysis* in rehearsals while fulfilling *Main Actions* and *Counteractions*. It is rediscovered during each moment of the performance before an audience. (See *Action*; also refer to Chapter 19: The Creative Life: Communion with Audience and Society for a further explanation of Stanislavsky's Diagram.)

Embodiment/Incarnation (Life of the Human Body in the Role): When the actor seeks to psychophysically connect both the inner thoughts and drives of the character to the specific physical expression of the character through *Physical Actions*. As the actor progresses along the *Through-Line of Action* during the rehearsal period and comes to understand the inner traits of his character, he then experiments to find their outer physical expressions in the form of active, transitive verbs. (See also *Transformation*.)

Emotional Memory: The imprint of past experiences, particularly their emotional content along the neural pathways of the body. (See *Affective Memory* and *Analogous Emotions*.)

Endowment/To Treat as If: The ability *To Treat* the stage sets, props, and costumes *as If* they were the real environment suggested by the play. *To Treat* other actors *as If* they were truly the characters they portray. *Endowment* is accomplished by selecting and fulfilling *Actions* that are fitting and typical toward objects, environments, and fellow actors. (See *Magic If*.)

A SELECTED GLOSSARY

Environment: The physical setting as described or implied by the playwright, interpreted by the director and designers, and inhabited by the actors. The *Environment* is part of the *Given Circumstances*. The *Environment* of the theatre, its stage, set, props, lighting, seating, and audience can also have a profound influence on the company of actors during rehearsals and performances.

Ethics: Professional behavior on- and offstage. *Ethics* include respect for equipment, sets, props, costumes, and for all those who work in the theatre or on a film. Punctuality, preparedness, and a joyful spirit that contributes to the working atmosphere contribute to an ethical environment. (See Chapter 17: Entering the Collaborative Process.)

Étude (A Study): An improvisational sketch created to explore a particular trait of character or *Event* using *Active Analysis* during the rehearsal process of a play. (See *Improvisational Études* and *Device*.)

Event: Something that happens; an important occurrence brought about by the combination of conflicting *Actions* in a scene, act, and play. It may be experienced by one or more characters and can be internal or external, but will always affect both. There can be several types of *Events*, each forming an important part of the structure of a climactic play. (See types of *Events* in Chapter 13: Active Analysis: Reconnaissance of the Play.)

Experiencing (Living Through): The ability of an actor to come alive through the imaginary *Given Circumstances* of the character in a specific play, the end result of the *Psychophysical Transformation* into character. While the performance is carefully planned and rehearsed, at the moment of performance the actor is infused with the life of the character, and this immediacy and *Presence* infects the audience.

Flow of Energy (Kinesthetic Awareness, Kinesthetic Response): The free *Flow of Energy* leads to the *Creative State* that invites *Inspiration*. The *Flow of Energy* involves the circulation of mental energy, physical energy, and breath, as well as healthy movement and communication among the other psychophysical systems of your body such as respiratory system, circulatory system, nervous system, and muscular system. The *Flow of Energy* dissipates tension by means of only engaging the necessary muscles to accomplish a simple *Physical Action*. It is closely aligned with *Kinesthetic Awareness*—the ability to sense what you are feeling within and around your body—and *Kinesthetic Response*—the natural reactions to stimuli.

Genre (and Style): A class or category of art. In theatre this would include the broad genres of comedy, tragedy, and musicals. Style is a more specific type of action, such as the different types of comedy, including farce, slapstick, restoration comedy, situation comedy, or satire.

Given Circumstances (Givens): These consist of the entirety of the imaginary world of the play as conceived by the playwright and given to the actors through the script (or conceived by the actors in the case of an improvisation). They also include the biographic and historical material, period, style, genre, epoch, and era. They are often called the *Givens*. In literary terms this is equivalent to both the exposition (background information) as well as all the information that is revealed or referred to throughout the play. In production terms it also includes all the elements given to actors by the director, the designers, the ensemble of actors, and all the other artists and technicians working on the production. We arrive at an understanding of the play's *Given Circumstances* by careful reading and rereading of the play and by asking the following questions at every step of work on a role: Who? What? When? Where? Why? With whom? What for? Where from? Where to? How?

Human Spirit: Stanislavsky sees each actor as a unique soul who brings a character to life thorough his or her individual psychological, physical, and spiritual characteristics. The actor's body is composed of his physical and vocal instrument and is not separate from his mind or spirit. For this reason each actor playing the same role and using the System will organically come to an entirely authentic interpretation of a character based on his or her own *Personal Theme* when working on a role. (See *Personal Theme*.)

I Am, I Exist (Presence): The state whereby the actor experiences being fully alive and present at each moment. It is the ultimate goal of the actor in performance and a requirement for an actor who strives toward the ideals of the *School of Living Experience*. *I Am* or *I Exist* is the willingness of the actor to live temporarily in a situation imagined or evoked by the senses. There are two I's that the actor must come to eventually blend into one: I, as myself the actor/creator of the role, and I, as the character living within the role. (See *Experiencing* and *Inspiration*.)

Imagination (Eidetic Images, Visualization, Film of Images): The actor's ability to create and see *Mental Images* at will (also called *Visualization* and *Creative Imagination*). Your *Mental Images* may be imaginary, personal, observed, or a combination of the three. They can be in any style from realistic to fantastic or grotesque. What is important is that they are *Eidetic Images*, vibrant and evocative, stimulating your mind and your body in ways appropriate for the character at a specific moment in the play. *Imagination* acts as a strong stimulus to emotion and leads the actor into the desired *Creative State* for acting. (See *Visualization*, and *Sensory Evocation*.)

Improvisational Études: In the System, an *Improvisation* is a planned sketch or narrative designed to explore the *structure of dramatic action* in both the training of an actor and the exploration of a play. *Improvisations* are used in the training of an actor in order to instill a practical use of each element of the System. Once the elements are understood and absorbed, i.e. become second nature, the actor can then use the entirety of his or her psychophysical instrument to explore the text through *Improvisational Études* and in the execution of *Actions* with a text. (See *Études* and *Second Plan*.)

Inner Monologue (Inner Dialogue): The term used to describe the character's private thoughts when not speaking. *Inner Dialogue* is an argument within the character's mind. The actor needs to have continuous thoughts as the character in the situation in order for the character to remain alive and responsive onstage. In a psychophysically trained actor, the thoughts are reflected through the body and thus expressed to the audience in the form of gestures and *Nonverbal Actions*. *Inner*

A SELECTED GLOSSARY

Monologue is also one of the most important techniques for film acting, as the experience of the character often must be conveyed in very subtle ways.

Inspiration: A *Superconscious* state; an experience whereby life is breathed into an artistic creation. In acting, insights and emotions are triggered in artist and audience. Stanislavsky wanted to develop concrete and repeatable techniques based in human behavior that would give actors tangible methods for entering into the *Creative State* to invite *Inspiration*. (See Chapter 1: An Invitation to the Quest for Inspiration and Chapter 3: The Creative State: Preparing for Inspiration.)

*****Intention:** An *Act of Will* behind what a character wants, needs, or desires. It is closely connected to the use of the term *Objective*—the *Aim* or *Goal* desired by a character in a scene. (See *Will* in *The Diagram of the Experiencing,* Chapter 18: The Actor of Living Experience.)

Justification: The purpose behind all actions as related to the *Active Facts* and *Given Circumstances* of a play. A *Physical Action* is said to be *Justified* and becomes psychophysical when it is imbued with purpose. To *Justify an Action* in a play, it is selected and fulfilled through a thorough analysis of the *Given Circumstances*. (See *Action*.)

Language of the Body: Different from but closely related to the popular idea of *Body Language*, it differs in that it is artistically chosen and executed to express and project to an audience nonverbal behavior, which may support or be in direct contrast to what is being said by the character. (See *Subtext of the Behavior*.)

Leitmotif: A *Theme* that is repeated throughout the sequence of action (also called a *Recurrent Theme*). *Themes* originate in the *Seed* or *Kernel* of a play and are brought to life through the action of the characters. In a well-written play each character also has his or her *Primary, Secondary, and Tertiary Themes,* which will repeat in the role. The *Themes* of a play and character converge during the final moments of resolution in a play to contribute to the playwright's *Ruling Idea*, the *Supertask*. (See also *Theme*.)

Life of the Human Soul: Stanislavsky refers here to the entire inner complex of human experience: psychological, physical, and spiritual. One of the primary goals of the System is to prepare an actor to reveal unique and universal truths of human life through a vivid theatrical form. (See *Life of the Human Spirit in the Role*.)

Life of the Human Spirit in the Role: The conscious and deliberate work on the psychic, physical, and emotional resources of the actor to bring a role to life. (See *Experiencing*.)

Logical Sequence and Consecutiveness of Actions: The *Inner* and *Outer Logic* of a character's psychology and physical behavior based on the *Active Facts* and sequence of *Events* of a play. By finding and fulfilling the *Logical Consecutiveness* of a character's *Physical Actions*, the actor will, through natural organic responses to those actions, find the logical sequence of the emotional score of the role as well.

Lure: A thought, *Image, Physical Action, Sensory Evocation,* or other *Device* used to excite the actor's imagination and bring him into the *Creative State*. In his later work, Stanislavsky suggested using a *Lure* to evoke a sense of *True Feeling* or emotion connected to what is happening now, rather than trying to evoke emotions based on past events directly through *Affective Memory*.

The Magic If: An evocative question that stimulates the actor's imagination and leads to the fulfillment of *Action*. It is the key to activating the *Given Circumstances* by stimulating appropriate thoughts and behavioral responses. When building an improvisation or actively analyzing the actions and circumstances of a play, ask, What would I do if today, here and now, for the first time, I were in this character's shoes, with this character's background, in these circumstances? This is used during conditioning exercises and training improvisations and rehearsals in order to discover the character's behavior. It is also used *Moment-to-Moment* during a performance to keep the actor alive and present while responding to obstacles through inventive and appropriate *Adaptations*.

Measure of Truth (Truth and Belief): Means that the actor must fulfill a realistic *Action* with the same degree of energy, tension, and *Tempo-Rhythm* as he would under similar circumstances in life. When an actor unduly rushes or retards time or tries to show an emotion (indicating) or force the emotion by more physical effort than required or through pushing with the breath, the results seem false to an audience. Whether acting in a realistic drama or one that is completely fantastical or absurd, the actor only needs to invest in the truth of his actions in order for the audience to accept even the most otherworldly or outrageous scenario. (See also *Control and Restraint*.)

Mental Action (Mind): *Mental Action* encompasses the psychic activities of the mind that make up the initial requisite states of *Willpower, Focus, Concentration, Imagination, Subtext,* and *Memory of Emotion* leading to and incorporated in all human behavior and stage action.

Method of Physical Actions: The name given to a *Series of Techniques* developed by Stanislavsky during the latter period of his work in the late 1930s, designed to analyze a play and assist an actor in the creation of a character through a series of rehearsal steps intended to discover the *Logical Sequence and Consecutiveness of Actions*. The emphasis of the technique is on finding the behavior of the character that is logical and sequential, leading to the evocation of emotion through *Physical Actions*. It is closely aligned with *Active Analysis,* and some experts in the field incorporate *Active Analysis* into the process but prefer to use the term *Method of Physical Actions* or *Method of Action Analysis*. (See *Active Analysis*.)

Milieu: Borrowed from the French to describe the totality of a place, including *Environment, Atmosphere, and Mood*.

Mise-en-Scène: A carefully selected orchestration of moving stage compositions that reveals the story nonverbally, moment-by-moment. The mise-en-scène in modern productions generally falls under the artistic guidance of the director but may also be developed collaboratively between the director and designers. It may be preplanned to the minutest detail or worked out in rehearsal. In Active Analysis it evolves through improvisations by the actors during the rehearsal process. (See Chapter 13: Reconnaissance of the Play; also *Subtext of Behavior, Blocking, Stage Business*.)

*Moment-to-Moment: The actor's ability to become fully engaged and remain in the present moment, reliving each word, action, and event as though experiencing them for the first time. Closely related to *Experiencing* and the state of *I Am/I Exist* and *Presence*. A term highly popular in contemporary American film and theatrical usage.

Mood: An emotional charge created by the playwright and interpretive artists for a scene or a play in order to affect actors and the audience. It is created through a combination of the external circumstances and interactions, the internal landscapes of the characters, and the perspectives and tone (serious; farcical, slapstick; quizzical; cynical) of the writer. *Mood* is often described in emotional terms: ominous, celebratory, frightening, anticipatory, dangerous, etc. The *Atmosphere* is one factor contributing to the impression of the *Mood* and vice-versa, and the terms are often used interchangeably. Characters also have *Moods* that can influence other characters and affect the *Atmosphere* of a scene, which are different from emotions triggered by specific incidents and more relevant to *Psychological Burdens*. (See *Atmosphere, Psychological Burden*.)

Motivation: The reason why a character, or person, behaves and speaks in a certain way. It is often unconscious for the character, while the actor may uncover it through rehearsals and text analysis. The *Motivation* can be triggered by many things; for example, an old wound, a current need, actions or words from the other characters, an insight or decision. This was not a term widely used by Stanislavsky, but the idea of various motivations was used. (See also *Intention, Objective*.)

Named Events, Episodes, and Units: A play contains a series of *Events* that are structured into scenes, and the scenes may include a number of *Episodes* (sometimes referred to as *Units*) made up of even smaller *Bits* (*Beats*). A character has a *Main Action-Task* and *Objective* in each *Episode*. The play, in its entirety, is also an *Event*. Each act is an *Event*, and each scene generally has one or more important *Events* that answer why that scene is in the play. The *Main Event* of the scene, which should be named, resolves the *Problem* of the scene one way or another, but not the *Problem* of the play, unless it is the climactic scene. In *Climactic Plot Structure* the author's careful arrangement of *Events* creates the structure of the *Plot* (how the author chooses to reveal the *Story*). However, in an *Episodic Play* the *Events* may not be linked by cause and effect or even similar characters but may be linked by being similar *Events* in completely different circumstances or with different characters or by *Theme* or other methods.

Nonverbal Action: *Actions* performed without speech and in justified silence. *Nonverbal Actions* are conveyed to an audience by means of expressive thoughts and physical behavior. (See *Language of the Body*.)

Novel: See *Telling the Novel*.

Objective (Goal, Aim, Solution): What the character wants or hopes to achieve. It is also what the character believes will solve his problem or fill his need. It is the *Aim* or *Goal* of a character's *Through-Line of Action* within an episode, scene, or act. The *Objective* provides a clear purpose that relates to the purpose invested in *Physical Actions* in order to make them *Psychophysical*. *Objective* is closely related to *Task* and *Problem*, in the sense that it is the character's hoped for solution or outcome as he grapples with the *Problem*. (See also *Task* and *Problem*.)

Obstacle (Object of Struggle/Conflict): An *Obstacle* is anything that impedes the character's progress. As a character attempts to solve his *Problem* and pursue his *Objective*, *Obstacles* arise. These *Obstacles* can be *External*, such as a *Physical Obstacle*, or an *Internal*, i.e., *Psychological*, *Obstacle*. The act of meeting an *Obstacle* creates conflict. In a play or scene, *external obstacles* often arise because another character has an opposing *Objective*. As the actor fulfills each *Action* toward his character's *Objective*, the other character(s) in the scene will have *Counteractions* to push toward his *Objective*. Opposing *Objectives* and *Counteractions* are *Obstacles*, which create a *Dynamic Conflict*, helping to bring energy to the scene.

Personal Theme (Your Own Theme): A state of self-realization when the actor discovers a deep and *Personal Theme* that is analogous to the main *Theme(s)* of his character. The actor arrives at this state through a very thorough analysis of his character and the play. The Personal Theme encourages the actor to more fully invest and arrive at a unique incarnation of his character. (Referred to by Sonia Moore in her books as Your Own Theme.)

Physical Actions: Physical behaviors or movement onstage, *Blocking*, or *Stage Business* given by the director. When they are *Justified* they become *Psychophysical Actions*. (See *Actions* and *Method of Physical Actions*.)

*Plot: The sequential development or revealing of the story of a play through a series of *events*, carefully selected and arranged by the author for dramatic effect. (See *Named Events, Episodes, and Units*.)

Poetic Reflection: *Poetic Reflection* describes artistic perspective brought to bear on past events, where distance enhances the artistic impression or usage. In acting it can refer to *Primary Emotions* that may be triggered as our pathways of emotion are evoked through thoughts, *Imagination* and other senses, *Physical Actions*, or *Obstacles* and that are carefully and artistically *Amalgamated* by the actor into a new landscape of *Secondary Emotions* for the character in the *Given Circumstances*. (See *Primary Emotions, Secondary Emotions*, and Chapter 12: Orchestrating Emotions.)

*Prana: Life force or energy that permeates the universe. Stanislavsky's actors were asked to concentrate deeply and then by means of strong inner intention to send "rays" of *Prana* energy to one another. The yogic techniques of pranayama are designed to access this energy within and outside the body using advanced breathing techniques. (See Chapter 2: The Actor's Palette: Interconnected Elements of Action.)

Primary Emotions: Emotions that are experienced in the actor's personal life. Stage emotions are *Secondary Emotions*, those created in the imaginary situation, and are *Poetic Reflections* of past emotions that are analogous to what is needed by the demands of a role. (See *Secondary Emotions*, *Poetic Reflection*, and Chapter 12: Orchestrating Emotions.)

Problem: An issue with which the character struggles, presented by a combination of the Given Circumstances and the character's background, perspective, and personality. It is helpful for actors to identify both a *Problem* and a *Task*. The struggle to solve the *Problem* almost always involves the other characters and is often tied into an *Event*. In order to identify the *Problem* in an *Episode*, *Unit*, or scene, the actor asks, How can I get . . . ? and then states the *Task*. For example: How can I convince the jury that I'm telling the truth? (See also *Task* and *Objective*.)

Psychological Burden: A *Psychological Burden* is an internal issue or problem that weighs heavily on the character's mind. Very often it is not spoken of immediately and may come to light in the course of the play's action. *Psychological Burdens* may be subtle yet strongly influence the thoughts, behavior, and feelings of the character. They are projected physically through the *Tonal Subtext* and *Subtext of the Behavior*. When they are extreme, it is called an *Idée Fixe* (fixed idea). (See *States of Being*.)

Psychophysical: Psychophysical is the inseparable body, mind and spirit (consciousness). A simple starting place with this concept in acting is that every thought or emotion has a physical expression, every physical act related thoughts and emotional responses. In acting you are always doing something physical, thinking something and feeling something. Origins of the word are as follows: Psycho is short for psychological and is derived from psyche, meaning an embodiment of the soul. According to the Oxford English Dictionary, Psyche was a character in Greek mythology considered the personification of the soul. She often took the form of a butterfly. She had a union with Eros, the god of passionate love. The preceding Greek word (psukhe) means breath, life and soul/spirit. The physical aspects include the body, its organic functions and movement, and the biological aspects of the brain.

Public Solitude: Allows the actor to deeply concentrate, as if he were completely alone and experiencing the life of the character while simultaneously inviting the audience into his innermost thoughts and feelings. It takes time, training, and practice for an actor to develop the *Dual Consciousness* necessary to both maintain a sense of being alone and yet aware that he is in public as well. (See *Dual Consciousness*.)

Reconnaissance of the Mind: The term used for the first steps of intellectual analysis and research of a play by a director, designer, or actor. It involves the gathering of facts and information, study of the *Events*, *Plot*, *Subject*, *Themes*, *Language*, *Actions*, etc., in search for the *Supertask* of the characters and of the play.

Relaxation: In addition to helping with acting and overall creativity, relaxation is a key to health by diminishing the effects of stress. The purpose of relaxation is to increase and learn to control the *Flow of Energy* in the mind and body. (See *Flow of Energy*.)

Representational Acting (Theatre of Representation): A philosophy and practice of acting whereby the actor creates in rehearsal and plays an image of a character, which is then repeated technically throughout a performance. No attempt is made to accomplish *"Living Experience."* *Representational Acting* perhaps reaches its height in the theatre of Molière, The Comédie Française.

Restraint and Control: The actor's conscious judgment and continual adjustment in performance to strategically, truthfully, and aesthetically reveal the character's life, circumstances, and emotion. The ability of an actor to distribute his physical, vocal, and emotional energy appropriately throughout a role without over- or underacting, and in the correct tempo-rhythm. Stanislavsky encourages actors to give full energy in rehearsals, and as the actor approaches performance to orchestrate energy according to the exact score of *Actions*. (See *Measure of Truth*.)

Reversal Points: A point in a scene where the character encounters a *Physical* or *Psychological Obstacle*, or *Counteraction* from another character and must *Justify* making an *Adaptation* and then decide to choose another *Action* and strategy to solve the *Problem*, possibly including focusing on a different *Task* or *Objective*. A *Reversal Point* also occurs when the *Initiator of an Action* then becomes the *Receiver of an Action* and vice-versa. (See *Counteraction* and Chapter 15: Active Analysis through Events and Actions.)

Secondary Emotions: Stage emotions prepared and selected during the rehearsal process. They can be repeated for artistic work onstage because they can be orchestrated and controlled. *Secondary Emotions* provide artistic perspective for the actor as they have been explored during the rehearsal period and conditioned through the selection of fitting *Actions* to arise spontaneously within the imaginary circumstances of the play. (See *Poetic Reflection* and Chapter 12: Orchestrating Emotions.)

Second Plan: The story that happens before, during (between the acts and when a character is not onstage), and after the play that is not seen by the audience. This includes incidents and events that are referred to by the character in the text. The *First Plan* is what is seen by the audience.

Seed (Kernel): The essence of the play and the character. *Seed* and *Kernel* are often used interchangeably; however, for simplicity we will refer to the *Kernel* of the play and the *Seed* of the character. The former is the germinating idea that triggered the playwright's impetus to write the play. The latter refers to the essence of the character expressed through motives, attitudes, traits, gestures, and specific behaviors. Used in the System as the *Seed* idea and motivating force behind all of a character's actions leading to its manifestation as the *Supertask* and message of the play.

Sensory Evocation (Sense Memory, Memory of the Body, and Sensory Creation): Involves not only seeing *Mental Images* but also assists in coloring and filling out *Images* by involving the other senses; thereby evoking smells, sounds, tastes, and textures. *Sensory Evocation* may utilize *Sense Memory*, which includes the memory of physical sensations and feelings as taken in through the five senses of sight, hearing, taste, touch, and smell. *Memory of the Body* and *Kinetic Memory* may include *Sense Memory* but also includes the memory of emotions and memory of physical behaviors stored in the body. (See *Affective Memory*.)

Social Purpose (Civic Duty): *Social Purpose* refers to a play, actor, director, or theatre company that is dedicated to the enrichment of culture and society (also called the artist's *Super-supertask*). Most important, it relates to an artist's desire to uplift and educate an audience through theatrical education in the form of entertainment.

Spine of the Play: See *Through-Action* and *Supertask*.

Spiritual Communion: See *Communion/Communication* and Chapter 6: Communion: Deepening Communication and Mutual Influence.

*Stage Business: Includes smaller, more detailed behavior, such as lighting a cigarette, making a drink, or hiding a letter. In Active Analysis the stage business is arrived at using sense memory and an exploration of action within the given circumstances while using stage props. (See *Blocking*.)

States of Being: There are three primary *States of Being: Physical, Psychological,* and *Emotional. States of Being* can vary in intensity and duration depending on the *Given Circumstances*. Examples of a *Physical State* would be illness, drunkenness, drug withdrawal, cravings, fatigue, wounded, a head- or toothache, or a physical disability such as blindness or deafness. *Psychological States* include worry, obsessiveness, and an overwhelmingly compulsive idea called an *Idée Fixe* (fixed idea). Also, included is a *Psychological Burden* that the character carries with him throughout a play. Emotional States are anxious, hyper, upset, fearful, grief-stricken, etc. (See *Psychological Burden* and Chapter 12: Orchestrating Emotions.)

Story (Telling the Story): An account of *Events* and the revealing of the people and details involved in and associated with them. This is a *Device* used by directors and actors in *Active Analysis* to assist in the understanding of the character and the role within the context of the entire *Story* of the play. Each actor tells aloud the *Story* of the play from his character's perspective by following the logical sequence of the *Plot*. (See *Telling the Novel*.)

Subconscious Creativity: A state of the actor's work that arises spontaneously through the conscious work on a role. (See *Inspiration* and *Superconscious State*.)

Subtext: The meaning under the text. The audience comes to the theatre or cinema to see and hear the *Subtext* (they can read the text at home). The *Subtext* must physically reveal a character's true thoughts, feelings, and motives through the *Subtext of the Body* and verbally through *Tonal Subtext*. Creation of the *Subtext* builds and reveals the character's subconscious mind. Stage *Action* springs forth from the *Subtext*. (See *Subtext of Behavior; Tonal Subtext*.)

Subtext of Behavior: The *Subtext of Behavior* is the specific behavior and bodily actions that an actor chooses for his character. It may align with or be in direct conflict with the words of the text, but it externally expresses the psychological and spiritual life of the character. (See *Language of the Body*. Refer to: *The Stanislavski System,* by Sonia Moore, Penguin, 1984, 68.)

Superconscious State: A term borrowed from yoga and practices of meditation by Stanislavsky, signifying the highest transcendent state of psychic awareness and creativity that can be achieved by the actor during performance. (See *Inspiration*.)

Supertask (Formerly called Superobjective): The play's ruling idea, message, or ultimate impression. It is the playwright's intention behind the play, the overarching impact he wants the play to have on the audience; the images, thoughts, and emotions he wants to be resonating in the audience long after they see the play. The production *Supertask* is the director and creative team's interpretation of the play's *Supertask* brought to life through a production concept that guides their creative solutions to the play's creative challenges and focuses the overall imprint that the team wants to leave on the audience. Each character also has a *Supertask*, a ruling idea that guides the formulation of scene *Objectives* and important thoughts, reactions, and choices—what that character wants most to achieve in the play. The combination of all the characters and their *Supertasks* in the play must lead to the fulfillment of the play's *Supertask*. (This search is at the heart of the explorations of *Active Analysis* in chapters 13, 14, 15, and 16.)

Super-supertask of the Actor, Director, or Playwright: The artist's desire to use his work for the education and edification of an audience and the greater society is called the *Super-supertask*. The System encourages each individual actor to ask what it is that he or she can best contribute to society through his artistic work. (See *Social Purpose* and Chapter 19: The Creative Life: Communion with Audience and Society.)

Task: Task is the active mental, emotional and physical struggle to overcome an obstacle and solve the problem. A *Task* is the tactical scheme, *Through-actions* the character actively engages in order to solve the *Problem*. To uncover the *Task* the actor asks, What can I do here and now, in these circumstances to solve this problem? It must be immediate. (See also *Problem, Objective,* and *Action*.)

Telling the Novel: A teaching and directorial *Device* to assist the actor during the *Active Analysis* of a role. As plays are written using only dialogue, the actor needs to re-create what might have been written by an author if the play were a novel, such as: the *Motivations*, reactions and *Counteractions*, physical and tonal subtext, characters' thoughts (*Inner Monologue*), etc. Telling the Novel aloud thus helps the actor fill out the inner and outer life of the role and find specific, interesting, and relevant behavior in the form of transitive active verbs, i.e., *Actions*. (See Chapter 15: Active Analysis through Events and Actions.)

Theme (Leitmotif, Thread): The *Theme* relates to the main idea and subject the writer is elaborating upon, or about which he is expressing a strong or moral perspective. Both the *Theme(s)* of the play and the *Theme(s)* of the character grow out of the *Kernel* and *Seed*, respectively. The *Themes* eventually flower into the *Supertask* of the character and the play. (See *Supertask, Seed/Kernel*. Refer to Chapter 2: The Actor's Palette: Interconnected Elements of Action.)

Through-action (Through-line of Action, Spine, Action Steps, Score of Action): Is composed of the series of steps the character takes to reach the *Objective*. It is also the link that ties the *Actions* to one another to create a consecutive line-through for the role and play. It involves taking *Action Steps* that the actor engages in moment-to-moment by initiating and responding with the scene partner(s). Collectively, the entire series of *Actions* for a role is referred to as the *Score of Actions* or the *Spine* of the role and culminates in the fulfillment of the *Supertask* of both the characters and the play.

Tempo and Rhythm: In the Stanislavsky System, *Tempo* is the speed or timing of your actions, and *Rhythm* is the inner intensity of an action. *Tempo* is primarily, but not exclusively, influenced by the external *Given Circumstances,* and *Rhythm* is primarily determined by *Mental Images*, thoughts, and emotional responses. *Tempo-Rhythm* serves as a bridge between the inner experience and its physical expression.

Transformation (Reincarnation into the Life of the Character): The process whereby an actor uses his or her own spiritual, mental, physical, and vocal resources to create the spiritual and physical life of another human being who lives within the imaginary circumstances of a play. When an actor achieves a complete *Psychophysical* absorption into character while simultaneously living the life of the human spirit, she is said to have achieved a state of *Transformation*. (See *Dual Perspectives*.)

Unconscious: For Stanislavsky, all the inner workings of the human mind that could not be consciously available to the actor but could influence an actor's creative process. (See *Subconscious* and *Superconscious State*.)

Verbal Action: A *Psychophysical Action* that is partially fulfilled through speech using the textual language of the play. It is named using an active, transitive verb in the infinitive form; e.g., to convince, to find out, to threaten, or to plead. (See *Action*.)

Visualization: The creation of a film of *Mental Images* that have been selected and organized by the actor and that run continuously through a role while speaking and in silence. (See *Imagination*.)

Volition (Will): The act of consciously exercising one's *Will*. *Will* is a conscious or unconscious decision, drive or desire to act. *Will* plus *Physical Action* evokes sensations that are experienced as feelings, and these in turn begin the process of *Living-Through* or *Experiencing*, which brings life to the physical *Embodiment* of the role. (See Stanislavsky's Diagram and Explanation in Chapter 18.)

*Yoga: An ancient technique, the name of which means the union of mind, body, and spirit, as well as the union of an individual spirit with the universal spirit. Yoga was one of the foundational influences in the creation of the Stanislavsky system. Some of the many techniques that Stanislavsky borrowed from yoga include meditation, *Concentration, Relaxation,* breathing techniques, and even the *Psychophysical* concept.

Appendix II
10 Yoga Poses

Iyengar Yoga Centre of Victoria

Restorative Practice ©2013

Hold all postures (except Bharadvajrasana) from three to five minutes, breathing softly and evenly through both nostrils. Focus mind on body and breath, bringing it back to the breath whenever it wanders off.

NOTE: Students already familiar with sirsasana (headstand) and sarvangasana (shoulderstand), may add these postures to the practice below, as follows:
a) Practise sirsasana after prasarita padottanasana (#5),
b) Practise sarvangasana after paschimottanasana (#8) followed by halasana (plough) and setubandha (bridge) if there is time—use support when needed.

1. SUPTA BADDHA KONASANA

Lie on back with buttocks against bolster, place blanket under head; bring soles of the feet together, separate knees.

(Optional) Tie a belt and place it around hip bones, between knees, and over outer edge of feet.

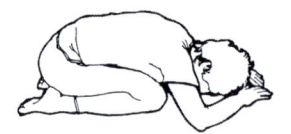

2. VIRASANA (forward bend)
Kneeling with legs apart,
bend forward,
rest head on floor, blanket or bolster.

3. UTTANASANA
(standing forward bend)

Stand with feet slightly apart,
legs straight,
bend forward from the hips and
rest head on a chair or brick.

4. ADHO MUKHA SVANASANA (dog pose)

Kneel down, place hands on floor, palms down, middle fingers parallel.
Lift knees off floor, straightening arms and legs, raise buttocks to ceiling.
Rest head on bolster or brick; adjust weight so it is evenly balanced on all four limbs; keep knees and elbows firm.

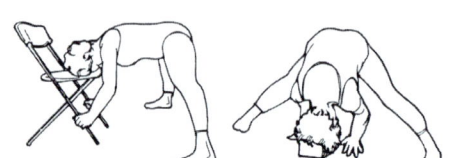

5. PRASARITA PADOTTANASANA

(standing forward bend)

Stand with legs wide apart, feet parallel, knees straight.
Bend forward from the hips, resting head on chair, brick, or floor (depending on flexibility).

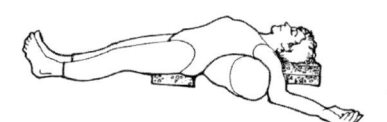

6. BACKBEND OVER BOLSTER

(a) for stiff people or with bad backs

Lie on back. Place a bolster horizontally across back. Place one foam block under buttocks. Place one or two foam blocks under head.
Keep legs together, rotate them internally, and move tailbone towards heels.

b) Criss-cross bolsters

Place one bolster horizontally and another vertically on top of it. Lie lengthways on top bolster, pelvis and back supported, back of head resting on floor, arms over the head, resting on floor, and relaxing.

If back is not comfortable, slide up and down until you find a restful position.

7. BHARADVAJRASANA (simple twist sitting in chair)

Sit sideways on seat of chair, feet and legs together.
When turning to left: place left hand flat against outside edge of back of chair, grip inside edge of back of chair with right hand.
Breathe, lengthen spine, and turn.
Repeat turning to the right side.

(Do pose three times each side, holding for three or four breaths.)

8. PASCHIMOTANASANA

(seated forward bend)

Sit on floor, legs stretching out in front of you, keep legs and feet together, rotate thighs internally and press out through inner heels. Bend forward from the hips and rest head on chair or brick.

9. VIPARITA KARANI

(legs against wall, buttocks raised, pelvis resting on bolster)

Lie on floor with legs against wall, raise pelvis and support buttocks on a bolster or several blankets, chest opening, back of head resting on floor, abdomen relaxed. Raise arms over head and rest them on floor (palms up, elbows bent).

Legs must stay touching the wall—if not, use elbows to wiggle closer in.

10. SAVASANA (deep relaxation)

Lie on floor, face up, shoulders back, shoulderblades resting on one or two folded blankets; place another folded blanket under head. Stretch arms out to the side, backs of arms and hands resting on floor. Place a rolled sticky mat or towel at top of buttocks (to support lower back); separate legs slightly and roll them out from the hips. Keep lengthening arms and legs, and let them rest on the floor. Use support of blanket to help open chest and facilitate relaxed breathing.

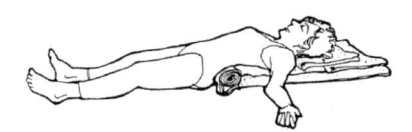

Please do not copy.
This sheet was produced by Derek French, MD, Shirley Daventry French, and Lauren Cox (drawings) with acknowledgement to their teacher, B.K.S. Iyengar.

©2013 by the Iyengar Yoga Centre of Victoria
202—919 Fort St, Victoria BC V8V 3K3 Canada
Telephone: (250) 386 - 9642 or Email: iyoga@telus.net

Appendix IIIa

Basic and Intermediate Improvisation Worksheets[1]

Purpose: To gain understanding of the structure of dramatic action and proficiency in creating it onstage

Guidelines: It is important to create in detail and not in general, so consider each nuance of the situation as suggested below.

(Many previously introduced terms and concepts are repeated here in italics for easy reference and review.)

Name Your *Event*: (noun, metaphor, title, or headline) _____
***Given Circumstances*:**

Who? _____

What is going on? (*active facts*)

What is the *problem*? _____

Where? _____

When? _____

With whom? *(Relationship)* _____

Where From? _____

Where to? _____

What do I want to do that will solve the problem in my favor? _____

---

[1] This worksheet created by Philip G. Bennett for his students at the TheatreLab & Conservatory.

(Similar to Why, but implies What you want to get, the Objective)

Why?_____

(Your reason, i.e., *purpose and motivation* for doing what you are doing. Sometimes *why* and *what* are the same, the *motivation* and the *objective*.)

How? (Always let the *how* take care of itself. Think of how? only when in the moment and while on your feet) _____

What can I do to reach this solution? These are your Action Steps and together they create a Through-line of Actions: Choose between two (2) and five (5) for improvisations and character *études*.

1. _____

2. _____

3. _____

4. _____

Obstacles: If it is a *Nonverbal* (silent) improvisation and you are alone, you need to choose an *obstacle* for yourself in order to create dramatic conflict. This is called the *Object of Struggle*. If two or more people are in a scene, then what they are fighting about is also the *object of struggle*, and/or the *Problem*. This creates dramatic tension and heightens the conflict.

Now you need to create *Weapons*. *Weapons* are *obstacles* that you choose to throw in your partner's way in order to win, as in a battle. Choose at least three (3).

1. _____

2. _____

3. _____

Images and Sensory Evocation: You need to have images for every person, place, or thing either seen or referred to in your improvisation. These can be personal or imaginary or a combination of both. This includes seeing the world of the scene around you and re-creating it with all your senses.

Physical and Psychological States of Being: Are you excited, fatigued, hurt, wounded, hyper, or anxious, etc.? Never play a *State of Being,* for that would be playing the result. You must find the correct psychophysical behavior using the *magic if*: If I was in this state what would I do? Put your sole attention to the *action* and *objective* and let the emotions arise out of that.

Analogous Emotions: Do not use this until you have thoroughly read and practiced the exercises in Chapter 11: Verbal Action: Communicating with Words and Subtext and in Chapter 12: Orchestrating Emotions.

Reflection: Use the reflection questions below the improvisation exercises in the chapters, particularly in chapters 9 and 11, when learning about silent and verbal actions. The reflection is an important step to solidify your learning.

Appendix IIIb

Intermediate and Advanced Improvisation Worksheet

Guideline: Follow all guidelines on the basic improvisation worksheet but add the following more challenging considerations:

The Arc of Dramatic Action

Every episode, scene, and good play has an arc. It is there because our lives have an arc. We are born; we become youths; as adults we rise to our peak, and we move into middle-age, arrive to our senior years, come to the last chapter of our lives, and then pass away.

This is the cycle of life and all physical matter; all living plants and creatures will experience it. Perhaps just as in a play, the characters have a before time and an after time.

Below is the structure designed to create brilliant improvisations, scenes, and plays:

Zone of Silence, or the Before Time: A *zone of silence* is used to establish the environment, atmosphere, mood, and relationships when there is a justification to remain silent. **Note:** When preparing an advanced improvisation, such as a Named Event, discuss with your partners beforehand how you can create a dramatic zone of silence. Then follow the Arc of Dramatic Action as outlined. It also helps to establish that something has just happened that leaves everyone speechless for a few moments or minutes. Anton Chekhov, a world-renowned playwright and storyteller, used long, silent pauses. Stanislavsky sometimes added zones of silence to immerse the actors and audience into deep thought and moods.

Reconnaissance: Go about your objective in a *circumvent manner*. That is, do not spring your action on your partners immediately unless the circumstances demand that you do so. It is far wiser to gather information by observation and action steps that will give you an advantage in the same way an army gathers as much information about the enemy so that it is able to attack at the best possible time and gain the best advantage in order to win.

When working on a play, the opening episode is usually, but not always, called the *exposition*. An exposition gives us information about the given circumstances of the story. Who, what, when, where, etc. However, it is important in your improvisations that you not come out and start to tell the exposition openly. A good exposition in a play and improvisation needs to be subtle and revealed gradually through the events, actions, and relationships of the characters.

Inciting Event: As you will see in Chapter 15: Active Analysis through Events and Actions, there is always an *initiator* of the action and a *receiver* of the action. Within your improvisations there also must be an initiator and a receiver of action. The inciting event can also be something that happens unexpectedly that ignites the action that sets the conflict in motion.

Building to a Climax: Once the action gets going, then you and your partners must battle it out until you build to a climax; then you will need to sustain the climax for a few moments until you sense that it is time to gradually bring it slowly down to a *logical conclusion*.

Logical Conclusion: *A logical conclusion* implies that you and your partner(s) either come to a resolve, stalemate, or a clear acknowledgment as to who has won and who has lost. There are exceptions; for instance, when an improvisation concludes with a character leaving the room abruptly. In fact, it is certain that you have already thought of other possibilities. That is very good; however, for the time being we suggest that you first learn the arc of dramatic action before venturing too far away from it. Once you have it down pat and can use your technique as your imagination dictates, then you are free to fly. In other words, "Don't put the cart before the horse."

Environment, Atmosphere, and Mood(s): Used to color an improvisation and each scene in a play.

1. **Environment:** The 360° physical surroundings.

2. **Atmosphere:** As if something were in the air, the less tangible environment. Very close to *mood*.

3. **Mood:** The feeling created by the *environment* and the *atmosphere* and what each person carries inside of them. For example: tension (personal and between people). Also, the *mood* you are in, your *Emotional State of Being:* depressed, happy, joyful, sorrowful, elated, etc.

Appendix IV

Additional Actions for Selection and Practice

Please continue to expand the list for yourself.

to Abuse
to Accuse
to Admonish
to Advise
to Allure
to Antagonize
to Appeal
to Astonish
to Bait
to Banish
to Befriend
to Beg
to Belittle
to Berate
to Beseech
to Boast
to Brag
to Break an engagement
to Break a promise
to Browbeat
to Chastise
to Cheer up
to Chide
to Claim
to Compromise
to Condemn
to Confess
to Consider
to Console
to Cut
to Damn
to Declaim

to Declare
to Defend
to Degrade
to Deject
to Demand
to Denounce
to Dissemble
to doubt
to Drop a bomb (metaphorically speaking)
to Encourage
to Enforce
to Enlighten
to Enlist
to Entertain
to Flee
to Force
to Forgive
to Frighten
to Gladden
to Goad
to Gossip
to Guard
to Guide
to Harass
to Harm
to Harry
to Help
to Henpeck
to Honor
to Humble
to Illustrate

to Incite
to Indoctrinate
to Infect
to Influence
to Injure
to Insinuate
to Insist
to Inspect
to Inspire
to Instigate
to Insult
to Intercede
to Intercept
to Interject
to Interrogate
to Interrupt
to Investigate
to Invite
to Invoke
to Jab
to Jeer
to Jilt
to Jostle
to Judge
to Justify
to Lash Out
to Laud
to Laugh at
to Lure
to Menace
to Mend
to Mesmerize

to Misdirect	to Puzzle	to Teach
to Mock	to Quell	to Tease
to Molest	to Query	to Tempt
to Nag	to Quiz	to Testify
to Needle	to Rally	to Thank
to Negate	to Reassure	to Threaten
to Obey	to Rebuff	to Train
to Observe	to Rebuke	to Trap
to Offend	to Reclaim	to Trick
to Offer	to Reconcile	to Unearth
to Order	to Recruit	to Unnerve
to Overpower	to Redeem	to Unburden
to Pacify	to Reflect	to Unleash
to Pamper	to Reject	to Unite
to Pardon	to Relinquish	to Upbraid
to Patronize	to Renounce	to Uplift
to Permit	to Report	to Upset
to Persuade	to Reproach	to Urge
to Petition	to Repudiate	to Use
to Placate	to Restrain	to Vanquish
to Plead	to Rid	to Victimize
to Poison (envenom)	to Ridicule	to Vilify
to Poke	to Rub salt into someone's wounds	to Violate
to Praise		to Vivify
to Pretend	to Sabotage	to Waken
to Probe	to Sanctify	to Warn
to Process (absorb, wonder, evaluate)	to Sanction	to Weep
	to Satirize	to Whine
to Proclaim	to Save	to Whip
to Prohibit	to Scold	to Win
to Promise	to Scorn	to Wonder
to Prosecute	to Slander	to Worry
to Protect	to Spurn	to Worship
to Provoke	to Support	to Wound
to Punish	to Surrender	to Wrong
to Push	to Swear	to Yield
to Put down	to Taunt	

Appendix V

Sample Text Analysis: *Three Sisters* by Anton Chekhov, Act 2, Scene 2 (Andrei and Ferapont)

Purpose: to demonstrate the logic of voice and speech analysis
Action, Inner Monologue, Subtext, and Image as notated on a script

S = Group of the Subject
V = Group of the Verb
C = Group of the Circumstances

Three Sisters **by Anton Chekhov, Act 2, Scene 2 (Andrei and Ferapont)**

Andrei: A: *To dismiss:* <u>Nothing.</u>^c *(IM: "Why does Protopopov bother me at home?").* ③ **A:** *To evaluate:* <u>Tomorrow is Friday.</u>^c ② **A:** *To complain:* **I don't** <u>have to attend</u>^v ② *(IMG: Andrei does not want to go, do you have such a place in mind?)* **A:** *To decide:* **but** <u>I'll go</u>^v ① <u>anyway</u>^c ... *(Notice the ellipsis, there must be a thought here.)* ① **A:** *To justify himself:* <u>to occupy</u>^v **myself.** ① *(IM: "I must get away from Natasha, and there is nothing to do here.")* **A:** *To complain:* **It's** <u>boring at home</u>^c …
Pause.

(This is a major pause in the scene, and there is no need to rush it. Take your time to really achieve deep thought and logically come to a decision to continue speaking. Ask yourself what Andrei is thinking and feeling. What analogies do I have in my experience, either personal or observed, to use as a source of images in the following section. What do I need to create and see in my imagination to be able to justify Andrei's self-ridicule and state of loneliness. How did my life end up like this? Maybe Andrei thinks something like this: All the dreams I had when I was younger are fading away. I married to hastily and made a mistake, and now life has cheated me. Ferapont is deaf so I can quietly get this off my chest by speaking my deepest feelings aloud.)

                              S   C   S   V
A: *To quietly implore:* Dear Grandpa! ① A: *To ridicule:* How strangely ① life ① changes and deceives
              C   C   V   V
us! ① A: *To cite an example:* Today, ① out of boredom, ① because I had nothing else to do, ① I picked
up ① *(IMG: Choose an image, either personal or imaginary, of something that has had a great meaning
for you in the past and now it doesn't, so it seems ironic to you.)* A: *To treat the book as if it is a lost
treasure:* this
       S   S   V
book—old university lectures—A: *To mock himself and Chairman:* and I wanted to laugh … *(Note the
                                        S
ellipsis.)* ① A: *To mock yourself:* My God, ① *(IMG: See an image of something menial that you look down
upon.)*
              S   S
I'm a secretary of the District Board, ① the Board ① where *(IMG: Andrei dislikes and distrusts the
                                                 S   V   S
Chairman intensely; what image would you choose here?)* Protopopov ① is ① the chairman. ③ I'm the
   S   C   VC   S
secretary, ① *(Andrei pictures himself as a nobody)* and the most ① I can expect is to be ① a member of
the *(IMG: Andrei sees a place and occupation that is far beneath him and repulses him. What images do
you
          S   S   S
have?)* District Board! ② I, ① a member of the District Board, ③ *(IMG: Take a slight pause here to
capture the image of an analogous dream, savor it, and let it affect you before you speak the line. Use your
                                          V   C   S   S
voice to express your feelings.)* who dreams ① every night ① that I am a professor ① at Moscow
University, (IMG: Choose an analogous image of a wonderful place that you'd really like to be right now!)* ①
    S   S   VC   V
a famous scholar ① whom all of Russia ① is ① proud of! ① Ferapont: I wouldn't know … ① I don't
V
hear well … *(Up to now Andrei has been speaking aloud; however, mostly to himself. Ferapont is a device
Chekhov uses to give Andrei a justification for speaking his private thoughts aloud.)*

Note: *Now it is your turn. Use the remainder of the text below to determine and write in the actions,
speech groups, underlined words, images, inner monologue and logical pauses.*

Andrei: If you could I probably wouldn't talk to you. I need to talk to somebody, but my wife doesn't
understand me. I'm afraid of my sisters for some reason. I'm afraid they'll laugh at me embarrass me. I
don't drink, I don't like salons, but with what pleasure I would be sitting now at Testov's in Moscow, or in
the Bolshoi Moscovsky, my dear fellow.

Appendix VIa

The Properties of Vowels (with IPA Vowel Articulation Chart)

Vowels are:

- voiced (the vocal folds vibrate to create sound)
- supported by a constant, uninterrupted stream of air, called *airflow* (which differentiates them from consonants); this is also why singers can release beautiful sustained sounds on the vowels
- differentiated by the shape and position of the tongue, lips, and jaw
- differentiated by *location* in the mouth—forward, middle, or back
- differentiated by *vertical location*—low, middle, or high
- differentiated by shorter or longer length of utterance
- differentiated by more tension, or less tension, called *lax*

The Properties of Diphthongs:
- Two vowel sounds slide together to create a new single-syllable sound called a *diphthong*. This can be true even if only one vowel is written, such as the *a* in *ate*. In terms of articulation, the tongue glides from one vowel position to another, but the second sound has less tension. There is vibration of vocal folds through both articulator positions to create a blended sound.

R coloration (also called rhotic): If an [r] follows the vowel(s) it colors the vowel sound by a either a bunching of the tongue in back or turning up the tip of the tongue. Generally in IPA, R coloration is shown by a little squiggle after the vowel symbol [ɚ] but some fonts also write it as [əʳ].

IPA Vowel Articulation Chart

IPA symbol	Sound	Sample Words	Location	Articulators
Front Vowels				
æ	aah	C<u>a</u>t, bl<u>a</u>ck, <u>a</u>sk	Front, low, tense	Lips tense, wide, bottom jaw lowered some (unrounded but more lemon-shaped lips) Teeth wide apart and showing Tongue tip almost touches lower teeth Tongue slightly tense against molars
e	ay	pl<u>a</u>ce, l<u>a</u>te,	Front, mid-height, tense	Lips open, wide with tension (unrounded) Teeth showing, wider than [ɛ] but not as wide as [æ] Tongue tip to lower teeth Tongue back against molars
ɛ	eh	m<u>e</u>t, b<u>e</u>d, f<u>ea</u>ther	Front, mid-height, lax	Lips open in middle but not as much on sides (unrounded) Teeth showing, slightly apart (less than [e] but more than [i], Tongue tip points at lower teeth Tongue back touches molars
i	ee	s<u>ee</u>, h<u>ea</u>t	Front, high, tense	Lips unrounded but open, wide, tense Teeth lightly closed like a smile Tongue tip points to upper gums (but not touching) Tongue back on upper molars
I	ih	h<u>i</u>t, s<u>i</u>t	Front, high, lax	Lips unrounded but open, wide and relaxed, Small space between teeth, Tongue tip points to top of upper teeth, Tongue back touches upper molars
Back Vowels				
ɑ	ah	f<u>a</u>ther, <u>a</u>rm	Back, low, lax	Lips unrounded but sort of heart shaped, Jaw lowered, teeth apart only few top front showing Tongue flat, relaxed base of mouth
o	oh	<u>o</u>pen, h<u>o</u>me, g<u>o</u>	Back, mid-height, tense	Lips very round. Far apart top to bottom, sides tense and pushing in, Teeth apart, lower jaw dropped Tongue tip points to lower teeth Tongue back raised
ɔ	aw	c<u>a</u>ll, f<u>ou</u>r	Back, mid-height, lax	Lips slightly rounded and forward, sides pushing in as far as possible Jaw lowered, only few front teeth showing, teeth slightly apart Tongue back raised
ʊ	oo	p<u>u</u>t, c<u>ou</u>ld	Back, high, lax	Lips rounded and forward Teeth slightly apart, only front top and bottom teeth showing Tongue tip touches lower teeth Tongue back raised
u	ooo	bl<u>u</u>e, f<u>oo</u>d	Back, high, tense	Lips rounded, tense and pushed forward like in a kiss, with only small opening Teeth apart Tongue tip touches back of lower teeth Tongue rounded in back

THE PROPERTIES OF VOWELS (WITH IPA VOWEL ARTICULATION CHART)

IPA symbol	Sound	Sample Words	Location	Articulators
Central Vowels				
ə (called the schwa)	uh unstressed	away, delicious, peaceful	Central, mid- height, lax, only unstressed syllables	Lips unrounded, lips and teeth slightly apart, Tongue relaxed
ʌ	uh stressed	cup, luck,	Central, mid, lax, stressed	Lips and Teeth slightly apart. Lips unrounded, Tongue relaxed
ɚ	er unstressed	power,	Central, mid, lax rhotic (r colored) Unstressed	Lips and teeth slightly open making a small square space, and pushed forward. Tongue tip curls back a little. Tongue back slightly rounded
ɜ˞	ur stressed	turn, learn	Central, mid, lax rhotic (r colored) Stressed	Lips and teeth slightly open making a small square space, and pushed forward. Tongue tip curls back a little. Tongue back slightly rounded
General American Diphthongs				
aɪ	ah-ih	five, eye	Back low to front high	Tongue glides from [a] to [i], dropped jaw pulls somewhat up as sound progresses
aʊ	ow-ooh	now, out	Back low back to back high	Lips go from open and rounded to more narrow, rounded, and pushed forward. Tongue glides from [a] to [ʊ].
eɪ	ay-ee	say, eight	Front mid to front high	Tongue glides from [e] to [I]
eəʳ	ay-ee-r	where, air	Front mid to Central mid	Tongue glides from [e] to [I] to [r]
Iəʳ	ee-ah-r	near, here	Front high to	Tongue glides from [i] to [ə] to [r]
iu	ee-ooo	due, union	Front high to back high	Tongue glides from [i] to [u]
ɔɪ	ow-ih	boy, join	Back low to front high	Tongue glides from [ɔ] to [I]
ʊəʳ	ooh-ih-r	pure, tourist	Back high to central mid	Tongue glides from [ʊ] to [ə] to [r]

Appendix VIb

The Properties of Consonants (with IPA Consonant Articulation Chart)

Consonants:
- may be voiced (vocal folds vibrate)—[v] [b]
- or unvoiced/voiceless (with a larger space in the glottis, air passes through without vibrating the vocal folds)—[f] [p]
- *cognates* are pairs of sounds where the shape of the articulators is exactly the same but one is voice and one is unvoiced—[b] [p]
- require an interruption of the stream of voiced sound vibration or unvoiced air vibration
- produced through friction [f], explosion [p], or sending the sound out through the nose [n]
- made by a particular combination of articulators, including one or both lips, the teeth, the tongue

The articulators shape the sound in different ways:
- *continuant* (a prolonged sound without a change in quality) [m]
- *glide* (articulators change shape during the creation of the sound) [w]
- *fricative* (friction and thus a kind of noisy turbulence is caused by only a narrow amount of air getting through) Examples are the cognates (f—unvoiced, v—voiced), (s—unvoiced, z—voiced),
- *plosive* (the air flow is interrupted completely and builds up to pop when released) Examples are the cognates (p—unvoiced, b—voiced), (k—unvoiced, g—voiced) (t—unvoiced, d—voiced)

The consonants are made in a particular location in the mouth:
- *bilabial* (labia= lips and bi = two, so this means made with the two lips, which also places the sound in the front of the mouth)—[m]
- *labiodental* (lips and teeth)—[v]
- *lingua-alveolar* (tongue and alveolar ridge, right behind top front teeth)—[t]
- *lingua-dental* (tongue and dental = teeth, made with the tongue between the teeth)—[th]

THE PROPERTIES OF CONSONANTS (WITH IPA CONSONANT ARTICULATION CHART)

- *lingua-velar* (lingua= tongue, velum = soft palate at the back of the roof of the mouth, made with the tongue touching the soft palate)
- Cognates mean the same mechanisms create a sound in the same location with one voice and one unvoiced. For example [b] (voiced) and [p] (unvoiced)

Affricates:
- Parts of two consonant sounds that combine to make a new sound—[th] [cr] [gl] [ch]

IPA Consonant Articulation Chart

IPA symbol	Written	Sample Words	Location/ Articulators	Manner of Production
Bilabials				
m	m	mother	Bilabial, nasal resonance	Voiced, continuant. Lips compressed
p	p	pop, dapper	bilabial	plosive, voiceless. Lips together, teeth apart. after air build up, explosion of air parts lips (cognate b)
b	b	best, stub	bilabial	plosive, voiced, lips together, teeth apart. after air build up, smaller explosion of air then with [b] parts lips (cognate p)
w	w	water, yellow	bilabial	Voiced, glide (cognate wh). Lips very forward like a kiss
hw	wh	where, awhile	bilabial	Voiceless glide (*not used much any more except in period or some very high class dialects*). More commonly wh is pronounced as its cognate [w] below, Lips very forward like a kiss
Labiodentals				
f	f, gh, ph	fast, laugh, phone	labiodental	Voiceless, fricative (cognate v). Upper teeth against lower lip only a little air through this space
v	v, some f	voice, have, of	labiodental	Voiced, fricative (cognate f). Upper teeth against lower lip only a little air/sound through this space
Lingua-dentals				
θ	Soft th	thanks, with	lingua-dental	Voiceless, fricative. Lips apart lax and not very wide, teeth slightly apart only few front teeth showing. Air passes through tip of tongue between teeth. (Cognate ð)
ð	Hard th	the, weather	lingua-dental	Voiced, fricative. Lips apart lax and not very wide, teeth slightly apart only few front teeth showing. Air passes through tip of tongue between teeth. (Cognate θ)
Lingua-alveolars				
s		cease, sing, dress, whisper	lingua-alveolar	Voiceless, fricative. Lips open, teeth only slightly apart. Tongue takes up a lot of the space of the opening. The natural [s] sound hisses as a fricative, as sound escapes through limited space, but it should not whistle. To avoid the whistling sound (called the sibilant S) make sure the tongue tip is pointed toward the gum ridge (but do not touch the back of upper front teeth) Lift the tongue and press the tongue edges firmly against the sides of upper molars. (Cognate z)

IPA symbol	Written	Sample Words	Location/ Articulators	Manner of Production
z		zoom, oz, dozen	lingua-alveolar	Voiced, fricative. Lips open, teeth only slightly apart. Tongue takes up a lot of the space of the opening with tongue tip pointing toward gum ridge and sound hisses through the narrow open space. (Cognate s)
t		taste, bitter, faced	lingua-alveolar	Voiceless, plosive. Lips open in lemon shape, teeth showing and slightly apart. Tongue tip pushes off of alveolar gum ridge (just behind front teeth) to released built up air explosively, tongue sides by upper molars. (Cognate d)
d		dance, closed	lingua-alveolar	Voiced, plosive. Lips open in lemon shape, teeth showing and slightly apart. Tongue tip pushes off of alveolar gum ridge (just behind front teeth) to released built-up air explosively, tongue sides by upper molars. (Cognate t)
l		laugh, call	lingua-alveolar	Lips and teeth apart. Lips lax. Tip of tongue against alveolar ridge. Tongue narrow so sides don't touch molars. Sound comes through mouth around sides of tongue. Sound is more forward (bright) on l at beginning of words and more back in the mouth (dark) when l at end of words.
n		neck, knight	lingua-alveolar	Voiced, nasal (velum directs sound through nasal cavity), continuant. Lips open, teeth showing and slightly apart. Tongue tip against alveolar ridge, sides against molars.
Lingua-Palatals				
r		risk, rapid	lingua-palatal	Voiced, sometimes fricative sometimes glide. Lips pursed open, few front teeth showing and look together but have a space between them with front overlapping but not touching back teeth (like a growl). Sides of tongue on upper molars but tongue tip near but not touching hard palate.
tʃ	ch	chess, catch	lingua-palatal	Voiceless, affricative (plosive and fricative sounds). Lips open pushed forward, teeth slightly apart, tongue touches hard palate, sides touch upper molars. Some sound slips out around shape (fricative) and the tongue pushes off ridge to release an explosion of sound (plosive). Cognate [dʒ]
dʒ	soft j, soft g	fudge, jam, gentle	lingua-palatal	Voiced, affricative (plosive and fricative sounds), Lips open pushed forward, teeth slightly apart, tongue touches hard palate, sides touch upper molars. Some sound slips out around shape (fricative) and the tongue pushes off ridge to release an explosion of sound (plosive). Cognate [ch]
j	yuh	you, amuse, view	lingua-palatal	Voiced, glide. Lips open, pushed forward but slightly different in anticipation of and sliding into different vowels. Teeth apart. Tongue top pressed on hard palate, sides on upper molars.
ʒ		range, pleasure, vision jump	lingua-palatal	Voiced, fricative. Lips with tension and pushing forward. Teeth almost touching with slight space. Tongue rounded and pushing on upper molars with tip toward hard palate. (Cognate ʃ)
ʃ		sheet, wish, ocean	lingua-palatal	Voiceless, fricative. Lips with tension and pushing forward. Teeth almost touching with slight space. Tongue rounded and pushing on upper molars with tip toward hard palate. (Cognate ʒ)

THE PROPERTIES OF CONSONANTS (WITH IPA CONSONANT ARTICULATION CHART)

IPA symbol	Written	Sample Words	Location/ Articulators	Manner of Production
Velars				
k		cry, kite, kick	lingua-velar	Voiceless, plosive. Tip of tongue lowered with back arched onto soft palate or velum, when it pulls away sound explodes. (Cognate g)
g		go, grow, bag	lingua-velar	Voiced, plosive. Tip of tongue lowered with back arched onto soft palate or velum, when it pulls away sound explodes. (Cognate k)
ŋ		lung, singing	velar, nasal	Voiced, continuant, nasal. Tip of tongue lowered with back arched onto soft palate or velum, as with k and g but sound emitted through nose instead of mouth.
Glottals				
h			glottal	Voiceless, glottal. Lips, tongue jaw anticipate vowel. Teeth apart.

Appendix VII

Full List of Exercises and Improvisations by Category

(The first number refers to the chapter where you can find it, the second the order it occurs in the chapter.)

Non-Verbal Exercises and Improvisations
Non-verbal, entire class, individual focus exercises (aware of others but focus on self)

- Exercise 2.1: A Habitual Activity
- Exercise 3.1: Watching the Breath
- Exercise 3.3: Shifting the Breath
- Exercise 3.4 Sunset on the Beach (visualization, relaxation)
- Exercise 5.1A: Progressive Relaxation
- Exercise 5.1B: Rising without Tension
- Exercise 5.3: Observing your Alignment
- Exercise 5.4: Standing in Alignment: Tadasana
- Exercise 5.5: Articulating and Activating the Spine
- Exercise 5.6: Disobeying Hands
- Exercise 7.3: Run, stop, and justify (Group)
- Exercise 7.4: Disobeying hands, with images and W.E.D.G.A.G.
- Exercise 8.1: The Apple, or "Trespassers Beware!" (guided visualization)
- Exercise 8.2: Run, stop, justify (with W.E.D.G.A.G.)
- Exercise 8.7: Walking to Class (guided visualization)
- Exercise 8.8: Take a Walk!
- Exercise 9.1: Optimal Alignment (for voice)
- Exercise 9.2: Releasing shoulders and neck
- Exercise 9.3: Extending the breath cycle
- Exercise 12.1 to 12. 5 Sensory Evocation Sight, Sound, Smell, Touch, Taste
- Exercise 12.6 Evoking the Sensory Hologram

Non-verbal, partner or small group exercises (interactive)
- Exercise 5.2: Mirroring Movement Patterns
- Exercise 6.1: Communicating mental imagery
- Exercise 6.10: Sharing Images with Prana

FULL LIST OF EXERCISES AND IMPROVISATIONS BY CATEGORY

- Exercise 7.5: Three Separate Movements
- Exercise 12.18 Working with Music without a Text (with emotions)

Non-verbal, entire class ensemble exercises (interactive)
- Exercise 6.4: Group Mirroring
- Exercise 6.5: Communicating relationships through the language of the body
- Exercise 6.8: Endowing imaginary objects
- Exercise 6.13 The Mystic Coin
- Exercise 9.4: Tai chi breaths

Non-verbal, solo improvisations (or individual focus 3–5 actors at a time)
- Exercise 2.2: The Burnt House
- Exercise 5.8: Simple physical actions with W.E.D.G.A.G. improvisation), To Sit in a Chair, To Treat a Chair As A Throne, To Treat a Chair as The Electric Chair
- Exercise 5.9: To Wait for the Jury's Verdict
- Exercise 8.3: The hospital visit (Improvisation)
- Exercise 8.4: Doors and windows (solo/small group improvisation)
- Exercise 8.5: To read (solo/small group improvisation)
- Exercise 8.6: Preparing for a date (Prepared Improvisation)
- Exercise 8.9: Improvisation: great news!
- Exercise 8.10: Improvisation: the job interview
- Exercise 8.11: Improvisation: awards banquet
- Exercise 8.12: Improvisation: the family heirloom
- Exercise 8.13: Additional improvisation actions for practice
- Exercise 8.14: Improvisation: my precious object
- Exercise 8.15: Additional 'to treat as' actions for practice
- Exercise 8.16: The important document
- Exercise 8.17: Additional sensory evocation actions for practice
- Exercise 12.7 Physical states of being
- Exercise 12.8 Psychological (mental) states of being
- Exercise 12.9 Psychological burden
- Exercise 12.10 Idée fixe
- Exercise 12.11 Emotional states of being
- Exercise 12.12 The Love Hologram
- Exercise 12.13 Targeting specific emotions
- Exercise 12.14 Targeting an emotion to an action
- Exercise 12.16A Fulfilling Physical Actions

Non-verbal, partner or small group improvisations
- Exercise 5.7: Predator and prey (nonverbal, ensemble)
- Exercise 6.11: Communicating relationships, events, and meaning – At the theatre, Two spies and a detective, the eleventh hour
- Exercise 8.18: The silent treatment
- Exercise 8.19: Secret agent
- Exercise 8.20: The elegant performance
- Exercise 12.16B Receiving Physical Actions

Non-verbal ensemble improvisations
- Exercise 6.12: The rope bridge

- Exercise 7.1A: Assuming and conveying status (ensemble)
- Exercise 7.1B: Endowing and receiving status (ensemble)

Verbal Exercises and Improvisations

Verbal, entire class, individual focus exercises (aware of others but focus on self)
- Exercise 10.1: Exploring the resonating chambers (entire class/individual practice)
- Exercise 10.2: Warming up the articulators (entire class/individual practice)
- Exercise 10.3: Vowel formation (entire class/individual practice)
- Exercise 10.4: Chanting the vowels (ensemble)
- Exercise 10.6: Consonant articulation (entire class or individual practice)
- Exercise 10.7: Shifting shape, location, and tempo
- Exercise 10.8: Combining consonants and vowels
- Exercise 10.9: Sounds with tempo variations
- Exercise 10.10: Vocal qualities and issues
- Exercise 10.12: Emphasis
- Exercise 10.16: Sounding out the text
- Exercise 19.2: Exploring Abhorrent Characters

Verbal, Partner or Small Group Exercises
- Exercise 10.11: Tonal subtext
- Exercise 19.3: Personal Monologues

Verbal, Ensemble Exercises
- Exercise 6.2: The numbers game
- Exercise 6.3: Communion through volume and tempo
- Exercise 6.6: Communicating attitude
- Exercise 6.7: Exploring space with movement and sound
- Exercise 10.5: Sound and space
- Exercise 19.4: Acting with Social Purpose
- Exercise 19.5: Investigating Other People's Perspectives (ensemble and community)

Verbal Partner or Small Group Improvisations
- Exercise 10.13: Projection by intention
- Exercise 10.14: Projecting intimacy
- Exercise 10.15: Vocal actions
- Exercise 11.1 The Eleventh Hour
- Exercise 11.2 A Wartime Farewell
- Exercise 11.3 Suspicion at the Doctor's Office
- Exercise 11.4 Black Market Border
- Exercise 11.5 The Two-Timer's Reward
- Exercise 11.6 Improvisation ; "Neither a Borrower nor a Lender Be," or, the Big Mooch
- Exercise 11.7 The Cover-Up
- Exercise 11.8 The Accusation
- Exercise 11.9 Blackmail!
- Exercise 11.10 Cheer Up!
- Exercise 11.11 Forbidden
- Exercise 11.12 The Interrogation

FULL LIST OF EXERCISES AND IMPROVISATIONS BY CATEGORY

- Exercise 11.13 The Reluctant Hero
- Exercise 11.14 The Secret
- Exercise 11.15 Additional Actions
- Exercise 11.16 Hidden Agendas
- Exercise 11.17 The Named Event
- Exercise 12.15: Words and analogous emotions

Verbal Ensemble Improvisations
- Exercise 6.14 Patterns and Cues

Outside of class Observations, exercises for further development
- Exercise 3.2: Observation of the fear response in you
- Exercise 7.2: Getting what you want
- Exercise 9.6: Personal speech habits
- Exercise 10.17: Guidelines for a comprehensive vocal warm-up
- Exercise 12.17 Physical Actions Re-created from Observation
- Exercise 18.1: Experiencing the Stanislavsky System
- Exercise 19.6: Artist's Manifesto

Active Analysis of a Role in a Play – Reconnaissance of the Mind
- Exercise 12.19 Working with Music with a Text
- Exercise 13.1: First reading of the play
- Worksheet 13.2A: Preliminary Theme Overview
- Worksheet 13.2B: Research the Playwright and the Playwright's Recurring Themes
- Exercise 13.3: Telling the Plot
- Worksheet 13.4: Climactic Plot Analysis
- Worksheet 13.6: Research on the Given Circumstances
- Exercise 14.1: Reading the play for character
- Worksheet 14.2: Subjective character analysis
- Worksheet 14.3: Subjective character autobiography
- Exercise 15. 1: Preparing your script for Active Analysis
- Worksheet 15.4: Initial observations about language
- Exercise 15.5: Script analysis—listing the active facts
- Exercise 15.6: The 'Three Wheres' and the ground plan
- Worksheet 15.6: Identifying the 'Three Wheres'
- Exercise 15.7: Marking and naming episodes (scene partners/director)
- Exercise 15.8: Identifying your character's problem
- Worksheet 15.10A: Finding images in the script (individual actor)
- Exercise 15.14: Identifying thought groups and types of pauses

Active Analysis of a Role in a Play—Reconnaissance of the Body
- Exercise 13.5: Named Events Tableaux (Plot and Spectacle)
- Exercise 13.7: Picture
- Exercise 13.8: Second Plan Improvisation on Main Events
- Exercise 13.9: Floating Image Landscape
- Exercise 14.5: Finding alternative behavior
- Exercise 14.6: Telling the Story of the play from your character's viewpoint
- Exercise 14.7: Character embodiment and movement dynamics
- Exercise 15.11: Telling the inner monologue/dialogue

- Exercise 15.12: Telling the tonal subtext
- Exercise 15.13: Naming your actions and reactions
- Exercise 14.8: A beginning for psychological gesture
- Exercise 14.9: Seed, theme, and supertask
- Exercise 14.10: Activating the seed, theme, and supertask in the text
- Exercise 14.11: Character interview
- Exercise 14.12: Relationship interview
- Exercise 14.13: Character second plan
- Exercise 15.2: Listening to the spoken words
- Exercise 15.3: Articulating punctuation
- Exercise 15.9: Text and subtext improvisations
- Exercise 15.10B: Actively finding and creating images
- Exercise 19.1: Preparing for Performance (creative visualization)

Bibliography

Allen, David. *Stanislavsky for Beginners*. New York: Writers and Readers Publishing, Inc., 1999.

Bartow, Arthur. *Training of the American Actor*. New York: Theatre Communications Group, 2006.

Beck, Aaron T., Gary Emery and Ruth L. Greenberg. *Anxiety Disorders and Phobias: A Cognitive Perspective*, rev. edn. Cambridge, MA: Basic Books, 2005.

Benedetti, Jean. *Stanislavski*. London: Methuen Drama, 1988.

Benedetti, Jean. *Stanislavski and the Actor*. New York: Routledge/Theatre Arts Books, 1988.

Benedetti, Jean. *Stanislavski: An Introduction*. New York: Routledge, 1988.

Benedetti, Robert. *The Actor at Work*, 9th edn. Boston: Pearson/Allyn and Bacon, 1970.

Berry, Cicely. *The Actor and the Text*. Revised edition. New York: Applause Books (1987), 1992.

Berry, Cicely, *Voice and the Actor*. New York: Macmillan, 1973.

Boal, Augusto. *Theatre of the Oppressed*. New York: Theatre Communications Group, 1993.

Bogart, Anne. *Viewpoints*. Lyme, NH: Smith and Kraus, 1995.

Bogart, Anne and Tina Landau. *The Viewpoints Book: A Practical Guide to Viewpoints and Composition*. New York: Theatre Communications Group, 2004.

Boleslavsky, Richard. *Acting – The First Six Lessons*. New York: Theatre Arts Books, 1991.

Brecht, Bertolt. "In Praise of Doubt," in *Poems, 1913–1956*. London: Methuen, 1976.

Brestoff, Richard. *The Great Acting Teachers and Their Methods*. Lyme, New Hampshire: Smith and Kraus, 1995.

Brook, Peter. *The Empty Space*. New York: Simon & Schuster, 1968.

Brook, Peter. *The Open Door*. New York: Pantheon Books, 1993.

Caldarone, Marina and Maggie Lloyd-Williams. *Actions: The Actor's Thesaurus*. Hollywood: Drama Publishers, 2004.

Caldwell, Robert and Joan Wall. *Excellence in Singing: multilevel learning and multilevel teaching*. Redmond, WA: Caldwell Publishing, 2001.

Carnicke, Sharon M. *Stanislavsky in Focus: Emotion and the Human Spirit of the Role*. Amsterdam: Harwood Academic Publishers, 1998.

Cazden, Joanna. *Everyday Voice Care: The Lifestyle Guide for Singers and Talkers*. Milwaukee, WI: Hal Leonard Corporation, 2012.

Chaikin, Joseph. *The Presence of the Actor: Notes on the Open Theatre, disguises, acting and Repression*. New York: Atheneum, 1972.

Chamberlain, Franc. *Michael Chekhov*. London: Routledge, 2004.

Chekhov, Anton. Trans. Jean-Claude van Itallie. *The Three Sisters*. Act Four. A revised edition. New York: Dramatists Play Service, Inc., 1995.

Chekhov, Michael. *On the Technique of Acting.* Revised by Mala Powers. New York: Harper Perennial, 1991.

Chekhov, Michael. *To the Actor.* New York: Perennial Library, 1953.

Cross, Wilbur L. and Tucker Brooke. *The Yale Shakespeare: The Complete Works.* New York: Barnes and Noble/Yale University Press, 1993.

Csikszentmihalyi, Mihaly. *Flow: The Psychology of Optimal Experience.* New York: Harper Perennial, 1991.

Csikszentmihalyi, Mihaly. *Creativity: Flow and the Psychology of Discovery and Invention.* New York: Harper Perennial, 1997.

Csikszentmihalyi, Mihaly and Barbara Schneider. *Becoming Adult: How Teenagers Prepare for the World of Work.* New York: Basic Books, 2000.

Damasio, Antonio. *The Feeling of What Happens: Body and Emotion in the Making of Consciousness.* Orlando, FL: Harvest Books, Harcourt, 2000.

Damisch, Lysann, Barbara Stoberock, and Thomas Mussweiler. "Keep Your Fingers Crossed! How Superstition Improves Performance," *Association for Psychological Science* vol. 21:7 (2010).

Davidson, Richard J. and Sharon Begley. *The Emotional Life Of Your Brain.* New York: Hudson Street Press/Penguin Group, 2012.

Deavere Smith, Anna. *Letters to a Young Artist: Straight-up Advice on Making a Life in the Arts: For Actors, Performers, Writers and Artists of Every Kind.* New York: Anchor Books, 2006.

Descartes, René. *Meditations On First Philosophy In Which Are Demonstrated The Existence Of God And The Distinction Between The Human Soul And Body* (1641). As reprinted online by Jonathan Bennett. First launched July 2004, last amended April 2007, accessed December 6, 2014. http://www.earlymoderntexts.com/pdfs/descartes1641_1.pdf.

Doidge, Norman. *The Brain that Changes Itself.* New York: Penguin Books, 2007.

Dubuc, Bruno. "Broca's Area, Wernicke's Area, and Other Language-Processing Areas in the Brain." http://thebrain.mcgill.ca/flash/i/i_10 i_10_cr/i_10_cr_lan/i_10_cr_lan.html. Accessed May 17, 2015.

Duhigg, Charles. *The Power of Habit: Why we do what we do in Life and Business.* New York: Random House, 2012.

Edwards, Christine. *The Stanislavsky Heritage.* New York University Press, 1965.

Ekman, Paul and Wallace V. Friesen. *Unmasking the Face: A Guide to Recognizing Emotions From Facial Expressions.* Palo Alto: Consulting Psychologists Press, 1975.

French, Shirley Daventry. "Reflections," *Iyengar Yoga Center of Victoria Newsletter,* Fall 2013.

Freud, Sigmund. *The Origins of Psycho-Analysis: Letters to Wilhelm Flies.* Ed. Marie Bonaparte, Anna Freud, and Ernst Kris, intro. Ernst Kris. New York: Basic Books, 1954.

Frost, Robert. *The Road Not Taken and Other Poems.* Mineola, NY: Dover Thrift Editions, 1993.

Geschwind, Norman. "Language and the Brain," *Scientific American* 226 (1972): pp. 109–122.

Gombrowicz, Witold. *Diary*, vol. 2 (1957–1961), ed. Jan Kott. Trans. Lillian Vallee. Evanston, IL: Northwestern University Press, 1989.

Gordon, Jon. *Training Camp: What the Best Do Better Than Anyone Else.* Unabridged audiobook. Hoboken, NJ: John Wiley & Sons, Inc., 2010.

Gordon, Mel. *The Stanislavsky Technique: Russia*. New York: Applause, 1987.

Grotowsky, Jerzy. *Towards a Poor Theatre*. Bury St. Edmunds: Methuen Drama, 1968.

Henry, Mari Lyn and Lynne Rogers. *How to be a Working Actor: The Insider's Guide to Finding Jobs in Theatre, Film and Television* (fifth edition). New York: Back Stage Books, 2008.

Iizuka, Naomi. *Polaroid Stories*. Woodstock, NY: Dramatic Publishing, 1999.

Iyengar, B. K. S. *Yoga: The Path to Holistic Health*. London: DK Publishing, 2001.

Iyengar, B. K. S. *Light on Prāṇāyāma: The Definitive Guide to the Art of Breathing* (1981). London: Harper Collins/Harper Thorsons, 2013.

James, William. *Principles of Psychology* (1890). Vol. 1. New York: Henry Holt & Co.

Jung, Carl G. *Modern Man in Search of a Soul*. Trans. W.S. Dell and Cary F. Baynes. London: Routledge, [1933] 2001.

Jung, Carl G. "The Concept of the Collective Unconscious." *Collected Works*, 9.1. Princeton, NJ: Princeton University Press, 1936.

Kandel, Eric R. *In Search of Memory: The Emergence of a New Science of Mind*. New York, W.W. Norton and Company, 2006.

Kandel, Eric R. *The Age of Insight: The Quest to Understand the Unconscious in Art, Mind and Brain*. New York: Random House, 2012.

Kapit, Wynn and Lawrence M. Elson. *The Anatomy Coloring Book*. New York: Harper and Row, 1977.

Kaplan, David. *Five Approaches to Acting*. New York: West Broadway Press, 2001.

Kelly, Edward F., Emily Williams Kelly, Adam Crabtree, Alan Gauld, Michael Grosso and Bruce Greyson. *Irreducible Mind: Toward A Psychology for the 21st Century*. Lanham, MD: Rowan & Littlefield, 2007.

Kemp, Rick. *Embodied Acting – What Neuroscience Tells Us About Performance*. London and New York: Routledge, 2012.

Kogler, Aladar. *Yoga for Every Athlete: Secrets of an Olympic Coach*. St. Paul, MN: Llewellyn Publications, 1995.

Korneva, Oksana. *Konstantin Stanislavsky, Selected Works*. Moscow: Raduga Publishers, 1984.

Lally, P., C. H. M. van Jaarsveld, H. W. W. Potts and J. Wardle. "How are habits formed: Modeling habit formation in the real world." *European Journal of Social Psychology* 40: 998–1009. doi: 10.1002/ejsp.674, 2010.

LaNae, Trisha. "A Conversation with Dr. Maya Angelou," *Beautifully Said Magazine*, 2012.

Lane, Eric and Nina Shengold. *The Actor's Book of Scenes from New Plays*. New York: Penguin, 1988.

Lecoq, Jacques, Jean-Gabriel Carasso and Jean-Claude Lallias. *The Moving Body*. Translated by David Bradby. New York: Routledge, 1997.

Levin, Irina and Igor. *Working on the Play and the Role: The Stanislavsky Method for Analyzing Characters in Drama*. Colorado Springs, CO: Meriwether Publishing Ltd. 1992.

Levin, Irina and Igor. *The Stanislavsky Secret*. Colorado Springs, CO: Meriwether Publishing Ltd. 2002.

Magarshack, David. *Stanislavsky – A Life*. London: Macgibbon & Kee, 1950.

Malaev-Babel, Andrei. *Yevgeny Vakhtangov: A Critical Portrait*. London: Routledge, 2013.

Marchand, Peter (based on the teachings of Harish Johari). *The Yoga of the Nine Emotions: The Tantric Practice of Rasa Sadhana.* Rochester, VT: Destiny Books, 2006.

Meier, Paul. *Accents and Dialects for Stage and Screen.* Lawrence, KS, Paul Meier Dialect Services, 2012. Available online at http://www.paulmeier.com/product/accents-and-dialects-for-stage-and-screen/. Accessed December 27, 2014).

Merlin, Bella. *The Complete Stanislavsky Toolkit.* London: Drama Publishers, 2007.

Miller, Arthur. *The Crucible.* New York: Dramatis Play Service Inc., 1954.

Miller, Henry. *The Wisdom of the Heart.* 2nd edn. New York: New Directions, 1946.

Miller, Richard. *The Structure of Singing: System and Art in Vocal Technique.* New York: Schirmer Books, 1986.

Mitter, Shomit. *Systems of Rehearsal: Stanislavsky, Brecht, Grotowshi and Brook.* London: Routledge, 1992.

Moore, Sonia. *Stanislavsky Revealed: The Actor's Guide to Spontaneity on Stage* (second edition). New York: Applause Books (1968), 1991.

Moore, Sonia (ed. and trans.). *Stanislavski Today – Commentaries on K.S. Stanislavski.* New York: American Center for Stanislavski Theatre Art, 1973.

Moore, Sonia. *The Stanislavski System: The Professional Training of an Actor* (second edition). New York: Penguin Books, Ltd (1960), 1978.

Moore, Sonia. *The Stanislavski System: The Professional Training of an Actor* (fourth edition). New York: Penguin Books (1960), 1984.

Moore, Sonia. *Training an Actor: The Stanislavsky System in Class.* New York: Penguin Books (1968), 1974, 1979.

Murphy, Shane M. "Models of Imagery in Sport Psychology: A Review." *Journal of Mental Imagery*, 14, (3&4), 153–172, 1990.

Nilsson, Jeff. "Imagination is More Important than Knowledge," *Saturday Evening Post*, March 20, 2013.

Novak, Michael. *The Joy of Sports: Endzones, Bases, Baskets, Balls, and the Consecration of the American Spirit.* Aurora, IL: Madison Books (1976), 1994.

Osanai, Kaoru and Andrew T. Tsubaki. "Gordon Craig's Production of *Hamlet* at the Moscow Art Theatre," *Educational Theatre Journal*. The Johns Hopkins University Press. Vol. 20, No. 4, Dec., 1968.

Patanjali, I. *The Yoga Sutras.* Trans. Sri Swami Satchidananda, Yogaville. Integral Yoga Publications, 1990.

Pink, Daniel H. *A Whole New Mind: Why Right-Brainers Will Rule the Future.* New York: Riverhead Books (2005), 2006.

Pinker, Steven. *How the Mind Works.* New York: Norton (1997), 2009.

Pitches, Jonathan. *Science and the Stanislavsky Tradition of Acting.* London and New York: Routledge, 2006.

Polyakova, Elena. *Stanislavsky.* Moscow: Progress Publishers, 1983.

Porter, Kay and Judy Foster. *Visual Athletics: Visualizations for Peak Sports Performance.* Dubuque, IA: Wm. C. Brown Publishers, 1990.

Radha, Swami Sivananda. *Kundalini Yoga for the West.* Boulder, CO: Shambala, 1981.

Reinking, Cathy. *How to Book Acting Jobs in TV and Film: Conversations with a Veteran Casting Director on Mastering the Audition Room … and Much More.* Los Angeles, CA: Cathy Reinking, 2009.

Schacter, Daniel L. *The Seven Sins of Memory.* Boston, MA: Houghton Mifflin, 2001.

Senelick, Laurence. *Gordon Craig's Moscow "Hamlet": A Reconstruction*. London: Praeger, 1982.

Shakespeare, William. *The Winter's Tale*, Act III, Scene 3. London: Routledge (1963 originally Methuen & Company, Ltd) third reprint, 1994.

Skinner, B.F. "Superstition in the Pigeon," *Journal of Experimental Psychology*, 38 (1948).

Spolin, Viola. *Improvisation for the Theatre* (third edition). Chicago, IL: Northwestern University Press (1963), 1999.

Stanislavsky, Konstantin (Constantin Stanislavski). *My Life in Art*. Trans. J. J. Robins. New York: Theatre Arts Books (1924), 1952.

Stanislavsky, Konstantin. *My Life in Art*. Trans. Jean Benedetti. London: Routledge (1924), 2008.

Stanislavsky, Konstantin. *Building a Character*. Trans. Elizabeth Reynolds Hapgood. New York: Theatre Arts Books (1949), reprint 1964.

Stanislavsky, Konstantin. *Creating a Role*. Trans. Elizabeth Reynolds Hapgood. New York: Routledge/Theatre Arts Books, (1961), reprint 2003.

Stanislavsky, Konstantin. *Stanislavsky – On the Art of the Stage*. Trans. David Magarshack. New York: Hill and Wang, 1961.

Stanislavsky, Konstantin. *An Actor's Work*. Trans. Jean Benedetti. London: Routledge, 2009.

Teck, Katherine. *Ear Training for the Body: A Dancer's Guide to Music*. Pennington, NJ; A Dance Horizons Book, 1994.

Trauth, Suzanne M. and Elizabeth C. Stroppel. *Sonia Moore and American Acting Training: With a Sliver of Wood in Hand*. Lanham, MD: Scarecrow Press, 2005.

Toporkov, Vasily Osipovich. *Stanislavsky in Rehearsal: The Final Years*. Trans. Christine Edwards. New York: Theatre Arts Books, 1979.

Tovstonogov, Georgi. *The Profession of the Stage-Director*. Trans. Bryan Bean. Moscow: Progress Publishers, 1972.

Trope, Y. and N. Liberman. "Temporal Construal," *Psychological Review*, 110, 2003.

Turok, Neil. *The Universe Within: From Quantum to Cosmos*. Toronto: Anansi, 2012.

Weber, Nance and Hubert Heinen. *Bertolt Brecht: Political Theory and Literary Practice*. Atlanta, GA: University of Georgia Press, 2010.

Wells, Lynn K. *The Articulate Voice: An Introduction to the Voice and Diction* (fourth edition).Boston, MA: Allyn and Bacon/Pearson Education (1999), 2004.

Wesp, Richard, Joshua Sandry, Anthony Prisco, and Pamela Sarte. "Affective Forecast Of Future Positive Events Are Tempered By Consideration Of Details," *American Journal of Psychology*, vol. 122 (2), 2009.

White, R. Andrew (ed.). *The Routledge Companion to Stanislavsky*. London and New York: Routledge, 2014.

Whyman, Rose. *The Stanislavsky System of Acting: Legacy and Influence in Modern Performance*. New York: Cambridge University Press, 2008.

Williams, Tennessee. *A Streetcar Named Desire*. New York: Signet/New American Library/Penguin, 1951.

Winkielman, Piotr and Jonathan W. Schooler. "Consciousness, Metacognition and the Unconscious," in *The Sage Handbook of Social Cognition*, ed. Susan T. Fiske and C. Neil Macrae. Los Angeles: Sage, 2012.

Woodcock, George and Julie Rak. "Doukhobors." *The Canadian Encyclopedia*, article published 8/22/13 last edited 12/17/13, accessed June 14, 2014, 2tp://www.thecanadianencyclopedia.ca/en/article/doukhobors/.

Wyke, B. D. (1974), "Laryngeal neuromuscular control systems in singing: a review of current concepts." *Folia Phoniatrica*. 26: 295–306.

Yogananda, Paramahansa. *Autobiography of a Yogi*. 12th ed. Encinitas, CA: Self-Realization Fellowship, 1946; 1981.

Yogananda, Paramahansa. *God Talks With Arguna: The Bagavad Gita*. Los Angeles, CA: Self-Realization Fellowship, 1995.

Zaporojetz, T. I. *The Logic of Speech on Stage*. Trans. and adapted by Sonia Moore. New York: The American Center for Stanislavski Theatre Art, Inc., 1981.

Index

Note: page references in *italics* indicate illustrations

accents 305
Accusation (exercise) 257
Acting with Social Purpose (exercise) 481–2
action(s) 5, 31, 276, 347, 540; additional list for selection and practice 562–3; bits/beats of 157; complex 262; consecutiveness of 155, 535, 547; indispensable 159; initiator and receiver of 359; internal and external 164, 510, 511; mental 120, 134, 188, 548; naming 375–6; Russian word for (derivation) 457; *see also* elements of action; nonverbal action; physical actions; psychophysical actions; through-action; verbal action
action steps 31, 144, 189, 254, 260; logical and consecutive 158–60
Active Analysis 35, 78, 299, 300–2, 346–85, 540; arriving at the supertask through 417, 456; and cold readings 423; compared to Method of Physical Actions 300–1, 361, 457; and embodiment 459; preparing script for 351–2; reconnaissance of the body 363–77; reconnaissance of the character 322–45; reconnaissance of the play 303–21; reconnaissance of the scene 347–62; in rehearsal 386–405; of speech 377–84; time and funding restraints 408; and traditional rehearsal process 430–1
Active Dynamics 453, 456, 457, 544
active facts 142, 542; listing 356–7

actors: A-list 39–40; and Active Analysis 301–2; auditions 419–20, 421–3, 447; blocking responsibilities 429–30; callbacks 423; casting 38–40, 419, 421–2, 424; coaching 431–3; firing rules 430, 441; headshots and résumés 420–1; input of 440; keeping to the script 349; of living experience 34, 281, 429, 450–64, 475, 504–5, 510; Palette 9, *16*, 156, 158; playing abhorrent characters 472–5; and rehearsal process 386–403, 407–8; relationship with character 323; and stage business 431
Actors' Equity Association 349, 421, 425, 430, 435–6, 441, 443
Actor's Studio 525, 526
acupuncture 80, 83
Adams, Tyler *73*, *419*, *441*
adaptation 32, 179–82, 508, 542; four qualities of 180
Adashev Studio 506
adjustment *see* adaptation
Adler, Stella 511, 524
adrenaline 55
aesthetic choices 453, 463–4
aesthetic distance 269
affective memory 34, 291, 508, 519, 524–5, 542
affricates/affricatives 224, 229–30
after time 148–9, 542
agreement 255–7
Akalaitis, JoAnne 413–14
Albee, Edward: *Who's Afraid of Virginia Woolf* 416

Alexander, F. M. 93, 193, 241
Alexander Technique 90, 93, 232, 242
Alexeyev family 493–4
Alfaro, Luis 484; *Bruja* 437; *Edipo* 483
alignment 90–95, 197–9, 238
Allen, Jennifer 68, 455
allergies 212, 213
alternative medicine 80
amalgamation 56, 105, 146, 330–6, 366–7, 453, 463–4
American Centre for Stanislavski Theatre Art (ACSTA), *later* American Stanislavski Theatre (AST) 527
American Laboratory Theatre 511, 524
American Repertory Theatre (ART) 413–14
amygdala 49, 55, 296
analogous emotions 34, 270, 281–7, 297, 542
Anderson, Gillian *311*
Andreasen, Nancy 52
Angelou, Maya 267
Ansky, S.: *The Dybbuk* 517
Anthroposophy 519
anxiety 83–4, 86
Apple, The (exercise) 161–2
archetypes 327
arena stage 409
Aristotle 313, 305–6, 338, 348, 414
Armstrong, Jannel *18, 285, 462*
Articulating Punctuation (exercise) 353–4
articulation 218, 219–20, 233, 239, 353–4; consonant 225
articulators 218, 219–20, 224, 225
artistic team 410; reconnaissance by 410–18; *see also* design team
asanas 64, 66, 67, 79–80
Association for Theatre in Higher Education (ATHE) 527
astanga (eight limbs) 64, 67
At the Theatre (exercise) 130
atmosphere 291, 542
attention: circles of 118, 133, 508; focus of 26, 98–101
audience: appropriate acting style for 434; collective experience of 4; collective insight of 466–7; communion with 468–76; expectations of 4–5; emotional response of 56, 79, 268; and fourth wall 132; gaining attention of 171–2, 232–3; including in circle of attention 133; influencing 120; origins of word 233, 307; response of 436, 468, 476
auditions 419–20, 421–3, 447; callbacks 423
Ausem, Dave *119, 314, 319, 363, 472*
Ausubel, Kenny 465
auteur director 414
Autobiographical Character Diary 328
autonomic system 82, 83
avant-garde theatre 513
Awards Banquet (exercise) 181–2
awareness of self 3–4, 38–47, 54–60, 69, 245, 337

backstage: atmosphere 70–1, 73, 259, 431; work 431
backstory 148
Ball, Margaret Joyce 212, 242, *440*
beats 158, 371, 382, 433, 542
Beaumarchais, Pierre Augustin Caron de: *Le Mariage de Figaro* 531
Beck, Aaron 43
Beckett, Samuel 356; *Endgame* 413–14
Bednarchik, Joseph *472*
before time 148–9, 542–3
beginner's mind 1, 52
Begley, Sharon 77
behavior: organic 16–17; subtext of 313–14, 553–4
Behavior, Finding Alternative (exercise) 329
behavioral science 109, 292
being, states of 157
belief 33, 183–4, 504
Benedetti, Jean 10, 377, 510, 522, 531, 534, 535
Benedetti, Robert 308
Bennett, Philip G.: in *The Cherry Orchard* 470–1; discovery of Stanislavsky's use of yoga 454; directs rehearsal of *The Crucible* 386, 392, 393–402; in *King Lear* 354; Sonia Moore's influence on 172–3
Berger, Henning: *The Deluge* 470, 517
Berlane, Angel *319, 363, 472*

INDEX

Berlane, Christi *119, 314, 319, 363*
Berliner Ensemble 159, 331, 356, 370
Berry, Cicely 237, 241, 243, 354
biomechanics 79, 99, 513, 533
bits 158; *see also* beats
Black Market Border (exercise) 252
Blackmail! (exercise) 258
Blake Street Hawkeyes 415–16
Blavatsky, Helena 507
blocking 427–30, 433, 435, 438, 514, 543; actor's responsibilities 429–30; body positions *430*; notation 429; organic 428; tableau 428–9; traditional 427–8; skeletal 427; Viewpoints 429
Boal, Augusto 484
body: alignment 90–5, 197–200, 238; anatomy of breath 200–3; anatomy of emotion 295–8; anatomy of speech 218, *219*, 220; anatomy of the voice *195, 196, 197*, 207, 216; communication pathways 82; connection with mind 17–18, 77, 78, 79–80, 82, 108–10, 292; creating a sculpture 284; importance of the spine 173; kinesthetic awareness and response 83, 429; kinesthetic memory 19, 27; language of the 80–1, 125, 245, 386, 547; pantomime of the 165*7*; positions in relation to audience *430*; as primary signal system 80–1, 195; reconnaissance of the 304, 329–44, 363–77; relationship with emotions 79, 269, 292, 293, *294*; spatial relationships 124–32; training 81–2; *see also* conditioning exercises; movement; muscles; proprioception
body language 80–1, 387
Bogart, Anne 81, 410, 416
Boleslavsky, Richard 491, 509, 511, 515, 524
Bolshoi Opera 522
Borderlands Theatre Company *437, 483*
Brach, Tara 43
brain 48–52, *49, 51*, 78; Broca's and Wernicke's areas 50–1, *51*; cranial nerves 82; and emotions 269, 292, 293, *295*, 295–6; fight or flight response 54–5; flashes of insight 184; and habit 102, 111–12; hemispheres 49–52, 159; importance of sleep 112–13; and movement 101, 102–3; neurons and synapses *101*, 102; rewiring 110, 111; and thought 101–102; tricks for memorizing lines 350–1; and visualization 120; *see also* mind; neuroscience
brain lateralization 49
brain plasticity 92, 110, 111
brainstorming 320
Brand, Phoebe 524
breakdowns (casting) 421
breaks, behavior during 446
breath: anatomy of 200–3; benefits of oxygen 467; breathiness 229; cycle 203–7; importance of alignment 197; and singing 203–4
breathing exercises 45–7, 57, 204–6, 238; *see also* pranayama
Brecht, Bertolt 11, 79, 159, 301, *528*, 528–9; exercises influenced by 331, 356, 370; Meyerhold's influence on 516–17; *The Threepenny Opera* 436, 479–80
Brehony, Douglas James *255*
Brestoff, Richard 79, 513–14
Broca, Paul 50
Broca's area 50, *51*
Brody, Jane 327
Brook, Peter 301, 304, 322, 362, 368, 414, 415, 487
Buddhism 43, 454
Bulgakov, Mikhail: *The Days of the Turbins* 530; *Molière* 534
Burnett, Elyse *330*
Burnt House (exercise) 22–6
buttons 436

Cabrera, Brandon L. *256, 282*
Caldwell, Robert 203
Cannon, Walter B. 54
cardiovascular system 295
Carnicke, Sharon M. 10, 361, 492; on affective memory 34; on "I am" 41; on mistranslations of Stanislavsky 532; and Stanislavsky's Plan of Experiencing 451, 453; and

Stanislavsky's use of yoga 63, 118, 453, 455, 458, 507, 508
casting 38–40, 419, 421–2, 424
catharsis 19
Cazden, Joanna 197, 212
Ceaușescu, Nicolae 480–1
censorship 483
Centrella, Christopher 466
cerebrum 49
Chaikin, Joseph 110, 415
chakras 65, 66, 454, 460, 461
Chamberlain, Franc 515, 517–18, 519–20
chanting 218; in Greek drama 348
Chanting the Vowels (exercise) 222–3
character 167–71, 183, 290, 314, 457; abhorrent 472–4; autobiography 430, 473; complex 262; creative challenges of 461–2; developing 141–2, 245–6, 358, 461–3; embodying 332–6, 337, 340–1; identifying problem of 361–2; improvisational études 329–44; inner landscape 104–5; inner monologue and inner dialogue 369–71; interpretation 306; and personal theme 469–70; perspective on the role 453, 461; reconnaissance of 322–45; seed, theme and supertask 337–42; transformation into 34, 172, 492, 524, 555
Character Analysis, objective and subjective (exercises) 323–8
Character Dichotomy Figure 325
Character Dynamics (exercise) 335–6
Character Embodiment and Movement Dynamics (exercises) 332–6
Character Interviews (exercise) 343
Character Relationship Map 324–5
Character Second Plan (exercise) 344
charisma 39–40, 41
Cheer Up! (exercise) 258–9
Chekhov, Anton 372–4, 500–3, 518, 523; adaptations 416; *The Cherry Orchard* 469, 470–1, 501, 505, 512, 523–4, 527, 530; *The Seagull* 372, 500–1, *502*, 530; *The Three Sisters* 328, 357, 372–4, 380–1, 501, 505, 523–4, 531, 565–7; *Uncle Vanya* 501
Chekhov, Michael 11, 79, 332, 336, 491, 509, *517*, 517–21; adaptation of the System 469–70; and atmospheres 291; disagreements with Stanislavsky 518–19; mental issues 474, 519; production of *Hamlet* 514, 519–20; roles at MAT 515, 518; Soviet disapproval of 301, 520; use of metaphor 327; in USA 520; and Vakhtangov 517–18, 520–1
childhood influences 140
Christmann, Shannon Leigh 254
Chronegk, Ludwig 496
Churchill, Caryl: *Mad Forest* 480–1; *Top Girls* 330, 368
circles of attention 118, 133, 508
circulatory system 82
circus 414–15
Cirque du Soleil 484
Classical theatre: language 348–9; *see also* Greek theatre
clichés 184
Climactic Plot Analysis (worksheet) 310–11
climax 313, 437
Clurman, Harold 524
cognates 224, 225
cognitive science 17, 43, 50–1, 184, 330
cold readings 369, 423
collaborative process 406–48
collective unconscious 3
Comédie-Française 504
comedy 33, 243, 314, 436, 437, 470, 528
Commedia Dell'Arte 11, 513
commitment 70–1
Communicating Attitude (exercise) 126
Communicating Mental Imagery (exercise) 121–2
Communicating Relationships, Events, and Meaning (exercise) 129–31
Communicating Relationships through the Language of the Body (exercise) 125
communication 28, 82–3; during rehearsal process 446–7; nonverbal 247; offstage 73–4
communion 28, 41, 64, 117–36, 543; with the audience 468–76; ensemble (Rope Bridge exercise) 131–2; group

INDEX

mirroring 123–4; and imagination 120–2; mental action 120; mutual influence 118–19, 120; spatial relationships 124–32; spiritual 28, 64, 67, 118, 469, 505, 553; through voice and speech 227–39; through volume and tempo 122–3
company business 425
compassion 69–70
Complete Works of William Shakespeare (Abridged), The (spoof play) 413
complication 171
compositions 427, 429
concentration 26, 45–7, 64, 68–9, 504, 543; exercises 98–101
conditioned response 17–18, 111
conditioning exercises 84–108; alignment 90–5; articulating and activating the spine 95–8; caution 84; disobeying hands 99–100; experiencing the given circumstances 149–54; mirroring movement patterns 90; optimal physical functioning 92–3; predator and prey 100; progressive relaxation 86–7; resting positions 85; rising without tension 87–9; science of 108–13; simple physical action with W.E.D.G.A.G. 102–4; To Wait for the Jury's Verdict 106–8
conflict 32, 145, 188–9, 254, *462*, *463*; dynamic 167–79, 253
consciousness 42, 484
Consonant Articulation (exercise) 225–6
consonants 221, 224–30; properties 571–4
Consonants and Vowels, Combining (exercise) 226–7
Constructivism 513, 533
contact sheets 425
context 331–2
control and restraint 172, 543
Coolidge, Calvin 532
copyright 349, 356, 409–10, 413, 414
costume 183, 332, 418, 426, 431–2, 445, 447, 500; dress rehearsals 443; in *Othello* 496–7; in *Tartuffe* 443, *444*
costume designer 439–40, 443
counselling 43, 72
counteraction 253–62, 543

Cover-Up (exercise) 256–7
Coward, Noel: *Blithe Spirit* 22, 254, 441
craft (stock-in-trade) 504
Craig, Bud 296
Craig, Gordon 511, 514–15
cranial nerves 82
Crawford, Cheryl 524
Crawn, Samantha 466, *472*
creative idea 337, 408, 543
creative impulses 453, 461–2
creative life, experiencing 484–8
creative space 62–3; ethics in 69–73
creative state 10, 37–61, 543–4; awareness of self 38–47; factors that help generate 52–4; in front of audience 54–60; scientific research on 47–53
Cristelli, Cynthia *390*
Crommelynk, Fernand: *The Magnanimous Cuckold* 513
Cubism 516
cue-to-cue 442–3
cues: learning 351; tech 442
curiosity, childlike 53
Csikszentmihalyi, Mihaly: on awe and wonder 52–3; on creativity 37, 48, 486; on curiosity 492; on effect of distractions 62; on flow 6–7, 476; on relaxation 53

Dali, Salvador 411, 412
Damasio, Antonio 42, 48, 268, 271–2, 292, 293, 297, 484
Damisch, Lysann 6
dance 81, 437, 455
Dark Knight, The (film) 474
Davidson, Richard J. 77, 291
Davis, Taneshia 70
del Toro, Benicio 39
Demyan, Michael *314*
Dennis, Mary K. 70, *285*
Descartes, René 41–2
design: concept 417, *418*, *419*; Cubist 516; implementation 418; and intellectual property 356; presentation 426; rehearsals and 431–2, 437; *see also* sets
design team 410, 411, 414, 437, 441–2, 468

devices 308, 347, 544
Devil's Music, The (musical) *418*
devising 415–16
dhyana 68–9
diagnostic exercises 20–6
dialectical materialism 454, 534, 535–6
dialects 209–10, 228, 231–2, 305
diaphragm 200, *201*, 203, 204
diction 348
diphthongs 221
director: and Active Analysis 301, 308; as *auteur* 414; and blocking 427–30; and casting 422; and designers 417, 437, 441–2; developing production concept 414–15; expanding the play 412–12; inexperienced 431; of music 437; notes by 440–3, 444, 447; preparing and studying the script 410–11; and rehearsals 386, 392, 393–402, 424, 426–30, 432, 433, 434, 436–7, 440–1; role of 158, 245, 323, 329, 331, 424, 426–7; and search for supertask 308, 342, 417; selecting 410; and stage business 431; and stage directions 356; and tech 441–4
discipline 70–1, 136
Disobeying Hands (exercise) 99–100; with Images and W.E.D.G.A.G. 150–2
distractions, effect of 62, 64, 75–6; *see also* personal issues
Dixon, Mrs. Alfred 246
Docherty, David 410
Doidge, Norman 110
Doors and Windows (exercise) 166–7
Dostoevsky, Fyodor Mikhailovich: "The Village of Stepanchikovo" 521
Dougherty, Dave *442*
Doukhobors 506–7
dramatic question 308, 310
dramaturg 410
Drescher, Fran 228
dress, personal 75, 446, 448
dual perspectives/dual consciousness 27, 44–5, 58, 112, 133, 172, 174, 269, 314, 544; interweaving of 453, 463–4
Dubuc, Bruno 49, 51
Duhigg, Charles 111
Duncan, Isadora 514
dynamic action *see* Active Dynamics

East Stroudsburg University: research into decision making 42–3; wall of envelopes 73; *Blithe Spirit* 22, 254, 441; *Polaroid Stories* 133, 277, 432, 435, 444, 466, 472; *Sold!* 70, 71, 259, 282; *Spike Heels* 18; *A Streetcar Named Desire* 363, 472; *Tartuffe* 443, 444; *Top Girls* 330, 368; *The Tragical History of Dr. Faustus* 439, *Twelfth Night* 406, 411
Edison, Thomas 492
Efros, Nicolai 497
eidetic images 105
Einstein, Albert 48
Ekman, Paul 288, 297–8
Ekman Facial Expression Chart 288
Eldee (Yunzhou Gao) *330*, *368*
Elegant Performance (exercise) 190–1
Elements of Action 22, 26–8, 368, 453, 462–3; applied to imaginary circumstances 28–35; and justification 157–8
Eleventh Hour (exercise) 131, 247–9
Eliade, Mircea 466
ellipsis 371, 382
Ellis, Albert 43
embodiment *see* incarnation
Embodying Biography (exercise) 334
emotional brain *see* limbic system
emotional memory 269–70, 271–2, 281, 297, 508–9, 521–2, 524–5, 544
emotions: analogous 34, 270, 281–7, 297, 542; anatomy of 295–8; appropriateness to given circumstances 458; arousing 79; controlling 268; danger of forcing 281, 291; distinguished from feelings 293, 296, 460–1; distinguished from inspiration 402–3; expressing verbally 218; facial expressions 288–9, 297–8; finding connections during rehearsal process 433–5, 436; impact of body on 79; James-Lange theory of 108; link with cognition 52; love 283–4; music and 289–90; obstacles and 290–1; orchestrating 267–302; passive verbs and (playing the emotion) 157; positive and negative 297; powerful 247; primary 297, 550–1; reawakened

during training 19–20; releasing 72; response through physical actions 287–9; response to imagined events 184; scientific studies of 42, 47, 291–8; secondary 268–9, 270, 281, 552; sensations aroused through 460–1; sensory re-creation of 271–6; and speech 210; Stanislavsky and 34, 269, 286, 291, 292, 298; states of being 277, 280–1; targeting 285–6; yoga and 455; *see also* triggers

empathy 69–70, 72, 298

Emphasis (exercise) 232

Endowing Imaginary Objects (exercise) 127

endowment 29–30, 142, 143, 183, 185–6, 544

energy: yogic 66; *see also* flow of energy

English language 220, 231–2

Enriques, Bryant 483

Ensler, Eve: *Vagina Monologues* 484

environment 545; artificial 16–20, 68, 138–9, 183, 268–9, 504; childhood 140; ethical 69–73; favorable 62–3; inner 120; for supertask 337

Epic Theatre 159

episodes 358–60, 364–5, 393, 433

Equity *see* Actors' Equity Association

ethics 68, 69–73, 136, 545

études, improvisational 158, 317–19, 329–44, 392, 545, 546

Europe: eastern 300, 408, 526; MAT tour of 511, 523, 533; Michael Chekhov in 520

event: context and perspective 331–2; definition 263, 545; naming 359–60, 391; *see also* Main Event; named event

exercises *see* conditioning exercises; diagnostic exercises; *and specific titles*

experiences, primary 297

experiencing 34, 44, 172, 331–2, 450–64, 476, 545; the creative life 485–8; Plan of 64, 65, 451–3, 452, 454, 456–64

experiencing the experience 42

experimental theatre 415–16

Exploring Abhorent Characters (exercise) 473–4

Exploring Space with Movement and Sound (exercise) 126–7

Exploring the Resonating Chambers (exercise) 217–18

exposition 148, 310

Extending the Breath Cycle (exercise) 204–6

external monitor 27, 44, 83, 164, 514

facial expressions 288–9, 297–8

Family Heirloom (exercise) 182

Fantastic Realism 159, 515, 517, 529

Farber, Selena and Shwanda 259

Fear and Loathing in Las Vegas (film) 39

fear response 54–5, 82, 83; exercises 55–6, 57–8

Fedotov, Alexander Fillipovich 495, 496

Fedotova, Glikeriya Nikolaevna 495

feedback 73–4

feeling: distinguished from emotion 293, 296, 453, 460–1

fencing 81

"fight or flight" response 55–6, 82

fight scenes 81

Fillmore, Kent 387, 389, 390, 393, 401

Film acting: audience response 466; auditions 423; building up resumé 407; changes to script 468; dialects 210; emotional scenes 433–4; importance of inner monologue 140, 164–5; learning lines 426, 447; producers 408, 411; special effects 438; spectacle 313; speech 218; takes 8; truth in 184; as visual medium 244

film of images 26, 104–5, 133, 164–5; exercise 106–8

first impressions 307

first plan 28, 148, 310, 317

First Studio 63, 506–8, 509, 511, 515, 517–19, 520

Fitzmaurice, Catherine 241

flexibility 53

Floating Image Landscape (exercise) 319–20

flow, concept of (psychology) 6–7, 67, 476

flow of energy 26, 56, 59, 67, 82, 82–4, 453, 461–3, 545; bidirectional 102–4

focus of attention 26, 98–101

Foley, Brian *314*
Forbidden Fruit (exercise) 259–60
form 158
Formalism 533
Foster, Ben *311*
Foster, Judy 120
fourth wall 132
French, Shirley Daventry 68, 83, 455
French, Stephanie: coaching by *432*; directing *Polaroid Stories* 444; motto on fear 56; production of *Twelfth Night* 411, *412*; and Stanislavsky's connection with yoga 455; *see also Sold!*
Freud, Sigmund 47
fricatives 224, 229–30
Fringe Benefits 484
Frost, Robert 53; "The Road Not Taken" 487–8
future events, anticipating 42–3

Gandhi, Mahatma 483
generosity 69, 71
genre 545
George Street Playhouse 418
Geschwind, Norman 50–1
Gest, Morris 523
gesture 342, 513; *see also* W.E.D.G.A.G.
Getting What You Want (exercise) 146–8
gibberish 231, 375
given circumstances 28, 33, 140–2, 143, 144–9, 165, 459, 545–6; conditioning exercises 149–54; emotions and 458; how 149; and indispensable action 159; research on 316; status 142–4; what (action/task) 144; when 145; where 145; where from and where to 148–9; who 141–2; with whom (relationships) 145–6; why and what for 146–8; *see also* three wheres
Glass, Philip 414
glottis 195, 197, 207
goal: artist's 48; *see also* objective
Goetz, Kendra *314*
Goldoni, Carlo 503; *La Locandiera* 501
Gombrowicz, Witold 386
Gorcharkov, Nikolai 534
Gordon, Jon 5, 418

Gordon, Mel 470, 519, 520
Gorky, Maxim 503, 506; *Children of the Sun* 505; *The Lower Depths* 523–4
gossip 71–2, 446
Gozzi, Carlo: *Princess Turandot* 516, *516*
Grable, Betty 179–80
Graham, Martha 38
grammar 378
Great News! (exercise) 181
Greek theatre 305, 309, 313, 348, 457, 465
Griboyedov, Alexander: *Woe from Wit* 510
grimacing 184
ground plan, creating 357, *358*
Group Theatre 524–5
grotesque 515–16
Grotowski, Jerzy 11, 159, 301, 415, 520, 528, *529*, 529–30
Gunn, Alida *483*
guttural consonants 230

Habima Theatre 517
habit: actors' 184–5; brain and 102, 111–12; cultural 210, 211; releasing 90; reprogramming 111–12
Habitual Activity (exercise) 22–3
hair 445, 447
Hamlet (Shakespeare): adaptation 413; advice to actors in 2, 193–4; and context 331; Craig's production 511, 514–15, 518; emotions and 269; Michael Chekhov's production 514, 519–20; Polonius quoted 358; psychological burden in 171; soliloquy 132; spectacle in 313; Wooster Group's staging 438
Hamsun, Knut: *The Drama of Life* 507
Hapgood, Elizabeth Reynolds 532
Hart, Roy 241
Harting, Carla *420*
Hartmann, Eduard von 458
headlines 264
headshots 420–1
health 80, 211, 212–13, 445, 446, 466
hearing 213
Helfand, Lev Borisovich 526

INDEX

Hello Dolly! (musical) 179–80
Henry, Mari Lyn 419
Herbert, Julie 332
Hermitage Theatre 501
Hero (film) 40
Hidden Agendas (exercise) 262–3
Hinduism 67, 519
Hoffman, Dustin 473, 474
hologram technique *see* Sensory Hologram
homeostasis 55
homework 70, 74–5, 76, 424, 426, 433, 434–5
Hospital Visit (exercise) 164
Howell, James 90
Hulme, Keri 406
human spirit 156, 546, 547
hypothalamus 49, 55, 295, 296

I am/I exist (presence) 27, 41–43, 141–2, 172, 296, 330–1, 546
iambic pentameter 349
Ibsen, Henrik: *The Enemy of the People* 503
idée fixe 277, 279
Iizuka, Naomi 356, 414; *Polaroid Stories* 133, 277, 354, 356, 432, 435, 444, 466, 472, 473
images 165, 365; communicating 121–2; emotional content 282; examining the text for 365–7; floating 319–20; maximizing effectiveness of 120; pictorial collage of 327; sensory 271–2; sharing (exercise) 128–9; *see also* film of images
imagination 26, 104–5, 106–8, 460, 546; effective use of 120–2; Einstein on 48; and emotions 271; exercises 23–4; *see also* "magic if"
Important Document (exercise) 186–7
improvisation 142, 149, 159, 535; and devising and experimental theatre 415; études 158, 317–19, 329–44, 392, 545, 546; event (preparing for) 355; Michael Chekhov and 518; obstacles in 171–2, 181–2; problems, main actions, and objectives 260–2; naming 261–2, 263–4; silent 187–91; Stanislavsky and 300, 301; structure 167, 247; worksheets 558–62; *see also specific exercises*
Improvising an Episode of the Text (exercise) 364–5
incarnation 453, 459, 463, 544
independence 53
India 465–6, 483
indication 139, 184, 329–30
inflection 208, 232, 377, 379
initiator 359
inner dialogue 33–4, 105–8, 140, 546–7; of character 369–71
inner environment 120
inner landscape 104–5
inner monologue 33–4, 58, 105–8, 139–40, 314, 500, 546–7; of character 369–71; importance in film acting 140, 164–5; speaking out loud 301
inspiration 2–4, 5, 7, 9, 38, 67, 69, 402–3, 453, 458, 463, 504, 547
instinct, learned 16–17
insula 296
intellectual property *see* copyright
intention 120, 547; and spatial relationships 124–5
internal critic 43–4
internal monitor 27, 44, 83, 84, 165, 314
International Phonetic Alphabet (IPA) 220–1; sample charts 565–7
Internet 420
interpretation 412–14
Interrogation (exercise) 261
interviews 181, 343, 477–8, 482
intimacy, projecting 235–6
intonation 208, 230, 231–2
intuitive sense 118
Investigating Other People's Perspectives (exercise) 482
Ivanov, Vsevolod: "The Armored Train No. 14-69" 531
Iyengar, B. K. S. 64, 66, 67, 68, 69, 80, 93, 96, 201, 202, 455

Jacobson, Edmund 86
James, William 42, 108, 109, 292
James-Lange theory 292
Jewish theatre 517
Job Interview (exercise) 181

Joint Stock Theatre Group 415, 480, 482
Jolie, Angelina 483
Jones, Guillermo *483*
Jones, Michelle *330*
Joseph, Esther *70*
Joseph, Jamil *18, 256, 462*
journals: artistic 476; creative/reflection 3–4, 246, 307; observation 148, 170; psychological benefits of keeping 54–5
judgment 453, 460, 474
Jules-Bois, Henri Antoine 10
Jung, Carl 3, 117
justification 17, 31, 139, 157–8, 547; exercises 149–50, 153–4

Kachalov, Vasili 515
Kandel, Eric R. 52, 53, 54–5, 109–10, 184, 292, 293, 296
Kashner, Patricia 73
Kaufman, Moises 415
Kedrov, Mikhail Nikolayevich 300, 534, 535
Kelly, Edward F. 108, 109
kinesthetic awareness 83
kinesthetic memory 19, 27
kinesthetic response 83, 429
Kirby, Vanessa *311*
Knebel, Maria Osipova 300, 534
Knipper, Olga 500, 501, 515
Komissarjevsky, Fyodor 495
Konnikova, Maria 112–13
Kris, Ernst 52
Kristi, Grigori 534
Kyoto, Japan *2, 12*

Laban, Rudolf von 335
Laboratory Theatre 529
Lally, Phillipa 112
Lambert, Sarah 443
Landman, Michael 352
Lange, Carl 106, 292
language 348–9; of the body 80–1, 125, 245, 387, 547; brain and 50–2, 110; in Classical theatre 348–9; initial observations about (worksheet) 355; poetic imagery 365; translations 413
larynx 195–7, 207
Lasater, Judith Hanson 68, 455

learning lines 74–5, 349–51, 360, 363, 426, 435, 447
Lecoq, Jacques 268, 269, 415
Lecter, Hannibal (character) 474
Ledger, Heath 474
leitmotif 158, 547
Lenin, Vladimir Illich 512, 530, 533
Lessac, Arthur 241
Lester, Julius: *Day of Tears* 259
Lewis, Aaqilah *282*
Lewis, Waylon 483
Liberman, N. 42–3
life of the human soul 172, 503, 547
lighting 426, 438, 442, *442*, 443, 500
limbic system 49, *295*, 295
Linklater, Kristin 241
Lip Trills (exercise) 208–9, 239
Listening to the Spoken Words (exercise) 352–3
Litwak, Jessica 332
living experience, theatre of 34, 281, 429, 450–64, 475, 504–5, 510
Lloret, Michael *439, 442*
logical sequence 509, 547
Loma Prieta Earthquake 168–70
Long, Adam 413
Love Hologram (exercise) 283–4
Lovegood, Luna (character, *as played by* Evanna Lynch) 228
Lucich, Joanne *388*
Luhrman, Baz 413
lungs *196*, 200; in Plan of Experiencing 451, *452*, 453, 458–9
lures 38, 269, 458, 548

McCarthy, Joseph 389
McGuinness, Merrill *277, 432*
McIntyre, Robert *441*
Mack, Rachel *314*
Mad Men (TV series) 75
Maeterlinck, Maurice 503
"magic if" 29, 137, 138–9, 140, 141, 171, 186, 318, 504, 548
Main Event: in *The Crucible* 404; improvisation on 317–18; naming 311, 315
major reversal 359
Malinovskaya, Maria 522
Maly Theatre 518

manifesto, artist's (exercise) 486–7
Manzi, Jenell *314*
Mapplethorpe, Robert 484
Marking and Naming Episodes (exercise) 359–60
Markov, P. 531
Marlowe, Christopher: *The Tragical History of Dr. Faustus* 438–9
martial arts 81, 455
Martinez, Janel *133*
Martinez, Julian *483*
Marxism 454, 520, 528, 530, 534, 535–6
Massachusetts Institute of Technology 111
massage 83, 238–9
material, selecting and developing 476–9
media, integrating 438
meditation 45–7, 57–60, 80, 86, 99, 339–40, 454, 507; *see also* yoga
Meier, Paul 231, 241
Melodic Intonation Therapy 110
memory: affective 34, 291, 508, 519, 524–5, 542; emotional 269–70, 271–2, 281, 297, 508–9, 521–2, 524–5, 544; of experiences 508–9; kinesthetic 19, 27; malfunctions 269; muscular 284; sense 27, 186–7, 271; *see also* learning lines
mental action 120, 134, 188, 548
mental game 120–1
metacognition 44
metaphor 264, 404
Method (Strasburg's) 524–6
Method of Physical Actions 300–1, 361, 457, 548; *see also* Active Analysis
Meyerhold, Vsevolod 11, 79, 301, 491, 500, 512–14, *513*, 515, 523; arrest and death 533–4; and biomechanics 513; and improvisatory exploration 506; influence on Brecht 528; and *plastique* 513
microphones 230
Midnight Cowboy (film) 473
Miele, Joseph 48, 111–12
Miller, Arthur 356; *The Crucible* 277, 283, 327, 378, *387*, 388, 388–404, *389*, *390*, *393*, *401*
Miller, Henry 1

Miller, Richard 203–4, 207, 216, 241
Miller, Robin 454
mime 21
mind: anatomy of 48–52; connection with the body 17–18, 77, 78, 79–80, 82, 108–10, 292; as judgment 453, 460; mental action 120, 134, 188; mental game 120–1; reconnaissance of the 304, 323–9, 410, 456, 551; *see also* brain; neuroscience; psychology
minor reversal 359
mirroring: group 123–4; movement patterns 90
mise-en-scène 313–14, 500, 548–9
Molière 503, 504; stage directions 356; *Georges Dandin* 496; *The Imaginary Invalid* 518; *Tartuffe* 11, *255*, 300, 301, *314*, 417, 443, *444*, 533, 533–5
moment-to-moment work 433, 549
monologue: for auditions 422–3; memorizing 350; personal 477–9; *see also* inner monologue
Monroe, Marilyn 39
mood 120, 549
Moore, Sonia 21, 99, 149, 166, 361, 525, *526*, 526–8, 534; on audiences 5; on ethics 136; experiments with the System 172–3; and gesture 342; gratitude to America 483; and importance of the spine 173, 452; on rhythm 522; and Stanislavsky's interest in yoga 454; translation of Zaporojetz booklet 377–8; and W.E.D.G.A.G. 103
Moore-Jaglom, Irene 470–1, 525, 527
Morozov, Sawa 499, 505
Moscow Art Theatre 11, 79, 128, 148, 491, 497–504, 521; Actor Training Studios 506–8; Anton Chekhov and 372, 500–3; Craig and 514–15; influence on Grotowski 415; Meyerhold and 512–14; Michael Chekhov and 518; and Peasant's Revolt 505; rehearsal processes 407–8; and Russian Revolution 512, 523; Second 519–20; Soviet Union and 300–1, 530–1, 533–6; summary of key events 538–40; tours abroad 503, 511,

523–4, 530, 532, 533; *see also* First Studio; Third Studio
Moscow Philharmonic School 498, 499, 513
Moskvin, Ivan 500, 534
Mota, Ariel Princeton *486*
motion, third law of 119
motivation 146, 549
Moved by Punctuation (exercise) 354–5
movement: exploring space with 126–7; importance of training 102; to music 289; patterns 90; neurophysiological impulses 101
Movements, Three Separate (exercise) 153–4
mugging (facial expressions) 184; *see also* indication
Murphy, Shane 121
muscles 101, 102–3, 164; memory 284; spine 173; tension 504; used in breathing 200–1, 203, 204
Muses 7, 48
music: brain and 110; collective experience of 3, 4; composition 377; and emotions (exercises) 289–90; expressing composer's vision 141; incidental 413–14; rehearsals and 426, 439; sampling 414; score 426; singing 203–4, 509, 522; speech as 509; training 5–6, 9; and voice 194
musicals 203, 436, 439
Mussweiler, Thomas 6
mutual influence 118–19, 120
My Grandmother's Attic (exercise) 128
My Precious Object (exercise) 185
Myers, F. W. H. 108
Mystic Coin (exercise) 134
mythology 3

named event 165–7, 263–5, 311, 372, 549; exercise 264–5; secondary 358–60
Named Events Tableaux (exercise) 315
naming: events 359–60, 391; improvisations 261–2, 263–4; seed idea 338
Naming Your Actions and Reactions Aloud (exercise) 375
Nanny, The (TV sitcom) 228

Nanus, Susan: *The Phantom Tollbooth 486*
nasality 228–9
naturalism 503, 513
neck, releasing 199–200
Neese, Dolores *387, 400*
"Neither a Borrower nor a Lender Be" (exercise) 255–6
Nemirovich-Danchenko, Vladimir 148, *498*, 498–500, 508, 513, 521, 523, 530, 536
nervous system 17, 65, 80, 101, 102, 110, 203, 271, *294*, 295, 451; autonomic 55, 82, 295, 296; central 65, 82, 95, 296, 461; peripheral 65, 82, 295, 461; somatic 82; sympathetic 55
neurons *101*, 102
neurophysical impulses 101
neuroplasticity 110
neuroscience 11, 42, 49–52, 101–2, 109–10, 268; behavioral 17; cognitive 17, 50–1
Newton, Isaac 119
Nicholas II, Tsar 505, 512
niyama 68, 69
nonconformity 53
nonverbal action 19, 20–6, 155–91, 549; active exploration of 164–7; two- and three- person improvisations 187–91; *see also* silence; W.E.D.G.A.G.
notes 445; director's 440–3, 444, 447
novel *see* telling the novel
Novitskaya, L. P. 534
Numbers Game (exercise) 122

object of struggle 167
objective 30–1, 146–8, 170–1, 254, 260, 326, 549–50
objects: endowing with meaning 127–8, 185–6; influencing through mental action 134
observation 146–8, 298, 476; of behavior 329; physical actions re-created from 288–9
obsession *see* idée fixe
obstacle 32, 171–2, 174, 177, 550; adjustment to 179–82; and emotion 290–1, 297
off-book, getting *see* learning lines

Olivier, Laurence 211, 483
Onegin Room 523
O'Neill, Eugene 356
opening nights 468
opening up 133
Opera Studio 522–3
organic acting 246
organic behavior 81
Osanai Kaoru 513
Ouspenskaya, Maria 491, 506, 509, 511, 524
Owstrovski, Ian 486

pacing 436–7
pain 297
Palette, Actor's 9, *16*, 156, 158
pantomime of the body 167
paraphrasing 301, 364
Pasteur, Louis 351
Patanjali 64; sutras 67–9
Patel, Ramanand 68, 455
Patterns and Cues (exercise) 134–5
Paul the Psychic Octopus 7, *8*
pauses 342, 353–4, 356, 371; connecting and dividing 379; identifying types of 379–80, 382
Pavlov, Ivan Petrovich 17, 111
peak performance 5–6, 8
Perevoschikova, Maria Lilina (wife of Stanislavsky) 496, 497, 498, 536
Period of Emotional Experience 510
Period of Physical Embodiment 510–11
Period of Study 510
personal background 140, 141
personal issues 19–20, 71–2, 281, 282, 291, 425, 434, 447, 475
Personal Seed, Theme, and Supertask (exercise) 339–40
Personal Speech Habits (exercise) 211
personal theme 340, 469–72, 550
perspective 331–2, 453, 461; *see also* dual perspectives
Peters, Jim *390*
pharynx 195, 200
philosophy 41–2, 457, 458
phonation 204, 206–7, 208
phonemes 208, 218, 220–1
phonetics *see* International Phonetic Alphabet

physical actions 17, 79, 101, 164–5, 270, 337, 524, 534, 550; exercises 102–4, 153–4, 274, 285–6; Grotowski and 415; verbal 157, 244, 250; *see also* Method of Physical Actions
Physical Actions, Emotional Response through (exercises) 28–9
physical states of being 276, 277–8
physiology, science of 17
Picon, Maria *435*
Picture Compositions (exercise) 317
Pink, Daniel H. 50, 51
Pinter, Harold 356
Pippin (musical) 415
Piscator, Erwin 517, 528
pitch 207–9, 231, 232, 239
Pitch Trills (exercise) 208–9
plan *see* first plan; second plan
Plan of Experiencing *64*, 65, 451–3, *452*, 454, 456–64
plasticity: of body 111; of brain 110
plastique 513
Plato 338
Platonov, Aleksandr Ivanovich 506
play: activating the seed, theme, and supertask 341–2; active exploration of 317–20; adaptations 413-14; expanding 412–13; plot analysis 309–13; reading 304–5, 306–7, 309–10, 313, 323, 411, 447; reconnaissance of 303–20; researching 307–8, 309, 316–17, 327; rights to 409–10; selecting 408–9; spectacle and mise-en-scène 313–15; telling story from character's viewpoint 331; telling the novel 355, 368–76; *see also* script
playwright: as designer of character 323; director as 414; germinating idea of 337; imagery 365; intention of 414; and pauses 382; researching 307–8, 309; respect for 412–13, 414; royalties 409–10, 413; and stage directions 356; and supertask 417, 456; viewpoint of 307
plosives 224, 229–30
plot 550; analysis 309–13; device 308, 324

poetic reflection 268–9, 270, 281, 291, 550
Polish Theatre Laboratory 415
Polykova, Elena 498
Poor Theater 159
Porter, Kay 105, 120
postmodern plays 159–60
posture *see* alignment
potentiation, long-term 102
practice, importance of 5–6, 18
prana 64, 65, 118, 202, 454, 459, 507, 508, 550; sharing images through 128–9
pranayama 64–5, 66, 67, 68, 201, 202, 507
pratyahara 68
Predator and Prey (exercise) 100
prejudice 75
premieres 411, 412, 414
preparation: for performance 466–7
Preparing for a Date (exercise) 175–7
preproduction 410–18
presence *see* I am/I exist
previews 468
privacy 70–2
problem 30–1, 260–1, 457, 532, 551; identifying 361–2
producers 408, 411
production concept 159, 414–15
production processes 407–19
production supertask 308
professional conduct 425, 445; *see also* ethics
Projecting Intimacy (exercise) 235–6
projection 133, 232–9, 469
Projection by Intention (exercise) 234–5
pronunciation 218
proprioception 17, 27, 83, 109
props 183, 431, 435, 446, 500
proscenium stage 409, *428*
psychological burden 171–2, 276–7, 279, 551
Psychological Gesture, A Beginning for (exercise) 336
psychological pauses 382
psychological realism 372
psychological states of being 276–7, 278–9
psychology 42–3, 44, 52, 108; behavioral 109 cognitive 43, 331; concept of flow 6–7, 67, 476; and voice 210, 211
psychophysical actions 10, 18–19, 31, 35, 457; motivators of 453, 460–1; selecting and naming 156–7
psychophysical instrument 78–84, 459; observing 164–5; sensory evocation 271–6; *see also* conditioning exercises
psychophysical science 108–13
psychophysical system 17
psycho-techniques 509, 510
public domain 409, 411, 413, 414
public/private dichotomy 145
public solitude 27, 118, 132–4, 165, 551
punctuality 70, 447
punctuation 353–5, 382–4
Pushkin, Aleksander 457; Aphorism of 453, 456, 457–8; *Miser Knight* 495–6; *Mozart* 509; *Onegin* 522

Q (design team) 411–12
Quakers 484
Quicksand (named event) 264

R coloration 221
Rabinowitz, Gabryal *22*, *254*
racial prejudice 75
Radha, Swami Sivanda 68, 455
Ramacharaka, Yogi 64
reading: exercise 174; play 304–5, 306–7, 309–10, 313, 323, 411, 447
Reading the Play for Character (exercise) 323
realism 503, 513; inner 502; psychological 372; spiritual 503; *see also* Fantastic Realism; Socialist Realism
Rebeck, Theresa: *Spike Heels* 18, 256, 285, 462
receiver 359
Red Director 533
Red Scare 388–9
rehearsals 424–48; Active Analysis in 386–403, 430–1; background 424–5; blocking 427–30; calls 425; of *The Crucible* 386–405; and design 431–2; dos and don'ts 445–8; dress 443; early 425–7; first reading 426;

INDEX

middle 432–5; scene 427–32; and search for supertask 417; stop-start 433; technical 441–5; ultimate phase 435–41; various approaches to 407
reincarnation 459
Reinking, Cathy 39, 419
Relationship Interviews (exercise) 343
Relationship Map 324–5
relationships 145–6
relaxation 26, 53, 56, 57–60, 83, 551; progressive 86–7; resting positions 85; rising without tension 87–9; *see also* breathing exercises; yoga
Reluctant Hero (exercise) 261
representation 460, 504, 552
reputation 425
research 307–8, 309, 316–17, 327, 473, 476, 480–1, 482; by director and designers 411; during rehearsal process 427
resonance 216–18, 228, 233–4, 237, 239
respect 72, 75–6, 136, 407, 422, 431, 446, 447
restraint *see* control and restraint
résumés 420–1
Reunion (named event) 264
Revello, Angelo, III *314*
Revero, Felicia 73
reversal 359, 552
reviews 468
rhotic 221
rhythm: of language 348–9; *see also* tempo-rhythm
Ribot, Théodule-Armand 34, 458, 508
ribs 201, 203
rights *see* copyright
ritual 6
Rodenburg, Patsy 241
Rodriguez, Herbert 88
Rogers, Lynne 419
role *see* character
Romania 480–1, 484
Romeo and Juliet (film) 413
Rope Bridge (exercise) 131–2
"Row, Row, Row Your Boat" (exercise) 122–3
Royal Shakespeare Company 315
royalties 409–10, 413
rudeness 72, 75, 76, 422

ruling idea 159, 307
Run, Stop, and Justify (exercises) 149–10, 162–3
run-throughs 435–6; stop-and-go 443
Russia: Active Analysis in 408; Peasants' Revolt (1905) 505; theatre traditions 500, 502; *see also* Soviet Union
Russian Revolution (1917) 512, 523, 530, 531

safety 445, 447
Salovey, Todd 477
Salvini, Tomasso 193, 494–5, 515
samadhi 68, 69
San Diego Repertory Theatre *436*, 477, 479
San Francisco Bay Area Experimental Theatre Movement 416
San Francisco State University 480
San Francisco Theatre Academy 283, 386, *387*, *388*, *389*, *390*, *393*, *401*, 454
San Jose Repertory Theatre *438–9*
Savasana (corpse pose) 86
Saxe-Meiningen, Georg II, duke of 496
scene: episodes 358–60, 364–5; ground plan 357–8; notes 433; reconnaissance of 347–62; rehearsals 427–32; selecting 305
scenery *see* sets
Schacter, Daniel L. 269
Schiller, Friedrich: *Kabale und Liebe* 496; *Maria Stuart* 496
School of Living Experience 34, 458, 504–5, 510
School of Representation 504
Schooler, Jonathan W. 109
science 11, 17; and concept of presence 412–3; and emotions 42, 47, 291–8; psychophysical 108–13; research on creativity 47–53; Soviet 534; *see also* neuroscience
score of actions 31
scoring the text 377–84
Scott, Brandon *412*
scrapbook, artistic 328
script: changes to 349; finding images in 365–7; graphic analysis of 378; initial observations about language

355; listing the active facts 356–7; preparing and studying 410–11; preparing for Active Analysis 351–2; production 425; punctuation 353–5; scoring the text 377–84; symbols for notation 376; *see also* learning lines
Sechenov, Ivan Mikhailovich 458
second nature 16–17
second plan 28, 148, 310, 317, 344, 552
Secret, The (exercise) 261
Secret Agent (exercise) 189–90
seed, theme, and supertask 337–8, 552; exercises 338–42
Seinfeld, Jerry 54
self-awareness *see* awareness of self; theatrical sense of self
self-consciousness 43, 58, 106, 139–40
self-criticism 43–4, 58, 106
Senelick, Laurence 514
sense memory 27, 186–7, 271
senses: exercises using 175–6, 272–4
sensory evocation 27, 186–7, 271–6, 552–3; exercises 23–4
Sensory Hologram (exercises) 275–6, 283–5
sets: changes 435; endowment of 183; ground plan 357–8; in Russian theatre 500; *see also* design
sexual harassment 446, 447
Shakespeare, William 39, 203, 233, 306, 309, 503; adaptations 413, 414; poetry 383; soliloquies 133; stage directions 355, 356; verse and prose language 349; *King Lear* 355; *Macbeth* 2, 277, 351; *The Merchant of Venice* 496, 501; *A Midsummer Night's Dream* 415; *Othello* 193, 211, 494–5, 496–7, 512, 515; *Richard III* 277; *Romeo and Juliet* 413; *Taming of the Shrew* 413; *Twelfth Night* 351, 406, 411, 412, 496; *see also* Hamlet
Shamanism 2, 466, 483–4
Shanghai Normal University 9, 300
Shankar, Raj 255, 314
Shepard, Sam: *Curse of the Starving Class* 475
Shifting the Breath (exercise) 57
shoulders, releasing 199–200, 238–9
sibilants 229

Sickels, Brian 411–12
Sight (exercise) 272–3
silence 247; zone of 189–90, 249, 253, 371, 561; *see also* nonverbal action
Silent Treatment (exercise) 188–9
Silicon Valley 471
Simonov, P. V. 536
Singer, Daniel 413
singing 203–4, 509, 522
Sino alla Morte (opera, kallisti ensemble) 124
Sit in a Chair (exercise) 102–4
SITI 81, 416; mission statement 487; *Bob* 429; *Going, Going, Gone* 416; *Who Do You Think You Are* 416, 417
Skinner, B. F. 6
Skinner, Edith 241
sleep 86, 112–13
Smash (TV show) 63
Smell (exercise) 273–4
Snyder, Naomi 330
social purpose 479–87, 553
Socialist Realism 300–1, 531, 533
Society of Art and Literature 495–6, 498, 499
Sold! (French and Zama) 70–1, 259, 282, 410
soliloquy 133
Sollogub, Vladimir 496
sound 426, 439; communicating through 218; design 411; exploring space with 126–7; mixing 439
Sound (exercise) 273
Sound and Space (exercise) 223
Sound with Tempo Variations (exercise) 227
Sounding Out the Text (exercise) 237–8
sourcing 410, 411, 427
Soviet Union 300–1, 411, 483, 530–1; Meyerhold's arrest and death 533–4; Michael Chekhov exiled from 520; science 534; Stalin's purges 526, 533–4; *see also* Russia
space: exploring 126–7, 223
spatial relationships 124–32
spectacle 313, 314, 315
speech 215–42; articulation 218, 219–20, 225, 233, 239, 353–4; communion through 227–39;

INDEX

components 216–27; dialects 209–10, 228, 231–2, 305; diction 348; emphasis 231–2; logic of 377–84; measures 379; as music 509; phonetic alphabet 220–1, 565–7; pronunciation 218; tonal subtext 230–1; training 219; vowels and consonants 220, 221–7; *see also* voice

Spider-Man: Turn Off the Dark (musical) 441

Spigelmyer, Kathi *412*

spine (of the body) 173; activating 95–8; in Plan of Experiencing 451–2, *452*, 453, 461

spine (of the play) 31, 44

spiritual communion 28, 64, 67, 118, 469, 505, 553

spiritual realism 503

Spolin, Viola 123

spontaneity 352, 387

sports: baseball stadium scenario *138*, 138; breathing 202; inspiration 8; training and practice 5–6, 78; visualization 105, 120; World Cup soccer 7, 8; the zone 67, 476

stage business 144, 431, 553

stage directions 356

stage formats 409

stage fright 54–8, 83, 233; tips for alleviating 57–60

stage layout *428*

stage manager 424, 425, 437, 442, 446

stakes, upping the 23, 244, 257–60, 290, 330

Stalin, Joseph 526, 530, 533–4, 535–6

stamina 83, 203

Stanislavski Ensemble 372

Stanislavsky, Konstantin (Konstantin Sergyevich Alexeyev): on acting as action 15; and Anton Chekhov 372, 501, 502; on audiences 4, 468; background 493–4; biography 493–526, 530–36; on "bits of action" 158; change of attitude to memory 271, 291, 520–1, 524; on charisma 39; and communication with oneself 133; and communion 28, 118; on controlling thoughts 54–5; and Craig 514; on creating character 141; on creative space 69; death 536; on distractions 71, 72; on elements of action 157; and emotions 34, 269, 286, 291, 292, 298; on experiencing 42, 450; and film of images 26, 104; on the "here and now" 149; on homework 74; on the human mind 62; illness 531, 534; and importance of technique 8; and improvisation 300, 301; on "in general" 21; influences on 9; and inner monologue 369; on inner realism 502; on inspiration 38; legacy 536–7; on "living the life of the human soul" 172; and "magic if" 137, 138–9; and Meyerhold 506, 513–14, 533; and Michael Chekhov 518–19; motivation 492–3; on naming a seed idea 338; notes 494, 531; and objectives 254; and opera 522; as Othello 193, 211, 496–7; on personal theme 469; and philosophy 457; on physical actions 155, 156; pictured *494*, *498*; Plan of Experiencing 64, 65, 451–3, *452*, 454, 456–64; and problem/task 30; and public solitude 27; on punctuality 70; and rehearsal process 427; on reincarnation 459; and relaxation 26, 53; and School of Living Experience 34; and science 11, 47; and scoring the text 377; self-criticism 494, 495, 497, 503, 509, 521; and social change 505; Soviet Union and 300–1; on speech as music 509; summary of key events 537–40; on superconscious 63–4; and supertask 456; and *Tartuffe* 417; on technique 346, 491; on tension 84; and term "psychophysical" 78; translations of publications of 531–2; on Vakhtangov 515–16; and yoga 41, 45, 63–6, 99, 118, 202, 454–5, 458, 460, 507–8, 536; *see also* Active Analysis through Events and Actions; Moscow Art Theatre; System

states of being 276–81, 553; emotional 277, 280–1; physical 276, 277–8; psychological 276–7, 278–9

status 142, 257–8; assumed/endowed 142–3; exercises 143–4, 259–60

Steiner, Rudolf 519
stillness 105, 164, 276
Stoberock, Barbara 6
Stoppard, Tom: *Rosencrantz and Guildenstern are Dead* 413
Strasberg, Lee 511, 524–5
Streep, Meryl 281
Streetcar Named Desire, A (Williams) *319*, *472*; Elements of Action 28–33; "Exploding Trunk" episode *362*, *363*; given circumstances 316; *idée fixe* 277; imagery *365*, *366*; improvisation on Main Events 317–18; listing key events 310; paraphrasing 364; relationship map *325*; researching 327; second plan improvisations 344; stage directions 356; tonal subtext 374; Young Vic production *311*
stress 55, 56, 82, 83; chronic 86–7
Strindberg, August 503; *Erik XIV* 470, 515
structure 158, 167
Studio on Povarskaya Street 506
subconscious 53, 245, 553; through the conscious 55, 80, 453, 456, 458
substitution 283
subtext 245, 553; of behavior 313–14, 553–4; of *The Crucible* 404; improvisation 364–5; physicalizing 387; tonal 230–1, 245, 374–5
Sulerzhitsky, Leopold Antonovich 63, 79, 128, 491, 506–8, *507*, 511, 514
Sunset on the Beach (exercise) 58–60
superconscious 10, 63–4, 458, 554
superstition 6
super-supertask 308, 483
supertask 159, 304, 307–8, 456, 554; finding through Active Analysis 417; in Plan of Experiencing 452, 453, 456, 460, 464; seed, theme, and 337–42
support wall 73
Suspicion at the Doctor's Office (exercise) 250
sutras 67–9
Suzuki technique 81
svadhyaya 69
Symbolism 506, 513
synaptic gap *101*, 102
synthesis 50

System, the (Stanislavsky's) 9–11; Anton Chekhov's contribution to 372; as basis for innovators 159; core training in psychophysical action 19; development of 79, 503–5, 507–11, 515, 522, 535; as organic behavior 17; role of conditioning exercises 78; Sonia Moore and 173; summary of key events 537–40; three bases of 453, 456–8; three stages of 510–11; in USA 524–7; yoga as key part of 41, 45, 63–6; *see also* Active Analysis; Stanislavsky, Konstantin

tableau vivant 313–14, 315, 317
Tables Turned (named event) 264–5
Tai Chi Breaths (exercise) 206
Take a Walk! (exercise) 178
Tanokura, Yoshinori *419*
task 30, 144, 554; *see also* supertask
Taste (exercise) 275
Teatro Campesino, El 484
technical rehearsals (tech) 441–5; conduct during 445; dry 442; notes 444; paper 442; stop-and-go runs 443; wet (cue-to-cue) 442–3
technique, necessity of 8–9
Tectonic Theatre Company 415
telegraphing 184
television: comedy 436; dialects 210; learning lines 426, 447
Telling the Inner Monologue/Dialogue (exercise) 370–1
Telling the Novel 355, 368–76, 554; and *The Crucible* 393–402
Telling the Plot (exercise) 310
telling the story 553
Telling the Story of the Play from Character's Viewpoint (exercise) 331
Telling the Tonal Subtext (exercise) 374–5
tempo-rhythm 32–3, 175–87, 429, 436–7, 555; musical 522; and sounds 227; and speech 231; *see also* beats
10 Things I Hate About You (film) 413
tension 56, 64, 81, 82, 83, 84, 209, 504; releasing 56–7, 58, 83, 86, 197–200, 238–9
text *see* script

INDEX

thalamus 49, *295*, 296
Theatre for Social Change 484
Theatre Studio *see* First Studio
theatrical sense of self: general 453, 463–4; internal/external 453, 463
theme 307–8, 337–42, 554; antithetical 472–5; personal 340, 469–72, 550; recurrent 158; as ruling idea 159, 307; worksheet 308
Theosophical Society 507
therapy 20
Third Studio 159, 172, 515–17, 526
thought (personal): anatomy of 101–2, 160–4; character's 105–6; expressing 120; identifying patterns of 379–80; relationship with emotions 292–3; *see also* inner dialogue; inner monologue
thought, play's 307; *see also* theme
three wheres 149, 166–7, 357
through-action/through-line of action 18–19, 31, 171, 307, 436, 555
thrust stage 409
Tiranti Anderson, Jennifer 411–12, 443
to treat as *see* endowment
To Wait for Jury's Verdict (exercise) 106–8
Tolkien, J. R. R.: *The Hobbit* 119
Tolstoy, Aleksei 503, 523; *Tsar Fyodor* 501, 523–4
Tolstoy, Leo 506, 507
tonal subtext 230–1, 245, 374–5; exercises 231, 374–5
tonsils *219*
Toporkov, Vassily 300, 534
Touch (exercise) 274
Tovstonogov, Georgy A. 300, 303, 313, 469, 525, 536
trachea 195, 200
training, importance of 5–6
transformation 34, 172, 492, 524, 554–5
transitions 350, 435
translation 413; of Stanislavsky's work 531–2
Trespassers Beware! (exercise) 161–2
triggers 111–12, 157, 268, 270, 271, 286, 290, 296–7; external 269, 296; internal 269, 296; music as 289
Trope, Y. 42–3

Trotsky, Leon 533
truth: enemies to 184–5; measure of 33, 167, 183–4, 548
Truth of Passions (aphorism) 457–8
Turgenev, Ivan Sergeevich 503
Two Spies and a Detective (exercise) 130
Two-Timer's Reward (exercise) 253
typecasting 38

unconscious 53, 458, 521, 555; collective 3
unions 421
United States of America: censorship 484; MAT tour of 503, 511, 523–4, 530, 532; Michael Chekhov in 520; production process 408, 412; System in 524–7
universality 3
University College, London 112
uvula 218

vagus nerve 82, 293, *294*, 295
Vakhtangov, Evgeny 11, 79, 491, 509, 515, 515–18, 523; at Adashev Studio 506; death 519; Fantastic Realism productions 159, 515; influence on Brecht 528; and Michael Chekhov 517–18, 520–1; Sonia Moore and 172–3, 526; succeeds Sulerzhitsky 508; and Third Studio 515–17
Vakhtangov Theatre (*formerly* Third Studio) 377, 517
Valdez, Luis 484
Veasey Laboratory 113
velum (soft palate) 216, 220, 228
verbal action(s) 156–7, 243–66, 555; with designated counteractions 253–7; with hidden agendas 262–3; named event improvisations 263–5; naming improvisations 261–2; with one spoken line 247–50; problem improvisations 260–1; selecting counteractions and negotiating status 257–60; with three spoken lines 250–3
verbs 156–7, 378; action 434–5; intransitive 157; passive 157; transitive 156, 157
verse structures 348–9
Vice (named event) 264

Victory (named event) 264
Viewpoints 81–2, 429, *429*
villains 472–5
visualization 26, 105, 120–1, 555; exercises 58, 127
Visualizing and Embodying Character (exercise) 333
Vocal Actions (exercise) 236
vocal folds/cords 195–7, 200, 206–8, 216; caring for 209, 212
Vocal Qualities and Issues (exercise) 228–30
voice 193–214; anatomy of 195, *196*, 197, 207, 218; caring for 209–13; communion through 227–39; components of 195–209; comprehensive warm-up 238–9; importance of alignment 197–200; importance of training 194, 211, 212, 228; onset 204, 206–7; pitch 207–9, 231, 232, 239; projection 133, 232–9, 469; quality and timbre 227–30; resonance 216–18, 228, 233–4, 237, 239; resources for training 241–2; as second signal system 195; tonal subtext 230–1, 245, 374–5; uniqueness 209–11; volume 233; *see also* speech
volition (will) 453, 460, 555
Vowel Formation (exercise) 222
vowels 220, 221–3, 226–7; properties 568–70
Vowels, Combining Consonants and (exercise) 226–7

Walker, Bill and Dolores 454
Walker, Patricia *388*
walking (exercises) 177–8
Wall, Joan 203
Walsh, Kirsten 22, *254*
Walsh, Lionel 327
Walters, Chris *419*
War (named event) 264
Warming Up the Articulators (exercise) 219–20
Wartime Farewell (exercise) 249–50
Washington, Destiny *439*
Watching the Breath (exercise) 45–7
Waters, Les 143

Watson, J. B. 109
Web (named event) 264
W.E.D.G.A.G. (Wonder, Evaluate, Decision, Gesture, Action, Gesture) technique 53, 160, 527; active explorations of 161–4, 165, 167; Disobeying Hands with 150–2; final gesture of 436; and obstacle 180; and pauses 371; simple physical action with 102–4
Wells, Lynn K. 195, 215, 220, 242
Wernicke, Carl 50–1
Wernicke's area 50–1, *51*
Wesp, Rick 43
West Side Story (musical) 203, 413
White, R. Andrew 10, 63
Whyman, Rose 451, 457, 458
Wilde, Oscar: *Salomé* 526
Wilder, Thornton: *The Matchmaker* 179–80
Williams, Tennessee: recurring characters 309; *Vieux Carré* 309; *see also Streetcar Named Desire, A*
willpower 120, 244
Winfield, Jess 413
Wing-Davey, Mark 480
Winkielman, Piotr 109
women, status of 75
wonderment 52–3; *see also* W.E.D.G.A.G.
Woodhouse, Sam 479
Wooster Group 438
words 218, 244; *see also* consonants; vowels
Words and Analogous Emotions (exercise) 286–7

yama 68, 69
yawning 216–17
yoga 18, 41, 45, 63–76, 84, 466, 555; alignment (Tadasana) 93–4, 187; asanas 64, 66, 67, 79–80; astanga (eight limbs) 64, 67; body-mind connection 79–80; chakras 65, 66, 454, 460, 461; flow of energy 67, 82–3; greeting (*Namaste*) 64; Hatha 64, 66, 507; non-religious nature 66; origins 66, 67; poses 556–7; prana 64, 65, 118, 128-9, 202, 454, 459, 506, 508, 550; pranayama 64–5, 65,

67, 68, 201, 202, 506; Raja 64, 507; Rolling Down from the Plow Position (Halasana) 96; Savasana (corpse pose) 86; Stanislavsky and 39, 45, 63–6, 99, 118, 202, 454–5, 458, 460, 507–8, 536; Sulerzhitsky and 507; sutras 67–9; twists 97–8; Watching the Breath 45–7

Yogananda, Paramahansa 10, 45, 64, 86, 454
Young Vic 311

Zakhava, B. E. 493, 536
Zama, Ahleea *see Sold!*
Zaporojetz, T. I. 377–8
Ziyi Zhang *40*